A HISTORY OF THE GOLD COAST
AND ASHANTI

A HISTORY OF
THE GOLD COAST
AND ASHANTI

from the earliest times
to the commencement of the
twentieth century

W. WALTON CLARIDGE

with a new introduction by

W. E. F. WARD

VOLUME TWO

FRANK CASS & CO. LTD.

1964

First published by John Murray in 1915 and
now reprinted by arrangement with them.

This edition published by Frank Cass & Co. Ltd.
10 Woburn Walk, London, W.C.1

First Edition   1915
Second Edition 1964

Printed by
Charles Birchall & Sons Ltd. London and Liverpool

CONTENTS

VOLUME TWO

PART V

THE DISSOLUTION OF THE ASHANTI KINGDOM

1873 TO 1896

CHAPTER I

THE OUTBREAK OF THE SIXTH ASHANTI WAR

1873

CHAPTER II

THE BOMBARDMENT OF ELMINA AND OTHER DISLOYAL
TOWNS

1873

v

CHAPTER III

THE OPENING OF SIR GARNET WOLSELEY'S CAMPAIGN

1873

CHAPTER IV

THE RETREAT OF THE ASHANTI ARMY

1873

CHAPTER V

PREPARATIONS FOR THE INVASION OF ASHANTI

1873

CHAPTER VI

THE INVASION OF ASHANTI

1874

CHAPTER VII

THE ASHANTIS AT BAY AND THE FALL OF KUMASI

1874

CHAPTER VIII

THE END OF THE WAR

1874

CHAPTER IX

THE EFFECTS OF THE WAR

1874

CHAPTER X

THE REVIVAL OF THE POWER OF ASHANTI

1875 TO 1880

CHAPTER XI

ALLEGED THREATENED ASHANTI INVASION

1881

CONTENTS   ix

CHAPTER XII

THE REBELLION AGAINST OSAI MENSA

1881 TO 1883

CHAPTER XIII

THE RIVAL CLAIMANTS TO THE STOOL OF ASHANTI

1883 TO 1884

CHAPTER XIV

THE BEKWAI-ADANSI WAR

1885 TO 1886

CHAPTER XV

THE ACCESSION OF OSAI KWAKU DUA III—PREMPI

1886 TO 1888

CHAPTER XVI

THE TAVIEVI REBELLION

1888 TO 1889

CHAPTER XVII

THE ADOPTION OF A NEW POLICY REGARDING ASHANTI

1888 TO 1891

CHAPTER XVIII

THE THREATENED ATTACK ON ATTABUBU

1892 TO 1894

CHAPTER XIX

THE ASHANTI EMBASSY TO ENGLAND

1894 TO 1895

CHAPTER XX

THE ARREST AND DEPORTATION OF PREMPI

1895 TO 1896

PART VI

EXTENSION OF THE SPHERE OF BRITISH INFLUENCE

1896 TO 1902

CHAPTER XXI

UNREST IN ASHANTI

1896 TO 1900

CHAPTER XXII

THE SIEGE OF KUMASI

1900

CHAPTER XXIII

THE GARRISON REINFORCED

1900

CHAPTER XXIV

ESCAPE OF THE GOVERNOR'S COLUMN

1900

CHAPTER XXV

THE RELIEF OF KUMASI

1900

CHAPTER XXVI

THE PUNISHMENT OF THE ASHANTIS

1900

CHAPTER XXVII

CONDITION OF THE COUNTRY AT THE BEGINNING OF THE TWENTIETH CENTURY

APPENDICES

LIST OF MAPS

PART V

THE DISSOLUTION OF THE ASHANTI KINGDOM

1873 TO 1896

A HISTORY OF THE GOLD COAST AND ASHANTI

CHAPTER I

THE OUTBREAK OF THE SIXTH ASHANTI WAR

1873

THE year 1873 witnessed the commencement of the sixth Ashanti war, a war that is noteworthy for several reasons. In the first place, it absolutely justified the predictions made by Governor Pine ten years earlier, and it was proved once and for all that it was possible to employ European troops on the Gold Coast for short periods, provided due precautions were observed ; and further, this was the first occasion on which a British force had ever attacked the Ashantis in their own country, thereby dispelling their belief in their own invincibility and laying the foundations for the overthrow of their kingdom and empire.

In considering the causes that led to this war, it must not be forgotten that, though generally regarded as a separate invasion, it was in reality a continuation of the war of 1863, since which no peace had been made. Governor Pine's refusal to surrender the fugitive Janin was, therefore, the primary cause ; for although ten years had elapsed and various circumstances had contributed to defer further action on the part of the Ashantis, this grievance had never been forgotten : the policy of Ashanti had undergone no change ; Kofi Karikari, when he succeeded to the stool in 1867, had sworn his " business should

3

be war," and he would, doubtless, have sent his army
against the Coast at once had it not been for the local
troubles that followed the murder of Asamoa Kwanta's
nephew. These disturbances were no sooner over than
plans had been made for another invasion, of which Adu
Boffo's expedition to Krepi and Atjiempon's march to
Elmina had formed a part, and it was only the supervention of unforeseen circumstances that had led to its
postponement. Adu Boffo had met with a quite unexpected
amount of resistance that had involved the loss of half his
army and a hundred and thirty-six Chiefs, besides the
expenditure of enormous quantities of ammunition, and
the negotiations for the transfer of the Dutch Possessions
to England had led to the removal of Atjiempon and the
frustration of his plans to organize a force in the west.
Thus the ten years that had elapsed since the last war
were accounted for and the original cause still remained,
which, considering the evidence [1] there is of the existence
of a definite agreement that was then broken, must be
admitted to be a just *casus belli.*

The King was inclined towards peace for the present,
though several of his Chiefs were clamouring for war,
and in all probability further action would have been
deferred until the losses of men and stores in Krepi could
have been made good, had not the transfer of Elmina
brought matters to an immediate head. This, therefore,
must be regarded as the actual cause of the resumption
of hostilities. As has been shown, the King undoubtedly
believed that Elmina was a portion of his kingdom and
had repeatedly protested against the transfer, and since
there is good evidence that this contention was perfectly
correct, and that the so-called renunciation of his claim
was not all that it purported to be, this second cause must
also be considered a just one.

Apart from the contention that Elmina really belonged
to the Ashantis, the transfer affected them in other ways.
The abolition of the Slave Trade had been a serious matter
to them, for they had thereby been deprived of the ready

[1] *Vide* vol. i., pp. 505-509.

and remunerative means of disposing of their prisoners of war that had been their principal source of revenue. The Kings had frequently complained of this, and the departure of the Dutch, who had still bought a certain number of slaves—nominally as soldiers for service abroad —had finally closed even this limited market. The abolition of the Slave Trade may therefore be cited as one of the more remote causes of the war.

In earlier times the Ashantis had traded largely at Accra ; but for the past half-century they had been dependent upon free intercourse with Elmina, and its possible closure to them was, therefore, a matter of vital importance. It was absolutely necessary for them to have free access to the sea, or they could find no outlet for their own trade and no means of obtaining a direct supply of powder, rum, salt and other articles that they needed. Their friendship with the Dutch had secured them hitherto ; but once Elmina passed into the hands of the English, they knew that the roads might be closed against them at any time, forcing them to use the distant market of Assini, and indeed striking at the very root of their power and independence : it is small wonder, therefore, that they objected to the transaction. The unwillingness of the Fantis to allow the Ashantis to trade directly with the coast, and the desire of the latter to avoid the large profits of these middlemen, had in fact been a contributing element in nearly every dispute with Ashanti. It has been maintained that goods destined for Ashanti, so long as it was an independent power, should not have paid duty, but have been passed through to the frontier in bond. Strictly speaking, this may be correct, but in a country such as the Gold Coast then was, it would have been practically impossible ; nor could it reasonably be expected that the English, who were on the Coast primarily for trade, would be prepared to relinquish the greater part of their revenue in order to treat a race like the Ashantis in an exactly similar way to a civilized nation. It was, however, the profits of the Fanti middlemen to which the Ashantis objected rather than the import duties imposed by the

Government. Some years later, in 1881, one of the
members of Buachi Tintin's embassy said to Ellis : " Give
us a town on the Coast, say Mori. Let it be ours ; let
us have a road of our own to it. If you say it is to be half
a mile broad, we will make it so. Then we can come there
to trade without having anything to say to those women,
the Assins and Fantis, who are really our slaves, and only
saved from destruction by you English. Do this, and
there will be no more trouble." [1]

Other minor causes of the war were the Ashantis'
alliance with the Elminas, who were now placed on equal
terms with their enemies the Fantis, and whom the Ashantis
felt bound to protect ; the interference with some of
their traders by the Assins, and the contempt they naturally felt for the power of the English after their long
series of victories over them, and especially on account of
the ridiculous conduct of the last campaign and the weak
and vacillating policy of Mr. Pope Hennessy. The most
effective means of securing peace is to show that one is
well prepared for war, and fighting power is, after all,
the argument that a savage understands best. The King's
words to Plange at the meeting of the Council on the 2nd of
September show plainly enough what his thoughts were.
The closure of the roads against them after they had once
been opened would, moreover, be regarded by the Ashantis
as tantamount to a declaration of war ; and the refusal
of the merchants, who it must be remembered were associated by tradition with the Government, to pay the
customary commission by which Ashantis gained free
board and lodging when they came to Cape Coast was
regarded by them as a withdrawal of the protection given
to lawful traders. Colonel Conran's absurd peace proclamation, too, had not been forgotten, and was regarded
as a flagrant attempt to take an unfair advantage by
putting a false complexion on the King's action. The
treatment of Atjiempon by the Hausa Police has been
alleged as a further cause ; they are said to have handled
him very roughly and to have robbed him of a number of

[1] Ellis, *Land of Fetish*, p. 311.

his gold trinkets, which they sold in Cape Coast. If this was so, it was no more than he deserved ; but it was not an actual cause of the war, although it may possibly have helped to precipitate matters. The army had been mobilized and left the capital before Atjiempon was released from Cape Coast, but news of his arrest could have been conveyed to Kumasi much earlier.

It is, moreover, uncertain what Plange really said to the King, who alleged several things against him in his interviews with Dawson and accused him of having caused most of the existing trouble. He asserted that Plange had told him that the Governor would not only take Elmina, but would give it to Kwaku Fram the King of Denkera, from whose ancestor the Ashantis had captured the Note. He also threatened that in four months' time the Governor would come and take away the King's power, that he would close the roads,[1] and that in limiting the ransom for the missionaries to a thousand pounds he had put his thumb-nail to his upper front teeth as though trying to force one out—a most insulting sign amongst all the Akan peoples—and said he would not pay what the King asked but what he himself thought proper. Plange was also suspected by the King of having misrepresented many things that had taken place in Kumasi, and was consequently in very bad odour there. Whether or not he really had ever said such things is, of course, uncertain. The missionaries, indeed, knew nothing of any such statements ; but they were not always present, and it is quite possible that he may have said something of the kind when annoyed by the difficulties he met with in his mission, and it is certain that any such threats or insults would greatly annoy the King and tend to precipitate hostilities, as he now alleged was the case.

The King, moreover, had every reason to believe that, in spite of his recent losses in Krepi, the moment was a favourable one for the renewal of hostilities with the English. He knew their weakness, and thought he saw convincing proof of it in the absence of any opposition to

---

[1] This he undoubtedly did say.

the march of Atjiempon's small force, in spite of his outrageous conduct. To his mind nothing but weakness could
have prevented them from attacking him or even the
Dutch, in whose Protectorate these atrocities had been
committed. He knew, too, of the dissensions between
the English and former Dutch tribes and was well able
to appreciate the helpless condition of a country divided
against itself, and he also knew that although the area of
the British Protectorate had been extended by the purchase
of all the Dutch Settlements, there had been no corresponding increase in the strength of the garrison maintained for its defence : it had, in fact, been reduced and the
3rd West India Regiment disbanded.

To recapitulate, therefore, this war was merely a continuation of that of 1863, which was now resumed because
of the occupation of Elmina ; but had the Dutch never
left the Coast, or had the English declined to take Elmina,
the invasion would have taken place just the same, if not
at this particular time, then at some future date. One of
the principal objects of the English in acquiring Elmina
and the other Dutch Settlements had been to put an end
to the warfare on the Coast, but now the common fate
of would-be peace-makers was theirs and they found
themselves seriously involved.

No matter what its actual exciting causes were, this
war was inevitable from the Ashantis' point of view, and
it was equally inevitable from the point of view of the
British Government. Whether or not matters might have
turned out differently if a wiser policy had been adopted
by the trading companies half a century earlier, it is now
impossible to decide ; but it is deeply to be deplored that
the Ashantis were not more fairly treated then and the
experiment at least made of trying to gain this fine race
as the friends instead of as the declared enemies of the
English. Could this have been done, they would have
proved invaluable allies, and a close and peaceful intercourse
with Europeans during a number of years, besides being of
great pecuniary advantage to both nations, could hardly
have been maintained without the higher civilization of

the English leaving its mark and the Ashantis being weaned from their more objectionable customs just as the coast tribes had been. This result might have been obtained as quickly, and with less cost in blood and money, by peaceable means as by the method of war, and without the birth of the unavoidable ill-feeling against and hatred of a conqueror. The experiment might, of course, have failed ; but even if this had happened, nothing would have been lost, and the Ashantis alone would then have been to blame. It is equally possible, on the other hand, that it might have succeeded. The benefits to both parties would then have been incalculable, and the necessity for the overthrow of the nation that has succeeded in establishing the only real empire that had ever existed in this part of Africa would never have arisen. Its failure or success would have depended mainly on the amount of tact exercised and the degree of intimacy between the two peoples ; for by these the rate of Ashanti progress would have been regulated. The time for such an experiment, however, was now long past, and the mutual feelings of distrust that had grown up had put it outside the range of practical politics ; while the conditions of life in Ashanti, the barbarous and despotic nature of its government, the enmity between its people and the British protected tribes, and the losses involved by the frequent quarrels and disputes consequent thereon, made some decisive measures necessary. The longer such measures were delayed and a weak and temporizing policy adopted, or any stronger policy was unbacked by the power to enforce compliance with legitimate demands, the greater the difficulties became and the more did the Ashantis learn to despise the power of the English and have increased faith in their own supposed invincibility. So far had this process already gone, and so peculiar and difficult would have been the situation, even if a treaty could now have been made between two nations so widely separated in the scale of civilization, the more barbarous of which was locally the more powerful, that the definite conquest of Ashanti could no longer be deferred.

The Ashanti army crossed the Pra on the 22nd of January 1873. So soon as the Chief of Yankumasi Assin heard of its approach, he had sacrificed three women and fourteen men to the god of the river to induce him to prevent the passage of the enemy, and when the Ashantis tried to cross at Prasu a few days later and some forty of their men, amongst whom was a sub-Chief of Bantama, were drowned, their loss was attributed by both parties to this sacrifice. The Ashantis then made further sacrifices, and, abandoning Prasu, went about half a mile higher up the stream to Atasi, where they succeeded in crossing without further loss. The strength of this army was estimated at 12,000 men ; it took five days to cross the river, using two ferries of two canoes each and sending thirty men over at each trip. The Ashantis then plundered and burned several Assin villages, and a skirmish took place between a portion of their force and a body of a thousand Assins, in which one Ashanti was taken prisoner and two more were killed, their heads being sent down to King Anfu Otu at Abakrampa as proof of the actuality of the invasion. It was from a letter from him and a message from Chibu the King of Assin, both of which reached Cape Coast on the 31st of January, that the Government learned the first definite news of the invasion, though there had been a number of vague rumours afloat for several days.

The Ashantis had so completely succeeded in blinding the authorities to their real intentions that Colonel Harley was even now disinclined to believe that an Ashanti army had really entered the Protectorate, and instead of immediately calling the tribes together and providing them with arms and ammunition for the defence of their country, wasted valuable time in sending Doctor Rowe as Special Commissioner to Anamabo, Abakrampa, and Assin to see how far these reports were correct, and, if true, to impress upon the Kings the necessity for united action. At the same time, fifty of the Hausa Police were ordered up to Dunkwa, but it was distinctly stated that this movement was not to be regarded as anything more than a demonstration in favour of the Protectorate, and they had strict orders not to fire unless they were attacked and then to retire at once upon Cape Coast.   Chief Bentil of Mumford, who had been elected Commander-in-Chief by the Fanti Kings during the last war, offered to collect an army of 20,000 men and was requested to do so ; the Cape Coast Volunteers were called out, and a proclamation prohibiting the sale of arms and ammunition to the enemy was issued. The Accras were not called up, but the eastern tribes were loyal with the exception of the Akwamus.

The Ashantis had caught the Government in its habitual state of unpreparedness.   There were but 160 officers and men in the whole country, and even these were broken up into small detachments and scattered along the coast as garrisons for the various forts, while the reserve store of arms available for distribution amongst the protected tribes amounted to only 190 Enfield rifles and 381 flint muskets.   Even after the Administrator had received convincing information that the Ashantis were marching towards the coast, Governor Hennessy, to whom every-thing was referred, refused to believe that the conciliatory policy that he had adopted could possibly have failed and tried to lay all the blame on Colonel Harley.   He even went so far as to write : " I do not believe that this is an Ashanti invasion, or the prelude to an Ashanti war, yet I think it quite possible that it may be converted into something of the sort by injudicious action, and even by injudicious words, uttered by the Administrator." [1]   What he really thought it was, or what else it could possibly have been, it is difficult to imagine, and he would probably have found it hard to explain.

Governor Hennessy was soon superseded by Mr. Robert W. Keate, who arrived in Cape Coast on the 7th of March and at first tried to evade all responsibility for giving assistance to the people by quoting from the despatch written by the Secretary of State on the 17th of May 1869, in which it had been laid down that " the wars in which

[1] Parliamentary Paper, *Ashantee Invasion, etc.,* 1873, part ii, p. 244.

they (the protected tribes) engage themselves are their wars, and not the wars of this country (Great Britain); that they must rely on themselves for success in their wars, and that the British Government is unable to make itself responsible for their defence in case they should prove unable to defend themselves." This principle, however, whatever might have been said for it in some circum stances, could not be applied in the present instance without the greatest injustice being done. In the first place, the Fantis, who were now threatened, had not " engaged themselves " in this war, nor had they done anything to cause it. It was due solely to the actions of the Government during the past ten or eleven years and to the foolish policy of Mr. Hennessy; and, secondly, the relations of the Government to the protected tribes were now very different from what they had been in 1869. Since that date the Authorities had broken up the Fanti Confederation and thus destroyed the organization upon which the people had relied for united defence; and though it is true that the scheme would have been unworkable without considerable modifications, the fact remained that the Government had never attempted to remedy its defects or improve upon it, but had promptly crushed it altogether. By thus depriving the people of the means they had devised for their own defence, the Government had made itself more than ever responsible for their protection, as the King of Mankesim did not forget to point out in his appeal for arms and ammunition. Governor Keate, however, fell a victim to the climate within ten days of his arrival, dying of fever at Cape Coast on the 17th of March. He was succeeded by Colonel Harley, who was promoted to be Governor-in-Chief.

The invading army was under the supreme command of Amankwa Tia the Chief of Bantama. Strictly speaking, it was his duty to remain in Kumasi and be responsible for the defence of the capital; but the continued retirement of Asamoa Kwanta, the real Commander-in-Chief, had rendered the provision of another general necessary, and Amankwa Tia, envying Adu Boffo the slaves and plunder he had acquired during his campaign in Krepi, had intrigued for this position and succeeded in obtaining it. His appointment, however, was most unpopular with the army as a whole, for he was known to be a confirmed drunkard, and his men had little or no confidence in or respect for him. His army consisted of three divisions, one of which was to advance into Akim, another under Adu Boffo was sent against Denkera, while the main body followed the Prasu-Cape Coast road.

The Assins collected at Yankumasi Assin and made a gallant attempt to check the enemy's advance ; but it was obvious that they could never hope to do so unaided, and though every effort was made to stir up some fighting spirit in the other tribes and cause a general advance to their support, the allies proved so dilatory in their preparations and acted with such a complete absence of co-operation, that the Assins were left to face the enemy alone, with the natural result that, when the Ashantis attacked them on the 9th of February, they were defeated and driven back and the enemy then camped in Yankumasi. Thus the old story of the earlier invasions was once more repeated and the enemy were allowed to engage and defeat the several tribes one after the other, driving before them the fugitives from the first battles to demoralize those whom they next had to encounter. Nothing, indeed, showed the impracticability of the scheme devised by the promoters of the Fanti Confederation more than this total absence of concerted action or agreement amongst the different tribes ; for the Confederation at best could only have existed by the suppression of all intertribal quarrels and disputes and the union of the whole Fanti race for one common purpose. It was this policy that was the real secret of the power of Ashanti. The Fantis however, even in the face of this great, common danger, were not only slow to combine, but were even quarrelling amongst themselves. Never a fighting race, but willing enough to do their best when necessary and then often fighting well, they never gave themselves a fair chance to repeat their victory at Dodowa, but by their own inaction and disunion constantly placed themselves in positions from which retreat was their only course and thus largely contributed to the growth of a belief, that is not altogether justified, that they are quite useless as soldiers.

Most of these quarrels that led the people to fight amongst themselves at this critical time, instead of marching to oppose the advance of the Ashanti army, owed their origin to disputes between those who had always been under British protection and those who had till recently been Dutch subjects. One such quarrel came to a head at Sekondi in the middle of January.

There had been a long-standing feud between the inhabitants of British and Dutch Sekondi on account of a dispute about the right to a palm plantation a short distance from the town on the Wassaw road, the ownership of which had been a subject of contention since so far back as 1856. In that year British and Dutch Commissioners —Doctor Sawkins the Commandant of Dixcove, and Mr. Bunckel the Commandant of Sekondi—had fixed a boundary to which the Chiefs had agreed, signing a document to that effect ; but in 1857 a further dispute had arisen and Commissioners—Mr. Lazenby the Commandant of Dixcove, and Mr. Kammerling the Commandant of Sekondi —had again been appointed by the English and Dutch Governments, who had confirmed the previous decision and the affair then seemed to have been finally settled. In 1868, however, when the Anglo-Dutch exchange of territory took place, the people of Ayim and other villages of English Sekondi had removed to Wassaw rather than accept the Dutch flag, and left the Impintin people, who had always been Dutch subjects, in possession of the town and this plantation. It was not until 1872, when the Dutch Possessions were ceded to Great Britain, that the English Sekondis returned and again availed themselves of their right to the plantation ; but in the meantime their rivals had been able to use it without restriction, and as they were unwilling to revert to the former state of affairs and continued to trespass and gather nuts in it, it once more became a cause of dissension.

On the 15th of January, Doctor Horton,[1] the Civil Commandant of Sekondi, summoned Andries and Inkatia, the Chiefs of the Dutch and English portions of the town, to the fort to discuss and settle the dispute. Inkatia first stated his case and handed in the documents affirming his right to the plantation. Andries was then called upon for his statement, but was frequently interrupted by Inkatia and his people ; high words ensued, and eventually Andries struck Inkatia in the face. The blow was at once returned ; but before matters could proceed farther the parties were separated and Andries was sent outside. A little later he was recalled ; but having once more struck Inkatia, was sent away altogether, while Inkatia and his people were detained in the fort for several hours before being allowed to go to their own quarter of the town.

The people of Dutch Sekondi had been disaffected ever since their former rulers left the Coast. Andries was known to be in close league with the King of Elmina, and although an English flag had been given to him in the previous September he had never yet hoisted it. On the 6th of the preceding May (1872), he had made a great hostile demonstration and surrounded the English town with nearly a thousand armed men, threatening the inhabitants and bidding defiance to the Commandant and garrison by hoisting Dutch flags and daring them to come out and remove them. Lieutenant Hopkins of the 2nd West India Regiment, who was then Commandant, had been publicly censured before him and his people, and the Government had undertaken to pay a fine which he (Andries) had imposed on the people of British Sekondi. Naturally this payment had greatly irritated them and increased Andries' opinion of his own importance. Had he been severely dealt with at the time for this flagrant breach of the peace and open defiance of the Government's authority, it is more than likely that this riot would never have occurred ; but the very lenient view that had been taken of his action, which can only be explained by re-

---

[1] A native of the Gold Coast.

membering that Mr. Pope Hennessy was then Governor-in-Chief, now bore fruit.

After the scene in the fort, Andries again prepared to attack the British quarter, and that same evening news was brought in that his people had already made a raid on several of Inkatia's villages. Dr. Horton, therefore, sent for him and his Chiefs, but none of them could be found. At half-past seven the next morning, a boy was brought into the fort by Inkatia's people, who they said had been shot by a man in the Dutch quarter, and a few hours later an organized attack was made on the English town by 700 or 800 of Andries' men. Before many rounds had been fired, the Wesleyan Chapel caught fire, and within a very short time the whole British quarter, with the exception of four houses, had been burned to the ground. Messrs. Swanzy's factory was plundered before the flames reached it, and at least five people were killed and many more wounded and taken prisoners.

The Dutch and English towns lay close together, being separated by a street less than twenty feet wide. The fort stood in the Dutch quarter, the houses of which surrounded it on two and a half sides, so that the English section could not be reached without passing through its narrow streets, which were now crowded with excited rioters. The fort was without fuel or water—the tank being in bad repair—and the garrison only amounted to twenty-one men of the 2nd West India Regiment. The fact that many shots were deliberately fired into it showed that the animosity of the Dutch Sekondis was not directed against Inkatia's people alone, and Dr. Horton wisely decided not to march this handful of men between two hostile forces, a course that would probably have resulted in the loss of every man, but fired a few rockets over the Dutch town and waited till he saw Inkatia hoist a white flag before sending a message to Andries calling upon him to cease firing. Inkatia having acknowledged himself beaten and given up two children as hostages, the Dutch Sekondis quickly dispersed. The same evening the Chief of Takoradi sent to Andries offering him assistance, and

300 armed men from Takoradi and Shama marched into the town early the next morning carrying Dutch flags, while the Commandant of Dixcove had the greatest difficulty in preventing the Butris from joining them also.

News of this riot quickly reached Cape Coast, and Colonel Foster was sent from Elmina with a detachment of the Hausa Police on board H.M.S. *Rattlesnake*. They landed at Sekondi on the 19th, and the two Kings and their Chiefs were then summoned to the fort and made their statements. Andries and Inkatia and nine of their Chiefs were then arrested on charges of riot and arson and removed to Elmina to await their trial. A large proportion of the goods that had been plundered from Messrs. Swanzy's store was recovered, and fifty-four guns were taken and destroyed by the police. Both Kings were subsequently deposed and deported to Sierra Leone, but were brought back and reinstated after the war was over.

A less serious riot occurred at Butri on the 13th of January. This arose out of the action of Mr. Hughes, the Civil Commandant of Dixcove, who had ordered a stay of all proceedings in a case in which the Chief of Butri had ordered a man to pay an extortionate fine to the King of Elmina and otherwise grossly ill-treated him. The people turned out, firing guns in the town and carrying a Dutch flag through the streets ; a constable and a bailiff who had been sent with the Chief to forbid the use of this flag were beaten and had their clothes torn, and next morning, when the Commandant went with more constables to arrest their assailants, the men took up a position on the far side of a stream just outside the town with guns in their hands. Mr. Hughes, however, led his men across, but the rebels scattered into the bush, where it would have been dangerous to have followed them, and only one man was arrested.

It was ascertained that the King of Elmina was exercising an undue influence over the Chiefs of many of the towns that had formerly been under Dutch rule, and was, in fact, encouraging a spirit of disaffection to the English flag with the object of carrying out the original scheme for which Atjiempon had been sent to Elmina—namely, a general rising of the western tribes led by the Elminas, which was to take place as soon as the Ashanti army reached the neighbourhood of the coast towns. He still had two of Atjiempon's sons and several other Ashantis with him in Elmina ; he had refused to accept a present of money sent him by the Governor ; he had never yet hoisted the English flag that had been given to him, and he was known to have sent his own brother to Kumasi with a message to the King. Always a bitter opponent to the English, he had been still further estranged by the tactless conduct of Colonel Harley, who had recently visited the town and made a speech in which he had said that many of the Elmina " customs " would have to cease. This was in direct opposition to what had been promised at the time of the transfer, and such a breach of faith had had the natural result of strengthening the hands of the King and bringing a number of recruits from among the previously well-disposed Elminas to augment his disloyal party. His conduct altogether had now become so suspicious that Colonel Harley deemed it advisable to test his loyalty in some way and try to ascertain how much truth there might be in the belief that he was really one of the instigators of the invasion and in close alliance with the enemy. Captain Turton, who was still Military Commandant of the town, was therefore ordered to summon the King and his Chiefs to a meeting in the Castle and find out how matters really stood.

This meeting was held on the 11th of March, and was attended by all the Chiefs and by every person of importance in the town. The oath of allegiance was read and interpreted, and Kobina Edjan was then called upon to set an example to his Chiefs by being the first to sign it. This he flatly refused to do, behaving in a most truculent manner, and in his speech said : " I am not afraid of your power. You may hang me if you like. I will not sign any paper. Myself and some of the people of Elmina have taken fetish oath to oppose the English Government coming to Elmina, and we have not broken that oath yet."[1] Two other Chiefs, Kwamin Ekum and Tando Mensa, also rejected the oath, and although Captain Turton took them to his own quarters and did his utmost to persuade them to listen to reason, they remained obdurate. They and Kobina Edjan were, therefore, arrested and sent to Cape Coast on board H.M.S. *Seagull*,[2] where they were imprisoned in the Castle and subsequently deported to Sierra Leone.

The policy of Kobina Edjan and his party had never undergone any change. They had offered no open resistance to the transfer of their town, because they had realized that they were helpless. The instructions sent from England had ordered that no force was to be employed to compel the people to accept the British flag; but though they had been obeyed literally, yet the Elminas had none the less been coerced morally when their position was pointed out to them by Sir Arthur Kennedy. At that time the Ashantis had not been ready to help and support them and they knew that they could not stand alone against all Fanti; they had, therefore, had no alternative but to accept the flag; but they had done so with many mental reservations, which, now that the position was beginning to look more hopeful, bore fruit in actions. Kobina Edjan, moreover, having been deposed by a large section of his people just before the transfer, was no longer recognized as King by Governor Fergusson when the ceremony took place, and had consequently never been required even to go through the form of accepting the flag and acknowledging allegiance to the British Government. Governor Hennessy had subsequently reinstated and recognized him without troubling to make any enquiry, so that Kobina Edjan, in truth, was in no way bound to the British.

In the meantime the tribes were slowly taking the field and concentrating at Dunkwa and Mansu, to which latter place the Assins had retired after their defeat. A little later, as the Ashantis continued their advance, the

---

[1] *Ashantee War, etc.*, part ii, p. 325. [2] A sloop.

1873
CHAP. I allies fell back to Yankumasi Fanti, where they were joined by the Cape Coast Volunteers and a force of 100 Hausas who had arrived from Lagos on the 23rd of February. Lieutenant Hopkins of the 2nd West India Regiment was in command, and his orders were " to give every moral aid to the Assins and the Fantees in arresting the progress of the Ashantees, and if he should find himself in a position to do so, to aid and succour the Assins in driving back the Ashantees beyond Mansu and holding that place," [1] but a little later it was pointed out that the " main object " of his command was " to cover and protect Cape Coast." [2] He was, therefore, placed in a difficult position and his hands were practically tied ; for he could not afford to run the least risk of having his retreat to Cape Coast cut off, and it was almost impossible for him to give any real aid to the Assins without risking something.

The Fantis had now mobilized in considerable numbers, and the camp at Yankumasi Fanti extended for some distance on either side of the road. Early on the morning of the 10th of March the allies advanced to attack the enemy, but failing to find him, sent out a few spies and returned to the camp, where they began cooking their breakfasts. Suddenly, firing was heard close at hand, the scouts came running in, and the allies barely had time to pick up their arms before the Ashantis were upon them. Kwesi Adu's detachment from Mankesim promptly fled, thus enabling the enemy to break through the line and get behind the Cape Coast men, who found themselves hemmed in on every side ; but in spite of this disadvantage they fought well, and though they lost many men killed, wounded or taken prisoners, eventually succeeded in cutting their way through the Ashantis and made good their escape. The Assins and Denkeras had held their own throughout the engagement, and even scored some slight successes, but finding themselves deserted and without any hope of support, they too were compelled to retire. Lieutenant Hopkins and the Hausas had come up while the

---

[1] *Ashantee Invasion* (Parliamentary Paper, 1873), part ii, p. 311.
[2] *Ibid.*, p. 315.

battle was in progress, but finding that some of the allies were already in full retreat, he considered it his duty to secure the safety of Cape Coast and fell back without firing a shot. The Chiefs complained bitterly of this inaction of the regulars, and with some reason ; for had they gone to the support of the Assins and Denkeras, the result of the day's fighting might have been very different, and time would have been given for some of the other allies to rally had they been inclined to do so.

This defeat brought the Ashantis to within thirty miles of Cape Coast and was the principal cause of a most disgraceful outrage in that town. A proclamation had been issued on the 17th of February setting forth that the Government would not guarantee the safety of any Ashantis living within the Protectorate, and warning them that if they remained they would do so at their own risk. It seems, however, that an exception was made in the case of those who had been living on the coast for any length of time,[1] provided, of course, that they behaved themselves. The news of the battle of Yankumasi Fanti and the near approach of the enemy, however, greatly alarmed and enraged the people of Cape Coast, who for some time past had been suspicious of Prince Ansa on account of his nationality, and believed, or professed to believe, that he was secretly supplying the Ashantis with ammunition, and at half-past two on the afternoon of Sunday the 16th of March a mob led by W. E. Davidson, James Brew and James Amissah[2] went to his house, seized some of his Ashanti servants—one of whom had been living in the Protectorate for more than twenty-two years—and dragged them to the beach. There the heads of four of these men were hacked off with cutlasses, one of the executioners being a woman. Some officers from the Castle were seen approaching the spot and the crowd dispersed, taking the heads of their victims with them ; but while the officers

---

[1] *Vide* letter from Civil Commandant, Elmina dated 2nd of March 1873, *Ashantee Invasion*, 1873, part ii, p. 336.
[2] The same three men who had taken so active a part in and been arrested on account of the Fanti Confederation.

were still standing over the bodies, they returned, dragging yet another prisoner with them, and before anything could be done to hinder them, he too had been beheaded. In the meantime another party had wrecked and plundered Ansa's house, and he and his wife and child had been compelled to barricade themselves in an upper room or they too would probably have been murdered. Armed police were sent out to protect him, and he was brought to the Castle and lodged there for safety; but public feeling against him ran so high that a strong escort was needed again the next day when he went to the inquest. A verdict of wilful murder was returned against some person or persons unknown, but nothing more was ever done to punish the perpetrators of this outrage.

Although it was known that Davidson, Brew and Amissah were the ringleaders who had headed the mob at Ansa's house, it was found that it would be impossible to prove their presence on the beach or that they were privy to any intention to murder when they went to the house. It was also felt that public feeling on the matter was so strong that there was no reasonable prospect of obtaining a conviction, even for riot, from any jury that might be summoned in Cape Coast, and consequently no proceedings were instituted against them. They were officially informed, however, that " Her Majesty's Government view with severe displeasure their participation in these disgraceful proceedings which led to the barbarous murder of five Ashantees ; that in ordinary times it would have been the duty of the Government to take steps to punish them for their part in the riot ; but that, looking to all the circumstances of the moment, and the natural excitement and anger caused by the invasion, the Government had refrained from giving directions for their prosecution." [1] How much effect this intimation was likely to have on the three men concerned must be a matter of opinion, but it speaks well for the King and goes a long way towards proving the honesty of his intentions that he did not immediately execute the missionaries and

[1] Lord Kimberley's despatch.

Fantis he had in Kumasi in revenge for these murders of his subjects. The people still had one of the wives of Kotiko the Ashanti ambassador, and a boy in their power ; but they were given up a few days later, and Prince Ansa was sent to Sierra Leone on the 16th of April for his own safety. Although his removal had been kept secret, it was discovered just as the boat put off to the steamer, and dense crowds of women assembled on the beach and denounced and cursed him with their customary force and fluency.

The allies had now formed a new and very extensive camp at Dunkwa, where about 25,000 men had been col- lected by the end of the month, and on the 20th of March a reinforcement of an officer and 100 men of the West India Regiment had arrived from Sierra Leone. The new camp had a frontage nearly seven miles in length, and the bush had been so well cleared that the enemy would be forced to cross a large stretch of open ground if they attacked it. Nothing, however, would induce the allies to make an immediate attack on the Ashantis : they preferred to think about it, and kept putting it off for two or three days at a time, thus enabling the enemy to receive a steady stream of reinforcements and several convoys of ammunition from Kumasi. The delay also allowed Adu Boffo—who had already defeated the Wassaws—time to bring his army over and join forces with Amankwa Tia.

The allies hesitated so long, that in the end it was the Ashantis who attacked them at about seven o'clock on the morning of the 8th of April ; but they then fought extremely well, and in a battle lasting five hours fully held their own all along the line. The firing was very heavy, and enormous quantities of ammunition were used. The Fantis always fire recklessly, and frequently over- load their guns, seventy of which burst in this action alone, so that it is difficult to keep them supplied with powder and lead. No prisoners were taken on either side, and the wounded were often most barbarously mutilated. The Hausas lost 17 men killed and wounded, and the allied tribesmen, whose strength was estimated at over 56,000, had 221 men killed and 643 wounded. What the losses of the Ashantis were is unknown, but they must have been considerable ; yet, in spite of this very satisfactory result, Lieutenant Hopkins could not persuade the Chiefs to renew the battle the next morning : they said they preferred to wait until the enemy should attack them. The Ashantis, however, had been greatly astonished at the amount of determined resistance that had been offered, and it was not until the 14th that they once more advanced and attacked along the whole length of the line. This battle lasted throughout the whole day, from nine o'clock in the morning till seven at night, but when darkness at last brought it to a close neither side could claim a victory. Most of the fighting took place in a thickly wooded valley to the north of Dunkwa, near Tetsi. Into this the enemy poured in great numbers ; but the allies advanced boldly, although they were at a distinct disadvantage in having to cross the open ground that they had cleared from their camp nearly to this valley. A rocket battery did good service in the centre of the line, and the losses on both sides must have been fairly heavy, although no figures are given.

The Ashantis were so disheartened after fighting these two hard battles and gaining nothing, that they destroyed a great deal of their baggage and began a retreat. Had the allies then fallen on their rear with but half the determined spirit that they had shown on the previous day, they must have inflicted a most crushing defeat, and the war would practically have been at an end. They knew nothing of this movement at the time, however, and having themselves had quite as much fighting as they cared for, also began to retire. News of this movement soon brought back the Ashantis, and the retreat became a rout as the allies neared Cape Coast.

The Chiefs excused their conduct by saying they could not fight so long as there was treachery in their own camp. They alluded to the case of George Blankson, the member of the Legislative Council, who was the same man who had opened the negotiations with Kumasi in 1865 before

Colonel Conran's peace proclamation was published. He had been accused on the 13th—the day before the last battle—of supplying the enemy with ammunition and information, and the greatest excitement had prevailed in the camp. He would probably have paid the penalty of his assumed treachery with his life, had he not been sent down to Cape Coast, where the investigation of the charges against him was postponed until the war should be over, with the result that they were never properly investigated at all. There seems, however, to have been some ground for these accusations, for a letter from the King dated the 12th of March is said to have been found on him, and it was freely alleged that he had been sending the Ashantis regular consignments of powder packed in bottles.

Nothing would induce the Chiefs to reorganize their army and return to Dunkwa, but several small detachments were mustered and stationed in the different districts to protect the villages and farms from pillage. Sixty Hausas under Mr. Loggie were sent to garrison the fort at Anamabo, where it was hoped they might form a nucleus around which the Anamabos, Kormantins, Winnebas and others would rally. The Assins, Abras and Akims occupied Asebu, but their numbers were very small, as most of their men had deserted. A cordon of lesser Chiefs was posted around Elmina and promised to oppose any attempt the Ashantis might make on that town. They could not have done more than make a show of resistance however, had they really been attacked ; and the Ashantis, had they chosen to do so, could have marched directly on Cape Coast and Elmina without meeting with any serious opposition. Fortunately, however, instead of following up their victory, they contented themselves with forming a large camp at Dunkwa, where they remained for some time. They were in a wretched condition ; food was scarce, and the half-starved troops suffered terribly from small-pox and dysentery ; the rains had set in, and their camp was crowded with wounded men ; while the whole of its surroundings were in an indescribably filthy

1873
CHAP. I

condition, and nearly every bush and hollow concealed the decomposing corpse of some wretched creature who had crawled away to die. The whole army was heartily sick of the war, and only longed to get back to Kumasi.

Meanwhile Atjiempon, who had so unwisely been released, had remained in Kumasi for a short time after the despatch of the main army, and had then been sent into Apollonia with a force of 3,000 men, principally Sefwis, to assist Amaki against Blay. Amaki had sent to Kumasi begging for aid, and the aim of this expedition, after defeating Blay, was to raise a large army from amongst the former Dutch subjects in Takoradi, Sekondi and Shama, and then cross the Pra to join the Elminas and Amankwa Tia.

About the middle of May the Ashantis broke up their camp at Dunkwa and began to move slowly in the direction of Jukwa, where the Denkeras had established their capital after their migration towards the coast. These people at once applied for assistance in arms and ammunition, and renewed efforts were made to induce the allies to reassemble and make another stand. For some time nothing could be done; every Chief excused himself by saying that he had to defend his own town, and the outlook daily became more and more serious. Eventually, however, a considerable force mustered at Abakrampa, whence it moved to Jukwa at the end of the month. On the 3rd and 4th of June some desultory fighting took place near the town, and on the 5th the Ashantis attacked the place in force. They met with only the most feeble resistance. Kwesi Ke, an unworthy successor of the former gallant Kings of Denkera, fled at the very beginning of the battle and took refuge in one of his villages on the road towards Cape Coast, so that when the Chiefs who had come to his assistance enquired for him he was nowhere to be found. The battle was very soon over, and ended in the total defeat and rout of the Fantis, who ran for their lives to Cape Coast. There the utmost alarm prevailed as the terror-stricken fugitives continued to pour into the town throughout the whole night. Panic soon seized the whole countryside, and between 15,000 and 20,000 people were estimated to have sought the protection of the Castle guns. The roads were blocked by the thousands of men, women and children who continued to arrive from all directions as the news spread. " It was a most piteous spectacle. Many were emaciated by famine or disease : some were carrying their aged parents on their backs, or leading the blind ; the wayside was littered with corpses, with the dying, with women bringing forth children." [1]

Early the next morning a rumour spread through the town that the Ashantis were advancing from the Sweet River and were already within five miles of the Castle gates. This proved false, but the mail-carriers sent to Elmina the next afternoon had to turn back because they found the road stopped by the enemy, and further false alarms constantly increased the generally prevailing panic. News was received that the Shamas and Elminas were preparing to attack Komenda, where, in the absence of the fighting men at Cape Coast, the old men, women and children were defenceless. A gunboat was, therefore, sent to bring them to Cape Coast, and more than a thousand were safely landed, but the surf was very bad at the time and many of the canoes upset, causing a loss of over forty lives.

On the 6th the Governor held a meeting with all the Kings and Chiefs, from which the only absentee was the King of Anamabo. He pointed out that their failure had been due to want of unity, and that the reason why the Ashantis were so consistently successful was that they acted under one head. He therefore suggested that they should adopt the same plan and elect one of their number to lead them before they formed their next camp. This, of course, was excellent advice ; but if Colonel Harley had been wiser, he would have given the people a little practical assistance earlier in the campaign when they were fighting bravely and well, instead of leaving them without support or leadership and merely offering platitudes and counsel now that they were defeated and disheartened. He had

[1] Reade, *Ashantee Campaign*, p. 106.

not given them a fair chance : there had been no nucleus of trained troops for them to rally round, and not even an officer to lead them. Lieutenant Hopkins' hands had been tied by the limitations put on him by his orders, and it is of very little use for a white officer to tell Africans to advance against an enemy so long as they see that he himself is not prepared to lead the way. Colonel Harley's mismanagement of affairs, indeed, had aroused the greatest indignation and, at a meeting of the European and African traders convened at Cape Coast, a resolution was passed condemning his conduct in terms that were probably plainer and more forcible than any that had ever been used in connection with a British Administrator since Governors began. The Chiefs retired to consider the Governor's proposition, and their reply, as given in the *West African Herald* of the 28th of June 1873—a paper published in Cape Coast—was a signal refutation of the statements that had been made by some of the promoters of the Fanti Confederation. After saying that " since the days of Governor Maclean there never has been such a large and complete assembly of the Kings and Chiefs as on this day," this paper gives a part of the Chiefs' reply as follows : " They do not feel able to take the management of affairs. It would be impossible for them to do so ; nor could they elect one to be their Chief King ; that power must come from the Governor, and if anyone has said that they wished to govern themselves, it was untrue." Amongst those who gave this reply were Anfu Otu the King of Abra, and Kwesi Edu the King of Mankesim, who had been put forward as Kings-President of the Confederation.

CHAPTER II

1873

THE condition of affairs after the flight of the allies from 1873 Jukwa was serious in the extreme. The Ashanti army CHAP. II was at Efutu, within a few miles of both Cape Coast and Elmina; but apart from the defeated and demoralized Fantis, the only troops available to oppose their advance were two or three hundred Hausa Armed Police and two hundred Volunteers. From Elmina came the disquieting news that the party that had sided with the deported King, consisting of Numbers 3, 6, 7 and 8 Companies, had revolted and openly joined the enemy; that Atjiempon had been seen with the Ashanti army in the immediate neighbourhood of the town,[1] and that the Castle yards were densely crowded with the hundreds of women and children who had sought the protection of the guns. That the Ashantis really were close at hand there could be no doubt; for they had been seen by reliable witnesses, and the women of the King's party were busily engaged in supplying them with food and water.

At this critical juncture reinforcements arrived. On the 8th of June, H.M.S. *Barracouta*,[2] Captain Fremantle, reached Cape Coast with 110 officers and men of the Royal Marine Light Infantry and Artillery[3] under Brevet Lieutenant-Colonel Festing, R.M.A. They had been sent out from England on receipt of the news of the defeat

[1] This proved to be incorrect.   [2] A paddle steamer.
[3] Transferred from the *Valorous*: fifty-two of each.

of the allies at Dunkwa, and were landed on the 9th. On the 10th, Colonel Festing went down to Elmina on board H.M.S. *Decoy*[1] to inspect, and on his return to Cape Coast a meeting of the Legislative Council was held on the 12th to consider the serious state of affairs. Elmina was now divided against itself : the old King's party in the quarter to the west of the River Benya had joined the Ashantis, while the mulattos and other inhabitants of the Garden Town remained loyal. It was decided that a strong garrison should be introduced into the town at daybreak the next morning, that martial law should then be proclaimed, and that two hours should be given the people in which to deliver up all arms before active measures were taken to enforce obedience. About fifty marines and an equal number of Hausas were told off for this duty and left Cape Coast soon after midnight ; these troops, with the men of the 2nd West India Regiment and Hausas already stationed at Elmina, brought the garrison up to 268. Twenty-three boats from the men-of-war were also detailed to Elmina to assist in enforcing compliance with the terms of the proclamation.

The troops marched into Elmina before dawn on Friday the 13th of June, and by the time day broke the disaffected portion of the town had been completely surrounded. This part of the town stood immediately outside the Castle, being built under its walls on what is now the parade ground. The Hausas and West Indians, with a few of the marines, formed a cordon from the River Benya to the sea on its western side, the Castle with its guns manned by Marine Artillerymen commanded it on the east, and a string of boats from H.M.Ss. *Barracouta, Decoy, Druid,*[2] *Seagull* and *Argus,*[3] under Lieutenants Wells, Bourke, Marrack and Young, was anchored in the river to cut off all chance of retreat in that direction, while the *Barracouta's* steam pinnace and the *Decoy's* cutter, under Navigating-Lieutenant Wonham, lay off the shore just outside the surf to prevent any escape by sea. Martial law was then proclaimed, and an order issued for the delivery of

---

[1] A gunboat.　　[2] A corvette.　　[3] A paddle steamer.

all arms and munitions of war at the Castle gate within two hours. The time passed ; but no arms were brought in, though many armed men could be seen in the town, and two deputations of Chiefs came to try to obtain some modification of the order with the evident intention of gaining time. They found it hard to believe that extreme measures would really be taken ; for as they themselves said, " The Dutch often threatened them, but always gave way at the last," and they doubtless expected the same kind of thing would happen now.

At the expiration of the two hours, a further proclamation was issued giving the people another hour within which to comply with the order, after which, they were told, their town would be destroyed without further notice and all women and children and unarmed men were warned to leave the neighbourhood at once. This notice, however, produced no more effect than the first one had done. At about noon, therefore, after a further extension of half an hour had been given, the Castle guns opened a heavy fire on the town. Flames quickly broke out in several places, and in less than twenty minutes little remained of the King's quarter but the bare walls of the houses. These were demolished soon afterwards, with the exception of two that were unusually well built and were kept for use as a police barracks and female prison.

The Elminas had fled through the back of the town, where they broke through the cordon of troops and took up a position on some rough ground encumbered with growths of prickly pear, whence they opened a brisk fire that was as promptly returned. While the Elminas and the troops were thus engaged, a report was brought in from Fort Conraadsburg that a number of Ashantis could be seen advancing to support the enemy. The seamen were therefore landed from the boats, and Colonel Festing led his men steadily forward, driving the enemy nearly to Ampeni before returning to the Castle. The King of Eguafo and his people fought on the British side in this action. The enemy had about twenty men killed, but the British loss was only 1 man of the 2nd West India Regiment killed and 3 wounded out of a total of 27 officers and 490 men engaged.

At about five o'clock another message was sent down from Fort Conraadsburg that the Ashantis were again advancing in force from the north. Fully 3,000 of them, some carrying scaling ladders, were seen moving across the salt plain at the back of the Government Garden with the evident intention of attacking the loyal portion of the town. It was now getting late, and all the boats, with the exception of those of the *Barracouta*, had already returned to their ships ; but every available man was mustered, and, after a small detachment had been left to guard the bridge, the remainder marched round Java Hill to meet the enemy. The *Barracouta's* boats, being still within hail, were recalled by von Hamel, the Dutch Vice-Consul, who had received the alarm from one of the Java pensioners, and the seamen followed the force from the Castle as soon as they could land again. The Ashantis advanced in a long line preceded by numerous skirmishers, and almost succeeded in turning the right flank of the British force, but Lieutenant Wells [1] came up with the *Barracouta's* men and, advancing under cover of the wall of the Government Garden, took them by surprise and caused them to waver. A general advance was then made and the enemy retreated in good order over the salt plain, firing steadily as they went. On reaching the edge of the bush about three miles from Elmina, they rallied and made a final stand ; but the steady volleys of the British troops soon drove them back again, and they broke and fled. Of the 15 officers and 318 men engaged, the British had only one marine killed and one officer—Mr. Loggie [2]—and three men wounded, but the Ashantis left about 200 dead on the field, amongst whom was one of the King's nephews, who had been in command, and several other Chiefs.

This defeat and the destruction of their town brought the Elminas to their senses, and, on the 18th, forty or fifty guns were delivered at the Castle, and seventeen

---

[1] Died on his way home to join the Royal Yacht.
[2] Acting Inspector-General of Police.

of the Chiefs took the oath of allegiance. Only seven Chiefs, three of whom were wounded, failed to appear, and by the 5th of July 250 guns had been given up. The battle was attended by other important results : it convinced the Ashantis that the prime object of their invasion, the capture of Elmina, was beyond their strength, and it showed the Ministers and the public in England that the invasion was a serious matter, and thus led to stronger steps being taken against the enemy.

A number of Cape Coast Volunteers had arrived in Elmina on the 15th, but the majority of them had to be sent back ; for, finding the fighting was over and having nothing better to do, they remembered their old enmity against the Elminas and began to pillage the loyal portion of the town.

On the 21st of June information was received from an Ashanti prisoner that the enemy intended to attack Cape Coast on the 28th. Colonel Festing therefore hurried over to make preparations for its defence. He found the place itself in a wretched condition, while the military stores were, if anything, worse. Quantities of Snider and other ammunition were quite unserviceable, and the very first cartridge he took out of the gun-limbers on Connor's Hill was " so sodden that water could be squeezed out of it like a sponge." [1] Many of the cartridges for the 6-pounders were absolutely useless, and " one limber contained a well-organized ants' nest." [2]

In the town itself the greatest distress prevailed. The place was still crowded with thousands of Fantis, cowed and despondent after their flight from Jukwa ; refugees from all parts of the country were gathered there in vast numbers, thousands of whom were unable to find any shelter in the already-overcrowded houses, and were forced to sleep in the streets ; food became scarcer and scarcer ; the supplies from the bush were cut off, and the terrified people dared not venture out even to cut firewood. The half-starved refugees were only kept alive by the distribution of rice by the Government ; but their numbers were

---

[1] Brackenbury, vol. i, p. 82.   [2] *Ibid.*

so great that although enormous quantities were issued, many died of starvation and exposure. At first twenty-five tons of rice were received by every steamer, and this quantity was afterwards greatly increased; but it was given out to the Chiefs for distribution, and it was not until it became known that they were keeping the bulk of it for their immediate followers that a proper system of relief by tickets was organized and a Sanitary Commission appointed. Upwards of a thousand people were supplied with rice daily, adults receiving a pint each and children under ten years old half a pint. To make matters worse the rains set in with unusual severity and there was an almost continuous heavy downpour for several weeks. The unfortunate refugees, homeless, underfed, and unable even to light a fire, sat huddled together shivering in the streets, seeking to obtain what little shelter they could under a thin cotton cloth or old piece of duck supported on a few sticks. A number of old sails were landed from the men-of-war for this purpose and did something to mitigate the sufferings of the people. The continued saturation so weakened the different buildings that many of them fell in : numbers of the mud houses of the people collapsed altogether, crushing their unfortunate occupants, and many lives were lost in this way. Even the ramparts of the Castle itself began to crumble away and fell down in two places, carrying platforms and guns with them, while of all the houses that had been hired in the town for use as public offices, Gothic House [1] was the only one in which there was a dry room. Small-pox, too, was raging at the time : the disease had broken out some time before and spread with frightful rapidity through the densely crowded and insanitary town and throughout all the surrounding country. The knowledge that the Ashantis suffered from it with equal severity was small consolation, and there were already over 200 patients in the hospital. Barbarous and disorderly scenes were of almost daily occurrence, for their troubles and reverses

---

[1] Occupied by the Customs, Treasury and Post Offices : there was also a gaol there.

had aroused the worst passions of the people, and the attack on Prince Ansa's house was but one incident among many. From time to time small parties of the bolder spirits among the Fantis would prowl about the bush in the direction of Elmina or conceal themselves near some path where they could lie in wait for any solitary Ashanti or Elmina who might come along. Then they would bring him down with a volley, hack him to pieces on the spot, and drag his head in triumph through the streets of Cape Coast by means of a string passed through a hole punched from the ear into the mouth. Occasionally they succeeded in taking a prisoner alive : they would then bring him back with them to be exposed to the insults and execrations of the mob, while he was secured " in log " with a jawbone hung around his neck as a reminder of what his own fate would be within the next few days.

In addition to their other troubles, the people were continually distracted by panic : scarcely a night passed without an alarm being given, and they lived in hourly dread of seeing the Ashantis pouring through their streets. Fortunately this never happened, for the enemy never suspected the true state of affairs in the town ; but marauding parties often passed near Cape Coast, and one night a village was burned within three miles of the place and the glare of the flames could be plainly seen and appeared so close that it caused the greatest alarm. Had the enemy really attacked Cape Coast nothing could possibly have saved it.

On the morning of the 29th of July, one of these bands of the enemy, about a hundred strong, attacked a party of about fifty Eguafos, only ten of whom were armed, near Ankwanda, a fishing village about two and a half miles to the west of Elmina. They took five of them prisoners, decapitated a sixth, and drove the remainder back to the village. The King of Eguafo and 200 of his men, supported by 20 Hausas, turned out to find the Ashantis and recover the prisoners, but they had already disappeared.

The greatest animosity still existed between the former
Dutch subjects and those who had always been under
British protection, and there were continual small disturbances between these two parties in the western
districts. Axim, Sekondi and Shama were hotbeds of disaffection, and a semblance of peace was only maintained
by frequent visits of the men-of-war which cruised up and
down that part of the coast. The presence of Atjiempon
and his force in Apollonia, where he and Amaki had destroyed several of Blay's towns, helped to keep up this state
of smouldering rebellion, and reinforcements had to be
sent to Axim, Dixcove and Sekondi, which were all being
threatened by Adu Boffo. Dr. Gouldsbury had visited
Beyin in April, and on the 26th Amaki and his Chiefs had
signed the oath of allegiance, protesting that they were
loyal in spite of all the reports that had been circulated
against them and even asking that the old fort might be
repaired and garrisoned. All the time, however, Amaki
was in league with the Ashantis, and had sent a messenger,
Kwamin Aisua, to Kumasi asking for help. A few months
later the Commandant's interpreter at Sekondi was captured by the Chief of Takoradi almost within sight of the
fort, and Captain Stevens momentarily expected to be
attacked. He was relieved by Captain Helden, who succeeded in obtaining the release of the interpreter, and
matters then quieted down for a time.

The Ashantis were still encamped at Mampon, Efutu
and the surrounding villages, and though better off
than the Fantis, were in a bad enough plight themselves.
They had free access to all the farms, and also drew supplies
regularly from Elmina ; but even with these advantages
food was none too plentiful, and the heavy rains, the
swampy ground, the insanitary condition of their camps,
and the ravages of small-pox and dysentery all combined
to dishearten them and make them thoroughly miserable.
Sitting there idle, one and all heartily wished the war was
at an end. Many deserted and gave themselves up at the
different forts, and were kept in the courtyard of Gothic
House until the war was over. In the end, the Chiefs and

their men became so dissatisfied that they compelled Amankwa Tia to send messengers to Kumasi asking the King to recall them ; but Kofi Karikari felt that he had been forced into the war by the ambition of these very Chiefs, and showed his resentment by saying, " You wished for war and you have it. You swore you would not return till you could bring me the walls of Cape Coast, and now you want me to recall you because many Chiefs have fallen, and you are suffering. . . . It was not I, it was you who wished it. . . . In due time I will send you an answer." [1]

On the 5th of July, Commodore Commerell arrived in the *Rattlesnake*, and on the 6th the *Himalaya* came in with 13 officers and 360 men of the 2nd West India Regiment under Lieutenant-Colonel H. J. Wise.[2] They had been ordered from the West Indies at the same time as Colonel Festing's marines had been sent out from England. This reinforcement relieved the marines who were garrisoning the Castle : those landed from the *Barracouta* and *Seagull* were re-embarked, and the detachment of Colonel Festing's men returned to Elmina. The *Simoom* also arrived on the 10th of August, bringing 170 more officers and men of the Royal Marine Light Infantry and Artillery, and was detained in the roads for use as a hospital ship. The climate had already begun to tell on Colonel Festing's marines, who by the end of July showed a percentage of 57·2 non-effectives, and these timely reinforcements enabled them to be spared and sent for a cruise on the *Himalaya* and *Barracouta*.

Early in August it was decided to try to find out if it would be possible to dislodge the Ashantis from Mampon and gain a better insight into their movements and intentions than had hitherto been done. Spies had constantly been sent out, but they brought in the most contradictory reports and were generally believed to conceal themselves in the bush on the outskirts of Cape Coast until their food was exhausted and then return for their pay, drawing upon their imaginations for any account they gave of the enemy's

---

[1] Ramseyer and Kühne, p. 239.
[2] Invalided soon afterwards, 18th of July.

proceedings. Lieutenant Gordon[1] was sent out on the
6th with ninety-seven Hausas and about the same number
of Volunteers and labourers, and chose a small hill at
Napoleon, on the Sweet River and about five miles from
Cape Coast, on which he cleared a site and began to build
a redoubt. A regular system of patrols was then organized,
by whom the surrounding country was properly explored,
and it was definitely ascertained that the main body of
the Ashantis was still encamped at Mampon and Efutu,
but that an advanced party was occupying Simio, and
maintained daily communication with Elmina.

A rumour now became current that Amankwa Tia intended to cross the Pra and join forces with Adu Boffo and
Atjiempon, and that a detachment of the enemy was
already in possession of an island some distance up the
river. The Shamas, moreover, were strongly suspected of
supplying the Ashantis with provisions, and Commodore
Commerell therefore left Cape Coast in the *Rattlesnake* on
the 13th of August to hold a palaver with the Chiefs of
Shama and ascend and explore the Pra with a view to
ascertaining if there was sufficient water for ships' boats
with guns and rockets to be towed up and dispute the
passage of Amankwa Tia's army if he attempted to cross.

At ten o'clock on the morning of the 14th the boats
of the *Rattlesnake* and *Argus* were manned and armed, and
the Commodore landed with Captain Helden the Civil
Commandant of Sekondi, and Commander Luxmoore of
the *Argus*. A palaver was held with the Chiefs, who denied
that they had given any assistance to the enemy, protesting that their one wish was to maintain an absolute
neutrality, and that they would therefore side neither with
the Government nor with the Ashantis. They gave this
desire to be strictly neutral as a reason for refusing to
furnish pilots for the boats that were to ascend the river,
and the meeting ended so amicably that any suspicions the
Commodore may have entertained were lulled, and he put
off and joined the boats that were waiting outside the bar.
The steam-cutter took the other boats in tow, the bar

[1] 98th Regiment.

was crossed, and the ascent of the river commenced. So confident was the Commodore of the good faith of the Shamas that, following their treacherous advice, he ordered the boats to keep close under the western bank lest any Ashantis should be lurking in the thick brushwood that fringed the opposite shore. A mile and a half of the river had been ascended in this way when, without the slightest warning, shots rang out on the Shama bank, and a hail of slugs came pouring into the boats at about ten yards range. The Commodore fell severely wounded in the right side [1] at the very first volley, and Captain Helden, Commander Luxmoore and several of the men were also badly hurt. The seamen returned the fire with their small-arms, though not a man was to be seen, but the rockets could not be used, as the steam-cutter was towing the boats. They at once put off into mid-stream ; but the number of the wounded compelled an immediate return to the ships, and it was mainly owing to the coolness and gallantry of Lieutenant Edwards, who was in charge of the steam-cutter, that they succeeded in getting out of the river at all.

In the meantime, another of the *Rattlesnake's* boats had landed ten Fanti policemen, who had been brought up to Shama from Sekondi to assist the single constable then stationed in the fort in protecting the town ; but they had no sooner set foot on the beach than the Shamas crowded round them in a hostile manner. The boat meanwhile had capsized in the surf while preparing to land the stores, and her crew and the midshipman in charge were swimming around and trying to right her. While they were thus engaged the Shamas opened fire on them and wounded several. Sub-Lieutenant Draffen tried to cover them by forming the Fanti Police into skirmishing order and was partly successful, but two of the police, one seaman and a Kru-boy were killed and several others wounded. Two more boats with rockets then came to their support and the Shamas fled into the bush, taking the body of the dead seaman with them.

[1] This wound necessitated his being invalided to the Cape of Good Hope.

So soon as the Commodore reached his ship, he ordered her to be cleared for action and opened fire on the town, which within two hours was reduced to a heap of burning ruins. The people, however, had all fled to the bush, so that few, if any of them, can have paid the penalty of their treachery. The British loss in this unfortunate affair was four men killed and six officers and fourteen men wounded.

The effect of this disastrous expedition to the Pra was soon seen. Those former Dutch subjects who had hitherto been hesitating in their allegiance and maintaining an outward semblance of loyalty now broke out into open rebellion, and the inhabitants of Takoradi, Dutch Sekondi and many other places threw off all further disguise, took up arms, and declared against the Government. It was most difficult to deal with these insurrections, for no troops could be spared and the punishment of the rebels had to be left to the Navy. All that the ships could do, however, was to cruise up and down the coast, shelling and burning a village here and there ; but such measures really caused very little loss or inconvenience to the people, who could always escape into the bush before the firing began and usually saw the ships in time to be able to remove their goods as well. The damage done to their houses, therefore, was the only loss they suffered, and a new grass roof and a few patches in the mud walls were, as a rule, the only repairs necessary.

At Sekondi the people of the Dutch town attacked the fort on the 16th of August, but were driven back with a loss of six men killed by the fort guns and the shells of the *Argus*. They then deserted the town and the loyal inhabitants took possession of their houses, which were nearer the fort and could be protected more easily than their own. At Axim the Dutch inhabitants retired to the bush, taking all their property with them ; but a skirmish occurred between them and some friendly natives, seven of whom were wounded, and in another encounter on the 19th one of the 2nd West Indian soldiers was killed and several others were wounded. This affair took place

within 300 yards of the fort while Dr. Gouldsbury and
Lieutenant Des Barres were engaged with a small escort
in searching for the shortest and safest route to the nearest
water supply, there being then but a few inches of water
left in the tanks at the fort. The town was bombarded
from the fort and afterwards burned. Dixcove and the
neighbouring villages were threatened by the Adjuas and
Shamas, but the rebels were beaten off and Adjua was
burned. On the 20th, Takoradi and several other towns
were shelled by H.M.Ss. *Barracouta* and *Argus* and parties
of seamen were landed to break up and burn the canoes.
At Takoradi about sixty men were employed in this duty,
but as they were pushing on to take some canoes lying
round the point, they were fired on by a number of men
concealed in the bush and had three officers and twelve
men wounded. The ships then passed on to Shama,
which was again shelled and set on fire to complete the
destruction commenced by the *Rattlesnake*. On the 22nd,
the Akwidas attacked Achowa, one of the Dixcove villages,
killing and wounding several loyal natives : they also
attempted to capture the Government post canoe, and
their town was accordingly shelled by H.M.S. *Druid* on
the 28th and completely destroyed.

Lieutenant Gordon at Napoleon was the first to organize
any systematic method of gaining intelligence. He sent
out small parties of the best Fanti spies he could obtain
in two or three directions daily, and each party was invariably accompanied by one or two reliable Hausas.
Care was taken to select Fantis and Hausas for this duty
who did not understand each other's language, and their
reports were taken separately and carefully compared.
The redoubt at Napoleon had been finished by the middle
of August, and Mr. Gordon had then intended to construct
a similar work on the summit of a hill near Simio. This
would have covered Elmina and prevented the use of the
village as a means of communication with the Ashantis ;
but when the time came to move over there and start work
on the new redoubt, the volunteers were seized with
panic and barely half-a-dozen of them fell in. They

regarded any movement towards Simio as involving them
in certain destruction by the enemy, and this idea had
gained so firm a hold on their imaginations that the original
scheme had to be abandoned and a redoubt was constructed
at Abi instead. This was three miles nearer Elmina, but
it gave the Fantis access to a fairly large area of fruitful
land, and, with the Napoleon redoubt, covered the approaches to Cape Coast from the north-west.

Colonel Harley was now most anxious to obtain what
he considered a sufficient force to march upon Kumasi.
He suggested that this should consist of 300 Marines,
600 West Indians, not less than 800 Rifles, 200 Volunteers
and 10,000 Native Allies. He proposed that this force
should march to Kumasi in November and accomplish
the journey in ten days. Colonel Harley, however, had
the not uncommon fault of being able to formulate schemes
without having the necessary grip of detail to enable him
to foresee the many possible contingencies that might arise
before they could be carried out.

Colonel Festing, when this proposal was submitted to
him, condemned it at once and showed how ridiculous it
was. He pointed out that it would be quite impossible
" that a march of this distance (170 miles) can be accomplished in a leisurely manner in ten days by an army
moving along a single, narrow track, in an unmapped
country, destitute of supplies, and covered with dense
forest, where every morsel of food must be carried with the
invading force from our base at Cape Coast Castle or
Elmina, and the climate of which all accounts agree in
affirming to be baneful to the European. My own judgment is, that such a march could not be accomplished,
even if altogether unopposed (but with the necessity of
taking military precaution), in much less time than a
month. As the troops advance, depots of ammunition
and provisions must be made at intervals. To provide
for the sustenance of even the bearers and other auxiliaries
attached to the army, would be an extensive undertaking.
. . In this case we must be guided not by speculation, but
by past experiences of similar undertakings. . . . As to

the notion of regulating the advance so as to be ' almost
a surprise,' I feel convinced that such a result could not
in any way be attained. . . . Allowance must be made for
sickness. . . . I should look with apprehension to the
impediment on the line of march (and, of course, with still
greater in immediate presence of the enemy) caused by
the crowding up of the only line of communication, and
that a single narrow track, by a totally unmanageable body
of natives, whose language we do not speak and who are
liable to panic-stricken terror. I do not offer any suggestion of my own, at present, as to the number and composition of the force competent to make a successful invasion of the Ashantee country and to seize its capital ;
but I would in the strongest manner deprecate any estimate which would leave it possible for a small band of
weary soldiers to arrive in front of Coomassie. It is not
only necessary to reach that place, but I hold it to be essential to arrive there with such a force that the native mind
shall be fully impressed with the power and resources of
England. . . . As an officer writing with responsibility,
I cannot permit myself to think lightly of an undertaking
involving unknown hazards ; that it is possible to assert
the Sovereignty of our country on this Coast I fully believe,
but not, in my humble opinion, with the insufficient means
proposed." [1]   Of the sound common sense of this criticism
there can be no two opinions, and subsequent events fully
proved its truth.

[1] *Ashantee War* (Parliamentary Paper, 1874), part ii, pp. 202–3.

CHAPTER III

THE OPENING OF SIR GARNET WOLSELEY'S CAMPAIGN

1873

WHEN the news of the Ashanti attack on Elmina was received in England, it made a profound impression. The knowledge that the Protectorate had again been invaded and overrun for many months by the enemy, that the sea-coast had been reached and the very forts themselves threatened, and that the most strenuous exertions of the local authorities had barely sufficed to save them, at last convinced the Home Government [1] that the time had come when something definite must be done and a real effort made to crush the power of Ashanti once and for ever. This step had, indeed, been inevitable for some time past; for the half-hearted and feeble military operations of the English upon the Gold Coast had naturally had the effect of causing the Ashantis to believe them incapable of offering any serious resistance to their inroads, and their former respect for them had long since been converted into profound contempt. But although the Home Government must have realized the impossibility of altogether escaping a great war with Ashanti, yet the terrible losses in the last campaign, the difficulty of raising any really effective army from amongst the protected tribes, and the dread of exposing white troops to the dangers of the climate had led to its repeated postponement. This had been made all the easier by the action of

---

[1] When questions were first asked in the House of Commons, the answer had been given that " ample measures had been taken " for the security of the forts.

the local officials, and it was only now that the danger 1873
could no longer be concealed that the Ministers at last
began to understand how serious the state of affairs on
the Gold Coast really was. Hitherto, Mr. Pope Hennessy,
Colonel Harley, and the other officers on whom they
had to rely for their information had persistently made
light of the matter and given anything but a correct view
of the case. This final disgrace, however, had brought
the prestige of the English to its lowest ebb, and made it
imperative that a signal victory over the enemy must be
gained if they were to remain any longer on the Coast.
Even now, many people were still opposed to the idea of
marching an army against Kumasi, fearing further heavy
losses with no corresponding gain. The general public
did not realize the danger the forts had been in, and
believed that whatever necessity for an expedition may
previously have existed, the victory of the marines at
Elmina must have done away with it, and it was not
until the news of Commodore Commerell's disaster on the
Pra was received that these illusions were dispelled. Fortunately, however, Lord Kimberley, who was Secretary of
State for the Colonies at this time, and the Minister for
War, Mr. Cardwell, who was himself a former Colonial
Secretary, both knew the history of recent British relations with Ashanti, and were, consequently, able to appreciate the importance of the present crisis at its true value,
and to insist, with a confidence inspired by an accurate
knowledge of the facts, upon the absolute necessity for
prompt and decisive action. Lord Kimberley, indeed,
went so far as to threaten to resign if the expedition did
not come off. These two Ministers agreed to appoint an
officer who should be both Civil Governor and Commander-
in-Chief, and their choice fell on Sir Garnet Wolseley. The
only stipulations he made in accepting the appointment
were that he should be given a force of European troops
if he considered their employment necessary, and that he
should not be required to remain as Civil Governor after
the military operations were over.

In July Commander John Glover, R.N., the late Administrator of Lagos, suggested that the eastern tribes might be organized and used to " cause a diversion in the rear of the Ashanti army, and at the same time to threaten Kumasi." He offered to lead such an expedition and to raise a force of Hausas to act with these eastern tribes, pointing out that he had already defeated the Ashantis at Duffo Island, that he was well known in the country, and that he would be able to enlist 100 Hausas where any-one else could raise but five. His plan was to establish a base depot at Adda, whence he proposed to ascend the River Volta and march against Kumasi from the east. Captain Glover had for years dreamed of reaching the unknown countries in the interior of Africa and opening up a great trade route between them and the coast : he had already tried the Niger in vain, and now hoped to discover in the Volta the route he sought. It was even suggested that the river should be ascended in steamers as far as Krachi, that Salaga should be used as a base for the final advance, and that the Dagombas and other tribes would readily be induced to revolt and join in it. Nothing, of course, was known of this country except from the merest hearsay, and the scheme as it stood was about as wild and impracticable as could well be imagined, nor could it ever have been carried out in the time. Even supposing that the many difficulties of the hundred miles or so of unknown and dangerous navigation between Pong and Krachi or Salaga [1] could have been overcome and the necessary stores safely taken up to the advanced base, the final march upon Kumasi from either of these places would have been fully as great an undertaking as that from Cape Coast. Nevertheless, this offer was accepted, and Captain Glover sailed for the Coast on the 19th of August. He was to be under the orders of the Adminis-trator, and the principal definite instruction given to him was that the general object that he was to keep in view was to create such a diversion on the flank and rear of the Ashantis as might force them to retreat from the Pro-tectorate, or, at all events, so to harass and alarm them

[1] The nearest places on the Volta to Salaga are Yegi and Pajai.

as to enable an attack on their front to be made with better

prospects of success.

Sir Garnet Wolseley submitted a rough outline of his scheme, and plainly said that he did not believe it would ever be possible to subjugate Ashanti without the aid of European troops ; but the Government was still so averse to their employment in such an unhealthy climate that it was very difficult to persuade the authorities to act on this recommendation, and the most they would consent to do was to hold two battalions in readiness in case they should be required. Sir Garnet further pointed out that whatever operations were carried out on the Gold Coast would have to be completed during the months of December, January and February, unless enormous risks were to be run by continuing in the field during the rainy season.

Nothing could better show how little the Colonial Authorities at home really knew of this country, which they had occupied and had under their protection for so many years, than the fact that in this emergency they found it necessary to send Sir Garnet Wolseley and his Staff out in September to inspect and report on the spot, and even sent materials for a line of railway and traction engines, which were intended to be used for the transport of military and commissariat stores to Prasu. These materials, some of which were actually landed on the Coast, were utterly useless : no railway could possibly have been laid in such a country within the limits of time imposed by necessity, and nearly as good a road would have been required for the traction engines as for laying a line of rail. The materials for the railway, indeed, never reached the Coast until the 7th of December.

Sir Garnet arrived at Cape Coast on board the *Ambriz*, with a staff of thirty-six specially selected officers, on the 2nd of October and landed the same afternoon. Colonel Harley did not come down to meet him, nor did he send any officer who could point out the various Chiefs who were awaiting him on the beach and whose presence was consequently ignored. Sir Garnet passed immediately into the Castle by the water-gate, while a salute was fired from the spur battery, and then walked out at the main gate and up to Government House, where the outgoing Administrator received him and he was sworn in by the Chief Justice. He found that Colonel Harley had removed to the Castle with Mrs. Harley some time previously, a step that had naturally been construed by the people as an open confession that the town was unsafe ; but Sir Garnet took up his residence in Government House and did everything he could to restore public confidence. Colonel Harley left on the *Volta* on the 6th.

Sir Garnet Wolseley had received very definite instructions from both the Colonial[1] and War[2] Ministers. He was ordered to address a letter to the King of Ashanti calling upon him to withdraw his forces from the Protectorate within a given time, to make adequate reparation for the losses they had inflicted on the protected tribes, and to give security for the maintenance of peace in future ; to threaten him that if he failed to comply with these demands he would be compelled to do so, and that such a defeat would be inflicted upon him as would effectively deter him from any repetition of such aggressions. He was further instructed to collect and organize native forces, and the terms of any peace that would be accepted as satisfactory were also defined. They included a renewal of the King's renunciation of any claim to Elmina or allegiance from any of the protected tribes, the release of the missionaries and all other prisoners, the keeping open of the roads through Ashanti for the purposes of trade, the surrender of hostages of distinction, the payment of an adequate indemnity, and, if possible, the diminution or cessation of human sacrifices and slave raiding.

The Secretary of State can have had but the very vaguest notion of the true state of affairs on the Gold Coast and of the disposition and resources of the Ashantis, if he ever seriously believed that the King would be influenced in the smallest degree by any letter that might be written in accordance with these instructions. The

---

[1] Brackenbury, vol. i, pp. 129–36.   [2] *Ibid.*, pp. 138-41.

Ashanti army was even then in occupation of and living 1873
on the protected territory ; the King had in his capital CHAP. III
numerous prisoners, including several Europeans, and
the lengthy negotiations for their release had convinced
him that they were persons of some importance ; moreover, a review of the whole history of his country's previous
wars with the English was unlikely to inspire him with
much dread of their power ; the head of one of their
Governors killed in battle was amongst his trophies, and
he would have found it hard to believe that any great
change had come over them now. This talk of compulsion, therefore, would have appeared to him to be mere
vain boasting and empty threats, for, so far as he knew,
the only Europeans who came to the Coast were persons
who rode everywhere in hammocks and feared the sun,
and this Governor would have to rely on the Fantis for
fighting men just as his predecessors had done, and these
his own troops had repeatedly and utterly defeated.
When these facts are remembered, the absolute absurdity
of expecting any result from such a letter is at once
manifest, and had it reached the King at this time he
would almost certainly have treated such threats with
absolute derision.

The instructions given to Sir Garnet not only defined
clearly enough what was expected of him, but also made
it abundantly plain that no European troops would be
sent out to assist him unless he was prepared to accept
the full responsibility of saying that their services were
absolutely indispensable, while even then they were not
definitely promised. Sir Garnet himself had never believed
that he could do what was required of him without these
troops, but before finally demanding them he was bound
to see what could be done with the material at hand. He
had expected to find at least 300 trained Hausas on
the Coast who might form the nucleus of a native force,
but he now discovered that all these men had been
sent down to join Captain Glover's expedition, and that
the only disciplined troops at his disposal were between
600 and 700 men of the 2nd West India Regiment, of

whom large numbers were on the sick-list, and a few Fanti Police.   These West Indian troops, moreover, were scattered along the coast in small detachments garrisoning the different forts, and since it was out of the question to withdraw them entirely from this duty, not more than about 300 of them were available for service in the field. Stores, too, were very deficient, and although large quantities of provisions were on their way to the Coast, the actual supply on hand on the 4th of October was only sufficient for four days' rations for the regular troops, and there were 19 Snider rifles and 400 Enfields available for issue.   It was essential, therefore, that an attempt should be made to raise a native force as quickly as possible, so as to enable the General to give an authoritative opinion as to the necessity of employing European troops before it was too late in the season for them to be sent out.

In order to avoid being wholly dependent upon the Fantis and other Coast tribes, efforts were made to obtain recruits from other parts of West Africa, who would be farther from their homes and, therefore, less likely to desert their posts. Officers had already been detached at Bathurst in the Gambia, and at Sierra Leone and the Sherbro to enlist recruits for the formation of two regiments, that were to be commanded by Lieutenant-Colonel Wood, V.C.,[1] and Major Baker Russell.[2]   An arrangement was also made with Captain Strachan, the Administrator of Lagos, for the transfer of 150 Hausas to the Gold Coast in exchange for half that number of men of the 2nd West India Regiment, and other recruiting officers were sent to Bonny and elsewhere.

It now remained to be seen what prospect there was of recruiting from the tribes on the Gold Coast itself.   On the 4th of October a great palaver was held in two marquees pitched together in the grounds of Government House.   In these the Kings and Chiefs and their Linguists were assembled, the remainder of their attendants and people standing outside.   Sir Garnet, being bound by his instructions, had once more to repeat the old ridiculous

---

[1] 90th Regiment.   [2] 13th Hussars.

assertion that the war was a purely native war and not **1878**
Her Majesty's, but promised that, if the people would chap. iii
only exert themselves, they should be given every possible
assistance against the enemy.   Ten pounds a month was
promised to each King and Chief for every thousand men
he put in the field, and the General undertook to supply
them with arms and ammunition, to issue a daily ration
of a pint of rice and a quarter of a pound of salt-beef to
each man or an allowance of $4\frac{1}{2}d$. in lieu thereof, and to
pay the men $1\frac{1}{2}d$. a day.   He told the Chiefs they would
have to make their own transport arrangements without
withdrawing any fighting men from their forces, and
finally asked them to say how many men they were prepared to raise.   After this speech the customary present
of gin was given to the Chiefs, who then retired to consult
together, promising to return with their answer on the
6th.   During the interval, various rumours were circulated that the Chiefs were dissatisfied with the terms
arranged, and that the people thought the pay offered
for fighting men compared very unfavourably with the
shilling a day that had been promised for commissariat
carriers ; but when they returned on the 6th, none of
them made any open complaint, but one and all expressed
their willingness to collect their men if they were given
English officers to accompany and assist them.   They
were in no great hurry to start, however, even after this
request had been granted.   Letters were also sent to those
Kings who had not attended the meeting summoning
them to collect their men and march to Dunkwa, where the
other contingents had been ordered to assemble.

The facts were that the Fantis had suffered so severely
at Jukwa, and their utter defeat and subsequent
privations were still so fresh in their memories, that they
had no great desire to meet the enemy again, while they
also knew perfectly well that the war was really at an end
and that the Ashantis were only awaiting their King's
permission to return to Kumasi.   They had no wish,
therefore, to stir their enemies up into renewed activity
by threatening to attack them, but infinitely preferred

1878 to let them retire in their own time and unmolested,
CHAP. III thankful that they went at all, and, with a typically
African want of foresight, caring very little about the
probability of their speedy return. It must be remembered, too, that they had heard similar appeals and promises made by other Governors in the past and had seen
very little come of them, and the General, wishing to make
the people do their utmost, had carefully avoided making
any allusion to the possible employment of European
troops and had only spoken of defeating the Ashantis
with an army of Fantis, a feat that the Fantis themselves,
whether they thought it possible or not, were certainly
not eager to attempt. The whole brunt of the present
war had hitherto fallen upon them, and the feeble support
that had been given to them during its earlier stages by
Colonel Harley had caused much dissatisfaction. Moreover, they knew well enough that the quarrel had not
been caused by them, but by the action of the Government in accepting the transfer of Elmina, and it is not
surprising, therefore, that the Chiefs were none too ready
to accept mere promises as proof that a different regime
was now to be inaugurated, and they can hardly be blamed
for having hung back a little at first. Sir Garnet Wolseley
himself admitted this, and wrote : " Seeing that we left
them almost entirely to themselves at the beginning of
this contest, it is scarcely to be expected that without
something more than mere verbal assurances the whole of
a much-dispersed and dispirited people will suddenly come
to believe in our serious intention vigorously to aid them.
To get the people to act with that rapidity which for our
purposes is essential we must act energetically ourselves." [1]

Persistent rumours were now current that the Ashantis
were planning an attack on Cape Coast, and the town was
accordingly put in the best possible condition for defence
under the command of Colonel Festing. Fort William,
Fort Victoria and Prospect Hill were all garrisoned ;
shelter trenches were dug and manned ; the bush in the
valleys was cleared ; the 2nd West India Regiment was

[1] *Ashantee War* (Parliamentary Paper, 1873-4), part iii, p. 248.

removed from the Castle to a camp on Connor's Hill, and 1873
a code of signals was arranged that would secure the CHAP. III
landing of bluejackets and marines from the men-of-war
at any hour of the day or night. Captain Buller [1] was
placed in charge of the Intelligence Department and collected and collated all available information, and surveys
and road sketches were undertaken in every direction.

The Ashantis encamped at Mampon and Efutu were
still drawing their supplies from the villages around Elmina.
Great quantities of smoked fish were constantly being
sent up from Ampeni and the other villages along the coast,
and cloth, rum and other goods passed by the same route
after being sent over by canoe from Elmina. The Am-
penis had, moreover, recently captured some Cape Coast
canoes, killing the crews and passengers and dashing out
the brains of their children against the gunwales. The
General had already summoned the Chiefs of these villages
to meet him in Elmina that he might warn them to desist
from such practices, but they had taken no notice of his
messages and were relying on the assurances of the Ashantis
that they had nothing to fear and could afford to defy the
Government, as the British would never venture to attack
them in the bush and could do them no harm if they did.
Parties of Ashantis had even approached within a few
miles of the town itself and fired on the surveying parties,
so that it was essential that something should be done
at once if any semblance of British authority and prestige
was to be maintained. The Fantis also needed some
encouragement before they would take the field again,
and nothing short of a success of some kind against the
enemy was likely to restore their confidence. Sir Garnet
therefore determined to make an attack on the Ashantis
quartered in these villages ; but the troops he had were
so few in comparison with the number of the enemy that
his only hope of success lay in the preservation of the most
absolute secrecy, so that the enemy might be taken by
surprise and defeated before these outlying detachments
could be reinforced from the main camps.

[1] 6oth Rifles.

1873   The attack was arranged for the 14th of October : 138
CHAP. III Hausas had arrived from Lagos on the 10th, and were
taken over to Elmina on the following day. Sir Garnet
accompanied them, and, after explaining his plans to
Colonel Wood, who was in command of the place, returned
to Cape Coast. It was now necessary to deceive the
Ashanti spies and give some excuse for the removal of
the garrison from Cape Coast, and it was therefore given
out that the General had received bad news from the Volta
River district, where Captain Glover was said to have met
with a serious reverse and to be hemmed in at Adda and
in urgent need of help. The men of the 2nd West India
Regiment were embarked on H.M.S. *Decoy* at six o'clock
on the evening of the 13th, and Sir Garnet and some of
his officers boarded the *Barracouta* three hours later. The
troops were replaced by bluejackets, who were landed to
garrison the Castle, and everyone, with the exception of a
very few officers on the General's personal staff, fully believed
that they were bound for Accra to relieve Captain Glover.

Soon after midnight, the ships sailed and reached Elmina
at about three o'clock. It was a pitch-dark night, but the
troops were got into the boats after some trouble and
towed towards the mouth of the River Benya. But there
an unexpected delay occurred, for the tide had been miscalculated, and nearly every boat grounded on the bar
and everyone got wet through ; much of the ammunition,
indeed, had to be changed. It was nearly five o'clock
before the last men landed and were joined by the Hausas
under Colonel Wood and the carriers whom he had kept
locked up in the Castle all night. A cordon of police had
been drawn round the town and no preparations had been
made in the Castle until after the drawbridge had been
raised for the night, so that it was tolerably certain that
no warning could yet have reached the enemy. Sir
Garnet gave Colonel Wood the command, and the column
marched at half-past five, accompanied by Chiefs Esilfi
and Ando [1] and twenty loyal Elminas as guides.

---

[1] These two Chiefs rendered valuable service during the war and
accompanied the army to Kumasi.

At about seven o'clock the neighbourhood of Esaman was reached, and the Ashanti outposts suddenly opened fire on the Hausas at close range. Nothing could be seen of the enemy, who had carefully concealed themselves in the thick bush and high grass near the road, and for some time the firing on both sides was very heavy, though wild ; but a gun and rockets were brought up and opened fire on the village, the marines were thrown out into the bush, and before long the enemy had been driven back and the place captured and destroyed. When entered, its only occupant was a small child, who had been abandoned or forgotten and was taken back with the troops, and the frequent explosions of powder and tremendous blaze of burning rum as the flames spread through the place showed plainly enough what a store-house it had been. The troops engaged were—2nd West India Regiment, 205 ; Hausas, 126 ; Bluejackets, 29 ; Royal Marine Artillery, 20 ; and Royal Marine Light Infantry, 129, making a total of 409 combatants, with whom were 300 carriers with food, ammunition and hammocks, and a rocket-trough and 7-pounder gun. The casualties, considering the closeness of the enemy, were very slight : one Hausa was killed, Colonel McNeill, V.C., and Captain Fremantle, R.N., were severely wounded, and one other officer, two marines, fifteen Hausas and three of the carriers were also hit. Colonel McNeill was Sir Garnet's Chief of Staff, but this wound, which divided all the tendons in his wrist, necessitated his being invalided, and he was succeeded by Colonel Greaves.

After an hour's halt, the column marched to Ankwanda, which was found deserted : the village was burned and the wounded were then sent back to Elmina. At two o'clock, the Hausas, with 150 of the 2nd West India Regiment and a few bluejackets and marines, pushed on to Brenu Akinim and Ampeni. Both these villages were found deserted, as the warships had been shelling them for some time ; a flag was flying behind Ampeni, however, and the recently decapitated body of a prisoner or sacrificed slave lay near the lagoon. The men were fired on by a

few small parties of the enemy hidden in the bush, but
no great damage was done ; a few Hausas were wounded,
and the rebels were then driven off by them and the Naval
Brigade.   Both places were burned ; water was landed
from the ships for the troops, and the men then returned
to Elmina, which they reached at eight o'clock the same
night, after having marched a total distance of about
twenty-one miles.

The success of this little expedition more than compensated for the trifling loss that it entailed ; for the
Ashantis were deprived of their main sources of supply,
and the people of other villages, upon which they might
otherwise have drawn, were now afraid to help them ;
public confidence in the Government was also restored to
some extent, and the Fantis, seeing their enemy beaten
in the bush, at last began to come forward and join the
allied camp at Dunkwa.   Their numbers, however, were
small, and it had been apparent for some time past that
there was very little hope of raising any really effective
force on the Coast.   There was no excuse for them now
that practical proof had been given that the General
really intended to attack the Ashantis in the bush and was
able to beat them ; but the Chiefs either could not, or
would not, induce their men to mobilize, and instead of the
thousands that had been promised, only a few hundreds
turned up, while the people of Cape Coast actually claimed
the disgraceful privilege of being the last to make a move.
The recruiting in the neighbouring Settlements had been
equally unsuccessful, and the only men obtained were
66 from Sierra Leone, 120 Kossus (Mendis) from the
Sherbro, 100 men from the Gambia, and 53 Opobos and
104 Bonnys who arrived a little later from the Niger
Delta : 100 Kru boys were also obtained as carriers.   These
men, with the Cape Coast Volunteers and those Fantis
who had been collected, were formed into two native corps
—Wood's and Russell's Regiments.   The actual composition of these regiments was as follows : Wood's Regiment
—No. 1 Company, Cape Coast Volunteers ; No. 2 Company, Elminas ; No. 3 Company, Kossus ; No. 4 Company,

Bonnys.   Russell's Regiment—No. 1 Company, Hausas;
No. 2 Company, Sierra Leonians ; No. 3 Company, Mumfords ; No. 4 Company, Winnebas ; No. 5 Company, Opobos;
No. 6 Company, Anamabos.   After this, an irregular and
undisciplined force of not more than 1,500 of the allied
tribesmen remained, and this was apparently all that
could be hoped for on the Coast.   Sir Garnet had, moreover, been warned by his experiences during the attack on
Esaman that the men were very liable to get out of hand
while fighting in the bush, where it was impossible for
their officers to supervise them properly, while the undisciplined natives were a positive source of danger, owing
to their habit of firing recklessly in all directions.   A few
Hausas, instead of being drafted into Russell's Regiment,
were handed over to Captain Rait [1] and trained as gunners.

It was obviously impossible to invade Ashanti with
such a force, and Sir Garnet, therefore, wrote home demanding the despatch of the European troops for whom
he had asked.   Knowing that there was even now a
possibility that they might be refused him, he made out
a strong case.   He showed that there was little or no hope
of securing peace except by inflicting a signal defeat on
the Ashantis ; that this certainly could not be done without the assistance of European troops ; that they would
not be required to serve on the Coast during the unhealthy
season ;   that everything would be prepared for their
reception before they arrived, and that the risk to their
health would be far less than was commonly supposed,
the losses in previous undertakings, especially during
the expedition in 1863, having been due mainly to causes
that would be effectively guarded against on this occasion.
His first request was for two battalions of Infantry and
small detachments of Artillery, Royal Engineers, etc. ;
but he soon afterwards increased these by a third battalion
in a letter dated the 24th of October, in which he wrote :
" I have seen the days pass by since I held a reception of
the native Kings and Chiefs, and no native levies of any
importance have taken the field.   Apathy, if not cowardice,

[1] Royal Artillery.

seems to have enveloped the people of these tribes. I had
hoped to raise large native levies from every portion of
the Coast ; but a few scores of men from each tribe,
amounting altogether to only a few hundreds, seem all
that I am likely to obtain. I have seen the danger of
depending on ill-disciplined levies in bush-warfare. I
have learned that the 2nd West India Regiment, on
which I had relied as an effective battalion, is unable to
furnish more than about 100 bayonets for the field." [1]

It was at this time that Sir Garnet, in accordance with
his instructions, sent his letter to the King. In it he
asserted that the invasion was without justification, but
that he was willing to discuss terms of peace provided the
King would comply with the following conditions within
twenty days : first, the withdrawal of all the Ashanti
forces from the Protectorate ; second, the immediate
surrender of all prisoners, and third, the giving of guarantees for the payment of compensation. The letter continued : " If you, in good faith, consent to these conditions
I shall be ready to treat with you in a friendly spirit, and
to consider any reasonable proposals you may make.
But if within twenty days I have not received from you
an assurance of your readiness to comply with Her
Majesty's wishes, or if you have not, within the date
already mentioned, withdrawn all your forces within your
own territory beyond the Prah River, having given such
guarantees as may satisfy me for the fulfilment of the
above-mentioned terms, I hereby warn you to expect
the full punishment which your deeds have merited. Rest
well assured that power will not be wanting to that end.
I can scarcely believe that you do not know how unequal
would be the struggle which you invite." [2]

Three copies of this letter were forwarded by separate
messengers on the 14th, 17th and 18th of October. Two
of them were intercepted and opened by Amankwa Tia
in his camp at Mampon, and the third also failed to reach its
destination. It would have been interesting to see what

---

[1] Brackenbury, vol. i, p. 229.
[2] *Ashantee War* (Parliamentary Paper, 1873–4), part iii, p. 203.

reply Kofi Karikari would have made to such demands 1873
and threats at this stage of the war, but Amankwa Tia, CHAP. III
instead of forwarding the letters to him—possibly because
the main road, by which Ashanti law prescribed that all
King's messengers must travel, was not open to him—
took it upon himself to reply, and sent the following remarkable document to the General.

"MAMPON, *October* 20, 1873.

" To his Excellency's Governor-in-Chief of Her Majesty's
Fort.

" SIR,
" I have received those two letters which you sent
to me in order to send them to the King of Ashantee.
For what purpose I came here is that : Assin, Dankra,
Akyem, Wassaw. Those four nations belong to the King
of Ashantee, and they refused to serve the King, and they
escaped away unto you. If the King sends his servants to
or to buy something at Cape Coast they catch them and
plundered their good to. And those nations ordered the
King of Ashantee that he may come and fight with them.
Therefore I said that they are not a friends with the King.
On account of that I shall come down here to catch those
four chieves who ordered the King of Ashantee to come
to fight with them.

" And they fought with me six times, and I drove them
away, and they escaped to be under you. But the King
did not send me into Cape Coast, and when you deliver
Assin, Dankra, Akyim and Wassaw unto me I shall bring
unto the King there is no any quarrel with you.

" I send my love to you.

" I am yours,

" (Signed) AMANKWATIA." [1]

Whether or not any of these Chiefs, relying on the
protection of the English, had sent insulting messages or

[1] *Ashantee War* (Parliamentary Paper, 1873–4), part iii, p. 210.
A facsimile of this letter forms the frontispiece to Brackenbury's
Ashantee War.

challenges to the King is unknown ; it is very possible, however, that they had interfered with his traders, for such occurrences were very common, and were made the grounds of complaint and proved to be true on more than one occasion. Amankwa Tia, for some reason, entirely ignored the main cause of the war—the cession of Elmina—and in spite of the direct attacks that he had made first upon the capital of the King of Denkera and then upon Elmina itself, elected to give this reason for the invasion. The Ashantis may have held that the treaty of 1831 had been broken and was invalidated by the failure of the English to keep the road to the Pra open and safe, by their non-surrender of Janin, and by the supervention of the last invasion, and now felt entitled to make their own terms, first among which would naturally be the return of their lost tributaries. On the other hand, it is, of course, possible that when once the cession of Elmina had brought about a resumption of hostilities, the Ashantis may merely have recognized the occasion as a favourable one for regaining their suzerainty over these tribes without troubling to justify it at all. The most plausible reason, however, that Amankwa Tia can have had for concealing the real object of this expedition was that in stating it he would have had to admit that he had failed, and that the victory was really with the English, in spite of the defeats he had inflicted on the allies. It was of special importance to the Ashantis to regain their power over Denkera ; for just as Elmina was necessary to them for trading purposes, unless they used the distant market of Assini, so an open road to it was equally necessary, and it could only be reached by passing through the territory of the now hostile Denkeras.

Sir Garnet Wolseley's letters however, in conjunction with his successful attack on Esaman and the discovery that both Mansu and Dunkwa were already occupied by his troops, so alarmed the Ashantis, who saw their line of retreat threatened, that Amankwa Tia decided to break up his camp and retire towards the Pra while there was yet time and without waiting any longer for the expected per-

mission from the King.   This retreat was to be carried out   1878
from Mampon along the road through Jukwa and Asanchi,   CHAP. III
and from Efutu through Ahonton, to join the main road to
the frontier at Dunkwa and Akrofu, and rumours soon
became current that it was Amankwa Tia's intention to
attack and destroy Abakrampa on his way north as a
punishment for the resistance offered by the Abras at the
commencement of the campaign.   Several Ashanti
prisoners had been taken wandering about in the bush,
with the apparent intention of inviting capture, and one
and all had told the same tale of sickness and despondency
in their camp.   None of these men, however, had been
taken in battle, and a strong suspicion arose that they
were merely repeating a lesson and had been sent out for
the special purpose of being captured and deceiving the
English, and, consequently, very little credence had hitherto
been given to these reports.   The news of the enemy's
retreat was now confirmed, however, by a Fanti woman
named Araba Bosuma, who had been living in the Ashanti
camp as the slave-wife of one of the Chiefs for the past
five months and had now contrived to escape.   She gave
a most circumstantial account of the beginning of this
movement.   The first column, with which were the
wounded and prisoners, had already left, having marched
by the Jukwa road on the 16th of October ; but the
occupation of Dunkwa by the allies under Colonel Festing
had compelled it to halt at Iscabio, a village a few miles
farther west.   The second column, under Amankwa Tia,
had left Efutu on the 25th, advancing directly towards
Abakrampa, and it was believed that its object was to
attack and destroy this place and then join the main road
at Akrofu and retire across the Pra.   According to the
statements made by Ashantis after the war was over,
however, Amankwa Tia's real object was to threaten
some of the British posts lower down the road, and thus
compel Colonel Festing, who would then be in danger of
being cut off, to evacuate Dunkwa and leave the road
open for the retreat of the Ashanti army.

Ever since the despatch of European troops had been

definitely requested, every effort had been made to hasten the construction of the road to the Pra, and posts were now held on it as far as Mansu, where a strong stockaded redoubt—Fort Cambridge—was built to hold a garrison of 200 men. This was ready by the end of October, and the road was then reported fit for the march of infantry in fours as far as that place.

Abakrampa had been occupied since the 15th of October by Lieutenant Pollard[1] with ten men of the 2nd West India Regiment, three Fanti Police and about eighty Abras, but the continued rumours of a projected Ashanti attack on the place now led to the garrison being reinforced by a number of Hausas from Cape Coast and Dunkwa and some more police. The village was built on the side of a hill : the houses were loop-holed, and the Wesleyan Chapel, which stood at the upper end of the street, was also loop-holed and its thatched roof removed as a precaution against fire. Here food, water and ammunition were stored in expectation of the attack.

[1] Royal Navy.

CHAPTER IV

THE RETREAT OF THE ASHANTI ARMY

1873

So soon as it was definitely known that the Ashantis were retiring, Sir Garnet Wolseley made every effort to maintain touch with them and keep them on the move, hoping in this way not only to inflict some loss on the enemy by harassing his rear-guard, but, more important still, to accelerate his departure, and, by appearing to be driving him from the Protectorate, to instil fresh courage and energy into the native allies. The posts on the road were strengthened, and the Dunkwa garrison was reinforced by fifty men of the 2nd West India Regiment and two 7-pounder guns. The forts at Elmina were garrisoned by men landed from H.M.S. *Druid* to enable Colonel Wood to move the whole of his men to Abi and thence to act against the enemy's rear in the direction of Mampon. Reconnaissances were ordered from all the posts, and on the 26th of October Sir Garnet himself left Cape Coast with 100 men of Russell's Regiment and 265 marines and bluejackets from the *Simoom* and the squadron, and marched to Asebu, at the junction of the roads to Abakrampa and Dunkwa. The column left Cape Coast at three o'clock in the afternoon, but the heat on the shadeless road was so great that numbers of the men fell out, and it was not until long after dark that Asebu was reached. There information was received that several bodies of the enemy were moving along the road through Iscabio towards Dunkwa, and Sir Garnet therefore decided to push on to Abakrampa in the hope that he might

take the Ashantis in the flank, while orders were sent to
Colonel Festing at Dunkwa to advance towards Iscabio
with i.. whole force.

At half-past ten on the morning of the 27th, Colonel
Festing marched out of Dunkwa with every available man.
His force consisted of 12 officers and 701 men, of whom
73 belonged to the 2nd West India Regiment, 7 to Rait's
Artillery, and 6 to the Fanti Police, while the remaining
615 were undisciplined native levies. The column advanced towards Iscabio in a drenching thunderstorm,
and, after traversing about three miles of the road, took a
prisoner, who was compelled to show the way to the Ashanti
camp. The Anamabos were leading, and at about two
o'clock the whole force charged into the enemy's camp. The
noise of the storm had covered their advance so well that
the Ashantis, numbering some 4,000 or 5,000 men under
Esaman Kwanta and Kwesi Dumfi, were taken completely
by surprise and fled into the bush : they rallied almost
immediately, however, and poured in a heavy fire from
the surrounding forest. This was as quickly returned ;
but the Anamabos were now at a disadvantage, being in
the open clearing while the enemy were all under cover.
A 7-pounder gun and a rocket-trough were brought into
action, and round after round of shrapnel, case, and rockets
was fired into the bush ; but the enemy replied as briskly as
before, and the incessant beating of their war-drums could
be plainly heard above the din. After the action had
lasted for nearly two hours, Colonel Festing advanced
with the West Indians, who poured in several volleys
and very soon dispersed the enemy. The camp was then
destroyed and the British force returned to Dunkwa.
The West Indians, on this and on many subsequent occasion, showed great nerve and steadiness and fully atoned
for their want of firmness at Esaman, which had been
their first experience of bush fighting. The fire of the
Ashantis throughout the action was very heavy, but " the
only natives who had fought at all well were the Anamabos,
the remainder having to be thrashed into action by the
officers, whilst numbers of them disappeared altogether

from the scene, or remained huddled up in small groups without fighting."[1] The casualties amongst the officers who had been trying to lead these men forward were proportionately heavy : five out of the ten officers engaged were wounded, including Colonel Festing and Captain Godwin,[2] whose wound was so severe that he had to be invalided to England. One Anamabo was killed, and four West Indians and forty-two natives were wounded ; of the latter, twenty-three were Anamabos, amongst whom was their King.

Next morning, Sir Garnet, who knew nothing of this engagement, advanced from Abakrampa towards Asanchi, where a large party of Ashantis was known to be encamped. He expected that Colonel Festing would advance simultaneously from Dunkwa, and that the enemy would thus be taken between two fires and utterly defeated. On reaching Asanchi, however, the camp was found deserted, and the troops halted and stood listening for any sounds of firing in the direction of Dunkwa before continuing the advance. Colonel Festing's native levies, however, had flatly refused to move, and after the stout resistance offered by the enemy on the previous day, he had not felt justified in making another advance with his handful of regulars only ; consequently, Sir Garnet had to return soon after midday and an excellent opportunity of inflicting a crushing defeat on the retreating Ashanti army was missed through the cowardice and apathy of the native allies. At this very time Amankwa Tia was marching along the road from Efutu towards Abakrampa, and, had he been aware of Sir Garnet's movements, might easily have taken him in the flank.

The General had to be constantly on his guard against unduly exposing any of the European troops in the bush ; finding, therefore, that the Ashantis made no immediate move against Abakrampa, and being unwilling to keep the Naval Brigade encamped there for an indefinite period, he returned to Cape Coast next day and re-embarked his men, leaving only 25 marines and 25 bluejackets to garrison

---

[1] Brackenbury, vol. i, p. 240.   [2] 103rd Bombay Fusiliers.

the village, with 200 men of Russell's Regiment, 80 Hausas, and about 300 Abras. This garrison was reinforced a few days later by the addition of 85 men of the 2nd West India Regiment and some Kossus, Mumfords and Winnebas belonging to Wood's and Russell's Regiments. Captain Sarbah's company of Volunteers—the Gold Coast Rifles— was also sent up and attached to the 2nd West India Regiment, and the Abras from Dunkwa were transferred to this post.

The Gold Coast Rifle Corps was a volunteer corps that had been enrolled on the 20th of June. None but British subjects or those who had been under British protection before and since the 31st of December 1867 were enlisted, and the officers and men paid monthly subscriptions for the purchase of arms and stores and also provided their own uniforms. The officers [1] of this Corps were : Captain John Sarbah, Lieutenants S. H. Brew and Thomas Penny, Sub-Lieutenants J. P. Brown (Adjutant) and Samuel Bannerman.

Sir Garnet's position was now most tantalizing. The enemy were in full retreat, yet he was unable to follow and harass them. The European troops had not yet arrived and could not be expected for some time ; the few regulars then on the Coast were insufficient for the work to be done, and the native allies, who might have provided an adequate force and inflicted a severe defeat on the enemy, either would not turn out or would not fight when they did. Any attempt to follow and attack the Ashantis with the small force at his disposal must have involved a terrible risk of bringing them to bay and repeating Sir Charles M'Carthy's disaster at Insamankow, and Sir Garnet therefore made a last despairing effort to put some spirit into the people, and, on his return from Abakrampa, published the following proclamation :

" To all Kings, Headmen, Chiefs and Tribes of the Gold Coast Allies of Her Majesty the Queen of England, greeting.

" I desire that you should know that immediately after

[1] All Africans.

the attack made upon Essaman and Ampinee and the **1873**
destruction of those places by the English troops under CHAP. IV
my command, your enemies broke up their encampment
at Mampon. Finding that they were unable to contend
with us either in the open or in the bush, they are now in
full retreat, endeavouring to return to their own country
by Prah'sue ; one of their retreating columns has been
attacked and dispersed by my troops near Dunquah.

" They are trying to carry with them in their flight
all the goods of which they have robbed you, all the wives
and children whom they have stolen from you.

" Men of the Gold Coast, will you allow this ?

" Will you let the hours slip by, whilst your wives,
your sons and your daughters are being driven off to
slaughter by the flying enemy ?

" Will you not pursue them ?

" Now or never is the time to show that you are men.

" I, for my part, shall hold no man as the friend of Her
Majesty or as the friend of this country who delays for
one moment.

" You have nothing to fear ; I hold the whole road
from here to Mansue, so that they cannot assail it. Gather
upon my strong forts of Dunkwa, Abrakampa and Mansue.
No one will venture to attack these points. Thence press
onwards to the Prah, and oppose your enemies as they
are endeavouring to recross the river. If you now act
quickly and with vigour, the fall of your enemy and the
peace of your country will be secured." [1]

This plain statement of the condition of affairs and so
stirring an appeal might have been expected to have an
immediate effect ; but the Fantis seem to have been
thoroughly cowed and quite unable to recover any portion
of the courage that they had undoubtedly shown on some
previous occasions. The General's comments in many
subsequent despatches clearly show that this appeal
failed to have the least effect upon them : on the 5th of
November he wrote : " It is impossible to exaggerate
the cowardice and feebleness of the conduct of our native

[1] *Ashantee War* (Parliamentary Paper, 1873-4), part iii, p. 232.

allies. They remain absolutely in the rear, abandoning our officers and firing wildly into the air at nothing ; then a sudden panic seizes them, and they rush panic-stricken home when no Ashantee is near them. Near Beulah a panic of this kind occurred because they came across some dead Ashantees. From Abrakampa similar scenes are reported." [1]

On the 3rd of November strong reconnaissances were made from Beula, Abakrampa and Dunkwa. The two latter alone came upon the enemy, and only Colonel Festing's force from Dunkwa found them in any great numbers. His column consisted of 9 officers and 1,111 men, of whom 1,011 were native levies. Advancing from Dunkwa soon after dawn in the direction of Iscabio, they soon came in touch with the enemy's scouts, who fired on the advance-guard and at once fell back. This, of course, precluded all possibility of again taking the Ashantis by surprise. A large camp was found a little farther along the road, whence a heavy fire was opened. The greater part of the allies, including whole tribes, immediately fled to Dunkwa and even beyond it, while of the 200 Anamabos even, not more than 60 or 70 stood their ground. Lieu-tenant Eardley Wilmot, R.A., pushed through to the front and opened fire with rockets, but was almost imme-diately severely wounded in the arm. He remained at his post, however, doing his best to put some courage into his men while his servant went back to fetch lint for his wound ; but before it could be brought he fell, shot through the heart. Colonel Festing dashed forward and brought in his body from the very front of the battle, and was himself wounded in the hip whilst doing so, while Surgeon-Major Gore, who came to his assistance, was also hit. The body was subsequently carried to Cape Coast and buried alongside that of Governor Keate. The steadiness of the West Indians alone saved the situation, and after the action had lasted two hours the enemy's fire slackened a little and the troops fell back upon Dunkwa. According to the accounts given by prisoners taken soon afterwards,

[1] *Ashantee War* (Parliamentary Paper, 1873–4), part iii, p. 250.

the Ashantis suffered very heavily in this engagement, 1873
and one rocket alone fell among a group of Chiefs and CHAP. IV
killed or maimed six of them. The British force engaged
and their losses were :

	Engaged.	Killed.	Wounded.	
			Severely.	Slightly.
Officers	9	1	5	—
2nd West India Regiment .	80	—	10	2
Rait's Artillery . . .	8	—	—	—
Fanti Police	12	—	—	1
Native Levies . . .	1,011	1	50	?
TOTALS	1,120	2	65	3 known

On the 5th, the long-predicted attack on Abakrampa
was made. At half-past three that afternoon the Ashantis
advanced against the western side of the town, driving
in the picket and opening a heavy fire on the advanced
skirmishers. The bush had been cleared for a distance
of about 100 yards all round the town, but the enemy had
evidently learned from previous experience not to expose
themselves in the open ; for though they made frequent
attempts to break out, shouting and cheering as they
advanced to the edge of the bush, they always recoiled
on reaching the clearing, and Major Baker Russell's efforts
to tempt them into the open by withholding his fire were
quite unavailing. In addition to the actual exposure, the
Ashantis were placed at a still greater disadvantage ; for
the bush had been so cleared as to leave all the stumps
as sharp stakes, several inches high. Anything approaching a rapid advance over such ground would have been
difficult enough even for men who were well shod ; but
for the bare-footed Ashantis, exposed as they were to a
galling fire while their own weapons were still outranged,
it was utterly impossible.

At about five o'clock, the enemy's fire slackened and a
party of scouts was sent down the Asebu road and found
the Ashantis advancing along several paths that they had
recently cut through the bush. A little later, a furious

attack was made on the western and south-western sides of the town, where the Ashantis charged boldly into the open and made a determined attempt to carry the position with a rush ; but they were driven back by the fire of the West Indians and Russell's Regiment and once more forced to seek the shelter of the forest. After two hours' heavy firing another lull occurred, but the attack was quickly renewed and maintained with but few intermissions until midnight, after which only a few occasional shots were exchanged between the enemy's sentries and some picked men on the British side. All the officers and the greater part of the garrison remained at their posts throughout the night, but by four o'clock on the morning of the 6th the firing had ceased altogether, and so soon as day broke scouts were sent out and reported that the enemy had drawn off but were again advancing from Adasmadi, where Amankwa Tia had his camp. The attack was renewed at eleven o'clock in a rather half-hearted manner.; for although the enemy surrounded the place on three sides, they never once left the bush, but hung about its edge and kept up a continuous fire, which only ceased at dusk.

Major Russell's first report had reached Cape Coast at nine o'clock on the evening of the 5th. It had merely stated that he was attacked, but had given the General no reason to believe that he was likely to require any assistance. At a quarter-past two on the morning of the 6th, however, a message was brought in from Akrofu that heavy firing had been heard until eight o'clock at night in the direction of Abakrampa and that the mail from that place had not arrived. Immediate preparations were then made to relieve the garrison. Captain Brackenbury was sent off to the *Barracouta* at three o'clock in the morning with a letter requesting the assistance of the Naval Brigade, and 22 officers and 303 men were landed from the squadron soon after daybreak. The General and his Staff marched with them, but the heat was so great and the men were so badly equipped—few of the marines having helmets, and the bluejackets wearing only low white-covered caps—that the road was soon dotted with

stragglers, and more than 10 per cent of the whole force
failed even to reach Asebu, only ten miles from Cape
Coast. There, although firing could be heard in the
direction of Abakrampa, it was found impossible to go
any farther until the remaining men, who were now
thoroughly exhausted, had had some hours' rest. At
four o'clock, when the march was resumed, only 141 men
were fit to proceed ; but the 50 marines who had formed
the Asebu garrison were taken on, and the party, advancing
by the Bateyan road, reached Abakrampa at sunset without having met with any opposition. The enemy had by
that time drawn off, and, though occasional shots were
exchanged throughout the evening, the attack was not
renewed.

Heavy as the enemy's fire had been during the two
days' fighting, the British casualties were most trifling :
one officer and one man of the 2nd West India Regiment
were very slightly wounded, one of the *Barracouta's* seamen was struck over the eye whilst looking out from the
Chapel roof, where a light naval gun and a rocket-trough
had been mounted, and about eighteen of the allies were
hit. The enemy, who were believed to have been at
least 8,000 strong, must have suffered much more severely.
The smallness of the garrison's loss was due to their
having fought from shelter trenches, or from behind the
loop-holed walls of the houses, and to the range at which
most of the firing had been carried on. The enemy having
been kept at a distance by the large clearing, their old
muskets had been outranged and most of their slugs fell
short, or were fully spent. The only real danger to the
defenders had been the impossibility of relieving any of
the men from duty, owing to their small numbers, and the
consequent risk that they might become worn out by
fatigue before they could be reinforced.

Next morning, the 7th, the garrison waited for the
attack to be renewed ; but when two o'clock came and
nothing had happened beyond a few desultory shots from
the forest, it was suspected that the enemy must be retreating, and the General ordered the Cape Coast levies,

of whom about 1,000 had arrived that morning with Colonel Wood, to advance into the bush. This, however, was the very last thing they wished to do, and, although they were driven to the edge of the forest, one and all then lay down and refused to move. Sir Garnet wrote : " My officers belaboured them with sticks and umbrellas, and Russell's fierce Kossus drove them on with their cutlasses from behind. Had I not witnessed this scene I could not have believed that the world contained such cowards. The Chiefs, if anything, were worse than their followers. But the bush in their front proved to be unoccupied, for the Ashantee army had already fallen back." [1] The Kossus, from their first arrival on the Coast, had been averse to carrying firearms, preferring to fight with the short swords to which they were accustomed.

Meanwhile, the Abras and Hausas had gone down the road to the camp at Adasmadi, where they took a number of Ashantis completely by surprise. This proved to be the rear-guard, for the main body had already left, taking Amankwa Tia, who was far too drunk to walk, with them. After exchanging a few shots, they also fled. The Hausas, under Lieutenant Gordon,[2] pursued them for some distance and took several prisoners, but soon left their officer and turned back to join the Abras in plundering the deserted camp. Here every sign of a precipitate flight was apparent : great heaps of baggage lay piled on every side, and more was strewn along the road ; even the chairs and stools of many of the Chiefs, including that of the King of Denkera, which had been captured and used by Amankwa Tia, and a number of war-drums [3] had been hastily abandoned. Brass pans, muskets, kegs of powder and baskets of goods lay everywhere. Many Fanti slaves, too, were found " in log " and liberated, and the headless trunks of others, who had been murdered to prevent their falling into the hands of the victors, lay around. One Komenda woman with her child was found

---

[1] Wolseley, vol. ii, p. 306.　　　　　　[2] 98th Regiment.
[3] Some of these drums are now in the United Service Institute's Museum.

with a great gash in her neck, her master having been 1878
shot as he was in the act of decapitating her. " The mark CHAP. IV
on her throat, and the terribly frightened look in the eyes
that had so recently looked death close in the face, were
the best witnesses to the truth of her tale." [1]

Next morning, the 8th, Sir Garnet, who was suffering
from fever, returned to Cape Coast with the Naval Brigade,
leaving fifty bluejackets and marines under Major Allnutt
as a temporary garrison in Abakrampa. Soon after his
arrival he had to be removed to the *Simoom*, and it was
not until the 20th that he was sufficiently recovered to
resume duty.

During the same morning, a reconnaissance was made
from Abakrampa towards Ainsa by a few Abras, about
100 Kossus of Wood's Regiment, and between 500 and 600
Cape Coast and Asebu allies, under Captain Bromhead [2] and
Lieutenant Gordon : [3] they were afterwards joined by
50 Hausas. From prisoners taken on the road they learned
that there were about 2,000 Ashantis at Ainsa under
Amankwa Tia. By this time nearly 300 of the allies had
already bolted, and the remainder would undoubtedly
have followed suit had they not been driven on by the
Kossus. As the party approached Ainsa, the enemy
fired a few shots from the bush on their left ; the Cape
Coast levies were immediately seized with panic and
began firing wildly as fast as they could load, and in their
excitement and terror even fired into the Abras. The
panic quickly infected the Abras, Kossus and Hausas,
and in a very short time nearly the whole of the ammunition was expended. This terrific fusillade, however, had
had the effect of silencing the enemy's fire, and at four
o'clock the order was given to retire. Very soon afterwards the allies were again seized with panic and ran down
the road, knocking down their officers and the Hausas,
after which the majority of them disappeared altogether.
The King of Abra and a few of his men alone kept their
heads. The Kossus and Hausas each had one man killed

---

[1] Brackenbury, vol. i, p. 270. [2] 24th Regiment.
[3] 93rd Regiment.

and two wounded, and another Hausa was reported missing ; he was believed to have been trampled to death by
the terrified Fantis while crossing a small stream. Seventeen Fantis came to have their wounds dressed, but their
sudden wholesale retreat to Cape Coast prevented any
accurate news of their losses being obtained ; it was said,
however, that they lost fifty men killed, many of them
probably by the slugs of their own men. Captain Bromhead, when passing along this road two or three days later,
found forty-five of their headless bodies on the path itself.
After this disgraceful affair Sir Garnet Wolseley wrote :
" Even the enemy's retreat cannot instil courage into
these faint-hearted natives, and they can neither be
counted on to ensure a victory nor complete a defeat.   They
were ordered to pursue the enemy, remain in the field, and
harass him in his retreat.   The road was strewn with the
débris of the retreating army, the bodies of murdered
slaves lay along the route, many prisoners were captured,
the enemy's fire was silenced ; and yet such is the cowardice
of this people that they had to be driven into action, and
after a success they became a panic-stricken and disorderly
rabble." [1]   The General then disarmed all the Cape Coast
men and employed them as carriers, saying that their
cowardice and duplicity surpassed all description.   The
Gold Coast Rifle Corps alone escaped this disgrace.

Soon after this, at a sitting of the Judicial Assessor's
Court held at Beula on the 14th, the Chiefs and Headmen
unanimously agreed that it was the bounden duty of every
able-bodied man not already engaged to assist in the
defence of his country in the present crisis, and that anyone who refused to do so without proper excuse should be
arrested and compelled to work without pay.   Cape Coast
was searched by the police, and every able-bodied man
who could be found, with the exception of those employed
by the trading firms or in other ways, was sent to work.

When Amankwa Tia, after his repulse from Abakrampa,
passed north to Ainsa, he had hoped to find the Dunkwa
garrison had been withdrawn to assist in the defence of

[1] *Ashantee War* (Parliamentary Paper, 1873–4), part iv, p. 20.

Abakrampa and the road to the Pra clear. So far from
this being the case, however, he now discovered that not
only was Dunkwa still occupied by nearly 3,000 allies
under Colonel Festing, but that strong posts had also been
established along the main road as far as Mansu. He
was, therefore, compelled to map out some other line of
retreat to enable him to strike the road to the north of
Mansu and promptly ordered paths to be cut through
the bush parallel to the road but some four miles westward
of it. This work, which owing to the density of the forest
took some time, was in progress when the rear-guard was
attacked at Ainsa. Altogether three paths were cut, a
centre one and two flankers. Sir Garnet expected the
Ashantis to strike the road just to the north of Mansu,
and the garrison of that place was accordingly strengthened,
but the most eastern column, composed of the pick of the
troops under Amankwa Tia, cut its way into the road at
Suta on the night of the 24th, the centre column debouched
at Fesu a little later, and the western division still farther
north. During this time touch with the enemy was completely lost, and the frequent reconnaissances that were
sent out from the various posts failed to gain any definite
information of his movements or position. On the 16th
Surgeon-Major Gore, while passing from Mansu to Dunkwa,
had been fired on by one of the enemy's foraging parties,
who killed one of his escort and wounded him and four
others ; but with this exception nothing was seen or heard
of the Ashantis until the 23rd. Rumours then became
current that they were at Suta ; but it was not until
Colonel Wood moved his force there on the 26th and found
the fires still burning in the camp they had vacated that
morning, and one of his scouting parties saw more fires
burning in the direction of Fesu, that it was definitely
known that Amankwa Tia had succeeded in reaching the
Prasu road well to the north of the most advanced British
post. " The army of a civilized nation need not have
been ashamed of a retreat conducted with such skill and
such success." [1]

[1] Brackenbury, vol. i, p. 302.

Colonel Wood had received orders to harass the enemy in his retreat, and on Thursday the 27th left Suta with the following force : 2nd West Indian Regiment, 23 ; Hausas, 93 ; Elmina Company of Wood's Regiment, 53 ; Kossu Company, 104 ; Royal Marine Artillery, 3 ; with a rocket-trough and 6 Assin scouts. On reaching Adobiasi soon after midday, information was received from a prisoner that a number of Ashantis were encamped at Fesu, and that Amankwa Tia, Kobina Obin of Adansi, and many other Chiefs were with them. The men's bundles were accordingly piled in the village under a small guard, and the advance was cautiously continued until the Ashanti pickets opened fire just south of Fesu. The Hausas and Kossus, advancing in extended formation, drove the enemy back to the village, across the clearing, and into the bush beyond. Several rockets were then fired into the bush, the Hausas halted in the clearing, and the Elminas and Kossus were sent forward ; but the undergrowth was so dense that it was impossible to move through it except along the path, and half an hour later it became evident that this party was being surrounded by the enemy. The men were therefore ordered to retire through the Hausas, who were extended to cover their retreat.

This movement was carried out in good order until panic suddenly seized the Hausas and spread to the Kossus. As these two detachments went flying down the road, they ran into No. 1 Company of Wood's Regiment, which, in spite of orders to the contrary, was coming up from Adobiasi, each man carrying his bundle on his head and escorting Assin carriers with the baggage that had been left behind in the morning. These two parties, crowded together in the narrow path, caused the utmost confusion : the Assins at once threw down their loads and disappeared, and a number of blankets and soldiers' kits, with a little ammunition, a box belonging to Lieutenant Woodgate, and a broken hammock fell into the hands of the enemy. The West Indians were not involved in this panic, and the marines with the rockets, of course, stood firm, though they were in imminent danger of being trampled under-

foot by the flying Kossus ; but the only natives who kept
their heads were the Elminas, who indeed behaved extremely well. Fortunately, the enemy did not press them
very closely during this retreat, or the result might have
been disastrous. As it was, the losses were small : one
Hausa was killed, four of Wood's Regiment were reported
missing, and two West Indians, one Hausa, four of Wood's
Regiment, and an Assin scout were wounded.

A great deal was made of this affair, which many people
tried to magnify into a disaster, and it was even reported
as such in England ; but although the conduct of the
Hausas and Kossus certainly made it a potential disaster,
the enemy never availed themselves of the opportunity
they undoubtedly had to cut up this little force, and the
trifling casualty list is the best evidence that it was really
the retreat of a small party from the presence of an overwhelming number of the enemy rather than a defeat.
With only partly disciplined native troops it is always
difficult to carry out any movement of this kind in an
orderly manner : their idea seems to be that if they have
to fall back at all the faster they do so the better, and it
is almost invariably done at top-speed, so that any retreat
with them is practically certain to become a rout. No
real harm would have been done, however, had it not been
for the accident of meeting the carriers on the road.

The Ashantis did not attempt to pursue, because they
were too occupied with the difficulties of their own retreat,
and this attack on their rear, after they had assured themselves that they had at length attained their object and
reached the main road well above the most northern
British post, considerably alarmed them ; so much so in
fact, that they immediately broke up their camp and,
marching all night with torches, barely stopped till they
reached the banks of the Pra. Here they were fortunate
in not being attacked ; for had any considerable British
force been available at the time, the whole Ashanti army
might easily have been destroyed. Hemmed in between
a hostile force and a deep and swiftly flowing river, encumbered by their wounded and demoralized by sickness

and defeat, they would have been at a terrible disadvantage, and must have fallen an easy prey. Even as it was, their haste to regain their own side of the river cost them many lives. Finding only one or two small canoes in which they could cross, and fearing every moment that they might be overtaken and again attacked, they felled a huge cotton-tree from either bank in the hope that their branches might meet and form a bridge ; but they failed to do so, and in attempting to cross by this means many men were swept away by the current and drowned. They worked day and night cutting out more canoes, thirteen of which were afterwards found by the British scouts, and forty men are said to have been drowned by the capsizing of one of these hurriedly constructed and overcrowded craft. In the end, the passage was made on the 27th, 28th and 29th of November at Prasu, Atasi and Kohia. Captain Butler,[1] who marched into Prasu on the 10th of December, was the first to reach the river after the enemy had crossed : two men of the 2nd West India Regiment arrived there soon afterwards, and were the first to cross into Ashanti. Colonel Webber had called for volunteers to follow the retreating army and ascertain what had become of it, and these two men had traced it to Prasu, where they crossed the river and nailed a piece of paper, on which they had written their names, to a tree on the north bank as proof that they had completed their mission faithfully. In the circumstances, these men performed a singularly gallant act : it necessitated a march of about twenty-five miles through the lonely forest with the knowledge that at any moment they might be pounced upon by over-whelming numbers of the enemy, and that, if not killed at once, they would be reserved for a slow and painful death in Kumasi. When the British scouts, who had been loath to approach the Ashantis after the affair at Fesu, did at length reach the river nearly a fortnight later, they found unmistakable signs of the precipitate nature of their flight. The road was strewn with the dead and dying, and many bodies were seen lying on the banks of the river, as many

[1] 69th Regiment.

as sixteen being visible from one point alone, while others were still entangled in the branches of the trees that had been felled across the stream.

Now that the enemy had gone, the site of his camp at Mampon was visited. It was nearly a mile square and covered with huts ; but the enormous number of graves, and the skeletons, skulls and bones that lay around on every side bore eloquent testimony to the truth of the reports that had been received of the number of men who had died from wounds, disease and starvation.

While these events were taking place along the road between Cape Coast and Prasu, Amaki was still giving trouble and receiving assistance from Atjiempon's force of Ashantis in Apollonia. On the 13th of October, H.M.S. *Druid* anchored off Beyin. Owing to the heavy surf, which made it unsafe for any of the ship's boats to attempt a landing, a letter was sent ashore in a small barrel, inviting the Chief to come on board and talk matters over. Amaki sent messages off to explain that his clerk was away in the bush and that he could not read the letter and made several other excuses for not visiting the warship, while his people were openly hostile. His town was, therefore, bombarded on the 16th, but the people, as usual, escaped into the bush. Arrangements had been made with Chief Blay for his people to make a simultaneous attack on the Beyins by land, and they had actually started along the beach for this purpose when they were recalled by messengers, who reported that their own town was being threatened by the Axims, otherwise the Beyins would have suffered far more heavily than they did. At about this time it became known that Atjiempon had died of consumption accelerated by a wound in the side caused by a fragment of a shell fired by one of the men-of-war. He had been making preparations to attack the Kinjabos, but the threatened invasion of Ashanti and the consequent increasing alarm in the capital led to the recall of his force to assist in its defence. On the 28th, Butri also was shelled and destroyed as a punishment for the repeated attacks that its people had made on Dixcove.

The Shamas had consistently aided the Ashantis throughout the whole time they had been encamped at Mampon,
and even now that they were retiring many of the people
had thrown in their lot with them and were accompanying
them as voluntary emigrants to Kumasi. They, with the
Elminas, had destroyed Komenda earlier in the war, and
the Komendas were now promised the assistance of the
men-of-war and encouraged to take their revenge. On
Christmas Eve, 635 Komendas, led by Sergeant Hughes
of the Cape Coast Volunteers, arrived on the east bank of
the Pra and were ferried across by the boats of H.M.Ss.
Merlin [1] and *Encounter*. After a successful skirmish with
the Shamas, which ended in the latter being driven out of
their town, the Komendas set fire to what remained of
the place and burned all the canoes ; but when the Shamas
threatened to attack them again next day, the Komendas,
who had expended nearly all their ammunition and were
without food, asked to be put across to their own side of
the river. This was done, and the next morning the ships
bombarded and burned Aboadi, whither the majority of
the Shamas had retreated with their property.

Meanwhile, Amankwa Tia's reverses had been causing
increasing alarm in Kumasi, even though their full extent
was not known. On the 27th of October a great meeting
of the Council had been held at Amankia, a suburb of
Kumasi, at which the Chiefs had once more urged the King
to recall the army ; but he again pointed out that it had
been they and not he who had clamoured for war, and now
refused to do as they asked unless they guaranteed to
refund the large sums of money that he had already expended on the campaign, which he estimated at 6,000
peredwins, equivalent to about £48,600. This they had
eventually agreed to do, and the message of recall had
then been sent, otherwise it is very doubtful if Amankwa
Tia, hard pressed though he was, would have dared to
recross the Pra. Afterwards, when the Chiefs were called
upon to fulfil their promise and defray the expenses of
the war, many of them were ruined altogether and others

[1] A gunboat.

had to sell nearly their whole families into slavery to make up the large sums demanded from them.

On the 1st of November, Sir Garnet had despatched another copy of his previous letter to the King, which he sent up by an Ashanti prisoner taken at Asanchi. In order to make as great an impression on this man as possible, and convince him of the magnitude of the preparations that were being made for the invasion of his country, he was sent out of Cape Coast on one of the traction engines ; the experience, however, had little or no visible effect on him, and he seems to have regarded the whole proceeding as a ponderous prelude to his own execution ; the engine, moreover, broke down at the first hill, and considerably detracted from the possible effect of the display. This letter did not reach Kumasi until the 20th of November, when the twenty days allowed for a reply had already expired. Dawson was called to read and interpret it to the King and his Council, who heard it in profound silence. The Queen-Mother, Efua Kobri, then made a speech, pointing out the threatening aspect of affairs, and finished by saying : " From olden times it has been seen that God fights for Ashanti if the war is a just one. This one is unjust. The Europeans begged for the imprisoned white men. They were told to wait until Adu Bofo returned. Adu Bofo came back ; then they said they wanted money. The money was offered, and even weighed. How, then, can this war be justified ? . . . Taking all into consideration, I strongly advise that the white men should be sent back at once, and God can help us." [1] The very next day Mrs. Ramseyer gave birth to a son, which the Ashantis regarded as a very bad omen.

The King's reply to this letter was to the effect that he had not sent his army against the white men nor to attack the forts ; he admitted the treaty of 1831, but said he had been incited to make war against the King of Denkera by hearing from Plange that Elmina was to be given to him ; but now that he had heard that Kwaku Fram was dead, he had recalled his army. In a second letter he complained

[1] Ramseyer and Kühne, p. 247.

of the attack that had been made on his army at Fesu when it was already on its way out of the Protectorate.

The army reached Kumasi on Monday the 22nd of December, but its entry was very different from the triumphal processions so often seen in former years. Instead of the usual long lines of prisoners and slaves loaded with valuable plunder and the numerous jawbones of the enemy's slain, only eighty persons now returned with the army, and the majority of these were voluntary emigrants from Shama or Fantis from the surrounding villages who had been given up to make some sort of show in the procession. The jawbones that were displayed were nearly all very old, and of the 40,000 men who had gone forth to war but half that number now returned. Nearly everyone in the capital was in mourning and sounds of lamentations filled the air : 280 Chiefs had fallen, and others who had gone out with twenty men now returned alone carrying their bundles on their heads.

The first phase of the war thus came to an end. The Protectorate was cleared of the enemy, and Sir Garnet was free to push forward his preparations for the invasion of their country and their final punishment ; for the Ashantis were still convinced that, whatever reverses their arms might have met with in the Protectorate, their own country was safe, and it was absolutely necessary not to miss this opportunity of finally undeceiving them. This first part of the war had been conducted mainly by Africans, and a few hundred seamen and marines and a West India Regiment had been the only regular troops employed. Although they had fallen off most lamentably towards the end, the people had turned out well enough at first, and many of them—notably the Anamabos—had fought with distinction on more than one occasion. This was by far the most arduous part of the campaign ; but it aroused very little interest at the time, and it was not until British regiments with well-known names were employed during the operations beyond the Pra that the public in England began to pay any serious attention to what was taking place on the Gold Coast.

CHAPTER V

1873

S<small>IR</small> G<small>ARNET</small> W<small>OLSELEY</small>'s main object, now that the Ashantis had retired across the Pra, was to push forward his preparations for the invasion of their country, so that he might have everything in readiness for an immediate advance so soon as the European troops for which he had asked should arrive on the Coast. Briefly, his plan was to make simultaneous advances with several columns, which were to cross the Pra at different points on the 15th of January and converge upon Kumasi. By this means he hoped to weaken the army that would be opposed to his main force by detaching the contingents of those Chiefs who would find their own districts threatened by the auxiliary columns. The main body, consisting of the European regiments, Naval Brigade, Wood's and Russell's Regiments and Rait's Artillery, under the General himself, was to advance along the road from Prasu ; Captain Glover was to lead his force towards Jabin from the east, and between this and the main body there was to be a third column composed of Akims under Captain Butler,[1] while on the western side Captain Dalrymple[2] was to advance with a force of Wassaws, Denkeras, and Komendas, and cross the Pra lower down than the main column. Pending the arrival of the European troops, these auxiliary columns now had to be organized, the road to the Pra completed, camps prepared on it for the troops, and transport and other arrangements made.

<small>1873</small>

<small>CHAP. V</small>

[1] 69th Regiment.   [2] 80th Regiment.

Captain Glover had gone to Accra immediately on his arrival in the country, and was already busy raising troops. Having interviewed the different Chiefs in the eastern district, he held a meeting with the majority of them at Akropong, at which he arranged that they should all deal directly with him, thereby frustrating the designs of the Accra Chiefs Taki and Solomon, who had hoped to act as intermediaries and distributing agents for the large presents he was making. On the 14th of October another large meeting was held in Accra, which was attended by every principal Chief in the eastern district with the exception of the Chief of Adda, who was being threatened by the Awunas and dared not leave his town, and the Akwamu Chiefs who were still in open rebellion. They all swore to be loyal and to assist Captain Glover, with the exception of Sakiti, one of the Chiefs of Eastern Krobo, who had formerly come under suspicion for having supplied the Akwamus with powder and now refused to take the Oath of Allegiance, but got up to leave the meeting, using rebellious and defiant language. His conduct so infuriated the others, especially his neighbours the Akims, Akwapims and Krepis, that they seized him and his followers and would undoubtedly have put them to death had not Captain Glover's officers interfered and rescued them. They were then removed for safety to Ussher Fort, but not before they had been subjected to some very rough handling. Feeling against the disloyal Krobos ran so high that fifty Hausas with ball cartridge were required to guard the fort throughout that day, and fifty more were marched down in the evening to assist in escorting the prisoners through the excited mob to James Fort, where it was thought they would be safer. Sakiti was kept a prisoner throughout the war.

Captain Glover had great faith in the Hausa as a soldier, and as the Hausa Armed Police sent down from Lagos formed the nucleus of his disciplined force, he was anxious to enroll as many more of these people as possible. There were a number of men from the Hinterland in Accra— Donkos—who were collectively and indiscriminately regarded as Hausas, although the majority of them were doubtless Grunshis, Dagatis, Gonjas, Dagombas, and others from the north who had been brought down by the Ashantis for sale after their wars. Captain Glover decided to complete his force by recruiting from amongst these men ; but a difficulty immediately arose similar to that which had occurred in 1851 when Governor Hill was forming the Gold Coast Corps. All these men were held as domestic slaves, and domestic slavery was still recognized as a regular and legal institution by the British Courts throughout the country. The slaves themselves were anxious enough to enlist, but their owners, with a singular want of loyalty, absolutely refused to permit them to do so, and in many cases even put them in irons to prevent their escaping to Captain Glover and joining the Armed Police. Even Government officials opposed the enlistment of their slaves, and though a few of the men escaped and reached Captain Glover, so much friction and ill-feeling was caused that open rioting took place, and on the 1st of October, when the Accras turned out armed and came into conflict with the Hausas on this point, one of the Chiefs of Ussher Town and a native trader were wounded. Eventually a temporary compromise was made, and Captain Glover undertook to pay £5 to the master of every Donko who enlisted, and though this arrangement was directly contrary to the instructions given by the Secretary of State in 1852, and was now again condemned by Lord Kimberley, it is very doubtful if the men could have been obtained by any other means.

Captain Glover's difficulties did not end here. The Awunas, excited by the warlike preparations that were being made on the River Volta, again broke out, and, early in October, burned several of the factories at Kitta. Captain Glover at once saw that if these people were not punished before he left for Ashanti, they would constitute a serious menace to the safety of his base ; in fact, the Addas, Krepis and Accras flatly refused to start until their old enemies had been subdued. They can scarcely be blamed for their unwillingness to leave their own towns undefended so long as the Awunas were threatening them, but there is little doubt that the conquest of Awuna was their main object, and that they took very little interest in the campaign against Ashanti, but were merely using Captain Glover's help to advance their own ends. This, too, was natural enough ; for the recent Ashanti invasion had not affected any of them, except the Krepis, and they knew, moreover, that it was now at an end, whereas the Awunas were an ever present and easily appreciable source of danger.

Meanwhile, Captain Sartorius,[1] who was serving under Captain Glover, had been sent into Eastern Akim and Akwapim to organize the forces of these tribes, after which he was to go to Pong and choose a site for a fortified camp and depot from which supplies could be drawn after the Pra had been crossed. On his way back he was ordered to clear the right bank of the river from Bato to Humi by burning the villages and compelling the inhabitants to cross to the opposite bank.

Blakpa was chosen as the base of operations against the Awunas, and stores and ammunition were gradually collected there ; but the time passed, and no sufficient force was available, owing to the dilatory manner in which the allies came in, so that although Captain Glover had intended to march against the rebels about the middle of October, and to have finished his operations against them early in November, it was not until nearly the end of December that he was ready to begin his trans-Volta campaign. But he had already promised Sir Garnet Wolseley that he would be established on the banks of the Pra by the 15th of January with a force which he had estimated at the lowest at 16,000 men and possibly as many as 30,000, and the General had made all his arrangements for the invasion of Ashanti on that date. Captain Glover had as last discovered that, well as he understood them, and in spite of the great influence that he undoubtedly exercised over them, the natives of the West Coast of Africa were utterly unreliable and apathetic,

---

[1] 6th Bengal Cavalry.

and that it was impossible to hurry them or to place any reliance on the promises they made. On the 22nd of December he had to write and tell Sir Garnet that he saw no possibility of reaching the River Pra in less than forty days.

This startling announcement reached Cape Coast on Christmas Eve ; but it was obviously impossible for the General to alter all his plans at the last moment, merely because Captain Glover had failed to realize his expectations. At the very most, only a delay of a few days could have been granted, and there was no reason to suppose that Captain Glover would be any more ready then than he was now. Any further delay, in fact, would have necessitated the abandonment of the projected invasion of Ashanti altogether, for the rains would then be setting in before it could possibly be carried out. Moreover, if Captain Glover was to be excused from taking part in the general advance, the whole labour and expense of his expedition would have been thrown away so far as its primary object was concerned. Peremptory orders were therefore sent to him to advance immediately to the Pra with his Hausas and any other disciplined troops he had, and to be on the banks of the river by the 15th of January whether the allies could be induced to follow him or not. This was to be his one object, and, if necessary, he was to break off all his operations against the Awunas. This despatch was accompanied by a private letter, in which Sir Garnet pointed out that it was absolutely essential to the success of his plans that a force should advance from the east upon Jabin ; that while the invasion of Ashanti could not be deferred, the settlement of the quarrels between the eastern tribes and the punishment of the Awunas were matters that could be dealt with at a later date, and that unless Captain Glover carried out the original plan and crossed the Pra on the date fixed, no success he might score against the Awunas could ever compensate for his failure to do so, for, so far as the war with Ashanti was concerned, he " might just as well be operating on the Zanzibar coast of Africa as in the Awuna district."

1878
CHAP. V

After sending off his despatch on the 22nd of December, saying he could not reach the Pra for forty days, Captain Glover had, on the 23rd, shelled and rocketed three or four villages opposite his intended landing-place. The next day the native levies were put across the river and a skirmish with the enemy ensued, which, after a few minutes' sharp fighting, ended in the Awunas being driven back by the Hausas and Yorubas, who then occupied the village of Adidomi. Next day more skirmishing took place and other villages were taken ; but on the 26th the troops were too exhausted to continue the advance till they had had a day's rest, and it was while they were resting in their camp that Sir Garnet's letter arrived, ordering Captain Glover to march at once to the Pra. This order was read out to the assembled Chiefs, and Captain Glover then called upon them to recross the river and follow him to the Ashanti frontier ; but they insisted that they must first defeat the Awunas, and that when they had been completely subdued, but not till then, they would be ready to accompany him to the Pra. Captain Glover therefore, finding it was hopeless to try to reason with the Chiefs, recrossed the Volta with his Hausas and Donkos and set out for the Pra on the 29th of December, leaving Mr. Goldsworthy [1] and Lieutenant Moore, R.N., in command of nearly 12,000 allies to complete the punishment of the Awunas. The orders he had received from the General were to cross the river on the 15th of January and advance towards Jabin. Should he feel strong enough, he was to push on to and occupy that town as quickly as possible, and there await the receipt of further instructions ; but in no circumstances was he to allow any of his men to cross the Oda River to the west of Jabin or advance towards Kumasi without distinct orders from the General.

The other officers who had been deputed to raise auxiliary columns were even less successful than Captain Glover. Captain Butler left Cape Coast for Accra on the 3rd of November and proceeded to Akim to collect levies.

[1] A Gold Coast Civil Officer ; late 12th Lancers.

On his way up from the coast he met Kobina Fua the
King of Western Akim, and ordered him to return with
him; but this he flatly refused to do, saying he must
first go to Accra to " make fetish." This was the result
of the reckless way in which Captain Glover had been
giving presents : he had been distributing gin, rum,
tobacco and other articles with a lavish hand, and every
Chief of any importance had received goods and money
to the value of £200 or £300 in addition to the ordinary
gratuity and pay and allowances for his men. Naturally
they had flocked to his standard on such terms as these,
though they failed him afterwards, and equally naturally
the other Chiefs who heard of these transactions and who all
regarded the war in a purely mercenary spirit, were anxious
to share the spoil. Kobina Fua, however, was disappointed and had his journey for nothing, for Captain
Glover had received strict orders from the General not to interfere with Captain Butler's mission by accepting recruits
from Akim and promptly sent him back to his own country.
It was not until towards the end of December, however,
that he arrived in Akim, and the opportunity of harassing
the retreating Ashanti army, which was at this time
the main object of Captain Butler's mission, had then
been lost. Captain Butler himself, with about fifteen
men, reached Prasu by way of Yankumasi Assin on the
10th of December and found the enemy had already
crossed the river. The apathy and greed of the Chiefs
having brought about the utter failure of this first object
of his mission, he next turned his attention to the collection of men for the invasion of Ashanti on the 15th of
January. Kofi Ahinkora, the Chief of Akim Swedru, had
already been told to collect his men, and the mobilization
was proceeding in the customary dilatory manner ; but
after seemingly endless delays a few hundred Akims were
at last mustered and led to the Pra.

Meanwhile, Captain Dalrymple had entered the Denkera country and was doing his best to raise a force of
Wassaws, Denkeras, Eguafos and Komendas, but with
very little success.

The construction of the road and the preparation of
the camping grounds had proceeded far more quickly
since the retreat of the enemy had left the country clear,
but the scarcity of labour was a constant source of difficulty, and troops had to be maintained to keep the gangs
in hand, while those sections of the road that were already
completed required constant attention, or they quickly
became overgrown, and the people even tore up the bridges
and other timber for firewood. In order to minimize the
risk to the health of the European troops, it was considered of the greatest importance that they should reach
the Pra dryshod and with the least possible fatigue, and
that they should be properly sheltered at night. The
road, therefore, was made 12 ft. wide, cleared of stumps
and roots and well drained, and every stream was bridged :
as many as 237 bridges of different kinds were built
between Cape Coast and Prasu.

While this work was in progress, camping grounds
had to be chosen and prepared for the troops. The sites
selected were as follows :

Camp.					Miles distant from Cape Coast
Inkwabim	.	.	.	.	6¾
Akrofu	.	.	.	.	13¾
Yankumasi Fanti	.	.	.	24¼
Mansu	.	.	.	.	35¾
Suta	.	.	.	.	46
Yankumasi Assin	.	.	.	58¼
Beraku	.	.	.	.	67¼
Prasu	.	.	.	.	73¾

The first two marches were purposely made as short as
possible, on account of the absence of any shade on that
portion of the road, and also because the men, coming
straight from on board-ship, could not be expected to be
in training for a long march in the heat, and would have
to be broken in gradually. At each of these places large
clearings were made and huts built to accommodate at
least 400 European soldiers and a proportionate number

of officers. Guard-beds of split bamboo or palm sticks were arranged along each side of the huts, so that the men would sleep 2 ft. from the ground, large (Crease's) filters were erected, and other huts for stores, ablution sheds and hospital built. Large supplies of dry wood were collected at every camp for fuel, and arrangements were made at Inkwabim, Akrofu, Mansu, Yankumasi Assin and Prasu for the provision of fresh meat—the cattle being specially imported from Sierra Leone, Madeira, and Lisbon—while bakeries were established at Cape Coast, Mansu, Yankumasi Assin and Prasu. Mansu, being the half-way depot, was a larger camp in every way than the others. Strict orders had to be issued that no natives were to be allowed to encamp on any of these sites, for it was found that wherever they had had one of their camps they had used nearly all the bamboo and other building material in the neighbourhood, thus causing great inconvenience and delay, and that whenever they had an opportunity of spending a few nights in one of the completed camps they used the huts for any purpose rather than that for which they were intended, and much labour was wasted in cleaning up after them.

The hospital arrangements, being of paramount importance in such a campaign, received very careful attention, and every preparation was made for the rapid removal and treatment of the sick and wounded. A hut was built for infectious cases in every station, for smallpox was always liable to break out, and a special hut was set apart for officers. At Prasu a hospital with a hundred beds was built and another with sixty beds at Mansu, but in all the other stations it was arranged that one of the ordinary barrack huts should be used as a hospital after the troops had passed up. At Cape Coast, Saint George's Church was taken as a hospital in addition to huts on Connor's Hill and elsewhere, providing beds ashore for sixty-six European soldiers and eighteen officers. This accommodation, however, was never intended for anything more than temporary use, for all sick and convalescents were to be treated on board-ship. H.M.S. *Victor*

Emmanuel [1] was specially fitted up as a hospital ship for
240 patients and sent out to Cape Coast, and H.M.Ss.
Himalaya and *Tamar* could take another 100 men each.
The *Simoom* was sent to St. Vincent, and convalescents
were to be transferred to her every ten days after the
arrival of the troops, there to await the arrival of the
homeward-bound liners from the Cape of Good Hope,
some of which were also to call on the Coast : the first of
these, the Union liner *Anglian*, came into Cape Coast on
the 15th of December. Arrangements were also made
for the detention at Gibraltar of such cases as were unfit
to be landed in England during the winter months. For
the removal of the sick and wounded from the front,
hammocks and ship's cots were provided in every station,
and others were set aside for use with the column. These
arrangements, at the lowest estimate, allowed for the
removal of the regular troops at the rate of 450 men a
month ; but these numbers could easily be doubled if
necessary, and could even be increased to as many as 1,425
men a month by working at extraordinary pressure.

That which caused the greatest difficulty and anxiety,
however, was the question of transport. Enormous
quantities of provisions had to be carried up to Prasu and
the intermediary camps, and the employment of European
troops, of course, greatly increased the amounts required,
while the number of labourers already taken for the construction of the road and camps added to the difficulty
of obtaining sufficient men as carriers. Transport also
had to be found for large trains of ammunition and other
military stores. At first the transport was in the hands
of the Control—a Department which in those days combined the duties of the present Army Service and Pay
Corps. Enormous numbers of carriers were constantly
being obtained and handed over to it, but without very
much result, for they deserted by thousands. Sir Garnet
Wolseley wrote : " This question of the desertion of our
carriers has assumed a most formidable aspect. Too
cowardly to fight their own battles, and too lazy, even

[1] An old line-of-battle ship.

when well paid, to help those who are risking their lives
in their cause, they have been deserting by whole tribes ;
and I do not hesitate to say that, were the most stringent
measures not adopted to force them to work, the successful
termination of the expedition might be endangered." [1]
The unwillingness of the Fantis to work, however, was
not wholly responsible for these desertions : they were due
in part to the mismanagement of those in charge. The
carriers were to be paid a shilling a day and to be divided
into gangs of 100 men under a Chief or Headman drawing
half-a-crown a day. Men supplied for this work, moreover, were allowed to count towards the gratuity of £10
per 1,000 men that had been promised to the Chiefs. The
officers of the Control Department really had far too much
to do, and were quite unable to devote anything like as
much time to the transport as was necessary for its proper
organization and management. The consequence was
that the whole arrangements were in such a chaotic state,
that the carriers were never under proper control and
had more than one quite legitimate grievance, so that
there was less cause to wonder that they ran away, more
especially when it is remembered that they took so little
interest in the war that they expected to be paid for
everything they did just as if the conquest of Ashanti
was to be undertaken solely for the benefit of the English,
instead of as much or even more for their own. The
carriers had been collected from all over the Protectorate
and even beyond it, but instead of keeping the men from
individual tribes and districts together and putting them
to work under their own Chiefs, the gangs were made up
indiscriminately of men who knew nothing of each other,
and then, to make matters worse, someone was chosen
as headman—usually because he could speak a little
English—who was probably a stranger to all the men
under him and had no control over them whatever. No
proper record was kept of the work done by the different
gangs, and it happened more than once that a party
coming in with loads would be sent off again on a fresh

[1] *Ashantee War* (Parliamentary Paper, 1873–4), part v, p. 66.

journey without even being given time for a meal. Instead of providing these men with rations, the old system of giving them a subsistence allowance was adhered to, which, though satisfactory enough in ordinary times for small numbers of men, was manifestly absurd in the present instance when they were working in a country that had been overrun and devastated by the enemy, so that there was no food for them to buy, and were, moreover, employed in such large numbers that even in time of peace the villages would have been unable to supply them all.   It was not altogether laziness or cowardice, therefore, that brought about these desertions—overwork and hunger were the true causes in many instances.

As has already been mentioned, the native levies were nearly all disarmed and turned into carriers soon after their disgraceful behaviour at Ainsa had proved their utter unreliability as fighting men, but even this accession of strength did not improve matters much, and the transport, up to the very last, was one of the principal difficulties of the campaign. The arrangements were much improved, however, by Colonel Colley [1] and a staff of combatant officers, who took over the management of this department on the 19th of December, and, by inaugurating a proper system of registration and way-bills, separating the regimental from the local transport, and dividing the road into four districts each with its own transport headquarters, soon evolved some semblance of order out of the absolute chaos that had previously reigned.

Matters were further complicated by the way in which many of the stores were sent out. Some were made up into packages that were far too heavy and had to be undone and repacked into loads of suitable weight before they could be moved, thereby entailing a great loss both of labour and time, while the rice, on the other hand, was sent out in 25-pound bags, which were too small for a man to carry, while two of them, though making the weight correct, formed such an awkward load that it could

---

[1] 2nd Queen's Own.   Afterwards Sir George Colley, the unfortunate hero of Majuba.

only be carried with the greatest difficulty. This, however,
was got over by collecting the children to carry these
bags : large numbers of women were also employed, and,
being both willing and strong, made infinitely better
carriers than the men.

From the foregoing account it will be seen that the
work to be done and the difficulties to be overcome before
the troops could enter Ashanti were considerable ; but
they were still further and quite needlessly increased by
the difficulty of enforcing the blockade of the Coast and
preventing arms and ammunition from reaching the
enemy. To their shame be it said that those who brought
the greatest proportion of these munitions of war to the
Coast were British traders, who seem to have been so
anxious to profit by the demand for such goods and the
high prices obtainable, that they exported and sold them
in enormous quantities, utterly regardless of the fact that
they would almost certainly be used against their own
countrymen. Ellis, writing of " vessels owned and
manned by Englishmen," says : " An officer commanding
a gunboat told me that he had chased vessels with contra-
band of war into the Assinee River, and had then been
obliged to lie-to and see keg after keg of powder landed
without being able to interfere,"[1] because these were
French waters. The officers of the French Navy, however,
did all they could to put a stop to this traffic. In March
1873 the Commander of the French warship *Curieuse*
reported to Colonel Harley at Cape Coast that he had just
come from Assini, and that large quantities of powder, lead
and muskets had been landed there by English vessels,
one ship alone having landed as many as 150 cases of
muskets and 2,000 barrels of powder. Many of these
ships belonged to Messrs. F. & A. Swanzy. One of their
vessels, the *Alligator*, was found to have sailed with 3,260
kegs of powder, 372 of which she had already landed at
Grand Bassam, only a short distance from the English
frontier ; and M. Verdier, the French agent at Assini,
who was ordered by Captain Mathieu, of the French sloop

[1] Ellis, *West African Sketches*, p. 137.

of war *Bregant*, not to sell munitions of war, disputed that officer's right to issue such instructions, and explained that his stores were full of such merchandise only because he had been " prevented from selling it because of the enormous quantity sold at a lower price by the English before, and more especially since, the declaration of war."[1] Another of Swanzy's vessels, the *Bryn-y-Mor*, brought out 2,000 kegs of powder, and, in defiance of requests made by the British Naval officers and the prohibition of the French, landed powder at Grand Bassam and lead at Assini and again at Apam on the Gold Coast itself. Another English barque, the *Jehu*, arrived at Assini in December, and was found to have 2,120 muskets and 30,000 pounds of powder on board, but was fortunately prevented from trading. Messrs. Swanzy's ships soon became so notorious in this traffic that the subject was mentioned in the English papers,[2] whereupon they tried to clear themselves by denying that they had ever supplied the Ashantis with arms or ammunition, either directly or indirectly, and even contended that it was impossible for such goods to reach them from the Ivory Coast. Such a statement was manifestly ridiculous : Grand Bassam was only twenty-eight miles from Assini, whence, as was well known, the Ashantis regularly obtained large quantities of ammunition, and there was a system of lagoons known to the natives and admirably adapted for canoe transport which connected them, so that Messrs. Swanzy, as interested parties, did not make their case any stronger by alleging that they were the only people who had the slightest knowledge of the trade and country behind Grand Bassam. Winwood Reade, who had been sent out in 1868 by Mr. Andrew Swanzy to explore these very districts, says : " The trade of Grand Bassam is not at ordinary times connected with Ashanti,"[3] thereby undoubtedly implying that at other times, as when the roads to the nearer markets were closed during time of war, it was so connected, or,

[1] Brackenbury, vol. ii, p. 313.
[2] *Pall Mall Gazette*, 3rd of October 1873.
[3] *Ashantee Campaign*, p. 121.

at least, that there was nothing to prevent it. It is, moreover, noteworthy that although this firm made great and repeated protestations of good faith, they did not take the one obvious and convincing step of ceasing to export powder and arms to the Coast, and their own returns show that their exports of guns from the 1st of January to the 10th of November 1873 were proportionately very much greater than they had been during the whole of the previous year, while the quantity of powder showed very little diminution.

Year.	Kegs of Powder.	Guns.
1872	15,199	7,630
1873 { To November 10	11,840	9,299
{ Same proportion to end of year . .	13,763	10,809

The French had always been anxious to obtain the Gambia, which lay in the midst of their Possessions and was of no great value to Britain. Had it been exchanged for their Possessions on the Ivory Coast, all these troubles would have been avoided and a long and uninterrupted coast-line would have been brought under British control. In 1869 its transference to France had only been prevented by the outbreak of the Franco-German war, and when the subject came up again in 1874-5 the French offered their Settlements in Grand Bassam, Assini and Gaboon in exchange ; but the offer was declined, mainly on account of the action of the Exeter Hall party, which used its influence to oppose the transfer of these people, some of whom had been brought up as Protestants, to a Roman Catholic Power.

In the meantime, the European troops had arrived. On the 9th of December, while Sir Garnet Wolseley was away in the bush, H.M.S. *Himalaya* had reached Cape Coast with the 2nd battalion of the Rifle Brigade and some detachments of Royal Engineers and other special corps. The *Tamar* arrived on the 12th with the 23rd Royal Welsh Fusiliers and further details ; and these were followed on the 17th by the hired transport *Sarmatian*, having on board the 42nd Highlanders (Black Watch) and a few more men of Departmental Corps.[1] The Highlanders had been sent out in compliance with the General's request for a third battalion, but the arrival of the troops at this particular time caused some difficulty. It was too late now to attack and defeat the Ashantis while they were still near the coast and to destroy their army before they could regain their own country, while the preparations for the invasion of Ashanti were still incomplete, so that no immediate advance could be made. Consequently, as it was of the first importance that the troops should not be exposed to the Gold Coast climate a moment earlier than was necessary, the ships were ordered to sea until the end of the year, by when it was estimated that everything would be ready for the march to the Pra. On the 27th of December the 1st West India Regiment[2] arrived from Jamaica, and Sir Garnet's first intention was to take it with him in the main column and not to land the Black Watch at all, especially as he had given an undertaking that he would not use any of the European troops unless he found their employment was essential to the success

[1] Ship.	Regiment.	Officers.	N.C.O.'s and Men.
Himalaya	Rifle Brigade	30	652
	Army Service Corps . . .		30
	Royal Engineers	4	68
	Army Hospital Corps . . .	2	26
	Medical Officers	13	
	Chaplains	2	
Tamar	Royal Welsh Fusiliers . . .	30	650
	Royal Artillery	3	61
	2nd West India Regiment . .		2
	Medical Officers	13	
	Chaplains	2	
Sarmatian	Special Service Officers . . .	15	
	Black Watch	30	652
	Army Service Corps . . .	1	12
	Army Hospital Corps . . .		26
	Staff Clerk		1
	Royal Engineers		2
	Medical Officers	15	

[2] 24 Officers and 554 N.C.O.'s and men.

of the expedition. Afterwards, however, this plan was
modified, and it was arranged that the 42nd should take
part in the campaign in Ashanti, while the 1st West Indians
were to be left as a reserve force garrisoning Cape Coast
and Elmina, and the 2nd Battalion was to guard the line of
communication to Prasu. It was felt that the advantage
of better fighting material thus obtained would fully
compensate for the additional risk to health involved by
landing the third European battalion.

CHAPTER VI

THE INVASION OF ASHANTI

1874

By the end of 1873 all the preparations for the invasion of Ashanti had been completed, and with the New Year the second portion of the campaign was entered upon. Sir Garnet Wolseley left Cape Coast on the 27th of December and reached Prasu on the 2nd of January. So well had the road been prepared that he was able to ride the whole of the way to Prasu in a light American buggy drawn by natives, but after the river was crossed he was carried in a Madeira chair slung between two bamboos and carried like a hammock on the heads of four carriers. The camp at Prasu had been prepared on a much larger scale than those at the intermediate halting-places, and was designed to accommodate a force of 2,000 Europeans in addition to the native regiments that were to be employed ; for it was the General's intention to concentrate his whole force there before crossing the river, as it was thought that the Ashantis would dispute its passage, or at least make a determined stand directly their territory was entered.

The transports had now returned to Cape Coast, and the disembarkation of the troops was begun. The Naval Brigade had already been landed on the 27th of December and marched into Prasu the day after the General arrived there without a single man having fallen out on the road. On New Year's Day the Rifle Brigade and Royal Engineers were landed ; the Black Watch landed on the 3rd and 4th ; and the disembarkation of the 23rd Fusiliers was begun on the following day. The troops landed by half battalions

very early in the morning, entering the warships' boats 1874
by moonlight and being towed in by steam-cutters before CHAP. VI
transhipping to surf-boats and landing. They were thus
able to march off from the beach by half-past three, and
reach their first camp at Inkwabim three hours later. The
Headquarters and Naval Brigade had required very little
transport, and this had easily been provided. The carriers
for the Rifle Brigade, consisting chiefly of Ahantas and
Elminas, were supplied from Cape Coast, and the Black
Watch were provided with Gomoas, who had been brought
down from Mansu. Large numbers of carriers were expected from the Aguna and Akumfi districts at this time to
furnish the transport for the 23rd ; but the Akumfis broke
away before they even reached the main road, and 500
Agunas deserted after their first trip, half of them not even
waiting for their pay. Other desertions were taking place
all along the line, and the movement of supplies to the
front, and even the advance of the troops, were seriously
threatened. In these circumstances the disembarkation
of the second half battalion of the 23rd and the Royal
Artillery was countermanded, and the first half battalion,
which had already reached Akrofu, was ordered to return
to Cape Coast and re-embark. Subsequently, however, in
order that this regiment might not be wholly unrepresented
in the march to Kumasi, a hundred men were landed and
replaced a hundred of the Black Watch who were specially
chosen as being the least likely to bear the fatigues of the
campaign. The loss of the third battalion was felt more
than the absence of the Royal Artillery, though it had
only been asked for in case serious resistance began at the
Pra. Captain Rait had trained his sixty Hausa gunners
so well that they could now be depended upon to work
their guns and rockets in the bush almost as well as European gunners could have done, and they had one great
advantage over Europeans, for they could carry their own
guns and ammunition if necessary, and as there was always
a possibility that the Fanti carriers might bolt if it came
to a hard fight, this work had been made an essential part
of their drill.

The Fantis, as a whole, seemed utterly incapable of realizing that any failure of the campaign now that it had been carried thus far must necessarily involve another fiasco like that of 1863 and have the inevitable effect of bringing down another Ashanti army to the coast. Even now that they had an army of Europeans to fight their battles for them, they would not assist in this matter of transport. Even the radical changes that had been made in the strength of the column did not reduce the number of carriers required sufficiently to counteract the enormous losses by desertion, and the absolute necessity of having a large reserve of stores at Prasu before the final advance on Kumasi was begun made it imperative that stringent measures should be adopted if the success of the expedition was not to be imperilled, or even its abandonment necessitated. As a temporary measure the men of the 1st and 2nd West India Regiments carried stores for a few days, work that they cheerfully undertook, though one man of the 2nd Battalion died under his load, and 150 Kru-boys from the fleet were similarly employed. The men of the Black Watch also volunteered to carry loads, and did in fact make one or two journeys before the General heard of it, and very rightly stopped it ; for such unaccustomed work was far beyond their strength in such a climate, and would certainly have impaired their efficiency for the purely military duties that they had been sent out to perform. These expedients, however, tided over the difficulty for a few days and gave time for the severer measures that were now being adopted for the collection of carriers to take effect. A cordon of troops was drawn round Cape Coast, and the town was then searched for deserters ; those men, too, who had hitherto been exempted because they were in the employ of the traders were now called up, and all public works in the town were stopped. Numbers of men soon found themselves carrying loads to the front : men who.had been pretending to be lame, and small store-keepers who would have been scandalized at the very idea of their performing any manual labour were astonished to find themselves on the road to Prasu with loads on their heads and an armed constable in attendance. Even a school-master who was missing was afterwards found to have been despatched with a box of ammunition. The pay of the men and the allowances to the Chiefs were also increased and frequent surprise visits paid to the different villages, which were then surrounded and carefully searched. These measures could not have been resorted to before, for that would have meant sending about a hundred West Indian soldiers into the bush to look for 8,000 carriers, and would, moreover, have stopped all work on the road, where the labourers would have refused to turn out without their escort ; but they now met with marked success, and the deserters soon ceased to feel safe anywhere and began to rejoin. On the 10th and 16th of January Mr. Marshall, the Judicial Assessor, held a Court at Dunkwa camp, where he sat with the Fanti Chiefs. They said that the punishment for desertion had always been death, but that since Sir Charles M'Carthy had deprived them of the power of inflicting capital punishment, flogging and fine had been substituted. They pointed out, however, that the crime of desertion had not been specifically mentioned. Kwow Kineboa was convicted of having advised and persuaded men to desert, with the result that twenty-three had done so, and Kujo Mensa, who had deserted with twenty-seven others, was found guilty on a similar charge. They and several others were condemned to death, but the sentences were never carried out. The men were imprisoned until the campaign was over, and then pardoned ; but these examples were not without their effect.

Within an hour of Sir Garnet Wolseley's arrival at Prasu, Ashanti messengers came in bringing the two letters from the King that have already been mentioned. They were lodged in one of the huts under a guard of West Indians. It was well known that no one dared to tell the King any bad news, and the tone of these two letters [1] fully bore out the supposition that Kofi Karikari had no

[1] Brackenbury, vol. ii, pp. 40-1, and *Ashantee War* (Parliamentary Paper, 1873-4), part v, pp. 56-7.

idea of the real extent of the reverses that his army had met with, and this belief was afterwards confirmed by the missionaries. As a matter of fact, the King knew nothing of the defeat of his troops before Elmina and at Abakrampa and Dunkwa, but had only heard of a brilliant victory that had been gained over the British at Fesu, in proof of which Lieutenant Woodgate's box and the broken hammock that had been lost there were shown to him. Amankwa Tia, of course, could not pretend that he had met with any great success in the Protectorate, for he would have been asked to show the spoil, and all that he had gained at the commencement of the campaign had been lost in his subsequent reverses or abandoned during his retreat. These trifling captures made at Fesu, therefore, were all that he now had to produce.

Sir Garnet, therefore, decided to send the King a plain statement of all that had happened in the Protectorate, and to show his messengers that what he had said about the invasion of Ashanti was no empty threat. Accordingly, in his reply, after denying that any such message as Plange was alleged to have delivered had ever been sent, he gave some account of the different engagements that had taken place and conclusively showed that the Ashantis had been badly beaten. Amongst other things, he wrote : " When Amankwatia attacked Abakrampa there were only fifty white men there ; yet, after two days' fighting, he was forced to retreat in confusion with great loss ; and many of your war-drums, Chiefs' chairs, and other military trophies, besides much baggage, were captured by my troops. As regards the attack upon your retreating army at Faisoo, it was made only by a small party of my undrilled black troops, who were ordered to fall back as soon as they found where your army was ; yet it caused the whole of the Ashanti army to retreat in the utmost haste and confusion, leaving their dead and dying everywhere along the path. . . . I wish to impress upon your Majesty that hitherto your soldiers have only had to fight against black men, helped by a few Englishmen. If, however, you should now be so ill-advised as to

continue this war, your troops will have to meet an army **1874**
of white soldiers. These white troops are now on their
march from Cape Coast for the purpose of invading your
territory, to enforce compliance with my just demands,
which I shall presently lay before you. . . . This war has
already entailed many defeats upon your armies ; you have
lost thousands of men in battle and from want and disease.
I am well aware of all these facts. You are surrounded
by hostile tribes who long for your destruction. Be warned
in time and do not listen to the advice of evil counsellors,
who for their own purposes might urge you to continue a
hopeless struggle against an army of white men, a struggle
that can only lead to the destruction of your military power,
and that must certainly bring great misery on your people
and danger to your Majesty's dynasty."[1] Finally, peace
was offered on the following terms :

i. The immediate release of all prisoners, both European
and African ;

ii. The payment of an indemnity of 50,000 ounces of
gold ; and,

iii. The conclusion of a new treaty of peace, to be signed
in Kumasi after the delivery of hostages for the safety of
the General and his escort.

While this letter was being written, the Ashanti envoys
had seen the nearly completed bridge over the Pra and
had been shown the gatling-gun in action. One of them,
whether from fear of these preparations, or more probably
because he dreaded the King's vengeance if an indiscreet
remark he had made was reported to him, blew out his
brains during the night. It had been proposed to send a
European to Kumasi with Sir Garnet's terms, and this man
had boastfully exclaimed that if that were done the King
would certainly kill him. This, of course, was strictly
against the Ashanti code of honour and the life of any white
man who had been sent as a messenger would undoubtedly
have been perfectly safe, as was at once pointed out by the
chief envoy, who threatened to report this remark to the

[1] Brackenbury, vol. ii, pp. 48–51 ; *Ashantee War* (Parliamentary
Paper, 1873–4), part v, pp. 61–2.

King. Others allege that the man had been so impressed by the sight of the gatling-gun, that he had said it would be useless for the Ashantis to attempt to fight an enemy possessed of such a weapon, and it is asserted that the surviving messenger also gave this opinion when he appeared before the King, with the result that he lost his head. The man was buried by his companions on the Ashanti shore of the river, and on the following morning, the 6th, the messengers crossed the bridge on their return journey. Russell's Regiment had been sent forward the day before to Esaman, a village some miles beyond the Pra, and the Naval Brigade had marched an hour before the Ashantis with orders to return as soon as they had overtaken and passed them and were well out of sight. The envoys, therefore, passed the Naval Brigade sitting by the roadside as though resting before resuming their forward march ; then they found Russell's Regiment busily entrenching their position at Atobiasi, and five miles farther on came upon Lord Gifford's Assin scouts. The sight of these white troops actually marching along the road to their capital, and of other soldiers already encamped beyond the Pra, greatly alarmed them and convinced them, more thoroughly perhaps than anything else could have done, that a crisis was at hand such as had never threatened Ashanti before.

When the General's letter was read before the Kotoku Council in Kumasi it produced a profound effect. Everyone seemed convinced of its absolute truth, and instead of the furious outbursts from the Chiefs that usually marked such proceedings, a gloomy silence prevailed ; while if an exclamation occasionally escaped one of the listeners, the King at once commanded attention. Even the date of the letter, the 2nd of January, caused increased alarm ; for on that day the great sacred tree of Kumasi, under which its founder, Osai Tutu, was said to have pitched his tent while his palace was being built, and from which the city took its name,[1] had crashed to the ground. Its shattered trunk still lay where it had fallen when the army entered

---

[1] Kum-asi—" under the kum-tree."

the capital, for none had dared to touch it. The coincidence was regarded as ominous. Kofi Karikari now knew, for the first time, how matters really stood, and the greatest alarm was felt. All the Chiefs who had been engaged in the war were in favour of peace, and none but those who had never left the capital, and who therefore failed to realize the position fully, now dared to counsel further resistance.

The King would probably have consented to surrender all the prisoners, and might even have agreed to pay the indemnity, for he was now thoroughly alarmed and sincerely anxious for peace ; but the suggested presence of a British force in Kumasi when the treaty was signed was too much for Ashanti pride, and would have threatened his empire with total extinction by proving to the tributary States and surrounding tribes that the power of Kumasi was on the wane. Affairs, however, were too threatening for any absolute refusal to be given : time was required to collect the defeated and disbanded army, which had been allowed to disperse immediately after its arrival in the capital, and it was therefore essential to prolong the negotiations and obtain some delay. The King was bound to temporize, and he also hoped to obtain better terms whereby he might gain peace without having to sacrifice his dignity and imperil the integrity of his empire. A letter, therefore, was written to Sir Garnet, in which he expressed his desire for peace and asked that a British officer might be allowed to return with his messenger to hear all he had to say on the subject. He said he was now quite satisfied that the message that had been delivered by Plange had never been sent by the Governor, and after once more asserting that Amankwa Tia had exceeded his instructions by attacking Elmina, asked the General to halt his army " for fear of meeting some of my captains as to cause any fighting." At the same time, he liberated the missionary Kühne, who was in an advanced stage of consumption, and begged him to intercede for him with Sir Garnet, assuring him that he would arrange everything satisfactorily if only the white ambassador was sent. He was anxious, however, to avoid any appearance before his people of having been coerced by threats, and Mr. Kühne, after being furnished with hammock-men late at night, was taken by torchlight to Kasi, a village three miles down the road, whence he continued his journey at daybreak and reached the camp at Prasu on the 12th. The King's messengers who accompanied him were detained at the most advanced post, so that they might not discover the deception that had been practised on the other envoys but still believe that Sir Garnet and the white troops were moving rapidly towards Kumasi and were indeed close at hand.

In acknowledging the receipt of this letter, the General explained that he could not consent to send any officer to Kumasi so long as the King detained two of the previous Governor's messengers, nor would he halt his army until the preliminary terms that he had imposed had been complied with.

Meanwhile, preparations for resistance were being made in Kumasi in case the General should persist in pushing on to the capital, and, on the 17th, the Chiefs assembled and swore to unite and march against the invaders. Kobina Obin, the King of Adansi, had shamed them into doing this against their better judgment by sending a message that the enemy were advancing and that if the Kumasis had no powder he at least had some. Had it not been for this taunt, all the missionaries would have been liberated at the same time as Mr. Kühne.

Russell's Regiment and Lord Gifford's Assin scouts had already crossed the Pra, and the latter had had a slight skirmish with the Adansis at Esaman on the 5th, in which one of the enemy had been killed and two women taken prisoners, while one of the scouts had been badly wounded. These Assin scouts were a valuable body of men, who did excellent work throughout the advance. They not only had an intimate knowledge of much of the country to be traversed, but were also desperately anxious to aid in the defeat of the Ashantis and thoroughly understood their tactics. Russell's Regiment continued to move slowly

forward, clearing the bush and fortifying the camping
grounds preparatory to the advance of the European
troops, while Lord Gifford's men reconnoitred still farther
ahead.   By the 17th Major Russell had occupied and
fortified the crest of the Monsi Hill, whence a small outpost of the enemy had been driven by the scouts, and the
next day Kwisa was reached and the scouts pushed on
to Fomana, which they found deserted. All along the
road they saw numerous signs of the work of the fetish
priests. A thread had been carried from tree to tree for a
long distance, presumably in imitation of the field telegraph,
which was regarded as a powerful English fetish ; a gun
carved out of wood and having a number of knives stuck
in it had been placed in the road, together with the corpse
of a man who had been sacrificed to induce the gods to
stay the advance of the British : he had been disgustingly
mutilated, and was found with the dissevered parts of his
body tied round his neck. Hitherto only a few Adansi
scouts had been seen ; for the country now being traversed
was the old Assin territory, which, since the migration of
that tribe to the south of the Pra, had been unoccupied
except by a few hunters, so that at this time the first
inhabited villages were those on the Adansi frontier.

Early on the morning of the 20th of January, the General
and the Headquarters Staff crossed the bridge over the
Pra. The Naval Brigade accompanied them, and the other
European troops followed. The Rifle Brigade crossed on
the 21st, and the Black Watch and detachment of the Royal
Welsh Fusiliers on the 22nd and 23rd. As the column
advanced, the posts on the road were garrisoned by detachments of Wood's Regiment and the West Indians, but the
remainder of the force was to be concentrated as quickly
as possible on the northern side of the Monsi Hill so that
the campaign might be brought to a close with the least
possible delay ; for although camping grounds and water
supplies had been prepared, the troops now had no proper
huts, but had to sleep on the ground and the sick-list was
daily increasing. The Naval Brigade had already sent
back 40 men out of 250, and the Rifle Brigade 57 out of

1874   650.   In view of these losses and their steady increase,[1]
CHAP. VI   combined with the information that was now obtained that
the Ashantis were preparing to make a desperate stand at
Amoafu, 200 more men of the Royal Welsh Fusiliers were
landed and marched to Prasu.

On the afternoon of the 23rd, while the Headquarters
were halted at Monsi, the remaining European captives
suddenly arrived in the camp. They had been released
on the 21st, and, as in the case of Mr. Kühne, had been sent
to Kasi by night and implored by the King to intercede
for him.   Two Ashanti messengers accompanied them bearing a letter from the King, in which he said he would himself pay the £1,000 to Adu Boffo rather than let so small
a sum stand in the way of the conclusion of peace, and
once again begged the General to advance no farther, promising to make Amankwa Tia pay the indemnity if he was
only given time, and saying he would liberate all the Fanti
prisoners directly the negotiations were completed.
These envoys corroborated the previous statements that
had been made by the King, saying that his instructions
to Amankwa Tia had been to march against Denkera,
instead of which he had gone by the Prasu road and
attacked Elmina, thereby incurring the King's displeasure.

As it was believed that Parliament was soon to reassemble, a message was sent announcing the King's
assent to the terms of peace and the liberation of the
prisoners. This was sent by the fastest steamer available
to Gibraltar to be cabled to England. By the time it
reached London, however, Mr. Gladstone and his Government had resigned office and a general election was in
progress, so that it came about that " this telegram was
sent to adorn a Queen's Speech which was never delivered,

[1] By the 25th of January the numbers were as follows :

Corps.						Officers.	Men.
Royal Welsh Fusiliers .	.	.	.	.	—	38
Black Watch	.	.	.	.	.	—	51
Rifle Brigade	.	.	.	.	.	3	78
Naval Brigade	.	.	.	.	.	—	48
TOTALS	.	.	.	.	.	3	215

for the opening of a Parliament which never assembled, 1874
to announce a promise of peace that was not fulfilled." [1] CHAP. VI

M. Bonnat reported that when the great fetish
tree in Kumasi fell down, the King had summoned the
priests to see what this portent might mean, and to enquire
what were the prospects of the war.   On their instructions
two men had been pierced through the cheeks with knives
and bound to trees in the forest, the priests saying that
their speedy death would mean victory to Ashanti.   One of
the unfortunate wretches, however, lived for five days and
the other for nine.   Bonnat, at his own request, remained
with the column and was attached to the Intelligence
Department, but the Ramseyers went on to Cape Coast,
where they arrived on the 2nd of February and were
accorded a great welcome after a captivity lasting four
years and a half.

Sir Garnet, in his reply to the King's letter, insisted
on the immediate liberation of the Fanti prisoners and
demanded the payment of half the indemnity and the
delivery of important hostages as preliminaries to the conclusion of peace.   He promised to advance but slowly for
the next few days in order that the King might have time
to comply with these conditions, and to halt his army
directly he had done so : he would then advance with an
escort of only 500 men to sign the treaty in Kumasi.   The
General made it perfectly clear that he was determined to
come to Kumasi whatever happened : all the King had
to do was to decide whether he came as friend or foe.   No
real delay was entailed by this promise, for it was necessary
to form a supply depot at Fomana before continuing the
advance.   Headquarters were therefore moved there, and
a four days' halt was made, which gave the troops time to
close up from the rear and appeared to the King as a
concession to his requests for delay.   The hostages demanded by the General were Prince Mensa the King's heir,
his mother Efua Kobri, and the heirs to the stools of Jabin,
Mampon, Kokofu and Bekwai.   They were, of course, the
most important persons in the whole kingdom and had

[1] *Daily News* Correspondent, *Ashantee War*, p. 297.

been chosen with the idea of impressing the Ashantis with the General's irresistible strength ; but it was unfortunate that their surrender should have been insisted upon, for, though Sir Garnet was doubtless unaware of the fact, it was absolutely out of the question that they could ever have been given up. United, they were far more powerful even than the King himself, and, whatever happened, neither the Queen-Mother nor the Heir-Apparent could ever have been surrendered so long as Ashanti remained a kingdom.

On the 26th a strong party[1] under Colonel McLeod[2] made a reconnaissance towards Atobiasi, which was found occupied by about 200 of the enemy, who, after a sharp skirmish lasting only a few minutes, broke and fled through the bush. Colonel Wood, with 105 men of his own regiment and a few of the Artillery and Royal Engineers, had in the meantime gone round by Kiang Boasu, where it was expected the retreating Ashantis would strike into the main path, but they saved themselves by passing north to Esian Kwanta. Two Ashantis were killed and two prisoners taken, and the village was then burned. From one of these prisoners it was ascertained that a force of at least 1,000 of the enemy had left Atobiasi the day before and were then at Boborasi under Kobina Obin the King of Adansi and six other Chiefs, that the King had sent them a supply of powder, and that he intended to make a stand at Amoafu. In a letter to the King, Sir Garnet informed him of this encounter and gave him a last warning, pointing out once more that it would be useless for him to attempt to oppose the advance of European troops and that the time of grace that had been allowed him had almost expired.

[1] Corps.					Officers.	Men.
Russell's Regiment	.	.	.	.	8	400
2nd West India Regiment	.	.	.	I	129
Rait's Artillery	.	.	.	.	I	14
Royal Engineers	.	.	.	.	I	17
Assin Scouts	.	.	.	.	I	60
TOTALS	.	.	.	.	12	620

[2] Black Watch.

By the 29th the reserve supplies had all been stored 1874
in Fomana and the column advanced to Dechiasu, where CHAP. VI
further letters were received from the King giving renewed
assurances of his peaceable intentions and repeating his
requests for delay. He finished thus : " My ancestors
never struggled with any European Power, and I cannot do
it if your Excellency do not mean to fight me whether I
meet your Excellency's demands or no. I shall only infer
your Excellency's evil intention towards me by the ad-
vancement of your Excellency's forces after receiving this
my letter. I therefore trust your Excellency will exercise
little more patience with me by giving me grace to negotiate
for peace." [1] The King, however, omitted to comply with
any of the demands that had been made upon him as
preliminaries to further negotiation, but excused himself
by saying that the near approach of Sir Garnet's force
had taken all the Chiefs away to guard their roads and
that he had no power to deliver hostages and prisoners, nor
to pay any indemnity until he had communicated with
and consulted them. This was certainly true to some
extent ; quite sufficiently so to be plausible ; but, as has
been mentioned, the conditions imposed were such as the
Ashantis could never have complied with, and, since the
steady advance of the invaders compelled them to fight
in defence of their capital, these subterfuges had to be
resorted to in order to gain time for the collection of an
adequate defending force. Dawson, the interpreter, had
cleverly contrived to warn the General not to put too
much faith in the King's protestations of peace by inserting
in a receipt for some money that had been sent him,
" The King's letter comes by the bearer of this. See,
please, 2 Cor. ii. 11 " ; [2] a valuable hint ingeniously conveyed in difficult circumstances.

The same morning, the 29th of January, Colonel McLeod
had marched against the Adansis at Boborasi with a mixed

---

[1] Brackenbury, vol. ii, p. 151 ; *Ashantee War* (Parliamentary Paper,
1873-4), part vi, p. 12.
[2] " Lest Satan should get an advantage of us : for we are not ignorant
of his devices."

European and native force.[1] They arrived before the
village at eleven o'clock, and taking the enemy completely by surprise, drove them into the bush and silenced
their fire.   The Adansis left about fifty dead behind them,
and fourteen others were taken prisoners, amongst them a
slave woman whose master had left her stark naked and
shot her twice to prevent her falling into the hands of the
British, but fortunately failed to kill her.   A number of
muskets and about a dozen kegs of powder were also
captured, besides a quantity of other property, including
the state umbrella of the old general Asamoa Kwanta, who,
in this last extremity of national peril, had been prevailed
upon to leave his retirement, and consented to accept the
command of the left wing of the army under Amankwa Tia,
who was his favourite pupil.   He had come down with a
convoy of powder to organize the Adansi forces and narrowly escaped capture.   The British casualties were slight,
though the enemy soon rallied and followed the troops
down the road, firing on the rear-guard, when the return
march was commenced.   Captain Nicol[2] was killed at
the very beginning of the fight as he was entering the
village at the head of the Anamabo company of Russell's
Regiment, and one man of that regiment and a carrier
were also killed : the Naval Brigade had four men wounded
and Russell's Regiment three.

   Captain Nicol's death was directly attributable to the
stringent orders that had been given by Sir Garnet Wolseley
that he was not to fire on the enemy unless he was first
attacked.   Lord Gifford, advancing in the extreme van
with his Assin Scouts had also been hampered by similar
orders.   Captain Nicol had, moreover, been forbidden to
burn the village.   These instructions had been given, partly
because the General was anxious to do nothing that might

---

[1] Corps.		Officers.	Men.
Royal Welsh Fusiliers	. .	1	79
Naval Brigade .	. .	14	209
Russell's Regiment	. .	1	57
Rait's Artillery .	. .	2 Rocket detachments.	

   [2] Hampshire Militia ; he raised the Bonny and Opobo Companies
of Russell's Regiment.

interfere with his peace negotiations with the King, and partly on account of an outcry that had been raised in England by the Exeter Hall party, which, though it might have weighed very little with Sir Garnet himself, yet influenced the authorities whom he was bound to obey. Nothing more ridiculous than such orders could well be imagined. If the negotiations with the King were deemed of sufficient importance, it would have been better to have postponed the attack on this village until it could be seen if anything was likely to come of them ; but if the necessity of continuing the advance and the impossibility of leaving this hostile force on the flank of the line of communications precluded this, they should have been left out of the question altogether. Many consider that, even in civilized warfare, it is more merciful in the end to carry it on with the utmost rigour ; but in a war with savages, at any rate, all concessions of this kind are certain to be misconstrued into signs of weakness. The burning of the farms and cottages of villagers in a civilized country seems unnecessarily cruel, but it really tends to shorten the struggle and thus saves further bloodshed and misery and does good ; but to spare places like these Ashanti villages is quite another matter. They are the equivalents of the magazines and fortified positions of a civilized race, and if the enemy are merely driven out and the places themselves left standing, they are reoccupied within a few hours of their evacuation by the victors, and nothing has been gained. Orders prohibiting the burning of villages that there is no intention of holding are therefore absurd, and orders forbidding men to fire on hostile savages until they are first attacked are almost criminally so, for they at once do away with the greatest advantage the troops have —the superior range and accuracy of their weapons—and place them at the mercy of the first volley at close range by greatly superior numbers. Captain Nicol lost his life while complying with such orders. He was endeavouring to withhold the fire of his own men and to parley with the Ashantis ; but they had been surprised and startled by the sudden appearance of this force in their midst, and, naturally enough, fired on the attackers the moment they realized what had happened and could seize their arms. Captain Nicol was the most conspicuous person in the open street, and fell dead at the first volley. The loss of this officer and the almost immediate reoccupation of the village by the enemy were not the only unfortunate results of these orders ; for the Adansis were so completely unprepared that, had the troops rushed the place in a determined manner, it is more than likely that both Asamoa Kwanta and Kobina Obin of Adansi would have fallen into their hands, and, by the proof thus obtained of the hostility of the latter, much subsequent trouble on account of Adansi would have been obviated.

Meanwhile, two out of the three auxiliary columns were advancing into the enemy's country. Captain Glover had crossed the Pra on the 15th with 750 Hausas, Yorubas and Donkos and advanced to Abogu, which was reached at about four o'clock the next afternoon. A slight skirmish took place, in which seven Hausas and a Yoruba were wounded, but the village was soon taken, and the enemy retired into the bush, whence they kept up an intermittent fire throughout the whole of that night and the following morning. The timely arrival of this force in Abogu saved the lives of forty slaves who were about to be sacrificed at a funeral custom. The Hausas had expended so much ammunition in this small action by wild and unnecessary firing that they now had barely ten rounds a man left, and Captain Glover was compelled to halt until a further supply could be got up. This detained him until the 26th, but the delay allowed the Chief of Asum to join him with 120 men on the 19th, and the next day Kofi Ahinkora of Eastern Akim arrived with 350 more.

Captain Butler had succeeded in persuading a few hundred Akims to accompany him to Beronasi on the Pra by the 15th, but nothing would induce them to cross the river into Ashanti. He, however, was determined to carry out his instructions and show these people that he, at any rate, regarded his promises as sacred, however little value they might set upon their own. Accordingly, on the appointed day, he and his officers crossed the river with a **1874** few Fanti Police carrying loads, while the chicken-hearted CHAP. VI Akims sat on the south bank and watched them. " They might well look ; the sight was a curious one. Three white men and six Fanti policemen carrying baggage had invaded Ashanti." [1] Even this example failed to induce the Akims to budge an inch : all they wanted was delay, and Captain Butler, after waiting three days for them to join him, started for Prasu. On the 25th, however, he was recalled by Daku the Chief of Akasi, who assured him, on behalf of the Akim Chiefs, that they were now ready to cross. The fact was that they were even more afraid of the General's wrath when their cowardice and duplicity should be reported to him than they were of the Ashantis. Even now it was not until one of Captain Butler's officers had crossed the river and kicked over every cooking-pot and knocked down every hut and shelter that he could reach, that they finally screwed up sufficient courage to cross the river and follow him along the Accra-Kokofu road. They received several reinforcements, who overtook them from day to day and brought their numbers up to about 1,400. On the 26th, while they were encamped at Enunsu, they were attacked by a party of Eastern Akims belonging to Captain Glover's force, who had been sent against the village in the belief that it was held by the enemy. Each party mistook the other for Ashantis, and a skirmish took place which ended in the rout of the Eastern Akims with a loss of three killed and several wounded. It was not until after the war was over that this mistake was discovered, the suspicions of the Eastern Akims, which they mentioned to Captain Glover on their return, being regarded at the time as a mere excuse for their defeat and flight. After this, Captain Butler's men moved to Akina, within ten miles of Amoafu, where they halted from the 27th till the 30th. There Captain Butler received a letter from Sir Garnet Wolseley telling him that he expected to engage the main Ashanti army at Amoafu on or about the 29th, and calling upon him to co-operate with his column by

[1] Butler, p. 201.

attacking the enemy in the flank ; but on the 30th a sudden and quite inexcusable panic seized the Akims, who, finding themselves so far advanced into the enemy's country, fled incontinently to the Pra, recrossed the river, and dispersed to their homes. They gave no excuse for this extraordinary conduct, and Captain Butler wrote : " So universal was the panic, that during the greater portion of the night bodies of men continued to move south, and early on the morning of the 31st Yankoma was reached and left behind. . . . No previous warning, no intimation whatever, had been given to me that it was the intention of the Kings and Chiefs to abandon Akina ; indeed, up to the very moment that the retreat began I was moving through the camps, endeavouring to get the Akims to move to Dadiasso, *en route* to Amoaful, and I had actually engaged a party of hunters to proceed through the bush to the main line near the latter place. Yet, so complete was the flight, that, within two hours, not a man was left in Akina, and long before midnight every Akim was behind the Ennoon River, ten miles distant. All this without a reverse having taken place, and after a loss of only two killed and two wounded in the entire force." [1] Captain Butler's force had thus ceased to exist by the end of January, and he had to abandon his march and strike across to rejoin the main column, which he met at Ajimamu on the 7th of February as it was returning from Kumasi.

Captain Dalrymple had been even less successful. When he had first set out for Jukwa, he had expected to find fully 1,000 allies there under Sergeant Hughes of the Gold Coast Volunteers, but found none at all. All his efforts to obtain men from the Kings of Wassaw, Eguafo, Komenda and the other Chiefs to whom he had been commissioned only resulted in the production of rather less than fifty men, and, as they absolutely refused to cross the Ofin River into Ashanti, Captain Dalrymple had no alternative but to abandon his task as hopeless, and rejoined Sir Garnet at Fomana on his return march. But though two out of three

---

[1] *Ashantee War* (Parliamentary Paper, 1873-4), part viii, p. 23.

of these auxiliary columns had utterly failed in their apparent object, they had not been without their uses. The news of the movements of these different forces had reached Kumasi, and, having lost nothing in transmission, had made a deep impression there. Moreover, the Chiefs of several of the outlying districts of Ashanti, finding their towns threatened by these columns, drew off their men from the main army to defend their own homes. The detachment from Jabin alone, which was preparing to oppose Captain Glover's advance, meant a loss to the King's army of fully 12,000 men, and Sir Garnet Wolseley's task of forcing his way up the main road was thus materially lightened.

CHAPTER VII

THE ASHANTIS AT BAY AND THE FALL OF KUMASI

1874

By the 30th of January 1874, the whole European force, together with the artillery and native regiments, had been concentrated at Insafu and Akankuasi : Wood's and Russell's Regiments, however, were now much reduced in strength, for they had been providing detachments to garrison the posts along the line of communications. The scouts had ascertained the presence of a strong force of the enemy a little to the south of Amoafu, and it was evident that a battle would have to be fought as soon as the advance was resumed.

It was almost certain that the enemy, who were present in immensely superior numbers, would try to carry out their usual plan of making flank attacks and surrounding the army opposed to them, and, as the British force was altogether too small to prevent this, Sir Garnet Wolseley decided to meet these tactics by dividing his troops into four columns to form a large open square. The leading column, which was to advance along the road and extend for some distance into the bush on either side of it, forming a line 300 or 400 yards or more in length, was commanded by Brigadier-General Sir Archibald Alison, Bart., C.B., and consisted of the Black Watch, with two 7-pounder gun detachments of Rait's Artillery and a party of Royal Engineers. The Headquarters and Royal Welsh Fusiliers were to follow in their rear. The right and left columns were to advance at some distance from, but parallel to the main road, keeping in touch with the centre column and cutting their own paths through the bush. That on the left consisted of the right wing of the Naval Brigade under Captain Hunt Grubbe, Russell's Regiment, two rocket detachments of Rait's Artillery and a party of Royal Engineers, and was commanded by Colonel McLeod, C.B. The right column, under Lieutenant Colonel Wood, V.C., consisted of the left wing of the Naval Brigade under Captain Luxmoore, Wood's Regiment, and similar detachments of Artillery and Engineers to those on the left. The rear of the square was closed in by the Rifle Brigade under Lieutenant-Colonel A. F. Warren. The total force, including Engineer labourers, amounted to 1,509 Europeans and 708 Africans.

The troops began to move off soon after daybreak on the 31st of January, and Lord Gifford's Assin scouts first came in touch with the enemy outside Ejinasi at a little before eight o'clock. The small party of Ashantis who occupied this place, after firing on the scouts, fell back, and it was taken with a rush ; but when two companies of the Black Watch began to advance along the path beyond, they quickly came upon the enemy's main force and the battle began in earnest. Asamoa Kwanta, who was in supreme command, had chosen his position with great skill. Soon after leaving Ejinasi the road descended into a swampy hollow filled with deep mud, through which flowed a sluggish stream, and then ascended a ridge on the opposite side. Beyond the stream, this ridge fell back on the right of the track ; but on the southern side it swept round in a semi-circle and covered the path descending into the ravine on the left, so that the Ashantis, who had chosen this ridge as their main position and occupied it in thousands, flanked and completely commanded, not only the path descending into the swamp, but also its continuation up the slope beyond. They could hardly have found a stronger place.

As company after company of the Black Watch, with their pipes playing, descended into the ravine, they were met with a terrific fire. So great was the hail of lead that it stripped the bark from the trees and almost bared them of leaves, while the smoke of the Ashanti powder hanging about in dense clouds in the still damp air of the forest added to its natural gloom. Fortunately it was a dull, cloudy day, so that the heat was less overpowering than usual. The enemy, none of whom were to be seen in the thick bush, maintained a continuous and deafening fusillade, and though the 42nd kept up a steady fire in return, they could make but little headway. As they entered the ravine, they were almost out of range of the Ashanti muskets and the enemy could do them very little harm ; but when they reached the stream and came under this heavy fire at close range as they floundered through the mud and water of the swamp, they offered an easy mark : man after man fell, and a continuous stream of wounded moved to the rear. By half-past nine seven out of the eight companies of the Black Watch were engaged, and a little later a company of the 23rd had to be sent up to their support. Still no progress could be made until the guns were brought up and poured a murderous fire into the enemy, fourteen or fifteen rounds being fired in quick succession at a range of only about fifty yards. The heaps of dead, torn and mutilated by the shells, that were afterwards passed, showed the fearful execution done by the Hausa Artillery. This was followed by a charge of the Black Watch, who drove the shaken Ashantis back. They did not go far however, but at once rallied on a second ridge behind their former position and fought as fiercely as ever. The guns had to be brought up again and again and other charges made, every short retreat of the enemy being followed by a corresponding advance of the Black Watch and Artillery ; but it was not until midday that a final charge of the 42nd took them into Amoafu after the battle had raged for over four hours.

The Ashantis had fought magnificently, as is evident from the fact that, even with the aid of artillery, one of the finest regiments in the British army had been unable to make headway against them for several hours. They had been greatly shaken by having their centre broken and could not withstand the steady advance of the Black

Watch, who kept them almost continuously on the move and prevented their taking cover ; but in spite of this, they not only disputed every inch of ground in front, but also delivered a succession of attacks on the flanks of the square. They were truly at bay : never before had they had so much at stake. Even at Dodowa they had had a clear line of retreat and their own country had not been threatened ; but here was an army of white soldiers not only in their country, but boldly pushing forward in spite of their utmost efforts to stay them, and already almost within striking distance of the capital itself.

Meanwhile, although Amoafu was occupied by the Black Watch, the battle was by no means over. Colonel McLeod's men had cut their way into the bush on the left, where they were met with a heavy fire from a body of men who occupied the summit and slopes of a small hill. Captain Buckle, R.E., was mortally wounded early in the engagement while directing a party of bush-cutters, and Captain Hunt Grubbe was seriously wounded in the hand. It was soon found impossible to keep pace with the Black Watch, owing to the density of the undergrowth, and the unpleasantness of having lost touch with them was increased by the impossibility of knowing how they changed their direction as they followed the turns of the path and the different parties more than once fired into each other. A path was therefore cut to the summit of the hill by the Opobos, one half cutting while the other half fired ; a clearing was made, and the enemy were then driven back by Russell's Regiment under cover of rocket fire. Just after Amoafu was taken, this column cut its way into the main road behind the Black Watch. In the same way, Colonel Wood's force was unable to advance against the terrific fire that was poured into it as it cut its paths to the north-east, and he, too, ordered his men to make a clearing in which they could lie down and return the enemy's fire.

While the main body of the Ashanti army was opposing the advance of these columns, other detachments had been making frequent determined attacks on the flanks and had even cut their way into the road behind the British troops. One of these parties nearly succeeded in rushing the village of Kwaman, whence Sir Garnet Wolseley was directing the operations, and even after Amoafu had been taken, the enemy again attacked it. About one o'clock heavy firing commenced from the bush on the eastern side of Ejinasi and all along the road as far as Amoafu, and though this road was lined by troops, who returned their fire, the enemy stood their ground till the Rifle Brigade advanced and occupied Ejinasi Hill, and it was not until a quarter to two that it finally ceased.

The British casualties in this battle were as follows :

KILLED

Officers
Captain Buckle, R.E.	1

Men
Black Watch	2
Wood's Regiment	1
TOTAL	4

WOUNDED

Officers
Royal Engineers	1
Naval Brigade	6
Royal Welsh Fusiliers	1
Black Watch	9
Rifle Brigade	3
Wood's Regiment	1
TOTAL	21

Men
Rait's Artillery	1
Royal Engineers	4
Naval Brigade	26
Royal Welsh Fusiliers	3
Black Watch	104
Rifle Brigade	6
Wood's Regiment	6
Russell's Regiment	17
Scouts	6
TOTAL	173

One of the men of the Black Watch, becoming separated **1874** from his comrades or losing his way as he fell back wounded, had been surrounded by the enemy, who killed him and cut off his head. It was their only trophy ; and when the body was found, the slashed hands and almost severed fingers bore silent testimony to the fight he had made for his life. When this head reached Kumasi late that evening and was exhibited by one of the princes, the people were far from pleased, regarding it rather as a misfortune that would surely bring trouble and retribution upon them. Of this regiment, which had had the hardest share of the work and whose losses were correspondingly heavy, Sir Garnet wrote : " It is impossible for me to speak in too high terms of that magnificent regiment, the 42nd Highlanders ; their steadiness and discipline, the admirable way in which they were kept in hand by their officers, and the enthusiastic gallantry with which every charge was executed, exceed all praise." The Ashantis must have lost heavily and were believed to have had between 800 and 1,200 killed and as many more wounded, but the exact numbers were never known. Amankwa Tia had fallen on the left, shot in the back as he was being carried off in his chair ; another great Chief, Appia, in the centre, and Kobina Jomo the King of Mampon, who had always counselled peace, was killed on the right. About 150 dead were found and buried close to the road, but there must have been many hundreds more in the bush, where there was no time to make any search, and the Ashantis invariably carry off their dead and wounded unless extremely hard pressed.

During the afternoon the enemy passed round and attacked the line of communications. At about one o'clock heavy firing was again heard in the direction of Kwaman, whither the wounded had now been sent. The attack was made from the south-west, and the enemy pressed hard upon the garrison of West Indians and Winnebas. A company of the Rifle Brigade was sent to their assistance and drove the Ashantis back, silencing their fire by four o'clock ; but about an hour later the attack was renewed. The baggage, reserve ammunition column and field hospitals had been left in Akankuasi and Insafu during the advance against Amoafu, but were now being moved up, and this convoy, five miles long, was passing along the road under escort of the 2nd West India Regiment. It arrived within some 1,000 yards of Kwaman at about five o'clock, during the second attack on the village, and the southern division of the enemy suddenly turned upon it. Many of the carriers, panic-stricken, threw down their loads and bolted down the road, and matters began to look very serious, when a welcome reinforcement of the Rifle Brigade and West India Regiment arrived from Kwaman. They had been sent out by Captain Dugdale, who had some suspicion of what was going on, and soon drove the enemy into the bush and enabled Colonel Colley's men to recover a great deal of the baggage. A great many loads, however, fell into the hands of the Ashantis, and the fighting on the road continued without any intermission until night set in, but only two of the Rifle Brigade and two West Indians were wounded. Another small convoy was attacked on the same day near Dompoasi, and £80 of Government money and a few loads were lost. Early the next morning the road from Insafu to Amoafu was lined by the troops, and the baggage that had been saved and the ammunition were safely passed up.

Many of the Ashantis had retreated to Bekwai, a large town situated about a mile to the west of Amoafu : it was the Bekwais, in fact, who had offered some of the most determined resistance during the battle. It was considered dangerous to leave this place on the flank, and orders were therefore given to destroy it before the advance was continued. This duty was entrusted to Sir Archibald Alison. At one o'clock Lord Gifford's Scouts marched out of Amoafu, followed by the Naval Brigade and a few Engineers and Gunners forming the advance-guard under Colonel McLeod, while the main body consisted of the detachment of the 23rd Fusiliers and five companies of the Black Watch. The Scouts reached Bekwai within twenty minutes and met with a vigorous opposition, sixteen or seventeen of them being wounded almost immediately, but they pushed **1874** on undaunted and succeeded in forcing their way into the CHAP. VII town. The Naval Brigade then came up and drove the enemy into the bush, so that the fight was all over before the main body arrived. For his gallantry in this attack and on many other occasions during the war Lord Gifford [1] was afterwards decorated with the Victoria Cross. Bekwai was burned and the force returned to Amoafu. The Naval Brigade had only one man killed and three wounded, but the Ashantis lost heavily. During the afternoon, yet another convoy was attacked at Dompoasi; one carrier was killed and two more were wounded, but though only twelve of the remaining eighty stood their ground, no loads were lost.

At daybreak on the 2nd of February the whole force marched out of Amoafu, and though the advance-guard was fired on as every village was reached, it met with no really serious opposition and reached Ajimamu soon after mid-day. The main body arrived a little later, and the General then decided to go no farther that day. In the afternoon, however, he sent Colonel McLeod on to Ajabin, which was occupied without opposition. The baggage was then ordered up from Amoafu and was brought in safely that evening under escort of detachments from each regiment, but it was not until after dark that the Naval Brigade, who formed the rear-guard, arrived in camp.

Meanwhile, the enemy from Boborasi, under Asamoa Kwanta and Kobina Obin, had made a determined attack on the post at Fomana. This place was occupied by two officers and 38 rank and file of the 1st West India Regiment and one officer and 102 men of the Mumford Company of Russell's Regiment. Besides these, there were two Transport and two Control officers and three surgeons in the town, and the King's house, which had been converted into a temporary hospital, contained twenty-four European convalescents. The village was large and straggling, and altogether too extensive to be properly defended by this small garrison, so that when the enemy attacked it from

---

[1] Lieutenant, 24th Regiment.

all sides at about half-past eight that morning, they soon forced their way into its southern end and set the houses on fire. The sick men, who had been armed and gallantly assisted in the defence, although some of them were so weak that they fell back fainting after they had fired, were removed from the hospital to a stockade that had been built for the stores at the other end of the village, the surrounding houses were pulled down, and the garrison was then able to hold the smaller position. All firing had ceased by one o'clock, and although a few shots were fired at some men who went out to fetch water, the attack on the post was not renewed. Fortunately no one was killed in this affair, but one officer [1] and two Europeans were severely wounded, and another officer,[2] several more Europeans, five West Indians and three of Russell's Regiment were also hit.

The most serious result of this affair at Fomana was the effect it had on the carriers, who were so frightened by the determined way in which the enemy had pressed into the town that they could not be induced to leave for the front with stores. The troops at Ajimamu had four days' rations with them, however, and Colonel Colley guaranteed to get up a further supply in five days' time, for he now had some 10,000 carriers on the road and the transport was so well organized under him that the mail was regularly brought up the whole distance from Cape Coast to Kumasi in thirty-six hours. The transport of the baggage, too, for the past few days had been a matter of constantly increasing difficulty ; for the roads had to be lined with troops while the convoy was being passed up and this duty continually kept the men out until late in the evening. Sir Garnet had, moreover, proved at Amoafu that the Ashantis could not withstand a continuous and determined advance, and therefore decided not to wait any longer, but to make a dash for Kumasi, where he had never intended to make a long stay, and which was now only about fifteen miles distant. He would then either make peace or destroy the place, and return as quickly as

[1] Captain Dudley North, 47th Regiment.   [2] Captain Duncan, R.A.

possible to Ajimamu, where further supplies would by then have been collected. Ajimamu itself was an important position, being situated at the junction of two roads, both of which led to Kumasi. It was now strongly entrenched, and all the weakly men were left behind to garrison it under Captain Cope of the Rifle Brigade.

At daybreak on the 3rd the final advance to Kumasi was commenced. Three-quarters of an hour after the start, the advance-guard came in touch with the enemy at a small stream, beyond which, on some densely wooded rising ground, the Ashantis were present in large numbers and at first disputed every inch of the way. Twenty-four rounds from a 7-pounder gun were fired into this position, and a few companies of the Rifle Brigade and Russell's Regiment then cleared the way. The British losses in this skirmish were one Scout killed, and seven Scouts, an officer and nine men of Russell's Regiment and six men of the Rifle Brigade wounded. The advance from this point, though steady, was very slow ; for parties of the enemy continually opened fire from ambuscades along the path and inflicted some slight loss at almost every discharge.

At half-past eleven messengers were met bearing a flag of truce and bringing two letters from the King and Dawson, in which the former complained that the General's rapid movements put him " into confusion " and begged that " regarding the hostages and the money " he might be allowed to " do it in the same as late Governor Maclean did. Because my old mother and my young brother are my both counsellors and helpers in every way." [1] Dawson added a note begging the General to halt, and saying, " No doubt we will all be killed if your Excellency do not stay." [2] In the second letter Dawson again begged for delay, and said, " I see now they have bend to do what is right, and trust your Excellency will not fight them again, as they intend to withdraw the forces." [3] He also

---

[1] *Ashantee War* (Parliamentary Paper, 1873–4), part viii, p. 20 ; Brackenbury, vol. ii, p. 201.   [2] *Ibid.*
[3] *Ashantee War* (Parliamentary Paper, 1873–4), part viii, p. 21 ; Brackenbury, vol. ii, p. 202.

sent a further message, saying that the King really wanted
peace, but would fight if the troops advanced. It was
quite evident that the King was very seriously alarmed,
and that Dawson was absolutely terrified, and it is fairly
certain that Kofi Karikari really would have been only
too glad to make peace at once on any terms that did not
necessitate the surrender of the Queen-Mother and Heir-
Apparent. This belief is borne out by the fact that his
messengers on their return were heard calling out to the
enemy not to fire, and a prisoner captured later in the day
said that although there were fully 10,000 Ashantis in the
immediate vicinity, they did not attack because they had
received orders from the King not to do so. It was known,
however, that a large force was being collected to the
north of the Oda River, where the King intended to make
a final stand if his negotiations failed. Sir Garnet never
realized how impossible was the surrender of the two
principal hostages for whom he had asked, and feeling that
the least show of weakness by making concessions now
would be most unwise, and suspecting, moreover, that the
King was only trying to gain time to collect more troops,
replied that he would not halt until the hostages were in
his possession ; but that, as time pressed, he was willing
to accept the Queen-Mother and Prince Mensa only, and
would halt for the night on the south bank of the Oda
River in order to give the King time to send them ; otherwise he would march straight to Kumasi. This short
delay cost him nothing ; for he knew it would be impossible for him to cross the river, fight another battle
and reach Kumasi that day. He was bound to halt therefore, but was able to appear to be granting the King's
request by so doing. Whatever may have been the King's
real intentions before, the receipt of this ultimatum decided
him : he could not comply with the General's terms, and,
therefore, had no alternative but to fight again in a last
effort to defend his capital.

The Oda River was reached by three o'clock : it was
fifty feet wide and waist deep, so the construction of a
bridge was at once begun, while Russell's Regiment

crossed over to the north bank to cover the Engineers at their work. The troops meanwhile made a clearing for their bivouac on the south bank. This was the first time they had been without proper shelter for the night, and, with the most extraordinary ill-luck, a heavy tornado came up soon after sunset and drenching rain continued throughout the whole night, against which the frail shelters of palm sticks and plantain leaves that the men had rigged up afforded not the slightest protection. Everything was soon soaked, and officers and men alike spent the night in the utmost misery, sitting huddled together in the cold and wet, unable either to keep their fires alight or to lie down and sleep in the streaming water and mud. The sappers worked at the bridge throughout nearly the whole night, and by seven o'clock the next morning it was finished. The rain had now ceased, and after the men had had time to dry their clothes a little and get some hot breakfast, the advance was resumed. The enemy opened fire almost immediately, and the Opobo Company of Wood's Regiment, who were in the advance-guard, suddenly fell flat in the road and began a wild and wasteful fire which their officers had the greatest difficulty in checking. Hitherto the men of these native regiments had behaved very well, but now that they found themselves so close to the capital of their dreaded enemy and with his army preparing to make its last desperate stand in its defence, they lost their nerve. A company of the Rifle Brigade and a 7-pounder gun were passed to the front, but met with such determined resistance that it was not until they had been reinforced by three more companies and the battle had lasted nearly two hours that they were able to push slowly on. For the first half-mile from the river the path rose tolerably evenly ; then, after a steep ascent, it passed along a narrow ridge with a ravine on either side, dipped again deeply, and then finally rose into the village of Odasu. The gun was brought up, a few rounds were fired to drive the enemy back, and the Rifle Brigade then made a short rush. This manœuvre was repeated again and again, until finally the village was reached soon after nine o'clock and occupied by the advance-guard. This advance, however, had not been made without loss : Lieutenant Eyre,[1] the Adjutant of Wood's Regiment, had been killed and was buried in the village while the battle raged around, Lieutenant Wauchope[2] was severely wounded, and seven out of the eleven Hausas who formed the gun's crew were also hit.

Meanwhile, although the village had been taken, the enemy was still holding the bush all around, and the main body was only just approaching that portion of the road which traversed the ridge. The Ashantis attacked it heavily on the right flank, and when the men reached the ridge they were met with a tremendous fire from both sides ; but the road was lined with troops from the river to Odasu, and at half-past twelve the Naval Brigade, which formed the rear-guard, was passed over with the baggage and along this covered way into the village. The slugs flew and whistled amongst the carriers all the way, and more than one dropped wounded ; but they were hemmed in by the troops, and the panting, terrified wretches were driven relentlessly forward until the whole convoy at last reached Odasu. The enemy then closed in on the road in rear of the column and overran the deserted camp. The Headquarters and Black Watch had arrived in Odasu soon after eleven o'clock, but the enemy surrounded the village on every side and maintained a continuous and fierce attack. At times they pressed up quite close to the houses, advancing in line and firing a regular volley, but they were driven back each time with terrible slaughter by the Rifle Brigade, who lined the bush all round the village.

Soon after midday, the General decided to make a dash for Kumasi. The honour of leading the way fell to the Black Watch. They were ordered to break through the enemy's lines in front and march straight to the capital, disregarding all flank attacks, while the remaining troops were to follow as soon as the attacks on the village had been finally repulsed and the place could safely be left in

---

[1] 90th Regiment.   [2] 42nd Regiment.

charge of a small garrison. Then followed the finest episode in the whole campaign. The Hausas brought up one of their guns and fired several rounds down the path, and then the Black Watch, with Colonel McLeod at their head, burst out of the village and charged down the road against and right through the astonished Ashantis. " On first debouching from the village, a tremendous fire was opened on the head of the column from a well-planned and strong ambuscade, six men being knocked over in an instant. But the flank companies worked steadily through the bush ; the leading company in the path sprang forward with a cheer ; the pipes struck up, and the ambuscade was at once carried. Then followed one of the finest spectacles I have ever seen in war. Without stop or stay the 42nd rushed on cheering, their officers to the front ; ambuscade after ambuscade was successfully carried, village after village won in succession, till the whole Ashantis broke and fled in the wildest disorder down the pathway on their front to Coomassie. The ground was covered with traces of their flight. Umbrellas and war-chairs of their Chiefs, drums, muskets, killed and wounded, covered the whole way, and the bush on each side was trampled as if a torrent had flowed through it. No pause took place until a village [1] about four miles from Coomassie was reached, when the absolute exhaustion of the men rendered a short halt necessary. So swift and unbroken was the advance of the 42nd, that neither Rait's guns nor the Rifle Brigade in support were ever brought into action." [2] Several officers and men of the Black Watch were recommended for the Victoria Cross for their gallantry in this advance, but it was only given to one man, Sergeant M'Gaw.

Meanwhile, the attack on Odasu had been maintained with unabated vigour ; but at a few minutes to two a message was received from Colonel McLeod that he would be in Kumasi that night. This news was at once com-

---

[1] Kasi.
[2] Sir Archibald Alison's description, Brackenbury, vol. ii, p. 215.

municated to the troops, who raised such a ringing cheer that the enemy knew it could have but one meaning and their fire immediately ceased. The order was then given for a general advance. A small but sufficient garrison was left to hold Odasu and the General marched out with the Rifle Brigade, followed by Colonel Wood with his own and Russell's Regiments and the Naval Brigade, forming the rear-guard in charge of the hospital, wounded and other impedimenta.

Two letters were received one after the other from Dawson frantically imploring the General to stop, but his only answer was to give the order to the troops to " Push on." These letters not only showed that the spirit of the Ashantis was broken, but that Dawson himself was reduced to a state of abject terror concerning his own fate. In one letter he wrote, " I find things have come to a crisis concerning the lives of us all here. . . . Plead with the Major-General to defer his personal coming, which frightens the people so much, and appoint an officer of rank. . . . Matters might be very well settled in this manner, and we may be saved, since the destruction of the whole blessed kingdom after we are killed would not bring us back. I know now the Ashantees will yield to all the terms of the Major-General for peace, except the sending their Royal lineage out of the kingdom, which is against their superstitious notions, so much so that they would rather die or perish foolishly than doing it ; I would not care a button if they could do it without us. . . . As it regards Ashantee power now being broken is very evident ; they now beg me, which they have never done before, to do all I can to save them. The King himself sent his step-father to tell me that he now acknowledges the superiority of the white men, and crave pardon that he may be allowed to treat for peace."[1] In a second letter he wrote : " For Heaven's sake, I pray your Excellency to halt the forces for to-day and to-morrow. All the Ashantee forces are coming back home. . . . If your Excellency do not halt,

---

[1] *Ashantee War* (Parliamentary Paper, 1873–4), part viii, pp. 21–2 ; Brackenbury, vol. ii, pp. 220–1.

and do not hear from me about 12 to-morrow noon, then all is over with me." [1]

As they drew near Kumasi, the Black Watch came upon a group of executioners on the point of putting a man to death as a sacrifice to stay their advance, but they met with no opposition and crossed the Suban swamp and entered the town at half-past five. Sir Garnet Wolseley, who arrived three-quarters of an hour later, found the troops drawn up in the market-place to receive him with a general salute, and at once called for three cheers for the Queen.

The scene in the streets of Kumasi after the entry of the troops was a strange one, and probably without parallel in the capture of a hostile capital. The whole place was full of armed men, who stood about the streets in great crowds watching the arrival of the soldiers, but without attempting to resist them or firing a single shot. Their only emotion seemed to be a mixture of pleasure and curiosity at the unusual sight of so many white men. Hundreds of fugitives from the field of Odasu, powder-grimed, blood-stained, and almost naked, continually poured into the town. Some of them were armed with double-barrelled guns and nearly new Enfields that were presumably the proceeds of recent trading at Assini. The Ashantis, now that they had been finally beaten, took their defeat very philosophically and made no further resistance : many of them came up to shake hands with the troops or brought them water to drink, and others showed such confidence in them that they were seen moving off quite openly, carrying their arms and ammunition into the bush. Some attempt was made by a few of the officers to stop this, but as it was getting dark and it was important to avoid any risk of street fighting that night, Sir Garnet decided that the men had better not be molested, and merely issued an order forbidding the removal of munitions of war. Dawson was met walking at liberty in the street and actually had the impudence to refuse to

[1] *Ashantee War* (Parliamentary Paper, 1873–4), part viii, p. 22 ; Brackenbury, vol. ii, p. 222.

point out the palace, saying he did not know where it was, and though he took Lord Gifford and his men all round the town, pretending to lead them to it, he eventually brought them back to the point from which they had started. He stated, however, that the King was not in town, but denied all knowledge of where he had gone to and said he could not possibly find out. He produced messengers, however, who were ready to go to the King, and Sir Garnet at once despatched the following letter :[1]

> " COOMASSIE,
> " *February* 4, 1874.
> " KING,
> " You have deceived me, but I have kept my promise to you.
> " I am in Coomassie, and my only wish is to make a lasting peace with you. I have shown you the power of England, and now I will be merciful.
> " As you do not wish to give up your mother and Prince Mensah, send me some other hostages of rank, and I will make peace with you to-morrow on the terms originally agreed upon.
> " If either your Majesty, or your Royal mother, or Prince Mensah, will come to see me to-morrow morning early, I will treat you with all the honour due to your Royal dignity, and allow you to return in safety. You can trust my word.
> " I am, etc.,
> " (Signed) G. J. WOLSELEY,
> " *Major-General and Administrator*,
> " *Gold Coast.*
>
> " *To His Majesty Coffee Kalkully*,
> " *King of Ashantee*,
> " *Coomassie.*"

The messenger, Awusu Koko, a nephew of the King, was at the same time assured by Sir Garnet himself that his

---

[1] *Ashantee War* (Parliamentary Paper, 1873–4), part viii, p. 22 ; Brackenbury, vol. ii, p. 228.

only wish was to treat with the King and make peace, and **1874**
that if his offer was accepted and any of the Royal family CHAP. VII
came in to see him, the town would be left untouched and
the troops march out, leaving everything exactly as they
had found it ; but he was warned that the first sign of
treachery or the first shot fired on the troops in Kumasi
would be the signal for the immediate destruction of the
whole place and the slaughter of every person in it.   As it
was almost dark when Sir Garnet arrived, pickets were
posted and orders issued against plundering, while an
Ashanti crier went round telling the people in the King's
name not to interfere with the troops.   The men were then
dismissed to find quarters in the houses on the main street.

It had been a hard day for the men after their night
of discomfort and sleeplessness in the rain ; but although
the Ashantis had fought bravely at Odasu, they never
pressed in so closely as they had done at Amoafu.   Their
signal defeat at the latter place seemed to have shaken
their confidence : their fire was wilder, and the attack
generally less determined, and the British casualties were
proportionately lighter.

KILLED

Officers
Lieutenant Eyre, Adjutant Wood's Regiment   1

Men

Wood's Regiment	.	.	.	.	1
TOTAL	.	.	.	.	2

WOUNDED

Officers

Headquarter Staff	.	.	.	.	1
Naval Brigade	.	.	.	.	1
Black Watch .	.	.	.	.	3
Russell's Regiment .	.	.	.	.	1
TOTAL	.	.	.	.	6

N.C.O.'s and Men

Rait's Artillery	.	.	.	.	. 12
Naval Brigade	.	.	.	.	. 4
Royal Welsh Fusiliers	.	.	.	.	1
Black Watch	.	.	.	.	. 14
Rifle Brigade	.	.	.	.	. 17
Wood's Regiment	.	.	.	.	. 10
Russell's Regiment	.	.	.	.	. 2
TOTAL	.	.	.	.	. 60

Until the defeat of their army at Amoafu, the Ashantis had firmly believed that their troops could destroy any force that might dare to cross the Pra, and the King had great faith in his own General's plan of campaign. His own wish had been to concentrate his army at the Monsi Hills, and he had never really approved their abandonment ; but he had been overruled by his counsellors and fetishmen, many of whom had no experience of war, who pointed out that if the invaders were defeated too near the frontier they would probably succeed in escaping across the Pra with nearly all their baggage, and much valuable spoil would then be lost. It had been arranged, therefore, that the Ashantis should retire towards Kumasi, drawing the British troops after them until they were at some distance from their base ; the main army was then to turn to bay in front, while the Jabins were to swoop down upon the line of communications, destroy the bridge over the Pra, cut off the supply of provisions and ammunition, and capture and hold all the British posts along the road. It was indeed fortunate that the Jabins were prevented by the advance of Captain Glover's force from carrying out their part of this plan ; for, had they done so, disaster might easily have overtaken the troops, who, at best, would have had to fight their way back to the Pra without provisions, while the sick and wounded would almost certainly have been captured and butchered by the enemy. Even as it was, Sir Garnet had not a man too many ; and had this happened, he would not have had enough, and the return march would have assumed a suspicious likeness to a retreat. The missionaries had purposely been released before the army began to concentrate at Amoafu. The King had known well enough that he held a strong card so long as he retained possession of these prisoners ; but although he had been loath to release them before, yet, when he found that his utmost endeavours would not procure much further delay and that he would have to fight since he could not comply with the terms imposed, so far at least as the delivery of Royal hostages and the entry of a hostile force into Kumasi were concerned, he sent them down at the last moment before his army concentrated on the road and cleverly used them to try to prove to Sir Garnet that no preparations had been made to oppose his advance, hoping thus to induce him to press forward still farther from his base and with fewer precautions, so that he might the more readily be taken by surprise and his army defeated and destroyed. Amankwa Tia and those Chiefs who had practical experience of war had advised the collection of the whole army, including the Jabin force, at Amoafu, and until he himself was threatened by Captain Glover, Asafu Agai the Jabin King had been equally anxious to march his 12,000 men there ; but Kofi Karikari had listened rather to the advice of his mother Efua Kobri and the fetish priests and refused his consent. It was not until after the decisive defeat of their army at Amoafu and the refusal of the Jabins to carry out their part of the arrangement when they found their own town in danger had upset their plans, that the Ashantis began in all sincerity to wish for peace, and it was only the utter impossibility of complying with the General's demand for the surrender of the Queen-Mother and Prince Mensa that then compelled them to make their last effort for the defence of their capital at Odasu. It had then been too late to gain the assistance of the Jabin force, and the plan of action had been to hold Odasu as the main position, and, should it by any chance be taken, to seize the road to the rear and threaten the invaders by cutting them off from their base. A large clearing had been made to the southwest of the village, where troops were posted for this purpose, and the plan was in fact carried out in its entirety ; but the determined advance of the Black Watch was a complication that had not been foreseen and upset all their calculations. It was so utterly opposed to their own methods of fighting that the Ashantis could never have believed that any army whose retreat was cut off would continue to advance and even disregard those attacks on its flank which they had always found fatal to any force. The King had been present at this battle in person, seated with a few attendants under his state umbrella on a hill in rear of his army. Early in the morning he had taken his seat, vowing that he would behead the first Chief who retreated, and it was only when the irresistible advance of the Black Watch brought the sounds of battle close to his own position and the bullets actually began to whistle past his ears, that he realized that the day was lost and fled to Breman, a village a little to the north of Kumasi, where he had one of his country residences. The Queen-Mother left the city only a few minutes before the entry of the Black Watch.

During the first night the troops spent in Kumasi, a number of fires, evidently the work of incendiaries, broke out one after another in different parts of the town, and the roar of the flames was punctuated by the loud explosions of the powder that was stored in nearly every house. Many of the troops, tired out with the day's march and fighting after their sleepless night at the Oda River, were again kept out for hours trying to extinguish these fires and pulling down the surrounding houses to prevent their spread. Strict orders had been issued against plundering ; but it was afterwards ascertained that the majority, if not the whole of these fires were caused by the Fanti prisoners who had been set free on the arrival of the troops and were now spending their first hours of freedom, torch in hand, in looting the houses all over the town. They all had a suspicious amount of property with them when they left Kumasi, especially Dawson ; far more certainly than men who had only just been released from captivity could have been expected to possess.

Several men who had been caught pillaging the houses **1874** were flogged, and a terrible example was made of one of CHAP. VII the Fanti Police who was taken red-handed and hanged in the middle of the night. Soon after midnight, when he came off guard, he had been found leaving a house with a cloth in his hand, and, on being taken before the Military Commandant, was sentenced to immediate execution. Those responsible for carrying out this sentence mismanaged the affair disgracefully by omitting to tie the man's hands before hoisting him up to the branch of a tree, so that he was able to seize the rope above his head and prolong his sufferings, while his agonized shrieks resounded all over the town and woke everyone up. Half strangled, he was lowered again, and a fearful scene then took place while the struggling wretch's arms were pinioned and he was again hauled up ; but his executioners only corrected one mistake to fall into another, and, in order to smother the terrified man's cries, adopted the extraordinary method of passing the rope from his neck to his mouth, so that it was fully a quarter of an hour more before death put an end to his sufferings.

Next morning, instead of the thousands of armed men that had filled the streets the night before, there were not more than thirty or forty Ashantis in the town. All night long a continual stream of people had been leaving the place, taking their arms, ammunition and valuables with them. Night had set in so soon after the troops arrived that there had been little opportunity to find and guard the exits from a strange town : even the palace had not been guarded, and the King's slaves had been removing treasure throughout the whole night ; but a guard of 100 men of the Rifle Brigade was now marched down, and sentries were posted around it so that no one could enter or leave it unobserved. This was no easy matter, for it was a large rambling building with a dozen or more courts leading one out of the other. A large two-storied stone building [1] with a flat embattlemented roof fronted on the

---

[1] This was the *Fort George*, that had been built by Osai Tutu Kwamina soon after the visit of Mr. Dupuis in 1820.

street, and behind this were numbers of houses clustered together with little attempt at order or arrangement. In the main building alone fully 1,000 men could easily have been quartered, and the principal courtyard was large enough to contain at least 200 more. The heavy door of the King's bed-chamber was covered with stamped plaques of gold and silver in a kind of chess-board pattern, and inside it was a big four-post bed covered with silks, beside which stood a large brass pan containing some evil-smelling mixture that had been compounded by the fetish priests. In spite of the quantity of property that had been removed during the night, an extraordinary number of curious and even valuable articles still remained. Heaps of boxes filled with silks and other costly materials were stacked in many of the rooms ; others contained numbers of drums, horns made from elephants' tusks, weapons, state umbrellas [1] and other things. There were tankards and cups and a breakfast and dinner service of solid silver, long strings of the valuable Aggri beads, stools and canes mounted in gold, and golden trinkets and ornaments of every kind, leopard skins and Persian rugs, and a great number of other valuables. In another part of the palace the great Death Drum was seen, decorated with human skulls and thigh bones. The stools that had belonged to the King's ancestors stood near it, and were now thickly covered with the blood of the countless human victims who had been sacrificed to swell their ghostly retinues : it stood on them in great thick clots, from which dense clouds of flies rose when anyone approached. The ancient crown of Denkera, captured from Intim Dakari by Osai Tutu in 1700, was also recovered and given back to his descendant then on the stool.

Another spot that was visited was the Death Grove, a gruesome hollow in the centre of a clump of trees and tall reeds, into which the bodies of the victims of human sacrifice were thrown : it was now nearly filled with their remains. The trees overlooking this spot were always crowded with

---

[1] One of these was brought to England, and is now in the United Service Institute's Museum.

vultures, and the pigs shared the foul feast with them.
" Grinning skulls and fleshless bones below ; and above,
bones not yet fleshless, skulls not yet deprived of their
covering ; and nearest of all, the bodies—we cannot say
how many, seven we count, and the nearest a woman—
bloated, swollen, discoloured, loathsome, and the whole
mass living, writhing, with the worms that feast in corrup-
tion." [1]

A messenger had arrived soon after daybreak saying
that the King would come in during the morning, and
another, who arrived a little later, said he would come later
in the day ; but the time passed and he did not appear,
while his messengers were caught collecting arms and
ammunition to take out of the town and were arrested
and the two chief ones subsequently taken to Cape Coast.
The King may or may not have meant to come in ; but
had he intended doing so, there were two reasons that
might well have induced him to reconsider his decision.
As he sat during the night watching the lurid glare of fire
in the sky over Kumasi, Kofi Karikari must have thought
the destruction of his capital had already been begun.
This sight and the conclusions he naturally drew from it,
coming while the General's message promising that his
town should not be harmed was still ringing in his ears,
would have been bound to make him hesitate before trusting his own person in his power, and the arrest of his
messengers in the morning would only have confirmed
his suspicions. Moreover, the constant arrival of numbers
of his people with the arms and ammunition that they
had removed from the capital could hardly fail to inspire
him with the belief that all was not yet lost, and that so
long as this momentarily increasing army was able to rally
round him, he need not give up all hope nor consider his
power irrevocably gone. Both these occurrences were
admittedly unfortunate, but they could hardly have been
prevented owing to the impossibility of properly guarding
the town when it was first entered.

The King having failed to appear or to send his mother

[1] Brackenbury, vol. ii, p. 242.

or heir, Sir Garnet prepared to carry out his threat of destroying Kumasi before he left. During the afternoon a report was circulated that the troops would advance in pursuit of the King at daybreak the next morning and that any Ashantis who were then found in the town would be shot. This was done to insure the departure of all the inhabitants before the place was set on fire. Prize agents were appointed, who visited the palace that night, and, opening box after box, collected as many valuables as could be carried by thirty men. These were taken to Cape Coast to be sold for the benefit of the troops and realized about £5,000. The Engineers spent the whole night in making arrangements for blowing up the palace and burning the town.

At six o'clock the next morning, the 6th, the troops were drawn up in the market-place in the reverse order to that in which they were to march to the coast, so that when the fiction about pursuing the King was abandoned, and they turned about, the Naval Brigade would be in front and the Black Watch form the rear-guard. They marched off at seven o'clock ; but the rear-guard stayed behind until the mining of the stone building in the palace was completed. By eight o'clock everything was ready, the fuses were lit, and the town set on fire. In spite of the heavy rain that had fallen the day before and throughout the whole night, the houses burned furiously, and the flames, fanned by a strong breeze, swept through the town, until, by nine o'clock, when the Black Watch took their last look at the place, all that remained of Kumasi was a heap of smouldering ruins.

CHAPTER VIII

THE END OF THE WAR

1874

SIR GARNET WOLSELEY's omission to destroy the celebrated mausoleum at Bantama before leaving Kumasi called forth a great deal of criticism. Certainly its demolition would have produced a most profound effect on the Ashantis, but it was spared because its destruction could only have been accomplished by incurring risks that the General did not feel justified in taking. There was his little army of Europeans, far away from its base, in a hostile country in which it was impossible to obtain suitable food, with barely sufficient supplies to enable it to reach its first fortified post, and already encumbered by the wounded from Odasu. The sick convoy had left on the morning of the 5th for Amoafu under escort of Wood's and Russell's Regiments and a company of the Rifle Brigade, and there were then no more hammocks or transport available. Any attack on Bantama would almost certainly have called forth renewed and most determined resistance, and, as it stood about a mile and a half outside the town, its destruction could hardly have been accomplished except at the cost of some, and probably many more casualties. The destruction of the mausoleum, moreover, had not been included in Lord Kimberley's instructions to Sir Garnet. These instructions had said that a " satisfactory state of things would be obtained " if he could " procure an honourable peace, or could inflict, in default of such peace, an effectual chastisement on the Ashanti force." This had already been done. Lord Kimberley, indeed, had foreseen the possibility of, and provided for the actual conditions that had now arisen when, in discussing the possible effect of the defeat of the Ashantis and the occupation of Kumasi, he wrote : " You might find yourself in possession of Coomassie, without any government or ruler to treat with, and as it would be wholly out of the question to keep European troops in a state of inactivity in the interior, you might be compelled to return without having obtained a full security for the establishment of a lasting peace." This state of affairs was to be avoided if possible, and Sir Garnet would have been acting directly contrary to the spirit, if not to the letter of his instructions, if he had done anything calculated to deter the King from coming in to treat. The object of the expedition, too, had been to obtain a definite peace and to show the power of the British to punish. This power was now fully proved by the capture of the capital and the flight of the King ; and the destruction of the mausoleum, while proving no more, would have threatened the very existence of the kingdom which it was the Government's wish, if possible, to preserve. Lord Kimberley had written : " If you should inflict a severe defeat on the Ashantee army near or beyond the frontier, the occupation of the capital might, perhaps, be effected without much difficulty ; but it is probable that the result might be a complete break up of the King's Government and power."

Throughout the 5th, Sir Garnet had been waiting for the King to come in : he could not therefore have made any move against Bantama on that day, and it was not deemed advisable to remain in Kumasi any longer. About midday a message had come in from Major Russell, who had gone down in charge of the convoy of wounded, that the Oda River had risen and was already a foot and a half over the bridge. This news, and a succession of heavy tornados which swept over the town during the afternoon and visibly raised the level of the water in the Suban swamp, caused some anxiety about the return march to the coast, and Sir Garnet had then and there decided to leave Kumasi the next morning. The remaining European troops were already showing signs of sickness after their wet night at the Oda River and subsequent want of rest, and the General dared not let them run the risk of further exposure to the climate and the continual drenching to which they would be subjected if their return march was delayed any longer now that the rains had set in.   Any attempt to destroy the mausoleum, therefore, could only have been undertaken at the risk of failure, and although its successful capture and destruction would undoubtedly have yielded much valuable plunder and have produced a prodigious effect both on the Ashantis and on all the surrounding tribes, it would at best have been but the destruction of a burial-place and the rifling of the tombs of the dead, acts from which the Ashantis themselves would have shrunk, and that few people, least of all British soldiers, care to commit unless compelled and justified by positive necessity. It was want of time, however, quite as much as anything else, that prevented anything more being done than the destruction of the King's palace and town.

The state of the road when the troops began their return march to the coast plainly showed what serious difficulties they might have encountered had the evacuation of Kumasi been further postponed. One stream, which on the upward march had been a mere rivulet three feet deep, had now became a sheet of water a couple of hundred yards wide, and several other swamps were waist and even arm-pit deep. The Oda River was swollen into a rushing torrent, but the bridge, which the Ashantis fortunately had not destroyed, still stood and allowed most of the troops to pass over it ; the footway, however, was two feet under water, and towards evening it gave way, so that half the Rifle Brigade and the whole of the Black Watch had to strip and wade or swim across while their clothes were passed over on the heads of carriers. Sir Garnet Wolseley and his Staff reached Ajimamu that night and remained there throughout the next day with the Rifle Brigade, Black Watch and Rait's Artillery, who were to continue the march to the sea as the stores were cleared out from the different posts ; but the Naval Brigade and

Fusiliers were pushed on to Cape Coast at once, where
they arrived on the 20th and re-embarked. The transport of the sick and wounded proved a tedious matter owing
to the enormous number of carriers that was required,
and it was not until the 10th that the General, having
burnt every village he passed through, arrived at Fomana.
There he remained with the native troops to see the last
convoy of sick passed down, but the Rifle Brigade and Highlanders continued their march to the coast and re-embarked
immediately on their arrival. The Fusiliers sailed in the
Tamar on the 22nd, and the Rifle Brigade, Royal Engineers
and other details in the *Himalaya* on the 23rd. The
hospital ship *Victor Emmanuel* left with invalids on the
26th, and the Black Watch, who had remained in camp
at Inkwabim until the *Sarmatian* arrived, embarked and
sailed in her on the 27th. Thus, by the end of February,
all the European troops had already left the Coast. Wood's
Regiment was disbanded at Elmina, and Russell's Regiment and Rait's Artillery at Cape Coast. The 2nd Battalion of the West India Regiment returned to the West
Indies, while the 1st Battalion was kept to garrison the
redoubts at Prasu and Mansu and the forts on the
coast.

While the General was at Dechiasu on the 9th, a messenger had arrived from the King with assurances of his
anxiety for peace and his readiness to accede to all the
terms imposed. He was told that, as hostages were no
longer necessary, they need not be sent, and that the terms
of a treaty could be arranged at once if the King would
send 5,000 ounces of gold in proof of his sincerity and as a
first instalment of the indemnity, and Sir Garnet promised
to wait at Fomana until the 13th to receive his answer.
This messenger also begged him to recall the forces under
Captain Glover, whose near approach so soon after the
main army had left Kumasi had greatly alarmed the King
and doubtless hastened his submission.

Captain Glover had left Abogu on the 26th of January,
and, overtaking Captain Sartorius, who had gone on with
200 men the day before, occupied Konomo. The same

day Lieutenant Barnard[1] took Odumasi, a village three **1874**
miles farther west, with a loss of three men wounded.
Captain Glover then remained encamped at Konomo,
awaiting the arrival of further supplies of ammunition
and sending out frequent reconnaissances in every direction. On the 1st of February Captain Sartorius led a party
along the banks of the River Enum, and, having crossed
the stream, suddenly came upon a small encampment of
fifteen of the enemy's scouts, who at once retired. Continuing his march for about two miles in a westerly direction, he found the enemy in some force, but they fell back
after firing a few shots and wounding two of the Hausas.
After marching another three miles along the river, he
discovered a large deserted camp ; but the next day, when
the place was revisited, he found it occupied by between
800 and 1,000 of the enemy, who came out to attack him
but almost immediately retired with the loss of one of their
number killed. This sudden retreat had been caused by
Lieutenant Barnard, who had attacked the position
simultaneously from the other side and lost four of his
Hausas killed during the skirmish. It was evident that
the Jabins were encamped all along the River Enum and
intended to oppose any farther advance of Captain Glover's
column.

Sir Garnet, after leaving Kumasi, had tried to communicate with Captain Glover, and, after receiving the
King's message on the 9th, had written to him again, telling
him what the main army had done and asking him to stay
where he was until the 14th, when he expected to leave
Fomana. He was then to fall back on the Pra. This
letter, however, never reached its destination, and Captain
Glover, having received fresh supplies of ammunition and
a reinforcement of about 4,000 Akims, Akwapims and
Krobos, who came up with Lieutenant Moore, R.N., left
his camp on the 8th and advanced to attack the Jabin
position. To his great surprise he found it abandoned, for
the Jabins had heard of the fall and destruction of Kumasi,
of which Captain Glover as yet knew nothing. Continuing

[1] 19th Regiment.

his advance without meeting the slightest opposition, he soon afterwards received a message from Asafu Agai the Jabin King, tendering his submission ; but he had been forbidden to undertake any negotiations for peace, and the King was therefore told he must deal directly with Sir Garnet Wolseley in Kumasi.

On the 10th, Captain Glover, believing he was then within about seven miles of Kumasi and that Sir Garnet was still there, sent Captain Sartorius with an escort of only twenty Hausas to open communications with him. Soon after leaving the camp, Captain Sartorius found that numbers of Ashantis were prowling through the forest all around him, and, on entering a village about five miles from Captain Glover's position, his men were fired on from the bush but no damage was done. His small escort had only forty rounds a man, so, not wishing to involve them in any fighting, he pushed on without returning the enemy's fire and soon afterwards met a woman and her slaves who were escaping from Kumasi. From her he learned for the first time that the place had been burned and that Sir Garnet had already left for the coast, while the King was said to be on his way back, vowing vengeance for the destruction of his capital. This news naturally caused Captain Sartorius much anxiety, and, finding he was still a long way from Kumasi, he halted for the night in a village, hoping that Captain Glover might come up to look for him. That night he was surrounded ; but the enemy drew off when they found the Hausas were on the alert, and in the morning Captain Sartorius explained the position to his men and put it to them whether they would fight their way back to Captain Glover's camp or risk pushing on through Kumasi to overtake the General. They pluckily volunteered to go on and reached Kumasi after a march of eighteen miles, instead of seven as had been expected. They found the place almost entirely razed to the ground : one or two tottering walls and part of a staircase were all that remained of the palace, and even they were so shaken that the first tornado was bound to bring them down. Passing through the still smoking ruins of the deserted city, they pushed on down the main road to Amoafu. The floods had now subsided, and, marching rapidly, Captain Sartorius entered the General's camp at Fomana at midday on the 12th, having completed a most remarkable march of fifty-three miles through the heart of the enemy's country, often surrounded or threatened, without provisions, and without having fired a single shot or lost a man of his small escort : altogether an unique performance. Captain Glover soon followed him, entering Kumasi with 4,700 men soon after midday on the 12th, and then marching by easy stages to Kwaman, which he reached on the 14th.

These two marches conclusively proved how completely successful Sir Garnet Wolseley's expedition had been. At any other time it would have been absolutely impossible for any such forces to have escaped extermination ; but now that the ruins of his capital still bore witness to his utter defeat and his principal tributary had already tendered his submission, Kofi Karikari at last realized that his power was broken ; and although he might have gratified his desire for vengeance by cutting up either of these forces with the Kumasis who had rallied around him, he desisted, partly because he was really anxious to see peace restored, and partly because he was afraid any such action might bring about the return of the dreaded European army that he had now got rid of. These were the reasons that had induced him to adopt the unusual course of seeking peace from a conqueror who had already done his worst and was on his way out of the country, and it was the withdrawal of the demand for impossible hostages that led to his prompt compliance with the General's order for the payment of a first instalment of the indemnity.

Late on the 12th, word was received from the King's envoys that they were at Dompoasi and wished to enter the camp and treat for peace : they added that they would not have come if they had not fulfilled the conditions imposed by Sir Garnet. Permission was immediately given them to come in if they had brought the gold, and the two envoys, accompanied by a long train of carriers, entered Fomana early the next morning. They said they had brought 1,000 ounces of gold with them, and explained that the King had found it impossible to collect more at such short notice. They also protested in the King's name against the demand made upon him, describing it as exorbitant and out of all proportion to the 600 ounces that Governor Maclean had required merely as a temporary security. Possibly pressure might have induced him to find a larger sum, but the main object now was to secure peace, and, as the payment of the gold was chiefly necessary as a sign of the King's complete submission, the amount actually obtained was a matter of secondary importance.   The envoys therefore were told to produce what gold they had brought. A large white Ashanti cloth was spread upon the ground : on one side sat the Government gold-taker, who had been brought up from Cape Coast to be ready for any emergency of this kind, and on the other sat five or six of the principal Ashantis. A heavy leathern bag was then brought forward and opened, disclosing a quantity of nuggets and gold-dust and a number of ornaments and trinkets in wrought gold. Gold plates and figures, knobs, bells, masks, brace-lets, jaw-bones and other articles were laid on the cloth and examined in turn by the gold-taker. These, with a few more trinkets that were afterwards produced by the envoys from the folds of their cloths, where they had perhaps concealed them in the hope of retaining them as a secret commission, amounted to 1,040 ounces of pure gold.

This practical sign of submission having been made, the envoys were given the following draft treaty to take back for the King's signature :

TREATY OF PEACE between MAJOR-GENERAL SIR GARNET JOSEPH WOLSELEY, C.B., K.C.M.G., acting on behalf of HER MAJESTY VICTORIA, Queen of Great Britain and Ireland, and SAIBEE ENQUIE, acting on behalf of HIS MAJESTY KOFFEE KALKALLI, King of Ashantee.

ARTICLE I

There shall be hereafter perpetual peace between the Queen of England and her allies on the Coast on the one part, and the King of Ashantee and all his people on 1874 the other part.

ARTICLE II

The King of Ashantee promises to pay the sum of 50,000 ounces of approved gold as indemnity for the expenses he has occasioned to Her Majesty the Queen of England by the late war ; and undertakes to pay 1,000 ounces of gold forthwith, and the remainder by such instalments as Her Majesty's Government may from time to time demand.

ARTICLE III

The King of Ashantee, on the part of himself and his successors, renounces all right or title to any tribute or homage from the Kings of Denkera, Assin, Akim, Adansi, and the other allies of Her Majesty formerly subject to the Kingdom of Ashantee.

ARTICLE IV

The King, on the part of himself and of his heirs and successors, does hereby further renounce for ever all pretensions of supremacy over Elmina, or over any of the tribes formerly connected with the Dutch Government, and to any tribute or homage from such tribes, as well as to any payment or acknowledgment of any kind by the British Government in respect of Elmina or any other of the British forts and possessions on the Coast.

ARTICLE V

The King will at once withdraw all his troops from Apollonia and its vicinity, and from the neighbourhood of Dixcove, Sekondee, and the adjoining coast-line.

ARTICLE VI

There shall be freedom of trade between Ashantee and Her Majesty's forts on the Coast, all persons being at liberty to carry their merchandize from the Coast to

Coomassie, or from that place to any of Her Majesty's possessions on the Coast.

ARTICLE VII

The King of Ashantee guarantees that the road from Coomassie to the River Prah shall always be kept open and free from bush to a width of 15 feet.

ARTICLE VIII

As Her Majesty's subjects and the people of Ashantee are henceforth to be friends for ever, the King, in order to prove the sincerity of his friendship for Queen Victoria, promises to use his best endeavours to check the practice of human sacrifice, with a view to hereafter putting an end to it altogether, as the practice is repugnant to the feelings of all Christian nations.

ARTICLE IX

One copy of this Treaty shall be signed by the King of Ashantee and sent to the Administrator of Her Majesty's Government at Cape Coast Castle within fourteen days from this date.

ARTICLE X

This Treaty shall be known as the Treaty of Fommanah. Dated at Fommanah this 13th day of February 1874.[1]

The treaty was read over and each article carefully explained to the envoys, who raised objections to only two of its provisions. First, they professed not to have understood that the indemnity demanded was so large as 50,000 ounces ; but when Sir Garnet pointed out that the King had already agreed to this sum, they withdrew their objection. The second point to which they demurred was the required acknowledgment of the independence of Adansi. This stipulation had been included in the treaty

---

[1] *Ashanti War* (Parliamentary Paper, 1873-4), part viii, p. 45 ; Brackenbury, *Ashanti War*, vol. ii, p. 269.

at the earnest request of Kobina Obin the King of Adansi,
who had come to Fomana on the 11th with some of the
Chiefs of Wassaw and Denkera, who, now that they heard
that Kumasi had fallen and that the fighting was all over,
crossed the Pra and advanced into Ashanti bravely
enough, though nothing would induce them to do so so
long as there had been the least danger and work to be
done. Obin had then begged to be allowed to come under
British protection and settle with his people to the south
of the Pra, where the Wassaws said they were willing to
have them. He professed to be much mistrusted by the
Ashantis, and said he detested their rule and had been
opposed to the war, in which he and his people had taken
no part, and he further pointed out that whether British
protection was extended to him or not, he would be compelled to emigrate now, as he would have incurred the
wrath and vengeance of the King by having opened these
negotiations. There was not an atom of truth in these
statements. Kobina Obin had from the very commencement of the trouble been one of the foremost of the war
party, and it had been due solely to his interference that
all the captives had not been released at the same time as
Mr. Kühne. It had, moreover, been he and his people who
had occupied Boborasi and made the attack on Fomana.
These facts, however, were either unknown or had been
forgotten, and although Sir Garnet was by no means
inclined to encourage the Adansis to secede, yet he felt
that he could not very well interfere in an amicable arrangement between them and the Wassaws and that any
refusal might possibly be equivalent to giving them over
to butchery by the Ashantis. Obin therefore was told
that he was at liberty to emigrate, and that he and his
people would be included in the treaty. It is a pity that
this special provision should have been made for the
exclusive benefit of the Adansis, for the Jabins had been
the first to tender their submission, yet, when they and
some other tribes applied to come under British protection,
it was refused them, and it is still more unfortunate that
the Adansis should have been accepted and officially

described as " allies of Her Majesty " without a definite treaty being made with them in which their exact position and duties might have been defined, and by which they would have been bound. It might then have been made clear that their protection by the British must be dependent on their removal, and much subsequent trouble which arose when they failed to carry out their promise might have been avoided. This article, in fact, gave the Adansis a most unfair advantage over the other Ashanti tribes and tributaries, which they had certainly done nothing to deserve. Sir Garnet, however, explained to the envoys that it had been inserted at the request of the Adansis themselves ; that he had taken no steps to persuade them to leave Ashanti, but that it was a private arrangement between them and the Wassaws with which he could not interfere. The messengers left the same afternoon, promising to get the treaty signed by the King and to produce it in Cape Coast within the prescribed time-limit of fourteen days.

The second article of the treaty had been very carefully worded, so that it might be open to the Government to insist on the payment of further instalments of the indemnity or not, as might be deemed advisable in the light of future events. Sir Garnet, however, gave it as his opinion that it was very doubtful if the full sum would ever be obtained, but pointed out that the right to claim it might be useful as a lever against the King. Although the seventh article provided for the maintenance of the road between Kumasi and the Pra by the Ashantis—from which it must be inferred that the Government undertook to keep the Prasu–Cape Coast portion of it in repair—yet the bridge over the Pra was for some inscrutable reason destroyed.

A letter was now sent to Captain Glover telling him that the King had paid the first instalment of the indemnity and asking him to retire with all his troops across the Pra. This reached him at Kwaman on the 14th and he left the next day. At Monsi a messenger from the King overtook him, bringing a present of fourteen ounces of gold

and a gold dish with a request that he would order the King
of Eastern Akim, who was doing his best to persuade the
King of Jabin to detach himself from his alliance with
Ashanti, to return at once to his own country. The
present was returned ; but the request was granted and
a letter was sent to the King of Eastern Akim ordering
him to recross the Pra with all his people. Reaching
Prasu on the 17th, Captain Glover there dismissed all his
native levies, who moved eastward to their own homes,
while he marched down the main road to Anamabo with
the Hausas.

Sir Garnet Wolseley had left Fomana on the 14th of
February, and, proceeding by double marches with his
Staff, entered Cape Coast on the 19th, when he was accorded
a tremendous ovation by the excitable Fantis. The streets
were thronged with women painted white in token of
rejoicing and waving palm branches : and well might they
welcome him, for the memory of their terrors and sufferings
during the earlier stages of the war was still fresh in their
minds, and he had truly accomplished more than any man
had ever done before and left indisputable evidence of his
victory in the ruins of Kumasi. Garrisons of the 1st West
India Regiment had been left at Prasu and Mansu, but all
the other posts had been evacuated and the stockades
destroyed. Martial law, too, was now removed from
Elmina. Sir Garnet had been asked to arrange, as far as
possible, for garrisoning the Coast after the war with
African troops, and he now requested Captain Glover to
detain 350 of his Hausas at Anamabo until Mr. Berkeley
the Governor-in-Chief should decide whether he would
keep them or not. This force formed the nucleus of what
subsequently became the Gold Coast Constabulary.[1]

The sale of the loot from Kumasi took place in the
Castle Hall and lasted several days. None of the gold
paid at Fomana was included in the sale : that was all sent
direct to England, and it was only the goods collected by
the prize agents from the King's palace that were sold
locally. The loot formed a curious collection when un-

[1] By Ordinance No 3 of 1879.

packed and laid out for exhibition and sale. Besides a
great number of gold- and silver-mounted calabashes,
stools, swords, pipes and canes, and a large collection of
gold trinkets and ornaments of every kind, silk cloths and
other goods, there were several fine old pieces of plate ;
dishes, salvers, tankards and other articles, including the
covered tankard said to have belonged to Sir Charles
M'Carthy, on which some faint traces of his initials could
still be made out. Other curious specimens were a crowded
group of small figures in bronze depicting a royal procession
through Kumasi, and a great silver casket fitted with a
Chubb's lock and weighing over nineteen pounds. The
universal desire to possess some relic of the expedition gave
most of the spoil a quite fictitious value, though much more
might have been obtained for the numerous Aggri beads
if the auctioneers could have allowed the bidders more
time to examine them. To the European officers these
beads were much like any others ; but the Fanti women
knew their value and were most eager to buy, but they
would not bid blindly, but wanted to weigh and examine
each bead as they were accustomed to do.

Towards the end of February, messengers from the
Wassaw Chiefs arrived in Cape Coast complaining that the
Adansis had not fulfilled their promise to migrate across
the Pra and requesting that an armed force might be sent
to compel them to do so. It was also rumoured that the
Assins were trying to induce the Adansis to settle in their
territory. Sir Garnet, however, declined to take any steps
in the matter, which he pointed out was one of mutual
arrangement between the Adansis and Wassaws only ; but
messengers were sent to Wassaw and Denkera to ascertain
the actual state of affairs.

When Captain Glover marched for the Pra at the end
of December, he had left Mr. Goldsworthy to continue the
campaign against the Awunas. After experiencing constant difficulties in inducing his men to advance and
attack, he had several brushes with the enemy, in which he
was more or less successful ; but on Sir Garnet's return to
the coast, orders were issued that these operations must

cease, and Mr. Goldsworthy was instructed to make peace 1874
with the Awunas and Akwamus. At the same time, Dr. CHAP. VIII
Gouldsbury was sent to the windward coast to accept the
allegiance of the Ahantas, Apollonians and other tribes
who had been in revolt. Mr. Goldsworthy failed in his
efforts to make peace with the eastern tribes, but Dr.
Gouldsbury's mission to those in the west was completely
successful. He first of all persuaded Blay and Amaki to
forget their feud and make friends at a meeting on the
15th of March, at which he explained to them that in
future they would be deemed of equal authority and that
each must be content to rule over his own district without
claiming any jurisdiction over that of the other. He
then went to Newtown, where the western frontier had
been fixed by a Franco-Dutch Convention, and succeeded
in preventing an attack that was about to be made on
Amaki by the King of Assini and a Chief named Amaka.
Other meetings were held with the people of Bushua, Shama,
Takoradi and other disaffected towns, at which fines
totalling 324½ ounces of gold were imposed on the Kings
and Chiefs and arrangements made for the mutual restoration of all prisoners and villages taken during the recent
hostilities. The Chiefs of all these places then signed
documents promising peaceful and obedient behaviour for
the future. When these fines fell due in August, Dr.
Gouldsbury had no difficulty in collecting all except the
56 ounces that had been imposed on the people of Bushua.
They made many excuses and tried to persuade him to
take half the required sum ; but this was very properly
refused. The Governor sent him back so soon as he heard
of this attempt at evasion, with a detachment of Hausas
and orders to increase the amount of the fine to 70 [1] ounces,
and to arrest the King and all the principal Chiefs and
bring them to Cape Coast if it were not paid by a certain
hour. This had the desired effect, and the whole 70 ounces
was paid over eight hours before the expiration of the
time-limit.

The people of all these places really wanted peace, and

[1] Or 72.

had already made overtures to the Government and supplied a certain number of carriers during the latter part of
the war, as had the Elminas also. Their hostility in the
first place had been due to a genuine belief that the British
would never be able to withstand the power of Ashanti
and a not unnatural desire to be on the side of what they
considered the stronger party, rather than to any actual
aversion to British rule.

Sir Garnet's mission was now accomplished, and he
sailed for England on board the *Manitoban* on the 4th of
March. Eighteen days had then elapsed since the treaty
had been sent to the King, but it had not yet been returned,
so the General, before embarking, wrote him a letter
reminding him that his messengers had promised to deliver
the treaty in Cape Coast within fourteen days. This letter
was sent by sixty-eight Ashanti prisoners, who were now
put across the Pra and released.

Sir Garnet had recommended as his successor Captain
C. C. Lees,[1] who had carried on the administration of affairs
on the Coast while he was away in Ashanti, but orders
were received shortly before he sailed that the Government
was to remain on the same footing as during his tenure
of office, with the civil and military administration in
the same hands, and he was told to hand over the Administratorship to some officer not under the rank of
Lieutenant-Colonel, and to arrange that no officer senior
to him should remain on the Coast. Great difficulty was
experienced in finding any officer who would accept the
appointment. It was offered in turn to Sir Archibald
Alison, Colonel McLeod, Colonel Greaves and Lieutenant-
Colonel Colley, but one and all refused it on account of the
climate ; " and this is the chief difficulty which even now
stands in the way of progress and prosperity on the Gold
Coast, for no really capable and first-rate man will accept
the Governorship, no matter what addition may be made
to the salary. Much of the confusion and mismanagement
that had occurred in the past was due to the fact that the
Administrators were usually men whose abilities were

---

[1] Late 23rd Regiment.

below mediocrity, and who had been thrust into the **1874**
appointment because no one better could be found to CHAP. VIII
accept it ; and there seems every probability of this state
of things being continued."[1] This statement is justified
in the main ; but there have been exceptions, and, at rare
intervals, a few really able men have been Governors of
the Gold Coast, but, if they survive the effects of the
climate, are promoted all too soon to some better appointment. In the end, Sir Garnet had to send to Prasu for
Colonel Maxwell, who commanded the 1st West India
Regiment and was bound to remain on the Coast, and
handed over the Administratorship to him.

On the 12th of March, a few days after the departure
of Sir Garnet Wolseley, an embassy from the King of
Ashanti arrived in Cape Coast. It was composed of one of
the King's sons, Kofi Intin, and representatives of every
tribe and province in the kingdom, who, with their followers,
numbered about 300 men. They were received by Colonel
Maxwell in the Castle Hall that same afternoon and produced the draft treaty that had been sent to the King, at
the foot of which there now appeared two crosses, which
the ambassadors stated had been placed there by Kofi
Karikari in token of his assent : they added, however, that
the King had been under the impression that the amount
of the indemnity was 5,000 bendas (10,000 ounces) instead
of 50,000 ounces, as stated in the treaty. Colonel Maxwell
therefore explained that the latter was the correct amount,
and asked them to retire and confer together before ratify-
ing the treaty, in order that there might be no possibility
of any mistake or subsequent disputes. Three days later
they returned, saying they were willing to ratify the treaty
as it stood, and it was then signed by Kofi Intin, eight
other Kumasis, and the representatives of eleven other
provinces on behalf of the King and the Ashantis, and by
Colonel Maxwell on behalf of Her Majesty.[2]

After the treaty had been signed, the envoys made

---

[1] Ellis, *History of the Gold Coast*, p. 347.
[2] For full list of signatures, *vide* Parliamentary Paper, *Ashanti War*,
1873–4, part ix, p. 11.

several requests in the name of the King, who apparently hoped that after he had duly humiliated himself by agreeing to everything that had been demanded from him, some leniency would be shown and concessions made. First, they asked that the stipend that had formerly been paid by the Dutch and afterwards doubled by Mr. Pope Hennessy might be continued by the Government ; secondly, they wanted the Adansis to be returned to them ; thirdly, it was stated that the Akim Chiefs had taken hostages from the people of Kwahu, Ashanti-Akim and Jabin and were intriguing with them to induce them to throw off their allegiance to Ashanti and migrate into Akim territory, and the King therefore asked that the Akims might be ordered to return these hostages and abandon their negotiations ; fourthly, the King wished to point out that the sudden total abolition of human sacrifices in his kingdom would be an extremely difficult feat and would tend to make his people think the nation was going down : while promising, therefore, to do his best to reduce their number and gradually abolish them, he asked permission to sacrifice two or three victims on the occasion of the death of any great Chief. This statement was true enough. Even a powerful and popular monarch would have found it almost impossible to abolish a custom that was not only dictated by the religion of his people, but had been in existence since the very foundation of the kingdom ; how much more difficult, therefore, would it be for a discredited and defeated ruler like Kofi Karikari to introduce and enforce so drastic an innovation. This, indeed, seems to have been realized by Sir Garnet Wolseley, who, in drafting the treaty, had merely stipulated for an attempt to check the practice " with a view to hereafter putting an end to it altogether." Had he thought there was the remotest chance that anything more than this could be accomplished, he assuredly would not have hesitated to demand it. Lastly, Kofi Intin was formally handed over to the care of the British Government in token of confidence and with a request that he might be sent to England and educated.

Few Governors would have hesitated to give an immediate answer to all except perhaps the last of these requests. Colonel Maxwell, however, declined to do so, but said he would forward the King's message, together with the treaty, to England. The Secretary of State replied that the previous misunderstandings as to the precise nature and significance of the stipend precluded its continuance, but that presents would shortly be sent to the King if he faithfully adhered to the treaty. As regards the Adansis, their secession from Ashanti having been a matter of private arrangement between them on the one hand and the Wassaws and Denkeras on the other, the Government must decline to interfere. Enquiries were promised concerning the complaints against the Akims, who would be compelled to give up any hostages who were being detained against their will and ordered to abstain from any attempts to promote defections amongst the King's subjects ; but it was pointed out that unless force had been used to induce them to renounce their allegiance no interference would be made, since they would then be in a similar position to the Adansis. Dr. Gouldsbury was sent to Akim on this mission and found about sixty Jabins, a dozen Kwahus, and a few Ashanti-Akims, but no restraint was being exercised over them. There were also nine Ashanti prisoners, and eight of these, who wished to return to their country, were given up. The Government, of course, refused to give any sanction, either direct or implied, to human sacrifices ; but the last request, that Kofi Intin might be educated in England, was granted. He was at this time about eight or ten years of age, and it was arranged that he should be kept at Cape Coast, living with the Colonial Chaplain, until he had learned enough English to be sent to England. He was afterwards educated at the Surrey County School near Guildford, and then given a junior appointment in the Customs Department of Trinidad. Later, he returned to the Gold Coast, and was given an allowance of £120 a year and several small appointments by the local Government.

The climate soon began to tell so severely on Colonel Maxwell that he sailed for England on the 29th of March, but died on the voyage home. Lieutenant-Colonel W. W. W. Johnston of the 1st West India Regiment acted for a few days, and a commission then arrived appointing Sir Garnet Wolseley's original nominee, Captain Charles Cameron Lees.

In June Captain Lees visited Jella Koffi, and after some delay, due to the Awunas' fears for the safety of their hostages in Ashanti, concluded a treaty of peace [1] with them on the 22nd, which provided that the River Volta should be kept open for all lawful traders, and gave the Government the right to occupy both Kitta and Jella Koffi and any other ports that might be deemed necessary in order to bring the whole Awuna country under the same jurisdiction as the Gold Coast. The eastern frontier was thus extended to Adafia, eighteen miles east of Kitta. This was a considerable gain ; for the Danes, by the purchase of whose Possessions and rights the British had acquired their first footing on this part of the Coast, had never claimed any such extensive jurisdiction, but had merely occupied their fort at Kitta.

Dr. Gouldsbury had, in the meantime, been negotiating with the Akwamus, and, on the 15th of June, completed a treaty of peace with them at Odumasi. [2]

The conclusion of these treaties with the Awunas and Akwamus finally brought the war to a close and restored peace throughout the whole Protectorate. This war had served to prove many things, but none more clearly than the deadly nature of the West African climate. Never before had there been such a number of Europeans on the Coast, and the medical returns of the troops, therefore, were of great value in demonstrating whether or not the unhealthiness of the climate had been exaggerated. These returns may briefly be summarized as follows :

---

[1] For full text of this treaty, *vide* Parliamentary Paper, *Affairs of the Gold Coast*, 5th of February 1875, p. 44.
[2] Full text, *vide ibid.*, p. 56.

	Officers.	Men.	All Ranks.
Total strength of force . . .	297	2,290	2,587
Casualties from engagements with the enemy :			
Killed in action	4	2	6
Died of wounds	1	10	11
Severely wounded . . .	6	49	55
Slightly wounded	21	109	130
Died of wounds in England . .		1	1
TOTAL	32	171	203
Casualties from disease :			
Died	11	33	44
Invalided	50	248	298
Died in England of disease contracted in Africa . . .	2	7	9
Left on board-ship or in hospital .		169	169
TOTAL	63	457	520

These figures clearly show how greatly the casualties
from disease exceeded those from wounds, and this in
spite of such hard-fought battles as that at Amoafu. Yet
even these statistics fail to show the full extent of the
loss, for they relate only to the European regiments and
Naval Brigade, and do not include the European officers
of the West Indian Regiments. In all, more than forty
officers died, but only six of them from wounds ; and out
of the twenty-four officers who were left on the Gold Coast
when Sir Garnet Wolseley sailed, eight died and seven were
invalided. Amongst the rank and file of the European
regiments 71 per cent of sickness took place, of which
59 per cent was due to fevers and 13 per cent to dysentery
and diarrhœa, and in the Naval Brigade [1] 95 per cent of
sickness occurred of which only 8 per cent was due to non-
climatic disease. It must be remembered, too, that this
terrible incidence rate occurred, not in a general population of old and young, weak and strong all together, but

[1] Of the 104 marines who landed with Colonel Festing, 2 had died
and 67 were sick at the end of the first six weeks. All but 20 were then
sent home in the *Himalaya* and 10 more died on the voyage, while of
the 20 that remained, all were dead or had been invalided before the
end of the war.

in a body of picked men in the prime of life, who had just
completed a sea voyage, each one of whom had had to pass a
searching medical examination, who had had every con-
ceivable care bestowed on them after they landed by giving
them constant employment, suitable food and clothing
and sanitary camps, and who were actually in the country
less than two months, while during that time any man who
became ill was promptly invalided. Yet, in the face of
these truly appalling figures, Lord Carnarvon, who had
succeeded Lord Kimberley as Colonial Minister, by quoting
only the deaths as amounting to just under 23 per 1,000,
actually attempted to show that the death-rate on the
Gold Coast was " about the same as the death-rate in the
metropolis, and lower than the death-rate in some other
English towns." A greater prostitution of the use of
statistics can hardly be imagined ; yet it is not uncommon,
even at the present day, to hear similar and equally absurd
statements made by those who apparently wish to prove
that West Africa is a desirable health resort rather than a
land cursed with a climate more fatal to Europeans than
any other.

There are a few other matters that must be mentioned
before closing the account of this war. It is questionable
whether Sir Garnet Wolseley's apparent vacillation may
not have encouraged the King to expect better terms if he
held out, though there was never any real change in the
General's purpose. As in other instances, Sir Garnet was
bound by his instructions, in which every possible contingency, with the single exception of the secession of
Adansi, had been provided for. He had to make peace
without fighting if he could ; but the changes he made from
time to time, and his very evident desire for peace, can
hardly have failed to appear to a savage king as signs of
weakness and probably went far to prolong Kofi Karikari's
negotiations and excuses. At Prasu he had declined to see
anyone but the King himself, yet in Kumasi he received
his messengers in person, and after insisting on the surrender of the Queen-Mother and Heir-Apparent, afterwards
offered to accept any persons of rank as hostages. He also

reduced the amount originally demanded as a first instalment of the indemnity and allowed his compulsory halt at
Fomana to appear as a concession to the King's demands
after he had repeatedly declared his intention of advancing
to Kumasi without delay. These frequent reductions of
his demands probably afford the true explanation of the
King's requests after the ratification of the treaty.

Another result of these instructions to avoid hostilities
if possible was the adoption of the unusual course of
showing the enemy the full strength of the invading force
and even trying to exaggerate it. Thus the King was
informed by letter of the disposition and routes of advance
of the different columns, and his envoys, besides being
shown the gatling-gun and detained to see the completed
bridge over the Pra, were made to believe in a rapidity of
advance that had been found impossible, by sending the
Naval Brigade along the road ahead of them and halting
the messengers who accompanied Mr. Kühne at the most
advanced post so that they might imagine the General was
already near at hand. The undoubted object of these
manœuvres was to frighten the King into an immediate
submission ; their effect, however, was to accelerate his
preparations for resistance. It may be contended that
the prolonged negotiations resulted in the release of the
European captives ; but it is very doubtful if anything
was gained by this. There is little likelihood that any
harm would have befallen them even had they been retained
until the fall of Kumasi, and, as a matter of fact, the Fanti
prisoners had by far the greatest claim on the Government if the question of colour is put aside ; for they were
British subjects, whereas the missionaries, and M. Bonnat
especially, had little or no right to expect official intervention on their behalf, and their only grounds for expecting it were the call of humanity and their common religion.

Perhaps the most remarkable feature of the whole war
was the anomalous state of affairs brought about by the
appointment of Captain Glover and the subsequent arrangement by which he was in one sense superseded by Sir
Garnet Wolseley, while in another he retained his inde-

pendent command.   There were many rumours current at
the time of personal ill-feeling between the two com-
manders, but they seem to have been absolutely groundless,
although there was undoubtedly a natural spirit of rivalry
between them, and if Captain Glover had found it possible
to reach Kumasi before the troops arrived for Sir Garnet,
he would probably have done so.   The absurdity of this
dual command was shown by what actually happened.   At
the time of Sir Garnet's arrival on the Coast, the Hausas,
who would have been invaluable to him, and on whose
services he had been relying, had all been sent east to join
the other expedition, and at the very time when they were
most needed and might have enabled the General to attack
and defeat the demoralized Ashanti army in its retreat,
they were actually sitting idle in Adda.   Moreover, the
force of Hausas and Yorubas collected by Captain Glover
utterly failed in its main object of inducing the eastern
tribes to rise and accompany him into Ashanti, and he
would probably have done just as well without this nucleus.
Most of the Hausa and Yoruba recruits he obtained were
sent up from Lagos by Captain Lees, and though it is
possible that no one else could have got so many, they
would have joined him in Cape Coast, had he been there,
just as readily as in Adda.   Captain Glover's presence
in the east, therefore, did little or no good, and even
hampered the General by absorbing nearly all the disciplined troops and closing these districts to him as recruiting grounds for native levies and carriers.   The two
things that he was able to accomplish were the detachment
of the Jabin force from the main Ashanti army and the
completion of the British victory when his advance
accelerated the King's submission : in fact, without him,
that submission might not have been made.

Had it been possible for Sir Garnet to have remained
in Kumasi for a few days until Captain Glover could have
joined him, and for the latter to have occupied the place
for a time with his native troops, the result would have
been far more striking to the Ashantis and their neighbours than the single though decisive blow administered by

Sir Garnet and immediately followed by his return to the
coast. This latter movement, though unavoidable, was
quite misunderstood by the Ashantis, who regarded it as
a retreat. However, whatever faults there may have been
in these arrangements, they were not those of the officers
concerned, but of the authorities at home who had sanctioned such a scheme.

CHAPTER IX

THE EFFECTS OF THE WAR

1874

THE Ashanti war had far-reaching results. The Government had undertaken the defeat of the Ashantis, and had accomplished it at an enormous cost in blood and money and with little or no willing assistance from the Fantis. By so doing it had freed the protected tribes from any possibility of attack for some time to come, and was justly entitled to expect something in return and to assume a greater part in the management of their affairs than it had hitherto claimed. The Earl of Carnarvon, then Secretary of State for the Colonies, put this very clearly when he wrote : " I hold and am desirous of pressing on the Fantee Chiefs that as by the costly and unaided efforts of the Queen they have been raised from the abyss of misery and defeat in which they lay to a position of peace and security, so Her Majesty, as their deliverer, is entitled to require of them a greater degree of deference and conformity to the known desires of herself and her people than she has in former times exacted."[1]

It is true that this particular war had not been brought about by any action of the Fantis, but the condition of affairs at its commencement had been such that the Government had had only two courses open to it—either to abandon the Gold Coast or to prove its power to inflict decisive punishment on the enemy. Had the former alternative been adopted, the inevitable result would have been the conquest of Fanti by Ashanti in the near future.

[1] Parliamentary Paper, *Queen's Jurisdiction, etc.*, p. 7.

A fearful revenge would then assuredly have been taken 1874
for past insults, and those who escaped alive would only CHAP. IX
have been reserved for enslavement, and enslavement in
Ashanti meant a very strong probability of sacrifice at
some future date. It may, therefore, justly be claimed
that Sir Garnet Wolseley's expedition had the double
effect, so far as the Fantis were concerned, of ensuring to
them continued protection and saving them from massacre
either immediate or remote.

Many people, indeed, urged the abandonment of the
Gold Coast when the war was over. The country did not
pay, and there was a constant risk of interruption to trade
and the necessity for costly expeditions. There was no
obligation to protect the traders ; for they dealt principally in gin and munitions of war, which they sold as
readily to the enemies of the Government as to anyone else,
and they had, moreover, proved in the past that they were
well able to maintain their position without Crown Government and with only slight assistance from Imperial funds.
Any obligation to protect the people had been discharged
by the recent conquest of Ashanti, and they had proved
themselves so utterly worthless and apathetic during the
war, and had, indeed, so nearly wrecked the expedition by
their unwillingness even to provide carriers, that their
claims to further consideration were at this time small
indeed. This had been fully recognized by Lord Kimberley,
who had written : " With respect to our relations after
the war with the tribes of the Protectorate, considering
that with some few exceptions the native tribes since
their first defeats have made very little effort to defend
themselves against the Ashantees, and that, practically,
the whole burden of the war has fallen upon this country,
it must be understood that when the present operations
have been concluded, Her Majesty's Government will hold
that they have discharged their obligations to the protected
tribes, and that they are entirely free to review their relations with those tribes and to place them on such footing
as the interests of this country may seem to require." [1]

[1] Parliamentary Paper, *Ashanti War*, part iii, p. 241.

The first result of the war was the issue of a new Charter, on the 24th of July 1874, by which the Gold Coast and Lagos were separated from the Government of Sierra Leone and jointly " erected into a separate colony under the title of the Gold Coast Colony." An Order in Council, dated the 6th of August 1874, gave the Legislative Council of the new Colony authority to give effect by ordinance to the powers and jurisdiction acquired by the Crown, to which was reserved a right of disallowance, and these ordinances were to take effect throughout the whole protected area. Captain George Cumine Strachan, R.A., was appointed Governor ; he had arrived at Cape Coast and assumed the duties of Administrator on the 25th of June, relieving Captain Lees, who was soon afterwards transferred to Lagos as Administrator.

The term " Gold Coast Colony " has been the cause of much heart-burning and outcry amongst at least a section of the people, who have protested most strongly against its use in connection with their country and insisted that the old term " Protectorate " is the only appropriate word. Their contention, of course, is that they occupy a unique position in the British Empire in that they have never been conquered, nor have they ever ceded their aboriginal rights in the country by treaty. The real ground of their complaint, however, is not so much the application of any special term to their country as the gradual extension of British authority that has followed or grown up with it, and the promulgation of laws modifying and regulating the powers and jurisdiction of their Kings and Chiefs, which they maintain are inherent in them, and, in the absence of conquest or voluntary renunciation, must necessarily remain so. This extension of authority, however, has not been the outcome of the use of the word " colony," but the two innovations owe their origin to a common cause.

The term " colony " was doubtless only used for convenience and in a technical sense. It had, in fact, been used in this way even in Maclean's time, for in the treaty of 1831 the passage occurs " signed with the Great Seal of the Colony." None of the many European nations that had been on the Coast had ever attempted or even contemplated real colonization. Their object had been trade, not settlement : first the gold and slave trades and afterwards general commerce. The nature of the Gold Coast climate is alone more than sufficient to prevent its ever becoming a British Colony in anything more than name. In fact, Lord Carnarvon, in a despatch written less than a month later, showed plainly enough that no territorial rights were claimed. He laid it down that such rights on the Gold Coast extended " merely to the forts, or at most to so much of the lands immediately adjacent as may be required for defensive, sanitary, or other purposes essential to the maintenance of the British position on the Coast. All beyond that area is foreign territory. . . . That country is foreign soil, divided amongst native Chiefs and rulers standing in no relation of allegiance to Her Majesty, independent of one another, and each presumably sovereign within the limits of his own domain. But within the territory of each such ruler, the English Sovereign has, by cession or sufferance, acquired a varying degree of authority and over the whole an undefined and somewhat anomalous jurisdiction." [1] The exact meaning of this statement as to the absence of any relation of allegiance between the Chiefs and the Crown is, at first sight, none too clear ; presumably, however, the passage is an acknowledgment of the fact that there had been no conquest of the Chiefs nor voluntary cession of their rights, and is also intended to imply that the debt of allegiance was dependent upon the acceptance of British protection, but that the acceptance or rejection of the latter was entirely optional. Later still, on the 11th of March 1887, another Secretary of State wrote that " the greater portion of the Gold Coast Colony still remains a Protectorate, the soil being in the hands of the natives, and under the jurisdiction of the native Chiefs." [2] There can be no reason to suppose, therefore, that the application of the word " colony " to the Gold

---

[1] Parliamentary Paper, *Queen's Jurisdiction, etc.*, p. 6.
[2] *Ibid., Affairs of the Gold Coast*, 1888, p. 33.

Coast was ever intended to imply the possession of territorial rights by the Government.

It is indeed difficult to understand what possible ground
of complaint the use of this term could afford, since the
promoters of the Fanti Confederation, the avowed representatives of that very section of the community who are
now loudest in their objections to it, had themselves
proposed to Governor Pope Hennessy, as an alternative
measure to their own scheme, that the Government should
" take over the whole country and govern it as vigorously
and on the same lines and principles as it does her other
Colonies."[1] This is a request that can only mean what
it says and at once voluntarily abandons any special
advantages accruing to such differences as exist between
the Gold Coast and other British Dependencies. In formu-
lating their own scheme, moreover, these men had proposed measures that altogether deprived their natural
rulers of their judicial rights, intending to assume these
powers themselves and merely to pay a sum of money to
the Chiefs to compensate them for the consequent loss of
fees and fines. It had been impossible to deal with this
request hitherto, because the Ashanti war had immediately
supervened ; but now, at the first opportunity, the
Government took the people at their word.

From this it is apparent that any hardship or grievance
brought about by the new conditions was of the people's
own seeking and introduced on account of, or at any rate
in accordance with, their own suggestions. Had it not
been for these propositions, emanating from the professedly
chosen representatives of the Fanti race, the position
would have been more difficult. It is an indisputable
fact that the Gold Coast had never been either conquered
by or ceded to Great Britain, and that, with the exception
of the ground on which their forts stood, the English
could claim no territorial rights. Strictly speaking, the
people had always been absolutely independent and had
at one time even been the landlords of the English. The
Government had only been able to claim the right to inter-

[1] *Vide* vol. i, p. 621.

fere with some of their customs in return for the protection
which it afforded them.   Such rights as it now enjoyed
were the gradual outcome of " sufferance, usage and tacit
assent."   The utmost that could have been urged would
have been that the Government, by prosecuting the recent
campaign in Ashanti instead of abandoning the Gold Coast—
their only other alternative—had saved the people from
certain conquest : but any claim that a saviour was entitled to equal rights with a conqueror would have raised
a very debatable point and one probably without precedent.

Up to this time, British jurisdiction on the Gold Coast
had been defined by the Bond of 1844, which was, therefore,
the only document to be considered.   This was really a
treaty with the Fanti Chiefs, wherein they had definitely
acknowledged the " power and jurisdiction " that had been
exercised by the Government up to that date, not merely
within the strictly legal confines of their " Forts and
Settlements," but also " within divers countries and
places adjacent " thereto.   They had also agreed that
" murders, robberies and other crimes and offences " should
be tried by the Queen's officers in conjunction with the
Chiefs, and judgment given in accordance with the native
law so modified as to conform to the general principles of
the law of England.   This document, therefore, while
preserving the judicial rights of the Chiefs, modified them
to some extent and distinctly tended to increase rather
than to limit the area within which the Government could
exercise jurisdiction ; and, without in itself conferring on
the people any right to protection, merely legalized that
extension of authority which had grown up by " usage
and tacit assent."

Within recent years, however, an amount of jurisdiction
had been exercised that was not fully covered by the
provisions of the Bond, and it was now desired to confirm
and legalize this also.   The Bond dealt only with criminal
cases and barbarous customs, but made no provision for
civil jurisdiction nor for the collection of a revenue and
other matters, authority for which had been claimed and

exercised [1] by the Government, though it had never actually been given.   In 1844, when this treaty was made, prudence had dictated the method of proceeding by negotiation with the Chiefs, and the question now arose whether the object desired should be attained in a similar manner or by proclamation.   Circumstances had altered considerably since then, and the local power and resources of the Government had steadily increased, culminating in the recent victory over the Ashantis.   The position of the English, indeed, was now so much stronger that it was decided that it would be undignified for the Crown to negotiate for and accept as a grant that which it already claimed and exercised as a right, and that an act of sovereign power, such as a proclamation by the Queen, would now be the only appropriate mode of procedure.   Besides the want of dignity, other considerations favoured this decision.   There was the possibility that some of the Chiefs might refuse to sign any document conferring such powers on the Government, and the Chiefs themselves were so numerous, and the extent of their jurisdiction and their relations to each other were so imperfectly understood by the authorities, that it seemed more than likely that some important persons might be left out who would afterwards claim that their consent was as necessary as that of the others.   In either case the Government would have found itself in a position of much embarrassment.

It is, however, apparent that, although the proposals of the promoters of the Fanti Confederation simplified the ethics of the case and disarmed criticism, yet the changes that were now introduced were none the less bound to come, whether by the invitation and consent of the people or not ; and, if nothing else had occurred to bring them about, they would have ensued naturally in accordance with the general principle that " if a white race, not decaying in itself, keeps a hold among and is brought into daily contact with natives it must . . . extend its influence and widen its empire." [2]   Had anything occurred to render the

[1] By the Supreme Court Ordinances of 1853 and 1866.
[2] *Vide* vol. i, p. 536.

introduction of these changes impracticable, there can be 1874
little doubt that the Government would have withdrawn CHAP. IX
from the Gold Coast altogether.

The proclamation declaring the Gold Coast a Colony
was published on the 12th of September 1874. By it, all
the rights and jurisdiction that the Crown had acquired
were transferred to the Supreme Court and defined to
include the preservation of public peace and the protection
of individuals and property ; the administration of justice,
both civil and criminal ; the enactment of laws with due
regard to native law and custom ; the determination of
appeals from the Chiefs' to the British Courts ; the supervision and regulation of Chiefs' prisons ; the maintenance
of an armed police force ; the settlement by the Governor
of disputes arising between the Chiefs ; the imposition,
with the assent of the Chiefs, of sanitary rates in towns
and villages ; the imposition of Customs and license
duties ; the provision of schools, and other matters.

The next great result of the war was the abolition of
slavery on the Gold Coast. The export Slave Trade had,
of course, ceased many years before : internal domestic
slavery, however, still existed, and it was this that was now
dealt with. This institution had been a thorn in the side
of the Government for very many years, and trouble had, on
more than one occasion, arisen from it. As has been shown
elsewhere, it was about the mildest form of slavery that
could exist, having but few objectionable features and
bearing no comparison with the conditions that had prevailed in the days of the Slave Trade proper. The very
name of slavery, however, had become so repugnant to a
large section of the British public that they refused to
tolerate it in any form. Men living on the Gold Coast
understood exactly what it was, were accustomed to it,
and had no false ideas on the subject ; but whenever it
was mentioned in England, the name conjured up visions
of a state of affairs that had no existence, and aroused a
degree of hysterical sentiment and horror that was quite
uncalled for.

Perhaps the most objectionable form of slavery now

in existence was that known as pawning. This, indeed, was the only way in which a free person could now become a slave ; for the sale of a free-born man and even the practice of buying and selling domestic slaves were discountenanced by the people and had quite fallen into disuse. The only slaves now purchased were new importations from the interior—the Donkos. Pawning was a custom by which a person became the slave of a temporary master as a pledge for debt. A man might pawn himself, or the head of a family might pawn any one of its members. A father could pawn his children with the consent of the mother, and a mother could pawn any of her children whether the father consented or not, provided only that he failed to give her the sum she required. If the pawn died, another, usually one of his or her children or another child, had to be substituted ; and although freedom was theoretically obtainable at any time by the payment of the debt and interest, in practice this was very rarely done. This was chiefly on account of the enormous interest charged, but partly because of the habitual carelessness of the people in such matters. The pawns, moreover, being well treated, were not dissatisfied with their lot. The most objectionable features of this custom, therefore, were the extreme rarity of redemption and the fact that the services of the pawn counted for nothing ; he neither earned wages, nor did his work reduce the original liability. On the contrary, although in the course of a few years the labour thus given in return for food, clothing and lodging only would, even at the lowest estimate of its value, have fully sufficed to pay both principal and interest, the whole amount was still recoverable and continued so indefinitely.

The subject of slavery in general had, within recent years, engaged the attention of more than one Secretary of State ; but no definite steps had hitherto been taken owing to the difficulty of dealing with an institution which formed a constituent element in the fabric of society on the Gold Coast. In 1866 Mr. Cardwell had pointed out to Governor Blackall that any ordinances such as he had then proposed for the registration of slaves, settling the

amount of compensation to be paid to the owners of runa- **1874**
ways, or dealing with slavery in any way as a recognized
institution, would directly violate an existing Act of
Parliament and therefore be illegal and void. He continued : " It will be for the Chiefs, therefore, to take precautions against their slaves entering British territory, and
for the Colonial Government to take care that no official
inducements are held out to fugitives, and to warn them
that, if after entering British territory they again quit it,
they must do so at their own risk. But the readiest and
most effective way of escaping from all these embarrass-
ments is to confine British territory within the smallest
compass which may be practicable, and . . . at the Gold
Coast to the land occupied by the Government Buildings."[1]

By this rather flimsy subterfuge the settlement of the
question had been shirked for the time. In 1872, however,
it cropped up again, and Lord Kimberley, referring especially to the alleged purchase of slaves from Ashanti,
then wrote : " The position of the British Government in
the Protectorate is that of influence over people who are
not British subjects, and whilst every means should be
taken to induce the natives to desist from such practices . . .
it does not appear to me that it is advisable to interfere
by direct legislation. Her Majesty's Government can give
no countenance whatever to the purchase of slaves, on
the ground that it may be an act of humanity, because the
slaves would be in a worse position if they remained in
the hands of their captors. It may be better for the individual slaves, but the general result of such mistaken
benevolence must obviously be to promote, rather than
discourage, the Slave Trade, and to lead the natives to
believe that in some circumstances it is justifiable to
engage in this atrocious traffic. The British Government
have succeeded, after great sacrifices, in putting a stop
to the exportation of slaves by sea from West Africa ; and
they are bound by every principle of their policy to prevent, if possible, the prosecution of the Slave Trade in
a territory for the Government of which they are in-

---

[1] Parliamentary Paper, *Domestic Slavery, etc.* (June 1874), p. 2.

directly responsible. I think the proper course would be
to endeavour to come to an understanding with the Chiefs
of the protected tribes to forbid the Slave Trade within
their several districts. If they enter into agreements with
the Gold Coast Government to this effect, that Government can then enforce those agreements, which will be in
the nature of treaties. It will, of course, be understood
that any slave imported into what is strictly British
territory must be at once set free." [1]

Lord Kimberley called upon the Administrator for a
report as to the best mode of giving effect to these proposals, but no answer was ever received. Nothing more
was done. The Ashanti war broke out, and it was not until
it was over that this question once more came into promin-
ence. The war had brought a number of Europeans,
including war correspondents, to the Gold Coast, and the
British public at last realized that slavery, no matter of
what kind, still existed as a recognized institution in a
British Colony, that British Courts were invoked to compel
runaway slaves to return to their owners, and that Government officials not only accepted slaves for debt, but had
even resisted their enlistment during the recent hostilities.
Slaves, too, were still said to be imported for sale from
Ashanti, though there seems to have been no real foundation for this assertion : it is, at least, extremely improbable
that the Ashantis, after their heavy losses during the war,
would have parted with any appreciable number of the
population, and they could obtain no new slaves themselves until they had so far recovered their strength as
to be able to undertake a war against some of their inland
neighbours. The public, of course, had no conception of
the true state of affairs : to them slavery was slavery pure
and simple, admitting of no modification or extenuation,
and affecting the honour and traditional policy of the
British nation, and their indignation was so great that the
Government was at length compelled to take some definite
steps to deal with it.

All previous attempts having come to nothing, it was

[1] Parliamentary Paper, *Domestic Slavery*, *etc.* (June 1874), p. 2.

decided that the timid policy imposed by force of circumstances in the past must now come to an end, and that advantage might be taken of the altered relations between the Government and the people to insist on the immediate abolition of slave dealing and the importation of slaves from Ashanti or elsewhere, to be followed as soon as possible by the final extinction of slavery of every kind. The Governor was warned, however, against exciting " needless fears, such as might arise if it were to be supposed that what is contemplated is some sudden and ruinous subversion of the existing social relations depending upon slavery, without regard to the various interests which have grown up and are clearly connected with it." [1] Several alternative proposals were made as to the exact form of regulations that should be introduced, and, in the end, two ordinances were drafted, sent to the Secretary of State, and approved.

Before passing these ordinances, the Governor summoned all the Kings and Chiefs in the western and central districts to a meeting held in the Castle at Cape Coast on the 23rd of November, at which, after recapitulating the leading points in the history of the relations between the Gold Coast and Ashanti and showing how the recent expedition had delivered them from defeat and misery, he told them what the Government expected in return. He carefully explained that there was no intention to force any slave to leave his master : those who were happy and contented might remain, but those who wished to claim their freedom and leave must be permitted to do so. On the conclusion of this speech, the Chiefs consulted together for a few moments, and King Edu of Mankesim then asked permission for them to retire and bring their answer on the following day. To this, however, the Governor would not consent ; but he volunteered to leave the Palaver Hall, so as to give them an opportunity for free discussion, and, on his return an hour later, the Chiefs said they were quite ready to give up buying new slaves, but expressed some doubt about the release of those they then held or of any

---

[1] Parliamentary Paper, *Queen's Jurisdiction, etc.*, p. 7.

pawns who might demand their freedom.   Many of them
held pawns for money they had lent and were afraid this
new arrangement might involve them in heavy pecuniary
loss.   The Governor therefore explained that the departure of any pawn who might elect to leave would not
imply the loss of the debt for which he or she had been
held as security, which would still be recoverable in the
Courts, and repeated once more that no slave or pawn would
be compelled to leave his master.   The Chiefs then withdrew
their objection and expressed their satisfaction with the
proposed terms and their willingness to abide by them.

It had been feared that this announcement might be
the cause of a serious disturbance, and arrangements had
been made for several warships to be in the roads and for
the temporary detention of a wing of the West India Regiment which had been under orders to leave.   The very
satisfactory conclusion of this meeting, however, dispelled
all anxiety, and the Governor left at once for Accra on
H.M.S. *Ariel*.   There a similar announcement was made
to the Chiefs of the eastern districts on the 6th, when they
also promised to do as they were asked.   The two ordinances were then passed : one [1] provided for the abolition
of slave dealing, and the other [2] for the emancipation of
existing slaves and the freedom of all children born after
the 5th of November 1874.   The provisions of these two
measures were made known by a proclamation published
on the 17th of December, in which attention was once
more specially drawn to the fact that it was " not intended by any of the aforesaid laws, or otherwise, to offer
inducement to any persons to leave any master in whose
service they may be desirous of remaining, or to forsake
the krooms [3] where they have been accustomed to inhabit,
and that it is intended to permit the family and tribal
relations to continue in all respects according as used
and wont, except only that of slavery and such customs as
arise therefrom and are thereon necessarily dependent." [4]

---

[1] Ordinance No. 1 of 1874.   [2] Ordinance No. 2 of 1874.
[3] Small villages or hamlets.
[4] Parliamentary Paper, *Queen's Jurisdiction, etc.*, p. 42.

As might have been anticipated, comparatively few
slaves availed themselves of the right thus given them.
They knew when they were well off ; they knew that so
long as they remained with their masters they were assured
of food, clothing and lodging at the cost of a moderate
amount of work ; they knew that they would be well
treated and, in fact, regarded as members of the family ;
and they also knew that if they left they would have to
provide for themselves, and might find great difficulty in
obtaining employment in a country where there was little
or no demand for paid labour of the kind for which they
were fitted. They realized, moreover, that now that the
choice of freedom or the continuation of their services lay
with them, there was even less likelihood than before that
they would be ill-treated. Practically all those slaves who
were worth holding, therefore, remained as they were,
and it was only the idle, useless and disorderly who claimed
their freedom ; and they, being unwilling to earn an honest
living, or unable to obtain employment to their taste,
added very largely to the criminal population. In fact,
this may be said to have been the principal effect of this
legislation, for, to this day, the domestic slaves on the Gold
Coast are a very numerous and contented class, and cases
of slave dealing and pawning, though much diminished
in frequency and severely punished whenever proved, are
by no means unknown.

The abolition of internal slavery had, however, at least
one other result, which, though less evident at the time
and certainly not foreseen, was nevertheless of considerable
importance. This was its effect on the trade with the
interior. All the large traders who brought their merchandize or gold to the coast and returned with European
goods used slaves as carriers. Many of them, indeed, had
none but slaves in their train. The cost of transport,
therefore, when once the initial purchase money had been
paid, only amounted to the maintenance of these people,
and any trader who had had to pay his carriers wages in
addition would have been quite unable to compete with his
rivals when he reached the inland markets. So long as

slavery had been a recognized institution in the Protectorate, these men had incurred no more risk by bringing
their slaves to the coast towns than in travelling with them
in any other part of the country ; but once it became
known that any slave on entering the British Protectorate
became nominally free and could, if he so wished, assert
his freedom and receive the protection of the law, these
traders obviously ran a greatly increased risk of loss.   The
majority of their slaves, like those on the coast, would
doubtless prefer to remain with them ; but there was
always the possibility that some of them, either because
they were tempted by their new surroundings, or because
they imagined that a life of freedom must of necessity
be a life of ease and luxury, might claim their liberty.
Their initial cost would then be a dead loss to their
owner, and he would, moreover, be unable to transport
some part of his purchases up country unless he was
prepared to pay for carriers at a rate that would involve the loss of all his profits.   Hence the new law
did undoubtedly act as a deterrent to that trade upon
which the prosperity of the Colony mainly depended,
and diverted an appreciable part of it to places beyond
the borders, which were outside the jurisdiction of the
British Courts, but where European goods were nevertheless obtainable.   On the other hand, the condition of a
number of slaves held by tribes beyond the frontier was
indirectly improved by the knowledge that if they were
ill-treated and fled into the Protectorate they could not be
recovered.

The people as a whole understood well enough that
the new law, by giving their slaves the option of remaining
with them or claiming their freedom, would not affect
their interests very seriously in practice, whatever it might
do in theory.   They therefore accepted the new conditions
quietly enough.   A few of the so-called " scholars,"
however, men of the same stamp as those who had brought
about the deposition of Aggri, began to agitate in the hope
of obtaining compensation for the loss of any slaves who
might chance to leave them.

It has been urged [1] that the term " educated African " should be employed instead of " scholar " ; [2] and rightly so, provided that it is reserved for those Africans who really are educated. Such men constitute an increasing, useful, and honourable section of the community on the Gold Coast, and are not to be confused with the class usually described as " scholars." This term, which, on the Gold Coast, is almost a term of reproach, though often falsely applied to " educated Africans," should rather be reserved for those who can hardly be said to have any real education at all, usually because they have lacked the energy and application necessary to acquire it, and who are so well described by Governor Strachan as " a class of natives who are found in Cape Coast and . . . in other towns on the sea-board of the Gold Coast, who have a smattering of education, but, being without industry or character, are incapable of following settled occupations, and who are ready to use the degree of knowledge they possess for any purpose, however mischievous, from which they can hope to reach any measure of selfish advantage. They have no real influence either with the native rulers of the Protectorate or with the population, but have occasionally in past times been able by misrepresentation and delusive promises to lead individuals or even sections of the community temporarily astray." [3]

These men now drew up and caused to be presented to the Governor a series of petitions purporting to come from the Kings and Chiefs of the Protectorate and others, in which they asserted that he had promised that, although no more slaves could be purchased, yet no existing slave should " leave his master or mistress without cause shown and proof of cruelty or maltreatment." [4] Of course, nothing of the kind had ever been said, and enquiry soon showed that, as on some previous occasions, the Kings and Chiefs had been misled into putting their marks to these documents without ever having understood the real nature of

---

[1] Sarbah, *Fanti National Constitution.* [2] *Vide* vol. i, p. 464.
[3] Parliamentary Paper, *Further Correspondence relating to the Abolition of Slavery,* 1875, p. 3. [4] *Ibid.,* p. 4.

their contents, which did not, in fact, represent their views at all. Some of the arguments contained in these petitions were sound enough, but the grossly false statements that were made quite overshadowed them, and nothing came of the appeal. The Kings, Chiefs and people perfectly understood what was required of them : they realized, moreover, what the " scholars " would seem to have forgotten, that this was a concession which they had been asked to make in return for their recent delivery, none of the cost of which had fallen upon them, and that if they refused and it was found impossible or not worth while to enforce obedience, it was more than likely that they would be left to their fate. It required very little imagination or foresight on their part to discern what that would be.

The third important result of the war was the disruption of the Ashanti kingdom and empire. Salaga, Attabubu, Krachi, Kwahu, and the other more distant provinces at once threw off the yoke, murdering and imprisoning any of the residents and their followers who had not been recalled to take part in the hostilities. The Attabubus, Krachis and the Brong tribes generally, with the exception of the Inkoranzas, were especially hostile. They had always longed for their freedom, and now refused to acknowledge any supremacy but that of Denti the great Krachi fetish. Before the war broke out, Kofi Karikari had sent to consult this oracle, and had been told he could not hope to succeed, since the very gunpowder he was going to use against the English was obtained from them. Denti, indeed, through his priests, expressed surprise that the King should have thought it worth while to make such an enquiry, and advised him to " purchase for himself and for each man in his army a pair of stout sandals, with which they may escape with facility and not have their toes sprained or their feet bruised when routed and pursued by the English." This prophecy had greatly enraged the King, who forced the Brongs to mobilize and fight in the van of his army. They had been in front in many of the hottest engagements. It was they who had faced the marines in the open at Elmina and who lost most men in the

attack on Abakrampa, and they had been in front again at **1874**
Amoafu and made the last despairing stand at Odasu.

The Krachis and confederate Brongs recognized the
right of the conqueror to their allegiance, and the tribute
they had formerly paid to Kumasi would now have been
paid to the Government, had it been asked for, as part
of the spoils of victory, just as some of the early ground-
rent notes for the forts had changed hands after a war.
They sent tusks of ivory to Accra in token of fealty, but
the meaning of this act does not seem to have been understood.

Kofi Karikari now sent messengers to Krachi to summon
the revolted people back to their allegiance ; but they
would have nothing to do with him, murdering his messengers and treating a second embassy that arrived a little
later in the same way. The people of Bassa and other
towns, fearing the King's vengeance, left their houses to
go to ruin and retired to Krachi ; but the precaution was
quite unnecessary, for the Ashantis had far too many
troubles nearer home to be able to undertake any expedition
against the recalcitrant Brongs. It was not until some
years later, however, that the latter ventured to return
and rebuild their villages.

Even in the kingdom itself disaffection was rife, and
province after province either seceded or made overtures
to the Colonial Government to be taken under its protection. The Home Government, however, was not prepared to incur any further risk or responsibility in the
country, and would not sanction any extension of the
limits of the Protectorate, nor enter into any relations
with the tribes of the interior that could give them a claim
upon it.

When the condition to which Ashanti had now been
reduced and the possibilities of the future are considered,
it seems almost incredible that this policy should have
been continued. The signal defeat of their army, assembled in a strong position and fighting as it had never had to
fight before, and the irresistible advance of a British force
through the forest upon whose obstructive powers they

had relied so much, had so thoroughly upset their most cherished beliefs and traditions, that the Ashantis were at last convinced that they must at least acknowledge the superior power of the English. Even the King and the haughty Kumasi Chiefs were now humbled and subdued In May Kofi Karikari had sent down another instalment [1] of the indemnity and voluntarily surrendered thirty-three persons belonging to the royal family of Assin, who were the descendants of hostages taken during the invasion of 1807. On the 3rd of July other messengers reached Cape Coast, bringing a third instalment of 400 ounces of gold, and the fact that 336 ounces of this was in ornaments and only 64 in dust and nuggets shows that the resources of the Ashanti treasury were at a very low ebb. The King, too, made an appeal, accompanied by presents, to Mr. Freeman and to Dawson to reopen the mission station in Kumasi ; but this was not done, because the Government, having decided not to interfere in the affairs of the interior and having profited by previous costly experience, would not guarantee the safety of the missionaries.

Had the stronger policy now adopted on the Coast been extended to the tribes in the interior and a wise and just administration been inaugurated while the Ashantis were in their present frame of mind, it is in the highest degree probable that it would have proved the foundation of lasting friendly relations between them and the Government, which would have become firmly established long before they had recovered from the blow they had received. It is possible, of course, that the experiment might have failed ; but had this happened, the want of success would more probably have been due to faults in its administration than to any inherent defects, and even if it had afterwards been necessary to use force, the Ashantis would not have been in a position to offer any very serious resistance. As matters stood, the very worst thing possible was done, and this absolute non-interference with their affairs even began to detract from the value of the victory gained by Sir Garnet Wolseley. The Ashantis had never been able

[1] Amount uncertain.

to appreciate the real reasons for his rapid return to the 1874
coast, and such methods were so entirely opposed to their CHAP. IX
own dilatory methods of warfare that, when they found
themselves left entirely alone, they soon began to believe
his retirement had been a retreat, that the English had
done their worst, and that they had nothing more to fear
from them.

The position, shortly, was this. The Ashantis, startled
and subdued by their unexpected defeat, were uncertain
how they stood. The majority of them, feeling their own
weakness and dissatisfied with the tyrannous rule of Kumasi,
to which they largely attributed their present misfortunes,
were anxious to live in peace and to enjoy the protection
and friendship of what they now realized was the stronger
power. This being refused, there were but two, or at
most three, possibilities open. One or other of these was
bound to eventuate, and every one of them could have
been clearly foreseen by the Government. Either the
individual tribes and provinces of the kingdom would
succeed in asserting their desired independence and
establish themselves as small separate states, or Kumasi
would, by force of arms or diplomacy, regain its supremacy,
and in the course of a few years recover its former power.
The only other possible solution of the problem was that
Jabin or one of the other more powerful provinces might
take the place formerly held by Kumasi. None of these
things was to be desired. If Ashanti was broken up into
a number of small independent kingdoms, they would
constantly be at war with one another, and the stoppage of
trade and its attendant losses to the British would be as
great as, and perhaps even more continuous than before.
If, on the other hand, the power of Ashanti as a whole was
revived, it would, in the course of a very few years, again
become a menace to the peace of the Gold Coast, and all
the money and lives that had been spent on its conquest
would, for any practical result, have been thrown away.
It is inconceivable that the Government can have desired
any of these things to happen ; yet one or the other was
so palpably inevitable that it is hard to understand the

persistency with which it still clung to its old policy of non-extension. With the Dutch gone, Ashanti defeated and disorganized, and the majority of its people seeking the friendship and protection of the British, the Government had an excellent opportunity to settle once and for all the one great difficulty that had always confronted it. The experiment was one that would have been well worth making, even if the risk of failure had been infinitely greater than it was.

Foiled in their attempts to gain British protection, the distracted and dissatisfied Ashantis were driven to rely on their own resources and began to reorganize themselves. Kofi Karikari prepared to return to his capital, and summoned all his principal Chiefs to meet him there. Asafu Agai the King of Jabin, however, had so recently committed himself by tendering his submission to Captain Glover in the hour of greatest national need, that he decided not to risk his personal safety by visiting Kumasi and determined never again to submit to its rule. He therefore not only refused to come in, but went further and made it plain that he would resist any attempts to coerce him into submission, and Karikari, equally unwilling to lose his most important feudatory or to have his country again devastated by war, sent messengers to the Governor begging him to interfere. Jabin ambassadors arrived at the same time ; but, although both parties were apparently anxious to avert war, the Jabins made it abundantly clear that they were determined to retain their newly asserted independence, while it was equally evident that Kofi Karikari's request that an officer might be sent to arrange matters had been made primarily with the object of bringing pressure to bear on them to compel them to renew their allegiance. The Governor, for a time therefore, refused to comply with the King's request ; but a more careful review of the situation soon afterwards induced him to alter his decision. Although Kofi Karikari was anxious for peace, and the Jabins, if unmolested, would doubtless remain quiescent, it was quite evident that the King could not afford to allow such defections amongst his people :

he would be bound to make an effort to prevent it, and at 1874 the first sign of this the Jabins would take up arms. The CHAP. IX two sides were believed to be fairly evenly matched, so that this would mean a struggle for supremacy that might last for years, during which the trade of the Colony would again be ruined. Looked at in this light, the prospect was so serious that the Governor decided to make an exception to the usual policy and intervene. Captain Lees was accordingly sent on a mission to both Kumasi and Jabin with instructions to mediate between the two parties and do all he could to prevent a collision, but it was specially impressed upon the Kumasi messengers that he would not use his influence to bring any disaffected tribes back to their allegiance.

Captain Lees left Cape Coast on the 14th of July and reached Kumasi on the 23rd, when he was received by the King with every possible honour. He soon learned that the whole kingdom was in revolt, and that not only Jabin, but Kokofu, Bekwai, Insuta, and other provinces were all trying to assert their independence. All communication with Jabin had ceased ; the King's messengers had been made prisoners, and the outbreak of hostilities was imminent. Kofi Karikari made repeated efforts to induce Captain Lees to use his influence on his behalf, but finding them of no avail, finally consented to make such reasonable concessions to the Jabins as might secure peace. Captain Lees then went on to Jabin, and it was arranged that the independence of the tribe should be recognized and that they and the Kumasis should bury all past quarrels and live in peace with one another, keeping their roads open for traders of any nation, and surrendering all prisoners then in their possession to Captain Lees, who would ascertain where they wished to go and arrange accordingly. Asafu Agai swore to these conditions in the presence of messengers from Kumasi on the 7th of August, and, on the 12th, Kofi Karikari also bound himself to observe them. It is much to be regretted that in arranging these terms nothing was said about the war indemnity, for the Jabins had been as actively hostile as anyone else until Kumasi fell, and should have been held equally liable. By the Treaty of Fomana the King (of Kumasi) was responsible for payment, but these negotiations greatly restricted his resources and it was most unjust thus to allow the Jabins to escape all liability and saddle the whole burden of this debt upon the King.

Jabin was joined by the kingdoms of Insuta, Afiduasi and Asuri ; but the Bekwais and Kokofus, who had also declared their independence, let it be understood that their action was due to their aversion to Kofi Karikari personally rather than to any special dislike for the rule of Kumasi. The absolute necessity of regaining the adherence of these important provinces, coupled with the discovery that Kofi Karikari had committed the unheard-of crime of desecrating the tombs of his ancestors at Bantama, overcame the reluctance of his immediate supporters in the capital, and, soon after Captain Lees' departure, he was deposed, and his younger brother Mensa enstooled in his place.

The rifling of the royal graves at Bantama had taken place very soon after the war, although it had only just been discovered. After his flight from Odasu, Kofi Karikari had lived for a time at Breman before returning to rebuild his capital, and it was during this period of retirement that he had run short of money and committed this crime to obtain it. Sending for the keepers of the royal mausoleum, he made them " drink fetish " that they would never divulge the secret that he was about to entrust to them on pain of instant death. This they did, and he then ordered them to exhume the bodies of his grandmother Efua Sapon, and some others, and to bring him the gold-dust, trinkets, rings, chains, Aggri beads, and other valuables that had been buried with them. They obeyed him, and the secret would probably have been well kept had not Karikari foolishly given a few of the rings and other ornaments to some of his favourite wives, on whom they were subsequently seen by his mother, Efua Kobri. She recognized them as jewels of ancient and unusually beautiful workmanship, but for some time could not imagine

how he had been able to obtain them. A little later,
however, some of these jewels were identified as having
been worn years before by Efua Sapon and the others from
whose graves they had been taken, and Efua Kobri then
denounced him to the Kumasi Chiefs. Karikari had now
returned to Kumasi, whither he summoned all his relatives
and Chiefs and informed them that, since his mother had
disgraced him by making these disclosures, he had decided
to blow himself and them up with gunpowder. The
threat, however, was an empty one ; and although the
Chiefs are said to have replied, " We are all ready to die
with you, but blow yourself up first," Kofi Karikari
preferred to live.

A king of Ashanti had the right, in times of great national
stress, to draw on the treasure at the Bantama ; but it
was regarded as an extraordinarily serious undertaking,
and, so far as is known, had never been done. But although this right existed, it could only be exercised with
the advice and consent of the Council, and even then it
would be unlawful for the King himself to look on the
gold. Kofi Karikari's action, therefore, was regarded not
only as illegal, but as unconstitutional and positively
sacrilegious.

CHAPTER X

THE REVIVAL OF THE POWER OF ASHANTI

1875 TO 1880

FROM the date of his accession, early in 1875, Osai Mensa had two main objects in view : he longed to wipe out the disgrace of the defeat of 1874 and revive the power and glory of Ashanti ; but, anxious though he was to retrieve the national honour, he was even more anxious still to avoid any conflict with the Colonial Government, and did his best to live on terms of friendship with it. A careful study of the whole of the literature and correspondence dealing with his reign must lead to this estimate of Mensa's policy. These two objects, however, were incompatible ; and he, like everyone else who tries simultaneously to attain two diametrically opposite ends, eventually fell between them. But, though he had no intention of opposing the Government, he knew that a struggle with some of his former subjects was a possibility that must not be lost sight of, and for which he must make some preparations. Before he could make any move, therefore, towards regaining the ascendancy of Kumasi over the surrounding tribes, he had first of all to make his own position as strong as possible and devoted himself for a time to replenishing his stock of powder, lead and salt, and reorganizing his army, so that he might be prepared for any contingency that should arise.

The point that rankled most was the independence of Jabin ; for this tribe, with the subsidiary kingdoms that had thrown in their lot with it, threatened to become a serious rival if allowed to gain any further accession of

strength. During the earlier months of 1875, therefore,
Mensa began to intrigue to win them back to their old
allegiance, and, in July, through the King of Mampon,
gained a promise of assistance from one of the principal
Jabin Chiefs, who, for some reason, was dissatisfied with his
position. Asafu Agai, however, discovered the treachery of
this Chief, and, having put him to death, took his revenge
on Mensa by seizing a number of Kumasi traders. Asafu
Agai, indeed, played into Mensa's hands.

Mensa was still afraid of becoming involved in trouble
with the Government, and, instead of taking immediate
action, sent down complaints of the King of Jabin's conduct
to the Governor, demanding that he should be required
to pay a fair share of the war indemnity, and asking the
Cape Coast traders to intercede for him with the Government on the grounds that the Jabins had closed the roads
and seized his people in defiance of the terms arranged by
Captain Lees. Mensa hoped to gain his object by these
diplomatic means without risk to himself, and prompt
action by the Government would have nipped his schemes
in the bud and settled the dispute at once ; but when the
traders forwarded the King's letter to Captain Strachan,
he declined to interfere, and replied " that he would act
with reference to the affairs of the interior as seemed to
him advisable." [1] Asafu Agai, elated by his sudden
accession to power, now sent insulting messages to Mensa
and openly invited the Akims to come and share the spoils
of Kumasi with him. Such conduct, of course, made war
inevitable and indirectly strengthened Mensa's hands and
brought about the first step towards the reconstruction of
his kingdom ; for the Bekwais and Kokofus, finding they
would have to throw in their lot with one side or the other,
now returned to their allegiance and joined Mensa.

When affairs had reached this stage and Mensa was still
hesitating between his thirst for revenge and his fear of
the Government, M. Bonnat suddenly arrived in Kumasi
with Prince Ansa. During his captivity he had heard of
the extensive trade that passed through Salaga, which at

[1] Ellis, *Land of Fetish*, p. 182.

that time had been under the subjection of Kumasi and occupied by an Ashanti resident with a large retinue. At the time of the Ashanti war, however, they, with many others similarly situated on the outposts of the empire, had either been recalled to take part in the hostilities or been murdered when news of the fall of Kumasi reached their stations. M. Bonnat was now engaged in a scheme for opening up a trade route to this important centre, which, though as yet unvisited by Europeans, was known to be only about eight days' journey to the north-east of Kumasi. Instead of confining himself to his business projects however, he mixed himself up in Ashanti politics, and, apparently forgetting all that he had formerly had to put up with in Kumasi, or possibly hoping to gain some important concessions from the King, warmly sympathized with Mensa in his feud with Jabin. He was even induced to visit that place and negotiate on behalf of the King for the renewal of the Jabin allegiance, but he was regarded with so much suspicion and disfavour that, though he himself escaped, about sixty Ashantis who were with him were put to death by Asafu Agai in obedience, so he afterwards said, to the orders of the Krachi fetish. Soon after this, in September, the inhabitants of five Jabin villages near the frontier intimated their desire to secede, and Mensa sent some Court officials with an escort from Kumasi to accept their formal submission. They were attacked by a Jabin force, but drove it off, and the people of the five villages migrated into Kumasi territory.

After these two events the Governor realized, when it was too late, that even Mensa's fear of his intervention and possible punishment of himself could no longer avert war, and Dr. Gouldsbury was sent into Eastern Akim with instructions to warn the Chiefs against taking any part in the quarrel and to proceed from there to Jabin and Kumasi and call on the two Kings to keep the oaths they had sworn before Captain Lees. The object of his mission, however, was well known on the coast, and before he left Accra on the 23rd of October Prince Ansa had already sent messages to his nephew, King Mensa, warning him that

" the white man was coming to palaver " and advising him, if he meant to fight, to do so at once. Mensa promptly took the hint and sent two armies against Jabin, which was attacked on the 31st of October. The Jabins made a gallant defence, and for two days the result of the battle was in doubt, but on the 3rd of November they ran short of ammunition and broke and fled in every direction. News of the impending attack had reached Dr. Gouldsbury while he was still at Kibbi and he had pushed on to Jabin with all speed, but by the time he arrived the battle was over and he found the town in the hands of the victorious Kumasis.

The conquest of Jabin was the direct outcome of the policy of non-interference that had been adopted by the Colonial Government, and its action in prohibiting the importation of munitions of war had only made the success of the Kumasis all the more certain. This embargo had not seriously affected them, for they could always obtain all they wanted from Assini ; but it greatly handicapped the Jabins, whose only chance of replenishing their stock was to smuggle powder from the Volta River. They did, in fact, succeed in bringing a large convoy as far as Akim, but it was seized by Captain J. S. Hay, who had been stationed there with a force of the Gold Coast Constabulary to keep the Akims quiet and disarm any Jabins who entered the Colony. The Jabins, having had less fighting than the Kumasis in 1874, had a good reserve of ammunition and fully held their own as long as it lasted, and even when compelled to retreat, carried away many of their valuables, while the King saved all his regalia and entered Cape Coast in great state early in 1876. Many of the people, however, chiefly women and children, fell into the hands of the Kumasis, and numbers of these captives were sent through Sefwi to French territory for sale, powder and lead being purchased with the money thus obtained. Asafu Agai, hearing this, sent messengers to the King of Sefwi asking him to cause his people to purchase and hold in pawn any of his subjects whom they might see in transit through their country, so that when in the future his fortunes should rise again he might be able to redeem them, whereas, if they were sold into French territory, they would be lost to him for ever. The King of Sefwi replied that if Asafu Agai would send duly authorized representatives to Wiosu to " drink fetish " with him, he would grant his request : this was done, and it was agreed that any persons bought by the Sefwis should be subject to future redemption by the Jabins on repayment of the original purchase money, together with the customary " redemption sheep." [1]

The fugitive Jabins were disarmed by Captain Hay as they entered Akim and settled on land to the north of Accra, where they founded New Jabin. Asafu Agai soon afterwards began to make plans with King Taki of Accra for the recovery of his kingdom, but this was stopped by the Governor at the time, Mr. Sandford Freeling, who summoned a meeting of the Chiefs at Accra on the 16th of July 1877 and warned them that they would not be permitted to use the Colony as a base of operations against Ashanti. Taki was fined, and all were told that at the first attempt to repeat the offence they would be punished by transportation. Asafu Agai's niece, Princess Afrakuma, escaped with him, and the stool and regalia were handed over to the Governor for safe keeping. Her son Yow Sapon, the heir-apparent however, and her sister were taken prisoners to Kumasi, but were afterwards released or escaped, and, on the death of Asafu Agai some years later, Yow Sapon succeeded him as King, but soon moved to Konengo so as to be farther from Kumasi.

The Government's policy of non-interference in the affairs of the interior might look very well in theory, but it was impossible to put it into practice with any hope of success. Mensa indeed seems to have realized this, although the Government did not, and it had only been his conviction that they would surely intervene that had delayed the outbreak of hostilities for so long. The Governor, moreover, acted inconsistently : he had intervened when he sent Captain Lees to Ashanti, and Mensa rightly expected him to see that an agreement made in the

---

[1] Equivalent to a fee of twenty-seven shillings.

presence of his representative was kept. Although it is true that Mensa himself was not entirely free from blame, yet the Jabins were the greater offenders. Mensa's long forbearance was solely due to his desire to remain on terms of friendship with the Government and to fear of the consequences to himself if he did not. British prestige had never been so great in Ashanti as it was at this time, and it should have been the policy of the English to maintain and foster it, instead of which they brought it into contempt and very soon nullified nearly all the advantage that had been gained by Sir Garnet Wolseley's victory. The Government, by sending Captain Lees as its representative, had made itself morally responsible that the agreement he arranged would be observed, and, in fact, stood in the position of a referee ; but when one of the parties lodged a formal complaint against the other, the Governor ignored it and matters were allowed to go from bad to worse, until, in the end, acts were perpetrated which could only be wiped out in blood, and the authorities realized too late that it was not only their duty, but distinctly to their advantage to interfere. They might advisedly have accepted the submission of the Jabins when it was first offered ; but from the day the independence of the tribe was acknowledged it was certainly to their interest to maintain it, supporting either party as might be necessary, for in no other way could the balance of power in Ashanti so easily be preserved and danger to the Colony averted, while the respect both parties then felt for the power of the English would have made this task all the easier. As it was, the opportunity to settle matters had been allowed to pass, and Dr. Gouldsbury's mission was sent too late to do any good and only made the Government look ridiculous. The outbreak of hostilities restored the important provinces of Bekwai and Kokofu to the Kumasi Confederacy ; the conquest of Jabin drove out the tribe that might have proved the Government's best lever and freed Mensa of his only serious rival ; Insuta, Afiduasi and Asuri returned to their allegiance on the defeat of their protectors ; the Jabins were dissatisfied at the absence

of any support, and Mensa, besides feeling indignant that
the Governor had not complied with his request and
insisted on the observation of the Kumasi-Jabin Agreement, found that he had regained nearly the whole of his
lost kingdom and power at one stroke and realized that his
fear of the Government had been groundless.   Probably no
one, before or since, has ever done so much for Ashanti as
did Governor Strachan and those who dictated his policy.

Dr. Gouldsbury advised that Jabin should even now
be occupied by a British force ; but it was too late to take
action of this kind, and the attempt fortunately was not
made : to have tried to snatch the fruits of victory from
the Kumasis in their hour of triumph would have been
nothing short of madness.   Mensa made no secret of the
contempt with which the Government's actions had inspired him, and Dr. Gouldsbury had to leave Kumasi
without having effected anything and without receiving
any of the customary marks of respect, while Captain
Baker, who arrived soon afterwards with an escort to
receive another instalment of the indemnity, was simply
told the gold was not ready and had to march out amid the
hootings and derisive laughter of the Kumasi mob, who
amused themselves by pelting him and his escort with
mud.   The gold, however, was brought by runners, who
overtook him at the Oda River ; but the incident so
alarmed the Government that it never ventured to demand
any further instalments.   " Thus, within less than two
years after the burning of Kumasi, the Ashantis had,
thanks to the Government's policy of non-intervention,
recovered the whole of their lost territory except Kwao
(Kwahu) and Adansi, and escaped the payment of the
greater part of the indemnity." [1]

During his journey, Dr. Gouldsbury visited Salaga and
Krachi on the Volta River.   He succeeded in making a
treaty [2] with the King, Fetish Priest, and Chiefs of the
latter place on the 8th of March 1876, by which they

---

[1] Ellis, *History of the Gold Coast*, p. 358.
[2] For full text, *vide* Parliamentary Paper, *Further Correspondence on
the Affairs of the Gold Coast*, 1882, p. 14.

bound themselves to put no obstacle in the way of free
trade between Salaga and other places in the interior and
the coast, and agreed to keep their roads open for the passage of all lawful traders and to encourage them to use
them so far as lay in their power.

Of the two former tributaries that still retained their
independence, Kwahu was too far away to be in any danger ;
but Adansi very nearly reverted to its old allegiance.
Kobina Obin had died in 1875, and the Adansis were then
divided into two parties, one of which wished to bring the
country again under Kumasi, while the other was equally
determined to maintain its independence. Feeling on this
question ran so high that a civil war very nearly broke out,
and the Adansis having asked for advice and assistance, the
Governor, fearing the obliteration of yet another mark of
the conquest of Ashanti, sent Captain Moloney up to
Kwisa. He stayed there some time and succeeded in
reconciling the rival factions, who, early in 1876, decided
to retain their independence and elected Inkansa Berofon
king : he was formally enstooled in Captain Moloney's
presence and recognized by him on behalf of the Government. The choice of this man, however, proved most unfortunate, and throughout his reign complaints were continually being made against his misrule. He was described
by Captain Lonsdale a little later as, " weak almost to
imbecility, avaricious and grasping, a bully by nature, and
a coward at heart, he would, if he dared, be the equal of
any native potentate in tyranny." [1] Such a man was the
very last person who should have been made King of
Adansi. The country needed a strong and wise ruler, for
its position was peculiar : although its independence had
been recognized by Ashanti, it was neither within the
Protectorate nor within the jurisdiction of the British
Courts, and there was, consequently, no appeal from the
decisions of Inkansa, which, as might be expected from
the character of the man and the fact that the greater part
of the fines he inflicted became his property, were often far

[1] Parliamentary Paper, *Further Correspondence on the Affairs of the
Gold Coast*, 1882, p. 58.

from just. His own Chiefs grew discontented and inclined to be rebellious, and the King of Ashanti was often annoyed by the way in which his people were treated when visiting or passing through the country, and by the fact that Ashanti criminals sometimes sought refuge there and could not be recovered. More than once there was danger that he would interfere to protect his own subjects, and he was only restrained by the belief that the British were bound to uphold the independence of Adansi.

Yet another incident occurred during this year that brought British prestige on the West African coast into still greater contempt with Europeans and Africans alike. Early in the year the King of Dahomi had caused an Englishman, Messrs. F. & A. Swanzy's agent at Wida, to be maltreated by the local Chief and sent under arrest to his capital Abomi, where he had been kept a prisoner for some time and treated with every indignity, being compelled to dance before the King's wives and dragged out daily bareheaded to be present at human sacrifices or the execution of criminals. It was not until he had been robbed of all he possessed that he was at last permitted to escape. Commodore Hewett,[1] who commanded the West African Squadron, demanded a fine of 1,000 puncheons of palm-oil in compensation for this outrage, and, on payment being refused, blockaded the coast from Adafia to Lagos. The blockade began on the 1st of July, and, in September, the King's troops advanced towards Little Popo, where they destroyed a number of villages and then threatened to attack the British post at Kitta. In 1877, however, a French firm whose interests were affected by the blockade paid a first instalment of 200 puncheons in the name of the King and the blockade was then raised ; but since the King himself had paid nothing and still refused to do so when further instalments were demanded in 1878 and 1879, nothing was gained. Even the 200 puncheons paid by the French firm were lost in the wreck of the *Gambia*, but the blockade was never renewed and the matter was allowed to drop.

[1] Afterwards Admiral Sir William Hewett, V.C., K.C.B.

During all the years that the English had been on the Gold Coast, the working of the gold that had originally given the country its name had been left entirely in the hands of the natives and nothing had been done by anyone but the Portuguese to introduce improved methods ; but now the first attempts were made to open up and explore the auriferous districts and several companies were formed. The first of these was a French company, the African Gold Coast Company, in which M. Bonnat was interested. These pioneers of what was destined to become an important industry landed at Axim on the 10th of April 1877 and went to Awudua. After spending several months in prospecting, they, in February 1878, obtained a concession at Takwa, a village situated among ranges of hills in the Apinto district of Wassaw. This was known as Bonnat's Concession. Other companies soon followed when the richness of the ore became known, but very little progress was made for some years owing to the natural difficulties attending mining operations in such a country.

In September 1877 [1] a quarrel arose between Numbers 1 (Bentil) and 2 (Anafu) Companies in Cape Coast over a question of precedence. The Bentils had always claimed the post of honour and marched in the rear, but the Anafus now disputed their right to do so and a fight followed in which firearms were freely used, six or seven men being killed and a great number wounded. Eventually the riot was quelled by the military and the ringleaders secured, four of whom, amongst whom were the rival captains, being sentenced to death and hanged.

As has been mentioned already, the eastern frontier of the Colony was removed to Adafia after the Treaty of Jella Koffi, and this new territory became the Kitta district. Only two-thirds of this district belonged to the Awunas, with whom alone the treaty had been made, the remaining third being occupied by the Agbosomis. They, however, had raised no objections at the time, and when they did protest two years later the new arrangement had already become firmly established and it was too late.

[1] One date given is 9–11th of September 1879.

The Kitta district is really on the Slave Coast and differs in its formation from the Gold Coast proper. The extensive system of lagoons, which is the leading characteristic of this part of the West African coast, commences immediately to the east of the River Volta, and the Kitta district really consists of a narrow sandy beach about forty miles in length and varying from a few hundred yards to about two miles in breadth. Behind this sandy ridge is the Kitta Lagoon, an extensive sheet of water communicating with the Volta River and containing a large number of islands on which the principal Awuna towns and villages are built. This lagoon extends eastward to within a few miles of Adafia, and the people were not slow to avail themselves of the exceptional facilities it offered for smuggling. The European traders aided and abetted them in this by establishing stores at Danu, a village about a mile beyond the frontier, where they landed all their goods duty free, but, when buying native produce at their factories in Kitta, gave the people orders for goods on these stores at Danu in payment. By these means they not only evaded the payment of duty on their imports and made a far larger profit than they could otherwise have done, but enjoyed the protection of the Government for the produce they purchased for export, while leaving all the risk of smuggling to their African confederates, who, after a short trip overland to the head of the lagoon, distributed the goods by means of canoes. The result of this was that spirits could be bought in Kitta for less than the amount of the duty chargeable on them, and the revenue of the whole district was not enough to cover the expense of its administration.

No one was more active in this dishonest trade than the notorious Geraldo de Lema, who, since the abolition of the Slave Trade had made his former occupation unprofitable, had been busy supplying the Awunas and other tribes with cheap spirits, powder, guns and other goods, all of which were smuggled in this way. It will be remembered that in November 1868 Sir Arthur Kennedy had offered a reward of £200 for his arrest, but without success, and had caused his house at Voji to be destroyed. Since

that time de Lema had openly visited Accra and Cape
Coast on at least two occasions, but the fact that he was a
wanted man seems to have been lost sight of during the
excitement of the Ashanti invasion and no notice had been
taken of him.   He had now returned to Voji and had other
establishments at Agbosomi and inland, and, in 1878, was
the cause of a fresh outbreak of the Awunas.

In January 1878 Lieutenant A. B. Ellis [1] of the 1st West
India Regiment was appointed Commissioner of the Kitta
district.   He quickly realized that something must be done
to stop this illicit traffic ; but, since there were but four
policemen in the whole district, only two of whom could be
on duty at any one time, it was obviously impossible for
them to patrol it effectively.   Mr. Ellis therefore organized
patrols of the Gold Coast Constabulary then stationed
there.   One night a party of 100 armed smugglers was
intercepted at Adafia, and a scuffle took place in which one
of the smugglers was killed and three Hausas were wounded.
The goods, however, were captured, and so many other
seizures followed in quick succession that the people soon
came to the conclusion that the risk was too great to be
incurred and that smuggling could no longer be made to
pay.   The consequence was that the trade of Danu was
practically ruined, and by June the revenue of the district
had risen from £200 to £1,200 a month.

This result, though highly satisfactory to the Government, pleased neither the traders nor the Awunas.   No one,
however, was more exasperated at this new turn of affairs,
or stood to lose more by it, than Geraldo de Lema.   He had
enormous influence with the Awunas, who at the best of
times were a turbulent and unruly people, and found little
difficulty in inciting them to action—a task in which he is
alleged to have been supported by the other traders, who,
though they were careful to act less openly, were equally
interested in the issue.   Towards the end of September, a
meeting of all the Chiefs was held in Awuna, at which the
question was fully discussed.   The younger Chiefs were

[1] The author of *A History of the Gold Coast of West Africa* and other
works.

anxious to declare war against the Government, but the older ones favoured the less perilous method of assassinating the District Commissioner, to whose personal actions they attributed their losses. Rumours of hostilities soon became current and there was a very noticeable increase in the quantities of guns and ammunition taken out of bond and sold by the traders, who, as usual, were quite ready to profit by the possibility of trouble. No open move was made, however, until towards the latter end of October.

On the 23rd of that month Mr. Ellis crossed the lagoon with Captain Laver, the master of a merchant ship then lying in the roads, for a day's shooting. They went in a boat manned by four Accra canoemen and took the Constabulary bugler with them to act as interpreter. On their way back during the afternoon, they pulled in towards an Awuna town, intending to buy some coco-nuts ; but the shore was fenced in by extensive reed-beds intersected by tortuous and shallow channels, and before they reached the landing-place the boat grounded. Thirty or more men were now seen charging down towards the boat armed with cutlasses, but, fortunately, as they had shore distance to cover, they did not all reach it at once. The first man to arrive wounded a canoeman in the head and then attacked Mr. Ellis, who promptly fired at him. The ball passed through the Awuna's chest and wounded another man who was coming up behind him, but the first man still came on and aimed another blow at the Commissioner, which caught him on the shoulder, but the point of the cutlass had fouled the flapping sail, which broke the force of the blow and probably saved his life. A hand-to-hand struggle then ensued, in which Captain Laver was also wounded ; but several shots fired into the advancing crowd made the Awunas hesitate and gave the canoemen an opportunity to jump overboard and push the boat off into deep water ; but, in the excitement of the moment, they missed the channel by which they had come and lost themselves among the reed-beds. This caused some delay, and when at last they reached the open water, they found themselves pursued by several canoes filled with armed men, who made frantic efforts to overtake them or to attract the attention of the inhabitants of some islands which they were bound to pass. The sail, however, gave the boat's crew an advantage, and they steadily drew ahead and reached Kitta in safety at sundown.

After this deliberate attempt to murder the District Commissioner, the hostility of the Awunas was no longer in doubt. Next day the market-place at Kitta, where thousands of people were usually busy buying and selling, was absolutely deserted, and, since the town was dependent for its food supply on what was brought across the lagoon, the position was becoming alarming. Runners were immediately sent to call in all the outlying detachments, but there were only 120 Constabulary in the whole district and a message was therefore sent to Accra asking for reinforcements. Shelter trenches were dug and sentries posted round the town at night, for the Awunas, unlike the Ashantis, rather favour night attacks.

At half-past two on the morning of the 27th, a number of canoes were seen creeping up the lagoon and the "alarm" was sounded : three rockets were then fired, and the enemy, finding the defenders were on the alert, drew off. Two days later Captain Hay, the Acting Colonial Secretary, arrived from Accra with 89 Hausas and a 7-pounder gun. The next afternoon, the 30th, fully 2,000 Awunas were reported to be encamped about four miles to the east of Kitta, and at half-past nine that night their drums were heard approaching and the fort was attacked. Torrents of rain were pouring down, the night was pitch dark, and the garrison had a most uncomfortable time when they turned out to man the trenches, which were all full of water. The Awunas fired several shots, but it was impossible to see them and they did no damage, for they were not firing at the men, but at the fort, the white walls of which were just discernible in the darkness, and after waiting two hours without any further sign from the enemy the garrison turned in again.

On the 2nd of November H.M.S. *Boxer* arrived in the roads, and efforts were made to arrange a meeting with the Chiefs, but for several days nothing was settled. The Awunas wanted the officers to go to their town unattended and unarmed ; but it was eventually agreed that the Chiefs should come to Kitta on the 7th, but should not be required to enter the fort, and that the officers should go into the town alone and unarmed. to meet them. At three o'clock on the morning of the 6th, the sentries on the east side of the town were fired upon and a number of houses were set on fire. These houses were all Government property, so that it was evident that the outbreak was the work of incendiaries in the town itself : the police barracks, too, were fired over the men's heads the next night. Nothing was arranged at the meeting with the Chiefs on the 7th, and, on the 8th, the Chief Justice, Mr. Jackson, arrived to hold an enquiry into the cause of the disturbances. With the aid of some of the Chiefs who were themselves engaged in trade and could not afford to incur the heavy losses they would suffer if it was interrupted by hostilities, the Awunas were induced to withdraw their forces, but nothing was done to punish them for their revolt.

In the following year, in order to increase the difficulty of smuggling, the eastern frontier was moved to Aflao. This step, however, although it made smuggling more difficult, did not wholly prevent it ; nor was Geraldo de Lema, the chief instigator of the recent disturbances, secured. A preliminary agreement was made on the 1st of December 1879 and a treaty signed on the 6th. At the same time a treaty [1] was made with the Agbosomis, whose exact relationship to the Government it was necessary to define, since they had protested against the annexation of their land after the treaty of Jella Koffi. This was signed at Kitta Fort on the 2nd of December. The Chiefs acknowledged the jurisdiction of the Queen over their seaboard and for a distance of two miles inland from high water-mark, and her right to impose duties and taxes. They also promised not to permit human sacrifices, slave dealing or murders within their territory, and to assist the

[1] For full text, *vide* Sarbah, *Fanti National Constitution*, p. 155.

officers of the Crown in the apprehension of offenders and escaped criminals. In return for these concessions they were to receive an annual payment of 1,125 dollars and permission to import twenty puncheons of rum and sixty cases of gin each year free of duty. They experienced great difficulty, however, in getting these terms fulfilled, and had to petition the Governor in February 1884 for payment of £937 10s. and the right to land eighty puncheons of rum and 240 cases of gin that were then owing to them. In the end, after certain payments had been made, the claims of the Agbosomis under this treaty were, in 1886, commuted by the payment of £1,400.

The Ashantis, ever since their conquest of Jabin, had been busily engaged in re-establishing their rule in that province and in improving their armament. Their experiences during the recent campaign had taught them the value of breech-loading rifles and disciplined troops, and great numbers of these weapons had been obtained from Assini, and others from Danu via the Kitta Lagoon, River Volta and Jabin. Mensa had also formed a corps of Hausas, the majority of whom were men who had been tempted to desert from the Gold Coast Constabulary by his offers of double pay, free rations, and other local privileges and advantages. A German named Neilson, who had been wandering about the interior for some time, also made himself useful by bringing down recruits for this force from Salaga. The knowledge of drill possessed by these deserters, though meagre enough, made them useful as musketry and drill instructors, and they taught the Ashantis how to handle their newly acquired weapons. By 1878 the Government had at last realized that the interdiction on the importation of arms and ammunition was really doing more harm than good ; for while it had never prevented the Ashantis from obtaining all they wanted, it tied the hands of the protected tribes and indirectly cost the Government a large sum in loss of revenue. It was accordingly withdrawn, and no sooner had this been done than the Ashantis openly imported rifles at Cape Coast itself. This was still by far the most

important trading centre on the Coast, although the headquarters of the Government had been moved to Accra in
1876, on account of its supposed better climate and the
proximity of the Akwapim mountains, where a sanatorium
was established.   As many as 300 Snider rifles were imported on one occasion, in December 1878, consigned to
Prince Ansa, who is alleged to have personally drilled sixty
men belonging to the bodyguard of Opoku the King of
Bekwai, and he handed these weapons over to Ashantis
who were already in the town waiting for them.   This
proved too much for the people of Dunkwa, who seized
the carriers and brought them back to Cape Coast : they
were greatly surprised when they were told they had
done wrong and saw the Ashantis set out with an escort
who conducted them and their purchases safely to Prasu.
Having completed the settlement of Jabin and strengthened
themselves by the acquisition of these improved weapons,
the Ashantis began to look round for fresh territory and
turned their attention to Jaman and Adansi.

Now Jaman was a fairly powerful state which had given
the Ashantis trouble on more than one occasion in the
past, and the Adansis, though weak enough in themselves,
were believed to be under the protection of the English.
It was decided, therefore, to proceed diplomatically and
not to resort to force until other means had failed.   There
was in Kumasi at the time an unprincipled and semi-
educated coast native named Huydecooper, who had formerly
been employed as a clerk in one of the Government offices
but was now making himself useful in various ways to
King Mensa.   This man now utilized his knowledge of
official forms to draw up fictitious despatches, and, accompanied by the German Neilson and a number of Court
officials from Kumasi, set out for Bontuku the capital of
Jaman.   The whole affair was arranged under the superin-
tendence of Prince Ansa, and the object of the embassy
was to inform the King of Jaman that " the Queen of
England had given the whole country from Kerinkando,
near Assinee, to Dahomey, to the King of Ashanti, and
that the King of Gaman was to swear to be subject to

the King of Ashanti."[1] Fortunately, Neilson died on the road, for it is impossible to estimate what might have been the effect of this mission had it arrived under the leadership of an European. The exact cause of his death is in some doubt : it is said to have been due to fever, but some accounts state that this fever followed wounds that he had received from some Jamans he met on the road and whom he had first attacked. Huydecooper, however, continued his journey and delivered his message, supporting it with his forged despatches, and then said he was authorized to accept the allegiance of the Jaman King on behalf of Mensa.

At this time, affairs in Jaman were in a very unsettled state. Ajiman, the King, was most unpopular with his Chiefs, not more than two of whom were loyal to him, and the majority wished to depose him and put his half-brother Kokobo on the stool in his stead. This stronger party had no wish to quarrel with Ashanti ; but Ajiman's following was strongly opposed to Kumasi rule and was to some extent supported by the Sefwis, whose country lay a little farther south, and who had thrown off the Ashanti yoke in 1874. Huydecooper's message, supported as it was by the documents he had brought with him, bore such a semblance of truth that the King's party and the Sefwis, to whom the news had immediately been sent, were at first filled with alarm ; but they were still suspicious, and sent a joint embassy to Cape Coast to ask whether Huydecooper was really the accredited representative of the Government or not. These messengers arrived on the coast in April 1879, and, so soon as they learned that Huydecooper was an impostor, alleged that Ajiman had already made him a prisoner and asked that an officer might return with them as a guarantee of the accuracy of the reply they brought. This request was granted, and Mr. John Smith was sent on a mission to Sefwi and Jaman.

Mr. Smith left Cape Coast on the 15th of May 1879, and reached Wiosu, the capital of Sefwi, on the 10th of June. After a delay of twelve days while the Chiefs were being assembled, the Governor's message, to the effect that

[1] Ellis, *Land of Fetish*, p. 191.

Huydecooper was an impostor, was delivered and gave unbounded satisfaction. The King, Kwaku Che, wished to take an oath of allegiance to the British Government, but this was refused and Mr. Smith left for Bontuku. He reached Apemanim, a village some twelve miles from his destination, a month later. There he was met by messengers from Ajiman asking him to wait until the arrangements for his reception were completed, and he accordingly halted ; but when the 24th of July came and he had heard nothing more from the King, he continued his journey and entered Bontuku the same day.

After several delays, a meeting was held on the 30th, but it was of a purely ceremonial nature. In the meantime, however, Mr. Smith had not been idle and was now in possession of private information of the real state of affairs. He had learned, too, that Huydecooper had never been a prisoner, but had left Bontuku when the messengers started for the coast and was now living with Kokobo at Banda, on the borders of Ashanti, whence a party had recently raided and burned several villages belonging to Ajiman. After further delays, a second meeting was held on the 3rd of August, at which the Governor's message was delivered to the assembled Jaman Chiefs ; but they showed no sign of enthusiasm, and, although Ajiman promised to hand over Huydecooper in thirteen days' time and publicly stated that he had full confidence in the fidelity of all his Chiefs, he failed of course to carry out his promise, because the man was not in his possession and it was no longer in his power to secure him, but came privately to Mr. Smith complaining that every Chief but one was against him, but that he had not dared to disgrace them by saying so at the meeting. Another meeting was held on the 21st, at which the Chiefs refused to take the oath of allegiance to Ajiman on the ground that one of their number was absent ; but when they met again two days later they threw off all disguise, openly denounced Ajiman as their enemy, and flatly refused to have anything to do with him. Mr. Smith then left for the coast, having persuaded Ajiman, who had been anxious to accompany him for protection, to remain in his country and try to assert his position. Messengers overtook him forty-five miles from Bontuku however, who said that Kokobo had entered the capital the day after the mission left and was trying to oust the King from the stool. They implored Mr. Smith to return and interfere on behalf of Ajiman, but he declined.

Simultaneously with the despatch of Neilson and Huydecooper to Jaman, Mensa, encouraged by a renegade Adansi Chief named Menta, had sent other emissaries to induce the Adansis to return to their allegiance. These messengers met with considerable success, and, by dint of bribes and promises, managed to win over many of the Chiefs ; but the King of Adansi no sooner heard of these intrigues than he sent messengers post-haste to the coast to inform the Governor of what Mensa was doing. The Acting Colonial Secretary, Captain Hay, was sent to Fomana with full powers, and a letter was addressed to the King of Ashanti protesting against the acts of his servants, calling upon him to observe the third article of the Treaty of Fomana, and warning him to desist from further interference in the affairs of Adansi. This prompt action had the desired effect, and Mensa, finding himself out-manœuvred, recalled his envoys to Kumasi. But although the Ashantis were foiled for the time, they did not give up all hope of regaining their authority over Adansi. No sooner had the envoys been recalled than large numbers of Ashantis appeared simultaneously in all the coast towns and bought up enormous quantities of salt. This caused great alarm and was regarded as a certain sign of impending hostilities, for the Ashantis can only obtain salt from the coast and cannot go to war until they have a sufficient supply in hand. In time of peace they buy it as they require it ; but this sudden increase in the demand was interpreted as meaning that they were laying in a large stock because they expected the source of supply would soon be cut off by the closure of the roads during war. It subsequently became known that the invasion of Adansi was indeed contemplated, but was postponed on account of the presence of the British mission in Jaman.

These two missions had been sent in direct opposition to the declared British policy of non-intervention in the affairs of the interior which had done so much harm during the administration of Governor Strachan ; but Captain Lees, who was now Acting Governor, had had a long experience of the country and realized that this policy was quite unworkable.　But although he took this more sensible course, he was censured by the Secretary of State, Sir Michael Hicks Beach, who, while expressing a hope that " the King himself will recognize the propriety of observing the treaty," wrote : " The action which you took upon this occasion was of a character which might possibly have placed the local Government, and ultimately the Imperial Government, in some embarrassment, should the Ashantis decline to comply with the demands made upon them.　In dealing with savages the refusal of a demand can seldom be safely left unnoticed ; and demands should not, therefore, be made, unless there is a settled purpose beforehand to enforce them, directly or indirectly, in the event of their being refused.　Adansi is not within the Protectorate, and the question of requiring the observance of the third Article of the Treaty of Fommanah is one of external policy, on which the Government of the Gold Coast should refrain, unless in case of urgent necessity, from definite action until Her Majesty's Government had decided whether the action proposed was proper and opportune, having regard to the general interests of the Empire.　I have to request that in future you will bear this caution in mind, and that you will take no further steps in the matter now under consideration without the previous sanction of Her Majesty's Government."[1]

This was all very well, and nothing can be truer than that it is always foolish to give a direct order to an African that is not backed by the power and intention to enforce it ; but if the circumstances that had called forth the Governor's action were not to be regarded as matters of " urgent necessity," it is difficult to understand what,

[1] Parliamentary Paper, *Affairs of the Gold Coast and Threatened Ashanti Invasion*, 1881, p. 198.

short of actual armed invasion, would have been allowed inclusion in that category. The mere fact that, thanks to this absurd policy, the independence of Adansi was now the only remaining trace of the conquest of Ashanti, was sufficient reason to necessitate opposition to the King's schemes for recovering his authority over it ; nor could the urgency of the matter be in doubt, for those schemes had almost reached their consummation, and further delay would have been extremely dangerous. Had the Governor waited to obtain " the previous sanction of Her Majesty's Government " before taking action, that Government might conceivably have found itself in a position of " some embarrassment " caused by the re-annexation of Adansi by Ashanti and the final obliteration of the last trace of the victory of 1874. Possibly the Secretary of State thought that, having allowed Ashanti to regain everything else and repudiate payment of the indemnity, it would be a waste of time to incur any risk in defending the little that still remained. Here, in fact, was a definite reversion to that old timorous attitude towards Ashanti that had been the cause of so much difficulty and loss in the past, but which it might reasonably have been supposed had been finally abandoned when Sir Garnet Wolseley was sent out. Of course, Adansi in itself was useless to the Government. By failing to carry out their promise to migrate south of the Pra, the tribe had forfeited all right to protection ; but the Ashantis were not sure of this, and the independence of their former subjects was a continual thorn in their side and served a very useful purpose as a lasting monument of their defeat. Fortunately, Captain Lees was strong enough to act on his own responsibility, and this prohibition arrived too late to be effective. The mission to Adansi was entirely successful ; and that to Jaman, though it failed in its object of securing Huydecooper, was the means of obtaining valuable information and proved the hopelessness of relying on that tribe for any effective aid in the event of further trouble with Ashanti. It also, indirectly, prevented the immediate invasion of Adansi.

The failure of his plans in Adansi did much to increase

the unpopularity of Osai Mensa, which had indeed existed for some time, although it was only now becoming acute. The war party, led by Awua of Bantama the Commander-in-Chief, Opoku of Bekwai and others, were annoyed by his unwillingness to declare war on Adansi. They knew, of course, that they could easily drive the Adansis across the Pra, and felt that they would thus wipe out the disgrace of their losses in 1874 and remove the last trace of the stigma of defeat. They had not forgotten the possibility that such actions might involve them once more in trouble with the English, but they had now so far recovered their strength and derived so much confidence from the possession of numbers of breech-loading rifles and the apathy hitherto shown by the Government, that they no longer feared such a conflict, but believed that, even if another expedition were sent against them, they would now be able fully to hold their own. Opposed to this party were the King, the Queen-Mother, and the Court, whose policy was to remain on peaceful and friendly terms with the Government. Mensa himself was fully as anxious to regain Adansi as any one of his Chiefs, and, had it not been for his belief that any open movement against it would involve him in war with the English, he would not have hesitated ; but he could not forget that he owed his present position to the overthrow of his brother by them, and was not prepared to incur the risk of losing everything he had thereby gained. These various causes combined to make his position precarious, and his people began to talk more and more of the good old days when Kofi Karikari had reigned and to say that, whatever his shortcomings had been, he had at least been a man and had not shrunk from measuring his strength with the white men.

Ashanti custom had demanded that Karikari should commit suicide on his deposition, but he had failed to see things in that light and had retired to Akropong, one of the smaller villages of Kumasi, where he lived quietly with a few of his wives and attendants. He had now outlived the contempt he had brought on himself by this defiance of established precedent, and, seeing the course events were taking, began to intrigue with the Kokofus to regain the stool. Mensa countered this move by converting his Hausa troops into a body-guard, whose fidelity he purchased with gifts and promises, and, by arming them and all his immediate attendants and retainers with breech-loading rifles, succeeded in making himself so strong that he could not lightly be interfered with. By these means he easily maintained his position ; but he knew that nothing could ever secure him so effectively as the conquest of Adansi and set himself to find out how much truth there might be in his suspicions that the Government would actively resent it.

In June 1879 Mr. Ussher was appointed Governor, and, in accordance with the usual custom, sent messengers with presents to Kumasi to notify the King of his arrival. Mensa seized the opportunity thus given him to instruct his return messengers, after they had been to thank the Governor for his gifts, to go on to Cape Coast, where they remained, living in Prince Ansa's house for many months, watching the course of events, collecting all the information they could, and giving various frivolous excuses for their continued presence in the town. These messengers were a Kumasi Captain named Busumburu and the Chief Captain Engwi, who had been one of those to sign the Treaty of Fomana on behalf of the Kumasis. They were in constant communication with the King by means of letters written by Prince Ansa.

In the meantime, Mensa had made another effort to acquire ascendancy over Jaman, where Ajiman had fought a few successful skirmishes with the Kokobo faction. In October or November 1880 he sent messengers to Ajiman representing that he (Mensa) had paid a large sum of money to the Queen of England in compensation, and that she had thereupon agreed that the whole Jaman territory should be transferred to his rule. On the 1st of December 1880 Governor Ussher died at Christiansborg Castle, and a few days later Jaman messengers arrived bringing this report to Mr. W. Brandford Griffith, the Lieutenant-Governor, who of course contradicted it.

The war party in Kumasi had now joined the Kokofus in their intrigues with Kofi Karikari, and Mensa's position was daily becoming more and more insecure. He was also greatly alarmed by the actions of Asafu Agai, the ex-King of Jabin, who was once more notoriously conspiring with King Taki of Accra to aid him in an attempt to regain his kingdom. The Jabins had always been one of the strongest tribes in Ashanti, and Mensa, in the midst of his other troubles, viewed the prospect of an attack by them and their coast allies with no small alarm. Asafu Agai was deported to Lagos and Taki was imprisoned in Elmina Castle, but Mensa still nursed a grievance against the Government for having allowed them to carry on these intrigues for so long while living under its protection.

During December 1880 various rumours reached the coast that Ashanti was going to war. Mr. Buhl, the Secretary of the Basel Mission, reported having heard from Mr. Ramseyer, who was then at Abetifi, that there was much talk of hostile preparations, and Chief Tabu of Adansi informed the District Commissioner at Cape Coast that Opoku the King of Bekwai had publicly sworn to restore to the King's rule first Adansi and then Denkera.

CHAPTER XI

1881

By the beginning of the year 1881 the tension in Kumasi
had become acute and an open rupture between the Court
and war parties was imminent. It was only averted by
the escape into the Protectorate of a person to whose
presence in Kumasi the Achantis attached much importance,
and whose freedom they feared might upset all their plans
and perhaps involve them in serious difficulties with Jaman.
This was one Awusu Tasiamandi, who presented himself at
the Castle at Elmina on the 18th of January and claimed
protection, saying that he had fled from Kumasi because
he had incurred Mensa's displeasure and feared the consequences.

This Awusu was a person of some importance. His
grandmother, Tambia, was the Queen-Mother of Jaman,
who had been brought a prisoner to Kumasi during the
Ashanti-Jaman war in 1818 and had there married Odu-
mata, an influential Ashanti Chief, and borne a daughter.
This daughter had afterwards married Prince Kujo of
Kumasi, who was then Heir-Apparent, and became the
mother of this Awusu, who had been left in Kumasi when
his relations were released and had lived there for many
years. His elder brother had been allowed to return to
Jaman, but had died very soon afterwards, not without
strong suspicion of foul play. Awusu, therefore, was a
prince of Jaman on his mother's side, which is the only
one of which the Akans take any account, and a possible
heir to the stool of that country. Hence the excitement

1881
CHAP. XI

and consternation at his escape ; for his presence in Jaman
at this time would have been fatal to the success of Kokobo,
who had the support of Ashanti. It was for this reason
that he had always been detained in Kumasi, although it
is alleged that the Jamans had once sent as much as 1,000
peredwins (nearly £8,000) to secure his release. Moreover,
being so nearly connected on his father's side with the
reigning house of Ashanti, he was in possession of much
information that it was important to keep from the Jamans
during the present unsettled state of affairs.

According to Awusu's own statement, he was charged
with having seized a man who had stolen his " gold book "
—probably one of the charms consisting of a verse of the
Koran encased in gold—and Mensa, having found him in
the wrong, had decided that he should be punished ;
whereupon he had run away to the coast. He asked to be
sent under escort to Jaman, and was told he was free to
go wherever he chose, but that the Governor could not
undertake to have him escorted anywhere. The anxiety
of the Ashantis to recapture him was undoubtedly due
more to their fear that he might reach Jaman than to any
wish to punish him for his offence, and his escape at this
critical time was just sufficient to upset the balance of
power between the Court and the war party by which
the latter had hitherto been held in check. Mensa, therefore, was overruled in his own Council, as more than one
of his predecessors had been ; but though Awua of Bantama swore the King's Oath that he would drive the
Adansis across the Pra and went to his town to call out his
men, Mensa afterwards brought all his influence to bear
on the principal Chiefs and succeeded in persuading them
to postpone any hostile preparations until he had first
lodged a formal demand with the Government for the
surrender of the fugitive.

The day after Awusu reached Cape Coast a messenger,
Anani, arrived with three Court criers bearing the Golden
Axe to demand his return. Busumburu and Engwi, the
two Captains who had been waiting in Cape Coast and
collecting news, followed Anani over to Elmina on the 19th,

when they demanded an audience with the Governor. This was immediately granted, and the messenger then stated that the King had sent him to inform the Governor that Awusu had been enticed by an Assin trader named Amankra to run away from Kumasi and enter the Protectorate, and that he therefore requested that he should be compelled to return and that Amankra should also be given up for having betrayed the friendship the King had shown him for so many years. It was further alleged that Amankra had recently visited Bontuku and obtained money from the King of Jaman by promising to persuade Awusu to go there. The Governor replied that since Awusu did not appear to have committed any crime and was now living under British protection, he had no power to give him up, nor even to prevent him from visiting Jaman; but that he was free to go whithersoever he pleased.

These charges against Amankra may possibly have been genuine enough, but there was no evidence to show that there was any real foundation for them and they were categorically denied by both Awusu and Amankra, neither of whom had any real interest in concealing the truth. According to them, Awusu only met Amankra when he reached Kwisa, and, having known him in Kumasi, appealed to him to conduct him to the Governor. Amankra, by acceding to this request, incurred the anger of the King, who considered that he had at least aided and abetted Awusu in his flight, and Mensa's resentment was turned against the whole Assin tribe.

What happened after this will never be known with certainty. Ellis, who, though he was not himself present at the palaver, arrived about ten days after it was over and seems to have interviewed everyone who was there, says: " As to what followed there was a serious difference of opinion. Some said that Enguie then stated that the Assins were people who always caused palavers between Ashanti and the Protectorate, and that the King said if the Lieutenant-Governor would not give up Awoosoo he would invade Assin. Those who held to this version further stated that Busumburu at once got up and confirmed this statement, and that the Lieutenant-Governor thereupon called Enguie's attention to the treaty of Fommanah, and pointed out to him that an invasion of Assin meant war with England. Other officers who were present at the audience positively declared that nothing of the sort had occurred, and that Enguie had at the audience made no threat of invasion ; but that, as it had been reported that he had said to the interpreter, informally, and in the course of conversation at the interpreter's house, that if Awoosoo were not given up the King would take Assin, the treaty of 1874 was shown to him. For my part, I am inclined to believe that this latter account is the correct one ; but it is a question which can never be satisfactorily settled, as the evidence is so conflicting." [1]

At the meeting of the Executive Council held in Cape Coast Castle on the 22nd, at which this subject was discussed, the Lieutenant-Governor stated that Engwi had said the King " would attack the Assins . . . if the Governor would not order the return of Awusu to Kumasi." But here again he was only speaking from memory, and all the contemporary papers show that great excitement, even approaching panic, prevailed amongst the Gold Coast officials at the time. It is therefore quite possible that Mr. Griffith may have been mistaken, and, in the light of subsequent events, it seems fairly certain that Mensa, at any rate, never authorized any such threat, but that an independent statement volunteered by the interpreter was erroneously believed to have been made by the Ashanti envoy. These interpreters are rather prone to offer comments and remarks of their own which, though only intended to assist and explain, often tend to confuse. On this occasion, moreover, the regular official, Davis, was not employed, but the interpretation was left to a young clerk in the Colonial Secretary's office named Quansah. Interpretation may appear to be an easy task ; but it requires a very extensive knowledge of both languages and much care on the part of those who undertake it to ensure a correct rendering of the meaning of all that is

[1] Ellis, *Land of Fetish*, p. 211.

said, and it is notorious that those not accustomed to the duty are, more than any others, liable to convey an erroneous impression. On a subsequent occasion, when both Engwi and Busumburu denied having made any such statement, the question was referred to the regular inter- preter Davis, who then said nothing about any formal threat having been made, but merely stated that Engwi had told him at his house that if Awusu was not given up the Ashantis would attack Assin.

Against this it may be said that when Mr. Griffith's letter to the King giving his version of what took place at the meeting was read over to the ambassadors they raised no objection to it, and Ellis says : " The axe was accompanied by an additional emblem which did threaten hostilities. This was a facsimile in gold of a portion of the earthen-nest of a mason-wasp, which escaped the notice of all Colonial officials, with but one exception, or was con- sidered by them unworthy of notice. This emblem denoted that if the affair on which the Golden Axe was sent were not settled to the satisfaction of the Ashantis they would use their stings, or, in other words, endeavour to attain their ends by force. So little was this symbol understood in Colonial circles that no explanation of its presence or meaning was ever at any time demanded from the Ashantis, not even when, later, they were protesting that they had never threatened or wished for war." [1]   This explanation of the meaning of the wasps' nest is approxi- mately correct. It is, however, an emblem of protest only, which, according to the Ashantis, is sent to any person or tribe, with whom there has been a former misunderstanding followed by peace, on the appearance of a fresh probable cause of dissension, as a combined protest and warning. It is not a declaration of war, but, as in the case of the Golden Axe, merely shows that the subject under discussion is deemed of great importance, and, consequently but indirectly, implies that the Ashantis, if they fail to get satisfaction peaceably, may think it worth fighting for.

On the other hand, it is quite possible that the message

[1] Ellis, *Land of Fetish*, p. 212.

may have originated in Kumasi without the King's knowledge. It was notorious that there was at this time a
strong war party in the Council which was opposed to Mensa
and the Court, and it is not impossible that they may have
made some such threat which was now repeated, though
their objective was Adansi rather than Assin. Even so, it
is not likely that the message was sent to the Governor,
but that Engwi, always a truculent individual, merely lost
his temper, either at the meeting or in the interpreter's
house, and boastfully repeated what he had heard from
the other Ashantis. Had the threat been sent officially,
whether by the King or Council, it would indeed have been
extraordinary if the official envoy himself had failed to
make it, but had left it to two men who had been living on
the coast for many months to complete the message that
he had been charged to deliver. Mensa indeed, in a later
message, distinctly stated that the axe had been sent
without his knowledge, and although it would be unwise
to accept as gospel all that an Ashanti might say on his
own behalf, there does not appear, in this instance at any
rate, to be any absolute reason for disbelieving him, since
his statements are in perfect accord with the conditions
known to have existed in the capital at the time. The only
other possible explanation of the facts would be that Mensa,
fearing to commit himself by making a definite threat,
had purposely arranged that it should be made by Engwi
instead of his own messenger, so that, when his plan failed,
he might be able to declare his own innocence and disclaim
all responsibility for the statement on the ground that
it was unauthorized. This, indeed, is exactly what some
accuse him of having done ; but the charge is based on
surmise only, and it is one of those instances in which
duplicity has been alleged against the Ashantis without
sufficient justification.

On one point alone is there no room for doubt. The
threat of invasion was made at one time or another ; but
whether in accordance with instructions from Kumasi or
as an irresponsible statement by Engwi can never now
be settled. Either Engwi's statement was quite un-

authorized, or some of Mensa's subsequent acts show
the most consummate diplomacy. On the whole, it seems
most probable that the King never sent any direct threat,
but bore in mind the possible alternative of resorting to
force if his demand was not complied with and circumstances seemed to favour a chance of success.

Be this as it may, it was firmly believed that a definite
threat of invasion had been made, and that the sending
of the Golden Axe was equivalent to a declaration of war.
The true significance of this emblem has already been
explained and will again be referred to later.[1] It had only
been sent because the point at issue was deemed of exceptional importance, and though it is true that if the
Ashantis thought a matter sufficiently urgent to require
the presence of this axe they might also consider it worth
fighting for if necessary, the axe in itself bore no such
menace. Alarm approaching panic seized all the officials,
who believed, or professed to believe, that the Ashanti
army might appear before the forts at almost any moment.
Their conduct was ridiculous and absurd to a degree, and
was, in fact, little short of disgraceful. The natives alone
kept their heads and remained quietly in their villages,
tilling their farms and carrying on their daily avocations
as usual. The slightest acquaintance with the previous
history of the country would have convinced anyone that,
had there been the least danger, or had an Ashanti army,
as was at one time believed, already marched towards the
coast, timely warning would have been given, and the
villagers would have been flocking into the towns to seek
the protection of the forts. The numerous Ashantis living
on or trading to the coast would at once have returned
to their own country, and others would not have continued
to come down as they now did. Moreover, the ambassadors
bearing the axe had only left Cape Coast on their return
journey on the 26th of January and could not have much
more than crossed the Pra by the end of the month ; yet
on the 1st of February an alarm was raised at dead of night
that the Ashantis were advancing and were already within

[1] *Vide* pp. 240–42.

three miles of the Castle walls. The garrison was got under
arms, a patrol was sent out, and, for some none too evident
reason, all the lights in the Castle were extinguished. No
refugees had yet come in ; it was well known that the
Ashantis never attacked at night, and it was absolutely
impossible that any army could even have left the capital
without some warning having been received ; nor were the
Ashantis at all prone to such rapid movements as those
with which they were now credited.

The Lieutenant-Governor's conviction that an invasion
was imminent was shown by other signs than these local
manifestations of nervousness. Troops were requisitioned
from Sierra Leone and the West Indies, and Mr. Griffith
even paid the large sum of 1,000 guineas to the Captain
of the *Corisco* to proceed direct to Freetown and thence
to Madeira with his telegram to the Secretary of State.
Four hundred men were ordered from the West Indies ;
two companies were sent down from Sierra Leone in the
Cameroon, arriving on the 2nd of February, and the
departure of the new Governor, Sir Samuel Rowe, was
hastened from England. Mr. Griffith moved into the
Castle, and the Europeans engaged in the gold-mines at
Takwa were officially warned to fall back on the fort at
Axim. Seventy-five men of the Gold Coast Constabulary
with three 7-pounder guns were sent under Mr. Newenham
to reinforce the existing detachment of forty men at Prasu,
where his orders were to act strictly on the defensive,
and a supporting force of forty more men was posted at
Mansu. At Elmina, the walls of the Castle, a fortress that
is absolutely impregnable to any force unprovided with
artillery, were heightened with sand-bags, and redoubts
were raised on Java Hill and in the Government Garden,
which it was proposed should be manned by men landed
from the fleet. The Senior Naval Officer, however, would
only consent to land his men if he himself were given the
command of the military operations ; but since it was
laid down in the Queen's Regulations that naval officers
should not command troops on shore, this created a fresh
difficulty, which was got over by giving him the command

of the Hausa Constabulary. About fifty seamen and
marines were then landed, but after sitting in Elmina Castle
for three days were re-embarked. The Naval Commandant, however, during his short term of authority, had
withdrawn the detachments of Constabulary from Prasu
and Mansu, and this movement had, moreover, been carried
out in such haste that carriers could not be found for a
large quantity of Snider ammunition, which had consequently been left behind for the Ashantis to seize or not
as they liked. The reason he gave for this extraordinary
proceeding was that the detachment might be in danger
of being cut off. " He did not seem to be aware that it was
the duty of outposts to delay the advance of an enemy
without compromising their own retreat, and to fall back
slowly, sending full information to the main body. . . . Had
the enemy advanced we should have had to depend on the
ignorant and panic-stricken natives for intelligence, and
should have had no reliable information as to the number,
line of march, and armament of the foe. In fact, it would
be difficult to imagine a more inexpedient step than this
withdrawal of our frontier post, for, in addition to weaken-
ing our military position, it naturally disheartened the
protected tribes and encouraged the Ashantis." [1]

At the suggestion of Captain Bolton of the 1st West
India Regiment, who was commanding the troops on the
Gold Coast, a request was sent to England that not fewer
than 7,000 men should be held in readiness for embarkation, although in the last war, when the Ashantis were fully
as strong as if not stronger than they now were, Sir Garnet
Wolseley had defeated them and destroyed their capital
with only two battalions and a few details totalling 2,587 of
all ranks. It was decided to defend only Axim, Elmina,
Cape Coast, Anamabo and Accra, and the Ashantis were
presumably to be allowed to ravage all the rest of the
country unmolested and take possession of and occupy
any other forts that took their fancy. Commissioners
were sent to the different tribes to organize their forces
and collect information, and 15,000 flint-lock guns were

[1] Ellis, *Land of Fetish*, p. 219.

ordered from England, with 50,000 spare flints, 400 quarter barrels of gunpowder, as much as 50 tons of buck-shot and 10,000 buck-shot cartridges.

News of these warlike preparations was, of course, sent post-haste to Kumasi by the King's agents on the coast. Their effect must be judged according to which theory of Mensa's attitude is accepted as the true one. If he really was meditating an attack on the Protectorate, he was now convinced that the Government was not to be taken unawares ; but if, as seems more likely, his intentions were peaceable, these preparations cannot have failed to annoy and surprise him. He at any rate made it appear that the latter was the case, and two messengers were immediately despatched to ask the Governor for an explanation. They arrived on the 8th of February and delivered the following verbal message : " King says what pass for some years ago that is all finished. He is looking all his people to come down for trade. A report reached the King, the officers and Haussa soldiers are making bridges to cross the Prah. The King has therefore sent his sword-bearer and Court cryer to ask his friend the Governor why he is going to fight." [1] These messengers stated that they had met the returning embassy with the Golden Axe one day's journey from the capital, and, unless both parties had travelled with most unusual speed, this must have been true. The fact therefore that Mensa had despatched these men before he had received the Governor's reply to his request goes far to support the belief that his astonishment was genuine, and that he, at least, was unconscious of having given any ground of offence. At the same time, it is possible that he may have heard the result of the mission before his messengers returned. Both the Ashantis and Adansis seem to have been convinced that the English were about to attack Kumasi, and the King sent messengers to Mr. Newenham, the officer commanding the detachment at Prasu, asking that he might be given timely warning of the advance. Moreover, two German missionaries,

[1] Parliamentary Paper, *Affairs of the Gold Coast and Threatened Ashanti Invasion*, 1881, p. 41.

Messrs. Buck and Huppenbauer, who were in Kumasi from the 5th to the 12th of February, reported on the 18th that they had found the King was averse to war and that they had seen no signs of preparation for it, though the Ashantis would doubtless defend themselves if attacked.

An exchange of words occurred at the meeting between the Governor and these messengers which by no means added to the dignity of the former. One of the messengers had stated, as showing hostile intent on the part of the Government, that the Adansis were clearing the road to Kumasi, and the Governor replied that they were required to do so by the Treaty of Fomana and expressed a hope that the Ashantis were keeping their portion of the road open also. The messengers laughed ; and Mr. Griffith, seemingly annoyed at this and knowing very well that the English had consistently neglected their own part of the road, then tried to cast doubts on their credentials and the authenticity of their message, asking how he was to know that they came from the King at all. They replied by pointing to the gold plaques they wore on their breasts— the insignia of their office—and Engwi and Busumburu both vouched for it that they truly came from the King ; but the Governor professed ignorance of the meaning of these emblems and said that Mensa should have sent him something he had seen before. This gave the sarcastic Engwi his opportunity, and he promptly retorted that, since the Golden Axe was the only portion of the Ashanti regalia that the Governor had yet seen, and that had not again reached Kumasi when the present messengers left, it was impossible for them to have brought it " even if his Excellency would like to see it again, which I doubt." [1]

On the 30th of January Prince Ansa returned from Axim, where he had been engaged in some mysterious business. It was strongly suspected that he had been arranging for the transmission to Kumasi of some three tons of gunpowder that was known to have been smuggled into the country through Apollonia ; for all the people of this district, with the exception of Blay's subjects, were

[1] Ellis, *Land of Fetish*, p. 222.

again in covert league with the Ashantis. The prospect of hostilities, indeed, had revealed a fact that had not been suspected before—namely, that the tribes of the Protectorate were no more united now than they had been in 1873. The loyalty of the Ahantas barely existed in name, and that of the Axims was open to serious doubt ; the Accras flatly refused to provide a single man for the defence of the country unless their King, Taki, was first released from Elmina, and the Awunas again became so openly hostile that the Addas would not have dared to leave their towns to join any force that might have been raised. Ansa lost no time in visiting the Governor and assured him that the Ashantis had no hostile intention, protesting that Engwi and Busumburu, both of whom were living in his house, had denied making any threat of invasion. No words of Ansa, however, could carry any weight now. There had been a time when he had been listened to with eagerness and even with respect on any subject relating to the country of his birth, but suspicions of his good faith had been growing steadily, and several facts had recently come to light that more than sufficed to discredit him as a true friend and adviser of the Government. Suspicion against him had, indeed, been so strong that it had been found necessary to take him into the fort at Axim for protection during the latter part of his stay in that town.

On the 17th of February, a third embassy arrived in Cape Coast consisting of a Linguist Bendi, with whom were a sword-bearer Atjiempon Daban. and three Court criers. They were accompanied by an aged priestess, who threatened to invoke the powers of the fetish utterly to destroy the English and Fantis if they did not at once abandon their project of attacking Ashanti. These dire predictions, however, were only the irresponsible vapourings of an old woman, and she formed no part of the embassy and did not accompany it to Elmina. On the following day, the ambassadors, with Engwi and Busumburu, met the Governor in Elmina Castle, and Bendi then delivered his message. He declared that the King had no quarrel with the Assins, and that if any threat of invasion had been made by Engwi he had made it on his own responsibility, since it had formed no part of the King's message to the Governor. He went on to point out that, since Engwi had been living on the coast, he was as much under the Governor as under the King, and hinted that, as the Governor was well aware that he could not have been entrusted with the King's message, he should have taken the words of his accredited envoy alone as authorized and official. There was a great deal of sound sense in these remarks. The King further expressed his determination to observe the Treaty of Fomana, and disclaimed all intention of attacking any of the protected tribes, saying that he would never bring a single gun across the Pra, and that his only wish was to live on friendly terms with the Government as his ancestor Kwaku Dua had done in the time of Governor Maclean. He also formally denied that the Golden Axe bore any such meaning as had been ascribed to it. After Bendi had finished his speech, both Engwi and Busumburu stood up and solemnly declared that they had never spoken the words of which they were accused, and it was then, as has already been mentioned, that the point was referred to the interpreter Davis, who admitted that the remark had been passed in his own house, but said nothing about any formal threat having been made at the meeting. The general tenor of the King's message was peaceful and apologetic, and must be considered eminently satisfactory.

Sir Samuel Rowe, the new Governor appointed in succession to Mr. Ussher, was now expected on the Coast within a few days, and Mr. Griffith, who was only carrying on the administration of affairs pending his arrival, therefore decided to give no reply to the King's last two messages, but to leave them for him to deal with. Sir Samuel Rowe landed at Elmina on the 4th of March, but, instead of at once dealing with the Ashanti question and bringing the misunderstanding to a speedy and satisfactory conclusion, as he might easily have done, he ignored the King's apologies and explanatory messages and continued the hostile preparations begun by Mr. Griffith. The policy he

adopted was as dangerous as it was ridiculous and ex-
pensive, and very nearly resulted in forcing the Ashantis
into a war which he should have done his utmost to avert.
There are limits to the forbearance and self-abasement of
a proud and warlike nation like the Ashantis, who, even if
they are savages, have a very fair knowledge of diplomacy
and are themselves eminently courteous in all their official
dealings. They therefore strongly resented the slights
now cast upon them, and the hands of the war party were
proportionately strengthened. Mensa, indeed, had the
greatest difficulty in restraining his Chiefs, and when the
news reached Kumasi that the Government was arming
the protected tribes and preparing to invade Ashanti, he
at last gave way and war would have been made at once,
had not a message been received from Prince Ansa next
morning declaring the rumour to be unfounded. This
turned the scale once more in the King's favour, and the
Queen-Mother even threatened to commit suicide " on the
heads " [1] of the principal Chiefs if they did not immediately
abandon their hostile intentions, while the Queen of Kokofu
sent in to say that if Ashanti made war on the Protectorate
she and her people would immediately join the English.
This left Mensa supreme, and in proof of the sincerity of
his peaceable intentions a remark made by him at a
meeting of his Council at about this time may be quoted.
He said : " It is said that white men are coming across the
Prah. We have done nothing, we have no quarrel with
them. Let us sit still ; and, if they wish to fight, let them
fire the first shot." [2]

It is hard to divine what were the Governor's real
reasons for his extraordinary conduct. He may, on his
arrival, have failed to grasp the true state of affairs ; he
may have wished to feel his way and see what else would
happen before giving his answer, or, again, he may only have
had a vague idea of imitating the dilatoriness of the African.

---

[1] In Ashanti anyone committing suicide " on the head " of another
names him as his murderer before taking his own life, and the person
so named is held legally responsible for his death and punished accordingly.

[2] Ellis, *Land of Fetish*, p. 242.

Yet the position was clear enough and Sir Samuel Rowe
was no stranger to the country, so that these reasons seem
singularly insufficient, and it is far more probable that the
real explanation of his actions and delays is to be found
in the theory that gained general acceptance among the
Europeans on the Coast at the time—namely, that he was
well aware that if there ever had been any threat of invasion there certainly was none now, but that he wished,
by prolonging the negotiations and postponing the settlement of the dispute for as long as possible, to maintain
the feeling of anxiety and an appearance of danger, so
that, in the end, he might get the credit of having averted
a really imminent peril. If this really was his object, he
succeeded so well that on the 13th of March the hired
transport *Ararat* actually put in at Cape Coast on her way
to England with sick and wounded from Natal to pick
up the wounded from the Ashanti war.

On the very day that the Governor landed, Kotoko, a
messenger from the King of Adansi, saw him and reported
that although the Adansis, from their position, must be the
first to feel any aggression on the part of the Ashantis,
there had been no trouble since 1874, and there were no
Ashantis then in Adansi ; that they had heard the King
was collecting an army in his capital, but this was merely
intended for defence should he be attacked, and had not
been called together until after the receipt of news from
the coast that troops had been sent to Prasu and that the
road from Cape Coast was being cleared. The King of
Adansi, therefore, had sent him to inquire what these
warlike movements portended.

Two days later, on the 6th, Sir Samuel Rowe met the
Ashanti ambassadors in the Palaver Hall of Elmina Castle ;
but the time was almost entirely taken up with the customary compliments, and no real business was transacted.
The Governor, however, made a few vague remarks on the
military resources of England, which can only have sounded
to the Ashantis like a thinly veiled threat, and they expressed a wish that Prince Ansa might be sent for before
they met again and that they might be allowed to make

their statement through him. Ansa arrived from Cape Coast two days later, and the Ashantis then asked permission to send three of their number with a special message to the King ; but Sir Samuel Rowe now insisted that this simple request must be made without the mediation of Ansa, and, when this was done on the 11th, replied that they might do as they wished provided they made it perfectly clear to the King that the message was from themselves alone and in no way emanated from him.

Nothing more was done, and no attempt was made to bring about a satisfactory settlement of the difficulty, but, on the contrary, an even greater parade of warlike preparations was made than before. Commissioners were daily meeting Chiefs and ascertaining from them what number of men they were prepared to put in the field ; troops continued to arrive, and an expedition to the Pra was talked of. Mensa, who was kept duly posted with the latest news by runners from the coast, found his difficulties daily increasing. He could not understand what was happening and became more and more convinced that the English, for some reason of their own, were bent upon making war on him : he had sent a humble, peaceful and apologetic message ; but had received no reply. There was no precedent in the whole history of Anglo-Ashanti relations for such contemptuous treatment, and Mensa was now more than ever put to it to restrain his Chiefs, who were burning to avenge the insult. But for his really sincere desire for peace, war must now have ensued. He, however, determined to make one more effort ; but realizing that it would be hopeless to make any further appeal to the Government, he despatched his next messengers to the traders of Cape Coast.

This, his fourth embassy, consisted of four persons— Osai Bruni, Yow Wua, Kwamin Insia and Dantando—who reached Cape Coast on the 10th of March. Their arrival and the object of their mission were duly reported to the Governor by the District Commissioner, but their presence was purposely ignored until, on the 13th, they went over to Elmina of their own accord and saw Prince Ansa, whom

they asked to introduce them to the traders and to the
Superintendent of the Wesleyan Mission, whom they were
instructed to invite to reopen a station in Kumasi. They
also begged permission to submit their message to the
Governor before delivering it to the traders, but it was not
until the 16th that they were allowed to do so. They were
then informed that while he had no objection to their
meeting the traders, they must clearly understand that
any negotiations with them would not affect any reply
he might decide to send to the King.

On the 18th they met the traders at Cape Coast and
delivered the following message : " The King has sent us to
come to Prince Ansa and say ' Let our family differences be
at an end.' He sent us to Prince Ansa for him to take us
to the merchants of Cape Coast Castle for them to help
the King, and say to the Governor that if he, the King,
had done anything wrong in the matter of the message
with the axe, that he, the King, asked that the Governor
would pardon his mistake."[1] They added assurances of
the King's desire for peace and asked that a European
officer might be sent to Kumasi who could see for himself
that no preparations for war had been made. The next
day they returned to Elmina and reported that their
interview had been most unsatisfactory, and that the
traders had refused to have anything to do with the matter.
They said that this was because the King had not sent
them any presents, but it is quite as likely that it was
because they, too, had come to the conclusion that further
appeal to the Governor would be a mere waste of time.
Sir Samuel Rowe then dismissed the messengers with a
parting warning that the difficulty between the Government
and the King had not yet been settled or cleared up, and
they set out for Kumasi on the 20th to inform Mensa that
his friendly overtures had once more been treated with
contempt, and to report the continued hostile attitude of
the Government, which had more than ever been impressed
upon them by the arrival of the 2nd West India Regiment
under Colonel Justice while they were at Cape Coast on

[1] Ellis, *Land of Fetish*, p. 249.

1881
CHAP. XI

the 18th. This addition raised the strength of the troops on the Gold Coast to some 1,200 men, consisting of 950 West Indians and about 250 Hausas belonging to the Gold Coast Constabulary.

Whether or not the Governor really appreciated the tremendous risk he was running it is hard to say ; but Europeans, Fantis and Ashantis alike were now more than ever suspicious that, for some mysterious reason of his own, he was bent upon forcing on a war. How widespread this belief was, was shown by the arrival of forty messengers with two state swords from the King of Sefwi on the 28th of March, saying that he had heard the English were about to make war on Ashanti and asking for arms and ammunition to enable him to call out his people to assist the Government. Other messengers had arrived a month earlier repeating the former petition of the tribe to be allowed to come under British protection, but their request had been refused and they had been advised to ally themselves with the Jamans for mutual defence.

On the 21st of March a meeting of the Executive Council was held in Elmina Castle to consider the state of the relations between the Government and Ashanti, and more than one officer ventured to express the opinion that it was high time that some settlement of the recent troubles was effected. Captain Hope suggested that a message should be sent to Kumasi to conclude the matter, and Colonel Justice pointed out that these needless delays involved a greatly increased risk if the Ashantis really meant to make war, by giving them further time for their preparations. He, too, proposed that one or more European officers should be sent up to negotiate, while the Chief Justice said that although he was convinced that the Ashantis were most anxious for peace, " they seemed to believe that the white man intended to take Kumasi, and that great care should be taken to prevent them from being driven into war through fear of our aggression." [1] Sounder advice never was given ; but Sir Samuel Rowe

[1] *Vide* Minutes of Council, *Affairs of the Gold Coast and Threatened Ashanti Invasion*, 1881, p. 122.

overruled all these suggestions and said he could not think 1881
of incurring the risk of sending any officers to Kumasi. CHAP. XI
The excuse he gave was that " the way in which natives
of Africa treated ambassadors was against it." If he
really believed this, he had not profited much by his long
residence in the country, and showed a singular and
lamentable ignorance of Ashanti history and custom ; but
if he only feared for their health, it is noteworthy that he
did not hesitate soon afterwards to expose numbers of them,
quite needlessly, to the unhealthy influences of Prasu at
the commencement of the rainy season. In the end,
nothing was decided, and the conduct of affairs was left
entirely in the Governor's hands, the meeting of the
Council having only served the purpose ascribed by Bosman
to the Dutch Council.[1] The Secretary of State fully endorsed the remarks of the Chief Justice and expressed
confidence that the Governor would do everything possible
to remove any such idea from the King's mind : he urged
a speedy termination of the difficulty, which, as he said,
was undoubtedly capable of a peaceful solution.[2] How
little ground he really had for such hopes the relation of
Sir Samuel Rowe's subsequent doings will show.

The Ashantis had sent peaceful and unusually humble
messages, and all that was now necessary was that a
suitable reply should be given. Instead of doing this, however, the Governor persisted in his former line of conduct,
and, on the 23rd, two days after the meeting of the Council,
interviewed a number of Chiefs and discussed with them the
number of fighting men and carriers they were prepared
to furnish ; and daily, after the 25th, quantities of stores
were sent up country to Mansu. On the 30th yet another
messenger, Yow Mensa, arrived from Kumasi to announce
that a most important embassy, with no less a person than
Buachi Tintin the husband of the Queen-Mother at its head,
was on its way to the coast with special instructions from

---

[1] *Vide* vol. i, p. 135.
[2] *Vide* despatches dated 29th of April and 6th of May 1881, *Affairs
of the Gold Coast and Threatened Ashanti Invasion*, 1881, pp. 125 and
129.

the King. Private information confirmed this news, and it was unofficially explained that Buachi was coming down to beg the Governor's pardon and sue for peace.

On the 4th of April Sir Samuel Rowe left Elmina and started up country, taking several Chiefs, Prince Ansa, and the two Ashanti Captains Engwi and Busumburu with him. He reached Prasu on the 13th, where a total of nearly 1,000 men, including as many as thirteen European officers and a hundred Hausa troops, besides other Police, was then encamped. This absurd and purposeless expedition to the Pra very nearly wrecked everything, and it was by the merest chance that another Ashanti war was not the result. The Ashantis had been kept continually informed of all that passed on the coast, and the news of the arrival of more troops, of the meeting with the Fanti Chiefs at Elmina and of the despatch of men and stores to Prasu, were duly recounted at a large meeting of all the most powerful Chiefs in the kingdom. The conviction was naturally forced upon them that the Government was undoubtedly about to attack them. All their internal differences were put on one side in face of this national danger, and they once more became a united people and determined to defend their country at any cost. Mensa, however, humiliated and insulted though he had been by the Governor's treatment of his conciliatory messages, determined to make one final effort to secure peace and had sent Buachi's mission from the capital on the 3rd of April charged with a message such as had never yet been sent by any Ashanti ruler. At the same time, in preparation for the probable need of defending his kingdom, a force of about 15,000 men was concentrated at Amoafu to guard the approaches to the capital, and arrangements were completed for the rapid mobilization of the rest of the army if the necessity should arise. Buachi, however, had barely started when the news was received that the camp and stores at Mansu were being moved up to the Pra, where a large number of men were collecting. This seemed to Mensa to confirm his worst fears, and, believing that further appeal would be useless and that in making it he would only be sacrificing his little remaining dignity to no purpose, he sent express messengers, who overtook Buachi at Akankuasi, ordering him to halt, and then turned his whole attention to preparing for the struggle that he felt could no longer be avoided.

Fortunately the Governor gained some inkling of the critical state of affairs, and was at last forced to admit that the position he had taken up was untenable. He therefore found himself compelled to abandon his peculiar policy, and was himself forced to reopen negotiations by sending the messenger Yow Mensa to inform Buachi that he was waiting to receive him. So soon as he got this message, Buachi came on and arrived on the opposite bank of the Pra early on the morning of the 16th. Having sent into the camp and obtained permission to cross, he entered Prasu soon after midday. The number and rank of those who composed it were sufficient proof of the extraordinary importance attached to this mission. In addition to Buachi and his brother and son, there were two other princes of the blood—Buachi Wiamani and Buachi Atansa sons of the late King Kwaku Dua, and representatives of the Kings of Bekwai, Kokofu, Mampon, and Insuta, and of the Chief of Bantama, Yow Bedu the King's personal attendant, Yeboa representing the other members of the royal family, and numerous other Court officials with about 400 attendants and followers. The Governor formally received the embassy that afternoon and had a private interview with Buachi the next morning.

Buachi then told the Governor the purport of his message, but added, somewhat satirically, that as he had met him " at his farm " he would prefer to deliver it officially in one of Her Majesty's forts. It was therefore arranged that everyone should return as soon as possible to Elmina, where the final palavers were to be held. Buachi further explained that the King had sent down to ask for the surrender of Awusu, believing that he was making a perfectly reasonable request ; that any threat made by Engwi or anyone else was wholly unauthorized, and that the misunderstanding had arisen through Mr. Griffith's ignor-

ance of the customs of the country and could not have
happened if Governor Ussher had still been alive ; that Mr.
Griffith had misinterpreted the meaning of the Golden Axe,
and jumped to the conclusion that the Ashantis were about
to invade the Protectorate, whereas nothing of the kind
had ever been intended, and that if, instead of sending this
false news to England, he had taken the trouble to learn
the truth by sending to ask the King the meaning of his
message, he would have found out his mistake and his
messengers would have seen for themselves that the
Ashantis were not preparing for war. The King readily
admitted however, that since Engwi was his servant and
was alleged to have made this threat, he must accept
responsibility for his acts, unauthorized though they
might be, and he had therefore sent the highest persons
in his kingdom to say that " he is exceedingly sorry and
ashamed for the mistake of his servant, but that in the
matter of the axe the mistake is the mistake of the
Lieutenant-Governor." Buachi continued : " I am old
enough to know the meaning of every symbol in my
country, and I know that on no occasion has the Golden
Axe . . . ever been used by the Ashantis as a sign of a
declaration of war. We have in Ashanti two symbols,
both of which are used when we declare war. There is a
certain sword in my country in the keeping of the King.
When that sword is sent to another tribe by the King of
Ashanti, that is a declaration of war by Ashanti. There
is also a certain cap in my country, which is in the keeping
of the King, and if a messenger was charged with certain
negotiations, and, in the event of their not being successful,
was empowered to declare war, he would be entrusted by
the King with that cap, and if he did declare war, he
would put on that cap, and that would be a proof that
the declaration came from the King and nation. The true
meaning of the axe is this, the axe is a fetish. We believe
that some mysterious power attaches to it. . . . When the
King Kwaku Dua sent a messenger to Governor Maclean
respecting runaways, this axe was sent, and the palaver
was settled. The axe is supposed to be brought down

when there is a difficult palaver, and if it accompanies a mission that mission will surely succeed, and if the road is blocked, with the help of the axe the road will be opened ; it is a fetish axe, but is never sent with a war message. . . . The bearer of the axe has never failed in any mission on which he has been sent, and we believe that whatever request we make, if that request be supported by the presence of that axe, that request will be granted. The mistake that was made by the Lieutenant-Governor was that, because he did not himself understand the meaning of the axe, or the ways of our country, he accepted the meaning which the Fanti interpreter gave to the axe, and the Fantis do not know the ways of my country. I beg your Excellency, in the name of my master and stepson, to intercede for my master with the great Queen of England, and . . . I, as representing my master and stepson and the whole Ashanti nation, kneel humbly before you in token of submission." [1]

On the 19th a start was made for Elmina, where, on the 28th, the Ashanti ambassadors met the Adansis and a number of the Chiefs of the Protectorate. At noon on the 29th the meeting for the settlement of the differences between the Government and Ashanti was held in the Castle. Buachi then formally delivered his message, the gist of which has already been given. He now stated that since the King found that " through somebody's foolishness or mistake " the Government had been put to some expense, he had sent down a gift of gold " not to pay for the expenses which they had incurred, but as a proof of his friendship." The sum which was thus voluntarily offered amounted to 1,000 bendas (2,000 ounces).[2] The assurances of the King's desire for peace were reiterated, and Buachi concluded his speech by a further allusion to the Golden Axe. " The axe," he said, " belongs to the fetish : it is a sign of the fetish. In the time of Governor Maclean there was a dispute concerning a man : the axe

---

[1] Parliamentary Paper, *Affairs of the Gold Coast and Threatened Ashanti Invasion*, 1881, p. 138 *et seq.*
[2] Equivalent to about £7,600 sterling or £8,000 currency.

was sent, and the end was peace. Under Colonel Torrane a difference arose and the axe was again sent. The matter was settled amicably. To two other Governors the axe was sent, and the end was peace. In the present case the axe was sent as belonging to the fetish, to obtain our desires peaceably. It is, in fact, a sign of an extraordinary embassy. There are those who have said the axe means war ; so the King has heard. It was not so. It is not so Take no heed of this ; the King of Ashanti only wishes for peace."[1] The Governor replied that he would consider the King's message and offer and give his answer another day.

On the 3rd of May a review of the troops and Constabulary was held, after which Sir Samuel Rowe told Buachi that if he would pay over the gold the whole question would be referred to the Queen for final settlement. Five hundred ounces were paid on the 23rd, and at a meeting in the big hall of the Castle on the 30th a second instalment was paid, which brought the total amount up to about 1,200 ounces, and Buachi, at his own request, remained as a hostage for the balance which had not yet reached the coast. It was nearly all paid on the 8th of June and completed a month later, after which the embargo on the sale of powder, arms and salt was removed.

At this meeting on the 30th, however, a far more important concession was made than the mere payment of gold ; for Buachi then offered in the King's name and as a further proof of his wish for peace no less important an object than the Golden Axe itself. It had been sent down from Kumasi by a special messenger after a long discussion in the Council, and was surrendered on the distinct understanding that it was not to be kept in any of the forts, where it might be seen and ridiculed by the Fantis, but should be sent direct to the Queen. Buachi now presented it with the following words : " I now lay before your Excellency something which I think will prove to you that the King, my master, is really in earnest in saying

[1] Ellis, *Land of Fetish*, p. 308 *et seq.*

that he wishes for peace. This axe . . . is one of the most treasured emblems of sovereignty in my country. In sending this axe for ever away from our country, we are sending away that which is associated with all the greatest glories of the Ashanti kingdom. But as this axe has been the cause of such serious troubles between the Ashanti kingdom and the Queen of England, the King begs Her Most Gracious Majesty to accept it, feeling sure that while it is in Her Majesty's possession she will not allow it to be treated with disrespect, and hoping that it will be to her a proof of the earnestness with which the King of Ashanti desires the cultivation of friendly intercourse with Her Majesty's Government."[1] Quite apart from its value as evidence of the King's sincerity, the surrender of the Golden Axe went far to prove the truth of Buachi's assertion that it was a fetish axe : its failure in the present instance had deprived it of its sentimental value and the Ashantis had lost faith in its power, otherwise it is hardly possible that it would ever have been given up except under compulsion.

Thus, after months of needless and dangerous delay, this difficulty, which had its origin in an unauthorized statement made by an Ashanti who was living on the coast and was not even accredited from the King for the matter under discussion, combined with a mistaken interpretation of the meaning of an Ashanti emblem, was at last brought to an end. The protracted negotiations had been caused solely by the ill-advised policy of Sir Samuel Rowe, who never tired of making ambiguous speeches, and, even to the last, after he had been compelled to abandon his attitude of what he considered dignified reserve, could not resist the temptation to put off the settlement of the dispute as long as possible, even going so far as to insinuate to Buachi that he had doubts about the authenticity of the message that he had brought. Such a policy should never be followed with uncivilized peoples, with whom nothing can ever succeed so well as plain, straightforward dealings.

[1] Parliamentary Paper, *Affairs of the Gold Coast and Threatened Ashanti Invasion*, 1881, p. 152.

How nearly the Governor's mismanagement of affairs ended seriously and precipitated the very war that it should have been his first duty to avert has already been seen. But the delay and attendant anxiety and alarm were not the only regrettable results of this policy. The Colony was put to an enormous and wholly unnecessary expense, and the cost of the absurd expedition to the Pra was doubled by the necessity of bringing everything back again to the coast. This foolish excursion and the treatment of the troops that had been sent out were managed in complete defiance of the teachings of experience. The rains were coming on, and Prasu was a no more desirable camping ground in 1881 than it had been in 1863. Its selection imperilled the health and even the life of every man who was taken there, and the Governor himself went down with fever and could not leave for the coast until some days after the departure of most of the other officers. The West Indian troops, too, were all landed instead of being kept at sea until it could be seen if they would be wanted, as had been done in the last war ; there was no accommodation for them, and they were quartered either in hired houses in the town or under canvas on the parade ground. The natural result was that during little more than a month, between the end of March and the beginning of May, out of 55 officers 1 died, 20 were invalided, and 9 still remained on the sick-list, while out of 27 European non-commissioned officers, 7 were invalided and 3 were still in hospital. The Ashantis had once more become an united people, and they and the protected tribes alike regarded the whole transaction with suspicion and distrust and firmly believed that the Government had only kept the question open to extort money as the price of peace. They, in fact, regarded the payment that had been made as so much blackmail.

Against all this, nothing whatever had been gained that could not have been secured as easily months before. The money paid by the King was not enough to cover the expenses that had been incurred, the surrender of the Golden Axe was only of sentimental value, and the King's

greater humiliation was no real gain. He had been ready
enough to prove his peaceable intentions and to apologize
for the acts of Engwi from the very first, and had he been
insincere, no amount of self-abasement and humiliation
would have changed him.

Meanwhile, Awusu, the original cause of dissension, had
been kept in Elmina, and, on the 17th of July, committed
suicide by leaping from the walls of the Castle, an act
that must have been a cause of much gratification to the
Ashantis.

During this year the first Roman Catholic missionaries
arrived on the Coast. They settled in Elmina, and, in
after years, opened additional stations in many other
places, since when they have, for reasons that are easily
appreciable, met with more genuine success than perhaps
all the other missions on the Coast combined.

CHAPTER XII

1881 TO 1883

1881–1883 THE earliest gold-mining companies at Takwa had been
CHAP. XII quickly followed by others. Swanzy and Company, the
Efuenta Gold Mining Company, and the Gold Coast Mining
Company all obtained concessions in the neighbourhood.
The Efuenta property was about a mile or so to the south
of the village, and that of the Gold Coast Company a little
to the north of it at Abontiakum. Swanzy's concession
lay still farther north at Crockerville and was afterwards
floated as a company, the Wassaw Gold Mining Company.
In 1881 a rich reef was discovered at Abosso, a few miles
from Takwa, and a French company—the Abosso Gold
Mining Company—and Messrs. Swanzy both took up
concessions there, while another company—the Tarkwa
Gold Mine Company—began making a clearing at Tamsu a
little to the south of Efuenta. In fact, by the end of 1881
concessions were being granted indiscriminately all over
the Apinto district of Wassaw and it was already foreseen
that serious complications would probably arise in the
future, for these concessions were granted for certain
distances from different centres and there could be little
doubt that many of the properties would be found to
overlap each other when the land was properly surveyed.
Swanzy's alone acquired not fewer than fourteen new
concessions in this district during October 1882.

Kru labour was employed on all these properties, with
the exception of Swanzy's mine, which was worked by
Fantis who received a third of the gold recovered. In

spite, however, of the undoubted richness of much of the ore, the enormous cost of transport and machinery made these undertakings unprofitable. Everything had to be landed at Axim and taken in boats up the Ankobra River as far as Tomento, whence it was carried on men's heads over bad roads and through extensive swamps to the Takwa valley. The cost of transport amounted to between £25 and £30 a ton, and, since no piece of machinery could be got up unless its heaviest section could be carried by four men, the possibilities of working the ore to the best advantage were seriously limited. A railway from Dixcove to Takwa was proposed, but though a survey was made, the project fell through. It was then suggested that a really good road should be built by the Government from Axim ; but since a road less than a mile in length made by one of the companies at Takwa had cost £500, it was estimated that such a work would entail an expenditure of some £17,500, and the finances of the Colony were not in a sufficiently prosperous condition to justify the alienation of so large a sum from the general revenue, even though the companies were willing to pay a heavy toll on all goods transported to their properties. This they could easily have afforded to do, for it was estimated that the cost of transport would be reduced from about £26 to between £7 or £8 a ton, and it would also have been possible to import much heavier and badly needed machinery. The Chiefs of the Axim district, however, were ordered to clear the bush and make as good a native road as possible, and this impoved matters to some extent. The unhealthiness of the Takwa valley was another serious disadvantage, and the death and invaliding rates amongst the Europeans sent out to the mines were appalling. In spite of all these difficulties, however, stamping machinery was put up and shipments of gold were made to England.

In 1882 two concessions were taken much nearer the coast in order to avoid this heavy cost of transport. The first of these was at Akanko about twenty-six miles from the mouth of the Ankobra River, and belonged to the Akanko Gold Mining Company, and the second, which was at Isra in Apollonia and only about six miles from the beach, was acquired by the Guinea Coast Mining Company.

The rapid growth of this industry naturally attracted a large number of people to the Takwa district. Many of them found employment on the different properties, but others, having no great liking for honest work, merely added to the criminal population or made their presence undesirable in other, if less objectionable, ways. They included several " scholars " from the coast towns, conspicuous amongst whom was the man Dawson who had been sent to Kumasi during the negotiations that preceded the outbreak of the last war. He was now in the employ of the French African Gold Coast Company, by whom he was styled " political agent," and, having considerable influence with the Chiefs of the district, occupied much of his time in holding courts and adjudicating on cases, at first nominally as the deputy of the Chief of Takwa, but afterwards apparently on his own account. There were many more of these " bush magistrates " who had assumed a certain amount of quite unauthorized and unconstitutional authority, but in 1881 a District Commissioner was appointed to Takwa and received special instructions to put a stop to these proceedings by himself undertaking the duty of adviser to the Chiefs.

The statements that had appeared in the papers during the early rush for concessions had given many people a very erroneous idea of the country, and it soon became known that many Europeans were thinking of leaving Cape Colony to come to the Gold Coast as diggers. A few even arrived in the country. In 1882 two men landed at Axim with a couple of donkeys and went up the Tano River. One of them died in the bush ; but the other succeeded in making his way back to the coast. Others came out in a similarly unprepared way only to return empty-handed and disheartened. The gold-fields of Wassaw offered no opportunities to men of this kind, and bore no resemblance to the auriferous districts of Australia, where, in a temperate and healthy climate, men with little or no capital could work small claims as diggers with a reasonable prospect of success. In the end it was found necessary for the Secretary of State to issue an official warning through the Governor of the Cape in order to save others from being deluded into making such useless and dangerous journeys.

After the settlement of the dispute about the Golden Axe, Buachi Tintin had asked that a European officer might return with him to Kumasi, and the Governor, thinking that this might prove a favourable opportunity for making an attempt to reach some of the tribes in the interior and extend trade, sent Captain R. La Touche Lonsdale to accompany the Ashanti embassy on its return journey. Having first visited Accra, they started for Kumasi on the 15th of October, being accompanied as far as Prasu by an escort of fifty Hausas.

Captain Lonsdale was the bearer of presents for the King and Queen-Mother, and was instructed to impress upon the Ashantis that it was the sincere wish of the Government that the friendly relations that had now been established should continue. Afterwards, he was to visit certain other tribes and try to convince them of the advantages of trading directly with the Europeans on the coast. It had always been the policy of Ashanti to prevent the tribes of the interior from visiting the coast towns, and they had only been able to obtain what they wanted in exchange for their produce from Ashanti traders. By these means the Ashantis not only secured a monopoly of the inland trade, but also obtained large middle profits and were able to exercise a wise control over the supply of firearms to their neighbours. The removal of these restrictions, therefore, was not likely to be looked on with favour in Kumasi ; but the abolition of these middlemen's profits was bound to increase the purchasing power of the people and the sales of the British traders on the coast. Since the war of 18; 3–4 this monopoly had been weakened by the interruption of trade between Kumasi and Salaga by the Brongs, who had closed the roads and refused to allow any Ashanti traders to go beyond Kintampo. As a result of their action, a large market had sprung up at the latter place, which then became the principal exchange for the products of the interior for goods imported from the coast. A certain amount of trade, however, passed in a direct line from Salaga through Krachi and Kwahu to Accra : this route avoided Ashanti altogether, and Captain Lonsdale was told to do all he could to increase and encourage the trade on it. He was also instructed to do everything in his power to convince the Adansis of the importance of keeping the road open to Prasu, and to point out to them that their safety largely depended on their refraining from interfering with traders or committing any other acts that might give reasonable cause of offence to the Ashantis. The Government also wanted to open another trade route in the west through Jaman and Sefwi. The Sefwis had already made friendly overtures, and were now communicated with through the medium of the Wassaws. A message was also forwarded through them to the King of Jaman. The Sefwis, Jamans, and Takimans all sent return messages to Accra, and were urged to keep a trade road open through their respective districts. Throughout these negotiations every care was taken to impress upon the different tribes that the English had settled all their differences with the Ashantis and had no intention of making any unprovoked attack on them ; and this was a very necessary precaution, for there was considerable risk that news of these transactions with their neighbours might reach the Ashantis and lead them to believe that the Government was forming a hostile confederacy against them.

Having interviewed the Adansis at Fomana, Captain Lonsdale went on to Kumasi, where he arrived early on the morning of the 7th of November and delivered his message and presents at a large public meeting on the 12th. He was then detained in the capital for several weeks, the principal cause of this delay being the anxiety of Buachi Tintin and his party that he should be accompanied to Salaga by some of the Ashanti Chiefs. Their object, of course, was to prevent those tribes who were still wavering in their allegiance from availing themselves of the presence

of a British officer in their country definitely to assert their
independence, and to persuade them and others that his
journey had, in fact, been undertaken to bring all those
who had already declared against Ashanti back under its
rule.   The King, too, was alarmed at the suggestion that
if these tribes consented to reopen the roads to Salaga
they would claim equal rights for their traders to pass
freely through Ashanti.   Captain Lonsdale, however, well
understood their motives and flatly refused to allow any
Ashantis to accompany him.   Excuse after excuse was
made ; but he stood firmly to his decision, and at last, on
the 5th of December, set out with three Kumasi Court
officials, who were sent back when the limits of Ashanti
territory were reached at Ejera.   The Amantins and all
the people beyond this point had renounced their allegiance
after the war and were now under the Krachi fetish Denti.
Salaga was entered on Christmas Day, and Yendi was
visited soon afterwards.   The trade of Salaga had greatly
depreciated, and its market, though still large, now occupied only a two-hundredth part of the space it had covered
before the trade was diverted to Kintampo.   Only a few
men now visited it, who left the main caravans from the
north at Yendi and rejoined them later by passing through
Brumasi to Kintampo.   The King of Kombi and all the
Chiefs beyond Ejera were unanimous in their wish to
maintain their independence and keep their roads closed
to Ashanti traders, but were favourably disposed to the
scheme of opening up and extending direct trade routes
between their countries and the sea-coast.

Leaving Salaga on the 20th of January (1882), Captain
Lonsdale went to Krachi, where he found the people
anxious to trade with the coast, and discovered that, in
May 1881, the Gonjas, Krachis and Brong tribes, with the
Insutas and Kwahus, had entered into a defensive alliance
to protect themselves against any future encroachments
of the Ashantis.   He then returned through the Krepi
district to Accra, having succeeded in establishing friendly
relations with many hitherto unknown Chiefs, as was shown
by the arrival in Accra on the 17th of July of messengers

from the King of Kombi and others with presents for the Governor and enquiries after his health.

On the 16th of November 1881, while Captain Lonsdale was living in Kumasi, Ya Affili, a sister of the Queen-Mother, had died. Knowing that human sacrifices were customary, and indeed compulsory on such occasions, he had tried to find out if any had taken place. What he believed to be the " death drum " was heard during the night and early the next morning, but though he fancied he noticed a special watchfulness over his movements on the part of the six Chiefs who had been told off to attend him and saw that the vultures in Kumasi made a sudden move towards Bantama, returning in the evening with every appearance of being heavily gorged with food, he could obtain no direct evidence of any of these religious murders having been committed. He was convinced, however, that sacrifices had been made, and there is no doubt that a certain number of slaves or criminals were, in fact, put to death during the funeral custom, and that further sacrifices were made and the blood mixed with the " swish " [1] when the Princess' grave at Bantama was afterwards closed.

This was only the ordinary procedure prescribed by the religious beliefs of the people, and the burial of any person of such importance without it would have been absolutely impossible. To have permitted any member of the royal family to have entered the next world without a suitable retinue of ghostly slaves and attendants would have been deemed absolutely sacrilegious.[2] However anxious, therefore, the King might be to mould his conduct according to the known wishes of the British Government, it would have been quite impossible for him to have omitted this essential part of the funeral custom ; but, in deference to the presence of a British officer in the town and a natural desire to give no avoidable cause of offence, these sacrifices were made with some secrecy and Mensa professed to Captain Lonsdale a determination to abolish them. He could, of course, hardly have said anything

---

[1] Puddled clay.   [2] *Vide* vol. i, p. 437.

else, whatever his private opinions and intentions might
have been, but there are grounds for believing that some
sacrifices at least were purposely concealed from him by
his mother and the Chiefs.

It was known, too, that Buachi had grossly misrepresented the Governor's message on this subject, and had told
Mensa that persons who spoke disrespectfully of any
member of the royal family, falsely swore the King's oath,
or were caught in adultery might be reserved for sacrifice.
The only ground for this was that when the subject was
under discussion Buachi had enumerated five offences that
were punishable by death by Ashanti law, and the Governor
had allowed the statement to pass without pointing out
that only wilful murder would be considered by the Government a sufficiently grave crime to justify capital punishment. Buachi's version of the message amounted to this :
that wanton decapitations for the mere purpose of " keeping customs " could not be permitted, but that there
was no objection to the execution of those who had been
condemned for transgressing their country's laws. He
himself really seems to have believed that this version was
correct. Possibly the interpreter had not made this
matter so clear as he should have done and a great deal was
left to be inferred. It would not be easy for an Ashanti
to realize that capital punishment for what Europeans
might consider minor offences, but which, according to the
laws and usages of his country were heinous acts, would
be regarded in the same light as the sacrifice of innocent
slaves or prisoners or war unless the fact was very plainly
stated. This must have been the view of the Government
interpreters also—unless they had been bribed—for Buachi
delivered his message in their presence and they raised no
objection to it. The Ashantis, moreover, would be supported in their belief by the remembrance of the hanging
of the policeman in the streets of Kumasi on the night of
its capture. This had always been, and still is, regarded by
them as a human sacrifice. The man's offence had been
disobedience of orders by looting a cloth ; but to an Ashanti
mind, and to most others, the taking of a cloth in a con-

quered town was no crime at all, and this execution could only appear to them as lawful punishment for disobedience of the order of a paramount Chief, as a " custom " to celebrate the victory and an offering to the gods, or as a combination of the two. With this incident within their own knowledge and recollection, they would naturally have scoffed at the idea that the English only resorted to capital punishment in cases of wilful murder.

Nor was the continuance of this custom an actual infraction of the Treaty of Fomana ; for the King had not undertaken to abolish it immediately, but only to " use his best endeavours to check the practice . . . with a view to hereafter putting an end to it altogether." When he subsequently asked permission to sacrifice a few victims on the death of any person of importance and pointed out that he could not very well avoid doing so, it had clearly been impossible for the Government to give any sanction, implied or otherwise, to so barbarous a custom ; yet everyone knew perfectly well that his statement of the case was quite true and fair, and that sacrifices would undoubtedly continue to be made, though, by the extension of British influence and the diminution of the supply of slaves if the Ashantis could be prevented from making further war on their neighbours, they would be bound to decrease in number. This opinion has, indeed, been justified ; and although sacrifices have year by year become increasingly more rare, and when made are carried out with the greatest secrecy, they are not even now entirely unknown on such occasions as the death of an important Chief.

But though their knowledge of African customs and African modes of thought enabled the officials on the spot to realize these facts and exercise a reasonable patience, it was otherwise with the British public, who, with their narrower outlook, regarded all such barbarous practices with uncompromising abhorrence, and, when a highly coloured account of some such custom reached England, raised a tremendous outcry of horror and indignation. It was reported that the King had wantonly put to death 200 virgins in order to use their blood to mix the " swish " for the repair of one of his houses. This was an obvious exaggeration ; for even the King of Ashanti was not so absolute a monarch that he could indulge in wholesale slaughter of this kind with no better object than the repair of a building. The Chiefs would not have permitted it at any time, much less while the country was in difficulties, the population greatly diminished by the recent war, and the supply of slaves almost entirely stopped by the secession of tributary States that had formerly paid 1,000 or 1,500 slaves annually as tribute. Sacrifices, even in Ashanti, were only made for definite and well-understood reasons ; and were it not for the commotion this story made at the time and the fact that it is often quoted against the Ashantis with various further embellishments even to the present day, it might have been treated with the silence it merits. The fact was, and is, that the Ashantis had been given a bad name, and many people were, and are, ready to believe anything that is said against them, no matter how improbable and absurd it may be. It is therefore as well to show on what insufficient evidence such charges have been made.

Ellis and others have attributed the origin of this report to the sacrifices made at the funeral custom of Ya Affili ; but this is obviously incorrect. Ya Affili did not die until the 16th of November, and her funeral custom, therefore, cannot have been begun before that date. This allegation, however, made its appearance in the columns of a local newspaper—the *Gold Coast Times*—on the 1st and again on the 22nd of October, and was printed in the (London) *Times* on the 11th of the next month, nearly a week before the death of the King's aunt. It was to some previous custom, therefore, that this rumour owed its groundwork of truth ; for funeral customs had, of course, been made for other persons, and it was also considered necessary to shed human blood during the regular customs for the King's ancestors at Bantama and before making any repairs or alterations to the royal mausoleum buildings. The repair of any damage by earthquake (attributed to certain spirits or gods—Sasabonsum) would also necessitate the preliminary shedding of blood to appease the supposed agents. That some unfortunate persons had recently been sacrificed was therefore morally certain, but none of these ceremonies would require more than a few victims, and there was not a scrap of evidence to support this tale of large numbers of young girls having been butchered ; nor is it in the least degree probable that such wanton atrocity would ever have been permitted. Captain Lonsdale, on his return to Accra, reported that he had gathered sufficient knowledge of the affairs of Ashanti during his stay in the country " to be able to say with a thorough conviction of the correctness of the statement, that nothing so conspicuously brutal took place," [1] and when, in response to Lord Kimberley's call for confirmation of the report, the Governor began to make enquiries, it at once became evident how little reliance can be placed on such tales. Mr. Laing, the editor of the *Gold Coast Times*, was asked for the authority on which he had published the statement, and could only adduce evidence which, being trebly hearsay, was no evidence at all. He wrote that he had " received the intelligence from a Mr. John Grant, a native of this town, who obtained it in conversation with a certain woman now living in Cape Coast. The latter it appears heard the news from the lips of one of the intended victims who escaped to the Colony, and whom she met in the village of Moree." [2] When, however, the District Commissioner of Cape Coast sought this girl in Mori and other villages around, she could not be found, and the Chief of Mori emphatically denied that any such girl had ever been in his town. Such, then, is the " evidence " on which this terrible accusation was then made, and on which it has been repeated and added to many times since.

Early in 1882 a fresh quarrel broke out between Ashanti and Jaman. Some three or four years earlier the Bandas had been driven from their original home in the north by

---

[1] Parliamentary Paper, *Affairs of the Gold Coast*, 1882, p. 43.
[2] *Ibid.*, p. 41.

the Chief of Bona and sought protection under the King of Jaman, who granted them land on the confines of his kingdom adjoining Ashanti, where they settled. Some time after this, Inkrusima, the Chief of Bedu, paid a long visit to Banda and began to intrigue with the new-comers. This Inkrusima had originally been under Jaman, but had seceded to Ashanti and was now seeking to regain possession of the lands he had originally held, but which had been confiscated when he left. Being unsuccessful in this, he began to intrigue with the Bandas. He first of all instigated them to plunder Jaman traders returning through their district from Salaga and Kintampo, and then prevailed upon their Chief to ignore the King's remonstrances and summonses. It is quite possible that Inkrusima may have been acting under instructions from some of the more warlike Chiefs in Kumasi, but, be this as it may, in the end he won over the Bandas to Ashanti. The Jamans naturally resented this and were anxious to regain their suzerainty over Inkrusima and Banda and to punish the former for his treachery. They believed themselves strong enough to do so by force of arms : threats of war passed, and the war party in Kumasi, glad of an opportunity of renewing the struggle with Jaman, sent instructions to the Chief of Banda, who, in January 1882, seized and murdered seventeen Jaman traders who were on their way back from Salaga. The King of Jaman, so soon as he heard of this last outrage, retaliated by sending one of his Chiefs, Passi, to attack Banda. On the 25th of May he destroyed the town and took twenty-nine of the inhabitants prisoners to Bontuku. Wanki was also attacked, and ten men and thirty-nine women were captured. After this, troops were mobilized on either side, and the outbreak of general hostilities was imminent.

Mensa himself seems to have taken very little part in these proceedings and to have been anxious to preserve peace, but unable to control his more turbulent Chiefs, and, in March, seeing that war was inevitable, sent messengers to the Governor to inform him of what was taking place. After entering a formal denial of and protest against the recent allegations against the King on the subject of human sacrifices, they complained that the Jamans had captured and killed certain people at Banda and that the King of Jaman had publicly proclaimed his determination to make war on Ashanti. The King had, therefore, sent to tell the Governor and ask his advice, because he regarded him as his master and felt he could not go to war without his consent. No mention, of course, was made of the provocation that had been given by the Bandas, but, apart from the fact that it had almost certainly been done at the instigation of the war party and against the King's personal wish, it was only natural that he should try to make his own case as good as possible. After some deliberation, it was decided that Captain Lonsdale should proceed at once to Kumasi and Bontuku and try to arrange a peaceful settlement of the quarrel.

On his arrival in Kumasi, Captain Lonsdale met with a great deal of opposition from the war party, who were anxious to see the old Ashanti policy of conquest and extension followed out in preference to this new plan of cultivating peaceful trade ; but after some difficulty he succeeded in obtaining a public promise from the King that he would refrain from hostilities and leave the adjustment of his quarrel with Jaman to be dealt with by the Government at some future date. He then went to Bontuku, where, as in Ashanti, he found everything in readiness for war and the Chiefs strongly opposed to any delay ; but, after several meetings had been held, he prevailed on the King to disband his army and leave the matter in the hands of the Government. Captain Lonsdale then sent one of his interpreters back to tell Mensa what had been arranged, while he himself returned to the coast through Sefwi. He visited the King, Kwaku Che, at Wiosu, where he and all his Chiefs voluntarily swore allegiance to the British Crown and received assurances that the Government would aid them in preserving their newly asserted independence, provided they did nothing to provoke the Ashantis. Nothing more, however, was done to settle the differences between Jaman and Ashanti.

Mensa's submissive attitude and his readiness, ever since the commencement of his reign, to conform as far as possible to the wishes of the Government had been a source of great annoyance to the powerful Chiefs of the war party. This feeling was now accentuated by his peaceable conduct in allowing the quarrel with Jaman to remain in abeyance and was the principal cause of his downfall. There were other reasons, however, which, in the aggregate, contributed materially to this result. Mensa had never been a really popular king, and like most weak men was inclined to be something of a bully. He was actuated by two motives : on the one hand, he was sincerely anxious to preserve friendly relations with the British Government, while on the other he wished to see the former power and grandeur of Ashanti restored and to make Kumasi once more renowned for the wealth and splendour of its Court. These two ambitions were irreconcilable. His patriotism dictated what coincided with the wishes of the war party— namely, the re-establishment of his rule over Adansi and other former tributaries, but any open attempt to do so was so fraught with danger of complications with the Government that he dared not undertake it, and such mild diplomatic measures as he was prepared to risk not only failed in their object, but also aroused the contemptuous anger of his Chiefs. His efforts to replenish his impoverished exchequer led him, moreover, to inflict unconscionably heavy fines for comparatively trifling offences. Charges were often made against men mainly because they were known to be wealthy, and these tyrannous acts did much to estrange his people. He has also been accused, but apparently quite unjustly, of having increased the number of human sacrifices to something far in excess of what it had been in previous reigns. It does seem, however, that when he saw the first signs of disaffection he tried to assert his authority by causing several of those who had offended him to be put to death without first obtaining the consent of his Chiefs. This was unconstitutional, caused a sense of general insecurity, and roused their anger. The delivery of Buachi Tintin's perverted message, too, had greatly flattered him, and he had certainly put many persons to death for offences other than murder ; but he was undoubtedly deceived by Buachi and cannot fairly be held responsible for this. Mensa has often been blamed and abused, and his conduct and motives have been grossly misrepresented ; but although the weakness of his character prevents any feeling of admiration for the man, he is really deserving of some pity. He was, to a large extent, the victim of circumstances. Called upon to rule Ashanti at a critical time when its fortunes were at their lowest ebb, he found the whole kingdom utterly disorganized and the people still smarting from their recent defeat, which, though it had shattered all their most cherished traditions and beliefs by conclusively proving that even the capital was not immune from attack, had yet been insufficient to break the spirit of the Chiefs. With a strong war party opposed to his pacific policy and the absolute necessity of avoiding any further dispute with a nation that had already amply proved its power, a stronger man than Mensa might well have failed to maintain his position. It was customary, too, for the Kings of Ashanti to have one or more descriptive secondary titles or " strong names," and Mensa, on his accession, had been given the name Bonsu, meaning a whale or large fish. This had been the principal title of Tutu Kwamina, who had adopted it during the attack on Anamabo Fort in 1807, when the sudden appearance of some such creature had been hailed by the Ashanti army as a good omen, and had, indeed, been almost immediately followed by the receipt of a flag of truce from the beleaguered garrison. The bestowal of this title had been a further handicap to Mensa ; for uncivilized peoples attach considerable importance to such names and would seem to believe that the recipients are actually endowed with the qualities of their sponsors. In accordance with this theory, the Ashantis had fully expected Mensa to emulate the deeds of Tutu Kwamina and restore their country to the proud position she had held when he reigned and Ashanti had been at the very zenith of her power and greatness. Their dis-

appointment and resentment, therefore, were all the
greater because they had expected so much. Another
trait in his character which contributed very largely to the
prevailing discontent and was the indirect cause of his
final disgrace, was his extreme licentiousness. The wife
of no subject was safe from his amorous advances. Those
of the people he took openly ; but with the wives of
powerful Chiefs he dared not do this, but gained his ends
just as surely by proceeding with greater caution and
secrecy. If the injured husbands dared to complain, they
knew that they were likely to lose their heads as well as
their wives.

About July or August 1882 Chief Awua of Bantama and
his brother Awukama, who had been with the troops on
the Jaman frontier, returned to Kumasi, and Awukama
then discovered that his wife had been unfaithful during
his absence. The guilty party was none other than Mensa.
The first report that reached the coast alleged that, since
the woman refused to divulge the name of her paramour,
she was taken before the King, and that she then said
that she did not wish to live with Awukama any longer
and completely turned the tables on him and Awua by
swearing the King's oath that they were plotting " to join
the Jamans and give the King up to the white men." It
seems, however, that nothing quite so dramatic ever took
place. The true version of what happened seems to be
that when the discovery was made, Awua, who had been
largely instrumental in the deposition of Kofi Karikari,
said they would now deal with Mensa in the same way,
whereupon the woman, hoping to save herself from punishment, reported this to the King and claimed his protection. Be the actual circumstances what they may,
there is no doubt the woman did give information of some
real or imaginary plot against Mensa and that he attached
great importance to it. He promptly seized Awua and his
brother, charging them with conspiracy to remove him
from the stool, and then made prisoners of numbers of his
Counsellors and Linguists, the Queen of Mampon and her
son, and about forty members of the royal family, all of

whom he believed to be implicated. In September, numbers of these people, amongst whom was Awukama, were put to death, and Awua himself would have shared their fate had he not been rescued by the people of Achima, one of his villages, who came secretly by night, took him out of log and carried him away to Inkwanta, the Chief of which had had a dispute with Mensa and declared his independence some months earlier.

These drastic measures terrorized the people into outward submission, but increased the general discontent, while the indignity that had been offered to so great a Chief as Awua was especially resented. The whole country was ripe for rebellion, and nothing but a leader was wanted to produce a general and immediate insurrection. Mensa himself provided the spark that produced the final explosion. He is alleged to have been in league with Osai Yow [1] the King of Kokofu and a relative of Mensa, who was in the habit of reporting to him from time to time the names of rich men in his province : they would then be fined heavily by Mensa on some more or less trivial pretext, and half the fine handed to Yow as commission. At the end of 1882, such a fine, amounting to 1,800 dollars, was imposed on Kofi Kra, a son of Amuafa the Chief of Dadiasi, one of the sub-districts of Kokofu. Amuafa at once rebelled and was joined by the Chiefs of Daniasi, Inkwanta, Takiman and others. On the 24th of February 1883, twenty-seven Ashanti messengers arrived in Cape Coast representing thirty-three revolted Chiefs and 6,000 fighting men, who were then collected at Inkwanta and sought permission to cross the frontier and settle within the Protectorate. Five days earlier a messenger—Yow Mensa—and fourteen followers had reached Accra from Mensa

---

[1] This name is given in some documents as " Assaya," which is presumably incorrect. The King of Kokofu, being of the Ashanti blood royal, would bear the title " Osai," and he is referred to elsewhere as " Yao." " Assaya " would therefore appear to be " Osai Yow " miswritten. In one single paragraph of one of Captain Barrow's despatches the names " Assaya " and " Amuafa " each appear with two different spellings, and further variations appear in some of his subsequent letters.

reporting disturbances in his kingdom and imploring the Governor to send an officer to help him to settle matters. All the sub-Chiefs of Bekwai now joined the rebels, and last of all, in March, the Kumasis rose also. On the 8th of that month the Chiefs removed all the stools and regalia from the stool-house, and Mensa fled to Abrodi, a village some five hours' journey to the north-east of the capital.

CHAPTER XIII

THE RIVAL CLAIMANTS TO THE STOOL OF ASHANTI

1883 TO 1884

NEWS of Mensa's flight had not yet reached the coast; but the state of affairs in Ashanti was known to be so critical, and the commercial outlook on the coast was becoming so serious, that, on the 31st of March, the Governor sent the Assistant Colonial Secretary, Captain Knapp Barrow, C.M.G.,[1] to Kumasi with an escort of fifty Hausa Constabulary under Assistant-Inspector Kirby. He was to report on the situation generally, but it was most urgently impressed upon him that he was being sent merely to obtain information, and that he must on no account say or do anything that might give colour to the belief that the Government either wished, or was in any way prepared to interfere in the internal affairs of Ashanti or to take any action regarding the quarrel between the King and his subjects.

Captain Barrow reached Kumasi on the 26th of April 1883, and was received by Asafu Buachi and Awusu Koko, who were in charge of the town. All the assembled Chiefs expressed the greatest satisfaction at his arrival. The golden stool lay on its side[2] on its raised dais at this reception; for Mensa was still living at Abrodi and the Chiefs had been afraid to send for him, because, so they explained, " they were afraid if they did so the young men

---

[1] Formerly an officer in the Royal African Colonial Corps. Appointed Colonial Secretary of Lagos in 1884 and died in 1888.

[2] Stools are always laid on their sides when not in use to prevent their occupation by evil spirits.

of the town might flog the King." Nothing could have shown better than this simple statement of the Chiefs how complete was Mensa's downfall, and the condition of the town itself told its own tale of bad government and a dissatisfied people. Instead of the wide clean open spaces and streets of former days, the whole place was overgrown with rank weeds and low bushes, and only narrow footpaths through them marked the streets. Many of the inhabitants had retired to the farms and bush villages, and whole rows of houses stood empty with their roofs fallen in and walls going to ruin.

Captain Barrow had met the Chiefs of Bekwai, Dadiasi and Daniasi at Amoafu, and they had one and all declared their determination never again to submit to the rule of Kumasi, no matter whether Mensa or any other King were on the stool; but his enquiries in the capital soon made it clear that the feeling there and in the other revolted provinces was against Mensa personally rather than against the dynasty. The Chiefs produced Kwaku Dua, a son of Ya Kia the sister of Kofi Karikari and Mensa, and explained that he was the rightful heir whom they wished to place on the vacant stool. Mensa's only adherents were the Kokofus and the King of Bekwai, who had been deserted by all his sub-Chiefs and people.

The ex-King Kofi Karikari, ever since his deposition, had been living quietly in Akropong. Hitherto he had been an interested but passive onlooker at the troubles which racked the kingdom he still regarded as his; but now at last he thought the opportunity had come for him to regain it, and he sent a small armed force against Kumasi. Fortunately it never reached its destination, for Captain Barrow had gained some inkling of his intentions and warned the Kumasi Chiefs to post unarmed pickets in all the villages along the road to Akropong. On the morning of the 2nd of May, Awusu Koko, Buachi Tintin and two of the Linguists ran into his quarters and told him that Karikari's force was already at Ofyim, a village just beyond Bantama, and within an hour of the capital, where they were plundering and slaying the inhabitants. They themselves immediately marched out to oppose them, and Captain Barrow sent one of his interpreters, Mr. Ashanti, to push on ahead of them and do his utmost to prevent a collision by assuring Kofi Karikari that Captain Barrow had not come to Kumasi to put anyone on the stool. He succeeded in turning back most of Karikari's men and accompanied them to Akropong, where he saw the ex-King and delivered his message. Some skirmishing took place, however, and four prisoners were taken by the Kumasis and seven by Karikari's people. The Kumasis readily gave their prisoners up to Captain Barrow, and, on the 5th, Mr. Kirby visited Kofi Karikari at Akropong and exchanged them for the seven Kumasis held by him, and whom he had intended to sacrifice. He also obtained a promise from Karikari that he would keep his people quiet and disturb the peace no more.

Captain Barrow's efforts to get the great provincial Chiefs to meet him either in Kumasi or at Fomana were unavailing, for they were all afraid to leave their towns while the country was in such an unsettled state. The majority of them, however, sent messages which showed they were quite willing to co-operate with the Kumasis in electing a new King and anxious to see a better system of government introduced, which should be " more like white man's law " and enable them to live in peace and enrich themselves by trade. They also wanted the Governor to help them in the choice of a new King, and proposed that he should meet them all at Prasu for this purpose.

On the 12th, Mr. Kirby visited Mensa at Abrodi. He found him living in great poverty, with only a few attendants and without a single Chief with him. Very little respect was shown him even by the people in the village. He bitterly complained of the treatment he had received at the hands of the Kumasi Chiefs and was most anxious to accompany Mr. Kirby on his return ; but this was, of course, forbidden, and Captain Barrow, having collected all the information possible, left Kumasi on the 27th of May and reached Accra on the 21st of the following month. His opportune arrival had temporarily prevented the outbreak of civil war between the Karikari and Dua parties ; but the stool was still vacant, and there were three claimants to it—Kwaku Dua, and the two ex-Kings Karikari and Mensa.

The respective claims of these three men may now be considered. Mensa's chances of again occupying the stool may be dismissed at once as hopeless. He was practically a state prisoner of the Chiefs, banished to Abrodi, and had neither money nor friends, the few who had remained loyal at first having long since deserted him. He even had difficulty in obtaining enough food and begged to be taken down to the coast : so bad was his case, in fact, that Captain Barrow reported that his removal and the grant of a small allowance for his subsistence would be no more than an act of charity. The only thing that could be urged in his favour was that he was in the direct line of succession ; but his brother Kofi Karikari was the elder son and had a prior claim.

Kofi Karikari had a certain number of supporters, chief amongst whom were the Mampons, Insutas, Agunas, Kokofus, Inkoranzas and Prince Ansa. They were largely of the filibustering type however, and but luke-warm in their loyalty, while his chances of reinstatement were much exaggerated by Prince Ansa, who was perhaps his most ardent partisan and did his utmost to paint his prospects in the rosiest colours. In August, a messenger was intercepted who had been sent by Ansa to tell Karikari that if he would provide a certain sum of money, several influential persons in Cape Coast could be induced to support his cause. Ansa's main contention was that the deposition of Karikari after the war had been unconstitutional, inasmuch as it had been carried out by the Chiefs of Kumasi rather than by a representative Council of the whole kingdom ; but by his flight and desertion of his people he had practically abdicated, and his subsequent misdeeds and the critical state of affairs at the time had rendered the collection of a representative gathering almost impossible, while there can be no doubt that the provinces had afterwards given their consent. Karikari, moreover, was a man of kindly disposition, and, up to the time of his disgrace, had been an undoubtedly popular King. Many of the people were of opinion that he had learnt wisdom from his misfortunes and profited by the severe lesson he had received ; but there were, nevertheless, grave objections to his reinstatement.   In the first place, he had shown personal cowardice, and afterwards, when he met his Chiefs, who had done their best for him and suffered heavily in his cause, he had accused them of cowardice also and blamed them for his defeat.   The taunt was quite un-merited and was especially exasperating to an Ashanti. The Chiefs therefore had deeply resented it, and even if this had been his only offence they might have found it hard to forgive.   There were, however, other grounds of objection to him.   One of these, which, though insufficient in itself to debar him from the succession, carried some weight, was his illegitimacy.   His mother Efua Kobri, when promised in marriage to Kofi Inti the uncle of Buachi Tintin, had listened to the amorous persuasions of a trader from Cape Coast, and Kofi Karikari was the offspring of their illicit intercourse.   Kofi Inti had, never-theless, married her afterwards and became the father of Mensa.   Since the Ashantis trace their descent through the female line, this had not prevented his succeeding to the stool ; but the princesses are not given in marriage to any but persons of birth and position, and this intrigue with a common Fanti of no standing whatever had been con-sidered specially disgraceful.   The event had, in fact, caused a great scandal at the time, but had been hushed up, and it was now dangerous to speak of it : it had not, however, been forgotten.   But by far the greatest objection to Kofi Karikari was his action in having robbed the royal graves at Bantama, and this was almost insuperable.

There were no such objections to the succession of Kwaku Dua, whose claims were by far the strongest and his following the most influential and important, including as it did all the Kumasi Chiefs.   Many of those who had at first favoured the re-election of Kofi Karikari soon espoused his cause, and the only objection raised by his few opponents was that they thought he was as yet too young to assume the responsibilities of government. He was in the direct line of succession, being the son of Ya Kia, who was a daughter of Efua Kobri and sister to Karikari and Mensa. His father was Kwesi Afriya, a son of Kwaku Dua I, who had married Tacheow the daughter of Tutu Kwamina.[1] Young Kwaku Dua, therefore, was of royal descent on both sides, and though the Ashantis, strictly speaking, only take the mother's side into account, they nevertheless recognized this fact and agreed that his pedigree was above all suspicion. Although his candidature had never been canvassed outside Kumasi, Captain Barrow reported that there were good grounds for believing that it would be almost universally approved. At the time of his grandfather's death young Kwaku Dua had not been more than three or four years old ; but the old King had nominated him as his successor,[2] saying that it would be useless to give the stool to either of the sons of Efua Kobri, because neither of them would be able to " keep his house in order." He was, however, far too young to succeed at once, and the stool had accordingly been held first by Kofi Karikari and next by Mensa ; but it is alleged that each, on his accession, paid a nominal subsidy of from twenty to twenty-four ounces of gold to Kwaku Dua in acknowledgment of the fact that they were only holders of the stool pending the time when he should be old enough to occupy it himself. He was now about eighteen or twenty years of age, and it was also believed that if he was made King the Jabins would return to their allegiance, while another point in his favour was that his party were in actual possession of the stool and regalia.

When Kofi Karikari found that Captain Barrow had left Kumasi and that the stool was still vacant, he conceived the idea that if he could gain possession of it he would materially strengthen his position. Accordingly, early in

---

[1] *Vide* genealogical tree, Appendix D.

[2] The dying Chief can appoint whom he wish to succeed him, and the families are obliged to elect the successor so appointed. This is called " Samansiw," the oath of a dying man. (Sarbah, 2nd Fanti Law Report—Toku *v.* Ama.)

August, he got together a small force and advanced towards Kumasi, and, on the 3rd, met a small party of Kumasis. A skirmish ensued, in which the latter were driven back with a loss of seven men killed. Karikari then continued his march on the capital, but was met by the Chief Stool-bearer, who assured him that Awusu Koko would destroy the stool rather than let it fall into his hands and urged him to turn back. This he did, and the Kumasis then collected a strong force under Chief Opoku, who, overtaking Karikari's men at Dadiem, defeated and put them to flight. They continued the pursuit as far as Breman and then turned off to Tafo, where they found the dead bodies of Awusu the King of Inkwanta, Kofi Poku and Osai Yow Head-Chiefs of Kumasi, and six others who had been sent to ask the Tafos with whom they would side and had been murdered. The Tafos had fled on the approach of this force, but were pursued to Kanyonasi, where a decisive defeat was inflicted on them. The fighting had lasted from eight o'clock in the morning until about five in the evening, and both Kofi Karikari and Kwaku Dua had been present. Besides Atahin the King of Aguna, who hanged himself, and Yow Akruma of Insuta, who blew himself up with gunpowder to avoid capture, Karikari lost some eighty men killed and sixty wounded, while the Kumasis had about sixty killed and fifty wounded.

Kofi Karikari succeeded in escaping with one of his Chiefs, and, though the latter was taken soon afterwards, he himself could not be found. A party under Chief Issi was therefore detached to hunt him down, and at length found him wandering in the forest near Berim, a small village on the Jaman road about six days' journey from Kumasi He was in a pitiful condition and almost starved, having been in the bush for fifteen days with nothing to eat but what he could find growing wild. Being of royal blood the Kumasis dared not put him to death, but kept him a close prisoner in one of their villages, though it was never expected that he would live after the severe privations he had undergone.

A rumour had been spread in August that the Kumasi

Chiefs intended sending the golden stool to the King of Denkera for safe keeping, and, though there was not the slightest probability that they would ever take such a risky step, the Government had taken alarm at the possibility, foreseeing that in that event the Karikari faction would almost certainly follow it with a hostile force into the Protectorate. Assistant-Inspector Brennan of the Gold Coast Constabulary had therefore been sent to warn the King of Denkera against mixing himself up in the disputes of the Ashantis, and he had afterwards gone on to Prasu and Fomana and learned a good deal of what was going on. The information he sent down was soon afterwards confirmed by messengers who arrived from Kwaku Dua on the 5th of September.

These messengers repeated the request already made by the Chiefs to Captain Barrow that the Government would interfere to restore order in their country by settling this question of the succession once and for all. They implored the Governor to send an officer who should place their nominee on the stool and advise him how to conduct himself as King ; but Sir Samuel Rowe was never the man to commit himself to any definite action and dismissed these messengers with a few vague remarks about the Government's desire for the restoration of peace in Ashanti, with the Government of which, however, it had no wish to interfere. In November, the Chiefs of his party elected Kwaku Dua King and formally put him in charge of the stool, but would not put him on it, as they were still hoping that the Governor would accede to their request and send an officer to be present at the final ceremony. These continual delays only made matters worse ; for Kwaku Dua's adherents, the only really powerful party, grew disappointed and discontented, while the followers of Kofi Karikari, who never had any real chance of success, were still encouraged to struggle on.

On the 1st of December, instructions were received from the Secretary of State authorizing the Governor to do as the Ashantis wished. He wrote : " It is, of course, not desirable that any premature action should be taken, but at the same time the re-establishment and maintenance of peace is of such vast importance to the trade and revenue of the Gold Coast Colony that no opportunity of furthering the attainment of that end should be lost. I think, therefore, that if you are able to satisfy yourself that Kwaku Dua is likely to be able to establish himself firmly in power, and to be acknowledged by the bulk of the Ashanti tribes as King, you would do well to take measures for at once attaching him to the British Government by making him suitable presents, and further express your willingness to meet him with the representatives of the nation at Prasu (or such other place as you may consider convenient and suitable), and there proceed to ratify his election and instal him on the throne." [1] Lord Derby advised the collection of all the Chiefs at this meeting, so that the Governor might arrange terms of peace between them, which could then be drafted into a short treaty, to be signed by them as the contracting parties and by the Governor as a witness of what had taken place.

Four days after the receipt of this despatch, further messengers arrived entreating the Governor to come up and settle the dispute, and, though messengers from Mampon stated their objection to Kwaku Dua, there can be no doubt that, had Sir Samuel Rowe acted on the instructions he had just received and arranged a meeting with the Chiefs, he would have found very little difficulty in restoring peace and harmony amongst them and could at once have ratified the election of Kwaku Dua and given him some sound advice as to his future conduct and government. But now, as ever, he shrank from committing himself to any action bearing the least taint of responsibility and dismissed the messengers on the 2nd of January 1884 with one of his customary speeches about the desirability of peace, merely promising that an officer should come up to inform the Chiefs who had sent to him that he wished them to settle their differences peaceably, but that he might, at some future time, consent to meet them at Prasu or elsewhere in the Protectorate.

[1] Parliamentary Paper, *Affairs of Ashanti*, 1884, p. 86.

In accordance with this promise, Mr. Kirby was sent up with the returning Ashantis, bearing written messages to the different Chiefs, which simply stated that the Government had no wish to force any King upon them against their will, advised them to settle their differences peaceably amongst themselves, and offered a meeting with the Governor at some future date if they thought it would assist them to do so. He visited the principal towns and districts in Ashanti, and found those of Kofi Karikari's followers in a very poor state. Kokofu had practically ceased to exist. The King, Queen-Mother, and most of the important Chiefs were prisoners in the hands of the Chief of Dadiasi, who, on pretence of paying a visit to his paramount Chief, had recently seized and carried them off and given the King to his son as a personal servant. This once important and powerful province was now represented by a ruined town and a population of some fifty starving people. The Mampons, too, had nearly all deserted their King, and he himself was only deterred from following their example and joining Kwaku Dua by his fear of punishment for his previous rebellion.

The supporters of Kwaku Dua were far more prosperous. Kumasi itself was fast being rebuilt, the population had nearly all returned, and the town was clean and surrounded by numerous farms. At the meeting in Kumasi, Kwaku Dua sat by the side of the golden stool, showing that it was only in his charge and that he was awaiting the permission of the Government before being placed on it. His party included the Kumasis, most of the Mampons, the Insutas, whose King had voluntarily renewed his allegiance, the Bekwais, who had deposed their King because he wished to retain his independence, and the Agunas. The latter had at first been divided, and at the time of Kofi Karikari's second advance, their King Atahin had been trying to drive out the Kwaku Dua faction ; but ever since his defeat and suicide they had been supreme and had now won over all the others.

There was also a small third party, comprising the Daniasis and Inkwantas, who wished to remain neutral, and asked to be allowed to come under British protection. A similar request was made by the Adansis, but was refused in each case.

After leaving Kumasi, Mr. Kirby visited Inkoranza and Kintampo. Atta Fua, the King of the former place, had always been a firm friend of Kofi Karikari and had severed his connection with Kumasi soon after his destoolment, on account of the tyranny and extortions of Mensa, and blockaded the road at Kofiasi. He had since died and been succeeded by Opoku who, however, continued the policy of his predecessor. The consequence was that all communication with the market at Kintampo was cut off, and this was now filled with French goods obtained from the ports on the Ivory Coast and brought up through Jaman. Mr. Kirby, however, succeeded in persuading the Inkoranzas to re-open the road and encourage the passage of traders.

Mr. Kirby returned to Accra on the 2nd of April and reported that the statements that had been made as to the number and strength of Kofi Karikari's supporters were gross exaggerations and that the party could never at any time have been a source of danger to the Kumasis. The latter, indeed, had only refrained from stamping it out altogether because they believed Karikari's candidature was favoured by the Government. This belief had been carefully fostered by Prince Ansa, who had not hesitated to spread the most mendacious reports. One of his messengers, indeed, had told the King of Bekwai, as from the Governor, that he (the Governor) was coming to proclaim Kofi Karikari King of Ashanti, and that if the King of Bekwai did not agree to serve him he would collect the Akims, Denkeras and Wassaws and attack and plunder him. The whole country was infested with " scholars " from the coast towns, who went about levying blackmail by pretending to hold authority from the Government to settle disputes : many instances of the mischief wrought by these men came to light, and they were often employed to spread the belief that the Government favoured the cause of Kofi Karikari. Cases of this kind are only too common even at the present day, and ever since the education of the Gold Coast African was first begun there have always been unprincipled men whose only use for the knowledge they acquired at school has been to impose on their more ignorant fellow-countrymen. There is a record of such a case as far back at 1841, when one Kwamina Mensa was sentenced by Governor Maclean to six months' imprisonment in Cape Coast Castle and the repayment of the money for " having procured forged summonses and gone through the country in the character of a constable and thereby extorted money from various persons."

Sir Samuel Rowe had now left the Coast and been succeeded by Mr. W. A. G. Young, who would probably have made immediate arrangements for the ratification of Kwaku Dua's election, had not Mr. Kirby brought word that when he left Kumasi on the 13th of March the Chiefs had already decided to carry out his public enstoolment on the 17th. They waited for more than a month, however, to see if their threat would have the desired effect of accelerating the despatch of a representative of the Government, and then, tired of the long delay and abandoning all hope of ever receiving the help for which they had asked, the Chiefs put Kwaku Dua on the stool on the 27th of April.

Kofi Karikari's following having dwindled to nothing, it was confidently expected that affairs in Ashanti would soon quiet down, and that the Inkwantas and other independents would return to their allegiance as soon as they found an improved form of government had been established ; but before any progress could be made, these hopes were dashed to the ground by the death of the young King on the 10th of June of small-pox. This left Kofi Karikari without a rival, and the Chiefs brought him to Kumasi ; but he was suffering from dysentery, as a result of the privations he had undergone during his wanderings in the bush, and succumbed to the disease on the 24th of the same month, eight days after his return to the capital. Prince Ansa, too, died of diabetes in Cape Coast on the 13th of November. Thus the two claimants to the stool, and one who had played not a small part in the affairs of Ashanti, were all removed from the scene within the short space of six months and without the lapse of sufficient time for any settlement of the quarrels and ill-feeling to which these troublous times had given birth.

Ashanti was as disorganized as ever. No immediate attempt was made to elect a successor to Kwaku Dua, and during the interregnum the Chiefs of Kumasi, who at such times considered themselves paramount, carried on such government as was possible in a country on the verge of civil war. Meanwhile, the Inkwantas, though maintaining their independence, used to resort to Kumasi in large numbers to trade, and the Kumasi Chiefs contrived to win over some of their leading men and began to intrigue with them to return to their allegiance. About August or September, however, the King of Inkwanta discovered what was going on and at once forbade his people to visit or hold any communications with Kumasi ; whereupon the Kumasi Chiefs, believing their influence in the district to be greater than it really was, and thinking they would be joined by a large section of the Inkwantas, marched a force against him. A battle was fought, in which the Kumasis met with a decisive defeat and lost eleven Chiefs and about eighty men killed and many more wounded, while twelve other Chiefs, amongst whom was Buachi Tintin, were taken prisoners.

The success of the Inkwantas, coming at such a time, had a most disastrous effect, and many Chiefs who had been wavering in their allegiance now openly abandoned it, until nearly every province had declared its independence and set up a separate government. The people once more deserted Kumasi, and the town fell into ruins ; a rumour indeed reached the coast that it had been sacked and burned to the ground. Many of the leading Chiefs had either died or been killed or taken prisoners in battle ; grass from twelve to fifteen feet in height grew in the streets, and whole rows of houses disappeared. Digging and washing for gold in the streets and market-place, once punishable by death, was now carried on extensively, the poverty of the people being so great that the old law against it was allowed to lapse.

But when affairs had reached this desperate state, and it seemed as though the Ashanti Confederacy had fallen to pieces for ever, Ya Kia, the Queen-Mother, made a last despairing effort to save it and sent messengers to all the provincial Chiefs begging them to come to Kumasi and elect a new King. This they agreed to do, only stipulating that his election and enstoolment should take place in the presence of, and be confirmed by, an officer of the British Government. Ya Kia therefore sent the Linguist Buatin and a suitable retinue to Accra to inform the Governor that it was proposed to place her sister's son Kwesi Chisi on the stool, and asking for an officer to be sent up. These messengers arrived in Accra and saw Governor Young on the 16th of October; but at the moment there was no officer available, and they were accordingly kept waiting until Mr. Kirby should come back from leave, when it was promised that he should return with them to Kumasi.

CHAPTER XIV

THE BEKWAI-ADANSI WAR

1885 TO 1886

EARLY in 1885 Geraldo de Lema, the man who for so many years had disturbed the peace of the eastern district and been the cause of so much bloodshed, once more incited the Awunas to rebel against the Government. After the rising in 1878, nothing had been heard of him for some years; but in 1882 he returned to Voji, and towards the end of 1884 began to make further mischief. He first of all tried to induce some of the Awuna Chiefs to intercept Captain Campbell, the District Commissioner, while he was on his way from Kitta to Ho, and, when this plan failed, urged them to massacre him and his whole party on their return journey. This plot also came to nothing, and de Lema then persuaded the Anyakos to blockade the lagoon and thus cut off the food supply of Kitta. As has already been explained, nothing but coco-nuts grew on the narrow strip of land constituting most of the Kitta district, and the people were entirely dependent on what was brought to their market from the islands and opposite shore of the lagoon. De Lema's action, therefore, speedily reduced them to great straits.

Governor Young, knowing that all former efforts to secure this man had failed, determined to make use of the few friendly Chiefs in the district and secretly caused them to be informed that a reward of fifty pounds would be paid for his capture. With the assistance of two loyal Chiefs, Tamaklo and Akolatsi, Captain Campbell succeeded in arresting de Lema in his house at Voji on the night of the

7th of January 1885 and took him to Kitta. There the charges against him were heard on the 14th, and he was then committed for trial at the Accra assizes.

Captain Campbell now made his first mistake and sent de Lema along the beach to Accra with an escort of only five men of the Gold Coast Constabulary. Considering the enormous influence of the man, the amount of trouble he had given, and the fact that the escort must pass the towns of his most ardent adherents, Captain Campbell's failure to send his prisoner by sea, or to provide an infinitely stronger escort if he went by land was, to say the least of it, most imprudent. It was an open invitation to the Awunas to attempt a rescue and they did not hesitate to accept it.

At seven o'clock on the morning of the 16th, a man arrived in Kitta and reported that the escort had been stopped and the prisoner detained by a party of Anyakos at Hwuti. Captain Campbell lost no time in going to the rescue of his men, and marched off at once with the very inadequate force of 38 Constabulary, to whom, moreover, he only issued twenty rounds of ammunition per man. The Chiefs Tamaklo and Akolatsi and some 60 or 80 of their men went with him. On reaching Hwuti he found the town full of greatly excited crowds of Anyakos; but, fortunately, they had not expected such prompt action and had not yet made up their minds what to do. The prisoner and escort were still safe, and Captain Campbell, having managed to free them, started them off for Accra at noon on the same day, while he and his party remained at Hwuti till the next morning, and then set out for Kitta, taking two Anyako Chiefs, Tamiki and Chiki, with them.

De Lema was safely lodged in Accra gaol on the 19th; but when Captain Campbell and his men began the return march to Kitta with their prisoners on the morning of the 17th, they had gone barely a mile and a half along the beach when they were attacked by a force of some 3,000 Awunas, who opened fire on them. It was now evident that the Constabulary would have to fight their way back against heavy odds, and Captain Campbell gave the order to return the enemy's fire and push slowly forward. The Hausas advanced steadily for nearly an hour ; but their small supply of ammunition was then expended, and they were compelled to retire. The Awunas then closed in upon them, and the order was given to fix bayonets, face about, and charge ; but the enemy constantly renewed the attack, and it was only by the frequent repetition of this manœuvre that they were kept off. Only one charge was actually carried home however, for after their first taste of cold steel the Awunas fell back each time the Hausas faced them, and an hour later gave up the pursuit altogether.

During this affray, the two prisoners made their escape and were seen urging on their own men. Captain Campbell received five wounds, some of which were serious, and two Hausas were killed, while a third died of his wounds before Kitta was reached and some twelve more were wounded. Throughout the engagement they had behaved extremely well, kneeling to fire and firing steadily and in good order. Chief Tamaklo's two sons were killed, and Chief Akolatsi and a number of their men wounded, while the enemy lost at least forty or fifty killed and had many more wounded. Kitta was reached the same day. The greatest excitement and alarm prevailed in the town ; all the women and children had sought refuge in the fort, and a reinforcement of twenty Constabulary was at once sent for from Danu.

When news of this outbreak reached Accra, Mr. Young immediately sought the assistance of Commander Parr of H.M.S. *Frolic,* who took down 100 Gold Coast Constabulary under Inspector Dudley from Accra and Elmina. This reinforcement brought up the strength of the detachment at Kitta to about 200 men. Thirty canoemen were also taken, as it was only by means of boats that the Anyakos could be reached and punished. The Governor demanded the surrender of the rebellious Chiefs and the payment of a fine of £1,000 : no attempt, however, was made to comply with these demands, and preparations were therefore made to destroy the Anyakos' towns.

Ten surf-boats were carried across the strip of beach and launched on the lagoon. In two of them Gardner guns were mounted, and two more carried 7-pounders. Each of these was manned by fifteen of the *Frolic's* men, while the other six carried twenty Hausas apiece. At half-past five on the morning of the 31st of January the two Gardner guns were posted on the flanks, the 7-pounders in the centre, and the boats advanced in line across the lagoon, preceded by Inspector Dudley and the Commander in the *Frolic's* gig and followed by an ambulance boat. The water was so shallow that the heavily laden boats frequently grounded and the men had to get out and push them off, so that it was half-past nine before they at last arrived in front of Anyako. The enemy, relying upon the security of their island home, had boastfully derided the possibility of their being attacked ; but when they saw the flotilla advancing they hastened to make their escape without offering any resistance. Several shells were thrown into the town, which at once set it on fire and it was utterly destroyed. Assistant-Inspector Stewart, with Native Officer Ali and sixty Hausas then landed and scoured the island from end to end. They found and burned another small village, and the whole force then returned to Kitta, which they reached a little before sunset without having suffered any loss.

On the 2nd of February, the *Frolic* cruised along the coast and threw shells over Jitta, Hwuti and Awuna, as a warning to the inhabitants that they were easily assailable from the sea. The bursting of these shells produced an astounding effect on the Awunas, most of whom had never seen anything of the kind before : they aptly described them as " the shot which made a tornado." On the 4th, two or three more shells were fired into Hwuti, and the ship then lay-to off Awuna to await the arrival of the Hausas, who had left Kitta at half-past three that morning and were marching against it by land. They found the town had been abandoned and burned it. The destruction of these places and the discovery that most of their towns could be shelled and destroyed by the gunboats without the least hope of resistance, completely cowed and subdued the Awunas, and those who had been wavering in their loyalty lost no time before sending in submissive messages and displaying British flags.

The extension of the eastern frontier to Aflao at the end of 1879, though it had done a great deal to check smuggling in the Kitta district, had not entirely put an end to it, and, in 1884, the authorities were considering the advisability of moving the boundary still farther east, so as to include the adjoining piece of coast known as Be Beach. But while they were still thinking about it, and before anything had been done, the German Government stepped in early in 1885 and declared a Protectorate over this and Togoland. Their territory, therefore, became conterminous with that of the British at Aflao and it was necessary to define the boundary with greater accuracy and for some distance inland. A commission was appointed for this purpose and the boundary agreed upon for a distance of two and a half miles inland on the 14th of July 1886, but it was not defined any farther. The Germans at the same time announced their annexation of the Agotime, Tavi and Kevi countries, which lay behind the Kitta district. This threatened to divert the Salaga trade from the Colony, and any further acquisition of territory by them would certainly have done so. This danger proved sufficient to overcome the Government's reluctance to extend the Protectorate and compelled it to take immediate steps to safeguard the commercial interests of the Colony in the interior. The Kriko district had been secured by a treaty, dated the 12th of November 1885, so soon as the first rumours of German activity in the hinterland had reached Accra, and now the Akwamus and Krepis were also included within the Protectorate. The Akwamus, through their King Akoto Ababio, had indeed petitioned the Government for protection, and the treaty [1] made between them and Mr. Griffith at Christiansborg Castle on the 27th of July 1886 sets forth that, in accordance with their expressed desire, " the country and territory

---

[1] Sarbah, *Fanti National Constitution*, p. 157.

of Akwamoo is hereby ceded and transferred to Her Britannic Majesty, so that the same shall become and form a part and portion of the Gold Coast Colony." Whether or not the Chiefs fully understood the literal meaning of this is open to some doubt; and this seems to have been appreciated at the time, for it was followed a few months later, on the 9th of May 1887, by the Akwamu Declaration, in which the King and Chiefs " freely and voluntarily acknowledged " that they considered themselves and their country part of the Protectorate, inasmuch as they had formerly " enjoyed similar protection from His Majesty the King of Denmark," who, they understood, had " ceded his right and title to their country to the British Crown in the year 1850." [1] Treaties were also concluded with the Agravis on the 12th of August, the Chiefs of Merpi, Bato, Mlefi and Blakpa on the 4th of September, and the Krepis on the 7th of October, 1886.

The western frontier had never yet been accurately defined with the French, whose Possessions on the Ivory Coast there adjoined the Gold Coast Colony. As has already been mentioned, the Dutch had made a convention with them soon after the exchange of territory in 1868, by which the boundary had been fixed at Newtown; but in 1880 the British had wanted to move it three miles farther west, and a commission had been appointed in 1882 to delimit it, but had separated a year later without having arrived at any agreement and the subject was still in abeyance.

During 1885 a number of serious riots occurred between different town companies on the coast. One at Winneba resulted in the death of several of the combatants, and ten of the rioters were tried, condemned and executed at Accra. In Cape Coast, the Bentil (No. 1) Company, unmindful of the lesson given them a few years earlier, insulted the Anafus (No. 2), Intins (No. 3) and Inkums (No. 4) by marching through their quarters of the town with a flag made of a piece of blanket, implying that they (the Bentils) used to feed and clothe the men of the other

[1] Sarbah, *Fanti National Constitution*, pp. 159–60.

companies, and the latter of course turned out and attacked them. Another such fight occurred on the 9th of November between the villages of Akrofu and Putubu, a few miles from Cape Coast, in which several men were killed and many more wounded.

Meanwhile, the Ashanti messengers of the 16th of October 1884 were still patiently waiting in Accra. They had been promised that Mr. Kirby should accompany them to Kumasi as soon as he returned from leave. He however first got an extension of leave and then retired from the Service altogether. The disturbances in the Kitta district then broke out and required the presence of several officers on the spot, so that there had been no one available to send in his place. This outbreak was almost immediately followed by the illness and death, on the 24th of April 1885, of Governor Young. He was succeeded by Mr. W. Brandford Griffith, the former Lieutenant-Governor, who said he did not feel justified in risking the life of any officer by sending him to Kumasi during the rainy season, which was then setting in. Other messengers had arrived in the meantime from Kumasi and elsewhere in Ashanti, who had repeated the original request for the presence of an officer and shown that the Ashantis still expected the Government to fulfil its promise. Most of these later messengers had returned ; but the original embassy still remained in Accra, partly in obedience to the late Governor's orders, and partly because Buatin was afraid to return to Kumasi with no result to show from his mission beyond a vague promise of future help. The state of anarchy in Ashanti had, moreover, unsettled the neighbouring tribes. The Sefwis had closed their roads and seized traders and their goods as they passed to Jaman ; while the Adansis, having fostered and industriously spread the belief that they were under British protection, and knowing the Ashantis were too disunited to be able to interfere with them, had for months past been plundering and kidnapping or murdering everyone who passed through their district, and had now closed the road altogether. This brought the trade of Cape Coast to an absolute standstill ; but a few Ashantis still resorted to Saltpond and Accra, which they could reach by other routes.

This was the state of affairs in January 1886, when the first rumours of impending hostilities between the Bekwais and Adansis reached the coast. The Bekwais, from their position, were looked upon by the Ashantis as the guardians of the trade route, and the King of Bekwai had complained to Sir Samuel Rowe of the misdeeds of the Adansis, but had obtained no redress, and had sent to Inkansa protesting against the frequent robberies and murders of Ashanti traders by his people. The latter, however, presuming on the belief that the Bekwais would never dare to attack him so long as they imagined him to be under British protection, had sent back insulting replies and in no way amended his conduct. The King of Bekwai at this time was Kari-kari, who had succeeded Osai Yow and was an ardent supporter of the movement for electing a new King of Ashanti and re-establishing the old Confederation. To these schemes the Adansis were, of course, opposed, and Inkansa had sent Karikari a message threatening him with punishment by the Governor if he did not abandon them. Karikari however met with considerable success, and was joined by several other provinces, which, in their turn, came under the ban of Inkansa's displeasure, and the Adansis seized and put to death any of their traders whom they could find. Early in 1886, 150 Ashantis who were returning from the coast were murdered by them for the sake of the goods they were carrying, and, in March, Yow Ampow the Chief of Fumsu treated four Insutas in a similar manner.

These continual outrages and insults in spite of his protests, and the apparent hopelessness of making any appeal to the Government, so exasperated the King of Bekwai that he retaliated by seizing and afterwards putting to death sixty-five Adansi traders who were returning from Jaman, and then called out his men and swore that he would inflict a terrible punishment on his enemies and drive them out of the country. Since the

Bekwai army comprised some 8,000 men, while the Adansis could only muster about a quarter of that number, it seemed highly probable that Karikari would find very little difficulty in carrying out his threat, and Inkansa, now thoroughly frightened, sent urgent appeals to the Governor for help.

The Adansis should, of course, have moved into the Protectorate after the Treaty of Fomana, and their failure to do so had been a constant source of difficulty and embarrassment to the Government ever since. They were a troublesome and useless tribe of filibusters, ruled by an incompetent bully, who lived by murdering and robbing the traders of the very people with whom it was of most importance to the English to be on good terms, but who believed the Adansis to be under their protection and the Government consequently responsible for their conduct. Their freedom from punishment hitherto had been due solely to the belief, carefully promulgated by themselves, that the British were bound to protect them, no matter what they did or what reverse they sustained. Had the Ashantis been told plainly that the Adansis had no claims on the Government so long as they remained north of the Pra, their immunity would have been very short-lived and most of the troubles caused by their misdeeds would soon have been at an end. The Ashantis would have ceased to blame the Government for conniving at acts for which it was in no way responsible, and the Adansis would either have had to amend their ways or would have had a punishment inflicted on them that they richly deserved, and have been driven south of the Pra, where they could then have been settled and properly controlled. The present situation was of the Adansis' own seeking, and they might very well have been left to make the best of it. The Government had nothing to gain by interference, and the natural and probable conclusion of the struggle was the one that would be most to its advantage. The only guarantee that had been given to the Adansis by the Treaty of Fomana was the preservation of their independence ; but since this had only been obtained on their representation that they would in any case be compelled to migrate into the Protectorate, it might fairly be held that it was conditional on their doing so, and that, so long as they chose to remain where they were, the Government was not bound to pursue the matter farther. Policy, however, had dictated otherwise ; for it was felt that the most must be made of this, which was practically the only outstanding memento of the victories of 1874, and that it must therefore be preserved at any cost ; but the Adansis certainly had no claim to general protection, and their independence was not even threatened. The Bekwais had no intention of making them subservient to Ashanti, but merely wished to take their revenge for past injuries and compel them to make the very move which they themselves had falsely represented as inevitable in 1874.

At this time the services of a tactful man would have been invaluable in Kumasi, where the Government certainly had everything to gain both politically and commercially ; but Mr. Griffith had just declared that he could not think of risking the life of any one of his officers by sending him there during the rains ; yet he did not hestitate to send Inspector Firminger of the Gold Coast Constabulary and thirty Hausas to the infinitely more unhealthy town of Prasu on account of this threatened expulsion of the Adansis. Mr. Firminger's instructions were to collect information regarding the relations existing between the Bekwais and other Ashantis and the Adansis, and between the Ashanti provinces and Kumasi, and to disarm the Adansis should they be driven across the Pra and " take measures to intern them by arrangement with the native Kings in those portions of the Protectorate bordering on Prasu,"[1] which was of course the very last place where they should have been put. Their character and tendencies were sufficiently well known to make it certain that, if they were left close to the frontier and trade route, they would not only continue their depredations on Ashanti traders, but would also use the Protectorate as a base for raids across the border. They should have been

---

[1] Parliamentary Paper, *Affairs of the Gold Coast*, 1886, p. 9.

settled in districts as remote as possible from the Pra and the main road, and, if possible, have been broken up into comparatively small parties settled at some distance from each other, so that they would find it harder to act in concert.

On his arrival at Prasu in March, Mr. Firminger found that Karikari had died on the 1st of February and been succeeded by Yow Janfi, who had been elected on the same day. No fighting beyond two slight skirmishes between reconnoitring parties at Odumasi and Akrokeri had taken place, and Mr. Firminger reported that both sides were eager for arbitration and that hostilities might even yet be averted. The Adansis, now that their punishment seemed imminent, were absolutely terrified ; but the Bekwais and Ashantis generally seemed ready to forego their vengeance if they could get a guarantee that the road to the coast would be kept open and safe for their traders. Inkansa sent to Mr. Firminger imploring him to intercede for him by sending a messenger to the King of Bekwai, who was then encamped with his whole army at Dompoasi near Amoafu. Mr. Firminger therefore sent to ask Yow Janfi whether he would agree to state his grievances against the Adansis for the information of the Governor and refrain from further action pending the arrival of his answer. The King replied that for a very long time the Adansis had been robbing and murdering his subjects, and that his messages to Inkansa had been answered by insults, till, in self-defence, he had called out his army and was now fully prepared to drive them out of the country. He pointed out that he had already complained to Sir Samuel Rowe, but without avail, but added that, as a mark of his respect for the Governor, he was willing to postpone further action until the 20th of March. He said he would be willing to leave the settlement of the quarrel in the hands of any officer the Governor might send, but that if he had heard nothing further by the 20th, he should open his campaign on that day.

Yow Janfi had been asked if he would be willing to state his grievances to the Governor and await his decision, and his answer, which in the circumstances was very moderate, made it plain that, although he was not prepared to do this unreservedly, because past experience had taught him that the arrival of that decision might be postponed indefinitely, he was nevertheless quite ready to submit to arbitration provided it was promptly arranged. He knew well enough that the Ashanti messengers who had been given a definite promise of an officer's aid in October 1884, were still awaiting its fulfilment, but were apparently no nearer gaining their object after a delay of a year and a half than they had been then. It was not to be expected, therefore, that he would commit himself to a similar and perhaps even longer delay now that he had made all his preparations and his army had actually taken the field, and he had therefore offered the alternative suggestion that an officer should be sent at once, who should settle the dispute on the spot, and fixed a time-limit within which a reply must be given. This message, however, only reached Prasu on the 15th, and Mr. Firminger then referred it to the Governor, but did not communicate again with Yow Janfi to explain what he had done and that he could not give an answer to this proposal on his own responsibility. Had he done so it is fairly certain that the King would have given a reasonable extension of time ; but as it was, the 20th of March dawned without his having heard anything further.

Meanwhile the Adansis, to the number of about 2,500 or 3,000, were encamped at Dompoasi near the Bekwai frontier, while, in expectation of defeat, all their women and children had been collected in the villages nearest the Pra ready to cross the river at the first rumour of a reverse. On the 23rd, Yow Janfi, thinking it useless to wait any longer for a reply to his last message, sent a party—alleged by the Adansis to have been 2,000 strong— to make a reconnaissance towards the Adansi camp. They came upon the main Adansi army at Akrokeri, and after a fight lasting several hours, fell back on their main body at about four o'clock in the afternoon. The Adansis had thirty men killed and sixty wounded, but succeeded in taking the heads of five Bekwais,[1] one of whom was a Chief.   The Bekwai force, being a mere reconnoitring party, would naturally retire towards evening or as soon as they had satisfied themselves of the position and strength of the enemy ; but the Adansis had been so convinced that they would be defeated, that they lost all sense of proportion, and, when they found themselves still holding their ground after this small action, foolishly imagined that they had scored a great victory, and, from being panic-stricken at the thought of punishment, now became insolent and defiant and declared their intention of pursuing the Bekwais and carrying the war into their country.

Before news of this affair reached Prasu, Mr. Firminger had received a letter from the Governor authorizing him, if he found it necessary, to cross the Pra.   He therefore sent messages to Inkansa and Yow Janfi saying that he was coming to see them with a view to settling their disputes, and asking the latter to postpone hostilities once more, or, if he had already begun fighting, to suspend all further operations pending his arrival.   The messengers arrived in Fomana on the 24th, the day after the skirmish at Akrokeri, while the Adansis were still so elated by their imaginary victory that Inkansa refused to allow the man to proceed to Bekwai, threatening to prevent him by force if he persisted, and sent him back under escort of two of his sword-bearers with the insolent message that the white man was too late and that the Adansis would follow the Bekwais wherever they went.   Any interference with an accredited messenger is at all times a gross breach of African etiquette ; but coming after Inkansa's frantic appeals to the Government to help him, and accompanied by such a message, it was an unheard-of piece of impertinence.   Mr. Firminger would no doubt have taken strong action at once had he not been hampered to some extent by the written instructions given him by Mr. Griffith. He had been strictly enjoined " on no account to adopt a harsh tone towards any of the Kings of independent coun-

[1] One version says these heads were taken at Odumasi, and that the Bekwais carried off their dead and wounded from Akrokeri.

tries," and in the case of Inkansa especially, in spite of his outrageous conduct, to " be careful to put what you say in a friendly though grave tone, so that he may see that it is a matter of regret to this Government to address him in the language of reproof."[1] Mr. Firminger, therefore, overlooked this insult altogether and, with a forbearance that showed more self-control than wisdom, sent another friendly message to Inkansa pointing out that he was allowing himself to be misled and putting himself in a false position. Inkansa, who by this time was able to take a more accurate view of the situation, then made a polite reply and sent the messenger under escort to the Bekwai frontier. He returned four days later and reported that he had seen Yow Janfi, who had promised to await Mr. Firminger's arrival.

Mr. Firminger crossed the Pra on the 5th of April, and on the 7th and 8th had meetings with Inkansa and his Chiefs at Fomana. On both these occasions the war party predominated, and Inkansa, now that he had a British officer and Hausas in his town, was once more inclined to be boastful of what he would do to the Bekwais and wanted to prevent any communication with them ; but, after a great deal of trouble, Mr. Firminger managed to instil a little common sense into him and persuaded him to leave the settlement of the quarrel in his hands. He then visited the King of Bekwai in his camp at Begroasi. Yow Janfi was at first inclined to agree to arbitration, provided a few villages to which he laid claim were ceded to him by the Adansis ; but when he began to consult with his Chiefs, he soon discovered that they would not permit any going back now, but were quite prepared to destool him rather than forego their vengeance on Adansi. He therefore explained that, although he personally would have been willing to submit to the Governor's arbitration, he was bound by the ruling of the majority of his Council, and, since they had declared for a continuance of the war and the expulsion of the Adansis, that must perforce be his

---

[1] Parliamentary Paper, *Affairs of the Gold Coast*, 1886, p. 25.
[2] *Ibid.*, p. 18.

answer. Considering the extreme provocation that they had received and the fact that they had at last discovered that the Adansis had been lying when they said that the Government was bound to protect them, their decision was not surprising. The Bekwais had the support of the Kumasis, and their force now numbered nearly 10,000 men, while 200 more, most of whom were armed with Snider rifles and had plenty of ammunition, marched into the camp from Kumasi while Mr. Firminger was there, and he, finding he could do no more, returned to Prasu, releasing on his way forty Mampon women and children and some Akims who had been seized by the Adansis and were about to be sacrificed. He was recalled to the coast very soon afterwards.

It now seemed that the final defeat and expulsion of the Adansis must follow within the course of the next few days ; but at the last moment Kwaku Inkansa succeeded in making an alliance with the King of Dadiasi, who was afraid that if Adansi were defeated by the Ashantis his own independence might next be threatened. This completely changed the outlook ; for Dadiasi at this time was stronger than either Bekwai or Adansi and could put a large army in the field, while the Bekwais were still further weakened by the sudden withdrawal of the Kumasi contingent. The reason for their recall is unknown ; but they had probably been thought unnecessary so long as it was believed that only the Adansis would have to be dealt with, and there may, moreover, have been difficulty in supplying food for so large a number of men. It was now, too, that the first signs of danger that the protected tribes might become involved in the struggle appeared. The Akims, who were on friendly terms with the Dadiasis, gave them permission to enter their territory and undertook to close their roads to Ashanti traders, while the Upper Denkeras sent offers of assistance to the Adansis ; but before the Akims had had time to do more than seize a few traders, these schemes were nipped in the bud by the despatch of British officers to the affected districts.

On the 23rd of April the whole Adansi army, about

2,500 strong, with 300 picked Dadiasi troops, advanced against the Bekwai position at Begroasi ; but the King of Dadiasi remained encamped with his main army on the Bekwais' left flank, whence he dared not move until he had " drunk fetish " with the Chiefs of several towns who he was afraid might side with the Bekwais and attack him in the rear. The allies first came in touch with a Bekwai outpost at Ahiman soon after midday and drove it in on Pampasu, where about 1,000 Bekwais were encamped. They had barely had time to burn Ahiman when they were attacked by this force and a battle ensued which lasted till dark without either side being able to claim a victory. The next day both forces remained in their respective camps : the Bekwais had been reinforced from Begroasi during the night, but the Adansis were too busy sending back their wounded and bringing up fresh supplies of ammunition to renew the attack. On the 25th however, they again advanced and fought throughout the whole of that day and the greater part of the next before the Bekwais at length began to fall slowly back. The Adansis then took and burned Pampasu, announcing their intention of capturing Bekwai itself within the next few days.

Both sides had lost very heavily, and the Bekwais had been greatly outnumbered ; for the greater part of their army had been drawn off to watch the Dadiasis on their left flank and had been unable to take any part in the action. The success of the Adansis, however, so alarmed the Chiefs of Kumasi and the other Ashanti provinces that they sent messengers to detach the King of Dadiasi from his allegiance, who, by threatening to invade his own district, soon prevailed upon him to leave the Adansis to their fate and join them in electing a new King in Kumasi. They sent a message to Inkansa ordering him to submit his dispute with the Bekwais to them for arbitration or war would be declared against him, while the King of Dadiasi at the same time sent to inform his ally of the step he had taken and advised him to retire from the Bekwai frontier and join him in going to Kumasi and helping to place a new King on the stool.

Inkansa however preferred flight, and sought safety in the Protectorate. The Adansis, to the number of 12,411 men, women and children, crossed the Pra on the 13th of June and two following days, and, in accordance with the instructions that had been issued by Mr. Griffith on the first outbreak of the disturbance, were distributed among · the villages near the frontier. Inkansa, with about 4,000 followers, settled in Assin; Chief Kotiko, with 600 more, went to Upper Denkera; and Chief Afakwa, with about 7,000 others, to Akim. The Bekwais burned Fomana and all the other Adansi villages, and then sent messengers to inform the Governor that in future the road to the coast would be kept open by them, and that the Ashanti Chiefs were about to assemble in Kumasi to elect a new King. So complete was the destruction of Adansi that not a house remained standing throughout the whole country, and in some places even the graves were opened and despoiled of the gold that had been buried with the dead.

CHAPTER XV

THE ACCESSION OF OSAI KWAKU DUA III—PREMPI

1886 TO 1888

NEARLY two years had now elapsed since the Queen- 1886–1888
Mother first sent her messengers asking for a European CHAP. XV
officer to be sent to Kumasi. The promise had been given,
but one cause and another [1] had postponed its fulfilment
until the Bekwai-Adansi war was over. Then it had been
proposed to send Assistant-Inspector Barnett, but he was
engaged at the time in settling a dispute between King
Sakiti of Krobo and the Akwamus, arising out of a claim
by the former to establish a ferry across the River Volta
in competition with the one worked by the Akwamus.
So soon as he returned from this duty he was invalided
to England, and, Captain Barrow being too unwell to
undertake the journey, the mission to Kumasi was once
more deferred, so that it was not until the 29th of August
1886 that anything was done. Then at last the messenger
for whom the Queen-Mother had asked in October 1884,
and for whom the Ashantis had been waiting so long and
so patiently in Accra, was sent ; but instead of a European
officer, as had been asked and promised, a native interpreter was chosen. The Governor, Mr. Griffith, tried to
excuse the long delay by representing that he had no
officer fitted for the duty, which, if true, was a singular
commentary on the efficiency of his staff or the arrangements whereby every officer of experience was on leave
at one and the same time.

Even now, Mr. Badger was only sent to tide matters

[1] *Vide* p. 284.

295

over for a few months, and not to comply with the Queen-Mother's original request.   He was told to visit the Kings of Bekwai and Kokofu, both of whom had sent independent messages similar to that of Ya Kia, and was given a letter to the Queen-Mother and Chiefs of Kumasi.   This letter and the messages to the two provincial Kings, after explaining the delay that had occurred, stated that the Governor had now sent to enquire whether the Ashantis still wished an officer to be sent up and promised, if so, to send one within two months.   Seeing that the original ambassadors had never been recalled but, on the contrary, had been repeatedly reinforced and their request confirmed by others, this enquiry was clearly superfluous and only made to gain time and minimize the danger of ignoring Ashanti any longer.

Mr. Badger was well received everywhere.   The long delay would not seem specially strange to the Ashantis, with whom, as with other Africans, promptitude of action is not a strong point : it goes far, however, to prove how much in earnest they were in seeking the help of the Government that they overlooked the fact that an African had been sent to them instead of the European for whom they had asked, a circumstance which, at any other time, would certainly have been resented as a slight.   He found that Kwesi Chisi had died, and that there were now two other candidates for the vacant stool, each with his own following ; that the question had been referred to the King of Bekwai for settlement, and that he was making arrangements for an election by the different Kings and was prepared to accept the decision of the majority, after which he would send down to the Governor to renew the request for an officer to represent the Government at the actual enstoolment.

The two claimants to the stool were Ajiman Prempi and Yow Achiriboanda.   The former was a son of Ya Kia and younger brother of the late King Kwaku Dua II, while Achiriboanda was a cousin of Ya Kia, being a son of Princess Ya Fre, the youngest sister of Efua Kobri, Ya Kia's mother.   Strictly speaking, on the deposition of

Mensa, Kwesi Chisi should have succeeded and been followed by Yow Achiriboanda ; but Kwaku Dua had been nominated by his great grandfather, and, as has already been explained, he succeeded in accordance with the custom " Samansiw " so soon as he was old enough to occupy the stool that had been held for him in the meantime by his uncles Karikari and Mensa. On his death, Kwesi Chisi, who was a son of Akosua Ode, Efua Sapon's second daughter, was the rightful heir, and had been so named by Ya Kia in her original message to Governor Young. His death left Achiriboanda the rightful heir, but there were objections to him. The Ashantis like a fine-looking man for their King, and Achiriboanda was not only ill-favoured by nature, but was also extremely careless and dirty in his habits. He was, moreover, prone to intrigue with other men's wives whenever he could, and had materially increased his unpopularity in this way. The Ashantis as a whole, therefore, were not inclined to regard his candidature with favour, and were the more ready to consider the claims of Prempi, who, as the younger brother of the late King, was undoubtedly the rightful heir if the nomination of the former by Kwaku Dua I was taken to exclude those who otherwise stood before him permanently from the succession. Prempi had the votes of the Queen-Mother, the King of Jabin, and most of the Kumasi Chiefs, and was also favoured by the King of Bekwai. Achiriboanda's chief supporter was Atjiempon, the Chief of Seiwa, who had been entrusted with 3,200 ounces of gold-dust by Mensa for safe keeping, repayment of which was now demanded by Ya Kia on behalf of her son. Ya Fre, however, had promised to remit this claim if her son succeeded. This promise had completely won him over to her side, and Yow Janfi the King of Bekwai reported at the end of November that his efforts to arrange for the election of a new King were only being obstructed by this Chief.

Yow Janfi's letter, which was received on the 17th of December, also contained a complaint against the Denkeras, who were charged with lying in wait for and robbing Bekwai traders. A party returning from Cape Coast had been attacked on the evening of the 18th of November soon after they had crossed the Pra, and three of them shot dead and four more wounded from an ambush by the path : others had been captured and robbed of their goods shortly before. This, of course, was exactly what might and ought to have been foreseen. The exiled Adansis, having been allowed to settle so near the frontier, were now using the Protectorate as a base for raids against their old enemies, and had induced the Denkeras, by bribes, promises, and the hope of loot, to join them. The folly of the arrangements that had been made was now apparent ; for no one could have blamed the King of Bekwai if he had sent his men across the border to avenge these wrongs. He, however, behaved with great moderation, and, laying his complaint before the Governor, asked what was to be done, adding that he was making preparations to punish the delinquents, but would not move until he had received his reply. The rebuke contained in the last passage of his letter was well deserved. He wrote : " It is to my surprise to hear of them to have the chance of crossing the River Prah from your Excellency's jurisdiction and act so offensively in mine, therefore I earnestly beg your Excellency to enquire about this or else the result will be very serious with the Denkeras and myself. If the Denkeras overtake Her Majesty's laws to be nothing, I should say that I value Her Majesty's laws over and over more than such people under her jurisdiction ; therefore your Excellency will kindly enquire about this if possible."[1] In his letter reporting these events to the Secretary of State, the Governor disclosed the fact that he was well aware that these attacks were being made by the Adansi refugees, yet he had made no attempt to prevent their repetition nor to arrest the offenders, but excused himself on the old pretext " want of reliable officers."

Soon after the receipt of this letter, however, Inspector Dudley, who had been on sick leave to Grand Canary, returned to the Coast, and instructions were at once issued to him to proceed to Denkera and warn the Chiefs against

---

[1] Parliamentary Paper, *Affairs of the Gold Coast*, 1888, p. 11.

mixing themselves up in the quarrels of the Adansis or
allowing their people to commit acts of war of this kind.
At the same time, Assistant-Inspector Stewart was ordered
up to Prasu, whence it was arranged that he should set
out every tenth day—commencing on the 10th of January
1887—with sufficient Hausas to protect and accompany
traders until the downward escort composed of the King of
Bekwai's men was met at Akrofum with the traders coming
to the coast : the two parties would then hand over their
respective charges and return to fetch others. Before this
arrangement came into operation, however, further outrages had been committed. At the end of December, an
Adansi Chief named Karsang crossed the frontier from
Upper Denkera at the head of a strong force and destroyed
two Bekwai villages, killing thirteen of the inhabitants and
carrying off more than a hundred others into Denkera,
and, at about the same time, another party attacked some
traders on the road near Kwisa and killed one man. It
also became known that the Adansis living in Akim had
induced the Chief of Akim-Swedru to espouse their cause,
and that they were planning a combined attack on Bekwai.

Inspector Dudley first visited Jukwa, the capital of
Lower Denkera, where the King, Bo Amponsam, denied all
knowledge of the doings of the Adansis. He said none of
their Chiefs were living in his country, and that, so far as
he was aware, there were none in Upper Denkera either.
Mr. Dudley was then taken ill and obliged to return to
Elmina, but afterwards visited Koshia and Babiensu in
Upper Denkera, where he found that the majority of the
refugees were not Adansis, but Inkwantas and Daniasis
who had fled with them. Karsang, however, and many
others were there, but it was impossible to recover any of
the captured Bekwais, as the few who had not been
slaughtered had already been sold to the Sefwis or any
other chance purchaser who would buy them. This was
freely admitted by Karsang, who, indeed, seemed quite
unable to realize that he and his people had done anything
to merit reproof, though it was also alleged that he had
murdered twenty-five Bekwai messengers some time

before.   Inspector Dudley was of opinion that the Denkeras themselves were less involved than had been supposed, as the refugees were present in such numbers—
estimated by Karsang at 20,000—that the local Chiefs were
quite powerless to control them and they were doing
exactly as they liked.   He found, however, that Bo
Amponsam had accepted bribes, and strongly suspected
that much of the trouble had been instigated by bad
advisers in Cape Coast.   Several of the refugee Chiefs,
indeed, were so independent that they had even omitted
to report their presence to the Head Chief of Upper Denkera, a gross breach of etiquette which had greatly annoyed
him.   Mr. Dudley alone seems to have realized the true
cause of the trouble and its only remedy.   He had written
before and now wrote again, urging the necessity for
immediately removing the refugees to some part of the
Protectorate nearer the coast, where they could be split
up into a number of small parties and kept under proper
supervision.

While these events had been taking place on the frontier,
Ababio, the Chief of Adukrum in Akwapim, had also been
giving trouble.   He had been in revolt against his paramount Chief, Kwamin Fori of Akropong, for some time
past, and now openly defied the Government.   In 1885 two
men had been killed in a disturbance in his town, which he
had neglected to report, and when he, as Chief, had been
called upon to arrest the murderers, he had failed to do
so or to appear before Kwamin Fori when summoned to
explain his conduct.   In December 1886 a bailiff was sent
to his town to serve a summons on one of the inhabitants,
who promptly tore it in two and attempted to strike
the officer.   Other police who went to arrest some of the
villagers were assaulted, and Mr. Riby Williams, the
District Commissioner at Akuse, then went to Adukrum
to enquire into the matter.   He was met with absolute
defiance.   On sending his orderly to ask the Chief to come
and see him, the answer he got was that he himself must
go to the Chief's house and salute him.   The orderly was
then sent back to tell Ababio he must come immediately,

which, after some delay, he did. Asked what he meant by sending such an insolent message, Ababio replied that " he was master of the town, and that the Commissioner must come and see him." [1] Mr. Williams then told him that some policemen had been assaulted in his town while in the execution of their duties, and that the Governor wished him to assist in having the offenders arrested. To this he replied with further insolent remarks, and finally told the Commissioner that, since he was the person who had been sent, he had better catch the men himself, after which he demanded payment as compensation for having been sent for, and, springing up from his chair, shook his stick in Mr. Williams' face and went off angrily, shouting, " Go and arrest the people yourself." A warrant was then issued for the arrest of the men who had assaulted the police, and a sergeant, a corporal, and four constables were sent to Biwasi, a neighbouring village, to execute it. They had no sooner caught and handcuffed the first prisoner however, than they were set upon by a number of men, who knocked them down, rescued the prisoner, and then drove off the police, declaring that no matter how many men the Government might send to arrest them they would beat them to death.

This outrageous conduct was at once reported to the Governor ; Captain Douglas was sent to Kwamin Fori at Akropong to request him to hand over Ababio, and forty-four Hausas were sent to assist him in doing so. This force marched out of Christiansborg at a quarter-past ten on the night of the 19th of December, taking sixty rounds of ball cartridge in their pouches, besides spare ammunition, a rocket trough, and two boxes of war rockets. At a quarter-past nine on the morning of the 21st they entered Akropong, where they met Mr. Williams and seven more Hausas whom he had brought with him. Kwamin Fori was at once seen and Ababio sent for. That night a message was brought in that the Chief was considering whether he would come in or not ; but the next morning

---

[1] This was strictly correct according to native custom, but it is seldom followed.

word was brought that he had refused to do so. Preparations were therefore made for an advance on Adukrum and the capture of the Chief. A message was sent warning him to send all the women and children out of the town, and Kwamin Fori was told to collect his fighting men and see that they all tied a piece of white cloth to the barrels of their muskets lest they should be shot by the Hausas by mistake. These preparations had the desired effect and convinced the people that the Government was in earnest. By daybreak the next morning Ababio had come in, and was formally handed over by Kwamin Fori on the morning of the 23rd, when he was taken down to Accra and deposed.

As far back as 1883 the Manchester Chamber of Commerce had pointed out that, while the imports of cotton goods into other parts of West Africa had shown a steady increase during the preceding five years, yet they had declined on the Gold Coast. They further complained that although the revenue of the Colony had greatly increased since the purchase of the Dutch Possessions, when an *ad valorem* duty of four per cent had been imposed, there were as yet no improvements to show for it. There were still no proper roads, and the streets in the coast towns were unlighted. They asked for a proper system of sanitation, railways, and the appointment of a British Resident in Kumasi. They also strongly urged the separation of the Gold Coast from Lagos, pointing out that the two Colonies were so far apart that it was quite impossible for them to be satisfactorily administered by a single officer ; while the upkeep of the Colonial steamer in which he used to travel to and fro involved an unnecessary expenditure of over £8,000 a year.

The Secretary of State said there were " strong reasons of policy and prudence " against the appointment of a Resident in Kumasi, the main reason, of course, being that the Government was at this time wedded to its policy of non-interference in the affairs of the interior and especially afraid of becoming involved in those of Ashanti. Moreover, since it had by this policy succeeded in breaking up

ie kingdom into a number of more or less independent
ictions, it would have been no easy matter to decide to
·hom such an officer should be accredited, and any officer
ppointed as Resident would have found it almost im-
ossible to avoid mixing himself up to some extent with
ishanti affairs.

Whether as a direct result of these representations or
.ot, however, new Letters Patent were issued on the 13th
f January 1886 whereby the Gold Coast and Lagos were
nade separate Colonies.

At the commencement of 1887, the Chambers of Com-
nerce addressed another memorial to the Secretary of
 itate complaining of the " apathy and inactivity " of the
iold Coast Government. They pointed out that although
wenty years earlier the annual value of the exports of
Iritish cottons to the West African Colonies had amounted
o £300,000, rising ten years later to £550,000 and reaching
,591,000 in 1884, they had declined in the following year to
£388,000, and in 1886 to only £318,000. This great falling
ff they attributed, and justly so, to " no serious steps
iaving been taken to maintain proper authority both
within and on our borders, and to keep a clear highway
or the trade into the interior," and alleged that much of
the trade was being diverted into other countries and that
British influence was declining. They contended that the
official returns gave a false appearance of prosperity by
showing an increased revenue, which was, however, really
due to the heavy duties on foreign spirits, tobacco, arms
and ammunition, the trade in which was almost entirely
in foreign hands and of little or no benefit to British
commerce. In support of their statements they instanced
the attacks on traders by the refugees in Denkera, the
stopping of the roads to Jaman by the Sefwis, and the
fact that a letter written by the Secretary of State in July
1885, asking for information about Ashanti and the future
policy of the Government towards it, had been allowed
to lie unanswered until April 1886, while even then no
opinion had been given on the important question of policy,
but the Governor had merely written that " he had not

sent up an officer, not having a man to spare," and tha therefore " no action had been possible."

There was undoubtedly a great deal of truth in these statements. The principal falling off in the trade wa in 1885, and it was in October 1884 that the Queen-Mothe had sent her messengers asking the Governor to send ai officer to assist in the election of a new King ; yet, as ha been shown, no one was sent until August 1886, and ever then only a native interpreter. This long and seemingly quite unnecessary delay had given time for the growth o many quarrels that would probably never have arisen, ox at any rate not have been allowed to last so long, if the kingdom had had a ruler at its head, and more especially one supported by the prestige of having been enstooled in the presence of an officer of the British Government sent up for the purpose at the request of the nation.

In January 1887 the only hope of a speedy settlement of affairs in Ashanti lay in the possibility that the King of Bekwai might succeed in his efforts to arrange for the election of a new King ; but he was thwarted by Atjiempon, who received some support from agents on the coast, who persistently spread false reports in Ashanti that the Government was opposed to the election of Prempi. The Prempi party now consisted of the Kumasi Chiefs, Awua of Bantama, and the Kings of Bekwai and Jabin. Achiri-boanda was supported by the Kings of Kokofu, Mampon and Insuta, led by Atjiempon.

During the last week in January, the rival parties met for a conference at Seiwa, when it was agreed that the question of the succession should be settled by vote, and the King of Bekwai then proposed that they should separate and meet again in a few days' time to complete the business. He seems, however, to have been thoroughly exasperated by the long opposition of Atjiempon and attacked him on his way home to his village. Atjiempon and his Chiefs, finding all hope of escape gone, sat down and tried to commit suicide, in which most of them suc-ceeded, but Atjiempon, though he shot himself in the throat, did not die at once, but was either killed by the

Bekwais or succumbed to his wound soon afterwards. Several other Chiefs are said to have been killed at the same time, amongst them the Chief Linguist to the King of Kokofu. The Bekwais then advanced against the Kokofus, who had sent out to demand an explanation, and having defeated them, burned their town.

At about the same time a large body of Inkwantas, who had been helped with guns and ammunition by the Denkeras, crossed the frontier into Bekwai. Inspector Dudley had already returned to Elmina, and Captain Lonsdale was therefore sent up to restrain them. He found, as Inspector Dudley had done, that the refugees were present in great numbers and were really lording it over the Denkera Chiefs, who, however, were proved to have given them assistance in return for bribes and pawns. He also heard that a battle had taken place on the 27th of January, in which the Inkwantas had been victorious, and that some Kumasi messengers had been murdered at Akwabosu, a village within the Protectorate. He endorsed the recommendation of Inspector Dudley urging the immediate removal of the Adansi and Inkwanta Chiefs and their followers to the coast. Mr. Griffith had now gone on leave, and Colonel White, who was acting, lost no time in carrying out this very necessary step and settled the Adansis near Insaba, in the Aguna district, where the Chief agreed to have them and gave them land. The Denkera Chiefs who had been aiding them in their forays were also punished.

The Kokofus, after the destruction of their town, fled to Tupretu, where they made preparations to avenge Atjiempon, and, on the 26th of April, attacked the Bekwais at Ahuri, but were defeated and driven off. Six days later the Bekwais succeeded in drawing the Inkwantas into an ambush, in which about 300 of them were killed and, driving the remainder across the Pra, enabled Captain Lonsdale to secure the Chiefs and send them down to the coast.

The Kokofus then attacked the Bekwais, and, on the 14th of May, drove them out of their camps, destroyed one of their villages, captured several of their Chiefs, and compelled them to retreat towards Kumasi. Osai Asibi, the King of Kokofu, then sent word to the Governor that he was in possession of the Bekwai country and was keeping the road open for traders, and asked that the Adansis might be induced to return to their own lands.

The Bekwais meanwhile had been joined by Awua of Bantama and a number of men from the districts to the south-east of Kumasi. This made them as strong as ever again, and the fact that they had Achiriboanda in their hands gave them a decided advantage, though they dared not put him to death because he was of royal blood. Both sides were really tired of fighting with such varying success, and Osai Asibi sent messages to Ya Kia saying that he and his people were ready to come to a settlement, while the King of Bekwai was reported to be suing for terms of peace. The moment, therefore, seemed a favourable one for intervention, and Colonel White authorized Captain Lonsdale to try to secure a cessation of hostilities and establish, with the consent of the people, a central government in the country. He was expressly ordered, however, to make it quite clear that the Government was only anxious to bring the existing unsatisfactory state of affairs to an end, and, though prepared to recognize any form of government on which the Ashantis might agree, had no wish to influence their choice, nor would Captain Lonsdale enter Kumasi until all the Chiefs had expressed their willingness to accept his assistance. The Secretary of State added instructions that any King of Ashanti who might be elected must be made to understand that the Government would accept no responsibility to help him if any of his people should revolt or secede.

Captain Lonsdale had recently returned from a tour through Lower Wassaw, Denkera and Sefwi, and, on the 8th of February 1887, had concluded a treaty with the latter tribe, the principal articles of which were as follows :

" II. The Governor of the Gold Coast Colony hereby takes the country of Sefwhi under the protection of Great Britain.

" III. The Government of Her Majesty the Queen of
Great Britain and Ireland, Empress of India, will not prevent Kwaku Inguan, King of Sefwhi, or his lawful successors either in the levying of revenues appertaining to
them according to the laws and customs of the country,
nor in the exercise of the administration thereof ; and Her
Majesty's Government will respect the habits and customs
of the country, but will prevent human sacrifices ; and
slave dealing, when brought to the notice of the Government, will be punished according to the laws of the Gold
Coast Colony." [1]

The Sefwis, therefore, in return for British protection,
agreed to abolish human sacrifices and slave dealing ; but
the other rights and judicial powers of their rulers were
preserved to them.

Captain Lonsdale was joined by Assistant-Inspector
Barnett and a party of Hausa Constabulary, and crossed
the Pra on the 10th of August. The effects of the long continued warfare were everywhere visible : from the river to
Ajaman, three days' journey, the whole country had been
laid waste ; not a house remained in any of the villages ;
even the trees had been cut down, and mutilated and decomposing bodies lay around. The King of Kokofu was
encamped at Ajaman with about 6,000 men, many of
whom were armed with Sniders. He was most anxious
that Captain Lonsdale should stay there ; but he insisted
on pushing on to Ajabin, which was a neutral village about
four hours south of Kumasi and about two hours' march
from where the King of Bekwai and Awua had their
camps. Numbers of dead were seen lying around, and as
both sides were ready to renew hostilities, it was evident
that he had been sent up none too soon. Some skirmishing,
indeed, had taken place on the 8th, and a general engagement had been expected on the 15th, but was fortunately
prevented by Captain Lonsdale, who sent messengers
forward from Akankuasi and prevailed upon the advancing
Bekwais to turn off towards their own town. They wanted
to come and see him, but as it was evidently their intention

[1] Sarbah, *Fanti National Constitution*, p. 110.

to march through the Kokofu camp, which would have been certain to provoke a fight, he went over to Bekwai on the 19th and extracted a promise from the Chiefs that they would advance no farther.

Captain Lonsdale's chief object now was to induce the Chiefs to return to their respective towns and recall their armies. The King of Kokofu had already given a promise to do so as soon as Awua of Bantama withdrew, and on the 24th Captain Lonsdale visited the Bekwai camp to try to persuade him to do so. Asafu Buachi and all the Kumasi Chiefs were there, but were most unwilling to leave the field, and finally made their departure conditional on the destoolment of the King of Kokofu, who, they declared, was responsible for there being no King on the stool of Kumasi. The next day, however, partly as a result of Captain Lonsdale's refusal to hold any communications with anyone out of his own country, they started for their homes. The Kokofus also returned to their town soon afterwards, and the women and children then began to come back to and rebuild the villages.

The hostilities had hitherto been confined to the Kokofus, Bekwais, and some of the Kumasis ; but reports now came in that several other tribes were preparing to take the field. This threatened to complicate matters further, and Captain Lonsdale therefore sent Mr. Barnett to persuade them to remain quiet. On reaching the other side of Kumasi, he found as many as four armies in the field, those of Mampon and Aguna being about to attack those of Ofinsu and Ejisu ; but after visiting the Kings and Chiefs, he was able to return to Captain Lonsdale on the 18th of October and report that they had all returned to their homes, that the prisoners had been exchanged, and that the country was again safe for travellers. During his absence, Captain Lonsdale had held numerous meetings with the Kokofus and Bekwais, and at length succeeded in inducing the Kings to " drink fetish " together by proxy, through their respective Princesses, that they would keep the peace. The King of Kokofu immediately broke this oath by putting to death all the Bekwai prisoners then in his hands, but fortunately this shameful act did not become known until some time afterwards. Peace having now been restored, the Chiefs began to prepare for the election and Captain Lonsdale left for Accra on the 18th of November to confer with the Governor on the policy to be followed in Ashanti in future, leaving Mr. Barnett in charge at Ajabin. While he was in Accra, however, his health broke down, and, in January 1888, he was invalided to England and died in Liverpool immediately after landing.

The peaceful state of affairs that had been brought about by Captain Lonsdale's negotiations did not last long. He had barely left for the coast when Achiriboanda escaped from the Prempi party and sought refuge with the King of Kokofu, who, believing the balance of power was now with him, ordered all his people to rejoin him in camp and once more prepared to attack the Bekwais. He next sent messengers to " drink fetish " with the King and Chiefs of Inkwanta, who were then in Upper Denkera and readily promised him their support. These Chiefs, who had been the cause of so much trouble before, had been allowed by Sir Brandford Griffith [1] to return to their own lands in Ashanti, and were then on their way there, accompanied by a police sergeant, whose presence naturally lent them some importance. This extraordinary step had been taken without any notification of it being sent to Mr. Barnett, who had considerable difficulty in bringing the alliance to an end and bitterly complained of having been kept in the dark about political movements that directly concerned the situation in Ashanti.

The renewed hostility of the Kokofus, just when their troubles seemed to be at an end, greatly alarmed the other tribes and made them more than ever anxious to get the election over without further delay, and, in the middle of January 1888, they sent to enquire from Mr. Barnett when steps would be taken to place a King on the stool, saying that it was now nearly three months since they had " drunk fetish " together for this purpose, but nothing more had been done. The King of Kokofu, indeed, was now the sole

[1] Recently promoted K.C.M.G.

cause of delay, and he was only holding out in the vain hope that something might turn up in his favour. The King of Mampon, hitherto a leading spirit of his party, had now left him and joined with Awua in inviting Mr. Barnett to come to Kumasi, saying they had agreed to send messengers to all the Chiefs summoning them to the capital to take part in the election of a new King. It was no longer in doubt who the successful candidate would be ; Prempi now had an overwhelming majority, and though the King of Kokofu still supported Achiriboanda, keeping up a camp of some 7,000 men, in which he collected all the criminals and scoundrels in the country, the latter had greatly damaged his cause by his notorious intrigues with married women, many of them the wives of Chiefs.

At last, early in March, Awua and the Kumasi Chiefs, wearying of the continued delays, formally nominated their candidate and placed him on the " Odum Stool " preliminary to the actual coronation ceremony when he would be placed on the " Golden Stool." News of this was sent to Mr. Barnett by the King of Mampon, who was afraid the coronation might be completed without the presence of any officer of the Government and urged him to come to Kumasi at once, which he did, arriving on the 15th. He was accorded a most enthusiastic welcome, and two days later sent messages to all the provincial Kings informing them that he had arrived and was waiting to see them elect their King. No African likes to be hurried ;[1] and though they all sent word that they were coming, it was some time before they began to arrive. Mr. Barnett, however, had received most definite orders that he was to leave Kumasi not later than the 10th of April whether a King had been enstooled or not. The Kumasi Chiefs implored him to postpone his departure, but he had to refuse, and they then did all they could to have everything ready by the 27th, which, according to their beliefs, would be the only propitious day before the 27th of April.

On the morning of the 26th, messengers arrived from the King of Kokofu saying that he could only come to

---

[1] And the more important the business, the more deliberate he is.

Kumasi on condition that everyone was forgiven for the crimes of rebellion, adultery with Chiefs' wives, murder, and other capital offences, a stipulation that showed more clearly than anything else could have done the kind of people he had been harbouring in his camp. After some discussion, so anxious were the Kumasis to get the election over, it was agreed that Ya Kia, Awua, and Asafu Buachi should meet him outside the town and there " drink fetish " with him to pardon all such offences of his followers. This had no sooner been arranged, however, and the King of Kokofu's messengers had not long left the town on their return journey, when fresh messengers arrived from him and the King of Mampon, saying they could not possibly be ready on that day and begging Mr. Barnett to postpone the election until the next Big Adaï. This fell on the 27th of April, and in view of the very definite orders he had received he had to refuse. The representatives of these two Kings were themselves astonished at the messages, and admitted that the ceremony could not be postponed, while the Mampon messenger added that they had no objection to offer to the enstoolment of Prempi. The real reason why these two Kings did not come in was because they were still uncertain what kind of reception might be awaiting them ; Kokofu, on account of his own hostility and the many serious crimes committed by his people, and Mampon, because it was known that, though now loyal to Prempi, he had previously been a leader of the Achiriboanda faction and had recently accepted a bribe of £100 from it. They also seem to have been encouraged to hold out by agents on the coast, who were bent on thwarting the Government's policy in Ashanti by spreading false reports and discrediting Mr. Barnett's authority. At midnight, therefore, the final enstoolment took place in the presence of Mr. Barnett, and Prempi assumed the title of Osai Kwaku Dua III. Ashanti custom required the presence of the Kings of Mampon and Kokofu at this ceremony, so that, strictly speaking, it was incomplete and hardly legal ; but their representatives were present and assured Mr. Barnett that neither would raise any objections and that the long-continued feuds might now be considered at an end. The new King then asked him to witness the " drinking of fetish," by which all past offences were wiped out, and celebrated his accession by liberating all prisoners both political and criminal.

Mr. Barnett left Kumasi on the 6th of April, accompanied by representatives of the King, who were sent to thank the Governor for what he had done and to request that, in view of the continued disaffection of the Kokofus, the passage of arms and ammunition over the Pra might be prohibited. The King also asked that any Ashantis living on the coast who were known to be meddling with Ashanti politics might be driven away, and sought permission to send down any doubtful persons who came to him representing themselves as Government messengers to be dealt with by the Governor. The sale of arms was soon afterwards prohibited for a time on account of a disturbance in Akim, and Yow Wua, the Kokofu agent in Cape Coast, was imprisoned as a political offender.

During these negotiations Mr. Barnett had frequently urged the necessity of appointing a British Resident in Kumasi after a King had been elected. He pointed out that, after the long period during which the kingdom had been torn by opposing factions, it would be no easy task for any King to restore peace and unity at once, and that no matter which candidate eventually proved successful, there might be a tendency to punish his former opponents, which would be likely to cause further outbreaks. The presence of a duly accredited officer of the Government would greatly minimise, even though it might not entirely abolish this risk, and his presence, advice and support would so strengthen the King's hands that he would be able to resettle his country, put down barbarous and corrupt practices, and encourage trade far more effectively than he could hope to do unaided. It would, moreover, have given confidence to the Jamans and others who were anxious to pass through to the coast to trade, but were at present afraid to do so ; it would have discouraged any persons inclined to delay the restoration of peace, and

would have put an entire stop to the intrigues of those
on the coast who were inclined to interfere in Ashanti
politics by at once exposing their false messengers. The
Cape Coast trading firms also renewed their appeal for
the appointment of such an officer in order to prevent
the trade routes being again closed, and pointed out that
" the destruction of the Ashantee power by the expedition
under Sir Garnet Wolseley having removed the central
authority which had previously kept the surrounding
countries and tribes in subjection and order, devolved
upon the destroyer the responsibility for peace and order.
The refusal of that responsibility by Her Majesty's Government has involved those countries in twelve years of war
and anarchy, and this Colony in a long period of anxious
dependence on a fluctuating commerce, which has finally
culminated in a large decrease in the import of British
manufactures." [1]

Sir Brandford Griffith was opposed to this, partly on
the ground of expense and partly because he failed to
appreciate the probable difficulty of the King's position,
and considered that, having been elected by a majority of
his people, he should be able to control them unaided.
His refusal was endorsed by the Secretary of State, but it
is to be regretted that this suggestion was not acted upon,
for the Government certainly stood to gain more than it
could lose by it. It was estimated that in order to ensure
the safety of a Resident and give him such moral support
as would make it fairly certain that his advice would be
followed, it would be necessary to maintain two officers, a
surgeon, and 100 Hausas in Kumasi, and that their pay,
together with the cost of transport, would amount to
£7,000 a year. This would appear, however, to have been
a very exaggerated estimate ; for the maintenance of a
large force of Hausas was only necessary on account of the
possibility of conflict with Ashanti, so that this small
detachment could easily have been spared from the Colony,
where their services were not really required. They would
have had to be paid equally whether they were stationed

[1] Parliamentary Paper, *Affairs of the Gold Coast*, 1888, p. 3.

on the coast or in Kumasi, and the only extra cost to the Government, therefore, would have been the duty allowance to the officer who acted as Resident, the transport, and possibly an extra surgeon, amounting certainly to not more than £1,500, or at most £2,000, a year. The moment was a most favourable one for making the experiment ; the Ashantis had for months past been imploring the Government to send an officer to aid them in " putting their country in order ; " at the enstoolment of Prempi they had freely acknowledged that the restoration of peace was solely due to the intervention of the Government, and there can be no doubt that they would gladly have welcomed a British Resident. Had a suitable man been appointed now, he might have gained their friendship and confidence, and much loss of commercial prosperity and the necessity for subsequent costly expeditions might conceivably have been avoided. At any rate, with so much to be gained, the cost of making the experiment was trifling.

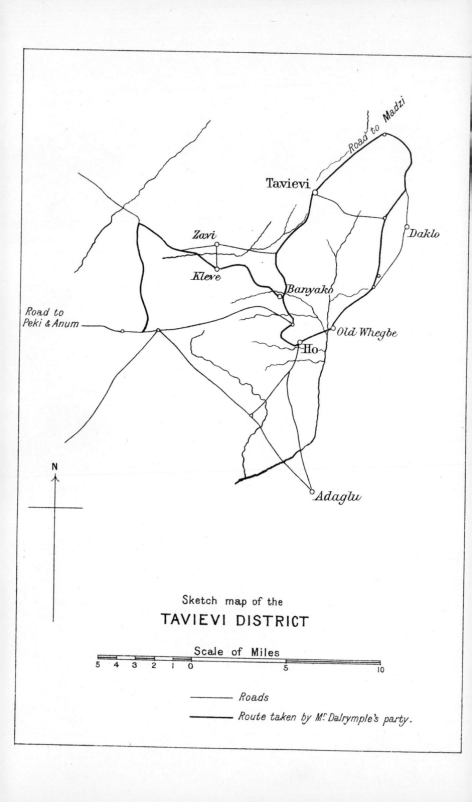

Road to Madzi

Tavievi

Daklo

Zavi

Kleve

Banyako

Road to
Peki & Anum

Old Whegbe

Ho

N

Adaglu

Sketch map of the
TAVIEVI DISTRICT

Scale of Miles

5 4 3 2 1 0   5   10

———— Roads

▬▬▬▬ Route taken by Mr Dalrymple's party.

CHAPTER XVI

THE TAVIEVI REBELLION

1888 TO 1889

THE troubles in Ashanti had no sooner been brought to end by the enstoolment of Prempi, than difficulties arose in the eastern district of the Colony itself. In April 1887 Kobina Achiri, the Chief of Wanki on the southern border of Eastern Akim, suddenly put forward a claim to the town of Insuaim, the capital of Atta Fua the King of Western Akim, and to the ferry over the River Birim which had always been worked by his people. Attempts had twice been made to settle the dispute, during one of which Assistant-Inspector Lethbridge had bound over the Chiefs of Eastern Akim in £1,000 to be of good behaviour, but without success, and in April 1888 the Assistant Colonial Secretary, Mr. Turton, was sent up to deal with it. He found the Chief of Wanki very truculent ; his arbitration was refused, and the Eastern Akims began to assemble in arms and were threatening to attack Atta Fua's people and take the river and town by force. Mr. Turton therefore sent to Accra for assistance, and 150 Hausas under Assistant-Inspector Brennan were sent up to preserve peace.

While these negotiations were going on in Akim, the Tavievis, a turbulent tribe in the Volta River district who had recently refused to meet the Commissioner and accept a flag he had brought them, and between whom and the Krepis there was a long-standing feud, suddenly attacked Zavi, a town belonging to the latter tribe, and killed seventeen of the inhabitants.

This feud dated back to the year 1870, when a dispute had arisen between the two tribes and the late King of Krepi [1] had been defeated by a combined force of Tavievis and Madzis. About 1876 he had invited the Chief of Tavievi to come to Zavi and make peace with him, and the latter, who was an old man, had sent between forty and fifty of his people, who had promptly been massacred by the Krepis. The recent attack on Zavi had been made to avenge these people.

Kujo De, the King of Krepi,[2] when sending word of this attack on his people to the Governor, intimated that he was about to take his revenge, and, as this seemed likely to lead to serious consequences, Assistant-Inspector Dalrymple was sent up with sixty-three men of the Hausa Constabulary to prevent him ; but he was specially enjoined not to use force unless actually compelled to do so.

Mr. Dalrymple was joined at Akuse by Mr. Bennett, the acting Commissioner of the Volta River district, who was to co-operate with him. On reaching Zavi on the 18th of April, they found Kujo De with an army of about 3,000 men, which was being hourly reinforced and was about to attack the Tavievis ; while the latter had ambuscaded all the paths and were murdering anyone who passed, so that it was impossible to go more than a few hundred yards outside the town without being fired on. The attack on Zavi had been accompanied by the most frightful atrocities. The Tavievis had seized a number of children, some of whom they had pounded to death in the great wooden mortars used for mashing yams ; others they had seized by the legs and, swinging them round, dashed out their brains against the trunks of trees. They had then lopped off the hands of the remainder and sent them back to carry the news to their people. The sight of their bleeding stumps and the terrible tale they told had naturally filled the Krepis with the fiercest longings for revenge, and Mr. Dalrymple had the greatest possible difficulty in restraining them. At length, however, partly by threats of force and partly by picketing the roads and

[1] Kujo De V.　　　　[2] Kujo De VI.

cutting off much of their food supply, he succeeded in dispersing the Krepi army, and then, in accordance with instructions received from Accra, went on to Tavievi to arrest those responsible for the attack on a charge of murder.

Belo Kobina, the Chief of Tavievi, met him at Peki and to all appearances was quite ready to do whatever he was told, but in reality he was secretly prepared to go to any lengths rather than submit to punishment for what he had done. As the Tavievis themselves expressed it, they knew " they had already put their necks upon the block and, therefore, they might do anything they liked " : in fact, it became known a little later that plans had been made to murder both officers during the night of the 10th and had only been prevented by heavy rain.

At a meeting held at Tavievi on the 11th of May, the fact was elicited that Belo Kobina himself and several of his Chiefs had been present at the attack on Zavi, and Mr. Dalrymple then formally arrested them and told them they would have to return with him to Accra. He then sent Mr. Bennett on ahead with the carriers, saying he would follow with the Hausas and prisoners ; but the short interval between the departure of the two parties enabled the Chiefs to issue secret orders to their men to conceal themselves near the path and fire on the escort if they should be with them.

Soon after two o'clock, the detachment of Constabulary started for Ho, the prisoners and their escort being at the head of the column. About two miles from the town, at the point where the road to Zavi branched off, the Hausas espied some men hiding in the bush near the path with their guns and warned Mr. Dalrymple ; but he, thinking they would never dare to fire on his party, told them to push on. One of the prisoners, however, called to the men to fire, because they were being taken away. Two or three snots were then fired from the bush, and Mr. Dalrymple only had time to order his bugler to sound the " Commence fire " when he was hit in the abdomen and fell dead. The Tavievis ran in to secure his head, but were driven off by the Hausas, who fired several volleys and a rocket, and then kept up a running fire while they put the body in a hammock and carried it to Ho : altogether they fired nearly 800 rounds.

The Hausas behaved extremely well, and though several of the prisoners, including Belo Kobina, escaped during the confusion and ten others were shot down while attempting to follow them, they brought the remaining five through to Ho. Seven Hausas were missing, two of whom were known to have been killed, and two more were wounded, while some of Mr. Bennett's carriers who had loitered on the road were also wounded by a party of Tavievis who had gone in pursuit of him. One of the missing men turned up nine days later, having lost his way and been wandering in the bush in the meantime. Mr. Dalrymple's body was buried in the Mission Cemetery at Ho, but was afterwards exhumed by the Governor's order and taken to Accra for burial at Christiansborg.

This murder created a profound sensation on the Gold Coast, for such a crime was almost unprecedented. Never before, with the exception of the historic but long-forgotten instances of Governor Hogenboom, Mr. Meredith, and a few others, had a white man's life being taken otherwise than in open warfare, and it was felt that unless prompt and drastic measures were taken to punish the Tavievis, this immunity would soon be at an end. It was evident, however, that since they had already gone to such extremes, they might be prepared to go to almost any lengths rather than submit, and since any want of success in an expedition against them would be fatal to its main object, it was decided to make the punitive force as strong as possible.

Assistant-Inspectors Brennan and Stewart were still in Akim with 130 Hausas, and orders were now sent to them to move to Pong on the River Volta, where they were to be met by Assistant-Inspector Akers, who was to march from Kitta with every man who could be spared from the district. No time was lost : in less than three hours after the receipt of his orders Mr. Akers was on the road with 120 Hausas and a gun, and entered Pong on the 20th, where he found twenty-seven Hausas and three 7-pounder guns that had been sent up from Accra awaiting him. His orders had been to await Mr. Brennan here unless he found that Mr. Bennett was in actual danger ; but being unable to obtain any news of the former, and fearing there might be great difficulty in getting the guns and ammunition over the road to Ho if he waited any longer now that the heavy rains had set in, he decided, since the road was perfectly safe, to push on at once, so as to give his men a rest before they were wanted for fighting. He reached Ho on the 25th, and was there joined by the remainder of Mr. Dalrymple's force, which brought the number of men in his command up to over 200.

Meanwhile, Mr. Turton was still at Insuaim. His efforts to settle the quarrel there had been unsuccessful, and he had sent an urgent message to Accra that an immediate outbreak of hostilities was probable and asked for reinforcements. Mr. Brennan, too, had sent him word that there were 2,000 or 3,000 armed men in Wanki ready to fight, and more were hourly arriving. His report, in fact, was so alarming that the expedition against the Tavievis was temporarily abandoned ; seventy-five Hausas were sent him from the coast, the Governor of Lagos was asked to lend 100 more, and Mr. Akers was ordered to leave a small detachment with Mr. Bennett at Ho and proceed at once to Insuaim with the remainder of his men. These instructions left Accra on the 24th of May ; but before they reached Ho, Mr. Akers, still unable to hear anything of Mr. Brennan's whereabouts, and believing himself strong enough to deal with the Tavievis without waiting for him, had already marched against them.

The Tavievi country was difficult to approach. It lay in an oval-shaped valley about eight miles long by two wide, and was surrounded on all sides by precipitous and densely wooded mountains attaining a height of some 2,000 feet. The only known approaches to this valley were by two narrow paths through the forest, one of which led over the mountains, and was, consequently, very steep and difficult, while the other and longer one passed through

a narrow gorge at its southern end and could have been
held by a few men against almost any number. There
were other paths ; but they were known only to the
Tavievis, who never used them except in time of war to
outflank an enemy or take him in the rear.

Mr. Akers marched out of Ho at one o'clock on the
morning of the 29th of May with 120 men. They took the
mountain path and reached the summit of the range two
hours later. Here they halted for half an hour, and then
descended into the valley and succeeded in getting within
two and a half miles of the town before they were discovered. The Tavievis then fired on the advance-guard,
but did no damage, and a quarter of a mile farther on again
opened fire and killed a lance-corporal, but were soon
driven back, and though they attempted another stand
at the branch road where Mr. Dalrymple had been killed
and kept up an intermittent fire as they retreated, the
Hausas pushed steadily on and entered Tavievi at a few
minutes before five. The town was quickly cleared, and
some of Mr. Dalrymple's property recovered. The remainder of the men and the stores were then brought up
from Ho, and at three o'clock that afternoon Kujo De and
the Chief of Ho arrived with 1,500 men, who were at once
set to work to clear the bush around the town. The place
had been won at a very trifling cost : the Constabulary's
only loss was the one lance-corporal killed, while the native
scouts had two men wounded. The enemy, however, were
believed to have lost about thirty men : they had never
expected a night attack, and had been taken almost
completely by surprise. The next few days were occupied
in sending out patrols, who scattered the Tavievis whenever
they attempted to assemble in any force, and in receiving
the Chiefs of the neighbouring towns, who all hastened to
come or send representatives to express their gratitude for
what had been done.

On the night of the 31st of May Mr. Akers received his
orders to proceed to Akim. He detailed a sergeant-major
and fifty men to hold Tavievi with 3,000 Krepis under
Kujo De, leaving them strict orders to act only on the

defensive, and then left with the remainder of his men on the 2nd of June, and, making forced marches, reached Aburi on the afternoon of the 5th. This place was in telegraphic communication with Accra, and, as it was now known that the state of affairs in Akim was far less serious than had been supposed, he was ordered to remain there instead of pushing on to Accra the same night, as he had intended to do. Kobina Achiri had now disbanded his army and was on his way to the coast ; he had been ordered to surrender himself at Insaba by the 31st of May, and, because he failed to arrive until the next day, Wanki had been razed to the ground, though it would appear that he had only been delayed by heavy rain. Eventually the matter was settled by Atta Fua, whose conduct throughout had been excellent, signing a document ceding the ferry at Insuaim to the Government. Achiri was allowed to return to his country towards the end of 1893 on his Chiefs signing a bond for his good behaviour.

On the 10th of June, messengers arrived at Aburi from Ho reporting that the Hausas and Krepis left at Tavievi had been forced to evacuate it, and were retreating on Ho. After the departure of Mr. Akers, all had been quiet until the 4th, when a party of Kujo De's men, who were returning with supplies, was attacked by a prowling band of the enemy and lost two men killed. On the 6th, the Chief, still thirsting for revenge and chafing under the inaction, led out his men to attack the Tavievis, who had now collected in the mountains in large numbers ; but he had no sooner engaged them than ten or twelve of his men were shot down and about twenty-five more wounded. Panic thereupon seized the remainder, who fled to Zavi, sweeping before them a few of the Hausas. The latter, in the meantime, had obeyed their orders and remained quietly in the camp, only firing a few shots and rockets when the Tavievis drew near the town. Kujo De himself, with about thirty of his men, the sergeant-major, and most of the Hausas were still in Tavievi ; but Mr. Bennett became alarmed for their safety, and sent them orders to retire at once on Ho, bringing all Government property with them. The Tavievis had thus secured a complete victory and undone all Mr. Akers' work, and, as if this were not enough, Mr. Bennett now proposed to evacuate Ho, where he was perfectly safe, and retreat on Pong, saying that if the Hausas did not come in he should go without them.

When the first news of this disaster reached the coast, Mr. Akers was staying with the Governor at Christiansborg, but his men fortunately were still at Aburi. No time was lost in beginning the return march, and Mr. Akers left Christiansborg at four o'clock the next morning with all the Hausas who could be spared from Ussher Fort : he was accompanied by Mr Riby Williams, who had just returned from a recruiting tour to Salaga and was to supersede Mr. Bennett. Picking up the Hausas who had been left at Aburi, they pushed straight on to Zavi, where they arrived on the 17th. Here they met the Hausas and Kujo De retiring upon Ho, as ordered by Mr. Bennett, and stopped them.

On the morning of the 18th, Mr. Akers marched out of Zavi with 150 Hausas and advanced on Tavievi. On arriving within a quarter of a mile of the town, a large camp was discovered on the hill above it, and the sergeant-major was sent round with forty men to take it in the flank while the main body advanced directly against the town. The enemy now for the first time discovered their approach and opened fire ; but they only stood for a moment and then fled in great disorder, abandoning all their property, including the Chief's state umbrella and chair. They were pursued for about two miles into the mountains and lost a great many men, but the only British casualty was one private slightly wounded. Kujo De arrived during the afternoon with 2,000 native allies, and during the next few days strong parties were continually being sent out to harass the Tavievis, who were dislodged from every position they attempted to occupy and soon became utterly demoralized : indeed, they barely attempted to stand when attacked, and at last, on the afternoon of the

23rd, showed a white flag on the side of a hill overlooking the camp and sued for peace.

Some of the Hos were sent out to see what they wanted, and brought in three Tavievi messengers, to whom the terms on which peace would be granted were explained. These were :

i. That they should become loyal subjects of the Queen, obey the commands of the Gold Coast Government, and acknowledge the suzerainty of the King of Krepi.

ii. That they should pay a fine to the Government.

iii. That they should surrender Belo Kobina and certain other Chiefs.

iv. That they should give up all their arms and ammunition.

v. That they should agree to keep the roads throughout their district open and free to all traders.

The next day Belo Kobina was given up, and his men came in daily after this and surrendered their arms and ammunition. They had been almost without food for the past six days, and estimated their total losses since the commencement of the war at from 500 to 600 fighting men, besides some 200 women and children, many of whom had been killed in some of the skirmishes, while numbers of others had died of starvation and exposure in the mountains. It was a terrible retribution ; but a necessary one. On the 3rd of July a great meeting was held, at which all the Chiefs of the district were present. The Tavievis then signed an agreement to pay a fine of £300 in two instalments, and another to keep their roads open or pay a further fine in default. At the same time, all the Chiefs of Krepi gave a similar undertaking about their roads, and those who had not already done so signed a declaration of fealty.

Meanwhile, in Ashanti, all immediate hope of a peaceful reign for Prempi was destroyed by the King of Kokofu, who, in spite of his professed anxiety for forgiveness and peace and the readiness of the authorities in Kumasi to grant it, had broken out into open rebellion even before Mr. Barnett had left the country. He was still occupying

his camp on the main road at Ajaman, and now began
raiding the farms and villages of all those who would not
take the oath to serve him ; he also rebuilt and garrisoned
several villages near the main road in Adansi for the purpose of robbing traders. Prempi, though sorely tried by
these acts, had given his word to Mr. Barnett that he
would take no steps against the Kokofus until after he had
recrossed the Pra, and he kept his promise.

During May, first the King of Kokofu and then the King
of Mampon unsuccessfully attacked the Ejisus ; but towards the end of the month the Kokofus, having been
reinforced by the Adansis and Dadiasis from the Protectorate, secured a victory over the Bekwais, who were
forced to retreat on Kumasi. Awua of Bantama, who so
soon as he heard that the Bekwais were threatened had
turned out his men and marched to their assistance, was
too late to help them, but defeated a part of the Kokofu
army that met and fired upon him. Turning back towards Kumasi, he halted for the night at Kasi, where he
was treacherously betrayed by some adherents of the
King of Kokofu, who seized him while he was asleep
and handed him over to Asibi, who immediately put him
to death.

The King of Bekwai declared that nothing would induce
him to turn against a King who had been installed by a
British officer and had never disobeyed the wishes of the
Government, and Prempi sent messengers to report to the
Governor what had happened, and to ask that the Kokofus
might be ordered to keep the peace. Before these messengers reached the coast, however, the continued advance of
the Kokofus compelled him to take action, and, in a two
days' battle fought at Ajimamu on the 26th and 27th of
June, the Kokofus, who were running short of powder,
were decisively defeated by a combined force of Kumasis,
Bekwais and Jabins and driven across the Pra. Their
total numbers were variously computed at from 18,000
to 22,000, including from 8,000 to 15,000 armed men. The
victorious army encamped on the north bank of the river
for a few days to prevent their recrossing, and was then

recalled by the King, who sent to tell the Governor what
had happened, and to ask him to prevent the exiled Kokofus
and their allies from using the Protectorate as a base for
operations against Ashanti.

Previous experience with the Adansis, and the fact that
the King's messengers had had to travel with a large
escort to protect them from the attacks of marauding
bands of Kokofus who were haunting the road, were
sufficient justification for this request. Instructions were
therefore sent to Prasu that the fugitives were to be disarmed as they crossed the frontier and told to go to Insaba,
where they would be allowed to settle on undertaking to
become peaceful subjects of the Queen and make no further
attacks on the Ashantis. Seeing that the Kokofus only
regarded the Protectorate as a temporary refuge and
wished to be as near the frontier as possible, so as to be
able to take advantage of the first chance that might arise
to regain their former position in Ashanti, it was not to
be supposed that they would carry out these instructions
except under supervision. There was only a Constabulary
clerk at Prasu, however, and but a small proportion of the
fugitives was there at all : the vast majority of them had
crossed the Pra at different points farther east, and were
now living in the villages close to the river, whence it
was quite certain they would constantly be making forays
over the border. It became necessary, therefore, to arrange
for their removal to the coast, and Mr. Akers was sent up
to carry it out.

He first went to Insaba and saw the Chief, Kofi Anti,
who had already promised to give the Kokofus land.
From him he learned that none of the refugees had yet
arrived in his district, but that their women and children,
to the number of about 10,000, were scattered about in the
villages between Essikuma and Insuaim, while the King
and Achiriboanda were at Kotoko near the Pra with an
army of 4,000 men, many of whom were armed with
Snider rifles. The scarcity of food had done more than
anything else to scatter them. They were said to be
preparing for another attack on the Kumasis, and to have

received a promise of 1,000 fighting men from the Inkoranzas.   From Insaba Mr. Akers went to Insuaim to see
Atta Fua, who had been ordered to assist in locating the
Kokofus, and found he had done nothing at all in the
matter.   The fact was that Atta Fua did not want the
Kokofus to go to Aguna at all, but was secretly doing all
he could to secure their settlement in his own country,
and had already promised them land.   Mr. Akers had
great difficulty in getting him even to send messengers to
them.   Eventually, however, he managed to collect Asibi
and his Chiefs at Insuaim, but this was only accomplished
by sending his sergeant-major for them, and telling them
that they must choose between coming to Insuaim and
returning to Ashanti.   On the 5th of September a meeting
was held, at which, in spite of the persuasive opposition of
Atta Fua, it was finally arranged :

i. That the Kokofu Chiefs and their followers should
at once pack up their things and go to Akrosu on the
borders of Aguna and Western Akim.

ii. That Asibi, Achiriboanda, and the Chief Linguist
Adom should accompany Mr. Akers to Accra to make any
complaints or requests they liked to the Governor.

iii. That Atta Fua should pledge his word not to allow
any Kokofus to return to live at Insuaim without the
express permission of the Governor.

Orders were at the same time sent to every Chief throughout the district not to allow any refugees to settle there,
but to pass them on towards Aguna.

Atta Fua, by his initial disobedience, had placed himself
in a difficult position.   Having promised the Kokofus
that they should settle on his land, he was afraid to incur
their anger by appearing to go back on his word.   He
was, moreover, really anxious to have them there ; for his
own country was very thinly populated, and he foresaw
that if they could be induced to settle down quietly under
him, his own power and dignity as a Chief would be greatly
increased.   At the same time, he could not blind himself
to the fact that any open defiance of the Government would
be extremely dangerous.   In the end   his attempts to

steer a middle course and please both parties very nearly brought about a serious disturbance.

Atta Fua had been very unwilling that Asibi should go to Accra ; but when he found Mr. Akers was determined on the point, he had obtained permission to go with him and entered into a bond to forfeit £100 to the Government if they failed to start by eight o'clock on the morning of the 10th of September. When the time came, however, he did all he could to gain an extension, but was eventually induced to start down the road. He had been drinking heavily and was greatly excited, crying out to his people as he left the town that he was being forced to go without being given time to wash or eat. Before he had gone far he made other excuses to stop, and finally made a spring at one of the Hausas who had just pushed an Akim man out of the way ; but Mr. Akers got between them in time to prevent his striking him. Atta Fua's drum was then beaten and immediately answered from the town, while armed Akims, whose numbers increased every minute, gathered round and were openly making ready to fire. The excitement was now at its highest pitch, and the accidental discharge of a single gun must have resulted in a serious riot, if nothing worse ; for the Hausas had already loaded, but were only 20 against 1,000. They, however, behaved admirably, and stood perfectly steady while Mr. Akers on one side of the road and the sergeant-major on the other went among the Akims and quieted them. Atta Fua was then persuaded to continue the journey quietly, and Asibi was found waiting for him a few hundred yards farther on.

The inclusion within the British Protectorate of Krepi and the other districts to the east of the Volta River, following the occupation of Togoland by the Germans, led to an agreement being drawn up between the two Powers at a conference at Berlin in December 1887, which was confirmed in March 1888. It provided for the establishment of a Neutral Zone between the 10th north parallel and a conventional line drawn on the latitude of the mouth of the River Daka, with lateral boundaries thirty-three

minutes east and one degree seven minutes west.   Both
Powers agreed to abstain from acquiring any exclusive
influence within this area, but admitted a mutual right to
make treaties with any of its Chiefs as to territories lying
outside it.

At the same time, it was realized that a definite arrangement must be made with the French regarding the western
frontier, which the Commission of 1882 had failed to
delimit.   Negotiations were therefore opened in 1888, and
on the 10th of August 1889 an agreement was signed at
Paris.   It was arranged that the frontier should start at
Newtown (from a point 1,000 metres to the west of the
house that had been occupied by the British Commissioners
in 1884) and follow a line drawn due north to the Tano
Lagoon : thence it followed the south shore of the lagoon
and the left bank of the Tano River as far as Nugwa,
above which point it was to be traced by Commissioners
on the spot in accordance with the treaty arrangements of
the two Powers with the natives and so as to leave Ashanti
to the British.   Provision was also made for the imposition
of minimum duties on spirits, tobacco and cotton goods.

In December 1888 it became known that the Dadiasis,
assisted by the Kokofus, were attacking and robbing
traders in the neighbourhood of Esaman on the Prasu-
Kumasi road.   These Dadiasis were a part of those who
had fled across the Pra with the Kokofus ; but no attempt
had as yet been made to remove them from the frontier,
although the Governor had to admit that he knew they
were there and that it would be dangerous to allow them
to remain.   Matters had now become so bad that a number
of Ashanti traders who were in Cape Coast were afraid to
return to Kumasi with their goods, on account of these
marauders, and trade threatened to come to a standstill.
The Governor, therefore, was forced to take action, and, in
January 1889, the Inspector-General of the Constabulary,
Lieutenant-Colonel McInnis, was sent up with 175 Hausas
to effect the removal of the refugees and intern them
nearer the coast : he was at the same time to order Asibi,
who was still living near Insuaim, to lose no more time

before removing to Akrosu. Many Dadiasis and Kokofus were found in Beronasi, and the houses in several villages beyond the Pra showed unmistakable signs of recent occupation, although at the time they were empty. Many more were living in Akim-Swedru, where they were encouraged by the Chief, Kofi Ahinkora, who had doubtless been conniving at what they had done. Altogether 596 Kokofus and 101 Dadiasis were collected, and 154 of the former and 28 more of the latter were afterwards found in Esaman. The Kokofus were handed over to Asibi at Akrosu and the Dadiasis to their King Amofa, who was settled about five miles to the north-east of Insaba.

CHAPTER XVII

THE ADOPTION OF A NEW POLICY REGARDING ASHANTI

1888 TO 1891

THE defeat and expulsion of the Kokofus did not end the troubles in Ashanti. The fact that Prempi, though nominally King, had not been properly enstooled with the full ceremony was a serious handicap to him in his efforts to restore order. He was little more than a boy, and certainly cannot have been more than sixteen or seventeen years old, for he had only been born shortly before the capture of Kumasi in 1874. He was, therefore, largely in the hands of his mother and the Chiefs, a fact that should be borne in mind when judging his actions. Even an older man, about the validity of whose position there was no doubt, would have found the task of reconciling the different factions in a country that had been distracted by civil wars for several years by no means easy ; but in the existing circumstances, and with some of the subsidiary rulers still in open revolt or brooding over their troubles in exile and constantly plotting to regain the positions that they had lost, it was almost impossible ; and, if the Gold Coast Government ever really believed that Prempi could accomplish it, it must have credited him with the possession of administrative powers far above the average. That he honestly made the attempt, however, there is little room to doubt, and it was only after he became first disappointed at his want of success and then distracted by the difficulties that inevitably confronted him, that, listening to the advice of those who were older than himself and who, but for their self-interest, were well able to have given him better counsel, he committed those indiscretions that led to his downfall.

Sencheri the King of Mampon, whose professions of readiness to recognize Prempi as King and to be present at his enstoolment had probably been sincere, was nevertheless afraid to go to Kumasi after Mr. Barnett had left, and made overtures to the King of Kwahu to intercede with Prempi on his behalf. The latter reported this to the Governor, asking whether he could do so, but was told not to mix himself up in the affairs of Ashanti. This finally decided Sencheri against making peace with Prempi, and he once more began to intrigue with the exiled Kokofus and the Insutas to gain the kingdom for Achiriboanda. In November Prempi and the Kumasis, finding these tribes still disaffected, and getting news of their secret negotiations with Asibi, attacked and defeated them. Some of the Mampons fled to Inkoranza, but Sencheri and most of his people, and the Insutas with their King Edu Tre, sought safety in Attabubu.

In November 1888 these events were reported to the Governor by messengers from Busum Fo the Head Chief of Krachi, and a month later a letter was received from Mr. Ramseyer, who was then at Abetifi, saying that the King of Insuta was seeking permission to enter the Protectorate, as the Ashantis would never consent to his remaining at Attabubu. The Insutas who brought this letter added that their King wanted an officer to be sent up to escort his people to Kwahu, as they were afraid they might otherwise be attacked on the road by the Jabins living under Yow Sapon at Konengo.

In accordance with this request, Mr. Badger, the interpreter, was sent up with an escort of a sergeant and six Hausas to bring the Insutas down to Eastern Akim, where it was proposed to settle them in some sparsely populated country between Kibbi and Insuaim. He reached Attabubu on the 11th of January 1889, and was received by the Kings of Attabubu, Mampon and Insuta. He soon discovered that the message had not been sent by the King at all—in fact, he knew nothing about it—but emanated from two of his Chiefs, Kofi Beng and Kujo Frempong, with whom he was furiously angry when he learned what they had done in his name, and was with difficulty restrained from putting them to death. Eventually, however, he was pacified, and then returned a message to the Governor thanking him for having sent, but explaining that he had never asked to enter the Protectorate and had no wish to do so, but intended to return to his own country as soon as possible.

Towards the latter end of 1888, messengers arrived in Cape Coast from King Ajiman of Jaman asking that his country might be taken under British protection, and at about the same time Prempi sent down a confidential message asking the Government to lend him eighty ounces of gold. This was an unprecedented request from a King of Ashanti, to whom in ordinary times this would have been a paltry sum, and the mere fact that it was made at all clearly shows to what an extent the long period of civil war and the interruption of trade had impoverished the people. Prempi wanted this money to pay the necessary expenses of his enstoolment ; for he realized that until this ceremony had been properly completed, his position would be very insecure and his authority next to nothing ; nor could he, until this had been done, draw upon the Royal Treasury at Bantama.

The Government decided to comply with this request on condition that Prempi gave a written undertaking not to place his country under the protection of any foreign Power without its consent. Inspector Lethbridge left Cape Coast on the 8th of December with Assistant-Inspector Ewart, Doctor Austin Freeman, and 100 Hausas of the Gold Coast Constabulary to pay the money to the King, and then visit Bontuku, the capital of Jaman, with a view to taking that country under British protection. Kumasi was reached on the 22nd, and on the 26th a palaver was held, at which Inspector Lethbridge told the King that he had been authorized to advance him the money for which he had asked. Prempi, however, had specially asked that the loan should be made secretly, as he was very much afraid that his people would not approve of such an arrangement and think it a disgrace; consequently, when Mr. Lethbridge, who was a soldier rather than a diplomatist, blurted it out in front of all the Chiefs in this way, he repudiated all knowledge of the matter, and contented himself with returning thanks for the visit. From a reference in a subsequent letter [1] to the King, it appears that the subject of a Treaty of Protection was also broached, but that Prempi objected to one of its conditions.

From Kumasi the mission went on to Bontuku. On their way they learned that there had recently been a dispute between one of Ajiman's sons named Diawusi, who was the Chief of Mo, and some of the principal Chiefs of the kingdom. The latter, who were led by an aged but powerful Chief named Papi, had caused Diawusi to be expelled from Mo, and it was he who had sent the message to the coast. He hoped that the arrival of a British mission, which he had evidently given out was being sent to support him, would be sufficient to induce Ajiman to restore him to his former position, and the Jamans were therefore inclined to regard it as hostile. It was also reported that two French officers were then in Bontuku, and that Ajiman had already signed a treaty with them and accepted a French flag.

It was fortunate that some idea of the true state of affairs was gained; for Diawusi arrived in the camp soon afterwards to establish friendly relations, but was very coldly received. When Bontuku was reached, Ajiman of course denied having sent any message, and said plainly that, as he had not sent for the English and did not want them there, he hoped they would return to the coast as soon as possible. Later, however, he became more friendly, and explained that, although it was true that he had signed a treaty with the French and accepted a flag from them, the treaty was merely to maintain friendly relations and encourage trade between his country and Assini, but that he had not accepted their protection. He said

[1] Parliamentary Paper, *Affairs in Ashanti*, 1896, p. 50.

that until 1874 his people had always traded to Cape Coast, and that he would prefer them to go there again if they could do so in safety, and finally offered to hand over the French flag and treaty to Inspector Lethbridge and execute a new treaty accepting British protection. This was signed on the 24th of January 1889, and Mr. Lethbridge then left for the coast to get it ratified, and to ask for instructions about the French treaty and flag, leaving the other officers and most of the Hausas in Bontuku to await his return.

Mr. Lethbridge returned by the road through Sefwi, and very nearly got into serious trouble at Wiosu, where one of his carriers took one of the King's wives. Her return was claimed through the interpreter Odonkor ;[1] but the appeal was ignored, and the King then sent men after the party to recover the woman by force. When he found himself threatened with attack, Mr. Lethbridge was more willing to listen to advice, and appealed to Odonkor to tell him what he had better do. The latter got him out of a difficult and dangerous position by taking the whole blame on himself, telling the Sefwis that his former interpretation of their complaint had been badly done and misunderstood by the officer. The woman was then given up and the affair settled.

Soon after Mr. Lethbridge's departure, Major Ewart and Doctor Freeman, finding that they would have at least two months to wait with little or nothing to do, decided to visit some of the neighbouring towns, and enquired of the King about the road to Kong. He, however, was so clearly opposed to their going there that the project was abandoned, and when, soon afterwards, they decided to visit Banda, they said nothing to him about it, but made all their preparations in secret. He soon heard of their intention however, and arrived with some of his Chiefs just as they were about to start. He told them quite politely but very plainly that he did not wish them to leave Bontuku, and found them ready enough to fall in with his wishes. All would then have been well, had not

[1] Afterwards Chief of Pong.

Papi, who was very drunk at the time, added some insolent remarks, saying that they were not wanted at Banda nor anywhere else, and had better remain quietly in Bontuku until the time came for their return to the coast, an event which he assured them would be hailed with rejoicing by the Jamans in general and himself in particular. This so annoyed Major Ewart that he determined to make an example of Papi at the first opportunity, though Doctor Freeman, considering the man's quarrelsome nature and the fact that he was far from sober, was not inclined to attach much importance to his conduct and evidently thought the Major was rather going out of his way to look for trouble.

A meeting was held with the King and Chiefs a few days later, when Major Ewart, after the conclusion of the other business, called Papi out, intending to inflict a fine of fifty pounds on him for the disrespect he had shown. Papi stood up and was about to come forward, but the King peremptorily ordered him to sit down, saying that he would undertake to settle that affair himself. To this Major Ewart would not consent, but, though Ajiman went down on his knees and implored him to forgive the man, who he said would never have behaved as he did if he had been sober, ended by ordering a native officer and four Hausas to seize Papi and bring him to where he was sitting.

This was the signal for a general uproar. Hundreds of Papi's people, many of whom were armed, crowded round him, so that it was impossible for the Hausas to reach him, while others ran into the town to fetch their weapons and summon reinforcements. Numbers of armed men were soon gathering from all directions, and a collision with the Hausas, each of whom had forty rounds of ball ammunition in his pouches, was narrowly averted. The men indeed, without waiting for orders, had come to the " ready " and were beginning to load their carbines, and were only restrained just in time. Ajiman renewed his apologies, but without effect. Dr. Freeman then approached Papi with the idea of persuading him to submit quietly, but was stopped by those around him, one of whom pointed a musket at his head. Ajiman and his principal Chiefs were clearly anxious to avoid a breach of the peace, and two of them drew Dr. Freeman away, while Ajiman finally volunteered to pay the fine himself in order to end the trouble. Major Ewart, seriously alarmed at the disturbance he had created, thought it wisest to agree to this ; but even then, so enraged was the populace, that the officers and troops were mobbed and jeered all the way back to their quarters, and would probably have been roughly handled had not Ajiman and the Chiefs accompanied them. A few days later, however, peace was restored, and at the end of March the party was recalled to the coast. They handed back the French treaty and flag before leaving, for the Anglo-French Boundary Commission, which was then delimiting the frontier above Nugwa, had arranged that, while Ashanti fell to the British, the French should have Bontuku. From a subsequent despatch [1] it appears that Major Ewart also gave a flag to the Bolis, who, if this is correct, must have sent to Bontuku for it.

Soon after his defeat and flight to Attabubu, Sencheri sent to Opoku at Inkoranza and demanded the return of those of his people who had fled there. Opoku, however, was anxious to preserve his neutrality and refused to send them back. Sencheri, therefore, tried to regain them by force, but, failing to persuade Kobina Ashanti the King of Attabubu to assist him, was defeated by the Inkoranzas and returned disgraced to Attabubu. After this, the majority of his people gradually left him and returned to Mampon, where his younger brother Osunchi was set up as King under Prempi early in 1889.

Inkoranza, though really one of the Brong tribes, had, as has already been mentioned, assisted Osai Opoku I in his war against Takiman, and, from an ally, gradually developed into a province of Ashanti, and when the other Brong tribes asserted their independence and formed the Brong Confederation after the war of 1873–4, Inkoranza

[1] Parliamentary Paper, *Affairs in Ashanti*, 1896.

had not joined them. Atta Fua[1] was then King of Inkoranza, and it was his ambition to remain altogether independent, but at the same time to avoid any open rupture with the King of Ashanti, for, situated as he was on the northern confines of the kingdom, he had little opportunity to retreat into the Protectorate in case of a reverse. To this end, while he carefully abstained from visiting the capital, he exchanged friendly messages with Kofi Karikari, who, in turn, knowing how precarious his own position had become after his defeat by Sir Garnet Wolseley, did everything in his power to win his friendship, and sent him a pair of gold-mounted sandals, a state umbrella, and other insignia of royalty. Atta Fua remained on terms of friendship with Karikari until his death, and his successor Opoku was one of the deposed King's most ardent supporters in his efforts to regain possession of the stool after the deposition of Mensa. After the death of Kwaku Dua II, Opoku had held aloof from both parties in Ashanti, partly because he would not support any candidate who had not been a favourite of his old friend, and partly in accordance with his policy to assert his independence by a gradual withdrawal from any participation in the affairs of Ashanti. Shortly after his enstoolment, Prempi, who may, or may not, have had some suspicion of Opoku's intentions, sent for him to come and " drink fetish " with him. This was a customary procedure for all tributaries on the accession of a new King, and was equivalent to a renewal of the oath of allegiance. Opoku, however, evaded compliance with this custom by averring that there was no reason to doubt his loyalty, and swearing that he would recover for Prempi the Ashanti suzerainty over the Brong tribes that had been lost in 1874. The obliteration of all trace of that defeat had ever been the dearest wish of the Ashantis, and the performance of this ceremony was, therefore, readily dispensed with and further presents were sent to Opoku, who had thus contrived, for the time being, to lull any suspicions the King may have had of his loyalty.

In September 1889 Sencheri attempted to recover his

[1] Or Atafa ?

kingdom, but was again defeated by the Kumasis and driven back to Attabubu. On the 20th of November, three of his messengers arrived in Accra asking that an officer might be sent up to bring him and all his people into the Protectorate, as they were afraid that if they remained at Attabubu, the King of Ashanti might attack them again. They also reported that the Insutas had now made peace with Prempi and returned to their own country.

This latter event had been mainly due to the position in which Edu Tre had placed himself by his conduct while in exile. He had refused to pay the customary fees when taking the oath of the Fetish Priest of Krachi, and the latter had retaliated by seizing some Insutas who were living in his town, and threatened to take similar steps against those at Attabubu. Edu Tre, therefore, knowing full well that Kobina Ashanti would do anything the Priest told him and that he himself might be seized at any moment, had no longer felt safe with him, and lost no time in making his submission to Prempi.

It was at first intended to comply with the King of Mampon's request ; but the fear that the message might be repudiated as that from Edu Tre had been, the cost of sending an officer and the necessary escort so far, and the risk that they might become embroiled with the Jabins on the way, coupled with the fact that the messengers had brought none of the usual insignia of office—which they explained by saying that they had been afraid to be seen carrying them—led to a letter being returned by them to the King instead. He was told that if he really wished to enter the Protectorate he might do so, and could avoid all danger from the Jabins by crossing the River Volta at Krachi and travelling down its left bank. He was also promised land on which he and his people might settle at a distance from the frontier, and that a message would at once be sent to the King of Ashanti asking him to leave him in peace.

This latter message was embodied in a letter asking Prempi to refrain from further persecution of the tribes

that had seceded from him, and advising him to turn his
attention to the improvement of trade. He was also told
that the Adansis would be allowed to return to their
country if he would guarantee that they would not be
molested. This letter was sent up by Mr. Badger, and
had been written mainly as an excuse to enable him to
visit Kumasi and find out and report what was going on
in Ashanti. In this it failed ; for when, on his return to
Accra early in January 1890, bringing two letters from
Prempi, one addressed to the Acting Governor Mr.
Hodgson, and the other to the Secretary of State, he
only saw the Governor for a few minutes. Mr. Hodgson,
noticing that his speech was thick and his manner peculiar,
thought he had been celebrating his return to Accra by
getting drunk and sent him away, but he was seized
by an apoplectic fit the same afternoon and died the
next day.

A great deal has been made of this letter from the
King to the Governor. It has been said that it is couched
in a grossly insolent tone, that it shows Prempi's determination to act antagonistically to the Government, and that
it was the beginning of all the troubles and misunderstandings that followed. The latter contention may well
be true, though in a different sense from that in which it is
usually meant ; but although the others may, of course, be
equally correct, there seems to be considerable room for
doubt on the point. It is perhaps largely a matter of
opinion, and for this reason, and because the King sets
forth his views very clearly, the letter is quoted in full.

"Coomasie, December 27, 1889.

" GOVERNOR,

" Your letter by your officer, Mr. Badger, came safely
to hand ; as you stated in the closing of your letter that
Mr. Badger should not be detained no longer than a week, I
take the little time to reply to you.

" 1. I am very sorry indeed to say that it is not my single
wish that the British Government should allow the King
of Mampon to come to the Protectorate ; and even those

that have come already, I am earnestly praying for their safe return.

"2. It is truly through the kind aid of the British Government that I ascended to the stool of my ancestors, those of my subjects who wilfully had opposed to my being placed on the stool took up arms against me, but were unsuccessful, they had to fly to you, which candidly and truly speaking should have been asked to return, for they had no respect for Her Majesty's Government ; for they knew it was through their kind assistance I am on the stool.

"3. Your true and firm friendship you stated in your letter with me I am sorry to say it wants wanting, for I believe that when two persons are keeping friendship each of them seeks the interest and welfare of the other, but it is not the case here. I thought that my subjects that had come to you came to solicit your intercession for their safe return, for I believe that when a friend's boy or servant offends his lord, he runs to his lord's friend to ask pardon for him, so when there is any punishment whatever, through the intercession of the other friend, the offended [1] servant is pardoned, and then he returns to resume his former duties ; this is real friendship, but I am extremely sorry it is not so with us ; I am deprived almost of all my subjects ; on whom, then, shall I reign ?

"4. You stated in the 6th paragraph of your letter that the King of Kwahu have signed treaty with the British Government ; may I ask, for what cause, have I had any palaver with him, or it is only the wish of the British Government that he should do so. The Sewhis I learn from them that during the late disturbances they have run to the British Government, and that if I seek for them they will gladly given in their allegiance to me, all these and many others I find that if it is the British Government's wish they all will return.

"5. The King of Bekwai has never send arms and crossed the boundary against the Inquantahs, for it is that wicked Quasie Mensa that is robbing, killing and troubling my subjects on my land, and so I send to check him, if he will

[1] *Sic.*

not serve me, and have taken shelter under you, I do not
see why he should not be kept within bounds.

" 6. Yes, I wish the return of the Adansis to their former
position, if they will understand as my loyal subjects
If they agree I shall send one of my influential Chiefs to
come and drink water with them, and if there is any
misunderstandings I trust and believe it shall be properly
settled, but if they wish to come and live on my lands
without serving me as before they may remain to where
they are, and I shall order my Chiefs to settle men on the
main road in order to have the roads properly kept.

" 7. When all my subjects have come to the Protectorate,
where is then trade ; for once they have crossed to you,
they shall fear to cross over and pass on my land to the
interior to trade.

" 8. I hope and trust that the British Government will
carefully and seriously consider this important subject, so
that peace and commerce may now freely take its course.

" Wishing you a merry Christmas and a prosperous and
blessed new year.

" I remain, etc.,

my
" QUACOE DUAH III X
mark
" King of Ashanti.

" His Excellency, F. M. Hodgson,
" Acting Governor." [1]

This letter may be considered first as regards its general
tone, and then as regards the actual statements contained
in it.   The former, it must be admitted, does appear at
first sight to be a little insolent ; but to what extent this
is intentional or accidental is quite another matter.   Mr.
Hodgson reported to the Secretary of State that, at their
one short interview, Mr. Badger had informed him that
he had told the King " that the letter he had written . . .
was not a properly worded one to send to the Governor,
and he also mentioned that the writer, a son of the late

[1] Parliamentary Paper, *Affairs in Ashanti*, 1896, p. 16.

Prince Osoo Ansah of Cape Coast, had nothing to do with the tone in which it was written, a Chief named Asafu Buaki being the most influential factor in the counsels of Kumasi." [1]

This Ansa was John Ossu Ansa, Prince Ansa's eldest son. He had received " an indifferent education at Cape Coast," had been for a time an acting master in the Government school there, and had afterwards been given a clerkship in the Audit Office, but had very soon been dismissed. He had then gone for a time to Southern Nigeria, and, on his return, had visited Kumasi, where he had remained ever since. He was described by Sir Brandford Griffith as " unscrupulous and unprincipled " and likely to lead the King into difficulties if he listened to his advice. He was at this time about forty years of age.

The King, of course, must have told Ansa what he wanted to say, or have actually dictated the letter to him in Ashanti, and he would then have written it in English, and probably have translated it again to the King before he put his mark to it. Now it would have been so absolutely contrary to all custom for Mr. Badger to have been present while this was being done that it is almost certain that he was not ; and he must therefore have been dependent for his information on this point upon Ansa, who was the only other person in Kumasi who understood the two languages, but whose uncorroborated evidence was of no value. A few very slight changes of expression are quite sufficient to make all the difference between a courteous and a discourteous speech, and words of the latter kind usually look worse still when reduced to writing ; but to a man like Ansa, these finer distinctions would not be so perceptible as to anyone having a more perfect knowledge of the English language. The King was evidently anxious to convey a clear impression and give an honest statement of his own view of the case, and a man with more than Ansa's education would probably have found it far from an easy task to make his letter as emphatic as he was told to do without at the same time

[1] Parliamentary Paper, *Affairs in Ashanti*, 1896, p. 14.

making it appear dictatorial and insolent. It does not
therefore follow that, even in the case of Ansa, the objectionable tone was intentional, and this is rendered still
less probable by the fact that a copy of the letter to the
Governor was enclosed in that to the Secretary of State, to
which no exception could be taken. It was as follows :

"ASHANTI, COOMASIE, *December* 27, 1889.

" MY LORD,
        " It is my greatest pleasure that I take the liberty
of writing you ; as I believe I am the first King of Ashanti
that ever have send a letter to England, and trust Her
Majesty's Government will give me all assistance and good
advice for the well government of my Ashanti Kingdom.
    " I find that the friendship existing between Her
Majesty's Government and my Kingdom of Ashanti, ever
since the time of my ancestors, is still now the same.
    " I believe if there is any grievance in me, Her Majesty's
Government is able to remove same, therefore I send the
accompanying copy of a letter to the Governor administering the Gold Coast Government, for your kind perusal,
and I trust Her Majesty's Government will assist me in
this important matter, as have been always done.
    " I wish Her Majesty's Government a merry Christmas
and a prosperous and blessed new year.
                " I remain, etc.,

                                    my
                " QUACOE DUAH III   X
                                    mark
                        " King of Ashanti.
" To the Right Hon. Lord Knutsford,
    " Her Majesty's Principal Secretary of State for the
        " Colonies."

The letter dealt mainly with subjects on which the King
evidently felt strongly, and about which he wished there
to be no room for doubt. He was also anxious to defend
himself against certain charges contained in the Governor's
letter to him. In the 1st, 2nd and 6th paragraphs he

shows a very natural objection to the continued absorption of his people into the Protectorate, but makes it clear that, although he is quite ready to allow the Adansis to re-occupy their country, and is indeed most anxious to have them back, he cannot consent to their doing so unless they are prepared to acknowledge their fealty to him : nor, since the Pra had always been the recognized frontier of his kingdom and their claim to independence after the Treaty of Fomana had involved Ashanti in much war and expense, could he reasonably have been expected to agree to any other terms. He also argues that those who had received the protection of the Government were really undeserving of it, since their need to seek it had only been due to their refusal to acknowledge him, whose enstoolment had been brought about by the assistance of that Government and sanctioned and recognized by the presence of one of its officers. This was a not unnatural view for him to take, and he equally naturally asks, in paragraph 7, how he is to be expected to comply with the Governor's recommendation that he should promote an increased trade, so long as the rapid depopulation of his country is being encouraged in this way. It is the custom amongst all the Akan peoples for anyone who offends another person in any way, or wishes to ask a favour of him, to go to one of that person's friends and solicit his influence on his behalf, or, as they themselves express it, to ask him to " beg him for them." It is to this custom that Prempi alludes in the 3rd paragraph of his letter after complaining that the Governor's protestations of continued friendship are not borne out by his actions, but it must be open to doubt whether he really believed that the refugees had sought asylum in the Protectorate with a view to availing themselves of it. The 5th paragraph is a reply to a charge made by the Governor that the Bekwais had recently invaded Denkera to attack the Inkwantas. There seems to be no definite evidence that they had really done so, and Prempi at any rate denies it, but admits that he sent to " check " the Inkwantas when he found they were making raids into his territory.

This they undoubtedly had done, and Mr. Hodgson justly
observes that the King's " action is perhaps not unnatural." Prempi was right enough in his contention
that, so long as the Government elected to harbour his
enemies, they should at least keep them within bounds : a
duty which it was notorious that they had repeatedly
failed in. In the following March (1890) the Government
had to send an expedition against this very Chief, Kwesi
Mensa, who was defeated and fled into the forest, where
he first murdered his son and nephew—boys of seven and
eight years of age—by hanging them, and then committed
suicide by the same means. His chief adherents, however, were captured and detained in Elmina Castle as
political prisoners.

Taking everything into consideration, therefore, although
it is possible that the tone of this letter may have been
intentionally insulting, the probabilities seem to be very
much against it. Both Mr. Hodgson and Sir Brandford
Griffith adopted the view that it was impertinent—mainly
perhaps because their own actions were criticized—but
the Secretary of State, in his reply, expressed no opinion,
but merely directed that the King should be informed
that " Her Majesty's Government hope that he will follow
the advice given him by the Governor of the Gold Coast
Colony, who is their representative and knows their wishes."

On the 25th of April a letter, dated on the 7th, was
received from the King, in which he stated that one of his
influential Chiefs, accompanied by representatives of every
Chief in the kingdom, was coming down to the Governor.
He asked that, as they and their servants would make up
a large retinue and the expense of subsisting so many men
in Accra would be considerable, the Governor would arrange
to meet them at Elmina and settle their business there.
As he was about to visit that town, Sir Brandford Griffith
wrote consenting to see the messengers there if they
arrived before he left, but said that otherwise they must
come to Accra. He was in Elmina from the 27th to the
30th, but they had not yet arrived, and he then returned
to headquarters.

It was not until the first week in July that these messengers reached Elmina. They consisted of Chief Kofi Appia representing the King, and a number of other Chiefs, Captains, and Linguists representing the principal people in Kumasi and the provinces, with upwards of 150 attendants. Mr. Holmes, the District Commissioner of Cape Coast, was deputed by the Governor to see them and ascertain what message they had brought. He met them in Elmina Castle on the 8th. Appia began by assuring the Government of the King's loyalty and desire for the maintenance of peace, and then stated the principal object of his mission, which was to ask the Governor to restore to the King all those Ashantis who had taken refuge in the Colony, and assist him in regaining his ascendancy over those of his former provinces that had declared their independence. He promised in the King's name that they should be received kindly and regarded as his loyal subjects, and, in support of his request, pointed out that so long as Ashanti was broken up into a number of small independent States there could never be any hope of permanent peace or a revival of trade ; whereas, if the whole country were restored to the King, he hoped to be able to end all troubles and keep his roads clear and open to encourage trade.

The Commissioner, after making a few general remarks on the subject of slavery and the desirability of peace, promised to convey the King's message to the Governor, and suggested that, as some little time must elapse before his reply could be received, they should return at once to Kumasi and the answer be sent after them by special runner. This Appia did not care to do, saying that he had been sent with a message to the Governor and would prefer to wait for his answer. He then said, " the Governor ought to come and meet them himself, as they had sent to tell him they were coming," but on Mr. Holmes reminding them that the Governor had been to Elmina to meet them in April, and that they had neither come nor sent any message to explain their delay, both he and Osai, the King's Captain, immediately stood up and apologized. They also asked to be excused for not having arrived when promised, and explained that the delay had been caused by the deaths of two of the Chiefs forming the mission while they were on the road which had obliged them to return to Kumasi to report to the King and get them replaced.

This remark of Appia was so much in accordance with the construction that had been put on the King's letter that, as had happened in 1881, the Governor seems to have immediately concluded that it had been made purposely and by instruction, in order to see how far he could safely go, and then withdrawn so as to appear to be a spontaneous statement made without authority. There seems to have been no ground for this suspicion, however, beyond the habitual distrust of everything said or done by an Ashanti, which was such an important dogma in the Gold Coast official creed. It had always been the practice of the Government to give a present for the subsistence of any messengers from the interior while they were visiting the coast ; but on this occasion the Governor had issued special instructions that this was not to be done. The cost of maintaining the large number of people that Appia had brought with him must have been considerable ; but when he asked for the usual subsistence it was refused, and it was immediately after this, and apparently as a direct outcome of his disappointment and annoyance, that he made the remark to which exception was rightly taken, but for which, as has been seen, he immediately apologized.

In his reply, the Governor complained to the King of what Appia had said, and told him that, since the refugees had come into the Protectorate of their own accord, they were free to leave it in the same way if they wished. The Government, however, would not try to influence them to return to him, nor would it recommend the Adansis to re-occupy their country unless their entire independence of Ashanti was guaranteed. So far as any other tribes who had declared their independence were concerned, the Governor explained that they were living beyond the sphere of British influence, and he could not, therefore, interfere with them at all.

Appia did not return to Kumasi, but sent the Governor's letter up by some of his men and awaited Prempi's reply in Cape Coast. It arrived early in October, and he then went down to Accra to deliver it in person. The King, after apologizing for Appia's conduct and begging the Governor to pardon him, explained that he had never intended that the Ashantis living in the Protectorate should be ordered to return, but only wanted them to be called in the presence of his messengers and told of his wishes and readiness to welcome them back. As for the Adansis, he said they were such troublesome people that he could only agree to have them back if they were prepared to serve him, otherwise he would infinitely prefer them to remain where they were. He also reminded the Governor of the promise he had made in his previous letter to let the Kokofus and Dadiasis know of the message he had sent down.

This promise had never been fulfilled, so Mr. Bascom, the chief clerk in the Secretariat, was sent on the 30th of October to Western Akim to tell the refugees that Prempi wished them to return and had promised to receive them kindly, and to inform them that they were free to go or remain where they were, as they preferred, but that the Government was not prepared to advise them in their choice. One Kokofu Chief, who was dissatisfied with Asibi because another Chief had been set up in his place, and five of his friends, elected to remain in Akim, and Achiriboanda was, of course, afraid to put himself in his rival's power ; but Asibi and the other Kokofu and Dadiasi Chiefs said they would return to Ashanti " in such manner and at such time as the Governor may direct." These Chiefs represented a total of 16,862 Kokofus and 3,920 Dadiasis.

Soon after this it became known that these people were under the impression that they would be sent back under the escort of a white officer, and, as the Government had no such intention, Mr. H. M. Hull was sent up to disabuse

their minds and emphasize the fact that the question of
their return was one that they must decide for themselves,
and in which they need expect no help of any kind from
the Government. This evidently surprised them, but they
adhered to their former decision, and Asibi promised to let
the Governor know when they were ready to start. Mr.
Hull also learned that Prempi had sent men to clean
Kokofu and prepare it for their reception, and that many
Kokofus from other parts had already returned there.

The Government really seems to have been anxious to
prevent the Kokofus from returning to Ashanti. They
were believed to have accumulated a large amount of guns
and ammunition, and it was feared that, whether they
sided with Prempi or not, they might cause disturbances.
While openly professing his readiness to let them go
therefore, the Governor was all the time secretly planning
to prevent it by getting Asibi and Achiriboanda to come
to Accra and then detaining them there.

The arguments that had been advanced by the King in
his letter were not referred to by the Governor in his
reply : they would have been awkward subjects to handle,
for there was a great deal of truth in Prempi's contentions.
It was manifestly absurd to expect him to do very much so
long as his authority was set at nought by nearly all those
who formerly owed allegiance to his stool, and it was still
more unreasonable to expect him to keep the road clear
and safe through the many miles of uninhabited country in
Adansi with the few people he had at his command. But
although his request had this much in its favour, it was
not one with which the Government could be expected to
comply. It had taken certain tribes under its protection,
and had done so with the best of motives, and, however
much the King might protest that such actions did not
harmonize with its professions of friendship for him, or
whatever the difficulties that might arise from them, it
could not withdraw that protection now and hand these
people back to him. The question could not arise unless
and until these tribes asked to be allowed to return.
That Prempi, instead of ruling over the Kumasis and his

few other adherents alone, should have aimed to restore his kingdom to some semblance of its former self, was natural enough and merely a continuance of the policy that had been followed by the Ashantis ever since 1874. This, however, was the first occasion on which it had been so plainly declared and supported by reasonable arguments. The importance attached to it by the King was shown by the number and rank of his messengers.

The position was a difficult one ; but it was only the natural outcome of the policy that had been followed by the Government. It was the invasion of Ashanti in 1874 that had originated the disorganization of the kingdom, but the Government had then declined to undertake any further responsibility in the matter, but had started with the fixed determination to leave the Ashantis to take care of themselves and manage their own affairs as they best could. This policy had been a complete failure. Each of the many European nations that had had Settlements on the Gold Coast had come there in the first place for trade in slaves and gold, and afterwards, when the slave trade was abolished and the profits from the gold trade had diminished, those who were left had remained for general commerce and to provide an outlet for their manufactures. It was trade and trade alone that had brought Europeans to the Coast, and it was trade that still kept them there. But on to this primary motive a secondary one had been grafted by the philanthropist, whose aim it was to introduce the Christian religion, to civilize the African, and generally to better his material and moral condition. Yet, though this desire was there and actuated the few, it was still trade that accounted for the presence of Europeans in a country that is utterly unsuited to them, and for the fact that the English had clung to it after the departure of all their former rivals. It was the traders, indeed, who had prevented its final abandonment many years before. Any policy, therefore, that was unattended by a profitable trade was a failure ; and no policy could be regarded as a complete success unless it advanced civilization and promoted the welfare of the African as well.

England's policy towards Ashanti since 1874 had signally failed in both respects and had been Ashanti's ruin. The destruction of the central controlling authority in Kumasi, and the weakness of the Government in declining all further responsibility and refusing to interfere for the preservation of order, had caused years of civil war, during which the suffering and loss of life must have been immeasurably greater than that attending the occasional wars of united Ashanti, while the naturally evolved civilization and arts of the country had been neglected and fallen into decay. Whether or not human sacrifices had diminished or increased, it is impossible to decide with certainty, because their number was never at any time exactly known, but could only be computed from native reports which were liable to the grossest exaggeration. It is probable, however, that they did diminish during this period ; but this was a result of the wars which made it impossible to spare the victims, and an indirect rather than a direct outcome of the Government's policy. The continually disturbed state of the country, moreover, made the roads so unsafe that all communication with the interior was constantly being cut off, and the once flourishing trade had been virtually extinguished.

On more than one occasion the authorities had been forced temporarily to acknowledge that this policy of non-interference was impracticable ; but, even when a really favourable opportunity was offered them, they had still shrunk from its permanent abandonment. The Ashanti question had been grossly mismanaged for years past, because a policy that was unwise from the start had been persistently followed even after it had been proved to be unworkable. This had now resulted in a state of affairs that had enabled the King to criticize the Government's actions, and to advance plausible, if not conclusive arguments against them. The King's case had, moreover, been greatly strengthened by the Governor's neglect to take reasonable precautions for the prevention of raids into Ashanti by the refugees, which, indeed, was so culpable that he would have been quite justified in thinking

it amounted to technical connivance.   It was impossible
to continue such a farce any longer, and a policy which
aimed at the inclusion of Ashanti within the Protectorate
was now inaugurated.

As far back as 1842 the Select Committee of the House
of Commons had recommended the establishment of a
model farm or botanical garden on the Gold Coast ; but
although the advantages of such an institution had again
been pointed out in the evidence before the Committee of
1865, nothing had ever been done.   Now at last, however,
in March 1890, a botanical station was opened at Aburi in
the Akwapim Hills.

Now that the Gold Coast Government had at last
realized that the inclusion of Ashanti within the Protectorate was the only reasonable course that remained
open to it, no time was lost in commencing negotiations :
in fact, the Governor did not even wait to submit his
proposals for the approval of the Secretary of State before
acting on them.   In December 1890 some messengers
from the King of Bekwai who visited Accra had been
sounded on the subject. They had thought that their
King would be only too glad to accept British protection,
and had been sent back to ascertain his views more definitely, and, a little later, returned with a message advising
the Governor to send an officer to broach the subject to
the King, and promising that the King of Bekwai would
use his influence to get the offer accepted.   Mr. H. M. Hull
was therefore sent on a special mission to Kumasi, accompanied by Assistant-Inspector Campbell and fifty men of
the Gold Coast Constabulary, Doctor Murray, and Thomas
Odonkor as interpreter.

Mr. Hull was given a letter to deliver to the King, in
which recent events were reviewed, and he was formally
notified that Attabubu had been taken under British
protection by a treaty concluded on the 25th of November
1890 by Mr. G. E. Ferguson on behalf of the Government.
Prempi was then reminded that the position of Ashanti
at this time was vastly different from that which it had once
occupied ; that whole tribes had left the country and

settled in the Protectorate ; that the allegiance of those
who remained was but half-hearted, and that large tracts
of once populous and fertile land were now empty and
uncultivated wastes.   It was admitted that the King had
done his best to restore order and prosperity, but, since
he had met with so little success, he was urged to consider
the advisability of adopting other measures, and was
offered a treaty of protection.

This letter contains a curious mixture of professions
of friendship and thinly veiled threats, and clearly shows
the absolute determination of the Government to carry
the new policy on which it had embarked through by one
means or another.   On the one hand, all desire to influence
the King in his acceptance or rejection of the treaty is disclaimed, and it is made to appear that the proposed extension of British protection over his country would be
made as a favour to the Ashantis rather than because it
was desired by the Government ; yet, on the other, passages occur that can only be construed as threats of what
will be done if he refuses.   In one place the Governor
wrote : " The British Protectorate is very extensive, and
Her Majesty's Government does not desire to add largely
to the enormous responsibilities it already has on the
Gold Coast.   Considering the position of Ashanti . . . and
looking to its business relations and friendly connexion
with the Gold Coast, it appears to this Government that
if Ashanti desired to come under British protection . . . it
would be the duty of this Government to yield to the
wishes of the King, and the Kings, Chiefs, and principal
men and people of Ashanti, that they should be allowed
to enjoy that protection." [1]   A little farther on it is declared that " this Government has no desire to force its
advice upon you, and it is quite open to yourself and to
your supporters to accept or decline the advice which this
Government, with the most loyal and friendly feeling
towards Ashanti, has tendered for your consideration." [2]
In contrast to these, however, other passages occur, in one

[1] Parliamentary Paper, *Affairs in Ashanti*, 1896, p. 49.
[2] *Ibid.*, p. 51.

of which the threat is held out that, since the King refuses to permit the Adansis to re-occupy their country without acknowledging his paramountcy, the Government may decide to take the district—a recognized portion of Ashanti territory — under its protection and send them back without his consent. In another, the Governor threatens that if the King does not follow the advice now given him and agree to place his country under the protection of the British, their friendship will be withdrawn, and writes : " Then you must not be surprised if this Government ceases to take that interest in Ashanti of which it has given such substantial proof in regard to your being placed on the stool, and in preventing at considerable cost your rebel subjects from making raids upon those who still adhere to you. . . . Rejection of the advice tendered to you will . . . be calculated to lessen confidence in the good faith and administration of the Authorities in Ashanti ; and it will become a question for the consideration of this Government, whether, in the circumstances stated, it would be any longer justified in continuing the confinement of Yaow Ewuah and the Denkera and Siahah Chiefs, and in incurring the expense of sending European officers to Kumasi." [1]

The proposed treaty, a draft of which was taken by Mr. Hull for the King's signature, consisted of nine articles. By the first of these the King was to place his people and country under British protection. The second accepted them. The third required the Ashantis to refrain from making war on their neighbours and to refer all disputes to the Governor for arbitration. The fourth provided that all disputes arising amongst themselves should be settled in a similar manner, and that the Governor's decision should be final and binding. The fifth secured to all British subjects free access to all parts of Ashanti, the right to build houses and hold property there in accordance with the laws of the Gold Coast Colony, and to carry on any trade that might be approved by the Governor or his deputy : it also stipulated that the authorities in Ashanti

[1] Parliamentary Paper, *Affairs in Ashanti*, 1896, p. 51.

should not confer similar rights on other persons without
the Governor's consent. By the sixth, the Ashantis were
to undertake to keep their roads in good order and encourage trade generally, and not to enter into any agreement or treaty with any other Power without the Governor's
permission. The seventh contained an undertaking on
the part of the Government that it would not interfere
with the customary collection of revenue by the King and
Chiefs, nor with their administration of the country and
the continuance of such of their laws and customs as did
not " militate against the dictates of humanity." The
eighth conferred on the Government the right to appoint
a Resident in Ashanti or to send a Travelling Commissioner
to visit the country at any time, who should assist the
King with advice for the promotion of law, order and
trade ; and the ninth reserved to the Home Government
the right to refuse to ratify the treaty within a year from
its date, but it was to come into force immediately on its
execution. Mr. Hull was authorized to make presents
amounting to £400 to the King, Queen-Mother, and principal Chiefs if the treaty was accepted in its entirety.

Sir Brandford Griffith seems to have felt confident that
this treaty would be accepted ; but the grounds for the
assumption were small indeed. The moment when the
Chiefs, without a head and wearied by continual strife,
were appealing to the Government for help to end their
troubles might very probably have found them willing
to enter into such an agreement ; but it had been allowed
to pass, and the condition of Ashanti now, though still
far removed from what it had once been, was nevertheless
improved. Those who had been most active in keeping
up the state of civil war were no longer there ; and the
country, though greatly depopulated and impoverished,
was quieter than it had been for years, and seemed likely
to improve still more with the promised return of many
of the rebels to their allegiance. But most important of
all, there was now a King, whose position, if not so secure
as it might have been, was nevertheless capable of improvement at any time if his enstoolment was properly

completed. He, moreover, had the support of the Kumasi
Chiefs, who were, and always had been the acknowledged
leaders in the affairs of the kingdom, while the remaining
provincial Kings and Chiefs, if not such ardent adherents,
were at least not opposed to him. His enemies were
fugitives in exile and could have no voice in the Council
until they chose to return and renew their allegiance. It
followed, therefore, that the acceptance or rejection of
this treaty would be decided by the King with the advice
of only those members of his Council who were, to a greater
or less extent, in sympathy with him and his aims, and
had some confidence in his ability eventually to carry
them out. The King's policy was well known : he had
never made any secret of it, and it did not differ from that
of his predecessors, who had always sought to consolidate
and extend their power whenever it was possible to do so.
He aimed to restore Ashanti to the position she had once
held, by winning back the revolted provinces and tributaries to their allegiance. He had already met with some
success in the return of the Insutas and many of the
Mampons, and now knew that the Kokofus and Dadiasis
were ready to follow them. It would have been hardly
credible, therefore, if he and those with him had now
consented, not only to resign all that they had already
gained and were momentarily expecting, but also voluntarily to abandon their own independence and accept the
protection of the very Power that was affording their
enemies an asylum. The King's recent letter had shown,
moreover, that he was beginning to doubt the sincerity
and disinterestedness of the Government's professed
friendship, and these renewed protestations, coupled as
they were with barely concealed threats to let his enemies
in the Protectorate loose upon him, to protect others in
the independent occupation of land that was his, and to
cut off all communications, were certainly not calculated
either to reassure him or to encourage him to put himself
more definitely in its power.

On the other hand, something had to be done. The
Government could not afford to sit down and see the

profitable trade with Ashanti diverted to the Possessions of rival Powers, the roads to the interior becoming impassable because there was no one to clear them, and ill-feeling and expense being incurred by the continual attempts of the refugees to make raids into Ashanti. Almost at this very time it had to take action against one of the Kokofu Chiefs, Maweri Opoku, who had taken a number of his men into Ashanti Akim, where he was attacking and robbing passing traders. He was arrested by Captain Lamb and a party of Hausas and sentenced to seven years' penal servitude in May 1892.

The Government was actuated mainly by a desire to establish peace and humane rule in Ashanti and to promote trade. Its motive was an excellent one, and the time had undoubtedly come when it was imperative for it to secure some definite control over the administration of Ashanti ; but this did not alter the fact that the necessity for such a step—now that it was too late to try the experiment of a friendly alliance—ought to have been realized before, when the difficulties in the way of its accomplishment were less, nor detract from the absurdity of expecting that the King would now be ready to give up his independence at the mere suggestion of the English conveyed in a letter that was obviously inspired by self-interest.

The mission arrived in Kumasi on the 2nd of April, and the Governor's letter was delivered and read to the King and Chiefs at a meeting on the 4th. They heard it quietly, and then separated to summon the provincial Chiefs and discuss it. It was not until the 28th, however, that they had all assembled and Mr. Hull met them. The King in the meantime had treated him coldly, but without actual insult, having put off a meeting that had been arranged earlier without excuse, and omitted to send the provincial Chiefs to call and salute him on their arrival. He therefore demanded and received an apology for these acts of discourtesy before proceeding to have the treaty interpreted to the Chiefs. The King of Bekwai then rose and begged the Council to consider the matter very carefully, at the same time declaring that he was ready to sign the treaty for himself and his people. He, in fact, was really anxious to do so, because he feared for his own safety if the Kokofus returned, well knowing that they might seize the first opportunity to attack him and wipe out the disgrace of their own defeat. After this the Council met daily ; but Mr. Hull could gain no hint of what decision they were likely to come to until the 4th of May, when he was privately informed by the King of Bekwai that the treaty would be rejected. He left for the coast on the afternoon of the 7th, and was overtaken at Kasi the same night by messengers bringing a letter for him to take down to the Governor.

Mr. Hull gained the impression in Kumasi that many of the people would have welcomed British protection, but that the Chiefs were all against the treaty, because they were afraid their own powers and authority would be curtailed. He also heard that some of the people were still in favour of Achiriboanda being made King, principally because they believed that he alone knew the exact spot where much of the royal treasure was concealed.

Be this as it may, the King's reply was only what might have been expected. After complaining that his message to the Kokofu and Dadiasi refugees had been communicated to them without the presence or knowledge of Chief Appia, who had been sent as his representative for this special purpose, he protested very strongly against the Governor's proposal to send the Adansis back to their country under British protection, saying that this would be " forcing and compelling him to receive in his land people whom he could not recognize as his subjects " and would ill accord with the Government's professions of friendship. He and his Chiefs, he said, were considering what measures they could adopt to ensure the road through Adansi being kept open, and begged the Governor to leave it to them to arrange. He then once more repeated his request that all his former subjects might be returned to him, basing it, as before, on the Government's alleged friendship for Ashanti, and saying : " I, whom you call as a friend, is it fair to take

all my subjects from me ? " [1]   He thanked the Governor
for what he had done in reference to the Kokofus and
Dadiasis ; but when he came to the subject of the proposed
treaty he wrote : " The suggestion that Ashanti in its
present state should come and enjoy the protection of
Her Majesty the Queen and Empress of India, I may say
this is a matter of a very serious consideration, and which
I am happy to say we have arrived at this conclusion, that
my kingdom of Ashanti will never commit itself to any such
policy ; Ashanti must remain independent as of old, at the
same time to remain friendly with all white men.   I do not
write this with a boastful spirit, but in the clear sense
of its meaning.   Ashanti is an independent kingdom, and
is always friendly with the white men. . . . I thank Her
Majesty's Government for the good wishes entertained for
Ashanti ; I appreciate to the fullest extend [2] its kindness.
. . . Believe me . . . that the cause of Ashanti is progressing
and that there is no reason for any Ashantiman to feel
alarm at the prospects, or to believe for a single instant
that our cause has been driving back by the events of the
past hostilities." [3]

The Secretary of State, so soon as he heard of what
had been done, expressed his disapproval, and censured
Sir Brandford Griffith for having taken so important a
step as offering a treaty to the Ashantis, about which, after
his own dilatory dealing with them, there could have been
no special urgency, without having first referred the matter
to him and obtained his sanction.

In September, Chiefs Buatin and Kwaku Freku arrived
in Accra with 240 followers bearing a message from the
King.   The first half of this referred to the recent mission.
The King complained that Mr. Hull had treated him with
contempt by rejecting all the presents of money and cattle
that he had sent him during his stay in Kumasi, and had,
moreover, left the capital without waiting for his answer
to the Governor's letter.   This refusal of presents was very

---

[1] Parliamentary Paper, *Affairs in Ashanti*, 1896, p. 71.
[2] *Sic.*
[3] Parliamentary Paper, *Affairs in Ashanti*, 1896, p. 71.

unusual and certain to be considered an unfriendly act :
it was, in fact, most unwise ; but it was due to no fault on
the part of Mr. Hull, but to the distinct orders of Sir
Brandford Griffith, who had hoped to keep down the
expenses of the mission by this means. Mr. Hull's departure, so soon as he had received private information
that his mission had been unsuccessful, had been hurried
on account of the state of his health. He left on the 7th ;
but the date fixed by the Governor as the latest for him
to leave, and of which the King had been notified, was the
11th. He had, of course, told the King that he was going ;
but the letter was not then ready, nor had the King made
any appointment for another meeting. Mr. Hodgson,
who was again acting during Sir Brandford Griffith's
absence in England, now explained that no discourtesy
had been intended. The second and principal part of the
message was a reiteration of the old request for the return
of all the seceded tribes, but the mere fact of its constant
repetition and the increasing importance of the messengers
clearly showed how much the King had set his heart upon
it. The answer given was a reference to the Governor's
former replies.

CHAPTER XVIII

THE THREATENED ATTACK ON ATTABUBU

1892 TO 1894

IN accordance with his policy of recovering all his lost subjects, Prempi, about the middle of 1891, had demanded from the King of Inkoranza the return of those Mampons and other Ashantis who had fled to and were still living in his country. Opoku had died during the war with Mampon, and Kofi Fua was now King. When they were attacked by the Mampons, the Inkoranzas had sent to Prempi asking for help, and he now called upon Kofi Fua to give proof of his loyalty by " drinking fetish " with him. Fua tried to evade this, as his predecessor Opoku had done ; but the King was suspicious, and there and then demanded the return of all Ashantis living in Inkoranza, and, when this was refused, made preparations to recover them by force. The Kumasi army attacked Inkoranza in August 1892, and inflicted a crushing defeat : 200 Inkoranzas were left dead on the field, 2,000 women and children were taken prisoners, Inkoranza was burned to the ground, and Kofi Fua, with the remnant of his people, was compelled to fly to Kumfa,[1] whence he sent messengers with £48 in gold-dust to the Governor, asking to be taken under British protection, as he was afraid he would soon be attacked again. The gold was returned, with a message that the Government was unable to take Inkoranza into the Protectorate, but that if the people were driven out of their own country and compelled to seek refuge south of the River Pra an asylum would be found for them.

[1] ? Kukuma.

On receiving this message, Kofi Fua sought aid else-where. He sent a present of twelve slaves and some gold-dust to the Fetish Priest of Krachi, who provided him with some charms and magic gunpowder, and Kobina Ashanti, the King of Attabubu, sent one of his Chiefs, Kujo Akojina, with a contingent of thirty men to his support. Kofi Fua also opened negotiations with the people of Mo for a defensive alliance. His fears were soon realized : early in 1893 the Kumasis again advanced against him, and, by a strategic movement, cut him off from his supports from Mo. The Inkoranzas, however, were successful, and drove back the enemy with consider-able loss after a battle fought in some swampy ground near Kumfa. The Kumasis, who had lost 300 men killed and captured, then retired, and the Inkoranzas, after a success-ful attack on the Bandas, who had been allied against them, returned to their town and began to rebuild it.

Meanwhile, the Kumasis had been making preparations to wipe out their defeat. Contingents were provided from Mampon, Insuta, Bekwai, Jabin, Ofinsu, Kumawu, Ejisu and other districts, and the supreme command was given to Amankwa Tia Kwamin, who swore that he would compel the whole of the Brong tribes to return to their allegiance. In June 1893 Kofi Fua on his side sent messengers to the Governor with four large elephant's tusks and twelve peridwins of gold (£97 4s.). This, by native custom, was equivalent to an acknowledgment of fealty, and Kofi Fua expected to secure the alliance, if not the protection, of the Government. He also moved his camp to Kintampo to guard against the possibility of being again cut off from his allies in Mo, and sent further presents to the Fetish Priest at Krachi, who closed the roads into Ashanti and called upon the Brong tribes to march to the assistance of the Inkoranzas. Kobina Kru of Abiasi, however, was the only Chief who obeyed this order. At the same time, Prempi sent messengers to inform the King of Attabubu that he was at war with the Inkoranzas, and to warn him and Sencheri, the ex-King of Mampon, not to mix them-selves up in the quarrel by assisting his enemies, or he would destroy them also. If the Attabubus were for peace, then he, too, was for peace. These messengers were stopped at Ejera by order of the Fetish Priest of Krachi, and, after some deliberation, in which the Attabubu Chiefs were not unanimous—two of them wishing to go to the support of the Inkoranzas—Kobina Ashanti replied that ever since he had severed his connection with Kumasi in 1874 he had held no communication with the Ashantis, and that he did not therefore understand why Prempi should send to him now. If he wanted peace, he should offer it to the King of Inkoranza, who, he understood, had applied to come under British protection as he himself had already done.

Early in August, the army under Amankwa Tia Kwamin defeated the Inkoranzas, Mos and Abiasis in two battles near Kintampo, and compelled them to retreat to Abiasi, whence they again sent to Attabubu asking for help ; but before their messengers returned they were once more attacked and defeated by the Kumasis. They are said to have run short of powder ; but they can have offered but feeble resistance, for, although the Kumasis lost a great number of men, they themselves only had five men killed and about 400 slightly wounded. Between 2,000 and 3,000 women and children, however, were taken prisoners, and the stool and state umbrellas of Inkoranza captured and carried to Kumasi. The survivors fled in every direction. Some ran to Brumasi ; others to Yegi and Prang ; and the people of these places, fearing the victorious Ashantis would follow them, buried their valuables and fled to Wiasi. Amongst those who went to Prang and thence to Wiasi was the Chief of Abiasi, but Kofi Fua made for Attabubu. Soon after crossing the River Pru he met a detachment of Kobina Ashanti's men coming to his relief ; but they were too late to be of any use to him, and he pushed on to Attabubu, where he remained a few days only before joining the other fugitives in Wiasi. The duplicity of the King of Attabubu, who he felt certain had been trying to keep terms with the Governor and with him at the same time, and whom he also suspected of having been in communication with the Ashantis, greatly annoyed him and was the cause of his refusal to remain any longer in his town.

The Ashantis pursued the Inkoranzas as far as Abiasi, where they encamped for nine days and then killed all their sick and destroyed the town and surrounding villages before returning to Kintampo. A small force was detached under Kunkurantumi, the King's Chief stool-bearer, to co-operate with Seidu Nji, the heir-apparent to the stool of Banda, in punishing the Mos ; but the latter were victorious, and both Kunkurantumi and Seidu Nji were killed : the former fell into a gold hole, but his body was taken out and beheaded.

Sencheri had now become tired of exile, and thought the war between Kumasi and Inkoranza might be turned to account to enable him to return to his country. He therefore sent secretly to Prempi, promising to try to gain the submission, not only of the Inkoranzas, but of the whole of the Brong tribes also. To this end, being unable to conduct his negotiations openly, he sent messengers to Kwesi Jantradu, the Priest at Krachi, and tried to persuade him to advise the Inkoranzas to send in their submission ; but the latter had already accepted presents from the Inkoranzas and seized Sencheri's messengers and their goods. After this all negotiations with the Inkoranzas were conducted through him.

The Ashanti army was still encamped at Abiasi when Prempi's messengers again arrived at Ejera, whence they sent Kwamin Agai, a subject of Sencheri, to tell Kobina Ashanti and Sencheri that he wanted them to " drink fetish " with him and return to their allegiance ; after which they were either to make peace between him and Kofi Fua or give the latter up. He included all the Brong tribes in his invitation, and said that he had heard that they were deserting their towns, but that if they were for peace, he, too, was for peace ; but if they wished for war they could have it. If they failed to send a favourable reply within five days, the King threatened to march his army against them. Messengers, including one from

the King of Inkoranza, returned to say that if the King of
Ashanti was sincere, his messengers must come on to
Attabubu ; but they, so soon as they heard that Kofi Fua
was at Wiasi, went back to Kumasi, saying that it was
sufficient for the present for them to know that he was
there and had sent a messenger, and that the Brongs
would hear further from Prempi. It was supposed that
these messengers had only been sent to find out where
he was hiding, for the Ashantis had lost all trace of him
after the last battle ; but they themselves explained their
action by saying that they had only been accredited to
the Brongs, and thought they might be asked what were
the King's intentions towards Kofi Fua, and, having received no instructions on this point, they would not have
known what reply to make, and had therefore gone back
to enquire.

News soon reached Accra from Mr. Hull, who had heard
it in Akim, that the Ashantis were planning an attack
on Attabubu, and Mr. G. E. Ferguson was then sent up,
ostensibly on a surveying expedition, to organize a system
of spies and find out what their intentions really were.
He reached Attabubu at the end of October, and found
the Inkoranza refugees were assuming a very domineering
attitude over the Brongs, whose weakness they had been
quick to discover. Kofi Fua hoped to be able to bully
them into acknowledging fealty to him, so that he could
then make his peace with Prempi and return to his own
country by bringing them back to their allegiance. They,
and a contingent brought from Krachi by the Fetish Priest,
were taking food by force and even shooting the owners,
and Kofi Fua had threatened to invade Attabubu after
his return to Inkoranza.

On the 18th of November the King's messengers returned from Kumasi ; but this time they came directly
to Attabubu instead of transacting their business from
Ejera as before. The message they now delivered was
that Prempi had no quarrel with the Brongs, but with
the Inkoranzas only ; it was long before his reign that
they had seceded from Kumasi, and he therefore knew

nothing about them ; he was at peace with them, but wanted the King of Inkoranza to say whether he would now return to his country and serve him. The envoys, however, admitted to Mr. Ferguson that the message first brought by Kwamin Agai, which he now repeated in their presence, had been correctly given.

Meanwhile, the information already in the possession of the Government had been confirmed by the arrival, on the 29th of September, of one of Kobina Ashanti's Linguists, who had been sent to inform the Governor that the Ashantis were preparing to attack him. He claimed protection and assistance, and though it was as yet too early to expect any news from Mr. Ferguson, affairs looked so threatening, and this rumour coincided so well with the King's known ambitions, that it was decided to make a demonstration of force in the Attabubu district, and to send a warning to Prempi without further delay. The former was to be made by 300 men of the Gold Coast Constabulary under the Inspector-General, Colonel Sir Francis Scott, and the latter was taken by Mr. Vroom,[1] the Native District Commissioner of Wassaw. At the same time, the sale of arms and ammunition in the coast towns was prohibited.

The letter taken up by Mr. Vroom informed the King that the Governor had heard he was contemplating an attack on Attabubu, and warned him that if it was made he would have to reckon with the Government, since the place was now under British protection. Mr. Vroom was also told to emphasize the fact that he would find himself embroiled, not with the Colonial Government alone, but with that of England also. He was to inform the King that British troops and guns had already been sent to Attabubu, and to protest against his action in having sent messages to Chiefs in the Protectorate otherwise than through the Governor, and practically to accuse him of having caused the King of Bekwai and his Linguist to be

---

[1] Vroom was a mulatto, who had originally been in the service of the Dutch Government and was afterwards appointed a District Commissioner under the English.

murdered because they had been in favour of the acceptance
of British protection and opposed the return of the Kokofus.
This charge was made in consequence of a rumour which
Mr. Hull had heard in Akim.

Mr. Vroom left Elmina on the 2nd of October and
arrived in Kumasi on the 14th, delivering the Governor's
letter and message the same day. The King denied that
he had ever had any intention of attacking the Attabubus,
but charged them with having sent men and arms to
assist the Inkoranzas in fighting against him, although he
had warned them against mixing themselves up in the
quarrel. He went on to explain that the only occasions
on which he had held communications with Chiefs in the
Protectorate had been when he had sent messengers to
the Kings of Eastern Akim and Assin. The first had
been sent to thank Amoaku Atta for having sent to inform
him of a case in which an Ashanti had violated his (Amoaku
Atta's) oath, and the second to accompany an Assin trader
back to his country and explain to his King that he had
been robbed and wounded in Ashanti, but that Prempi
had heard the case, recovered his property for him, and
awarded him damages against his assailants. These were
mere acts of courtesy. When any person swears the oath
of a King, "it is the duty of the King to whom the fact of
the taking of the oath is reported or represented to in-
vestigate the matter, whether the person be his subject
or not, and then having done so to inflict fine on the
guilty one. If the oath appears to have been violated or
perjured, the person taking it is fined, which, when collected, is sent to the person whose oath was taken." [1]
Prempi was undoubtedly speaking no more than the truth
when he protested that he had meant no discourtesy to the
Governor by what he had done ; in fact, he must have
thought the latter was rather going out of his way to seek
a ground of complaint against him. The charge of conniving at the murder of the King of Bekwai completely
fell to the ground ; for he himself had received Mr. Vroom

[1] G. E. Ferguson, Parliamentary Paper, *Affairs in Ashanti*, 1896,
p. 136.

in his town. This was Yow Buachi, who had been King for about eighteen months, having been placed on the stool after the deposition of Kwaku Ababresi for tyranny and extortion, and for having put two of his Chiefs to death without consulting his Council. Ababresi, however, was still living in one of the neighbouring villages. The death of Attobra,[1] the Linguist, was explained by Yow Buachi, who said that the deceased and a Headman named Yamua[2] had quarrelled and the latter had shot himself, but " swore by Attobra's head "[3] before he died. Attobra had then been " put in log " and appealed to the Chief of Esumeja to settle the case for him, but, while it was still pending, took the Great Oath that he would die as Yamua had done, and had accordingly been put to death.

A few days after Mr. Vroom's arrival, Prempi sent to recall the army, which had now returned to Kintampo. He sent four times altogether ; for the Chiefs said they were bound by their oath to bring back the King of Inkoranza and compel the submission of the Brongs, and in the end the King had to send an important Chief to swear his Great Oath that the white man was on his way to Kumasi, but that it was not yet known what he was coming for. The army then returned, but destroyed Kintampo before leaving.

Captain Aplin, with the advance-guard of the expeditionary force, left Accra on the same date as Mr. Vroom set out from Elmina—the 2nd of October—and Sir Francis Scott followed with the main body a few days later. He arrived in Abetifi on the 21st, but remained there so long that it was not until the 17th of December that he reached Attabubu. The Jabins, Agogos and Inkoranzas all asked to have their countries taken into the Protectorate, and their appeal was supported by Sir Francis Scott and the Basel missionaries at Abetifi, who were all anxious that an ultimatum should be sent to the King demanding an indemnity for the loss of trade and the expense to which the Government had been put in sending troops to Attabubu. The Chambers of Commerce of London, Glasgow

[1] ? Atta Bra.   [2] ? Yow Amoa.   [3] *Vide* note p. 232.

and Liverpool also wrote urging the inclusion of Ashanti within the Protectorate and the extension of Government administration over it.

Mr. Hodgson, however, though he fully recognized that this was a desirable step, and that if the Ashanti Confederacy was still further weakened by the defection of these tribes and the Bekwais, little, if any opposition could then be offered by the Kumasis, could not overlook the fact that the latter might, and probably would, make some resistance, which might be more than the forces he had at his disposal would be able to cope with. He had already written fully on the subject to the Secretary of State and asked for authority to adopt this course, and that European troops might be held in readiness to come to the assistance of the local Government if necessary. This, however, had been refused, and it had been left to him to decide whether or not he would take action with nothing more than the Gold Coast Constabulary to support him—a responsibility that he very naturally refused to take, even though Sir Francis Scott was confident of success. The different tribes were told, therefore, that their application could not be granted, although the Inkoranzas, having been driven into the Protectorate, would be found a place to settle in if they wished. The Protectorate, however, would not be extended to include their own country.

Mr. Ferguson, in the meantime, had been authorized to conclude treaties of friendship and freedom of trade with such tribes on the right back of the River Volta as were not under Ashanti nor within the Neutral Zone, and with Inkoranza. This latter treaty was signed on the 25th of January 1894.

After Mr. Vroom left Kumasi for the coast, the King sent messengers to follow him and repeat what he had said about his war with the Inkoranzas and the action of the Attabubus. They were given a reply telling him that the Government expected him to preserve peace, desist from further war against the Inkoranzas, and see that the lives of the captured women and children were spared. It was further alleged against him that, in spite of his assurances that no atack on Attabubu had been made or intended, Abiasi and other villages belonging to it had been destroyed, and he was warned that any alliance with Salaga, such as he was rumoured to be contemplating, would be regarded as an unfriendly act.

There had been war in the Salaga district for several months, arising out of a dispute about the succession to the stool of Kabachi, and Kabachi Wula, the successful claimant, had recently defeated the King of Kombi and driven him out of the country. Kabachi Wula was very jealous of the increasing importance of the Kintampo and Attabubu markets at the expense of that of Salaga, and it was therefore of special importance to prevent any alliance between him and Prempi, which would almost certainly have resulted in the ruin of both these places and the diversion of much of their trade to French and German territory at Bontuku and Keti. It also became known that Prempi was trying to persuade the Bolis to aid the Bandas in continuing the war against Inkoranza, and Mr. Ferguson was sent from Attabubu to remind them that they had accepted a flag from Major Ewart in 1888 and concluded a treaty of friendship with the Government when he himself visited their country in June 1892. By the time he reached Kintampo, however, they had already heard of his approach and left the Banda camp.

That the invasion of Attabubu had at one time been intended there can be no doubt. Amankwa Tia Kwamin had definitely included it as one of the objects of his expedition in the oath he swore before leaving Kumasi ; the King's first message to the Attabubus pointed to the same end, and a reserve had been kept in Insuta, Kumawu and Agogo to co-operate with the army sent against the Inkoranzas when it reached the Attabubu frontier. Prisoners and deserters from the Ashanti camp all told the same tale, and it was, moreover, well known that the recovery of his suzerainty over the Brong tribes was one of the King's dearest wishes. He had made repeated applications to the Government to have them given back to him, and, quite apart from the question of extension of territory, it meant a great deal to him by reopening the direct road to Salaga : nor was it altogether surprising that, having failed to regain them by negotiation, he should have decided to resort to arms ; for he argued that since the English had taken no action when the Adansis were driven out, they would not be likely to do so in the case of any other remote tribe with whom they might happen to have treaty relations.

Prempi was undoubtedly in the wrong in so far as his intentions were concerned, and it was the timely despatch of the troops to Attabubu that had alone prevented its actual invasion ; for their real destination and object were unknown, and the army had at once been recalled to defend the capital. So nervous, indeed, were the Ashantis at this time, and so great was their anxiety to hear Mr. Vroom's message, that they even forgot a portion of the ceremonial etiquette, about the strict observance of which they are usually most punctilious. Yet, as matters turned out, it was the protected Chief Kobina Ashanti rather than Prempi who appeared in the wrong ; for the latter's charge against him was quite correct. Mr. Ferguson discovered that the detachment under Kujo Akojina, which Kobina Ashanti tried to make out had only been sent to guard his frontier, had really been sent to aid the Inkoranzas, and had not only fought with them against the Kumasis, but had afterwards accompanied them on their expedition against the Bandas also. Kobina Ashanti, too, had accepted a present of two slaves and a wicker state palanquin from Kofi Fua in recognition of their services. This was long before any move had been made against the Attabubu frontier, and although the Governor wrote telling Prempi that he should have complained to him instead of sending to warn the Attabubus against mixing themselves up in the war, it was rather too much to expect that he would be ready to incur the delay that this course would have involved when he found a protected tribe already in the field against him. There was, in fact, nothing whatever against Prempi except his intention ; for his troops had neither entered Attabubu territory nor done the least damage to anything belonging to the tribe. Abiasi and the other villages that had been destroyed, and which the Government at one time believed belonged to Attabubu, were afterwards proved to be quite independent of it, and, even if this had not been so, the Abiasis had been in the field with the Inkoranzas and were actually pursued into the town.

A little later, in February 1894, further messengers arrived in Accra bringing a letter from the King, in which he protested that although he had explained everything in connection with the charges that had been made against him, yet the troops had not been recalled from Attabubu and Ashanti-Akim, where he alleged they were frightening the people and compelling them to sign treaties of protection with the Government, and molesting passing Ashanti traders.

The first part of this complaint was, of course, utter nonsense. The treaties that the tribes in those districts were signing were treaties of friendship and trade, and came far short of the protection that they had asked for and would have been only too ready to accept without any need for compulsion. They were, in fact, tentative and half-hearted measures designed to satisfy the people for a time without committing the Government to any increased responsibility. They were intended to tide matters over until such time as its new policy could be carried out. It by no means follows, however, that Prempi knew what these treaties really were ; for it would have been hard for him—and must, indeed, have been hard for the people themselves—to understand how a Chief could receive a British flag and sign a treaty with the Government without coming under its protection. This was all that the Attabubus had ever done, and if these others, who had been repeatedly begging for protection, really understood the difference between their position and their own, they must have thought the arrangements most unfair. The explanation seems to be that when Attabubu was given protection it was not foreseen how matters would turn out ; but when others came forward with similar requests, the authorities found the responsibility was likely to be greater than they cared to undertake, even in the case of those tribes who were independent of Ashanti, while in the case of others, such as the Jabins, they were afraid to provoke the King's hostility by appearing to encourage the defection of his subjects ; for although they were now anxious to acquire administrative powers in his kingdom, they aimed rather at dealing with it as a whole.

The second complaint, however, though one that is frequently made and for that reason alone very often discredited, was probably not without foundation. It was, of course, denied that traders had been interfered with in any way ; but no one who has ever travelled ten miles in the bush with carriers or troops can be unaware that cases of this kind are not only extremely common, but also very difficult to detect or prevent. The sufferers are too often afraid to report them, lest worse should befall them. Although these allegations may have been exaggerated, therefore, they doubtless rested on a very real foundation of fact. In this case, too, there was all the more probability of the truth of the charge, because there was great difficulty in getting supplies for the troops, so much so in fact, that Sir Francis Scott found it necessary to detach an officer and 100 men and send them to Amantin, where food was comparatively plentiful, as it had not been approached by either party during the war. As Amantin was a day's march along the road to Kumasi, this unexplained movement and the town's occupation by troops must have had a very hostile appearance to the King. Mr. Vroom, too, had reported when on his way to Kumasi that the Assin ferrymen at Prasu were in the habit of taking goods from returning Ashanti traders, and it is hardly likely that the soldiers and carriers in the remote Attabubu district did less.

During the whole of this time, Sir Francis Scott had never ceased to urge the desirability of making an advance upon Kumasi and taking the whole country under British protection once and for all. He was confident that this could be done without firing a shot ; but still there was the risk that the King might elect to fight, and Mr. Hodgson could not take it unless he had a definite promise that Imperial troops would be sent out if he needed them. Since this had first been refused, he had written more than once and used every possible argument in his efforts to prevail on the Secretary of State to alter his decision, but without success. At last, in January 1894, Lord Ripon wrote that the Government was not inclined to adopt the policy advocated, because it thought it would cause too great an increase in the responsibilities of the Gold Coast Government, nor could it sanction any course which might involve a necessity for the employment of British troops. The risks attendant on the existing conditions, however, were recognized, and it was suggested that the King should be asked to receive a British Resident at Kumasi in return for stipends for himself and his principal Chiefs. The King was to undertake not to make war on or disturb any of the tribes living beyond a certain frontier, which was to be defined so as to exclude from Ashanti the Bekwais, Inkoranzas, and other tribes who had asked for British protection ; and the Resident was to live in Kumasi with a strong guard of Hausas, and to enquire into any disputes that might arise between the King and these outside tribes, referring all questions in which the King was found to be in the right to the Governor for final adjustment, but was to interfere as little as possible with the internal affairs of the country.

The troops were now withdrawn, leaving only a small detachment in Bompata, with supports at Abetifi, and Mr. Vroom was once more sent up to Kumasi to make this new proposal to the King. The letter in which it was set forth resembled Sir Brandford Griffith's previous communication in one respect ; for while it professed only to advise the King to fall in with the Government's wishes and to leave him perfectly free to act as he thought best, yet it contained a hidden threat. This time it was his rival Achiriboanda who was made use of, and Mr. Hodgson wrote : " This arrangement now proposed is in every way so advantageous to you and your people . . . that you will,

I feel sure, not hesitate to agree to it. There is no wish to force you to do so. Prince Achiriboanda, who is now living here with the King of Kokofu, a loyal friend to the Governor, would, I doubt not, subscribe to the arrangement, and would loyally carry out the wishes of the Queen in the event of his succeeding to the Golden Stool, for which step he has, as you know, very powerful supporters."[1] Mr. Vroom also had instructions to impress upon the King that Achiriboanda was in constant communication with the Governor, " and that a word from me, if I like to give it, would bring the Kokofus, Dadiassis, Inkwantas and Daniassis back to Ashanti, in support of his claim from the South, the Kings of Juabin and Mampon, with their people, from the East, and the King of Nkoranza, with his people, as well as the Mos, from the North ; that his present condition is, under the circumstances, a hazardous one ; and that it is to his interest to draw close to the Governor of the Gold Coast in the manner which he has now been requested to do."[2] A form of agreement was sent up for signature, but no mention of the stipends was made in the letter, lest it should rouse the King's suspicions and lead the Chiefs to believe that he was being asked to sell his country or his independence. Mr. Vroom, however, was authorized to promise £600 a year to the King, £200 a year each to the Kings of Mampon, Kokofu, Bekwai and Jabin, and £80 a year to the Queen-Mother.

This was a makeshift arrangement at best, and was only resorted to because the Government, having decided to adopt a certain policy, yet shrunk from taking the small risk entailed by seeing it through properly. Nor had it even the merit of probable success. It was perfectly well known that the main objection to the treaty that had been offered before had been the proposal to establish a Resident in Kumasi, and it was not likely to be regarded any more favourably now. It was not that the Ashantis were seriously opposed to such an appointment in itself ; but they were afraid that it would prove the preliminary step

[1] Parliamentary Paper, *Affairs in Ashanti*, 1896, p. 167.
[2] *Ibid.*, p. 166.

to the loss of their independence and the abolition of their slave-holding rights. They were neither fools nor blind : they had watched the way in which the English on the Coast had gradually risen from the position of tenants of the local Chiefs to that of paramount overlords, and, profiting by what they had seen, recognized that such an appointment as was now proposed might prove to be the thin end of the wedge that was to reduce Ashanti to a position similar to that now occupied by Fanti.

The withdrawal of the troops from Attabubu had, moreover, strengthened the King's position ; for all the surrounding tribes, and even the Kumasis themselves, had felt certain that they would eventually march to the capital, and were said to be prepared to submit peaceably to whatever terms were dictated to them ; but their failure to do so now enabled the King to persuade the people that it was he who had got rid of them. He represented, and very possibly believed, that the English were afraid to risk an advance on his capital. Those Chiefs, too, who had been negotiating to come under British protection came to the conclusion that the Government was too weak for them to rely on with safety, and saw that they would be driven to renew their allegiance to Prempi. The movement, in fact, gave the last blow to British prestige, which had been waning through the tentative and vacillating policy of the Government ever since 1874. Prempi, therefore, was almost certain to regard these fresh proposals as an admission of weakness and a sign of his own moral victory, inasmuch as the Government were reduced to asking for that which he and everyone else had fully expected it to take. He had already expressed his opinion of the real value of the Governor's professions of friendship, and their mere repetition was not likely to make him change it ; still less so when accompanied by threats actually to incite a simultaneous attack on him by all his enemies from every side.

Mr. Vroom had barely started on his mission when messengers arrived with a letter from Prempi, in which he once more complained of the continued interference of the

Ashanti refugees in the Protectorate with his traders. This was admittedly true, and the Governor had already made arrangements for Mr. Hull to go to Prasu and find out exactly what was going on there. The responsibility for preventing occurrences of this kind lay, of course, with the Government ; but no regret was expressed for it in the reply sent to the King ; on the contrary, it was utilized as a further excuse for pressing on him the necessity for accepting the offer just made him and agreeing to accept a British Resident, so that the country might be settled and the tribes who were perpetrating these outrages encouraged to return to their own homes.

Mr. Vroom arrived in Kumasi on the 17th of March, and found the King engaged in celebrating the funeral custom of his sister Ekua Bedu, who had died on the 13th. His arrival at such a time was most inconvenient ; for this was one of those occasions on which the sacrifice of a certain number of human victims would be considered indispensable. The King, indeed, had sent messengers to meet him at Esumeja and ask him not to come any farther at present ; but he had only consented to march more slowly. The reading of the Governor's letter was postponed until the 28th, when the Kings of Mampon, Bekwai and Insuta were represented by their Linguists. The subject of the stipends was introduced at the next meeting, held on the 7th of April, and the King then asked Mr. Vroom to return to the coast, promising to send his answer on the arrival of the provincial Kings, who were expected shortly to take part in a custom. This he declined to do ; but undertook to send any letter to the Governor whilst he himself awaited further instructions in Kumasi. Two days later, however, this request was repeated by the Chiefs, and, after a time, endorsed by the King, whereupon Mr. Vroom replied that he must " take his request as a modest command," and agreed to leave at once. It was evident, however, that Prempi had made this request with considerable reluctance, and was most anxious to avoid creating the impression that he was driving him away.

There were several reasons for all this. No one knew better than Prempi that his position would never be really secure until he had been placed on the Golden Stool with the full customary ceremonial, and it was with this end in view that he had recently set up two insignificant Chiefs to replace the exiled Kings of Mampon and Kokofu: They, as his tools, would be ready to perform their part in the ceremony, and he had no reason to fear any opposition from the Kings of Bekwai or Jabin. Before this could be done, however, it would be necessary to complete the funeral custom for the late King, and it was for this that all the provincial Kings and Chiefs had been summoned to attend in the first week of May as a preliminary to the enstoolment, which was to take place immediately afterwards. The presence of an agent of the Government in the capital while these ceremonies were being performed was to be avoided if possible ; for human sacrifices would form an essential part of both, and Prempi's position was far too precarious for him to dare to dispense with them, however much he personally might wish to do so. Had Mr. Vroom remained, he could hardly have helped knowing something of what was going on, and would, moreover, have seen the puppets that had been set up as Kings of Mampon and Kokofu, and have been a witness that the whole proceeding was something of a farce. It was for these reasons that he had been asked to return to the coast without receiving any answer to the message he had brought ; but he was in Kumasi long enough to feel certain that it was Ansa and a few self-interested Chiefs who were at the bottom of these arrangements. Their power and importance would have disappeared at once with the arrival of a British Resident in Kumasi, and they were determined to oppose it by every possible means. They had the ear of the King, and knew that they could influence him as they liked ; but they were afraid of the provincial Kings and Chiefs, many of whom they thought might be favourably disposed towards the Government's proposals. As matters stood at present, it would have been easy for these provincial Chiefs to overrule the King in Council ; but so soon as he was placed on the Golden Stool he would acquire more right to veto their decisions, and their success, though not absolutely impossible, would become far more difficult. Hence the anxiety of Ansa and his party to have this ceremony completed before the Governor's letter came up for consideration.

Ansa knew that Mr. Vroom had a shrewd idea of the part he was really playing, for the latter had spoken to him about it and warned him. He now tried to lull suspicion and justify himself by sending a long letter to the Governor filled with plausible statements and explanations and representing that he was actuated solely by a desire to promote peace and the spread of civilization in Ashanti. He admitted, however, what does not seem to have been known before, that he had been present at one of the battles during the war with Inkoranza, but said he had gone to the camp to try to induce the army to return, and had been present at the battle only out of curiosity. This letter was sent down by Mr. Vroom, and Ansa tried to persuade him to support his statements, and, when he refused, followed it up with another long letter to the Governor, which was sent down by special messengers, who travelled with Mr. Vroom. This letter purported to come from the King, but it was strongly suspected that he knew nothing about it. It was an attempt to discredit anything Vroom might say to the effect that he had been driven out of the country ; complained that he had been very impatient while in Kumasi, and explained that the delay had been caused by the absence of the provincial Chiefs. Whether this letter emanated from Ansa alone or was merely inspired by him is open to doubt ; but the Governor at once wrote to the King warning him against the man, and telling him of the letters that had passed ; but, since Ansa himself was the person who would read any letter to him, it is more than probable that Prempi never heard its true contents. Rightly or wrongly, the conviction grew that, but for Ansa, there would be little difficulty in carrying the Government's plans through, and the letters purporting to emanate from Prempi at this time—which were all in

Ansa's hand-writing—show so much internal evidence of his composition in their canting tone and general plausibility, that it is quite impossible to decide to what extent they should be accepted as faithful representations of the King's views, written at his dictation, or merely as the unauthorized attempts at diplomacy of Ansa himself. In fact, Ansa's connection with him in all probability did more than anything else to bring Prempi into a discredit that was largely undeserved.

Reports of human sacrifices in Kumasi now became frequent, but, as usual, there was no real evidence of their occurrence, and these reports were little more than rumours and statements founded on hearsay. So long as the religious beliefs of the Ashantis remained what they were, however, it was quite certain that ceremonies of such importance as the funeral custom of one King and the formal enstoolment of another would be attended by these rites. But although human sacrifices had undoubtedly taken place, it is almost certain that, as had happened in 1881, their numbers were greatly exaggerated. When Mr. Hull was in Kumasi to offer the treaty of protection and the Governor's letter was being read out, the Chiefs had interrupted when the passage reminding them that the continuance of this custom would not be permitted was reached, and eagerly asked whether sacrifices or executions were meant. Mr. Hull had replied that the Governor meant exactly what he had written, and this seemed to please them very much. As has been explained elsewhere, the great majority of these sacrifices had never been anything more than public executions, though slaves and prisoners of war had of necessity been used when the number of criminals was insufficient. Nowadays, however, every man was of value to the state, and it was unlikely that any more victims would have been sacrificed than was absolutely necessary. A diminution in the number of sacrifices was, therefore, bound to take place naturally, even if there was no desire to conform as far as possible to the known wishes of the Government. In a kingdom so unsettled as Ashanti was at this time, crime was not

likely to decrease, and would supply a sufficient number of
victims for all ordinary requirements, and quite as many
as the Ashantis could afford ; hence the satisfaction of the
Chiefs when they understood, as they undoubtedly did,
that no exception would be taken to executions.   There
is no evidence whatever that the sacrifices that took place
during these ceremonies were anything more than this,
in which case the Chiefs were quite possibly acting in good
faith.   The best authenticated instance seems to be one
reported by Mr. Vroom, in which a man was put to death
for adultery with a Chief's wife, which, by Ashanti law,
was a capital offence.   All others were founded on the
merest hearsay.   These reports, however, were eagerly
seized upon as additional reasons for urging the inclusion
of Ashanti within the Protectorate, a measure that was now
universally recognized in the Colony as the only solution of
the Ashanti problem.

Prempi was formally enstooled on the 11th of June,
when 400 persons were rumoured to have been sacrificed.
It was reported that the King of Bekwai alone brought
gold-dust instead of victims, declaring his intention to do
nothing to encourage the practice.

CHAPTER XIX

THE ASHANTI EMBASSY TO ENGLAND

1894 TO 1895

For some time after Mr. Vroom's return from his unsuccessful mission to Kumasi, nothing definite could be learned of what was going on in Ashanti. It was rumoured that after Prempi's enstoolment the Chiefs had been in conference for two weeks, deliberating on the steps to be taken for the settlement of the affairs of the kingdom, and doubtless considering the proposals that had been made in the Governor's letter, no reply to which had yet been given, though the King wrote in June to say that he was about to send one. A little later it became known that a poll tax of ten shillings was being collected throughout Ashanti. This, it was said, was to pay some debts that had been incurred by the Kokofus during their stay in the Protectorate, so as to expedite their return, and some colour was lent to the report by the fact that about a ton of powder and large quantities of lead and guns were crossing the ferry at Prasu every week and passing principally to the Bekwais, who would naturally wish to be prepared against possible attacks by their old enemies. Ansa at this time was reported to be in disgrace, under suspicion of having misappropriated some of the money thus raised.

The money, however, was intended for a very different purpose. As might have been foreseen, the King and Chiefs had decided that, whatever other concessions they might be prepared to make in order to secure the friendship of the Government, they would never willingly relinquish their independence. They could plainly see that the inclusion

382

of their country within the Protectorate was the Government's ambition, and they were at their wits' end to know how to prevent it without an open rupture, which, above all things, they wished to avoid. The veiled threats contained in the recent letters had made them suspect the sincerity of the professions of friendship and good-will with which they were interlarded. They could not believe it possible that the same people who, after inflicting upon them a succession of defeats, invading their kingdom and burning their capital, had left them severely alone, could now wish to take over their country, unless their sentiments towards them had undergone a radical change. So far as they were aware, they had done no more than refuse to enter into a treaty that was distasteful to them, and they were at a loss to understand this new attitude taken up by the Governor, against whom they considered they had legitimate grievances for having harboured the disaffected tribes and then failed to keep them in order. The King's suspicions of double dealing, too, were to some extent justified ; for while the authorities were professing to accede to his request and allow the Kokofus to return, they were at the same time making secret preparations to detain Asibi directly they discovered that he was ready to go.

It is, of course, not surprising that the Ashantis could not understand the situation ; for the explanation of it lay not so much in anything that they had done, as in the altered policy of the Government. It had at last chosen the right one ; but it had been so long in finding it out and in deciding to accept the responsibilities that it involved, and had allowed so many favourable opportunities for its adoption to slip by, that it was hardly to be expected that the Ashantis would be able to understand it now. It had at last been recognized that the annexation of the country or the extension of British protection over it afforded the only reasonable solution of the Ashanti problem ; but the most favourable opportunities had been allowed to pass, and the Ashantis were sufficiently astute to be able to appreciate this : they had succeeded in retaining their

independence then and were not likely to relinquish it
readily now. In truth, the greater part of these troubles
was due solely to the Government's timidity and hesitation,
although the whole blame was, of course, cast upon Ashanti.
Moreover, the English were now so anxious to carry out
their new policy that they tried to force it through at once.
They traded on the fact that they had assisted to place
Prempi on the stool to exercise a hold over him, keeping
up the fiction that everything they did in relation to
Ashanti was done at great inconvenience to themselves
and solely in the interests of the King and his people,
whereas it was mainly undertaken in the interest of the
commercial prosperity of the Colony and with a view to
avoiding the risk of further troubles. That which had
really brought matters to a head was the discovery by the
authorities that they could not, except at great inconvenience and expense, prevent the Ashantis to whom they
had given protection and for whose conduct they were
therefore responsible, from making raids against those of
their countrymen who still remained loyal to their King.
The improvement of the condition of the Ashantis themselves by the suppression of their least desirable customs,
and other philanthropic aims, occupied a very secondary
position.

The Ashantis, therefore, being quite unable to grasp
the situation, and having failed to obtain any satisfaction
from the Governor, who they believed was secretly conspiring against them, had determined to make their appeal
to the Secretary of State himself, and it was to defray the
cost of sending a special embassy to England that this
money had been raised.

The King himself seems to have been far too perplexed
at this time to be able to decide on any definite course of
action. He was a mere puppet in the hands of Ansa, at
whose suggestion this plan had been adopted, and who was
to be the interpreter and leading spirit of the mission.
Ansa, who like most plausible rogues was certainly no
fool, was actuated by self-interest as much as by any desire
to help his countrymen. He recognized the present as an

excellent opportunity to visit England at the expense of the Ashantis, and foresaw that, whether he was successful or not, he personally had everything to gain and nothing to lose. He was also a sufficiently good man of business to think he would be able to turn his position as an African Prince and Chief Ambassador of an African King to account, and gain that credit in England which he had lost on the Gold Coast, where his ventures had all turned out badly and he was deeply in debt. It by no means follows, however, that he was not actuated by some patriotism also and anxious to see his country advance and improve. Being to some extent enlightened by his long residence on the coast, it would have been but natural for him to have entertained such hopes, and it is quite likely that he gave an erroneous idea of his real intentions by the use he made of such education as he possessed to forward them : he may, in fact, have injured himself by his clumsy employment of a tool in the use of which he was not proficient.

The Ashanti embassy consisted of John Ansa and his younger brother Albert, Chief Kwamin Buatin, a Linguist Kwaku Freku, Kwaku Inkruma a Chamberlain, Kobina Bonna a court crier, Atjiempon Daban a sword-bearer, and Kujo Tufu an armour-bearer. They were accompanied by a large retinue of servants, and arrived in Cape Coast on the 10th of December.

This Albert Ansa had accompanied Sir Samuel Rowe to Prasu in 1881 as an extra clerk, and continued to receive temporary employment in various minor capacities until March 1883. He was then given an appointment as telegraph clerk, and, in 1884, after having been previously reported to the Governor and reprimanded for inattention to his work, had been dismissed by Governor Young for " insolence, irregularity and disobedience of orders." On the intercession of some of his friends, he had been re-instated, but only to a lower grade, and, taking umbrage at this, had sent in his resignation. The Governor, however, refused to accept it, and ordered that he should be dismissed. Since then he had been trading, first at Cape

Coast and subsequently in partnership with a man named Johnson at Axim.

The Governor received the Ashantis two days after their arrival, on the 12th, when the King's view of the situation and his intentions were at once made clear. He had sent no answer to the letter that had been taken by Mr. Vroom, but had merely authorized his messengers to report themselves to the Governor and " give his compliments to his good friend " before proceeding to England to carry out the mission with which he had entrusted them. The Linguist of the party explained that this course had been decided upon because the Ashantis had realized the futility of continuing negotiations with the Colonial Government. He said : " The King is very anxious that perpetual peace be effected in Ashanti. His Majesty thinks that if he keeps writing to your Excellency that will not settle matters for good. Therefore he has deputed them to Her Majesty the Queen, so that every matter may be entirely settled. Mere letters will not settle matters, so His Majesty has sent them to go and see the Queen so that peace may be perpetually effected in Ashanti." [1] The Governor protested that the King had promised him an answer to the letter and that he was treating the Queen's representative with discourtesy and disrespect, but nothing further could be elicited from the messengers and the interview then terminated. The proceedings after this were unfortunately too often marred by puerile excuses, quibblings, and attempts to justify their conduct by both parties.

The next day a second meeting took place, at which the Governor did everything in his power to discredit Ansa in the eyes of the other Ashantis, hoping that they would then return to Kumasi to ask for further instructions ; but without success. He then delivered a telegraphic message that he had received from the Secretary of State warning them that the Queen would only communicate with the King of Ashanti through the Governor of the Gold Coast,

---

[1] Parliamentary Paper, *Further Correspondence relating to Affairs in Ashanti*, 1896, p. 4.

and that if they persisted in going to England they would not be received there. " In no case would Her Majesty receive a mission from a ruler who was accused on apparently good grounds of allowing human sacrifices." To this they replied in writing that they had been commissioned to go to England and intended to carry out their instructions. Their decision was communicated by cable to the Secretary of State, who sent instructions that the ambassadors should be forbidden to proceed to England, and a note to this effect was accordingly sent to them. This was addressed to " Mr. John Ossoo Ansah. . . . Messengers from the King of Kumasi," and Ansa refused to receive it because he was not addressed as " Prince." It was once more sent with an intimation that it contained a message for them from the Home Government, but he still refused it unless the King was described as " King of Ashanti," instead of King of Kumasi only, and, since the messengers declined to attend at the Castle, it was again sent down to them, and they were told that the King would not be recognized as King of Ashanti until he had replied to Mr. Hodgson's letter, though it is difficult to understand how it could be maintained that the mere writing of a letter could alter the limits of his kingdom. Captain Stewart and Mr. Vroom were the bearers of the letter on this occasion, and were told to open and read it to the Ashantis if Ansa still refused it ; but he now accepted it after some hesitation, saying that he did so under protest.

At another meeting held at Government House, Cape Coast, on the 15th, Ansa read a paper protesting against the Governor's action in having refused to acknowledge the King as King of Ashanti, but only as that of Kumasi, and in having stated that he and his brother had been dismissed from the Government Service.

It was with the full concurrence of the Secretary of State that the Governor had not only declined to admit that Prempi was anything more than King of Kumasi, but also refused to acknowledge Ansa and his companions as ambassadors or " anything more than special messengers." This decision was based on the grounds that the King was not a " Chief of sufficient importance to be allowed to send ambassadors to the Queen," and that he was reasonably suspected of allowing human sacrifices.

Ansa also complained of the " spirit and passion " with which the Governor had addressed his party at their last meeting with him, which Sir Brandford Griffith now denied and attempted to disprove by calling upon all those who had then been present to confirm this accusation if they thought it was true. Quite possibly it was groundless ; but the mere fact that no one ventured to stand up now and side with the Ashantis against the Governor does not in itself disprove it. Such action would have required considerably more independence of character than is commonly met with.

He further complained that since they had been forbidden to go to England " the liberty and courtesy that are always accorded to British subjects " were being denied them. When it suited their purpose, however, the Ansas had strenuously denied that they were British subjects. They had quoted Lord John Russell's despatch to Governor Maclean to prove that their father's receipt of an allowance of £100 a year had not made him a British subject, since it left him free to live in Ashanti or wherever else he chose, the only condition attached to it being that he should from time to time come to Cape Coast and communicate personally with the officer administering the Government. This was admitted ; but the grounds on which his children were claimed as British subjects were very different. Their mother was a Cape Coast woman, and Albert had been born in that town and was, therefore, by English law a British subject. John had been born in Kumasi and brought to Cape Coast when he was a month old, and, according to English law, if nothing more had happened, would have been deemed an Ashanti subject. He, however, had served in the Gold Coast Rifle Corps as a sergeant-major and held the medal for the last campaign, so that he must have taken the oath of allegiance to the British Crown on his enlistment, though he now tried to deny having done so. But, quite apart from this, they would

both have been considered British subjects by Akan law, 1894–1895
because all children are held to belong to their mother and CHAP. XIX
take her nationality.

The Government tried to argue that Prempi was not
King of Ashanti, but of Kumasi only, because Senkiri and
Asibi had not taken part in his enstoolment, and the
newly appointed Kings of Mampon and Kokofu, who had
taken their places in the ceremony, were likely to be
deposed again whenever they returned. This argument,
however, was ridiculous, and can only have been advanced
because the Government was at a loss to find any justification for its action. It might with just as much reason
have refused to recognize the deposition of Kofi Karikari
and the accession of Mensa,[1] and, even according to its
own argument, must have granted that Prempi was paramount ruler over those provinces whose Kings had been
present at and taken their part in his enstoolment. Moreover, so far as Ashanti was concerned, Senkiri and Asibi
were rebels in exile, and there was no guarantee that they
would ever be anything else ; nor would Prempi have been
bound to pardon them even if they had returned, were it
not that he had voluntarily undertaken to do so and would,
indeed, have been only too glad of the opportunity to keep
his word if they had tendered their submission. The
implied suggestions, therefore, that their stools should be
kept vacant indefinitely and that the acts of persons who
had been set up in their places must necessarily lack
validity were absurd. Even assuming that it was a fact
that the new Kings were only appointed temporarily and
would be required to give up their stools on the return of
the former holders, it only reduced them to the position
of Acting Kings, and the King of Ashanti might as reasonably have refused to accept any letter from an Acting
Governor on the ground that he was not the true holder
of the position and would revert to a lower appointment
on the Governor's return. Such arguments came especially
badly from the Government, since it was by their act that
Asibi was still being detained on the coast. The true

[1] *Vide* p. 267.

test of whether or not a man is king of a country is his recognition as such by its inhabitants rather than the opinion of foreigners. Ashanti itself had never been a very large country, though at one time it had had a great empire. The latter had now been lost ; but Ashanti itself remained, and its inhabitants, discontented though some of them might be, recognized Prempi as their paramount King, for the provincial Kings still supplied him with contingents for his army or came in person to Kumasi at his bidding. Those Ashantis who had fled to the Protectorate were rebels and exiles, and could have no voice in the affairs of the kingdom ; it was only those who still remained whose opinion mattered or could carry any weight. The Government had, moreover, acknowledged this. Sir Brandford Griffith had written to the King when proposing the treaty of protection in 1891 : " I can only recognize yourself and those Kings, Chiefs and principal men who have remained loyal to you as the existing authorities in Ashanti. The heads of other tribes will not be allowed to return and question your action . . . unless they are prepared to agree to the arrangement." It is unnecessary, however, to go farther back than Mr Hodgson's letter of the 23rd of February—that very letter which had given rise to the present altercation. In it he definitely refers to the King's position as " King of Ashanti," and the draft treaty which was enclosed in it is drawn up between the Queen by Hendrick Vroom and " Kwaku Dua III, King of Ashanti." Whether the Government was now prepared to recognize him as King of Ashanti or not, therefore, it had at least been ready to make a treaty with him as such, and would presumably have been perfectly satisfied with it if it had got it. It was therefore too late now to turn round and say that he was King of Kumasi only. Messengers from Kings of Ashanti, moreover, had frequently been recognized and referred to in despatches by Governors and Secretaries of State as " ambassadors," and in the copy of the minutes of the meeting of the 12th of December, which was forwarded by the Governor to the Secretary of State, the present mission

is described as " The Ashanti Embassy." It is only too
evident, therefore, that the position now taken up on these
points was assumed for convenience rather than from a
love of accuracy.

But although some of the excuses and arguments now
advanced by the Government were indeed mere quibbles,
and a most unusual haste was being shown to arrive at
some final settlement of the Ashanti question, it was really
necessary that something should be done. The Government was certainly to blame for having dallied with the
matter for so long, but the time had now come when further
delay, besides being as inconvenient and costly as ever,
was fraught with positive danger and threatened to ruin
the position and prospects of the English on the Gold
Coast for ever. The old risks of misunderstandings, wars
and temporary interruptions of trade were unaltered ;
but to these was now added the new and far greater danger
that if the English failed to establish some kind of control
over Ashanti, some other Power might do so instead.
That trade with the interior, upon which the prosperity
of the Colony almost entirely depended, would then be
cut off for ever. The French for some years past had been
making great advances in West Africa, and were rapidly
extending their sphere of influence farther and farther
inland. They were already firmly established on the
western frontier of the Gold Coast, and the Germans were
on the east, so that it was only towards the north that
the English had any prospect of expansion. But the
continued advance of the French into the interior was now
threatening to close this to them also, and it seemed likely
that the Gold Coast would soon be surrounded, and that
the French might succeed where the English had hitherto
failed and include Ashanti itself within their sphere of
influence. This would have been absolutely fatal to the
Colony, and it was the fear of it that had at last compelled
the Government to act with such unusual vigour and
determination.

As regards the actual message from the Secretary of
State, the Ashantis said the King would still wish them

to go to England, even if he knew the purport of this message, since the charges that it made against him were unfounded and could not be proved.

Lord Ripon's telegram had ordered that a European officer, accompanied by Mr. Vroom, should be sent to Kumasi to inform the King that his messengers had been stopped, and to ask for a definite reply to Mr. Hodgson's letter of the 23rd of February. He was to assure Prempi that his independence would not be interfered with farther than was involved by the terms laid down in that letter, and to warn him that, if he rejected those, equally favourable ones might not be offered again. This message resembled the letters in containing a request accompanied by a threat, and was not likely to reassure the King, who, having no knowledge of cable messages, must have supposed it emanated from the Governor and that he was merely trying to prevent him from communicating with the Government in England and continuing the line of conduct that had made him wish to do so.

Captain Donald Stewart was sent up with Mr. Vroom on this mission. They were given a letter from the Governor instructing them to explain to the King what had happened and to deliver the Secretary of State's message, especially emphasizing the fact that no communications could be held with him except through the Governor, and that any message he might have entrusted to Ansa and the others for delivery in England could not therefore be accepted as a reply to the letter. They were not to remain in Kumasi longer than a week, unless they were both of opinion that the desired result would be attained by a slightly longer stay.

On their arrival at Kasi on the 2nd of January, they were met by some of the King's messengers, who asked them to wait there until the 7th, when he would be ready to receive them. They, however, refused to stay longer than one night, and entered Kumasi the next afternoon. Only the formal reception took place then ; but the next day the King fixed the 7th for hearing their message, explaining that he could not give an earlier date because his

Chiefs would not have arrived. When the 7th came, he tried to postpone the meeting until the 10th, and it was not until one o'clock the next morning that it was held. The Governor's letter was then read, and the meeting adjourned to the 15th for the attendance of the provincial Kings ; but on the 15th they were still not ready, and the King then promised his answer, first in four weeks, then in three, then in two, and finally in one ; but even this was refused.   Next morning, however, the Linguists arrived just as the officers were about to start for the coast, and assured them that if they would only consent to wait another week they would be able to take back a satisfactory reply.   They therefore agreed to remain until the 21st.

The reason for all this delay was that the King and Chiefs, having relied upon Ansa for so long, were uncertain what to do now that he was away and had sent to ask his advice. Until the 19th the Council was divided, some being willing to sign the treaty and others opposed to it ; but the runner then returned from Cape Coast with his answer, and the success of the mission was doomed.   Ansa was not going to be deprived of his trip to England at the last moment.

On the 21st the promised meeting was held in the palace, and, after the Governor's letter had again been read, Captain Stewart asked for the answer to that brought up by Mr. Vroom ten months earlier.   The King of Ofinsu then demanded that the letter should be handed over, but the officers explained that it contained their private instructions and was not addressed to the King.   A tremendous uproar followed.   The Chiefs insisted that the letter must be given up, or they would receive no answer, while Amankwa Tia said that since the King had sent his reply to the Governor's letter by his messengers and the Queen had refused to receive them, so should it be in Kumasi also.   Finding it impossible to get any other answer, or even to make themselves heard, the officers asked permission to withdraw, but were again told that they must first give up their papers.   They therefore asked if they were being detained as prisoners, to which the Chiefs replied, " No, not as prisoners, but you must give up the papers before you can go," and the King said, " If you refuse to give up the papers, then you must tell me what answer to send." In the end however, they were allowed to retire, much to the annoyance of the War Chiefs, who were most anxious to detain them. Some Linguists and other officers of the Court overtook them on their way to their quarters and told them to return ; but knowing that this would only involve a renewed attempt by the Chiefs to gain possession of the Governor's letter, they refused, and said the King could send any answer he had to give by the Linguists. The messengers returned soon afterwards saying that the King had already sent his answer by Ansa and the other messengers ; that they would go to England and deliver it to the Queen, and that this was the only message he had for the Governor.

The anxiety of the Chiefs to gain possession of the letter was probably not due to wanton insolence, though their manner throughout the meeting was insulting enough. It is easily explained in one or other of two ways. Either they must have thought that it would be of some use to them, or they honestly believed that they were entitled to receive it and that Captain Stewart and Mr. Vroom were purposely keeping it from them. It is this latter explanation that is the most likely to be true. The letter could be of no use to them personally, for none of them could have read it, and Ansa cannot have known that it contained confidential instructions to the officers of the mission, though he may have suspected it and have hoped to make use of them to forward the success of his mission in England. Hitherto, when British officers had visited Kumasi they had always brought a letter for the King, which, after being read to him, was, of course, handed over. The Chiefs would naturally have expected that the same procedure would be followed on this occasion, and have considered that the King had a right to the letter, and that its non-delivery was an insult to him. Ansa would have thought so too, and, consequently, if the demand was made by his orders, it is most likely that he merely asked that the letter, which he expected would be sent to the King, should be sent down for his information and to give him an opportunity of changing the advice he had given if he thought it necessary.

The mission left Kumasi on the 22nd of January and reached Fumsu in Adansi on the 25th. About a quarter of a mile outside this place one of the Hausas in the advance-guard was shot dead from behind a tree a few yards from the path. His body was carried into Esaman and a message sent back to the Chief of the village to try to find the murderer. He soon produced an Ashanti named Yow Apon, who was the only man who had been out that day with a gun, and he was taken down to Elmina. It was believed that he had had no intention of shooting any of the Hausa escort, but one of the officers, and that the man, having been discovered by the Hausa, had shot him to prevent him from giving the alarm or securing him. The intended victim was probably Mr. Vroom, against whom the Ashantis were greatly incensed, because they attributed much of the present difficulty to the advice that he had given to the Government.

At the meeting on the 15th of December the Ashantis had promised to send to tell the King the message that had been sent from England, and on the 3rd of January, while Captain Stewart and Mr. Vroom were away at Kumasi, his answer was received and forwarded by Ansa. It was that it was true that he had written and promised a reply to the letter of the 23rd of February after he had conferred with his Chiefs, but " after due consultation with them and prior to the appointment of the embassy now at Cape Coast, the Council was of opinion that the question raised . . . was so grave and sweeping, touching as it does the constitution and construction of His Majesty's Independent Kingdom, that considering the unfriendly attitude already assumed by Her Majesty's Government on the Coast to the kingdom of His Majesty (and His Majesty deeply regrets this should be the case), it is impossible that mutual sympathy and understanding could be looked for, or arrived at in this Colony, to prevent war and bloodshed.

And that, therefore, a special embassy should be sent to England, to lay before Her Majesty and Council this and other important matters connected with the peace and progress of His Majesty's Kingdom, and her beneficial co-operation with Her Majesty's settlement on this Coast, for full discussion and final decision. That the envoys were asked to see your Excellency, and to say that they have been thus empowered to go to England to see Her Britannic Majesty." [1]

On the 7th of April 1895 Mr. W. E. Maxwell, C.M.G., took over the Governorship of the Colony from Sir Brandford Griffith. Before his arrival, however, on the 28th of March, the Ashanti ambassadors or " special messengers " had sailed for England in the S.S. *Accra*. Their guide, Kofi Assam, had preceded them by the boat before. He had been a barrister in practice in Cape Coast, but had recently been disbarred for mal-practices. On their arrival in England they communicated with the Foreign Office, explaining that they did so on the ground that Ashanti was an independent state and therefore not under the Colonial Office. They also enlisted the aid of several Members of Parliament and others, including one J. H. Brew, who had formerly been a solicitor on the Gold Coast, but had been suspended from practice by one of the judges. They also forwarded a long written statement of their case, which, though not entirely accurate, was certainly drawn up with some skill ; but, as they had been warned, both Lord Ripon and his successor, Mr. Chamberlain, refused to receive them. Whether he thought an interview might have some advantage or not, the Secretary of State could not go back upon what he had already said without making it appear that the prohibitions that had been given in his name had been invented by the Governor in order to prevent communication with him. Ansa, as had been expected, employed his spare time in business of his own, trying to obtain credit from manufacturers and tradesmen and to grant con-

[1] Parliamentary Paper, *Further Correspondence relating to Affairs in Ashanti*, 1896, p. 40.

cessions.   In the end the Governor had to ask that a warning might be published that he had no credit on the Gold
Coast and no property to secure liabilities of any extent.

Instructions were now given to Mr. Maxwell to send an
ultimatum to the King, and at the end of September a
letter was taken up by Captain Stewart and Mr. Vroom, in
which he was told that the Government was satisfied from
the evidence before it that he had violated the Treaty of
Fomana by encouraging the practice of human sacrifices,
placing hindrances in the way of trade, and failing to keep
the road open from Kumasi to the Pra. He was also
charged with having made attacks upon tribes who were
in friendly relation with, and had sought the protection of
the Government.   These acts, it was alleged, had kept the
country in a state of war and deprived the Colony of its
trade and could no longer be tolerated. The King was
therefore required to receive a British Resident at Kumasi
without further delay, who would see that he carried out
his treaty engagements and refrained from making war
on his neighbours, but would not otherwise interfere in
the administration and institutions of his country. He
was also told that the Government had decided to extend
its protection over the Inkoranzas, Mos, and all other
tribes who had asked for it, and was warned not to interfere
with them, and was reminded that the indemnity stipulated for in the Treaty of Fomana still remained unpaid.
Captain Stewart and Mr. Vroom were to return at once,
and the King was to send his answer by the 31st of October
at the latest, or meet the Governor at Prasu by the same
date if he preferred it.

The reception of this mission was very different from that
of the last ; the road from the Pra to Kumasi had been
specially cleared, and the tone of the Chiefs was much
improved. On his way up Captain Stewart offered protection to the King of Bekwai, but he had only recently
renewed his oath of allegiance to Prempi, and, not wishing
to break it without some reasonable excuse, refused to sign
any treaty at present, though he emphatically declared
that in no circumstances would he take up arms against

the English.   He was, in fact, anxious to throw in his lot with the Government, but afraid to declare himself at present.   It was also discovered that Samori, a Sofa free-booter and slave-raider, had recently attacked and de-feated King Ajiman of Jaman because he had refused to let him open a trade route through his country to the coast. It was believed that Prempi had asked Samori to help him to recover all those countries from Jaman to the coast which had formerly belonged to Ashanti, and that he had refused.   Samori, however, sent to tell Prempi of his victory over Jaman, and it was known that the latter had sent return messengers to say that he was glad to hear of it. Captain Stewart could not find out whether any private message had been sent in addition, though this was strongly suspected, because a large present, consisting of a hundred loads each of kola, salt, and gin, a hundred sheep, and two hun-dred ounces of gold-dust [1] had been sent by his messengers.

On his return journey Captain Stewart concluded a treaty with the Adansis at Prasu on the 18th of October. It consisted of eight articles.   By the first and second Kwaku Inkansa and his Chiefs, for themselves and their successors, placed their country under British protection ; by the third and fourth they agreed not to make war on their neighbours, and to refer all disputes to the Governor for arbitration ;   while the fifth and sixth provided for freedom of trade throughout the country and the mainten-ance of roads, and the seventh for the abolition of human sacrifices and slave dealing, but preserved the other laws and customs of the country and the Chiefs' rights to levy the ordinary dues.   The last article reserved to the Crown the right to refuse ratification within a year.   The Adansis were now free to return to their own country so soon as they were ready to do so, but they preferred to wait until the present trouble between the Government and Kumasi had been brought to an end.   Like the Bekwais, they were not at all sure of the Government's power to protect them from the King's vengeance if they really needed it.

---

[1] These figures were, of course, based on native reports, and there is good reason for believing that they are exaggerated.

Prempi's position on the receipt of the Governor's
ultimatum was a difficult one. He had relied upon Ansa
and followed his advice in everything for so long that he
was now afraid to act without him. He had, moreover,
spent a large sum of money in sending his messengers to
England, and, even though he had been told that they
had not been received, was still hoping against hope that
they might accomplish something, and loath to take any
decisive action until he had news from them. While he
was thus waiting for the news that did not come however,
the time slipped by and the end of October found him as
uncertain as ever what course to take. He dared not
commit himself to a definite answer until he had heard
from Ansa, and when his messengers at length arrived on
the 12th of November, the only reply that they brought
was that Ansa and the others had already left for England
with the King's proposals.

Meanwhile, so soon as it was known that the 31st of
October had passed without any reply having been received
from Prempi, preparations were hurried forward for the
despatch of a military expedition to enforce the demands
that had been made. This seriously alarmed Ansa, who at
last realized that the Government did not intend to be
trifled with any longer. He at once enlisted the aid of a
barrister named Sutherst, who began a long correspondence
with the Secretary of State and certainly did his best to
gain a hearing for the Ashantis. He alleged that Ansa
held a document signed by the King and giving him the
widest powers to act on his behalf, and that he was ready
to agree to the terms that had been dictated by the Government and to sign a treaty at once. He contended that,
since Ansa and his companions were but semi-civilized,
it was unreasonable to refuse them a hearing merely
because they had come to England without permission.
Mr. Chamberlain's suspicions, however, were at once
aroused by the fact that this was the first mention that
had been made of the existence of these credentials or the
willingness of the Ashantis to accept the Government's
terms. They had always been represented as coming with

" proposals," and this sudden change of tone directly they heard that an expedition was to be sent out was too obvious to be overlooked or misunderstood. This was borne out by the testimony of Lieutenant - Colonel O'Gorman of the Royal Dublin Fusiliers, who had been in communication with them ever since their arrival. He produced a letter from them refusing to give him any definite proposal to lay before the Secretary of State, and said that in his conversations with them they would hear of nothing but war.

Mr. Chamberlain therefore declined to negotiate any treaty with them, and advised them, if they were sincere, to telegraph at once to inform the King that he could only avert the expedition by immediately concluding the required treaty with the Governor and then to return to the Coast themselves. In the meantime, however, the military preparations would be proceeded with until the treaty had been completed, and the Ashantis would be required to pay all expenses incurred thereby. To these conditions Ansa agreed, with the exception of the payment of expenses. This he contended was like firing on a flag of truce, since the demands of the Government had now been agreed to by him in the King's name, and military preparations were therefore needless. Mr. Chamberlain replied that while he was glad to accept the statements of Ansa for what they might be worth, he could not order these preparations to be discontinued until the King had completed the treaty, nor could he consent to make it with Ansa because he was not satisfied that he had any real authority to pledge the King's word.

This view was justified. Ansa's so-called credentials were submitted and found to consist of the following document :

(Seal)

" To the Most Gracious and Illustrious Sovereign, Victoria, Queen of Great Britain and Ireland.

Kwaku Dua III, King of Ashanti, wisheth health and prosperity

We pray your Most Gracious Majesty to know that we have appointed our trusty and well-beloved grandson, Prince John Ossoo Ansah, son of the late Prince Ansah, of Ashanti, on our behalf to lay before your Majesty divers matters affecting the good estate of our kingdom and the well-being of our subjects with full power for the said Prince Ansah as our ambassador extraordinary and minister plenipotentiary to negotiate and conclude all such treaties relating to the furtherance of trade and all matters therewith connected as your Majesty shall be pleased to entertain.

We therefore pray that your Majesty will be pleased to receive the said Prince Ansah on our behalf and to accord to him your Majesty's most royal favour.

Given at our Court at Kumasi this 8th day of September 1894.

my
Kwaku Dua III, X
mark
King of Ashanti." [1]

It would have been absurd to have trusted to the authority of such a document, which might at any time have been repudiated by the King. Putting on one side the fact that no mention was made of any person but Ansa, and that it was questionable how much might be included in a treaty "relating to the furtherance of trade," the mark that purported to have been placed there by Prempi in Kumasi on the 8th of September was not witnessed, and the other members of the mission, who preceded the Ansas on their return journey to the Coast, emphatically told the Governor that they had no knowledge whatever of any documents whereby Ansa was invested with full powers. In fact, they regarded themselves as the real ambassadors and the Ansas as their clerks and interpreters. When Ansa himself arrived on the 27th of December however, the worthlessness of this paper was no longer

[1] Parliamentary Paper, *Further Correspondence relating to Affairs in Ashanti*, 1896, p. 122.

in doubt. He was forced to admit that it had never been signed by Prempi at all, but that the mark said to be his had been placed there by Ansa himself in Cape Coast while Kwaku Freku held the pen. The so-called King's seal had been added as a finishing touch later still, having been impressed with a die that had been made after their arrival in London. It was apparent therefore that Ansa, in addition to trying to usurp whatever powers had been given to the others, had himself concocted these false credentials after his arrival in Cape Coast and completed them in London. Who it was who helped him [1] is doubtful ; but he must have had some assistance, for the wording is quite above all samples of his unaided composition.

[1] Possibly Kofi Assam.

CHAPTER XX

THE ARREST AND DEPORTATION OF PREMPI

1895 TO 1896

THE command of the Ashanti force was given to Sir Francis Scott, the Inspector-General of the Gold Coast Constabulary. The three principal officers of the Headquarter Staff of the Army at this time, Lord Wolseley, Sir Redvers Buller and Sir Evelyn Wood, had all served in the last campaign and knew exactly what was likely to be required, a fact that did much to facilitate the preparation and organization of the expedition. Instructions were at once sent out to the Governor to arrange for the construction of camps and the enrolment of carriers, and the Admiralty was asked to have several warships in readiness off the Coast should they be required.

The force was made up as follows : a Special Service Corps of Infantry, consisting of 12 officers and 240 non-commissioned officers and men ; the 2nd Battalion of the West Yorkshire Regiment, 20 officers and 400 men ; a wing of the 2nd Battalion of the West India Regiment from Sierra Leone, 20 officers and 380 men ; and a number of special service officers and details of the Royal Artillery, Royal Engineers, Army Service Corps, and Army Medical Staff Corps, amounting in all to another 250 officers and men. There was also a hospital ship and its establishment, which was to lie off Cape Coast and could accommodate 10 officers and 100 rank and file. In addition to these white troops there were nearly 1,000 Hausas and between 600 and 800 Native Levies. These Native Levies consisted of 300 Krobos under Chief Matikoli, 100 Mumfords under

Chief Brew, and a company of Elminas under Chief Ando ; they were joined at Prasu by 100 Adansis, and a little later by a detachment of Bekwais. Major Baden-Powell was in command, and it was the duty of the Levy to scout ahead of the main column as Lord Gifford's men had done in 1874. The other arrangements were also very similar to those in the last war. The main column was to advance by the Prasu road and cross the Adansi Hills, Captain O'Donnell was to follow practically the same route as Glover with 200 Lagos Hausas and about 800 Native Levies, while Captain Dehamel was to advance from Elmina with a small force of Hausas and West Indians. Lieutenant-Colonel Kempster was second in command, H.R.H. Prince Henry of Battenberg, K.G., Military Secretary, and H.R.H. Prince Christian Victor of Schleswig-Holstein, G.C.B., Aide-de-Camp. Captain Donald Stewart accompanied the force as Political Officer.

Previous experience had taught that one of the principal difficulties was likely to be the provision of a sufficient number of carriers for the transport, and that it would be unsafe to rely too much on the Chiefs to supply them. This, of course, was not entirely their fault, for the Government had, in recent years, assumed so much of the authority originally possessed by the Chiefs that the latter now had but little power or control over their people and could not always enforce obedience to their orders even when they really wished to do so. A Compulsory Labour Ordinance [1] was therefore passed, by which Head Chiefs were compelled to call out their men to act as carriers when served with a notice requiring it. They were liable to a heavy fine if they failed to comply, and the people to punishment if they refused to obey. Kujo Imbra, the Head Chief of Cape Coast, was, in fact, imprisoned and fined £100 under this ordinance, but the conviction was quashed on appeal.

On the 16th of December most of the Ashanti envoys landed at Cape Coast ; the Ansas, however, did not accompany them, but waited for a later ship. They were probably nervous about their reception by the King, and

[1] No. 9 of 1895.

hoped that he would have expended most of his wrath at their failure before they arrived. The envoys, before they left for Kumasi, told the Governor that the King would accept a Resident and asked to be allowed to take him back with them; but were told to tell the King that if he was sincere he must prove it by meeting the Governor on the frontier, signing a fresh treaty with England, and paying the expenses to which the Government had been put by his disobedience and delays.

On the 24th the West African squadron, consisting of H.M.Ss. *St. George, Philomel, Blonde, Racoon* and *Magpie,* under Admiral Rawson, anchored off Cape Coast. A hundred Lagos Hausas under Captain Reeve Tucker, landed the same afternoon. On Christmas Day the transports *Coromandel* and *Manilla* arrived with the white troops, but the men were kept on board until everything was in readiness for them to march up country. This and the camps on the line of march were arranged in much the same way as in the last war.

The Headquarter Staff left on the 27th. The next day the Special Service Corps was landed, and, though many fell out during the first day's march to Inkwabim and two men actually died on the road from the heat, they marched into Prasu on the 3rd of January in splendid condition. The West Yorkshire Regiment disembarked on the 29th and reached Prasu on the 5th of January. This regiment had been serving for several years in India and Aden, and had been ordered to the Gold Coast from Gibraltar while on its way home. It was thought that the men would be able to withstand the heat better than troops newly sent out from England, but they were already worn out by continued fevers after their long service in the East and not in a fit state to undertake the arduous work of active service in West Africa. They suffered terribly, and numbers fell out daily. On the first day over eighty fell out, many of whom had to be carried, and the road was strewn with stragglers; while during the sixteen miles' march into Prasu alone thirty fell out.

In the meantime, so soon as it was known that his

envoys were on their way back, Prempi had summoned all his Chiefs to a meeting in Kumasi to hear their report and decide what was now to be done. Yow Buatin the King of Bekwai, however, refused to attend, and, when Prempi sent further messengers to bring him, ordered his people to drive them out of the town. Such open defiance was not likely to be overlooked, and Buatin sent an urgent message to Sir Francis Scott at Prasu tendering his submission, asking to be taken under British protection and begging for immediate help. These messengers arrived in the camp at Prasu on New Year's Day while the Ansas were there on their way to Kumasi. They had landed at Cape Coast on the 27th of December : both seemed weighed down with anxiety, and were probably wondering how they would be received on their arrival in Kumasi now that their advice had only put the King to great expense, and, instead of removing all his difficulties, as they had promised, resulted in the despatch of a British military expedition to his capital. The Bekwais were terribly alarmed lest the Ansas should report their double dealings to the King, so while the latter were detained on some pretext outside Headquarters, they stripped off their badges of office and hurriedly recrossed the Pra on their return journey to tell their King that the assistance for which he had asked would be given.

If this help was not to arrive too late, it was evident that prompt action must be taken, and a flying column was therefore ordered to proceed at once from the British outposts at Dompoasi to Bekwai under Major Baden-Powell. The force was composed of two companies of Hausas and the Native Levies, and, in order to render it independent of the main column should it be cut off in the defence of Bekwai, took with it a week's supplies, necessitating the addition of 450 carriers. The distance was about twenty miles ; but Esian Kwanta, where the Bekwai road branched off, was known to be held by an Ashanti picket, and it was therefore decided to make a secret flank march through the bush by night to Obum, whence the Bekwai road could be reached at Himan. The force was to parade at moonrise (9 p.m.), and no orders were given as to its destination, so that any Ashanti scouts who might be prowling around would see the camp settle down for the night and retire satisfied at dark. The march was painfully slow, for, despite the moon, it was pitch-dark in the dense shadow of the forest, and the men had to grope their way step by step over rough ground encumbered by the roots and fallen branches and trunks of trees. Nothing was seen of the Ashanti scouts, though the still glowing embers of outpost fires were twice discovered, but it was long past two o'clock the next morning when Himan was reached : a distance of only nine miles in six hours. Here it was learned that there had as yet been no attack made on Bekwai, so, as everyone was thoroughly tired out, a halt was called for four hours, and then, while one company of Hausas pushed on to Bekwai with the carriers, the rest of the force turned down the main road to dislodge the Ashantis from Esian Kwanta. The scouts soon discovered that, though their camp fires were still smouldering, the Ashantis had already retired towards Kumasi, and, after detaching a small party to hold the place, the force marched for Bekwai. The King was greatly relieved by the arrival of the troops, and, on the next morning, the 5th, the Union Jack was hoisted with as much ceremony as possible. The flag was run up in a ball, and Yow Buatin then pulled the halyard and released it, while the troops presented arms, the band of the Hausas played " God save the Queen," and the King rested his head on his hand and feigned sleep as a sign that he could now rest peacefully beneath that flag until he died.

The next morning a business meeting was held, at which the King was asked to make some return for what the British had done for him by providing some fighting men for the Native Levy and a number of carriers. Carriers, he said, were out of the question ; he could not get them and they would not know how to carry loads if he did, as they had never been accustomed to such work ; but after a great deal of argument and a threatened withdrawal of the force, he undertook to provide 1,000 fighting men, and most of these were employed as carriers. The Bekwais' refusal to act as carriers was probably due to unwillingness to do what they considered menial work instead of fighting, as they were accustomed to do, rather than to ingratitude. They saw that the fighting men of the Native Levy then in their town belonged to the coast tribes, whom they as Ashantis had conquered and despised, with a handful of the Adansis whom they had driven out of their country not long before. It was hardly to be expected, therefore, that they would show any great enthusiasm in volunteering to perform for them a duty that in their own army was always undertaken by slaves : it would, indeed, have been a curious sight to see 1,000 Ashantis acting as carriers in such a column, and they were probably unaware that it would be with the white troops that they would work. The next day messengers arrived in Bekwai from the coast and from Kumasi, but the King was asked to hand them over, and he promptly did so before they had any opportunity to communicate with him.

On the 11th of January the Kings of Bekwai and Abodum came into the camp at Esian Kwanta to sign formal treaties with the Government : they were treaties of friendship and trade very similar to that which had just been made with the Adansis. Yow Buatin seemed disposed to prolong the proceedings indefinitely by arguments about the abolition of capital punishment for all crimes except murder ; but the King of Abodum, who was a mere boy of about fourteen, was ready to sign at once, and Yow Buatin, fearful lest this subordinate ruler should sign before him, then hastened forward and made his mark.

The Special Service Corps had crossed the Pra on the 5th, followed by the Staff the next morning and the West Yorks a day later. North of the river, all the villages were found deserted, and the column now advanced very slowly with its various units often separated by several days' march.

On the 8th, envoys came down to the outposts bringing two small boys heavily bedecked with gold, and said to be sons of Prempi, whom they offered as hostages for the King's submission in the hope of averting the entry of the troops into Kumasi. These boys, however, were believed to be only slaves, and, whether the King's sons or not, were of no value as hostages. They were therefore sent back with a message that the expedition must come to Kumasi, where the Governor would arrange terms with the King, but that he would not be deposed if he agreed to them. A more important embassy was then sent down, consisting of Kwaku Freku and Buatin at the head of a number of lesser Chiefs and some 200 followers, which reached Odasu a few days later. While these messengers were waiting for their interview an unfortunate incident occurred. They were sitting in a part of the road that it had been ordered was to be kept clear, and the Hausas told them to move. Whether they understood what was wanted or not, they made no attempt to comply, and the Hausas then attacked them with sticks and drove them away. They scattered and fled in all directions, dropping most of their property as they went, which, of course, was taken by the Hausas and men of the Native Levy. With some difficulty the officers quelled the disturbance, collected the Ashantis, and restored to them as much of their property as could be found after a search through the camp. Captain Stewart apologized for what had happened and promised that the Governor would arrange to compensate them for the insult and their losses, and Kwaku Freku then stood up and said that they were authorized by the King to say that he would pay the indemnity and " come under the white men's government." Captain Stewart once more told them that the troops would certainly come to Kumasi, where the King would be required to make his submission to the Governor, but would not be deposed if he complied with the Government's demands— namely, the appointment of a British Resident, the payment of an indemnity, and the surrender of hostages until he had done so.

By the 16th the whole force was encamped in and around Odasu preparatory to the final advance into Kumasi. During the night, as had happened here in 1874, the troops were drenched to the skin and unable to get any rest. A terrific storm burst over the camp about midnight and the whole place was soon flooded, while the wind and lightning brought down many huge trees all around, and several carriers, who were sitting huddled together under a cotton-tree in a vain attempt to find a little shelter from the rain, were crushed by it in its fall. After lasting for two hours, the storm passed over, and the men began making what fires they could and drying their clothes, but at four o'clock another tornado burst over the camp, and the rain never ceased until after eight. Such breakfast as was possible in such miserable circumstances was hurriedly eaten and the final march began at six o'clock. The advance was very slow, however, for the men were quite done up after their sleepless and uncomfortable night. All the hammocks were soon full, and many men fell out on the road.

The Native Levy and a company of Hausas with their drums and fifes entered Kumasi soon after eight. Captain Stewart was with them, and the Engineers with the cable followed close behind. Pickets were at once posted on all the approaches to the square, where the flag was then planted and the men awaited the arrival of the other troops. They soon began to come in, and by three o'clock they had all arrived and were billeted in the houses along the Bantama road. Prempi had turned out with his Chiefs and attendants to watch them arrive, and sat under his state umbrella, with the Queen-Mother at his side, from nine in the morning till five. With him were the two Ansas, who were evidently much alarmed, and spent most of their time running from one official to another. At five o'clock Sir Francis Scott and his officers took their seats in the square, while Captain Stewart went across to tell Prempi that the commander was ready to receive him. The Ashantis then filed past, and Prempi, who of course came last, was told that the Governor was on his way to Kumasi and would arrive the next day, when he would arrange a date for a meeting at which he would be required to make his submission according to the usual native custom.

The royal procession then set out for the palace. " Hundreds of torches were lit, while the crowd of nobles, courtiers, captains, citizens, and slaves went mad with transports of joy, excitement, and rum. . . . They leaped, they squirmed, shouted and screamed, directing all their frenzied motions to the royal litter. . . . Wearing European costume, and patent boots fit for Bond Street, were the two Ansah Princes. They squirmed and shouted with the rest, looking perfectly ridiculous in their civilized attire. Prince Christian and Major Piggott appeared on a bank watching the proceedings : both Ansahs danced furiously to the rear of the litter, and then walked quietly behind with the greatest nonchalance ; but directly the procession turned the corner, thinking they were free from European observation, they again danced and yelled with redoubled vigour."[1]

On Saturday the 18th the Governor arrived. He was received by all the troops drawn up on the parade ground, while the artillery fired a salute, and Monday the 20th was fixed for the meeting with the King.

There were rumours that an Ashanti army was collected and concealed not far from the town, and that the palace and palaver ground had been mined, and it was thought possible that Prempi and some of his Chiefs might attempt to escape during the night. A cordon was therefore drawn around the palace after dark, and several men and Chiefs, including John Ansa, who came out were quietly secured and only released in the morning. They may have been sent out to see if the path was clear, but, if Prempi had ever contemplated flight, their failure to return evidently alarmed him and caused him to abandon the idea, for he never gave any sign. The Queen-Mother left the palace at about three o'clock in the morning with a long procession of attendants, and was allowed to pass unsuspectingly through the line of watchers to her own house, which was then quietly surrounded.

Prempi had been told to be on the parade ground at six o'clock ; but though the troops were all formed up by seven and the Governor, Sir Francis Scott, and Colonel

---

[1] Musgrave, p. 164.

Kempster were seated waiting on an improvised dais of biscuit boxes, surrounded by the other officers, there was no sign of the King or Chiefs. Captain Stewart therefore went to the palace to summon him, and, after a few minutes' delay, his procession joined that of the Queen-Mother and made its way slowly to the square. The King was, of course, followed by his Chiefs and an enormous crowd of stool and umbrella bearers, musicians, guards, and other attendants ; but with the exception of the principal Chiefs and a few personal servants, all these retainers were cut off from their masters by a flank movement of the Hausas, and any who attempted to take up their usual positions were rather roughly handled. Prempi then seated himself, with his mother and the Chiefs, on the side of the square facing the Governor. One Chief was still missing ; but he was soon seen approaching, hurried on by the escort of Hausas that had been sent to fetch him. He was unceremoniously separated from his attendants and pushed into the square, where his indignant expostulations were cut short by a sergeant who seized the nearest stool and pushed him down on to it.

Mr. Vroom then stepped forward to interpret the terms offered by the Governor, while Albert Ansa stood up to act for the King. Prempi was first of all reminded that the arrival of a British force in his capital had been brought about by his neglect to answer the ultimatum that had been sent to him and his persistence in sending envoys to England after he had been warned that they would not be recognized or received. The neglect of the Ashantis to fulfil the terms of the treaty of Fomana was then touched on, the Governor pointing out that the indemnity had never been paid, that no proper road had been maintained from the Pra to Kumasi, and that human sacrifices had not been abolished. Since, however, the Government had taken many of his former subjects from him and definitely refused to recognize him as anything more than King of Kumasi, it was manifestly unfair to expect Prempi to pay an indemnity that had been imposed on Ashanti as a whole ; and while it was true that no proper road had been kept open, it was equally true that the Government had neglected the southern portion. It was not true, however, as has already been shown, that the total abolition of human sacrifices had ever been stipulated for by the treaty of Fomana. Finally, the conditions that were now to be imposed were stated, and Prempi was told that the Government had no wish to depose him provided he made his submission as required and paid an indemnity of 50,000 ounces of gold. The Governor added that he was waiting to receive that submission at once.

This, of course, was a terrible blow to Prempi's pride. It was a thing that no Ashanti King had ever done before, except when Mensa voluntarily made his submission by deputy in 1881, and was the one thing above all others that he would have avoided if he could. For a few moments he sat irresolute, nervously toying with his ornaments and looking almost ready to cry with shame and annoyance ; but Albert Ansa came up and held a whispered conversation with him, and he then slipped off his sandals and, laying aside the golden circlet he wore on his head, stood up with his mother and walked reluctantly across the square to where the Governor was sitting. Then, halting before him, they prostrated themselves and embraced his feet and those of Sir Francis Scott and Colonel Kempster. " The scene was a most striking one. The heavy masses of foliage, that solid square of red coats and glistening bayonets, the Artillery drawn up ready for any emergency, the black bodies of the Native Levies, resting on their long guns in the background, while inside the square the Ashantis sat as if turned to stone, as Mother and Son, whose word was a matter of life and death, and whose slightest move constituted a command which all obeyed, were thus forced to humble themselves in sight of the assembled thousands." [1]

Prempi had barely regained his seat when, prompted by the Ansas, he rose again and said, " I now claim the protection of the Queen of England." He was reminded by the Governor, however, that the second condition, the

[1] Musgrave, p. 177.

payment of the indemnity, still remained to be fulfilled. The King replied that he had not forgotten it, and was quite ready to pay, but, as he had not got so large a sum in hand, he would pay 340 bendas (680 ounces) at once and the balance by instalments. The Governor answered that he could not sanction this arrangement, that he did not believe that a King who could afford to send envoys to England could really have any difficulty in paying the sum demanded, that the failure of the Ashantis to pay the indemnity for the last war prevented him from trusting them again, and that he must therefore receive the whole amount, or at least a considerable part of it, at once and ample security for the payment of the balance. Prempi again protested his inability to pay more than he had already offered, and the Governor then said, " The King, the Queen-Mother, the King's father, his two uncles, his brother, the two War Chiefs, and the Kings of Mampon, Ejisu and Ofesu [1] will be taken as prisoners to the Coast. They will be treated with due respect."

This was an utterly unexpected demand, and the Ashantis for a few moments sat as though paralysed. Then the Chiefs jumped up and earnestly begged that their King should not be taken from them, while Kwaku Freku, pointing to the Ansas who were standing by looking half amused and half nonplussed at the result of their handi-work, angrily asked what was to be done to them, since they had been the cause of all the trouble. The Governor answered that they would be arrested and taken to the coast to stand their trial on a charge of forgery. They were at once handcuffed, while several officers and warrant officers who had been detailed for the duty drew their swords and closed round the King and Chiefs. The latter were then removed to a house near by, and the Ansas marched to the Hausa guard-room in a state of mingled fear, rage and astonishment.

Meanwhile, the cordon had not been withdrawn from the palace, and two companies of the West Yorks were now marched down to seize it. Every door was closed and

[1] Ofinsu.

barred ; but the hum of many voices could be heard within, so, while one company strengthened the cordon, the other burst open a small door and forced its way in. The men found themselves in a large empty courtyard, but, on breaking down another inner door, they entered a smaller court in which were a number of Ashantis. They offered no resistance, and were quietly disarmed and placed under an escort outside while the palace was searched. A number of articles was collected, including several rings, trinkets, and gold-mounted swords ; but very little of real value was found, for the Golden Stool and other regalia had been removed and concealed elsewhere long before the arrival of the troops.

Immediately after the palaver was over and the palace had been seized, the Native Levy was marched to Bantama and surrounded the fetish houses ; but when the Royal Mausoleum was broken into, nothing but a row of empty brass coffins was found, for the skeletons of the Kings and the treasure that was kept there had all been removed to a safe hiding-place before the town was occupied. The customary offerings of food still lay outside the plastered-up door of the Mausoleum however, so that it was evident that this removal had been carried out with great secrecy, and that the people still believed their dead Kings were there. The village was burned to the ground, the great fetish-tree blown up, and the sacrificial bowl that stood under it taken as a trophy by Sir Francis Scott. The fetish-trees in Kumasi itself were then blown up and the houses burned or razed to the ground, while the Ashantis, equally terrified by the fear of what their gods might do to avenge such desecration and wonder and alarm at their failure to do so, gathered up as much of their property as they could carry and fled to the forest. Many of them were attacked and robbed by the carriers, but some of the latter were caught, tied up, and flogged, and the fugitives were not again interfered with.

That night strong pickets were posted all round the town to guard against any attempt that might be made to rescue the King ; but nothing happened ; the Ashantis were too cowed and awed by the events of the day to act for themselves, and their leaders were prisoners in the town.

Next morning, the 21st, a report was brought in that an Ashanti army was collecting in a village near Mampon, and Major Baden-Powell left with a flying column at midnight to scatter it. He found, however, that there had never been more than about 400 Ashantis in the village, and that they had left shortly before he arrived, for their camp fires were still burning. Prempi's summer palace was then visited, for it was thought that many of his valuables might have been stored there; but the troops found nothing but a litter of rubbish and rifled boxes, and it was said that the King's slaves had fled there immediately after his arrest and taken everything worth having before continuing their flight to their own countries.

On Wednesday the 22nd the white troops left for the coast with the prisoners, leaving the Governor and Captain Stewart with the Hausas and West Indians to follow later. The Ansas were made to march in handcuffs, but the other prisoners—except Prempi, who preferred his own litter—were carried in hammocks under escort of the West Yorkshire Regiment.

The first camp at Dede Sewa had barely been reached when the sad news of the death of Prince Henry was telegraphed up from the coast. He had been taken ill with fever on the 10th of January and invalided from Kwisa the next day. On his arrival in Cape Coast, he had been put on board H.M.S. *Blonde* to proceed to Madeira, and had then seemed so much better that, when the ship sailed on the 17th, he was fully expected to recover; but two days later a change for the worse set in, and he died the next morning off Sierra Leone.

The downward march was delayed by the number of sick who had to be carried the whole way in hammocks, and by the necessity for scouring the bush ahead of the column to guard against attempts to rescue the King or perhaps to kill him rather than allow him to be taken away; but although Ashantis were found lurking in the bush on many occasions, no attempt was ever made, and they seemed to be waiting in the hope of catching a last glimpse of their King before he was taken from them rather than with any other object. Asibi, the exiled King of Kokofu, was met on the road returning to his own country, and Inkansa of Adansi turned out to meet the troops and said he should soon return to his own land and re-establish his capital at Fomana now that the power of his enemies had been broken.

Sir Francis Scott and his Staff reached Cape Coast on the 1st of February, and Major Piggott of the 21st Lancers, who had been appointed the first Resident in Kumasi, returned almost immediately with a force of Hausas to relieve the troops who had been left behind. The West Yorks marched in early on the 5th with the political prisoners, but the Ansas had been left at Prasu until they could be brought to trial. For days before their arrival people had been pouring into the town from the surrounding country to see their once dreaded enemy, and now that they could hear the drums of the white troops who guarded him, formed a dense crowd on every available building and piece of ground on the road to the Castle gates. As they caught sight of the hammocks with the prisoners, they set up a tremendous shout of mingled triumph and hate, which rolled on as an ever-increasing roar as the column passed through the town. Prempi was completely unnerved by his reception, and cowered back in his litter almost livid with fear. He could have no doubt what his fate would have been but for the strong escort that marched with fixed bayonets on each side of him. The procession passed through the main gate into the Castle, and then, after a short delay, the water-gate was thrown open, the West Yorks came out and lined a path from it to the shore, and the prisoners were led down and embarked in the surf-boats that were waiting to take them to H.M.S. *Racoon* for removal to their prison in Elmina Castle. What with their hopeless despondency at their position, their alarm at the hostile yelling crowds that swarmed over the beach, the house-tops, and the sacred rock outside the Castle, their fear of the vast expanse of rolling sea which they had never seen before, and the discomforts of sea-sickness that soon followed and convinced them that they had been poisoned, the wretched prisoners must have found this the unhappiest hour of their lives : nor can Prempi have been any more reconciled when he discovered that the irony of Fate had decreed that that very fortress for which the Dutch had paid ground-rent to his ancestors for nearly two and a half centuries, and for which his uncle had afterwards fought and lost his kingdom, was now to be his prison.

Immediately after the prisoners had been put on board the man-of-war, the embarkation of the troops was begun, and within two or three days they were all on their way back to England. The expedition had thus been brought to a close without a single shot having been fired, yet there had been a very high rate of sickness amongst the troops : 40 per cent of the officers were treated, 42 per cent of the European rank and file, and 32 per cent of the Native troops, while nearly twenty Europeans had died on the Coast and several others never lived to reach England.

This expedition had been brought about by the Government's recent change of policy regarding Ashanti. The chief difficulty of the Gold Coast Administration had always been its relations with this tribe, and since it had at last been decided that the Ashanti question could only be settled by taking the country under British protection and establishing a Resident in the capital, action had to be taken without further delay, lest the French should succeed where the English had hitherto failed. Proposals had been made to the King, but had remained unanswered, and it was quite evident that, whatever else he might agree to, he would not willingly relinquish his independence. Prempi was young and inexperienced, and allowed himself to be led away by the self-interested advice of the Ansas, who, with the aid of a disbarred barrister and a suspended solicitor, had now brought about his downfall. It was they, and perhaps the Queen-Mother and the older

Chiefs, who were to blame rather than he. His failure to reply to the Governor's ultimatum and his persistent attempt to appeal to and negotiate with the Government in England after he had been driven to mistrust the professed friendliness of the local authority, were entirely due to their advice, and were the immediate cause of the expedition. But the remote and original cause of all the trouble was the action of the Government in having destroyed the power of Ashanti and overthrown a great native organization in 1874 without making any attempt to provide another means of maintaining order. Its neglect in this matter and the subsequent timorous policy that led to the refusal of the very condition at which it now aimed, when it had been voluntarily offered and even begged for by the Ashantis themselves, had enabled the latter to regain much of their lost power and caused them to hesitate later when the Government had altered its policy. Prempi, so soon as he realized that he had been deceived by the Ansas and was assured that he would not be deposed, stopped the mobilization of his army, made no attempt to resist the entry of the troops into Kumasi, humiliated himself by making full public submission to the Governor, claimed British protection, and agreed to have a Resident installed in his capital. It was his non-compliance with the demand for the immediate payment of the whole or at least the greater part of an enormous sum as a war indemnity that had been made a pretext for his removal. Mr. Chamberlain, in his despatch to Governor Maxwell, had written in reference to the treaty that it was proposed to make : " It will be necessary to include a provision with regard to the payment by the King of the expenses of the expedition, an estimate of which I shall send you as soon as possible. If it appears to you that the finances of Ashanti make it impossible to pay the whole amount, you may arrange to compound the claim for a sum proportioned to the resources of the King. You will also consider whether it will be desirable that the sum in question shall be paid at once, or be divided into fixed instalments to be paid at intervals, the period of which should, of course, be definitely fixed. In consideration of the payment of the cost of the expedition, Her Majesty's Government will not insist upon the discharge of the debt of 50,000 ounces of gold stipulated for in the treaty of Fommanah." [1] There is no record in the published correspondence of any estimate of the cost of the expedition or any further instructions as to the amount to be demanded from the King ever having been sent to the Governor, who may therefore have demanded 50,000 ounces on the precedent set in 1874 or because the amount had been referred to in the ultimatum. The point is immaterial, however, for the question of how the indemnity was to be paid had been left to the discretion of the Governor, who had also been authorized to reduce the amount if necessary, so as to make it "proportionate to the resources of the King." Mr. Maxwell assumed that the King could pay the enormous sum demanded of him, and, when he protested that he could not do so, seized him and all the principal persons in the kingdom as security. This, however, is one of those occasions when the Ashantis have been accused, apparently without any real justification, of making excuses in which there was no truth. The only ground the Governor could advance on which to base his theory was that the King had been able to afford to send messengers to England. This, however, had only been done as a last resource, and it was well known that the cost of the mission had had to be met by the imposition of a special tax, which had taken some time to collect; it was also known that the last instalment of the 1874 indemnity had nearly all been paid in worked gold and not in gold-dust, that the trade of the country had been at a standstill for years owing to civil wars, that the defection of large numbers of his people had still further impoverished the King, that their wars were a source of expense and not of profit to the Ashantis now that the slave trade had been abolished, and, lastly, that the King himself had but recently been reduced to begging the loan of a paltry sum

[1] Parliamentary Paper, *Further Correspondence relating to Affairs in Ashanti*, 1896, p. 128.

from the Government to defray the expenses of his enstoolment. At all times of threatened war or invasion,
moreover, it was customary to remove valuables to some,
possibly distant, place of security, and it was therefore
extremely unlikely that either Prempi or his people could
have found anything approaching this sum on such short
notice. Proof, almost positive, is afforded by the fact that
even the arrest and deportation of the King failed to
extort it ; for, had the people been able to collect the
money, or had the King or any of the other prisoners had
it in hiding, it would assuredly have been forthcoming.
It must be accepted as a fact, therefore, that the Governor,
whether from ignorance as a comparatively new arrival in
the country, or from a determination to settle the Ashanti
question and establish the Government's new policy in
the way that he believed to be best, did make demands
with which the King could not comply and then arrested
him, ostensibly as security, when he failed to achieve the
impossible. It was doubtless difficult for him to decide
when to compromise and when to insist ; but if his aim
was to bring Ashanti under his administration and induce
its people to live peaceably and contentedly under British
protection, the removal and imprisonment of their King
was the very last measure he should have resorted to. It
has been a cause of dissatisfaction with them ever since,
and they still complain bitterly of what they describe as,
and fully believe to be, an act of deliberate treachery.
The absence of all resistance to the advance of the troops,
though sometimes attributed to the fact that they followed
so quickly on the heels of the Ansas, was really due to the
repeated promises that the Government had no intention
to depose the King provided that he acceded to the terms
that would be imposed. This, so far as the Ashantis
knew, he could and was willing to do ; but had they known
that impossible terms would be demanded, or had the
least suspicion that their King would be carried away into
captivity, there is not a shadow of doubt that they would
have fought most determinedly. They therefore regard
this act, following immediately on the promises by which

they were lulled into a false sense of security, as deliberately treacherous.

The arrest of the Ansas on a charge of forgery was fully deserved, but it was soon found that there was not sufficient evidence against them to secure a conviction.

The net results of this expedition, therefore, were the overthrow of the Ashanti dynasty and the loss of that country's independence, its acquisition as a valuable hinterland to the Gold Coast Colony under British protection, and the birth of deep and lasting feelings of anger and resentment in the hearts of the Ashantis at the way in which these ends had been attained.

PART VI

EXTENSION OF THE SPHERE OF BRITISH INFLUENCE

1896 TO 1902

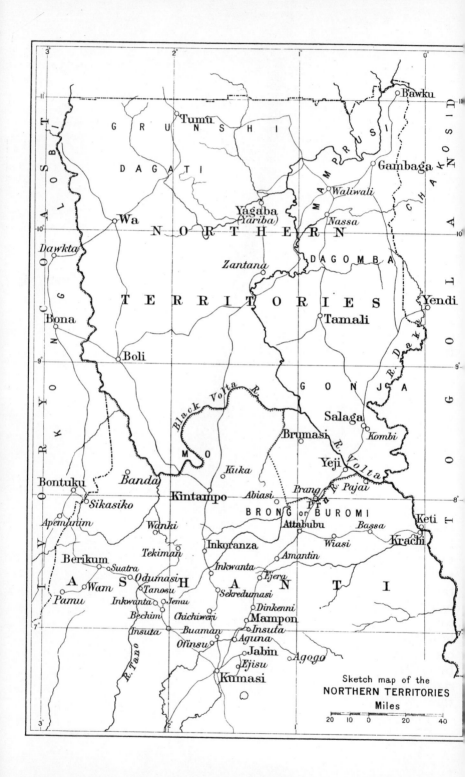

Sketch map of the
NORTHERN TERRITORIES
Miles

CHAPTER XXI

UNREST IN ASHANTI

1896 TO 1900

AFTER the deposition of Prempi, the Government was just beginning to congratulate itself that its troubles were at an end, and that it had acquired an extensive and valuable hinterland throughout which to extend its trade, when fresh trouble broke out a little farther north with a Mahommedan free-booter named Samori. Born in Segu, zeal for the Moslem faith had gained this man a large following of his co-religionists, whose first object had been the conquest and conversion of the pagan tribes around them. After subduing those on both banks of the Upper Niger, he had gradually extended his operations until he reached the hinterland of Sierra Leone in 1881 and came into conflict with the French in Senegal, who, after an unsuccessful attempt to come to some arrangement with him, defeated him in several engagements. By 1886 they had so crippled his resources that he sued for peace, and a treaty was made by which Samori undertook to confine his operations to the right bank of the River Niger. This gave him time to recruit his army, and he then began a long series of raids to the south to capture slaves to attend on his fighting men, and entered into an alliance with the Sultan of Segu to resist the encroachments of the French. The latter, however, defeated his ally, and then, thinking it best to come to terms with Samori, made a fresh treaty with him by which he once more bound himself to remain on the right bank of the Niger. This, however, he repudiated three months afterwards.

Nothing more was done until 1891, when the French again attacked Samori ; but though they defeated him on many occasions between then and 1893, they could not succeed in taking him prisoner. At the end of 1893 he was again raiding in the hinterland of Sierra Leone, and a column of 500 men of the West India Regiment and Frontier Force, under Colonel A. B. Ellis, C.B.,[1] was sent up to attack him. On the 23rd of December this force was encamped at Waima in the Konno country, when it was suddenly attacked by the French, who had been pursuing Samori and were unaware that there was a British force in the neighbourhood. The English on their side believed that it was the Sofas who were attacking them, and a fierce engagement ensued before the mistake was discovered. Three British officers and five men were killed and eighteen more wounded, while the French Commandant, Lieutenant Maritz, received wounds of which he died soon afterwards.

This unfortunate affair enabled Samori to get clear away, though, had the two forces known of each other's presence in time and been able to co-operate, they would have had him between them and must almost certainly have captured him. After this nothing more was heard of him until just before the Ashanti expedition, when he was known to be on the frontier with his headquarters at Bontuku. His refusal to help Prempi when he asked him may have been due to the fact that the latter was a pagan, or because Samori was unwilling to embroil himself with the English. He, at any rate, always professed to be friendly towards Europeans, whom he acknowledged were his superiors, but he had very little hold over his Sofas.

Samori's presence in Jaman led to the despatch of a small expedition to the neighbourhood of Bontuku in February 1896. It found that the whole country-side had been so devastated by the Sofas that the only food obtainable for the troops was a little cassada flour. Samori was

---

[1] The same officer who was District Commissioner at Kitta in 1878 ; vide p. 205. Author of *History of the Gold Coast, Land of Fetish*, etc. Afterwards made K.C.B.

then at Boli ; but though he professed friendship for the 1896–1900
English, he would not come down to meet the officer com- CHAP. XXI
manding the expedition, and the latter therefore returned,
concluding treaties with Bechim-Ahafo, Asurafo-Ahafo,
Borumfu and Wam on the way.

On the 20th of November 1896 Lieutenant Henderson,
late R.N., left Accra with Assistant-Inspector Irvine,
Doctor Part, Mr. Ferguson and 100 Hausas to visit a
number of Chiefs to the north of Ashanti with whom
treaties had been made during the past few years by Mr.
Ferguson and others, and with the intention of occupying
Bona and Boli. The object of this was to ensure that the
caravan route to the north should be kept open, and to
counteract the efforts of French and German explorers to
divert the trade of the hinterland into their own Pro-
tectorates. The French had refused to recognize the
Anglo-German Agreement establishing the Neutral Zone,
and Mr. Ferguson in 1894, Lieutenant Henderson in 1896,
and Captain Armitage in 1897 were sent to conclude fresh
treaties guarding against any action by a third Power,
while Captain Donald Stewart at the same time visited the
Mamprusi country to the north of the Neutral Zone and
concluded treaties with its Chiefs.

On approaching Bona, with the King of which Mr.
Ferguson had made a treaty, the mission heard that the
place had recently been captured and burnt by some of
Samori's people, and found Boli occupied by some 2,000 or
3,000 Sofas, who, however, evacuated it on the approach
of the British. The mission remained in Boli until the
beginning of January 1897, trying to open negotiations
with Samori's son, who was in command at Bona, and then
went on to Wa, which was also occupied by some of Samori's
troops, and, entering it without opposition, hoisted the
British flag. A small mud fort was built, and at the end
of February Mr. Henderson, leaving fifty Hausas under
Captain Irvine and Doctor Part to garrison the place,
took Mr. Ferguson and the rest of the force with him to
Dawkta on the road to Bona. From there he sent a message to Samori's son that if he continued to raid the

pagans his actions would be regarded as hostile. The Sofa commander replied that he had no wish to quarrel with the white men, but that his soldiers were short of food and he intended to capture Dawkta immediately, so that if the English did not wish to be killed he advised them to retire across the River Volta. Mr. Henderson decided to fight, and was attacked within a few hours by 8,000 Sofas, who completely surrounded the place and kept up a heavy fire on the little garrison for two days and nights. On the third day the firing suddenly ceased, and a messenger came in from Samori's son saying that he did not wish to kill the English and asking them to retire quietly. Mr. Henderson, however, replied that he had no intention of abandoning the position. The firing was at once resumed, and on the fourth day the townspeople, finding the water supply was giving out, surrendered to the enemy, who then succeeded in capturing a portion of the town, which made the British position almost untenable.

Mr. Henderson therefore determined to cut his way through their lines and retire on Wa. In the meantime he had lost two of his men killed and Mr. Ferguson and five others had been wounded ; but at sunset there was a lull in the firing, a hollow square was formed with the wounded in the centre, and the attempt was made. It was not until the British force was actually passing through their lines that the Sofas discovered it and opened fire from every side ; but it was now dark, and after firing a couple of volleys to clear the path in front, the force got through without further trouble and reached Wa the next day.

On the road they met a reinforcement of fifty Hausas under Captain Cramer, with two 7-pounders and two rocket troughs, that had been sent up from Kumasi. The Sofas then surrounded Wa and, owing to the treachery of its King, the water supply ran short. Mr. Henderson, therefore, seeing that it would be almost hopeless to attempt to hold the place against such overwhelming odds, decided to visit the Sofa camp and try to arrange an armistice. Having left instructions with Captain Irvine to evacuate the fort and retire without him if he did not return, he took two interpreters and left for the Sofa headquarters, where Samori's son received him politely, but refused to listen to any terms unless the British surrendered. Mr. Henderson, of course, would not hear of this, and was detained in the camp as a prisoner of war, but was allowed to send a note to Captain Irvine in Wa telling him the result of his negotiations. Wa was evacuated the same night, and the force, harassed from time to time by the enemy, met a small body of French troops on the road and succeeded in reaching Yariba on the 20th of April. During the retreat, Mr. Ferguson was abandoned by his carriers, and, being found soon afterwards by the Sofas, was shot and beheaded.[1]

The Sofas greatly admired Mr. Henderson's courage in visiting their camp alone, and, at a council of war held the next morning, it was decided that he should be treated with every respect, and, after seeing Samori, given safe conduct to the coast. He was therefore sent under a strong escort to Haramakoro in the Jimini country, where Samori then had his headquarters. He arrived there on the 29th of April, and after being treated as a guest, shown a review of the troops, a cartridge factory and an ammunition store, was given a pair of gold anklets as a present from Samori to the Governor and despatched on his journey to the coast on the 4th of May. Samori's troops were well supplied with modern rifles and revolvers, and he had a cartridge factory and ammunition stores.

After this, Samori moved westwards into the hinterland of the Ivory Coast, where he came into conflict with a small French force in August 1897; but it was not until 1899 that they at last succeeded in capturing him.

At this time there was another slave-raiding Chief named Babatu in the Wa district also. He and Samori were at one time inclined to have a trial of strength the one against the other, but they thought better of it, and agreed not to interfere with each other, but to raid separate parts of the country. Several towns successfully withstood their sieges, but the havoc and desolation they

[1] 6th of April.

caused was widespread, and the charred ruins of places they burned may still be seen in many parts of the district.

In 1897 the approach of the French in pursuit of Samori to the immediate neighbourhood of British territory, combined with the necessity for keeping the trade routes open beyond Kumasi, led to the countries to the north of Ashanti being constituted a separate district called the Northern Territories. Major H. P. Northcott was appointed Commissioner and Commandant with the local rank of Lieutenant-Colonel.

The extension of the spheres of influence of the two Powers into the hinterland also made it necessary to draw up a new frontier agreement. That signed in 1889 had only delimited the frontier for a short distance inland, because at that time the advanced line of British and French posts had been so far apart that it had not seemed probable that boundary disputes could arise for many years to come. Another convention signed on the 12th of July 1893 had defined the frontier as far as the ninth parallel. But, while England's policy had until quite recently been merely to retain what she had without extending her Possessions, the French had constantly aspired to the establishment of a great West African Dependency, and had been pushing rapidly forward into the interior by every possible means, both by military expeditions and specially accredited emissaries. They had already succeeded in surrounding and completely shutting in the Gambia and Sierra Leone, and, since they had now reached a considerable distance north from the Ivory Coast to the west of the Gold Coast, and had gained a fresh base by their conquest of Dahomi in 1892, from which they could extend into the interior from the east of Togoland, it seemed only too certain that they would soon sweep round to the north and deprive the Gold Coast of its only road for expansion also. France aimed at making the hinterlands of Algeria, Senegal, the Ivory Coast and Dahomi coterminous, and Samori had served a useful purpose by furnishing an excuse for many expeditions that would otherwise have aroused suspicion earlier. It was

not until now, when the mischief was almost done, that the
Gold Coast Government realized the danger of its position.
To the north, both nations now had a line of fortified posts.
The British occupied Wa, Nassa, Waliwali, Gambaga,
Bawku and other places, while the French held Tumu and
a number of other posts only a short distance to the north
of the British line, and also had a station at Wa, where the
two lines therefore touched. Many of the French posts,
moreover, were established in countries to which Britain
had a prior claim by right of treaties.

Boundary commissioners were therefore appointed, and
a new convention was signed in Paris on the 14th of June
1898 by which the northern boundary was delimited. It
left Bona, Lobi and Moshi to France ; and Dagati, Wa,
Mamprusi and the southern part of Grunshi to England.
On the 14th of November 1899 an agreement was signed
with Germany for the partition of the Neutral Zone and
the demarcation of the Anglo-German frontier of the
Northern Territories so that Salaga, Gambaga and Mamprusi should fall to Great Britain, and Yendi and Chakosi
to Germany.

The end of the disturbances in Ashanti and the prospect
of a much improved trade began to attract an increased
amount of capital and a number of prospectors for gold,
timber and rubber to the Gold Coast, and it was foreseen
that, as the country became more settled, this would
still further increase. Legislation was therefore proposed
with a view to protecting the Chiefs and others from unscrupulous prospectors who might contrive to obtain
concessions of land for a fraction of its value, and an
ordinance known as the " Lands Bill " was introduced in
1897 " to regulate the administration of public land,
and to define certain interests therein, and to constitute
a Concessions Court." This measure caused the greatest
indignation and alarm amongst the people of the Colony,
who contended that there were no public lands on the
Gold Coast for the Government to administer, since every
acre, with the exception of the actual sites of the forts and
a few plots that had been acquired for public purposes,

belonged either to some Chief's stool, to some family, or to an individual owner. Just as the Anglo-Dutch transfer of territory in 1868 had led to the formation of the Fanti Confederation, so now, when the people thought that the Government was about to usurp the right to deal with their property as its own, they united to oppose it, and formed what became known as the Gold Coast Aborigines' Rights Protection Society. In 1898 this Society sent a deputation, consisting of its President J. W. Sey, T. F. E. Jones and George Hughes, to England, where, on the 5th of August, they and their counsel had an interview with Mr. Chamberlain and the question was fully discussed. In the end the rights of the people were admitted, the Lands Bill was withdrawn, and a Concessions Ordinance passed a little later in its stead, which gave a marked impetus to the gold-mining industry.

Meanwhile, Lieutenant-Colonel Piggott had acted as Resident in Kumasi from March to October 1896, and Captain Donald Stewart, C.M.G., had then been appointed. Sir William Maxwell visited the place again in 1897, but returned in December shattered in health and sailed for England, but died [1] on the voyage. He was succeeded by Mr. Hodgson, the former Colonial Secretary.

At first the Kumasis had all withdrawn to their bush villages, and practically the only Ashantis in the town were the few Chiefs and their followers who had been ordered by the Governor to remain to assist the Resident. Most of the town was altogether abandoned, and that part of it which lay to the south of the Bantama road was cleared and a strong fort built on rising ground. It was about fifty yards square, with rounded bastions at each corner and loop-holed walls about thirteen feet in height. It was built partly of brick and partly of the stone used in the buildings of the old palace, was entered by a single steel-faced door,[2] and, in addition to quarters for the Resident, contained store-rooms, magazines and a well,

---

[1] On the 14th of December.
[2] This door was originally on the eastern face of the fort under the Residency, but has since been moved to the northern face.

and mounted five machine-guns and four 7-pounders. The country was administered by the Resident through a Native Committee of Chiefs, of which he was the President, and Chiefs Opoku Mensa—better known by his title Obu Abassa, the Arm Breaker—Kwaku Nantwi, and Kwamin Efilfa were the members.

The policy of the Government aimed at keeping the trade routes open and preventing the Ashantis from re-asserting their authority over the outlying districts, and they outwardly appeared to be settling down under the new conditions. In reality, however, they were far from content, and although the exiles returned to their lands, very few Kumasis came back to the town. They never forgave the loss of their King, and felt especially disgraced because he had been taken from them without their having fired a single shot in his defence. They had a large store of ammunition that had been prepared in 1896, but not used when it was decided not to oppose the expedition, and soon afterwards they took a solemn oath that they would fight again at the first favourable opportunity, with the object of compelling the Government to give them back their King, and began to collect arms and ammunition secretly. The Kumasis, Ejisus and Ofinsus especially got together enormous quantities, which they obtained in Saltpond and brought up through Akim Swedru.

In 1896 it was reported that the people of the Achima country, in which are the Kumasi bush villages, were meditating an attack on the British post, and a detachment of Hausas which was on its way to the coast was diverted from Northern Sefwi to reinforce the garrison. Nothing happened, however. In the following year, 1897, Mr. Vroom, C.M.G., was sent up by Sir William Maxwell to gauge public feeling in the country, and reported that the Ashantis were still unsettled and had not yet acquiesced in British rule. In 1898 some local trouble was appre-hended in Wam, and towards the end of the year the Abodoms " drank fetish " with the Kumasi Chiefs that they would fight against the Government. In 1899 there was a disturbance in Aguna, and part of the town was

burnt, but Captain Davidson Houston, who was then
Acting Resident, visited it with a small force and arrested
the ringleaders, and nothing more was heard of it.   By this
time, however, it was common knowledge among the
Ashantis that they were to fight again as soon as a favourable opportunity arose if they did not get their King back,
and in November 1899 Captain Houston thought the
rumours of disaffection among the Kumasi tribes so
authentic that he sent for all the Kumasi and Achima
Chiefs and made them swear oaths of loyalty to the British
Government through the Native Committee.   Prempi
himself had been removed from Elmina to Sierra Leone,
so as to be farther away from his people, but they still
contrived to communicate with him.

In December 1899 an Ashanti boy arrived in Accra and
offered to reveal the whereabouts of the Golden Stool,
which, with other Ashanti treasure, had been concealed in
the forest and closely guarded for the last four years.   He
represented that its guardians were tired of their duty, and
had sent him to say that, if the Government would ensure
their safety and reward them handsomely, they were now
willing to give these things up.   It was this proposal that
seems first to have given Sir Frederic Hodgson the idea of
attempting to gain possession of the stool, and he sent his
Private Secretary Captain Armitage, with the boy and
an escort of Hausas to fetch it.   Great precautions were
taken to guard against discovery : the boy was disguised
as a Hausa soldier, and was constantly attended by
Captain Armitage's orderly, who, in order to aid the
deception, was dressed in a cloth and carried his carbine
and valise, while, as a further precaution, the boy was
carried in a hammock when passing through villages, so
that he might be taken for a sick Hausa who was being
helped with his equipment by one of the carriers.

The nearer the party arrived to their goal, however,
the more alarmed did the boy become lest he should be
discovered and killed, and eventually, while they were at
Bisiasi, he escaped by night during a tornado and made his
way to a neighbouring village—Ahunjo—but was found

and brought back the next morning. The Chief of Ahunjo
and some of his people came in with him and explained
that he had come to them during the night and asked why
they were sleeping when the white man had come to bring
war into their country, and, when they had said that since
he had come with the white man they should detain him
until they had communicated with the officer, had offered
to bribe them to let him go, and finally told them that he
had been sent by Achiriboanda from Accra to show the
Government where the Golden Stool was hidden. Fortunately, he was not known in the village, and Captain
Armitage apparently succeeded in persuading the Chief
that the boy was a soldier, who had had sunstroke and
did not know what he was talking about.

Bali, near which the treasure was supposed to be hidden,
was reached on the 5th of February 1900, and just as
it was getting dark the boy was taken round the village
and pointed out the path that led to the spot. Later in the
evening this was followed ; but the boy was now almost
mad with fear and either could not, or dared not point out
the correct road. Threats and persuasions were alike of
no avail, so the quest had to be abandoned, and Captain
Armitage returned to Accra.

There is little doubt, however, that the treasure was
really concealed close to Bali at that time. The party had
no sooner started down the side path than they were
followed by one of the Linguists, who told Captain Armitage
that he was on the wrong road and that the track only
led to some farms. He begged him to turn back, and
became absolutely frantic in his appeals when he refused.
Bali was deserted when they returned, and it was not until
some hours later that the people came back and explained
that they had gone away because they were afraid that
the white man would be lost in the bush, and they wished,
if enquiries were made, to be able to say that they had not
been there at the time. It was afterwards discovered,
however, that they had sent three urgent messages
through to Kumasi during the night to tell Opoku Mensa
that a white man had come to Bali, and to ask what they

were to do. The village, moreover, was built differently from
other Ashanti villages and inhabited by a different class of
people. The houses were so arranged that it was possible,
by passing from one to the other, to traverse the whole
length of the place without being seen from the street,
and the men all carried guns and wore their " war-coats."
Captain Armitage's orderly, too, who had been present at
Prempi's submission, recognized three men who had then
attended him. They were in the village when the party
arrived, but disappeared soon afterwards.

The cost of maintaining the garrison in Kumasi and
provisioning it from the coast was, of course, considerable,
and had to be borne by the Colony, for the Ashantis contributed nothing beyond a certain amount of free labour.
Sir Frederic Hodgson therefore contemplated levying some
kind of tax or payment from them that might defray this
expense, and had decided to visit Kumasi in March 1900.
After the failure of this attempt, therefore, he determined
to take the boy with him when he went, and have these
villages visited in force while he was there.

The Governor, who was accompanied by Lady Hodgson,
Captain Armitage, Doctor Chalmers and Mr. Wilkinson the
Acting Director of Public Works, left Accra on the 13th of
March with an escort of only twenty Hausas under a
sergeant to look after the carriers, and crossed the Pra on
the 22nd. At Kwisa he was met by Inkansa, now very
old and blind, who handed in a long list of grievances, chief
among which was a complaint that the Bekwais had taken
a strip of land that had formerly belonged to Adansi, and
which Inkansa now wanted the Governor to compel them
to return to him. This land was auriferous and the most
valuable part of the old Adansi territory, a fact well known
to the Bekwais, who, when they drove out the Adansis,
had annexed it to their own country by right of conquest
and in strict accordance with native custom. On their
return after the last expedition, therefore, the Adansis
had found themselves deprived of their most valued possession, and now appealed to the Governor to interfere and
order the Bekwais to surrender it. Inkansa, however, was

reminded that in 1899, while he was still an exile at Insaba, he had sent a Linguist to Accra to enquire whether, in the event of his returning to his own country, this land would be given up to him, and had then been told that the Government would not take any steps to disturb an arrangement that was in accordance with established native custom. Inkansa apparently hoped that the lapse of ten years would have caused this decision to be forgotten, and showed much annoyance and some tendency to open truculence when reminded of it.

Kumasi was entered on the afternoon of Sunday the 25th, when the Acting Resident Captain Davidson-Houston, the other officials, Basel missionaries, Kings, Chiefs and Members of the Native Committee turned out to welcome the Governor as he passed up the road to the fort. There was no sign of anything unusual; yet the majority of those present were secretly chafing under the present condition of affairs, and had been nursing their grievances until the first injudicious or tactless act was now all that was needed to incite them to open rebellion against the Government. Even while the Chiefs were filing past the fort to salute the Governor as he stood on the verandah, one of them, Kofi Kofia, pushed his way through the King of Jabin's attendants and, placing his hand on the side of his palanquin, told him that if the Governor had not " brought them a good message " they intended to fight. Such an act is enough in itself to show how strong was the feeling of discontent; for to approach a man of importance at such a time or otherwise than through his Linguist was a gross breach of etiquette.

Four o'clock on Wednesday the 28th was fixed for the Governor's meeting with the Kings and Chiefs, which was held in front of the fort. First of all he told them definitely and finally that neither Prempi nor Achiriboanda, who was still living under surveillance in Accra, would ever be allowed to return to rule over them; but that the powers of the King Paramount would continue to be vested in the Resident, acting under the Governor as the Queen's representative. That he claimed the right to call out the people at any time, not for war as in the past, but for peaceful purposes, to work as carriers or in building houses and making roads. Next he referred to the unpaid war indemnity under the Treaty of Fomana and the expenses that had been incurred by the Government in the last expedition, and said that although he had no intention of demanding the immediate payment of this money, yet an annual sum of 2,000 peredwins—equivalent to about £15,000—must be paid as interest, which would be apportioned among the different tribes as follows. The Kumasis would have to pay 125 peredwins ; the Mampons, Adansis, Bekwais, Inkoranzas and Mansu-Inkwantas 150 each ; the Insutas, Kokofus and Agunas 110 each ; the British Jamans 100 ; the Jabins, Tekimans, Bechims, Inkwantas, Wams and Bompatas 75 each ; the Ofinsus, Ejisus, Kumawus, Wenkis, Abodoms, Ahafus and Obogus 35 each, and the Agogos 20. These sums were to be collected and paid in by the Chiefs, who would receive 10 per cent of the amount for their trouble. Lastly, the Governor demanded the delivery of the Golden Stool, and then, after a few words of advice about the advantages of peace and good government, money presents were made to the Kings and the meeting broke up.

In less than a week after this meeting the Ashantis rose in armed opposition to the Government, and it is necessary, therefore, to consider what were the causes of the outbreak.

Now, as has already been shown, the Ashantis had always held that Prempi's removal had been accomplished by treachery, and that the expedition of 1896 was unnecessary. They may not, indeed, have been anxious to see a British Resident and his military guard permanently established in their capital ; yet when they found that the Government was determined on the point and that all their attempts at negotiation to avoid it were fruitless, they had acquiesced. They had protested against the expedition being sent and had offered no resistance to it, although they were by no means short of war materials at the time. The avowed intention of the Government had been to establish a British Resident in Kumasi, and the Ashantis had never dreamed that it had any ulterior motive and was, in fact, secretly plotting to remove their King. Apart from the fact that any such intention had been definitely and repeatedly repudiated by the Governor, the precedent of Sir Garnet Wolseley's expedition and promises was against it. They had, therefore, been taken entirely by surprise, and the final scene had found them unprepared with that resistance which they would undoubtedly have offered had they had the least suspicion of what was going to happen, while the arrest of their Chiefs had deprived them of the leaders who would otherwise have mobilised them when the discovery was made. They had thought it possible that a reasonable fine might be inflicted and would have been ready to pay it ; but the demand for the immediate production of an enormous sum of money had been quite unexpected. It was, of course, made merely as a pretext for the removal of the King, for the Governor must have known that no such sum could possibly be collected and paid on such short notice. Sir Frederic Hodgson, indeed, plainly admits this in his letter to the Colonial Office dated the 29th of January 1901, in which he says, " the Kumassis and the Kings of those of the confederated tribes who supported Prempeh, found that they had entirely miscalculated events, and that the British Government not only intended to remain, but made demands which were unexpected, and which, without previous preparation, they could not comply with." [1]

The main cause of the discontent of the Ashantis, therefore, was the removal of their King ; but in addition to this, British rule was in itself distasteful to them, because it abolished many of their old-established customs and at the same time introduced new conditions that they disliked. Slave raiding and holding especially was now rendered increasingly difficult. If their slaves ran away, they could neither recover them nor obtain others to replace them ; yet they were required to furnish labour for transport and building purposes. The influx of large numbers

[1] Parliamentary Paper, *Ashanti War*, 1900, p. 110.

of Fanti traders and others from the coast was also deeply resented.

These original causes of dissatisfaction are well summed up by Major Nathan, who succeeded Sir Frederic Hodgson as Governor. In his despatch to the Secretary of State dated the 19th of March 1901, he wrote : " I should say that the real origin of the rising is a profound dislike on the part of the Chiefs and leading people of Ashanti to British rule. This dislike is not unnatural. We take away from them all they care about and give them in place conditions of life which have no attractions to them. We have deprived them of the power of making war on each other and on neighbouring tribes, of the power of keeping their people in order by barbarous punishments, and of the power of recruiting their labour with slaves. We try to give them protection from external aggression, peace within their own boundaries, law enforced by our own civilized methods, and opportunities of making wealth by labour. The Ashanti was perfectly able to protect himself from the aggression of the surrounding tribes before we came to his country, having for 200 years prosecuted a series of success- ful wars against his neighbours, all the facts of which are well known to him. Peace within the country has no attractions to a man whose title to respect and whose recognized source of power and wealth are in feats of war. Humane punishments for offences and particularly for offences against the power and dignity of big men are to his mind ridiculous as well as unsatisfying to the pleasure he derives from seeing blood flow. Personal labour of any kind is beneath the dignity of the Ashanti, and a wage which has to be slowly accumulated before it reaches a sum such as he could obtain from a day's loot in an enemy's town is no compensation for labour. I fear that the only things which European civilization have brought him which he really appreciates are spirits and powder. The Chiefs like, no doubt, velvets and silks, but the use of these is confined by custom to a comparatively few leading people. The toga, which forms the sole dress of the bulk, is rightly regarded by the ordinary Ashanti as superior when made of native cloth to when it is made of Manchester cotton. Native custom, as a rule, restrains them from building any but the simple huts in which their race have always lived. It is true they like jewellery, but of this the big men have plenty made by native workmanship from their accumulated hoards of gold. A complicated system of administration, hallowed by antiquity and historic precedents, which our ignorance and policy have alike tended to break down, and a deep-rooted superstition which we are unable to understand, and from which our presence in the country has detached a portion of the people, further help to make our rule distasteful to the Ashanti." [1]

These, then, were the causes that had reduced the Ashantis, and especially their Chiefs, to a state of discontent and unrest which had only been held in check by the existence of the fort and its garrison, and was bound, sooner or later, to end in open resistance. Exactly when this happened was merely a question of opportunity and the occurrence of some special event to act as a directly exciting cause.

They thought they saw the opportunity now in the arrival of the Governor himself in their midst with so small a staff and an escort of only twenty Hausas under a sergeant ; in the absence on leave of the Resident, Captain Stewart ; in the military difficulties in which they well knew Great Britain was involved at the time ; and in the smallness of the garrison in the fort, which had been allowed to fall below strength, and, with detachments away in Attabubu and British Jaman, numbered only about 130 men instead of 300. They thought very little of a Governor whose dignity and importance were not maintained by the usual show of power ; but they had a very wholesome feeling of mingled fear and respect for Captain Stewart, whom they had known for years as a strong but just man, who, besides understanding them better than anyone else did, would deal with any trouble promptly and severely and stand no nonsense. They knew, too, either by report

[1] Parliamentary Paper, *Correspondence relating to Ashanti*, 1901, p. 12.

or from information received from educated Fantis, that
the war in South Africa was taxing the military resources
of Great Britain to the utmost, and they may also have
known that she had troops engaged in China also.   The
whole of their past history justified the belief that they had
nothing to fear unless white troops were sent against them,
and they did not believe that these could be spared.

The immediate exciting cause of the rising, however,
was Sir Frederic Hodgson's speech on the 28th.   The
Ashantis had hitherto been content to wait, because they
firmly believed that the return of Prempi was merely a
question of time, and the definite announcement that he
would never be allowed to come back had dismayed and
shocked them.   Then followed the demand for the payment of interest on the indemnity imposed by the Treaty
of Fomana and the cost of the last expedition.   This
demand was made by instruction of the Secretary of State
on the recommendation of the Governor and Resident,
but, whether the Ashantis were willing to pay tribute
towards the upkeep in their country of an administration
that was distasteful to them or not, the reasons given for
it were certainly not such as would commend themselves to
them.   The greater part of the indemnity had remained
unpaid mainly because the Government, by its own inactivity, had allowed the matter to lapse.   It had afterwards hesitated so long to interfere in the internal affairs
of Ashanti, even when implored to do so, that the country
had been torn by civil wars and impoverished by long years
of strife and tribal defections to such a degree that it had
become a physical impossibility for the Ashantis to collect
and pay any very large sum.   The whole circumstances
had, moreover, been altered by the removal of Prempi
and the establishment of British administration in the
country.   By its own acts, therefore, the Government had
allowed the Ashantis to look upon this question of the
payment of the indemnity as forgotten and a thing of the
past, while they not unnaturally regarded the demand
that they should contribute to the cost of an expedition
which they had always protested was unnecessary and to

which they had offered no resistance as unjust. Lastly, came the demand for the surrender of the Golden Stool, and it was this that finally convinced them that the time for armed resistance had arrived ; for to them, the possession of the stool meant even more than the presence or absence of Prempi.

This stool was held in great reverence : it was symbolical of the power of Ashanti, and was, in fact, a " fetish " in which the sovereign power was held to be embodied, to be exercised by its temporary holder the King. The whole history of the country was bound up with the stool, and none but the person placed on it could be acknowledged as King or exercise sovereign power. So long, therefore, as the stool remained in their possession, the Ashantis could always enstool another King if Prempi died or failed to return ; but without it, even the return of Prempi would avail them but little. Nothing would ever have induced the Ashantis to surrender it voluntarily, for to have done so would have been to surrender their national integrity. Captain Donald Stewart, in his report to the Governor in January 1891, says of it that it " is looked upon as the great Fetish of Ashanti, and I don't believe that any Ashanti King, Chief, or man, even if they knew where it was put, would ever give the Government the slightest help to seize it. Even our most loyal Chiefs and Kings dislike immensely any allusion to the stool, invariably try to turn the conversation if it is alluded to, at the same time denying all knowledge of its whereabouts." [1]

It is evident, therefore, that the loss of the Golden Stool would have meant a great deal to the Ashantis, and that its possession might have been of some importance to the Government ; but if the latter wanted it and had been able to obtain it, the proper time for its removal would have been in 1896, when Prempi was arrested. For Sir Frederic Hodgson to ask for it now, and, moreover, to ask for it in the way he did, was, to say the least of it, a great mistake. He led the Ashantis to believe, not so much that he wished to deprive them of it, as that he wanted it for

[1] Parliamentary Paper, *Correspondence relating to Ashanti*, 1901, p. 4.

his own use, and that the Government aimed at installing its officer as King Paramount of Ashanti.

This has been denied. Lady Hodgson writes: " It has been said that the Governor demanded the delivery of the Golden Stool, and insolently claimed to be regarded as the King Paramount of Ashanti. This is again absolutely untrue. . . . The Governor said that the Queen, being now the paramount power, should have the stool belonging to that power as the symbol of her supremacy. He added that the Kings were sitting upon their tribal stools, and that he hoped they would evince their loyalty by producing the Golden Stool and handing it over, not, of course, for him to sit upon, as was recorded by this calumnious correspondent, but to show their recognition of the Queen's position." [1]

This may very probably represent what the Governor meant ; but unfortunately it is not what he said. Lady Hodgson, it is true, was present at the meeting with the Kings and Chiefs, but presumably she did not write this passage until after her return to England. The speech, however, had been taken down in shorthand at the meeting, and the Governor forwarded a transcript copy to the Secretary of State on the 7th of April, and it is not to be supposed either that he neglected to read it through or sent it as a report of what he had said if it was not. This, then, is the best evidence of what he really did say, and the portion referring to the Golden Stool is recorded thus :

" There is one matter which I should like to talk to you about. I want first to ask a question of the King of Bekwai.

(The King comes forward.)

" King, I want to ask you this question. You were put on the stool not very long ago. What would you have done to a man sitting on your right hand who kept back part of the stool equipment when you were enstooled ?

" *A.* I have no power myself : my power is the Government.

" *Q.* Then you would have reported the matter to me to deal with ?

---

[1] Lady Hodgson, *Siege of Kumasi*, p. 81.

" *A*. Yes.

" *Q*. And you would have expected me either to get you the equipment or to punish the man ?

" *A*. Yes.

" Now, Kings and Chiefs, you have heard what the King of Bekwai has said upon the point I raised. What must I do to the man, whoever he is, who has failed to give to the Queen, who is the paramount power in this country, the stool to which she is entitled ? Where is the Golden Stool ? Why am I not sitting on the Golden Stool at this moment ? I am the representative of the paramount power ; why have you relegated me to this chair ? Why did you not take the opportunity of my coming to Kumassi to bring the Golden Stool, and give it to me to sit upon ? However, you may be quite sure that although the Government has not yet received the Golden Stool at your hands, it will rule over you with the same impartiality, and with the same firmness as if you had produced it." [1]

This is perfectly plain and is not likely to have been understood either by the interpreter or by the Ashantis in any other sense. But although this demand for the Golden Stool was in itself a great mistake, yet the Governor made it infinitely worse by breaking the primary rule in dealing with such people ; for he had made a definite demand without having the power to enforce compliance.

[1] Parliamentary Paper, *Ashanti War*, 1900, p. 16.

CHAPTER XXII

THE SIEGE OF KUMASI

1900

THE Governor's speech on the 28th of March had been received in silence, and the Kings of Jabin, Kumawu and some others had afterwards tried to summon a meeting of all the Chiefs to discuss the question of the payment of interest ; but the Kumasis flatly refused to attend, saying that now that they knew that their King was not going to be given back to them, they declined to so much as consider the question of any payment, but intended to arm themselves forthwith and rise against the Government. They were promptly joined by the Ofinsus and Ejisus, and then won over a section of the Kokofus by promising their King, Asibi, who was the nearest blood relative to Prempi, that they would place him on the Golden Stool.

This was the state of affairs on the 31st of March, when the Governor sent Captain Armitage, with forty-five Hausas under Captain Leggett, to visit Bali and Inkwanta in the very district where the malcontents were then arming themselves. With them were Mr. Erbyn the Resident's interpreter, a dispenser, sixty-four hammock-men and carriers, and the Ashanti boy whom the Governor had brought up with him from Accra. Captain Armitage was to try to gain possession of the Golden Stool, and if he found any large quantities of guns and ammunition in the villages, to capture them and either destroy them on the spot or bring them back to Kumasi. He reached Ofinsu that afternoon, where he was met by two Hausas, who had been sent out in civilian clothes by the Acting

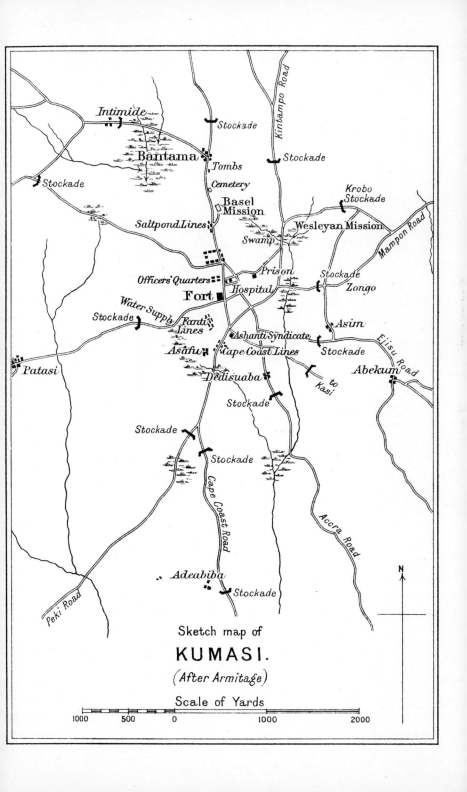

Sketch map of

KUMASI.

(After Armitage)

Scale of Yards

Resident to see what was going on in Bali and Inkwanta. They reported that the people were very much excited, and saying that the time had now come when they must make war on the white man, who, not content with having taken Prempi away, was now demanding money in addition, and that a meeting had been arranged to take place at Inkwanta that very afternoon at which the Balis were to be present. The men were therefore sent back to Inkwanta to see if they could find out what had happened ; but when they returned at ten o'clock that night they reported that they had found the village quiet, though a great many people had been there quite recently.

Inkwanta was reached and surrounded early the next morning ; but only about fifty men were found in it, and when Captain Armitage, after telling them that the Governor had heard of their disloyalty and was determined to put a stop to it, proceeded to search the houses, he only found twenty-five guns and a very small quantity of powder, which he did not think it worth while to retain. Bali was surrounded in the same way soon after midday ; but the people had been warned of their approach and there were only six old men in the village, while a thorough search of all the houses failed to reveal more than seventeen old guns and half a keg of powder.

Next morning, Captain Leggett was left with nineteen Hausas in Bali, while Captain Armitage set out with the remainder of the detachment to search for the Golden Stool. The boy led them down a barely discernible track through dense forest, which, after a march of nearly four hours, brought them to two houses in a small plantation of kola and plantain trees. It was beneath the floors of these houses that the boy said the Golden Stool and other treasure were buried, but, though the floors were dug up and a thorough search was made, it was quite evident that the ground had never been disturbed, and, as nothing more could be got out of the now terror-stricken boy, the party returned to Bali.

Meanwhile, at about two o'clock that afternoon, one of the Hausas left in Bali, who had chanced to walk about a

hundred yards away from the houses, reported to Captain
Leggett that the bush was full of armed men, and he
barely had time to extend his men across that end of the
village, when the noise of a large party was heard in the
forest, and some thirty or forty armed Ashantis were seen
close to a fetish temple that stood in a small clearing about
sixty yards from the end of the street. They were very
excited, shouting and dancing and pointing their guns at
the soldiers, while the fetish priest was running about
knocking up their guns and evidently doing his best to
pacify them. The Hausas were ordered to take what
cover they could, but on no account to fire, while Captain
Leggett tried to attract the attention of the priest in the
hope of using him to parley with the Ashantis. He had
just succeeded in calling him over when the search party
returned. On nearing the village, Captain Armitage had
heard a tremendous uproar, and some of the carriers had
run out to meet him, calling out that the Ashantis had
surrounded the place. On its eastern side was the fetish
temple and a large grove of plantains that grew almost
up to the walls of the houses, and in this numbers of armed
Ashantis were now collected with Captain Leggett's Hausas
extended across the end of the village facing them. The
Ashantis were still very excited and kept shouting all sorts
of abuse, so Captain Armitage told the priest to try to
induce the Chiefs to come and state their grievances to
him. He promised to do so, but they never came.

Meanwhile, the carriers were ordered to cut down the
plantains, and had cleared about twenty yards of ground
when the Ashantis suddenly opened a heavy fire on them,
which was returned by the escort. The troops were
therefore withdrawn into the nearest houses and ordered
to loop-hole the walls and pull down the neighbouring
huts, but not to return the Ashantis' fire unless they tried
to rush the village. These arrangements, however, took
time, and the officers' chief difficulty was to control the
fire of their men, who had only brought sixty rounds of
ammunition each, but were most anxious to expend it
against the enemy. One man, indeed, succeeded in firing

all but eight of his rounds within the first twenty minutes. Both officers, Mr. Erbyn, six Hausas and two carriers were slightly wounded. The Ashantis kept up a continuous fire until dark, and then retired down the road leading to Kumasi, leaving a cordon of sharpshooters round the village, who maintained an intermittent fire throughout the night. A heavy tornado broke over the place soon after dark ; but the Ashantis down the road and around the fetish temple could still be heard talking and singing their war songs, the burden of which was that the Governor had demanded large sums of money from them and sent two white men to find the Golden Stool, but that instead of the money they would send him the white men's heads, and the Golden Stool should be well washed in their blood.

It was now evident that the detachment would have to fight its way back to Kumasi against heavy odds. No one slept that night, and an hour before dawn the men were quietly assembled in one of the compounds and told off to their positions in the column, while the carriers were given their loads and implored to keep cool. Captain Armitage took the advance-guard and Captain Leggett the rear-guard. Then, as day began to break, the party passed from one house to the other without being seen and stole quietly through the morning mist down the road towards Kumasi. On leaving the village, the path led down into a small swamp and then rose sharply on the other side. The advance party had almost reached the swamp, when a volley was poured into them from the bush on either side of the road at a range of only a few yards. This spread panic amongst the carriers, who, instead of lying down behind their loads as they had been told, threw them down and bolted. Some, indeed, dashed into the bush into the very arms of the Ashantis ; but the majority fled wildly down the road, carrying away most of the advance-guard and knocking Captain Armitage down in their mad rush. His orderly, however, stood by him, and he succeeded in collecting three more Hausas, who silenced the enemy with a few volleys and enabled the column to push on again. The whole of the baggage, however, had been lost,

and one Hausa and seven carriers were missing. The
party then pushed on as rapidly as possible, while occasional shots could be heard away in the forest, which told
of fugitive carriers being hunted down, and a few shots
were fired at the advance-guard from a plantation outside
the next village.

Many of the carriers now came hurrying back with news
that the Ashantis were waiting for them at the Ofin River,
and, on nearing it, a large party was seen posted on the
bank.   They were all talking loudly however, and not
keeping any special look-out, so that it seemed they did
not expect to have to do more than cut off a few stragglers
who might have succeeded in escaping from Bali.   Several
volleys were fired into them by the advance-guard, which
at once scattered them, and, when the river was reached,
it was found that they had fled across it, leaving their
Chief, Kwesi Buachi of Kumasi, lying dead beside his chair.
Twenty guns, six kegs of powder, and a number of other
articles had also been abandoned.   Fortunately they had
been so disconcerted by the suddenness of the attack and
the death of their leader, that they made no attempt to
hold the opposite bank, for the tornado of the previous
night had flooded the river and it was neck deep as the
column forded it.   Three more villages were passed, at
each of which the column was fired on, and then, after
passing through one deserted village, Chiasi was reached.
This was the mobilisation headquarters of the Kumasis,
and about a hundred stools that lay around in a circle
showed that a big meeting had been held there recently.
On leaving, the column was exposed to a heavy fire at close
range, and two men in the advance-guard fell seriously
wounded, another in the main body was killed, and a
carrier was also wounded.

From this point on the column was almost continuously
under fire, and the situation momentarily became more
desperate.   The men, who had now been fighting and
marching for thirty hours, were worn out, and it was
difficult to fill the gaps in the advance-guard ; the ammunition was running short, and some of the men were already

without any ; the column was hampered by its wounded, some of whom were now being carried in hammocks improvised from the carriers' cloths, and there was a constant danger that the remaining carriers would drop and abandon them ; while the fire from the bush was so well maintained that it was impossible to advance more than a few yards at a time. Soon after midday, therefore, Captain Armitage decided to halt, and ordered a space to be cleared in a plantation to the left of the path in which to encamp. A little later a sergeant and four men were sent down the road to see if it was clear, but had to turn back almost immediately, while a carrier who volunteered to take a letter through to Kumasi, which was only an hour away, started off at about five o'clock, but was captured by the enemy. Towards evening the remaining ammunition was collected and found to amount to only 480 rounds.

That night was spent within a small circular stockade of plantain stems surrounded by a cordon of sentries. The want of water, however, was sorely felt, especially by the wounded, and at dawn the next morning Captain Leggett was given eight men of the advance-guard and nearly all the ammunition, and told to push through to Kumasi at all costs and return with reinforcements, food, water, ammunition, and assistance for the wounded. Fortunately, he was not fired on, and reached Kumasi in safety. Four Hausas under a corporal, who had met him near Kumasi, joined Captain Armitage without meeting with any opposition, and he, too, then marched in, being met on the road by Captain Leggett and Doctor Tweedy with hammocks for the wounded.

The total casualties during this march were one Hausa killed, one missing, two dangerously wounded, and both officers and seventeen men slightly wounded. Two carriers were severely and four slightly wounded, while seven more were missing. What the losses of the Ashantis were was never known ; but they themselves afterwards estimated the strength of their total force on the road between Bali and Kumasi at from 5,000 to 6,000 men, and admitted to some 200 killed and many more wounded.

Meanwhile it had become known in Kumasi soon after
Captain Armitage left that the Kumasis, Ejisus and
Ofinsus were arming themselves in the Achima villages,
and Hausas had been sent to warn him ; but they were never
heard of again, and were doubtless done to death by the
Ashantis on the road. The next day, Sunday the 1st of
April, the Governor's anxiety for the safety of the party
was still further increased by the discovery that Kumasi
was almost deserted, and that two out of the three members
of the Native Committee, Efilfa and Nantwi, had joined
the rebels ; while the Basel missionaries took fright during
the afternoon, and, led by Mr. Ramseyer, came pouring
down the road from Bantama to seek safety with all their
belongings in the fort. They were stopped, however, outside the house where the Governor was staying, and told
very plainly that until such time as he found it necessary to
retire into the fort they would not be allowed to do so, nor
to increase the general alarm and add to the confidence of
the Ashantis by such movements. On the 3rd, the Kings
of Mampon, Jabin and Kumawu sent a letter to the
Governor telling him that the Kumasis had threatened to
fight if they came to see him, and that they were going to
fetch their guns ; but when the news of the fighting on the
Bali road reached them the next day, they and the King
of Aguna came at once to the fort to declare their own
loyalty and explain that they had had no knowledge that
this attack was contemplated.

It was now evident that the rising was a serious matter,
and there seemed every probability that it might spread
unless prompt action were taken to crush it. This, however, was more than the Governor could attempt ; for the
small garrison in Kumasi was barely sufficient to ensure the
safety of the fort, and he had been unable to send help to
Captain Armitage, because he could not send enough men
to be of any service without leaving Kumasi practically
defenceless. Orders were therefore telegraphed to Accra
for all the available Constabulary to march at once to
Kumasi, and another telegram was sent to Kintampo
asking that runners might be sent to Major Morris, the

Commissioner and Commandant of the Northern Territories, requisitioning troops from there also. The Secretary of State was also telegraphed to, and ordered reinforcements to be sent as quickly as possible from Lagos, Northern Nigeria and Sierra Leone. At the same time, a message was sent to Yow Buachi the King of Bekwai, calling upon him to join the loyal Chiefs, and asking him to send his fighting men to assist the Government. He, however, sent two of his Linguists under escort to Kumasi to explain that, while his loyalty might be relied upon, the Adansis were threatening him, and he therefore begged to be allowed to defend his own country. This was the first actual intimation of the disloyalty of the Adansis that had been received, and, since the reinforcements from Accra and any further relief columns would have to pass through their country, it was of great importance that they should be held in check, and the King was therefore given the permission that he had asked.

Pending the arrival of reinforcements, the Governor could only try to settle matters quietly by negotiation. He therefore sent for the loyal Kings to meet him in the fort with Opoku Mensa, who had been brought there and given a room as soon as the defection of the other members of the Native Committee was discovered. They suggested that, since the demand for payment was one of the principal grievances of the Kumasis, he should cancel it, and it was eventually arranged that he would refer the point back to the Secretary of State and make no attempt to collect any payments until he had received further instructions. They then asked the Governor to assure them that if the malcontents came in he would spare their lives, and he promised that, since the young men had only been led away by their Chiefs, they should not be punished, but said that the conduct of the Chiefs themselves would have to be investigated, and that the action taken with regard to them would depend upon the evidence in each case.

The Kings then sent messengers to the Kumasi leaders and opened negotiations ; but though many messages passed between them, the Kumasis remained obdurate,

declaring their fixed determination to fight against the
Government, and demanding that the loyal Kings should
join them forthwith. The King of Kokofu had now come
in to declare his loyalty, and joined the others on the
afternoon of the 11th, when they came to report the failure
of their negotiations to the Governor. He thanked them
for the efforts they had made and for their protestations
of continued loyalty to the Government ; but told them
that they must stay with him in Kumasi instead of returning to their own districts to arm themselves, as they had
asked to do, so that their own people and the Kumasis
might all see that they were on the side of the Government. Next evening, however, the King of Aguna returned
with Linguists representing the other Kings, and said that
they were afraid to stay, as they had heard that the
Kumasis intended to attack their people ; but the Governor
told them plainly that any King who left would do so as
the declared enemy of the Government, and they made
no further demur.

On the 13th, the Governor heard that Osai Kanyasi,
the Chief of the Owiku or Royal Tribe, and some of the
other Chiefs were anxious to come in and make their peace,
and his nephew Kofi Sencheri, one of the two Kumasi
Chiefs who had remained loyal, came to the Governor to
treat on his behalf, and was told that if Osai Kanyasi
would send his Linguist terms would be offered him. Two
days later Yow Wua, who had formerly been detained in
Elmina as a political prisoner and released in 1893, mentioned that he had seen Osai Kanyasi in the town that
morning, and later in the day reported that he had again
come in and was then in his house. A Hausa guard under
Captains Houston and Armitage was therefore sent down
to arrest him, and he was removed to the fort. He was
released on parole the next day and handed over to the
Kings of Mampon, Jabin and Aguna, who undertook to be
personally responsible for him.

The day before the arrest of Osai Kanyasi, the loyal
Kings had been given permission to attend a meeting of
the insurgent Chiefs to which they had been invited, and

they now returned and reported that the Kumasis and their adherents were at present divided into two parties. A certain number of them, led by Osai Kanyasi, were anxious to surrender and return to their allegiance if they were assured of pardon, while the others, who were the more numerous, were determined to continue hostilities unless the Government agreed to their terms. These were —first, that Prempi should be given back and regulate the collection of any annual payment that was to be made ; second, that they should be allowed to buy and sell slaves, as in the past ; third, that no further demands should be made on them for the supply of carriers ; fourth, that they should no longer be required to build houses or supply thatch ; and fifth, that all the strangers and petty traders in the town should be sent away.

These terms, of course, were ridiculous ; but they are of interest as showing the chief causes of Ashanti discontent. The Governor, after expressing surprise that the Kings should have allowed themselves to be made use of to bring such a message to him at all, told them that so far as Prempi was concerned he had already given his final decision at the meeting on the 28th ; that slavery in Ashanti had been definitely abolished in 1896, and that whether they thought human beings no better than cattle to be bought and sold as suited their convenience or not, the Government never did, and never would so regard them ; that they would still be required to supply carriers and find labour and materials for building, but that, since his arrival in Kumasi he had found that some hardship was caused in this way, and that he would therefore find a remedy and alter the regulations accordingly ; but that, so far as the traders from the coast were concerned, Kumasi was now a part of the British Empire, throughout which all were free to live and trade in peace, and he had no intention of making any local exception to this rule. The Kings were then forbidden to hold any further communication with the Kumasi party, and told to refer any messengers who might arrive in future to the Governor. The next day messengers did arrive, and were duly sent away by the Kings.

Nothing more could be done until after the arrival of reinforcements. The Governor had now removed to the fort, and the Ashantis had established themselves in large camps around the northern, eastern, and southern sides of the town beyond the swamp, where they could be heard singing and drumming every night ; but they had not yet closed the roads nor interfered with traders. Food was still brought to the market, though in daily diminishing quantities, and Messrs. Daw and Leslie Gordon of the Ashanti Goldfields Corporation at Obuasi were able to visit the Governor and returned unmolested on the 18th, with Mr. Wilkinson and Captain Houston, who was proceeding on leave. Captain Armitage was appointed Acting Resident in his place. Very little definite news could be obtained of what was going on outside the town ; but it was rumoured that Captain Parmeter had been attacked at Sekredumasi on his way down from the Northern Territories and been compelled to return to Kintampo, that the Basel Mission native catechist at Sekredumasi and his wife had been seized and " put in log," and that a number of other isolated individuals had been either murdered or made prisoners. It was also rumoured that the Kokofus were divided in their allegiance, that his Chiefs had compelled Asibi to reject the offer of the Golden Stool, and that they intended to depose him immediately the present troubles were over. He himself was said to be contemplating flight to Asamoa Kwami, the Chief in command of the Ashanti camp at Kasi, and was therefore kept under strict observation. Later, on the 21st, it was reported that he intended to escape during the night, and he was therefore arrested and brought into the fort. The Kokofu Chiefs then in town came to thank the Governor for having thus rid them of Asibi, and elected Kwamin Esil to succeed him.

When the Governor arrived in Kumasi, there was a long-standing dispute about the succession to the stool of Insuta, which was one of the matters that he had intended to settle during his visit. The claimants were Kobina Intim and Kwesi Berikum. Both were of royal blood, and on this ground, at any rate, Kwesi Berikum had the better claim ; but his rival had the stronger following and was much the finer man. Kwesi Berikum, in fact, was rather deficient in intellect. As neither party would give way to the other however, the Governor had suggested to the Chiefs that they should bring forward a third candidate, and they had produced Yow Mafo. Kwesi Berikum's party then gave way, and said that they had no objection to offer to Yow Mafo's enstoolment ; but Kobina Intim, after some hesitation, refused to withdraw his claim. It was then suggested that Yow Mafo should be enstooled and that Kobina Intim should " stand next to the stool " and succeed him. The King of Mampon was asked to use his influence with Intim to secure his consent to this arrangement, but failed, and matters were at a standstill when the first signs of rebellion broke out, and Intim settled the question of the succession once and for all by joining the rebels, while Yow Mafo stood loyally by the Government. Fortunately, the whole of the regalia of Insuta had been brought into the fort for safe keeping during the negotiations, and Yow Mafo was soon afterwards duly enstooled.

On the 18th of April the first reinforcements, 100 Hausas under Captain J. M. Middlemist the Acting Inspector-General of the Gold Coast Constabulary, marched in from Accra, and it was decided to try to drive out the insurgents from Kasi and the other villages close to Kumasi, or, if these places were found deserted to burn them. On Monday the 21st therefore, Captains Marshall and Leggett, with a Native Officer, Medical Officer, and seventy-three non-commissioned officers and men went to Asim and Abekum, two villages distant fifteen and twenty-five minutes respectively from Kumasi, and burned them without meeting with any opposition. The next morning Captain Middlemist went out with Captains Marshall and Bishop, Doctor Hay, and 100 Hausas to Kasi, which they burned and levelled with the ground. They saw only one armed Ashanti, whom the advance-guard shot, and then went on to Adeabiba, which was also burnt, and brought back twenty Ashantis whom they found there prisoners to Kumasi.

On the 23rd Captains Marshall and Bishop, with Doctor Hay, Native Officer Akere, 104 Hausas and 50 carriers, left Kumasi soon after daybreak to destroy Kwaman ; but Yow Wua, who accompanied the column as guide, misunderstood his instructions and took them along the Ejisu road towards another village called Kwamo. The Governor, however, had information that the rebels were in force on this road, and, so soon as he discovered the mistake that had been made, sent a soldier with a letter to recall Captain Marshall. The warning was sent too late however, for the messenger had not long been gone when heavy firing was reported on the Ejisu road. A number of wounded civilian Hausas began to straggle into Kumasi soon afterwards, and a little later the column returned by the Mampon road. Captain Marshall, who was carried in wounded, then reported that he had been ambushed just outside Fomosua, where the Ashantis had suddenly poured in a terrific fire along the whole length of the column, which they maintained for three-quarters of an hour, in spite of the steady volleys of the Hausas. Many of the men had now been either killed or wounded, and the greatest confusion was caused by a number of civilian Hausas from the Zongo, who, contrary to orders, had followed the column armed only with spears and swords in the hope of loot, and now rushed in amongst the men for protection. A retreat was therefore ordered to Odomu ; but the enemy maintained their fire throughout the whole length of the road, and were found to be holding the outskirts of that village also. They were dislodged, however, in about ten minutes, and no further opposition, beyond a few shots fired at the rear-guard, was then met with. The casualties were very heavy : Native Officer Akere, three corporals and one private had been killed, and all three officers and fifty-five rank and file wounded. Akere's body, over which Doctor Hay and Sergeant Amadu Fulani had stood under a heavy fire and fully twenty yards from the head of the column until a hammock could be brought up, was carried back to Kumasi and buried in the Government cemetery at Bantama.

This unfortunate affair naturally encouraged the enemy, who drew in closer to the town and sent a detachment round to close the Cape Coast road and cut the telegraph wire : not, however, before the Governor had got another urgent message through asking for further reinforcements from Northern Nigeria.

On Wednesday the 25th of April it was evident that the town was completely and closely surrounded. People going down to the water supply in the early morning had been fired on and some of them captured. The Basel missionaries also sent down a letter reporting that the Ashantis were closing in on Bantama and were already within a few hundred yards of their house, and, when Captain Armitage started up the road to see for himself what was happening, he met Mr. and Mrs. Ramseyer on their way to the fort. They and the four other missionaries who followed them were temporarily lodged in the officers' quarters near the cantonments ; but later in the day they were removed to the fort, and Messrs. David and Grundy of the Ashanti Company, who were staying in the town, were also called in. An outpost that had been stationed at Bantama to reassure the missionaries was withdrawn, and Captain Middlemist extended his men across the road and as far as the prison, while the soldiers' wives and children from the cantonments and the people living in the Saltpond, Cape Coast, and Fanti Lines [1] left their houses with everything they could carry, and sat down under the walls of the fort.

The Ashantis had now occupied the Basel Mission buildings and Saltpond lines, whence they poured in a heavy fire on the officers' quarters, while a larger party tried to pass round between the cantonments and the swamp, in order to get into some long grass between the fort and quarters and cut off the retreat of the defenders.

[1] The Saltpond lines were houses on the left of the Bantama road beyond the cantonments ; the Cape Coast lines were on the road to Cape Coast in Asafu, and the Fanti lines between them and the fort.

This party, however, was driven back by volleys from the road.   About midday the King of Aguna and Yow Mafo volunteered to lead their loyal Ashantis against the enemy. They were accompanied by Captain Armitage, and quickly drove the rebels out of the Saltpond lines, but were then exposed to such a heavy fire from the Basel Mission buildings and the bush on the right of the road that they were compelled to retire.   They fell back slowly, while a maxim-gun at the officers' quarters covered their retreat, and the Ashantis then re-occupied the Saltpond lines and part of the cantonments.

Meanwhile bodies of the enemy were pressing in on other sides of the town.   One strong detachment forced its way into the civilian Hausa Zongo beyond the swamp and set it on fire, while its inhabitants fled terror-stricken to the fort for shelter.   A few rounds of shrapnel from a 7-pounder soon drove the enemy back, and Kobina Kokofu, one of the few loyal Kumasi Chiefs, was then sent with a party of his men to see if he could save at least a portion of the Zongo ; but it was too late, the dry wattle and grass huts burned like tinder, and the whole place was quickly destroyed.   Another detachment crossed the swamp from the Cape Coast road and occupied the Fanti and Cape Coast lines, but was temporarily driven back across the swamp by Kwachi Inkatia the Chief of Mansu-Inkwanta and his men, with heavy loss to themselves and at the cost of twenty of Inkatia's men killed and twice as many wounded. Night was now closing in, and the troops were all withdrawn ; the gate of the gaol was thrown open and the prisoners, forty-three in number, were released, and the hospital and officers' quarters evacuated, leaving the enemy in possession of everything except the fort itself and the cleared space around it that was covered by the guns.   During the day's fighting two Hausas had been killed and Captain Leggett again slightly wounded.

Earlier in the day the gate of the fort had been left open and the refugees merely kept back by the guard ; but as their number grew and the gradual retirement of the

troops increased their alarm, the order was given for it to
be closed and barred. This was only accomplished with
difficulty ; for at the first sign of what was intended, the
refugees, of whom there were now fully 3,000, made a mad
rush for the gateway, carrying Captain Middlemist along
with them and nearly crushing the life out of him in their
terror, before the Governor succeeded in dragging him
inside, and the guard, after a tremendous struggle, closed
and secured the gate. A cordon of sentries was then
posted round the crowd of refugees, while others had to be
brought up to the verandah of the fort to beat back with
the butts of their carbines those who tried to enter by
climbing the posts supporting it.

" The scene which was presented from the verandah
of the Residency that night beggars description. The
blazing houses in the cantonments and Fanti and Cape
Coast lines, some of which the rebels had fired, cast a lurid
light upon the surging mass of humanity clustering round
the fort walls, from which arose the wailing of women and
the pitiful crying of little children, who wept with their
mothers out of sympathy, without knowing of the danger
realised by their elders. Beyond and around this terror-
stricken crowd stood the Hausas, seemingly indifferent to
their surroundings, but, in spite of their long day's fight,
as alert as ever. Occasionally a Hausa woman would force
her way through the crowd to bring food and water to
her lord and master, while round the cordon walked the
white officers, and that fine old native officer, Mr. Hari
Zenoah, who had grown grey in the Government service,
praising here, reprimanding there, while keeping up the
spirits of his men. Every now and then, amid a whirlwind
of sparks, some thatch roof would fall in, converting the
four ' swish ' walls of the house into a white-hot furnace.
Away across the swamp glowed the embers of the burned
civilian Hausa town, occasionally lighting up the Wesleyan
Mission buildings, as yet untouched by the Ashantis. Behind all towered the blank wall of forest which surrounds
Kumasi, from which were borne the triumphant shouts of
the rebels, who had at last caged the white man within the

narrow limits of his fort walls. It was a night never to be forgotten." [1]

The next day it was expected that the attack would be renewed ; but although the Ashantis could be seen passing backwards and forwards in the cantonments and towards Bantama, they made no movement against the fort, and the carriers were therefore sent out under escort to save the drugs, dressings and other medical stores that had had to be abandoned when the sick were removed from the hospital. The water-bottles, clothing and other equipment were removed from the military store at the same time. Water also had to be fetched from the spring below the fort, for to have supplied all the refugees from the well with a windlass and bucket would have been impossible. Fortunately, the Ashantis made no effort to prevent this, being satisfied that they were bound to starve out the garrison, and therefore unwilling to take unnecessary risks, and water was fetched twice daily throughout the siege. Sanitary arrangements, too, had to be made for the refugees, and, since no food was now obtainable, the issue of the reserve rations to the troops was begun. Trenches were also dug around the fort, with shelters behind them for the Hausas, and the men told off to their positions for the defence.

That night a tornado, accompanied by a deluge of rain, burst over the fort and still further increased the misery of the unfortunate refugees. Warned by this, they spent the greater part of the next day in building themselves shelters of any materials they could find. Some of the more daring even went as far as the Fanti or Cape Coast lines, and, lifting the thatch bodily off the huts, staggered back and propped it up on forked posts. Others used cloths, hides or anything else they could find that would afford a little protection. A miniature town thus sprang up in a few hours, the only restrictions being that the gate of the fort must be left clear, that the shelters must be kept low enough not to interfere with the working of the guns, and that no fires must be lit in the houses, but all

[1] Armitage and Montanaro, p. 32.

cooking done outside on the road. Some difficulty was experienced at first in enforcing this last order, but the demolition of a few shelters as a punishment soon showed the people that it would have to be obeyed. The Ashantis meanwhile had been seen still busily moving about in the direction of Bantama and in the cantonments, though it was impossible to discover what they were doing. Later in the day a party came down and set fire to the thatch roofs of the prison buildings and evidently intended to destroy the hospital and officers' quarters also ; but these were within range of the fort, and they were easily driven off. Others were seen to have occupied the Wesleyan Mission house near the swamp on the Kintampo road, and to be making a large camp behind it.

Next morning, Sunday the 29th of April, the Ashantis were found to have loop-holed the walls of the houses in the cantonments that faced the fort, and to have occupied the prison, hospital and officers' quarters, from which they were busy removing the beds, doors and shutters. A few shots, however, cleared them out from the European buildings, and they then retired into a hollow behind the hospital, where they were screened from view and kept up an intermittent fire on the fort throughout the morning. Later however, they re-occupied these buildings and com- menced a heavy fire from them and the cantonments on the fort and the Hausas drawn up in front of the loyal natives. They were evidently determined to push their attack home, and came out more than once into the open, but were repulsed each time with heavy loss by the fire of the maxims. Several rounds of shrapnel fired into the prison and cantonments, and maxim fire directed against the hospital and quarters having failed to dislodge them, the troops advanced at midday and soon drove them out of these buildings, across the hollow behind the hospital— where it was found that they had built small stockades with the hospital beds, doors, shutters, and furniture from the Basel Mission—and half-way through the cantonments, before they were recalled to the trenches on account of an alarm of attack from the direction of the Cape Coast road. This however proved false, and the King of Aguna, representing the loyal Chiefs, then asked to be allowed to follow up this victory with their men and drive the Ashantis out of the cantonments and Basel Mission. They were engaged by the enemy about half-way through the cantonments, and for about half an hour could advance no farther, until Captain Armitage, who had accompanied them, passed round with a detachment on the swamp side and surprised and outflanked the Ashantis, who were found massed behind the houses in the Saltpond lines. The allies then dashed forward and, having once got the enemy on the run, gave them no chance to rally, but, after clearing them out of the Basel Mission buildings, swept right on into Bantama before they were recalled by a note from the Governor, who expected to be attacked by the Queen of Ejisu's men.

It was now seen what the Ashantis had been so busy about for the past few days ; for besides building their stockades behind the hospital and loop-holing the houses in the cantonments, they had broken large holes through the party walls of these houses, so that they could pass from one to the other without exposing themselves, and had completely gutted the Basel Mission house. The missionaries had evidently been well supplied, for " hundreds of empty wine and beer bottles lay scattered about, while tins containing preserved meats, vegetables and groceries had been battered open and their contents either eaten or strewn over the ground. The furniture was broken up into matchwood, and two harmoniums had been disembowelled. Window-sashes and doors torn from their hinges, books and papers rent to fragments, plates and glasses smashed to bits, told of the wild orgy enacted during the night of the 25th." [1] The Ashantis, as usual, carried off many of their dead, amongst whom was Osai Kujo Krum, one of the Kumasi Chiefs, but left 150 on the field and must have had many more wounded. The Hausas, however, only had two men killed and ten wounded, and the losses of the loyal Ashantis did not amount to

[1] Armitage and Montanaro, p. 41.

more than twenty wounded, while they also captured about 200 loads of plantains and yams in Bantama and carried them back in triumph to their camp in the Resident's garden outside the right face of the fort.   Another result of this action was to keep a large body of the enemy occupied and thus prevent any possibility of their joining the Ashantis on the Cape Coast road ; for the arrival of the Lagos column was hourly expected.

Meanwhile a dozen or more wounded Ashantis, whom their comrades had been unable to remove when they were driven out of the European buildings, had taken refuge in the Constabulary store-room,[1] and, while the fighting was going on at Bantama, a crowd of Hausas, civilian refugees and carriers had followed the firing-line in search of plunder. The carriers had discovered these wounded men and, entering the store, hacked them literally to pieces with their blunt machets until the place was a perfect shambles, with blood and brains spattered all over the floor and walls and even on the ceiling.   They were just completing this barbarous business and setting fire to the Ashantis' cloths when Captain Armitage, on his way back to the fort, was attracted by the women and children who had crowded round the windows and door cheering and applauding them.   He dashed in and scattered the murderers, but was too late to save any of their wretched victims ; for the last survivor, at whom they were hacking as he sat propped up against the wall feebly trying to defend himself with one maimed arm, rolled over dead just after he entered.

[1] The present orderly room.

CHAPTER XXIII

THE GARRISON REINFORCED

1900

At six o'clock on the evening of the action at Bantama, the 29th of April, the sound of firing was heard on the Cape Coast road and the Lagos column marched in. Immediately the requisition for troops had been received, 250 men under Captain J. G. O. Aplin, C.M.G., the Inspector-General of the Lagos Constabulary, with Captains E. C. Cochrane and B. M. Read, Lieutenant Ralph, Doctor Macfarlane and two maxims and a 7-pounder had been got ready and sailed in the *Lagoon* to Cape Coast, where they arrived on the 19th of April. An officer and fifty men had been landed at Accra, which had been practically depleted of troops when Captain Middlemist left, but at the last moment a telegram had been received reporting the serious state of affairs in Kumasi, and these men had been brought back from the cantonments—nearly four miles from the landing-place—and re-embarked. No time was lost at Cape Coast : carriers had been got ready in advance, and the troops landed at once and marched at nine o'clock the same night. In spite of all precautions, however, some of the carriers managed to abandon their loads and desert ; but the column pushed on, leaving a non-commissioned officer and twenty-five men to bring on these loads as soon as fresh carriers could be got. Prasu was reached on the 23rd, and a halt was made to allow these carriers and their escort to close up. They came in the next day, and on the 25th the column crossed the Pra and entered Esumeja on the evening of the 27th. Here Mr. Branch, the Acting

Director of Telegraphs, was found swathed in bandages and lying on a native bed in the rest-house.

Mr. Branch had been inspecting the line and, on his arrival at Prasu, found that communication between there and Kumasi was interrupted and located the break at Esiagu, a village just beyond the Oda River. Leaving his baggage at Esumeja, he had gone out with his eight hammock-men and two native linesmen to repair the damage and had nearly reached Esiagu when the Ashantis suddenly poured in a volley from the side of the path. The four men who were carrying him fell, either killed or seriously wounded, while the others at once ran into the bush and made their way to one of the Kokofu villages, where they reported what had happened to the Chief. A slug passed through Mr. Branch's helmet, but beyond a bad shaking by his fall he himself was unhurt. As he stood up, however, he was seized by the Ashantis, who cruelly beat him on the soles of his feet with lengths of telegraph wire that they had cut from the line. At last they left him, and he managed to escape into the bush ; but they fired after him and wounded his dog, which, running off yelping in a different direction, drew them away and allowed him to escape. Though in great pain, he managed to crawl a little way back towards Esumeja, and then hid himself in the bush while he bound up his bruised and bleeding feet with strips torn from his shirt, and found a stout stick before continuing his journey. As he passed through the next village he was mobbed and jeered at by the men and pelted with stones and filth by the children, but not otherwise molested, and soon afterwards met a party of loyal Kokofus. They had been sent out by the Chief to find him, and carried him back to Esumeja in a hammock improvised out of their cloths.

The next morning, the 28th, Mr. Branch was provided with a hammock and taken on with the column. The Chief had warned Captain Aplin that the Ashantis were preparing to attack him at Esiagu, but when a halt was made at the Oda River, the scouts could find no trace of the enemy and he pushed on. Suddenly a terrific fire was poured into the main body from all sides, and though this was returned by the Hausas, maxims, and 7-pounder, it was fully twenty minutes before any advance could be made. Then the Ashantis made another determined stand about a quarter of a mile farther up the road and, when driven back, retired to and tried to hold Esiagu, from which they had to be driven with the bayonet. One Hausa had been killed, and four officers and seventeen rank and file wounded, two of them mortally, and, as it was now two o'clock and the wounded needed attention, Captain Aplin decided to put Esiagu in a state of defence and halt there for the night.

The next day no opposition was met with until, after crossing another stream and passing through the ruins of Kasi, the rear-guard was heavily attacked about three miles from Kumasi. The enemy, estimated to be about 8,000 strong, occupied the bush on both sides of the path, while others were posted in trees, and the whole column was surrounded. Fortunately, the Ashantis fired wildly and most of their slugs flew high; but they disputed every inch of ground, and after fighting continuously for between five and six hours, the column had only advanced about a mile. Then the Ashantis' fire suddenly slackened and the Hausas dashed forward, only to find that the enemy had retired behind a huge cotton-tree that had been felled across the path about fifty yards beyond its next turn. Fire was opened on this with a maxim and the 7-pounder, but the range was so short that the men serving them were shot down almost at once and had to be repeatedly replaced. The rear-guard was therefore brought up and ordered to charge. Captain Read, who was leading, received four wounds and had his right arm badly broken, but struggled on to within a few yards of the tree before he found that nearly the whole of his men had been shot down and he was forced to retire, being wounded once more in the head a moment later. The men were now tired out and getting disheartened, and both maxims jammed; the men's carbines, too, were so hot that they could hardly hold them. The ammunition for the 7-pounder too, was exhausted, and the gun had to be loaded with stones and gravel hurriedly scraped up from the path. In fact, the position was becoming momentarily more desperate, when Captain Cochrane, though severely wounded in the shoulder, volunteered to lead a flanking party through the bush, and, taking twenty-five men with him, succeeded in getting close to the enemy without being seen and poured in three well-directed volleys. These so startled the Ashantis that they hesitated for a moment ; but before they had time to recover from their astonishment, the Hausas on the road had taken advantage of the lull in their fire to charge up and were scrambling over the tree into their midst with fixed bayonets. This proved too much for the enemy, and they turned and fled.

Unfortunately the Hausas pushed on so rapidly after carrying this position that the gun had to be abandoned, for, with Captain Read and the gunners all severely wounded and no one to help them, it was found impossible to lift it over the tree. The expenditure of ammunition, too, had been so enormous that the column arrived in Kumasi, where ammunition was sorely needed, with less than forty rounds a man and no 7-pounder ammunition at all.

No further opposition was met with, and a few minutes later the column, advancing at the double, was met at the entrance into Kumasi by Captain Armitage and Doctor Chalmers at the head of the loyal Ashantis and passed up to the fort. The casualties were very heavy : three officers wounded, two of them severely ; and two non-commissioned officers and men killed and 130 wounded. This brought the total casualties for the two days' fighting to six officers wounded, five rank and file killed or since dead, and 139 wounded out of a total force of six officers and 250 men. The enemy's losses must also have been very heavy, for the bush was reported to be strewn with their dead, and several of their Chiefs had been either killed or wounded.

The terrible expenditure of ammunition, amounting to 70,000 rounds or over 260 rounds a man, in the two days'

fighting, together with the desertion of many of the carr
which had made it impossible to bring on 6,000 pound
rice that had been ordered up, rather detracted from
advantages of the arrival of this reinforcement ; for t
were now all these extra men to be supplied with amm
tion and food from the rapidly diminishing reserve in
fort.   The successful engagement of the 29th, howe
had cleared the Ashantis away from the town itself
enabled many of the buildings to be re-occupied and s
improvements to be made in the immediate surround
of the fort.   Half the cantonments were still undama
and the Gold Coast Hausas now returned there, while
Lagos Constabulary occupied the prison stockade.   F
these positions were further strengthened by sh
trenches, which were manned night and day, and ano
trench was dug commanding the hollow behind the hos
and protecting the officers' quarters, which were also
occupied.   The refugees, too, were moved away from
walls of the fort and camped on the ground betwee
and the quarters.   The awful stench which arose from
large a concourse of people crowded together in a s
space for many days, combined with their constant cha
by day and night, had made their presence so near the
absolutely intolerable.   For days past it had been
possible to open the windows of the Residency, and
removal of these people to some other camping gro
within the protected area was therefore imperative.   F
daily grew scarcer and scarcer ; for the Ashantis, fin
that their fire was quite ineffective against the fort,
that any attempt to advance over the open ground
take it by storm was impossible in the face of maxim
had now changed their tactics and settled down to c
every road and, by cutting off the supply of food, st
the garrison out.   A small daily ration of corned beef
hard biscuit was served out to the Europeans and troo
but after having been stored for four years in a trop
climate, the beef was often found covered with a t
layer of green mould when the tins were opened, and
biscuits were full of weevils.   The only livestock at

commencement of the siege consisted of five cows and two sheep, which were slaughtered at intervals of three days and did not last long. The auxiliaries and refugees had to find food as best they could : the supplies they had captured at Bantama were soon exhausted, and they were then dependent on such edible roots and leaves as they could obtain in and about Kumasi, and anything their foraging parties could raid from the surrounding plantations. These plantations, however, were so well watched by the Ashanti pickets that the men who ventured out on such quests were more often than not either killed, or had to be helped back by their comrades wounded and bleeding ; yet from time to time they were successful, and thus contrived to save themselves from actual starvation.

On the day after the arrival of the Lagos column, spies reported that the Ashantis had not re-occupied their stockade on the Cape Coast road, nor even removed their dead, and Captain Armitage therefore proposed to the Governor that 100 men should be left to hold the fort, while the remainder of the force escorted him and Lady Hodgson to Prasu and then returned to keep the road open for the relief column. After some discussion, however, the suggestion was rejected, mainly because it was thought that the relieving force must arrive within a few days, and that it was not therefore worth while to incur any risk of being attacked on the road.

The Governor's refusal to leave when he had the chance, however, was not allowed to blind the garrison to the possibility that it might even yet be necessary for them to fight their way out of Kumasi if the expected relief failed to reach them in time, and in preparation for such an emergency some reserve of ammunition and food had to be kept. After the arrival of the Lagos Constabulary, however, there were only 78,000 rounds available for the 480 Hausas in Kumasi, and the necessity for making this last as long as possible, and at the same time keeping a reserve for a possible march to the coast, naturally had the double effect of preventing the garrison from pushing home their attacks on the enemy when they were forced to go out in search of food, and encouraging the Ashantis in the belief that they were at least fully able to hold their own.

On the 2nd of May it was decided to attack the Ashantis who held the Wesleyan Mission house and the stockade they had built to the right of it. Five shells were thrown into the stockade from the gaol, and the loyal Ashantis, who had previously marched down to a spot near the swamp with Captain Armitage, then advanced against the position, while a party of twenty-five Hausas guarded the Mampon road. They had got within about a hundred yards of the mission house when they suddenly found themselves exposed to a heavy fire from a second stockade which had been built across the road on its left, but was invisible from the fort. They pushed on, however, for another fifty yards, keeping up a steady fire, but could go no farther. Captain Armitage therefore sent for a 7-pounder, which arrived just as his men were about to retreat, and, after firing a few rounds of shell, the Hausas from the Mampon road were called up and ordered to fix bayonets and lead a charge against the position. They got within twenty yards of it; but the enemy's fire was so heavy and continuous that they were forced to halt, and, as it was evident that the Ashantis were bringing up reinforcements and threatening to cut off their retreat across the swamp, they were ordered to retire. Only one loyal Ashanti was killed, but fifty more and five Hausas were wounded. Two days later the Ashantis burned the Wesleyan Mission and moved their stockade farther up the road.

On the 6th Captain Middlemist died. He had been ill with fever for several days, and it was believed that his end was accelerated by internal injuries that he may have received when he was caught in the mad rush of the terrified refugees at the fort gate. He was buried the same afternoon under a small clump of trees behind the fort.

On the 9th, the loyal Ashantis, supported by twenty Lagos Hausas under Captain Cochrane, attacked the enemy on the north-west of the town in the hope of obtaining food ; but they were driven back, and a rather stronger party that was sent out the next day was equally unsuccessful, principally because it was impossible to spare sufficient ammunition to enable such attacks to be pressed home by a large enough force.

On the 11th, the loyal Chiefs asked permission to open negotiations with the enemy, saying that they thought they might be able to restore peace. This was considered extremely doubtful ; but they were allowed to make the attempt, more especially because it was hoped that they might succeed in obtaining some supplies of food. They chose the mother and father of the King of Kokofu as their messengers, and sent them to the camp on the Mampon road, where Bodu, the Ejisu War Captain, had his headquarters. They were to tell the Chiefs that the loyal Kings begged them to lay down their arms so as to save Ashanti from being overrun by the Government troops, who must assuredly arrive before long, and to say that the Acting Resident was willing to meet them and lay their grievances before the Governor. The messengers returned the next morning with Bodu's answer, that for the present the Ashantis' terms were identical with those that had been offered through the King of Mampon, but that he was sending to all the camps summoning the Chiefs to a meeting, which he hoped the loyal Kings would attend. They, however, refused to visit the camp, but offered to send representatives, at the same time pointing out that it was for the Kumasis and their supporters to save their country from being ravaged by fire and sword by accepting the Governor's terms, rather than to dictate terms themselves. The Chiefs agreed to receive the Kings' representatives and " drink fetish " with them preparatory to declaring an armistice, and the chosen men, each of whom was a near relative of the King he represented, crossed over to the Mampon road camp on the morning of the 13th.

Fetish was then drunk and an armistice declared, while the Chiefs sent several loads of food to the Kings, and promised to supply more, saying that they were fighting against the white man only, and did not want them to

suffer.   That evening a refugee who had gone out in search
of food was fired on and killed ; but the Ashantis at once
sent in messengers to explain that the men who had shot
him were unaware of the agreement that had just been
made, and that instructions were being sent immediately
to all the camps.   With this single exception, the explanation of which was perfectly reasonable and doubtless true,
the Ashantis, with their customary honour in such matters,
faithfully observed the armistice.   The refugees and
carriers brought in large quantities of food from the
Bantama side without any attempt being made to interfere
with them, and the Ashantis themselves began to come in
with the promised supplies at noon on the 15th.   This was
the signal for a wild rush of carriers and refugees, who,
half maddened by the sight of food in their starving condition, ran down towards the swamp in such haste that the
Ashanti women who were carrying it were frightened and
turned back.   Order, however, was quickly restored by a
few Hausas under Captain Marshall, and fully 200 loads of
plantains must have been purchased, when suddenly the
sound of the discharge of a 7-pounder gun was heard on
the Kintampo road, and within a few minutes the head of
a column of Hausas appeared on the brow of the hill.
These were the men from the Northern Territories under
Major Morris, D.S.O., who had arrived long before they
were expected, and were welcomed with the wildest enthusiasm by the refugees as they marched up to the fort.

It was the attack made on Captain Parmeter that was
responsible for the early arrival of this force ; for the
District Commissioner at Kintampo had then sent to inform
Major Morris that there was a general rising of the Ashantis
and that he feared his station might be attacked.   Major
Morris had then started with every available man to
reinforce Kintampo, and had already reached Zantana
when he received the Governor's telegram asking for help
in Kumasi.

Captain Parmeter had been invalided from Gambaga,
and was on his way home.   By the time he reached
Kintampo at the end of March he was very much better,

and, after a few days' rest there, left for Kumasi with
Dresser Lampty, reaching Inkoranza on the 3rd of April.
There he met Mr. Rainsford, the District Commissioner,
who was on his way up from Kumasi to Kintampo. On
the 4th he resumed his journey to Kumasi, and, when he
halted for lunch at Inkwanta, found a large meeting just
breaking up, while the Chief was insolent when asked to
supply a man to replace one of the carriers who was sick.
After lunch the carriers were sent on ahead, and Captain
Parmeter followed about a quarter of an hour later in his
hammock ; but on reaching the stream that forms the
boundary between Inkoranza and Ashanti, he found all
the carriers sitting down, and they told him that they had
stopped because they had met two traders who said they
had been robbed at Sekredumasi, while they themselves
had caught sight of three men with guns on the path ahead.
Captain Parmeter ordered them on again, but on reaching
a stream near Sekredumasi called a short halt to rest them
and let them drink while the headman went on as usual
to prepare a house for him. The others soon followed,
but the carriers again halted before the village was reached,
saying that they had seen more men with guns on the path
in front, and while Captain Parmeter was trying to start
them again four shots rang out in the direction of Sekredumasi. Though it was not, of course, known until afterwards that these shots announced the murder of the
headman, they were enough for the carriers, who at once
turned back, dropped their loads, and ran away.

Even now Captain Parmeter did not suspect that anything was wrong. Nothing really unusual had happened :
carriers are ever ready to make excuses to loiter on the
road, and the duty of carrying a sick man's load for him is
never sought after ; meetings in villages are of constant
occurrence, and neither insolence from a small village
Chief nor highway robberies are very unusual, while small
parties of hunters with their guns can be met any day on
the roads in Ashanti. Captain Parmeter therefore collected what carriers he could with the help of his hammock-
men and then sent his orderly back to find the others. He

never saw him again ; but sufficient carriers had now been collected to take up all the loads but two, and he started to look for the orderly and missing men. Two carriers who were sent back to fetch the loads that had been left behind came running back with them, and reported that there were now large numbers of armed men on the road and that others were moving off into the bush on either side. Lampty then turned round and saw them coming, while Captain Parmeter jumped out of his hammock and was at once greeted with a volley, the slugs whistling over his head. A couple of shots from his revolver sent the Ashantis into the bush, but only to reappear as soon as they had had time to reload, when they again advanced down the path. Captain Parmeter therefore fired his remaining four shots, and then, finding that the barrel of his revolver had burst and that there was nothing else to be done, turned and fled. Round the first bend in the path he fell heavily, and this, in his weak condition, quite knocked him out. He tried to struggle on, but had to sit down twice, and finally turned into the forest and lay down about twenty yards from the path utterly exhausted. Lampty very pluckily stood by him, and finding that he really was incapable of going any farther, lay down by his side. He had barely done so when a number of Ashantis dashed past : a few went on ahead and could be heard firing for some time, while others broke open the loads and began to share the loot. Others, again, who had noticed the tracks where Captain Parmeter had first rested at the side of the path, turned into the bush to look for him. Fortunately, the ground where he finally left the road was rocky, and he had left no traces of his present whereabouts. It was now getting dark, and the searchers soon returned to claim their share of the spoil, while Lampty heard them say that their failure to find the fugitives did not matter, as, after the meeting held at Inkwanta that day, the people of the three villages that they would have to pass through in order to reach Inkoranza were all sworn to kill them.

The Ashantis now went back to Sekredumasi, and Captain

Parmeter and Mr. Lampty, after waiting to see if this was
merely a ruse to draw them from their hiding-place,
cautiously struck deeper into the forest and then turned
to the left in the hope of being able to keep parallel to the
road. They made painfully slow progress, however :
every moment they were either tripped up or caught by
the throat or clothes by creepers and undergrowth, and
their faces and hands were soon scratched and bleeding,
while their clothes hung about them in rags. Over and
over again Captain Parmeter sank down utterly exhausted,
and implored Lampty to leave him and try to save himself,
since he could go no farther ; but Lampty always helped
him to his feet again and flatly refused to move without
him. In the end the only way in which they could make
any progress at all was by Captain Parmeter leaning his
head against Lampty's back and hanging by his hands
from his shoulders, while the latter ploughed a way through
the undergrowth by using his arms like a swimmer. At
last they came to a spot where the bush was so thick that
they could find no way out of it, and sat down to be a
prey to the ants and mosquitoes until day broke.

With the first streaks of dawn they moved off to the
left, hoping to strike the path far from Sekredumasi, and
although they crossed it once by mistake they were fortunately turned back by an unusually dense patch of bush,
and then saw the telegraph wire high up amongst the trees.
Following the path, they soon reached the stream where
the carriers had first halted the day before, and were
eagerly drinking the stagnant water, when they heard the
sound of voices approaching, and barely had time to slip
behind the buttresses of a large cotton-tree before about
eighty armed Ashantis came down the path, crossed the
stream, and ascended the rocky slope on the other side.
It was evident that they were tracking the fugitives by the
prints of Captain Parmeter's boots, and that they would
miss them when they got off the rocky ground. There was
no time to be lost : slipping quietly into the stream,
Captain Parmeter walked backwards for a little distance
on some sand and then, plunging higher up stream, swung

himself up on to a tree that had fallen across it, took off
his boots, and turned into the forest.   It was fortunate
that he did so, for the Ashantis returned almost immediately, and seeing the foot-prints on the sand, began searching through the bush in the opposite direction.

All that day the two fugitives lay hid, with neither food
nor drink, while the Ashantis were scouring the forest all
around them.   From time to time a party of searchers
would pass within a few yards of them, and twice they
moved and lay down again nearer the road.   At seven
o'clock they got up and started along the road by moonlight ; but it was very trying work, for the shadows in
the forest glades deceived them over and over again by
their resemblance to figures.   A little later, however, they
came on real figures, for they suddenly found themselves
in the midst of a party of searchers, who, thinking that
they would never dare to move by moonlight, had stopped
to rest and were sleeping on both sides of the path, and
even on it.   The fugitives, however, picked their way
cautiously through them, and at about two o'clock in the
morning reached a stream, where they had their first drink
for nearly twelve hours and a short rest.   While they were
sitting there a man came down the path, but, when Lampty
tried to stalk him, he ran away.   Lampty, however, called
out to him in the Accra language asking who he was, and
he then came back and proved to be one of the missing
carriers, four more of whom joined them a little later.

Captain Parmeter had been marching all this time
without his boots, in order to avoid being tracked, and was
now so exhausted that he was continually falling, while his
feet were so swollen and tender that he could hardly get
along at all.   The men at first tried to carry him on their
shoulders ; but they were too weak, for they, too, were tired
out and had had nothing to eat.   A little later they found
a small ladder that had been left by the side of the path
by one of the telegraph linesmen and tried to carry him on
that, but he fell asleep and tumbled off before they had
gone far.   However, two of the three villages through
which they had to pass before reaching Inkoranza had now

been got through in safety ; but when they came to the 1900
third they found that some of the carriers who had been CHAP. XXIII
in front had been talking and thus roused the people, who
could be seen moving about outside the houses. Concealment was impossible, for they had already been seen ;
so they put on the boldest front they could and walked
straight on. On reaching the farther end of the village,
however, they found three paths leading out of it, and
Lampty had to ask a man which was the Inkoranza road.
He said he would " ask the Chief," and moved off, while
they, being afraid to risk taking the wrong road, sat down
under a tree in the village street to wait. Everyone
whom they asked for food, water or anything else gave
them the same answer, that he would " ask the Chief," and
last of all Lampty went to his house and fetched him. He
was asked to supply four men and a hammock to carry
Captain Parmeter to Inkoranza, and after seemingly
endless delays a cloth was at last brought and tied to a
pole, but it was so old and rotten that it split as soon as he
got into it and let him fall.

All these excuses and many others were made in order
to allow time for the people to communicate with the last
village ; for the Chief was overheard by one of the carriers
to say that he could not understand how it was that they
had been allowed to pass after the message that had been
sent from Inkwanta. Presently another carrier heard
orders quietly given that they were to be shot as they left
the village, and men with guns were seen stealing off into
the bush on either side of the road. Lampty called out
warning Captain Parmeter what was being done, spelling
out the word " guns " for fear it might be recognized.
He had now found a strong cloth, and the carriers set about
rigging up a hammock, while Lampty, realizing that their
position was desperate and that their only chance lay in
making a bold move at once, went up to the Chief and
said : " There are plenty more white men and plenty more
clerks like myself, and it is very foolish of you to go and
kill us. We know the message you have received, and
we have seen your men go out into the bush to shoot us

on the road. All right, do so ; we are not afraid, my master and I. But you are fools, for remember there are other white men and other clerks, and they will come with soldiers, and who, then, will get the blame ? You in this village, of course. Did those who sent you the message dare to do this thing ? No, of course not." The Chief then asked if they had been seen in the other villages, to which Lampty replied : " Yes, the Chief of Inkwanta was at Kumasi, but I saw the headman in charge, and the Chief of the other village too." [1] This statement so staggered the Chief, and seemed to explain so well what he had hitherto been unable to understand, that he at once sent to recall his men from the bush, and the party, starting about ten minutes later, reached Inkoranza without further trouble.

At Inkoranza the Basel Mission native catechist, Hansen, reported that news of the attempted seizure of the Golden Stool, of the fighting at Bali, and of a general rising of the Ashantis, who had hemmed the Governor in in Kumasi, had already reached the town, and that the King, who had arrived too late for the meeting with the Governor and had left Kumasi soon afterwards, had sent orders to his War Chiefs to join the rebels at once with all their men. A telegram was therefore sent to Mr. Rainsford at Kintampo, warning him of the rising and asking him to send runners at once to Major Morris. The wire was cut outside Inkoranza just after this message got through.

During the King's absence in Kumasi, Inkoranza was, of course, left in charge of the Queen-Mother, who was opposed to her people joining the Ashantis in declaring war against the Government. She and her following, however, were not strong enough to countermand the definite order that had been sent by the King, nor to hold in check the War Chiefs and their party, who were looking forward to gaining possession of several thousand pounds in money and the large quantities of valuable stores that were known to be at Kintampo. She was in a very difficult position, and, consequently, when she was sent for by Captain

[1] Armitage and Montanaro, p. 228.

Parmeter, her answers were evasive and gave him a very false impression of her loyalty. That afternoon, however, a meeting of the Chiefs was held, at which the position of affairs was fully discussed, and it did not take them long to realize that their carelessness in having neglected to cut the wire earlier had now led to the premature discovery of their plans and prevented any possibility of their taking Kintampo by surprise. Several Chiefs, therefore, came over to the Queen-Mother's side, thereby making her party the stronger, and enabling her, when she next saw Captain Parmeter, to tell him that her people would remain loyal and that she had already sent orders to the Inkoranza villages through which he had passed that they were to release any of his carriers whom they had captured and not to close the road.

A message had been sent to Kintampo by the telegraph clerk some time before Captain Parmeter arrived reporting, on the word of his head hammock-man, that he had been lost in the bush, and, the line having now been repaired, the answer was received that Captain Benson was on his way down with an escort of thirteen Hausas and would arrive that night. Captain Parmeter then returned with him to Kintampo, where the officers in the station had a most anxious time preparing the place for defence and keeping guards, for the whole of the surrounding country was very unsettled.

It was not until the 21st of April that the Governor's telegram to Major Morris reached Kintampo, after having been ten days in transit, and even then all the roads to the north were guarded by armed men, and five runners were sent off before one succeeded in getting through. Fortunately, however, Major Morris had already acted on receipt of the first message. This reached Gambaga on the 18th of April, and preparations were at once made for the 340-mile march to Kumasi. In three days everything was ready, and Major Morris left Gambaga on the 22nd with Captains Maguire and Berthon, Doctor Garland, and 170 Hausas of all ranks. They took a 7-pounder and a maxim with them, with 71 shells and seven boxes containing 480 rounds of maxim ammunition in belts, while the men carried 180 rounds of carbine ammunition each, with 11,250 more in reserve.   At this time there was a corps of volunteer native cavalry in the Northern Territories, known as the Moshi Horse, which had been raised by Major Morris and used with success on several occasions against unfriendly tribes.   A troop eighty strong, under Chiefs Derri and Kru Wongara, now accompanied the column.   The march was a very trying one ; for it was terribly hot by day in the shadeless open country through which they had to pass, while tornados accompanied by torrential rain occurred every night.   Nevertheless, with only one day's halt, the column marched into Kintampo in pouring rain on the 5th of May, having covered 238 miles in thirteen marching days.   The runner with the Governor's telegram, as has already been mentioned, had been met at Zantana, six days out from Gambaga.   At Kintampo they were met by a column from Wa under Captain Digan, for a duplicate of the first message to Major Morris had been telegraphed to Boli and sent on from there by runner.   Captain Parmeter, Doctor Graham and Mr. Lampty also joined here, and the full strength of the column was thus brought up to five European officers, one native officer, two medical officers, three native subordinates, 230 Hausas of all ranks, and 82 Moshi Horse, while 214 carriers were employed for the transport.

The King of Inkoranza had now returned to his town. He had been stopped by the Kumasis on his way back and compelled to " drink fetish " with them before they would release him, and his arrival had now strengthened the hands of the war party, who were anxious to attack Kintampo.   The Queen-Mother, however, was still staunchly loyal, and was doing her best to hold the King and his followers in check ; but her own party had been weakened, and pressure was being brought to bear on the King by the Sekredumasis, who had come to Inkoranza and of whom he seemed to be much afraid.   On the 8th a message was brought to Kintampo from the Queen to the effect that, unless help arrived soon, she would be unable to hold out any longer, but would be taken a prisoner to Kumasi. Major Morris therefore telegraphed to her that he was coming to her support with a large force, and asked her to do her utmost to impress upon her people the importance of their remaining loyal.

The column left Kintampo on the 9th and reached Inkoranza soon after midday on the 11th, being met at the entrance to the town by the Queen-Mother and about 300 of her supporters, who expressed the greatest delight at the arrival of the troops. The King was in hiding in the bush, and the Sekredumasis had returned to their village so soon as they heard that soldiers were coming down. Hundreds of men, however, were standing about on the outskirts of the town, and Lampty reported to Doctor Garland that he had discovered a number of loaded guns concealed in the long elephant grass just outside it. It was fairly evident, therefore, that the majority of the Inkoranzas were wavering in their loyalty, and that the force had arrived only just in time to enable them to decide what course they would adopt. The Silver Stool of Inkoranza had been seized by Major Morris immediately on his arrival, but was now formally handed back to the Queen-Mother at a big meeting, at which she was thanked and complimented for her loyalty, and assured that the column required no assistance, but would easily be able to cut its way through to Kumasi. Major Morris afterwards reported to the Governor as follows : " No words can express and no reward be too great for the admirable way in which the princess behaved. The whole of the credit of the non-rising of the Nkoranzas is due to her unswerving fidelity to the British Government, even at the risk of her own life." [1] Events proved that the Inkoranzas remained loyal throughout, and it is indeed fortunate that they did so ; for had they attacked Kintampo with the least determination it must almost certainly have fallen.

On the 11th, after burning Inkwanta, which was found deserted, and destroying the crops, the Ashanti scouts were discovered at about half-past one, but fell back after ex-

[1] Parliamentary Paper, *Ashanti War*, 1900, p. 86.

changing a few harmless shots. Half an hour later the column became engaged just outside Sekredumasi, where the Ashantis occupied a position in some long grass; but the maxim was brought into action, and they retired with heavy loss after about half an hour's fighting. The column, whose only casualties had been one of the Moshi Horse killed and four wounded, then camped in Sekredumasi, where quantities of half-cooked food were found on the fires. The next morning a flying column of 150 men was sent to burn the unfriendly village of Franti, while the remainder of the day was spent in destroying Sekredumasi, including the fetish grove, where the remains of quite recent human sacrifices were discovered. Yenasu was similarly destroyed the next day, and the column camped for the night at Chichiweri and burned it before leaving. Next morning, the 14th, about two and a half hours after leaving Chichiweri, the Moshi Horse, who were at the head of the column, were suddenly attacked by a strong force of Ashantis who were lying in ambush behind the trunk of a large fallen tree. Both their Chiefs fell dead and nine men were wounded, which so demoralized the remainder that they fell back in disorder. The Hausas then opened fire and, with a loss of only two men wounded, cleared the road for the advance. Every village on the road and all the farms were destroyed, but no further opposition was met with, for the Ashantis had decided to concentrate nearer the capital before making another stand. Soon after leaving Buaman on the morning of the 15th, however, a strong stockade was discovered across the road and shelled by the 7-pounder. The Ashantis replied with a heavy fire from the stockade and the bush all around, but after this had been kept up for an hour without intermission it was found that the enemy had been driven from all points except the stockade itself, and Major Morris determined to take it by storm. Ordering his men to fix bayonets, he and Captain Maguire put themselves at their head and charged down the path. Major Morris fell badly wounded, but the position was carried, and the men went on without a check past two more stockades that had been built at short distances behind it, but which the rapid advance of the troops had prevented the enemy from holding. Kumasi was now only twelve miles distant, so after Major Morris and seventeen of the men who had also been wounded had been attended to, the march was resumed, and the Major directed operations from his hammock. No further opposition was met with ; for as they drew nearer to Kumasi they came within the zone of the armistice and found all the stockades unoccupied. Major Morris stayed in the fort, but his officers occupied the Ashanti Syndicate house, and the men were quartered in the Cape Coast lines.

These were the last persons to enter Kumasi before it was relieved, and brought the number of Europeans who had to endure the rigours of the siege up to twenty-nine— or thirty if Captain Middlemist is included—and the strength of the garrison to about 750 of all ranks. The Europeans were :

His Excellency Sir Frederic Hodgson, K.C.M.G., Governor,

Lady Hodgson,

Major Morris, D.S.O., Commanding the troops,

Captain Marshall,[1] West Kent Regiment,

Captain Digan,[1] Connaught Rangers,

Captain Armitage, Travelling Commissioner, Acting Resident,

Captain Parmeter, Inspector, Gold Coast Constabulary,

Captain Bishop, Assistant-Inspector, Gold Coast Constabulary,

Captain Leggett, Assistant-Inspector, Gold Coast Constabulary,

Captain Berthon, Royal Munster Fusiliers, Assistant-Inspector, Gold Coast Constabulary,

Captain Aplin, C.M.G., Inspector-General, Lagos Constabulary,

Captain Cochrane, Assistant-Inspector, Lagos Constabulary,

Captain Read, Assistant-Inspector, Lagos Constabulary,

[1] Special Service Officers.

Mr. Ralph, Assistant-Inspector, Lagos Constabulary,

Dr. Garland, Senior Assistant Colonial Surgeon, Gold Coast,

Dr. Chalmers, Acting Chief Medical Officer, Gold Coast.

Dr. Tweedy, Assistant Colonial Surgeon, Gold Coast,

Dr. Graham, Assistant Colonial Surgeon, Gold Coast,

Dr. Hay, Assistant Colonial Surgeon, Gold Coast,

Dr. Macfarlane, Assistant Colonial Surgeon, Lagos,

Mr. Branch, Clerk-in-charge, Telegraph Department, Gold Coast,

Rev. F. Ramseyer, Basel Mission,

Mrs. Ramseyer, Basel Mission,

Mr. Yöst, Basel Mission,

Mrs. Yöst, Basel Mission,

Mr. Weller, Basel Mission,

Mrs. Haasis, Basel Mission,

Mr. David, Ashanti Company,

Mr. Grundy, Ashanti Company,

and already dead—

Captain Middlemist, Acting Inspector-General, Gold Coast Constabulary.

CHAPTER XXIV

ESCAPE OF THE GOVERNOR'S COLUMN

1900

THE unexpected arrival of the column from the Northern
Territories during the armistice, and at the very moment
when they were supplying the beleaguered garrison with
food, not unnaturally led the Ashantis to believe that the
whole of the negotiations had been purposely arranged
with a view to enabling this strong reinforcement to enter
Kumasi without opposition. They had no idea that the
arrival of the force so soon had been as unexpected by the
Governor as it was by them, but, regarding the whole
arrangement as deliberately treacherous, were furious with
the white men for having deceived them. The civilian
Hausa refugees, too, apparently interpreted the absence
of any opposition to the entry of the column as meaning
that the Ashantis had decided to raise the siege and rushed
up the road to loot their camp. This, however, was more
than the already infuriated Ashantis were likely to put
up with, and the men soon returned even faster than they
had gone, and reported that the enemy had fired on and
killed six of them. Messengers were at once hurried over
to the camp to explain that these men had gone out without
the knowledge of the white man ; but it was too late, the
Ashantis refused to believe it, and told the messengers that
if they came again they would be shot without further
parley. It was most unfortunate that the negotiations
had been broken off in this way, just as there seemed every
prospect of obtaining a good supply of much-needed food ;
for, although the Gambaga Hausas had brought in about

200 rounds of ammunition a man, this was nothing like as much as was needed, and they had only brought enough food to last them for a day or two. Thus, at one stroke, the garrison was increased by over 300 men who must be dependent on its already slender store of food and deprived of the best opportunity it had yet had of increasing the supply.

After consultation with the Governor, Major Morris withdrew the Hausas from the trenches round the fort and re-occupied Asafu and the Basel Mission buildings, but decided that, though he now had a sufficient force, it would not be possible to make any very determined attacks on the enemy, owing to the shortage of ammunition and the necessity for saving most of it in case the garrison had to fight its way out when the rations were exhausted. There were only 170 rounds a man left in Kumasi, and the rations had already had to be reduced. Europeans received one pound of meat and one biscuit daily, while the Hausas had a third of a pound of meat and a biscuit and a half, and the carriers a quarter of a pound of meat and half a biscuit each. On this meagre allowance, eked out with any leaves or roots they could find, they had to subsist ; but the refugees, of course, were entirely dependent on their own efforts, which, however great, could not provide much, and they suffered terribly. It was heartrending to see them day after day carefully turning over the same ground in the hope that some small root might have been overlooked, and Major Morris therefore decided to expend a limited quantity of ammunition in testing the strength of the besiegers and trying to obtain a little food for these starving people.

On the 20th, therefore, a reconnaissance in force was undertaken against the Ashantis holding the eastern approaches to the town. Four 7-pounders were taken down to the prison, and the camp on the Mampon road was shelled for about an hour. Scouts were then sent out, and reported that the Mampon and Krobo stockades were being held in force, so Captain Marshall took 120 Hausas, a 7-pounder and a maxim to attack the Mampon road

stockade, while Captains Armitage, Leggett and Bishop,
with 150 Hausas, 300 loyal Ashantis and another 7-pounder
and maxim, went down the road leading to Lake Busumtwi
to attack the stockade at Dedisuaba, which was held by a
force under Amankwa the Kokofu Chief of Kwantanasi.
Both parties were met by a heavy fire from overwhelming
numbers of the enemy, who held the stockades and bush
around them. They therefore reported that there was
no hope of their being able to capture the positions without
expending a large amount of ammunition, while the
Ashantis at Dedisuaba were being further reinforced from
the Cape Coast road. They were therefore recalled without having been able to accomplish anything more than
locate the stockades and form some idea of the strength of
the forces holding them. This reconnaissance cost over
thirty rounds of 7-pounder and nearly 4,000 rounds of
maxim and carbine ammunition, while one Hausa had been
killed, Captain Leggett and four others severely wounded,
and twenty-one more slightly wounded. Captain Leggett
had been shot while firing the maxim, he and the gun
rolling over together, and had received his second and
severer wound while he was righting it.

The next day Opoku Mensa, who was suffering from
pneumonia and had been sinking fast for several days, died
in the fort. Shortly before he passed away he sent for
Captain Armitage and assured him, as he had repeatedly
done before, that he had known nothing about the rising
that had been fomented by his fellow Chiefs on the Native
Committee. The news of his death soon reached the
Ashantis, for they were heard singing dirges for him the
next day.

On the 24th a force was sent to attack the Ashanti camp
at Intimide, but took the wrong road and missed it altogether. The Governor also held a review of the troops to
celebrate the Queen's birthday.

The next morning Captain Cochrane marched out before
daybreak with Mr. Ralph, 140 Hausas and a maxim to make
the deferred attack on Intimide. They came on the
stockade just as it was getting light. It was a formidable

structure, built right across the road and extending into the bush for fifty yards on either side ; but was held by only a small force and captured without difficulty. Enchi Ajai the Chief of Inkawia, who was in command of the stockade, on being awakened and told that the Hausas were upon him, left his men and fled. It was in his village that a European, Mr. Branksome, had been brutally murdered, and he was probably afraid of what might happen to him if he were taken. He was afterwards tried for cowardice by the Chiefs and deprived of his stool, in addition to being made to pay a heavy fine. A passage was made through the centre of the stockade, and the carriers were left to pull it down while the troops pushed on towards the village. The enemy, however, rallied outside it and poured in a heavy fire, on which the volleys of the Hausas had no effect. Captain Cochrane did his utmost to induce them to charge and take the place with a rush, but they flatly refused to move,[1] and, as it was evident that a number of the enemy were creeping round towards the rear of the column and threatening to surround it, the retreat was ordered. It was specially unfortunate that the men held back here ; for the Ashantis had been taken entirely by surprise, and when the village was first reached many of them could be seen running out of their houses unarmed to see what was the matter. It was known, too, that there were very extensive plantations around this place, from which a large supply of food might have been obtained : as Major Morris rightly commented, it was a chance that was not likely to occur again. The casualties were one Hausa dangerously, Mr. Ralph and seven men severely, and three more slightly wounded, while, judging by the wailing that arose from their camp during the night, the Ashantis must have lost heavily.

The enemy had been found so unprepared at Intimide in the early morning that it seemed probable that a night attack on one of their camps might prove successful. Early in the morning of the 26th, therefore, after heavy rain

[1] They were Yorubas of the Lagos Constabulary.

had been falling all night, Captain Armitage, with a coast man named Anderson and thirty Hausas who had been specially instructed in what was required, moved quietly down to the Mampon road, while a large force of Hausas was held in readiness to come to their support and wheel round into the camp so soon as they had rushed the stockade. They soon discovered, however, that the Ashantis had taken precautions against surprise ; for, when they had nearly reached the stockade, the leaders suddenly tripped over a long cord hung with bells and empty gin bottles that had been stretched across the path about two feet from the ground. Nor was this all ; for the ground beyond had been carefully strewn with broken pots, calabashes, and dried sticks, which, with the bells and bottles, made a tremendous noise in the stillness of the forest when trodden on. The Hausas behind were now tripping over the bells also, and the sentries at the stockade challenged. Anderson called out in Ashanti that they were some of the King of Jabin's men who had deserted from Kumasi, and they were told to come on quickly ; but on looking round, Captain Armitage found that he and Anderson were alone. Their men were found round the next bend in the path, huddled together in a frightened group and hurriedly loading their carbines. The unexpected jangling of bells and other weird noises in the darkness and quiet of the forest had proved too much for them in their weak and half-starved condition, and they had lost their nerve. The non-commissioned officers were alternately ordering and begging them to go on, but without avail, and though Captain Armitage succeeded in persuading them to follow him once more, he reached the front of the stockade only to find that they had failed him again. The Ashantis by this time were thoroughly awake, and their drums and horns were sounding the alarm in every direction : the opportunity had been lost, and there was nothing to be done but to return to the fort. That evening the Ashantis on the Cape Coast road exploded a quantity of powder within sight of the garrison, which at first was thought to be accidental ; but it was done out of pure bravado to show that they at least had munitions enough and to spare.

Despite these failures, the urgent need of food induced Major Morris to order another attack on Intimide, where it was known to be plentiful. The force employed consisted of 220 Hausas under Captain Marshall, with Captains Digan, Maguire and Bishop and Doctors Graham and Hay. Leaving Kumasi about an hour before dawn on the 29th, they arrived in front of the stockade at half-past five. It had been repaired and was strongly held by the Ashantis, who at once opened a heavy fire. They had doubtless been warned by three men who had been seen running down the road. Any possibility of taking the place by surprise, as had been intended, was therefore out of the question, and Captain Marshall, who had been wounded, ordered the guns to be dismantled before retiring, while he went back to have his wound dressed. A few minutes later, Captain Maguire [1] fell mortally wounded, and the column had to retire for some distance under fire, and was again attacked from an ambush just outside Bantama. Captain Maguire and one man were killed, and Captain Marshall and twenty-three rank and file wounded, two of them mortally.

The total amount of ammunition expended in these unsuccessful attacks was 40 rounds 7-pounder, 820 rounds maxim, and 8,117 carbine. Apart from locating the stockades and ascertaining the strength of the enemy, their only, and by far their most important object was the capture of food, and it would seem that this might have been accomplished had the ammunition been used in one determined attack by a strong force, instead of being expended in driblets in a number of attacks by small detachments, none of whom had enough to enable them to follow up any advantage they gained. The lessons of 1874 had already been forgotten, and the men who had faced the Black Watch and Rifle Brigade at Amoafu and Odasu were now expected to run from far stronger positions when attacked by small detachments of half-starved and

[1] Essex Regiment.

partly-trained black troops.   These continual reverses, too, disheartened the men, who knew well enough that the ammunition was running short.   That they held back occasionally when they should have gone on must be admitted ; but there was every excuse for them : many of them were mere recruits, and the majority had less than two years' service, while it is notoriously hard for any man, black or white, to fight bravely on an empty stomach.

A period of forced inaction now ensued, and with the exception of a reconnaissance that was made on the 11th of June to discover the exact position of a stockade that the Ashantis had built about a mile down the Cape Coast road, no attempt was made to harass the enemy.   The plight of the garrison and refugees grew daily worse and worse : everything that could by any possibility be turned into food was eagerly seized upon and sold at fabulous prices. Some of the traders outside the fort who had managed to conceal and save small quantities of stores now produced them : biscuits were sold at ten shillings apiece, a two-pound tin of beef fetched £2 16s., and a seven-pound tin of flour £3, while whisky was retailed at two shillings a small spoonful, matches at two shillings a box, and red peppers at three pence each.   Parrots, dogs and pets of all kinds had long since disappeared, while even lizards were now difficult to obtain.   A palm cabbage or a rat fetched ten shillings, and on the day after the second unsuccessful attack on Intimide the already scanty ration was still further reduced.   A proclamation was issued at the same time putting the Hausas under the Army Act.   A soup kitchen was also opened on the 7th of June, from which some 200 children were supplied every morning with a small meat tin full of warm fluid made by boiling the crumbs left in the biscuit tins and the few small scraps left from the Europeans' tables with sufficient water to make it go round.   The rains had now set in in full force, and to add to their other miseries and dangers, small-pox broke out among the refugees.   The cases, however, were so quickly isolated that it fortunately did not spread. But want, exposure, anxiety, and the unwholesome and innutritious, and sometimes even poisonous food, had already made everyone, Europeans and Africans alike, more or less ill, while the refugees were dying daily of pure starvation. Men walking along or sitting on the road outside the fort would suddenly fall forward dead, while others, wasted almost to skeletons, went mad, and either wandered about the place raving and shrieking, or sat picking at their cloths with a vacant smile on their faces. The carriers were continually employed in burying the dead, cutting the weeds and long grass that grew up around the fort, and keeping the ground clean ; otherwise the mortality must have been even greater than it was. About 1,200 refugees deserted to the enemy, preferring the certainty of slavery and the possibility of execution to slow death by starvation. By the second week in June the people were dying at the rate of over thirty a day, and Doctor Chalmers reported to the Governor that " estimating the population of Kumasi at about 4,000 persons on June 4th 1900, and at 3,000 persons on June 18th (many having left the camp), the death-rate rose from ·75 per 1,000 per diem (*i.e.* 273·75 per 1,000 per annum) to 10·6 per 1,000 per diem (*i.e.* 3,869·0 per 1,000 per annum) ; or, in other words, the population would have ceased to exist in about 94 days from June 18th at the rate of mortality on that day." [1]

Meanwhile repeated efforts had been made to gain some news of a relief column. The reports brought in, however, were most contradictory, and as time went on and the people became too weak to go far away, it was almost impossible to get any news at all. The spies, however, persistently reported the presence of a white man and troops at Esumeja, while a little later it was said that wounded Ashantis were being brought back to Kumasi. It seemed, therefore, that help must come soon, yet day after day went by and the watchers in the fort still saw no sign of it. At last, on the 15th of June, it was decided that the last desperate step for which preparations had all along been made, but which everyone had hoped would

[1] Parliamentary Paper, *Ashanti War*, 1900, p. 66.

never be necessary, must be taken on the 23rd. The rations, already reduced to the absolute minimum, would last no longer, and on that day three officers and a hundred Hausas were to be left to hold the fort with a little ammunition and sufficient food to last them until the 15th of July, while the remainder were to try to cut their way through the enemy's lines and reach the coast. Preparations were made early, though no one but the Governor and Major Morris knew the actual date of departure, as it was of importance to take the Ashantis by surprise. Even now it was hoped that the long-expected relief might come in time. Rockets and star shell were fired on the night of the 16th to attract the attention of any column that might be on its way up, but they had been so long in store that they were of very little use. After this a 7-pounder was trained nearly vertically at night and common shell timed to explode high in the air fired from it; but though it was afterwards ascertained that these signals were once heard at Esumeja and answered with a similar number of rounds, the reply was not heard in Kumasi. This was perhaps fortunate ; for had it been, the garrison might have been tempted to delay their march out until it was too late. A number of notes, too, were written in French on small pieces of tissue paper, and a large reward offered to anyone who should succeed in delivering one to the officer commanding the relief force and bringing back an answer. Several men volunteered, but only one got through, and that not until after the Governor's column had already marched out.

At about this time Asibi made a desperate attempt to escape to the besiegers' lines. He succeeded in eluding the sentry and got outside the fort, where he hid in an empty shelter, but was seen by a servant, who raised the alarm. Asibi then darted out of his hiding-place and ran down the road towards the Mampon road camp, but was overtaken and brought back by some of the Hausas. After this he was kept in irons and constantly watched.

Several alternative routes were discussed for the column that was to break out. At one time it was suggested that it should take the Kintampo road and then pass through Attabubu to the Volta River, but this plan was afterwards abandoned. The Cape Coast road was known to be so strongly guarded between Kumasi and Esumeja as to be out of the question, while this route would also involve passing through the hostile Adansi country. The road through Peki to Bekwai, too, was so close to the Cape Coast road that it was thought too dangerous, and finally that through Patasi to Inkwanta was chosen, partly by a process of exclusion, partly because, so far as was known, there was only a single stockade on it, and partly because the loyal King of Inkwanta was in the fort and could furnish guides who knew the road well and ensure a plentiful supply of food directly his own territory was entered.

Although it was generally known that the garrison was to break out, both the date of departure and the actual route chosen were still kept secret. Major Morris, indeed, let it leak out, as though by accident, that the column would leave by the Cape Coast road as everyone expected. On the night of the 22nd, there being still no sign of relief, everyone was warned that the march would be begun at dawn ; but, though they had been expecting it, it was not without dismay that the worn-out garrison realized that the time had really come when they must stake every-thing on this last desperate venture : so hazardous was the undertaking, indeed, that few of them can have felt any confidence of success. The Governor's last words to Captain Bishop were : " Well, you have a supply of food for twenty-three days and are safe for that period, but we are going to die to-day," and this probably expressed the general feeling.

The force left to hold the fort consisted of Captain Bishop, Lieutenant Ralph and Doctor Hay, with Native Officer Hari Zenua, 109 Hausas, and 25 carriers. They were given 160 rounds a man, besides ammunition for the guns, and although most of them were invalids, it was hoped that they would be able to hold out as long as their food lasted. All the other Europeans, 600 Hausas, and carriers and the loyal Chiefs and their followers to the number of about 800, were to leave with the Governor ; while as many of the civilian refugees as were able to travel, numbering about 1,000, were to be allowed to follow behind the rear-guard.

The carriers, who had been made to sleep inside the fort for several nights past, so as to prevent the actual date of departure becoming known, were awakened at four o'clock, and, of course, made a tremendous noise. They were given their loads, which, owing to their weak state, had been kept down to thirty-pounds weight, and passed out with them to wait in the road. Presently the troops came up through the mist to take up their places in the column, the hammocks were got out, the loyal Ashantis were guided to their places, and by five o'clock everything was ready. The column had been formed up as if to march out by the Cape Coast road ; but now the advance-guard, under Captains Armitage and Leggett, which all those not in the secret had of course thought was the rear-guard, turned about and moved quietly down the hill past the water supply towards Patasi, followed by the rest of the column. The road led down through dense bush into a swamp, and was so narrow and muddy that the men could only pass along it in single file. They proceeded cautiously for nearly half an hour, and then, round a bend in the path, came upon the stockade, from which a heavy fire was at once opened on them. The men pushed on however, but Captain Leggett, the Inkwanta guide, and several Hausas having been wounded, Captain Armitage called a halt and left Captain Leggett with instructions to continue firing volleys while he took twenty men round through the bush to get behind the stockade and take the Ashantis in the flank. This he succeeded in doing, and then, sending back for Captain Leggett and more Hausas, and ordering the sergeant in charge of the men on the road to cease firing, charged in behind the stockade. It was easily taken, for there were very few men in it at the time, though numbers were seen streaming back across their camp from the bush on the other side. It had originally been held by about 300 men ; but while Captain Armitage's party had been working its way through the bush, the Ashantis had also detached a large force to make a flank attack on the column. This had fortunately passed round on the opposite side, and the stockade had been taken before they got into position.

The enemy had cut a circular path right round Kumasi connecting all their camps, so that they could bring up reinforcements quickly. There was no time to be lost therefore, and the men were at once set to work to make an opening in the stockade large enough to allow of the passage of the hammocks and guns. Altogether four Hausas had been killed, and Captain Leggett, nine Hausas, and the guide wounded, and, as Captain Leggett's wound proved to be serious, he was now sent back to the main body and temporarily relieved by Captain Marshall until Captain Berthon, who was some distance farther down the column, could get up to replace him. The advance was then continued until, when just outside Patasi, the Ashantis opened fire from an ambush on the right, and Captain Marshall and several Hausas fell. They were soon driven off, but one of Captain Marshall's wounds was serious, and a short halt had to be made to enable Doctor Graham to come up. The village was then entered and found to have been burnt.

Another short halt was made in Patasi to allow the column, which was about two miles long, to close up and Captain Berthon to join the advance-guard, and soon afterwards, after silencing two more ambushes, another small village was entered. This was evidently the camp of the Ashantis holding the Patasi stockade, and was well stocked with food. As the troops entered it, plantains were cooking over the fires in front of the huts, and other large bunches lay around on every side. The sight of all this food proved too much for the famished men, who, forgetful of Ashantis, discipline, and everything except their craving hunger, dashed away to chase fowls and collect whatever they could. After about ten minutes, however, they were got together again, and the march was then resumed to Tekiman, which was reached after two

more short skirmishes with the enemy.   Here Major Morris
ordered a halt to give the men a chance to eat a little of the
food they had taken ; but very little time could be allowed,
lest Asamoa Kwami should send a force from the Cape
Coast road to intercept them, while there was also great
danger that the men would make themselves seriously ill
and be unable to go on if they were allowed to eat too
much after their long privations.   At half-past one, therefore, the advance-guard moved off, and just before dark the
column reached Terabum, a village of about twenty houses,
where it was to halt for the night.   The main body was
ambushed just outside the village, and the advance-guard
was fired on from the loop-holed houses as it entered the
place ; but a square was formed round the clearing and
a few volleys sufficed to clear the Ashantis into the bush,
while the pouring rain that then began to fall silenced them
altogether.

The first day's march was over, but not without heavy
losses.   The flanks of the column had been harassed by
parties of from thirty to fifty of the enemy throughout the
whole day, and, in addition to the men who had been
killed and wounded at the stockade and on the road,
numbers of carriers and refugees were missing.   They
had either been killed while hunting for food in the first
village beyond Patasi and in the plantations outside
Tekiman, or had failed to rejoin the column when it moved
on and fallen a prey to bands of the enemy who were
prowling round the rear of the force.   Many more, again,
too weak and emaciated to keep up on the march, had
fallen out on the road and been killed or captured.   Months
afterwards, over a hundred dead bodies were counted on
the first two miles of the path itself, and very many more
must have lain undiscovered in the bush.   Most of the
loads, too, had been thrown down and abandoned : beds,
bedding and blankets, boxes of clothing and hardly saved
food, medical stores and instruments—nearly all had been
lost.   A camp bed was found for Lady Hodgson, but the
Governor, on this and many subsequent nights, had to
get what rest he could in a borrowed chair, while most of

the other Europeans were even worse off. Not a filter remained, and Lady Hodgson and many others had nothing but the clothes they were wearing. Captain Armitage describes the scene after the village was entered as follows : " Our loads lay about in utter confusion, where they had been dumped down by the carriers, who came staggering in like drunken men. The Governor and Lady Hodgson sat upon boxes waiting for the tent which never came, and finally sought shelter in the wretched hut I had kept for them. The crush was so great that two huts, filled with wounded, collapsed from the pressure on the walls from without, and the occupants were with difficulty rescued. Fires had been lit everywhere, and from them arose suffocating volumes of smoke, as the damp wood spluttered and cracked. The many trampling feet had churned the ground into a sea of mud over ankle deep. And upon this steaming mass of humanity the torrential rain fell silently, pitilessly, as though determined to extinguish the wretched fires, around which squatted shivering groups of natives." [1] With nearly 3,000 people crowded into a space not more than 120 yards in circumference on such a night, with men squabbling for room, with children crying, with the enemy's drums sounding at intervals from the bush, and with the carriers and refugees chattering the whole night through, there can have been little rest for anyone.

The next morning, it was still raining hard when the column moved off at seven o'clock. The men, wet, dejected, tired and thoroughly miserable, advanced cautiously, expecting every moment to walk into an ambush ; but there was much less undergrowth in this part of the forest, and after several likely looking places had been passed in safety it soon became apparent that the Ashantis had not headed the column, and the men cheered up and pushed on at a good pace. The rear-guard, under Captain Aplin, however, was attacked about two hours out of Terabum and had some heavy fighting. The panic-stricken refugees ran in amongst the Hausas, knocking them down in their

[1] Armitage and Montanaro, p. 102.

anxiety to seek safety higher up the column, and considerably hampered the men.   Only one Hausa was killed however, and seven more were wounded; but the refugees lost heavily.   Mr. and Mrs. Ramseyer and the other two missionary ladies had been abandoned by their hammock-men and were now obliged to walk, often wading for hours at a time through mud and water that, after the heavy rains, were waist deep or more in the swamps. That night was spent at Hiakesi, and a strong guard was posted at the entrance to the village to keep out the civilians, who were ordered to camp on the road, thus avoiding much of the noise and discomfort that had been experienced at Terabum.

The next morning the rain had fortunately ceased, and, the Ashantis having abandoned the pursuit, the column reached Inkwanta, Kwachi Inkatia's village, unmolested. Here they found the British flag flying and food in abundance.   The drums thundered out a welcome, and men with a hammock and guns at once started down the road to meet and salute their King.   First came the advance-guard with its Inkwanta guide, who, in spite of his wound, had kept up throughout the whole march and now received a tremendous ovation from his countrymen.   Then came a detachment of Hausas with Major Morris and other officers, and behind them the Governor, who arrived on foot, and was so overcome with fatigue and anxiety that the relief of finding the danger practically over proved too much for him, and he had no sooner taken the salute from the Hausa guard than he fell forward in the street unconscious.   He soon recovered however.   Kwachi Inkatia, after being received by his people with the wildest enthusiasm, sent them out to get food for the troops, who were given a much-needed rest for the whole of that day and the next.   Fires were lit everywhere, and all were soon busy cooking and eating.   The Governor sent a letter from here, by Kofi Yami the King of Bekwai's Linguist, to the officer commanding any relief column, telling him what had happened, and that it was essential that Kumasi should be relieved by the 15th of July.   He also sent off a Hausa runner to Cape Coast with a telegram to the Secretary of State.

On the 28th the column moved to Edubia, whence men were sent forward to the Ofin River to build rafts. Captain Marshall died of his wounds that night, and was buried the next morning, while Captain Leggett was sinking fast, and died at Takorasi on the evening of the 29th. At Takorasi the men who had been sent to the Ofin returned and reported that the river was in high flood, with the surrounding country under water for miles, and that it would be impossible for the whole column to cross it in one day. The Lagos Hausas were therefore left behind with the missionaries to follow a day later, while the others crossed on the 30th. They had to wade through water sometimes five feet deep for several miles before reaching the river, which was then crossed by means of two rafts carrying five men each and drawn across by means of a stout cable of creepers that had been stretched from bank to bank. A small canoe was found and sent back to a spot where a deep stream had to be crossed on a fallen tree trunk to bring Lady Hodgson over; but the Hausa who took it made a mistake, and told the Governor that they were to cross the river in it, which they eventually succeeded in doing, but not before they had had a narrow escape from being drowned; for the canoe was far too small to be safe, and was whirled away by the current when the river was reached and almost capsized on a submerged snag.

After crossing the Ofin, there was of course no further danger of attack, and the column was split up into three detachments for the march to the coast. The Governor's party reached Cape Coast on the 10th of July, and proceeded to Accra on board H.M.S. *Dwarf* the next day, being accorded a great welcome at both places. The missionaries got in a few days later, but Mr. Weller, who had been very ill, had died at Akwabosu the first day after crossing the river. Yow Mafo had also died on the way down, but Asibi was brought through in safety and sent to join Prempi in Sierra Leone before both were removed to the Seychelles. During the march, in addition to the

two officers who had died of their wounds and one who **1900**
had been slightly wounded, twenty-three of the rank and
file had been killed, sixteen had died of wounds, thirty-seven
had been wounded, and thirty-nine more were missing.
These casualties amounted to twenty per cent of the whole
force, while those amongst the carriers and refugees were
very heavy, though the actual figures were never known.

During all this time Ya Bremawua, the Queen-Mother of
Mampon, who, in the absence of the King in Kumasi had
been in charge of the town, had been staunchly loyal.
Early in April, Doctor Montgomery, the Acting District
Commissioner at Attabubu, had sent 200 pounds in specie
to Kumasi under escort of two Hausas, but on reaching
Mampon they were told by the Queen of the rising and
that they could not get through. She had then provided
a strong escort of her own people to accompany them
back to Attabubu, lest they should be attacked and robbed
on the road while the country was in such an unsettled
state. She also begged Doctor Montgomery to send some
troops to her assistance, as the Ashantis were troubling
her and her people and doing everything in their power
to compel them to join in the rising. This, however, he
could not do, as he only had a very small detachment at
Attabubu, but he continued in almost daily communication
with her by means of messengers. The Chief of Ejera,
who was under her, had been detained by the Ashantis
and compelled to join them, and his Sub-Chief, so soon
as he heard it, collected all his men and marched towards
Kumasi to join the insurgents. But they, again, were
ordered back by Ya Bremawua, who declared that none
of her people should fight against the Government, and,
when the Kumasis sent to demand powder from the
Mampons, her only answer was that she had 500 kegs, of
which she had just issued 200 to be used in the defence of
the rest if they cared to come and try to take it. They
declined to accept this challenge however, and from the
middle of June she caused them much inconvenience by
preventing any food or salt being taken to Kumasi.

At the same time, there were other small detachments

of Hausas at Asafu with Captain Hobart, the Acting District Commissioner of Sefwi, and at Sikasiko with Captain Soden, the Travelling Commissioner in British Jaman. Captain Hobart was at Pamu when he first heard of the rising, and at once ordered Pong Yow, the King of Wam, to summon all his Chiefs to a meeting, at which he told them what had taken place at Kumasi, warned them not to join, or in any way aid the Ashantis, and accepted their oaths of fealty to the Government. The country was very unsettled however, and it was doubtful in whom it would be safe to place much faith. The King of Ahafu sent in messengers to say that his people had joined the Ashantis and that he was coming in to Wam for protection ; but the next news received was that his people had taken him with them by force to Kumasi. The King of Berikum also sent an urgent message asking for help and support, as the Ashantis were threatening to burn his town and put his people to death if they did not join them. This was more than Captain Hobart could give ; but he sent asking Captain Soden to visit Berikum, and he, by continually patrolling the district, managed to prevent any further defections, though the Odumasis and Wankis had already risen, and Kobina Cherri, the Chief of the former place, which was a great rubber centre, had put seventy-six Krepi rubber collectors and brokers to death with frightful tortures, and extorted large sums of money from many others by threatening them with a similar fate. Captain Hobart stayed in Pamu until the end of the first week in June, by which time the district was fairly settled and he thought it safe to visit Berikum, where he stayed until the 21st. He then received news of the death of Atta Kwesi the King of Sefwi, and, knowing that this would be likely to unsettle the district, hurried back to arrange for the election of his successor. He reached the capital, Wiosu, on the 22nd of August, and Kwamin Tando, the Chief of Asafu, was then enstooled King of Sefwi. He was an extremely loyal, able, sensible, and very influential man, and it was fortunate that he succeeded at this time. He soon afterwards informed Captain Hobart that the Ashantis were planning an attack on Asafu, and asked to be supplied with guns and powder, so that he might arm his people and assist in its defence. Captain Hobart, however, had no arms available, and the attack, fortunately, was not made ; but the people all left the town, and small parties of the enemy occupied the roads and kept watch on his movements.

Surprise has often been expressed that the Governor and his party ever succeeded in getting out of Kumasi and reaching the coast. That they did so at all in their weakened condition was indeed marvellous ; but their success was due to the secrecy of their preparations, combined with some good luck. But perhaps the most marvellous thing of all is that many more of these weakened Europeans did not die on the road from the exposure and hardships of travelling in such weather and in such a climate with absolutely no comforts whatever. In the first place, the Ashantis, after their attempts on the 25th and 29th of April, never tried to take the fort, but contented themselves with cutting off supplies and sitting down until starvation should do their work for them. This was partly because the ground around the fort had been well cleared, and they knew by experience that they were seldom successful when fighting in the open, but mainly because they had conceived a very wholesome respect for the fighting qualities of the Hausa troops. The determined way in which the small detachment had fought its way back from Bali, and the great losses that had been inflicted on them, both then and during the fights on the Bantama and Cape Coast roads, had greatly impressed the Ashantis, and convinced them that these troops, though black, were, by their natural courage and endurance, as well as by their superior armament and discipline, very different from the Native Levies from the coast tribes on whom the English had had to rely in the absence of white troops in their other wars. For these reasons, and because they thought starvation would soon accomplish their object, they did not risk coming in close enough to interfere with the use of the water supply. Then, again, the secrecy that had been maintained as to the road the column was to take did much to ensure its safety, for the Ashantis fully expected it to leave by the Cape Coast road, on which they had prepared several stockades and had an overwhelming force in readiness. Its appearance before the Patasi stockade, which was only one of the minor defences and held by quite a small detachment, came as a complete surprise, and so fully occupied the few men there that they had no time to send for reinforcements. Even then, it was by the purest chance that the enemy's flanking party did not pass to the other side of the column and meet Captain Armitage's party in the dense bush, when, in a hand-to-hand fight under such conditions, the Ashantis' superior numbers would in all probability have won them the day. Captain Bishop, too, had been ordered to open a heavy fire with the 7-pounders on all the camps around Kumasi directly he heard firing on the Patasi road, and this contributed very largely to the delay in reinforcing the detachment there. The rank and file of the Ashantis were heartily sick of camping out day after day in their miserable huts during the rains ; but the Chiefs had imposed a fine of sixty pounds on any man who left his post, and no reinforcements would therefore leave for Patasi without definite orders to do so, more especially as no one knew what was happening there or expected it was anything more than another sortie in search of food. By the time the Chiefs discovered that the Governor himself was escaping with a large party, the stockade had already been taken and the column had passed. There was then nothing to be done but to pursue it, and here again luck favoured the fugitives ; for the Chief who was sent was unreliable. Chief Antoa Mensa was detailed to follow the column with a force of 1,500 men, and, if possible, prevent its escape from Ashanti, but in any case to bring back the Governor's head. He was a comparatively unimportant man, who had only come to the front during the rising by the zeal with which he had espoused the cause of the Kumasis, and, finding that the watchfulness of the rear-guard made his task more difficult than he had expected, but that he could easily capture numbers of refugees and carriers and their loads, soon gave up the pursuit and turned back, hoping that those who had sent him would be as well pleased with loot and slaves as with the Governor's head. In this, however, he was mistaken, and was promptly degraded ; but it was then too late to send off a fresh party, and it was, moreover, still uncertain how many of the garrison still remained in the fort.

Meanwhile, the little force that had been left behind had been assured by the Governor, when he was leaving, that he had authentic information that the relief force was already at Esumeja and would arrive within five days at the latest. Buoyed up with this hope, the time at first passed quickly enough ; more especially as there was plenty of work to be done. The Governor's column had barely left when a number of Ashantis came down from the Bantama stockade, evidently thinking that the fort had been abandoned altogether ; but the fire of the maxims soon convinced them of their mistake, and it was the last attempt of the kind that they made. Soon afterwards, however, they burned the Basel Mission and Wesleyan Chapels in revenge. The men were all told off to their posts, and those who were to man the guns were ordered to sleep by them, so as to be ready for any emergency. Only about 150 refugees, who had been too weak and ill to follow the column, now remained, and the stench from the abandoned huts soon became overpowering, while the numbers of vultures that hovered round some of them made it only too certain what they contained. Within the first few days, therefore, these huts were all searched to make sure that they were either empty or their inmates already dead, and then burnt. Day after day went by with no sign of the expected relief, until the garrison began to despair. The men, now reduced to little more than skin and bone and covered with foul sores, grew weaker and weaker and more and more apathetic : some could no longer stand up to receive their daily ration of food, and hardly a day passed without one or more deaths. The survivors no longer had the strength to dig graves, and the dead were carried out every evening and buried in the trenches. At last the rations were reduced to a cup-full of linseed meal and a block of tinned meat about two inches square, and on more than one occasion the mere effort of crawling up to receive it proved too much for the strength of some wasted man, and he dropped dead while taking his share. Others ended their misery by committing suicide. Enormous prices were paid on the rare occasions when any women brought a little food to sell outside the fort : a piece of coco yam, usually worth a fraction of a penny, fetched fifteen shillings, and the same price was paid for a tiny pineapple, while bananas were sold for eighteen pence apiece. The officers, too, would give any man three shillings for half a biscuit if he could be per-suaded to part with it at all. Last of all, small-pox broke out in the fort, and the patients had to be removed to one of the shelters outside, Doctor Hay clambering over the wall daily to visit them. So the time passed, and the day when the last rations would have to be issued drew nearer and nearer, until hope was almost abandoned. Should this day arrive before the long-expected relief came, the remaining ammunition was to be divided and an attempt made to escape during the night. The three white men, each with a dose of poison in case he should be captured, agreed to keep together ; but the men were to be allowed to do the best they could, each man for himself.

CHAPTER XXV

THE RELIEF OF KUMASI

1900

On the coast, the news of the rising in Ashanti caused the greatest alarm, which increased almost to panic after the telegraph wire was cut and no further communications could be received from Kumasi. No one knew what was happening there, and the wildest rumours were circulated in Accra and Cape Coast. A Committee of Defence was formed, and later still the Volunteers were called out in anticipation of an attack on the coast towns. Trade, of course, was at a standstill, and the coast tribes had been warned by Ashanti messengers not to aid the white man, and were almost paralysed with terror. In the meantime 1,400 troops had been ordered to the Gold Coast, and the command of the Ashanti Field Force was given to Colonel Willcocks, C.M.G., D.S.O., the Commandant of the West African Frontier Force. Owing to the distances that many of them had to come, however, it would be some time before they could arrive at the base at Cape Coast.

On the 8th of May, Captain Hall, West Yorks Regiment, landed with two companies of the 1st Battalion West African Frontier Force 450 strong under Captain Wilson and Lieutenant Beamish, and one 75-millimetre gun from Northern Nigeria. Captain Edwards also arrived with fifty Sierra Leone Frontier Police, and Captains Anderson and Elgee with ninety-eight more Lagos Hausas. Captain Hall assumed command pending the arrival of Colonel Willcocks, and decided to leave for Prasu at once; but so great was the panic amongst the coast tribes that it was

most difficult to get carriers, while the local authorities
would not pass a Compulsory Labour Ordinance for fear of
upsetting them and causing them also to join in the revolt.
Only sufficient carriers, therefore, could be obtained to
transport the supplies and ammunition for the force itself,
and Captain Hall left for Prasu, hoping that, as confidence
was restored by the presence of his troops, the people would
come forward to carry the stores necessary for the garrison
of Kumasi. At Prasu, the Sierra Leone Police were detached to reassure the miners at Obuasi, who were panic-
stricken and momentarily expecting to be attacked, while
those at Ahuri had already fled to the King of Bekwai for
protection. The main column then pushed on in the hope
of ensuring the loyalty of the Adansis, who were known
to be wavering. Progress was difficult, however, for the
desertions of carriers necessitated the soldiers carrying
ammunition and provision boxes in addition to the 200
rounds in their pouches.

On the 20th Captain Hall arrived at Fomana, and, with
Captain Haslewood of the Gold Coast Constabulary, who
was acting as his Staff Officer, held a meeting with Kwaku
Inkansa, who made great protestations of loyalty, signed
a treaty, and promised and even supplied a number of
carriers. Two miners, Messrs. Jones and Cookson, who
had come over from Bekwai to meet the column, brought
news of the disloyalty of the Kokofus, and Captain Hall
therefore left them in Kwisa with a small escort to await
the arrival of Captain Slater and some Gold Coast Hausas
who were coming up the road, while he, at the urgent
request of the King of Bekwai, pushed on to occupy
Esumeja. He reached it on the 22nd without meeting
with any opposition. This was an important post, for it
was situated on the main road a day's march south of
Kumasi and within a short distance of both Bekwai and
Kokofu. The presence of this force, therefore, inspired
the loyal Bekwais with confidence and enabled a close
watch to be kept on the movements of the Kokofus.

The next morning, the 23rd, Captain Hall made a reconnaissance towards Kokofu with 200 men, and although

opposed by large numbers of the enemy, succeeded in burning an out-lying village and getting within a short distance of the town. But the Ashantis were then threatening to surround him and cut off his retreat, and he therefore fell back on Esumeja with the loss of Lieutenant Edwards, Sergeant Griggs,[1] and six men wounded. On the same day the Bekwais drove a small detachment of the enemy out of Abodum and burned it.

The vaunted loyalty of the Adansis proved very short-lived ; for on the 24th they attacked Messrs. Jones and Cookson at Dompoasi while they were on their way back to Bekwai. Their carriers at once threw down their loads and fled, while the white men only just succeeded in escaping to Kwisa, where they reported what had happened to Captain Slater. He could not understand why this attack had been made, and set out with twenty-five men to discover the cause, but had not been more than about two hours on the road when he, too, was heavily attacked from all sides. This attack was so sudden that two of the Hausas were panic-stricken, and, seeing their officer and several men fall at the first volley, fled for their lives and barely halted until they reached Cape Coast, where they reported that Captain Slater had been killed and his whole force cut up. For this act of cowardice they were afterwards arrested and sent back for trial by Court Martial. Captain Slater, however, struggled to his feet, and, finding that the firing was heaviest in front, pushed on to help his advanced party, losing another man killed and five more severely wounded. The dead were therefore abandoned, and two men told off as an advance and two as a rear-guard, while the remainder quietly slung their rifles and retired with the wounded to Kwisa. These men behaved splendidly ; for they well knew that if one more were wounded there would be no one left to carry him, and they would either have to abandon him or make a final stand in the forest until the last man was shot down. Fortunately, however, the Adansis made no attempt to follow the party, but contented themselves with collecting

[1] Royal Artillery, attached to the West African Frontier Force.

the carbines and ammunition of the dead. Captain Hall, meanwhile, knew nothing of the defection of the Adansis, and sent two parties of carriers on the 26th and 28th to fetch stores and ammunition from Prasu, where Lieutenant-Colonel Wilkinson, Northumberland Fusiliers, the newly appointed Inspector-General of the Gold Coast Constabulary, had just arrived with two officers and 160 men. They, too, were attacked near Dompoasi and lost four men and a carrier killed and fifteen more wounded. However, Lieutenant Beamish, who was in command, managed to rush and burn Dompoasi and then pushed on to relieve Captain Slater in Kwisa.

The rising of the Adansis and the attack on Messrs. Jones and Cookson so frightened the miners at Obuasi that many of them left for the coast. A party of Adansis came upon two of these fugitives, one of whom they captured alive and tortured to death, while the other, who was a big powerful man, made such a good fight for his life that they despaired of taking him, and he was decapitated from behind during the struggle. There were still about sixty white men left at Obuasi however, and Police Commissioner Donovan left Cape Coast with fifty men on the 24th of May with arms for them, and reached the camp in safety.

This was the state of affairs when Colonel Willcocks landed at Cape Coast on the 26th of May. The few troops that had yet arrived had been pushed up towards Kumasi without any settled plan, and were now practically isolated in different posts on the road, with insufficient supplies and ammunition, surrounded by the enemy, and only able to communicate with each other with difficulty. Kumasi was entirely cut off, and neither bribes nor promises of reward would avail to get a message through. It was not even known for certain whether the fort had fallen ; for news of the arrival of the column from the Northern Territories had not reached the coast, and the garrison was believed to be very much smaller than it really was. Nor was there much hope of improving this state of affairs for some time, for no preparations had yet been made on the coast : no stores had been collected, and there was very little ammunition ; there was no organized plan of operations, and not a single record of Sir Garnet Wolseley's campaign ; no carriers had been got ready, and there seemed very little prospect of obtaining them locally. Colonel Willcocks, therefore, set about restoring order out of the chaos that prevailed. He telegraphed for more troops and guns, ammunition, hospital and other stores, bought up all the rice that could be obtained on the coast, and cabled for a monthly supply of one hundred tons, and, realizing the hopelessness of attempting to reach Kumasi with Fanti carriers who would need more than half his troops to drive them on and prevent them from deserting, ordered large numbers from other parts. Hundreds of Mendis and Timanis were sent from Sierra Leone, while others were supplied from Northern Nigeria or sent round the Cape of Good Hope from Zanzibar, Mombasa and Zomba. These men, besides being excellent carriers and more valorous than the timid Fantis, had the additional advantage of being in a strange country with no home to run to and no friends to help them if they deserted. Orders were also issued for the concentration of the troops that were already in the country. There were some 200 men of the Southern Nigerian Battalion of the West African Frontier Force under Lieutenant-Colonel Carter, C.M.G., in Cape Coast when Colonel Willcocks landed, and they were sent up to join Colonel Wilkinson's force preparatory to concentrating at Esumeja and Bekwai and attempting to open communication with Kumasi.

Although on every occasion when it has been necessary to undertake military operations against the Ashantis this same difficulty has been experienced with the transport, it must be admitted that the lot of the West African carrier is not to be envied. At all times he has to carry a load of about sixty pounds weight for long distances, over all sorts of ground and obstructions, in all weathers, and often without a rest for many days in succession. If his load happens to be of an awkward shape or, like a gun, so heavy that two or four men have to carry it slung on a bamboo frame, his ordinary difficulties are still further increased. Fortunately, he is a simple creature and does not require many comforts or an extensive wardrobe. A spare cloth which he rolls into a pad to intervene between his head and the load, a grass mat on which to sleep, and a water-bottle, complete his equipment. His outlook is not a bright one as he follows the narrow winding track through the monotonous forest with men exactly like him in front and behind, and the principal changes he gets are when he comes to a specially bad or swampy piece of ground, a fallen tree across the path, or a frail bridge over some deep and swiftly running stream. At such times he may be seen with muscles outstanding, teeth clenched, and perspiration streaming down his body, straining in the effort to keep his footing in the greasy mud or on a narrow tree trunk, and avoid the risk of being crushed under his load if he fails. Such is the lot of the carrier at ordinary times, when he accomplishes the day's march more or less in his own time. But when employed on a military expedition he must keep his place in the column, is hustled on by the soldiers guarding him, is sniped at by the enemy, and runs many of the risks of the fighting man without any of the compensating glory and excitement. There is every excuse, therefore, for an unwillingness to serve on such occasions ; though not sufficient to absolve the Fanti, who gained more than anyone else by the conquest of his hereditary enemy, but who is constitutionally not a brave man, and regards the prospect of finding himself under the fire of an Ashanti force, with no chance of running away, with absolute horror.

On the 1st of June, eleven Europeans and 280 more men under Captains Melliss [1] and Beddoes [2] arrived from Nigeria, and Colonel Willcocks left with them on the 5th for Prasu, which was to be made a base for the collection of stores for the final advance. Soon after his arrival

[1] Indian Staff Corps.
[2] Royal Dublin Fusiliers.
[1] and [2]. Both these officers were made local majors soon after reaching Bekwai.

there on the 8th, news was received that Colonel Carter had joined Colonel Wilkinson at Fumsu on the 31st of May, but had met with a serious reverse in attempting to reach Captain Hall at Bekwai and Esumeja. He had first been attacked on the 2nd of June just beyond Sheramasi and lost four men killed and seven wounded ; but on the 6th, after leaving Kwisa for Bekwai with a force of 380 men, his column had been ambushed by the Adansis near Dompoasi and forced to retire with heavy loss.

This attack near Dompoasi came as a complete surprise, for, beyond an unusual number of footprints on the path, there was no sign of the enemy until a tremendous fire was poured into the column from the bush, upon which neither the fire of the 7-pounder and maxim nor the volleys of the men had any effect whatever. Officers and men were falling all along the line, and the guns' crews were nearly all shot down. Lieutenant Edwards continued to work the 7-pounder, ramming home the charges with his walking-stick, until he himself fell wounded ; Lieutenant O'Malley was badly wounded while working a maxim, which was soon afterwards put out of action by a bullet which pierced the water-jacket ; Captain Roupell, who had been with the advance-guard and had been knocked over at the first volley, was soon wounded again, but, though shot through both wrists, continued to bring up ammunition by carrying it between his forearms. Colonel Carter, too, fell severely wounded over the left eye, and had to hand over the command to Colonel Wilkinson, at the same time giving the order to retire. The hail of lead had now cleared away much of the bush and leaves that had concealed the enemy's position, and through the haze of smoke from their black powder it was now possible dimly to make out the lines of a huge stockade, behind which they were entrenched. So secure were they behind this defence that it was no wonder that the Hausa's fire had had no effect on them. There was nothing for it but to retire ; for the guns were out of action and ammunition was running short. But with all the wounded to be removed and the probability that the enemy, elated by their success, would follow and harass the flanks and rear of the column, it seemed quite likely that the retreat might degenerate into a panic-stricken rout.

While Colonel Wilkinson was wondering how he could best carry out this movement, Colour-Sergeant Mackenzie of the Seaforth Highlanders, who was with the Yoruba company of the 1st West African Frontier Force and had trained all the men himself, came up to him and obtained permission to charge the stockade. Calling up his men from their position in rear of the column, he ordered them to fix bayonets and dashed forward at their head against the stockade, followed by all the unwounded officers and men in the vicinity. The men had been thoroughly exasperated by the long fight and their heavy losses, and would not be denied, while the sight of the advancing line of gleaming bayonets proved too much for the Adansis, who broke and fled without making any attempt to rally. The battle was over after having lasted two and a half hours, and a probably disastrous retreat had been averted by the gallant action of Colour-Sergeant Mackenzie. He had won the Medal for Distinguished Conduct in the Field a year before in Nigeria, and for this act was awarded the Victoria Cross and given a commission in the Black Watch.

The enemy's stockade, like the majority of those built by them, was a formidable work set about twenty or thirty yards back from the road and running roughly parallel to it. It was nearly a quarter of a mile in length, six feet high and six feet thick, and provided with a continuous loop-hole. It was built of two rows of green tree trunks firmly bound together and with the space between them filled with timber, stones, and rammed earth, while behind it were trenches, in which the men loading the guns were perfectly safe. The stockade itself, however, was sufficient protection, for not only was it quite proof against rifle fire, but even the shells from the 7-pounder could make no impression on it. Moreover, it was built in a zig-zag line, so that a cross fire could be maintained throughout its whole length, and was furnished with large wings at each end to prevent its being turned. All the materials

had been collected from behind, where a path had been
cut to facilitate retreat, while the bush in front, being
quite untouched, gave no indication of the presence of
the enemy. These stockades formed quite a new feature
of Ashanti warfare. During the expedition of 1896 the
laagers made at various places are said to have impressed
the Ashantis very much, and they made notes of them,
subsequently improving their knowledge under the instruction of Mendis, numbers of whom had been imported
in 1897 as transport carriers and deserted at different
times.

In this action the men had fought in close formation
along the road, which was the method then employed in
Nigeria ; but it was the last time it was used against the
Ashantis, though the experience was bought at heavy cost.
Colonels Carter [1] and Wilkinson, Captain Roupell,[1]
Lieutenants Edwards [1] and O'Malley,[1] Surgeon-Captain
Fletcher, Colour-Sergeant Mackenzie, and eighty-six men
had been wounded, many of them severely, and six others
were either killed or died of their wounds. It was perhaps
on account of these casualties and the difficulty of trans-
porting so many wounded men, as well as because not less
than 40,000 rounds had been expended, that, although the
position had now been won and the way lay open to
Bekwai, the order to retire was not countermanded and
the column fell back on Kwisa.

On receipt of the news that a force of nearly 400 men,
led by Europeans and practically unencumbered by baggage
and carriers, had not only been stopped, but forced to retire
with heavy loss while still more than thirty-five miles from
the enemy's main position outside Kumasi, Colonel Willcocks at once telegraphed to the Secretary of State asking
for 800 more troops and special service officers, carriers,
and extra supplies of all kinds. Captain Melliss was then
ordered to proceed at once to Kwisa with 150 men and all
the available store of food and ammunition to help Colonel
Carter, and the last reserve of 100 men was moved up
from Prasu to Fumsu. Captain Melliss took orders to

[1] All invalided.

Colonel Carter to remain at Kwisa, while a message was
sent round through Obuasi to Captain Hall at Bekwai
asking him to send down the largest force he could spare
to meet Colonel Carter and assist him on his march north.

Captain Melliss was attacked by the Adansis, but soon
drove them off with the loss of his bugler killed and one
British non-commissioned officer, six men and several
carriers wounded, and joined Colonel Carter at Kwisa.
Meanwhile, one of Sir Frederic Hodgson's letters had been
brought through, and, after being read by Colonel Carter,
was sent on to Colonel Willcocks. It described the sufferings of the garrison, and urgently appealed for help.
Colonel Carter therefore, believing that he had already
proved the impossibility of marching north by the road
he was then on, and apparently failing to understand that
Colonel Willcocks' orders to him to hold Kwisa and await
the arrival of reinforcements were definite, decided to
retire to Fumsu and try to reach Bekwai by the road
through Obuasi.

This movement was carried out on the 14th of June,
and unfortunately led to yet another disaster ; for although
Colonel Willcocks sent an urgent message to Captain Hall
directly he heard of this further retreat, it arrived too
late to stop the reinforcement from Bekwai. Captain
Wilson, Royal Irish Fusiliers, had already left on the 16th
with two white non-commissioned officers and 112 men of
the Nupi company of the Northern Nigerian Frontier
Force. This force met with no opposition until it reached
the fatal stretch of road near Dompoasi, where the Adansis
had their stockades. Here the enemy, emboldened by
their success in having turned back a far stronger column
only a few days before, poured in a tremendous fire ; but
the Nupis, young soldiers though they were, returned the
fire steadily and pushed on. The enemy's position, however, extended for a long distance down the road, and
men soon began to drop. Before they had gone far,
Captain Wilson fell mortally wounded, and the Adansis
began to close in in the hope of securing his body. The
men, however, fixed bayonets and gathered round their

officer while he was placed in a hammock, and then fought their way ahead once more, carrying him in their midst. Staff-Sergeant Payne, Royal Army Medical Corps, twenty-five men and sixteen carriers were also wounded, and some of these unfortunately had to be abandoned with the bodies of six more men who had been killed. But although Captain Wilson, as he lay dying in his hammock, implored the men to leave him and help the other wounded, they stuck bravely to their task, and at last fought their way through with his body to Kwisa. Here, of course, they had expected to join Colonel Carter's force, but found to their consternation that the post had been abandoned. It almost seemed that the force must now be annihilated, but Colour-Sergeant Humphries, Royal Irish Fusiliers, upon whom the command had now fallen, pushed straight on to Fumsu, which was reached that night after a march of thirty-three miles, the greater part of which had been made under fire. Captain Wilson's body was buried there, and the wounded were sent in the morning to the advanced hospital at Prasu. Six days later one of the abandoned Nupis, who had been wounded in nineteen places, crawled painfully into Fumsu. He had covered the twenty miles from where he fell by slowly dragging himself for short distances by night, lying hid in the forest by day, and keeping himself alive on a few plantains that he found.

The letter from the Governor had stated that the garrison could hold out on reduced rations until the 11th, but it was already the 12th when it reached Colonel Willcocks. Thinking that the Governor would make for the friendly town of Bekwai therefore, he sent orders to Colonel Wilkinson, who was now in command at Fumsu—Colonel Carter having been invalided to England on account of his wound—to move there with his whole force and all the available reserve of ammunition, so as to be ready to help him if he succeeded in breaking out of Kumasi. Captain Beamish and fifty men were at the same time sent to hold Obuasi, where the mine manager Mr. Webster, and a few members of his staff had been abandoned in the most cowardly way by the European miners, some twenty of whom had left for the coast on the 14th. . Colonel Willcocks issued orders for their arrest, but they had sufficient sense of shame left to make them careful to avoid the British posts on their way down.

The departure of this column left Colonel Willcocks once more without a reserve ; but 400 men of the West African Regiment, with about twenty officers under Lieutenant-Colonel Burroughs, had just landed at Cape Coast from Sierra Leone, and Captain Wilkinson was also on his way with another company of the West African Frontier Force from Jebba. Officers were also despatched to raise Native Levies, with the double object of proving to the Ashantis that the coast tribes were still loyal and providing a force that, while useless for actual fighting, could be depended upon to do valuable work in following the column and plundering and destroying the villages and crops. The King of Denkera provided 3,000 men, and others were sent from Akim Swedru, Dengiasi, Mampon, Jabin and Inkoranza. They were given a certain number of Dane guns, with powder and lead, but were required to find their own food by plundering the enemy's farms.

On the 22nd of June Colonel Burroughs' force marched into Prasu and left the next day for Fumsu on its way to join Colonel Wilkinson at Bekwai. Captain Eden came in three days later with another 150 men of the 2nd Battalion of the West African Frontier Force, and it was known that 300 more men and a detachment of 70 Sikhs were on their way from British Central Africa. With Colonel Burroughs' force were the men who had deserted Captain Slater : they were now tried by Court Martial, pleaded guilty to having shown cowardice in the presence of the enemy, and were sentenced to death. In confirming the finding of the Court, however, Colonel Willcocks commuted the sentence to one of twenty years' penal servitude on the ground that this was the only occasion upon which any man of the Ashanti Field Force had behaved otherwise than with the greatest gallantry, and in recognition of the services of the remainder of the rank and file. They were

then stripped of their uniforms in the presence of the 1900
assembled troops and sent down to Elmina gaol.

Colonel Wilkinson's force had reached Bekwai by the
flank road through Obuasi without firing a shot, but
Colonel Burroughs and the West African Regiment were
to march by the main road, so as to clear both routes and
at the same time leave the enemy in doubt which would
be chosen for the final advance on Kumasi. Some newly
erected stockades on the Monsi Hill were located by careful
scouting, and carried after an hour's fighting with the loss
of one man killed and three wounded, and, after a halt at
Kwisa, where a small detachment was left, the force arrived
before Dompoasi on the evening of the 30th of June.
Heavy fighting had been expected here, but it was already
getting dark and pouring with rain, and the choice lay
between camping in the forest in close proximity to the
enemy and trying to carry the position at once. Scouts
were sent on through the bush and soon returned to report
that the stockades were unoccupied ; for the Adansis,
though they knew that the column had left Kwisa that
morning, had decided when night began to fall that no
attack would be made that day, and, disheartened by the
rain, had gone back to the village to cook their evening
meal. Captains Stallard and Tighe, therefore, who were
with the advance-guard, decided to rush the place at once,
and, calling in the scouts, gave the order to charge. The
Adansis were taken completely by surprise, for the noise
of the falling rain covered all sound from the bare-footed
troops, and they were still busy over their cooking fires
when the leading company dashed into their midst. The
utmost confusion followed : the Adansis sprang up from
the fires and ran to the houses in which they had stacked
their guns or fled panic-stricken into the forest, while
the West Africans poured volley after volley into them as
they showed up in the flickering firelight. Some, who had
secured their arms, ran down through the bush to man the
stockade and opened fire on the main column, but were
soon driven off, and in a very short time the village had
been completely cleared and half a company was scouring

the bush in pursuit. This half-company remained out all night, and could be heard from time to time firing on the stragglers, while thirty dead were found in the village and large numbers of guns and a quantity of ammunition and food were captured. Several carbines and 3,000 rounds of ·303 ammunition were also recovered. This was the first real success the troops had had, and the day was spent in Dompoasi destroying the stockades, clearing the bush in front of them, cutting down the fetish-trees, and burying the dead. Amongst the latter, many headless corpses of soldiers and carriers who had fallen in the earlier fights were found, and on the 1st of July Bekwai was reached.

Meanwhile, one of the letters in French that had been sent out by the Governor had reached Captain Hall at Esumeja and been sent on to Colonel Wilkinson at Bekwai. It said that the garrison could hold out until the 20th, but it was midnight on the 21st when Colonel Wilkinson received it. He, however, left at once for Esumeja in drenching rain with every man he could spare to form a rear-guard for the Governor's column if he should succeed in breaking out ; but when nothing happened by the next evening he returned to Bekwai, where messengers arrived a few days later with news of the Governor's escape through Inkwanta.

Colonel Burroughs was so elated by his success at Dompoasi that, contrary to his instructions and not knowing that Colonel Willcocks intended to use the other road, he determined to attack and destroy Kokofu, which threatened the flank of any force advancing by the main road. By drawing on Colonel Wilkinson's and Captain Hall's men as well as his own, he got together a force of 650 men with one 75-millimetre gun and five maxims, and, keeping 150 men and a maxim in reserve, advanced with the remainder against the town. This time, however, the enemy were fully prepared, and were Ashantis, and not the Adansis who had already suffered defeat. The head of the column had got within about half a mile of Kokofu, when a tremendous fire was opened on it, and the enemy quickly worked their way round until they had the whole

force engaged. Although the guns were brought up and 1900
literally swept the bush in front again and again, yet the
Ashantis held their ground and no advance could be made.
When absolutely forced to retire under the storm of lead
from the maxims, they did so in the most orderly manner,
one rank falling back through another, and renewed the
attack almost at once. All attempts to deploy the troops
outwards to meet these attacks failed : companies lost
touch and more than once fired into each other ; the
Ashantis were rapidly enveloping the whole column and
threatening to cut off its retreat ; the rear-guard was
already heavily engaged, and the wounded were falling
fast. Colonel Burroughs, therefore, after three hours'
desperate fighting, gave the order to fall back on Esumeja.
The Ashantis then followed the column right up to the outskirts of the village, harassing the rear-guard and pressing
in so close that the men even killed some of them with their
machets. This disastrous fight entailed a heavy list of
casualties : Lieutenant Brounlie of the 3rd West India
Regiment, who was attached to the West Africans, and
six men were killed, and six other officers, one European
non-commissioned officer, and seventy-two rank and file
wounded.

With the arrival of a number of Mendi carriers from
Sierra Leone, the Commandant had now collected sufficient
stores at Prasu to enable him to advance to the relief of the
garrison that he felt sure must have been left in the fort,
although he had as yet had no intimation of it. His plan
was to leave small garrisons in Bekwai and Esumeja, but
temporarily to abandon all other posts on the line of
communication, trusting to the Ashantis to concentrate on
Kumasi to oppose his advance, instead of cutting in behind
him on the road, while he made a dash on Kumasi by an
unknown route. In no other way could he assemble a
sufficient force to accomplish the relief ; for, although he
now had 1,500 troops, three 75-millimetre guns, five
7-pounders and eight ·303 maxims in the country, at least
750 men would be required for the actual fighting, and not
less than 250 more to guard the 1,750 carriers, which was

the lowest number with which it would be possible to transport the hospital, sufficient food and ammunition to relieve the garrison and feed the troops, and six weeks' rations for the men who were to replace those in the fort. There was to be no repetition of former tactics, which had merely resulted in filling the fort with men without ammunition or food.

Colonel Willcocks and the Headquarter Staff left Prasu on the 1st of July and reached Fumsu the next afternoon. On the 4th he received the news of the Governor's escape, which had been sent on from Bekwai by Colonel Wilkinson. This was the letter that Sir Frederic Hodgson had sent off by the King of Bekwai's Linguist from Inkwanta, and contained the first definite intimation that a garrison had been left in the fort and could hold out until the 15th of July. Colonel Willcocks at once telegraphed to the Secretary of State guaranteeing to relieve Kumasi by that date, and sent runners with an urgent message to the Governor asking him, now that he had reached friendly country and did not need the troops with him, to detach as many as possible to assist in the relief. This message unfortunately failed to overtake the Governor; for a few hundred extra men would have been invaluable at this time, by freeing others who had to be left to hold posts on the line of communications.

There were only one and a half companies to escort all the carriers from Prasu, and Colonel Willcocks had therefore sent orders to Colonel Burroughs to come down with 300 men and meet him at Dompoasi, so that the Adansis, if they intended to make another attack there, would be caught between two fires. This caused the enemy to retire to one of their camps, and the column entered Bekwai on the 9th without having fired a shot. A detachment of 150 men and one gun were left at Kwisa to await the arrival of the last troops from Fumsu, who were to march up as rapidly as possible, and, after evacuating Kwisa, join the main column at Bekwai.

A runner who was sent off from Bekwai with a letter telling the garrison that relief was coming and a promise of

fifty pounds if he got through with it was never heard of
again ; but a message was received from Kumasi. This
was brought by a half-starved Hausa soldier, who had been
struggling through the forest for two days in momentary
peril of his life, and crawled into Esumeja on the morning
of the 10th, covered with sores and dazed with hunger and
fatigue, and produced from his cloth a scrap of paper on
which was written : " From O.C. Kumassi to O.C. Troops
Esumeja. His Excellency and main troops left for Coast
seventeen days ago ; relief most urgently wanted here.
Remaining small garrison diminishing : disease, etc.
Reduced rations for only few days more. F. E. Bishop,
Captain G.C.C." This last despairing appeal from Kumasi
probably did more than anything else could have done to
stimulate all ranks in their final effort to break through
the enemy's cordon. It was answered that night by firing
six star shells, but they were not seen from the fort. The
bearer of it was sent in a hammock to Bekwai, where Colonel
Willcocks promoted him to the rank of sergeant on the
spot and presented him with a sum of money, but he
afterwards expressed his regret in writing that he had not
recommended him for the Victoria Cross.

The remaining troops entered Bekwai at ten o'clock
that night, after an exceptionally fine march carried out
under great difficulties. Before leaving for Kumasi,
however, it was necessary to make a demonstration against
Kokofu, partly to reassure the King of Bekwai, who was
afraid the Ashantis there would attack him as soon as the
troops left, and partly to keep the Kokofus on guard in
their own town, and if possible draw some of the enemy
from their main position outside Kumasi to help them in
repelling the expected attack. This feint was made on
the 11th. Colonel Willcocks moved out to Esumeja with
a strong force, and then sent Captain Carleton of the West
India Regiment down the Kokofu road with 400 men and
two guns to clear the bush in places and build two rough
stockades, so that the enemy might be deceived into thinking that preparations were being made to attack them a
day or two later. His orders were, if possible, to avoid

becoming engaged, and at any rate not to run any risk of casualties. The ruse was completely successful ; for the Kokofus felt so certain that they were about to be attacked that they sent for and obtained a reinforcement of 2,000 men from the main stockades outside Kumasi, and the Ashantis were left in doubt until the very last moment whether the column would advance by the main road or through Kokofu, or by the less frequented track from Bekwai through Peki.

The night of the 12th of July was one of drizzling rain, and the 1,750 carriers required for the final march spent it within the bamboo palisaded enclosure that had been built at Bekwai, surrounded by the troops. Soon after two o'clock in the morning Colonel Willcocks sent for the King and obtained a few of his men as scouts, while others were provided by the War Captain of Peki. Final orders were then issued, and it at last became known that the advance was to be made through Peki. This route, though a little longer than the main road through Esumeja, had the advantage of running for a greater distance through the friendly Bekwai country and avoiding some of the enemy's most formidable stockades. The relieving force marched out at six o'clock ; it consisted of 60 Europeans, 700 men of the West African Frontier Force, 200 of the West African Regiment, 50 Sierra Leone Frontier Police, and 50 gunners with two 75-millimetre guns, four 7-pounders and six maxims. The only troops now left to hold posts on the road were 200 men in Bekwai, 100 at Esumeja and 50 at Obuasi. The honour of leading the way fell to Captain Eden's [1] company, on the ground that he had volunteered to remain in the fort after it had been relieved. It was essential that Peki should be reached that night ; but it was a terrible march, and although the distance to be covered was only fifteen miles, it took the main column nineteen and a half hours to get in and the rear-guard two hours longer. The rain poured in ceaseless torrents throughout the day, and the whole road was little better than a swamp, while the swollen streams and other bad places

[1] Oxford Light Infantry.

continually delayed the transport and necessitated frequent halts. " The few hammocks allowable in a column some three miles in length were reserved for the sick and wounded, so that one had to foot it both going and returning. Some hours before our destination was gained night came on. Thenceforward, worn out, we struggled along, holding on to each other in the inky forest-darkness. Nothing broke the deathlike silence, save the dropping of water from the trees overhead and the squelch of filthy mud churned up by three thousand feet. Soaked with rain, the column was forced at times to wade waist-deep in water. The exhausted carriers fell out by dozens, one even died ; others injured themselves and caused much delay. When a carrier dropped from sheer collapse, his load would be cheerfully picked up and shouldered by some soldier ; so that, wonderful to relate, not a single one was lost. Frequently some jaded white man would fall asleep when a short halt was necessary to help the transport over a particularly bad spot. In the small hours our immediate goal was reached, and, too fatigued either to undress or take food, we turned into the native huts to get a few hours' rest. But even then sleep was not for all, for sentries had to be posted and pickets thrown out round the village." [1]

The Chief of Peki produced two Ashanti prisoners whom he had captured ; but they maintained a stony silence when questioned, and Colonel Willcocks therefore told them that he intended to pardon and release them on condition that they took a message from him to their camp at Treda. This was a large fetish village a short distance farther up the road, which was known to be strongly held. They were then taken outside the lines and ordered to tell their Chiefs that the Colonel would halt in Peki throughout the next day, but would attack them without fail on the day after if they did not abandon their position. Partly to keep up this deception and partly to give the men a much-needed rest, the start the next morning was delayed until eight o'clock. Moreover, rapidity had not been a distinguishing

[1] Biss, p. 183.

feature of the column's advance hitherto, and this, combined with the message of the night before, quite deceived
the enemy, so that, when the advance-guard reached the
slope on the top of which Treda stood, they found the
Ashantis quite unprepared and dashed in among them
with the bayonet. The place was cleared within a few
minutes, before the tail of the column had even left Peki,
and at a cost of only one man dangerously and two slightly
wounded. Large quantities of food were captured here,
together with one of Lady Hodgson's boxes and Major
Morris' saddle. After a halt to destroy the place, the
column left ; but it was now passing through the thick of
the enemy's country, and progress was slower than ever,
partly because of the necessity for careful scouting, and
partly on account of numerous delays caused by attempts
by small parties of the enemy to get at the carriers. It
was already four o'clock when Inkwanta was reached, and
it was dark before the rear-guard got in, so a halt was made
there for the night. This was not the village through
which the Governor had passed, but a small place of the
same name [1] situated six miles from Treda and five from
Kumasi. During the last march on the 15th the enemy
continually harassed the flanks of the column, but were
kept off by the maxims. They then tried to rush the
hospital and rice carriers, who became panic-stricken, threw
down their loads, and caused a great deal of confusion.
The rear-guard was delayed for some time in repelling this
attack and fell about a mile behind ; but the enemy were
at last beaten off, and the column closed up. Colonel
Willcocks had intended to fortify the last village roughly
and leave the baggage and carriers there under a sufficient
escort, while he pushed on with the fighting men and
returned for the transport after Kumasi had been entered.
These attacks and the bad condition of the path, however,
had delayed the column so much that there was no time
to carry out this arrangement. At a little after four o'clock
the stockades were found : they were situated at a point
a little before the path debouched into the Cape Coast road

[1] A very common name. It means a cross road or junction of roads.

about a mile outside Kumasi. One was built right across the path, with smaller works on either side, while still larger and stronger ones lay away to the right across the main road. When the Ashantis found that the column was advancing by the Peki road, they hurriedly cleared the ground to the right, so as to bring a cross fire on it from the main stockades, and a heavy and continuous fire was now opened from the front and both sides. That on the left, however, was quickly silenced, and Colonel Wilkinson, who was in command of the advance-guard, had the guns brought up, while Colonel Willcocks moved up to the head of the column and gave orders for a heavy fire to be maintained while the men of the advance-guard and main body were extended across the front. The three millimetres were directed against the stockade in front, with one 7-pounder on the left and the others on the right ; and their continuous fire at a range of only about a hundred yards, not only compelled the Ashantis to keep behind their stockades instead of attacking the flanks, but also prevented them from looking over the tops of their defences, which were not loop-holed, and made them fire high.

The men, clearing the bush as they went, soon formed a line about six hundred yards in length, and the bugles then sounded the " cease fire " and the whole line sprang up with a shout and dashed forward against the stockades. The sudden silence, after the roar of the guns and carbines, was so startling that the enemy also stopped in astonishment, but, though they recovered almost immediately, they could not withstand the determined charge of the troops, who charged headlong at and over the stockades and drove the discomfited Ashantis up the road.

The troops had behaved splendidly. It must be remembered that they were nearly all young soldiers, that they had hitherto had no big success, but only a series of reverses, and that they knew they were greatly outnumbered by an enemy famed for his fighting qualities, flushed with victory, and entrenched in a strong position ; yet they charged forward without the least hesitation and would not be denied. Even the Commandant's escort

joined in, and he was left standing with no one but his two
orderlies near him. Only two men were killed and two
officers and twenty men wounded, but the Ashanti Chief
afterwards estimated his dead at 200. The stockade
across the road was pulled down to allow the transport
to pass, and the terrible havoc created by the millimetre
shells was then evident on every side. They had gone right
through the stockade and burst beyond it amongst the
crowded Ashantis, whose mutilated bodies lay around.
" A pile of mangled forms, some still breathing, lay in
confusion, many having fallen across one another, some
disembowelled, another with the whole face blown off—
all variously mutilated. Limbs had been carried yards
away into the bush beyond, and the ground was slippery
with blood." [1] A few minutes' march then brought the
troops into the broad road leading into Kumasi. They
pushed on almost at the double ; but it was impossible
to see the fort until within a few hundred yards of it, and,
though everyone listened intently, no sound was heard, and
there were several moments of suspense lest the relief should,
after all, have come too late. Everywhere was desolation.
The only living things visible were the vultures that rose
lazily from the decomposing corpses lying on the path or
in the long grass beside it, while over all hung a depressing
silence and a sickening stench. On reaching the top of
the slope, however, just after six o'clock, the fort burst into
view and all doubts were set at rest by the notes of a bugle
sounding the " general salute." The gates opened and the
three officers [2] of the garrison, with the few emaciated men
who still survived and had strength enough to walk, came
out to welcome the column.

Soon after the relief of the fort, the disappointed Ashantis
set fire to the Basel Mission buildings, but were driven off
by a party of a hundred Hausas, and at eight o'clock a pre-
arranged signal of five star shells was fired to let the garrison

---

[1] Biss, p. 190.
[2] Captain Bishop was given a D.S.O., Mr. Ralph a direct commission
in the Royal Fusiliers, and Doctor Hay a C.M.G. for their share in
the defence of the fort.

at Bekwai know that the column was in and that the news of the relief of Kumasi could be telegraphed to England.

The column was now to return to Bekwai with those of the old garrison who were fit to be moved, leaving Captain Eden with two other officers, a medical officer, two British non-commissioned officers, 155 men of the 2nd Battalion West African Frontier Force, and twenty Gold Coast Constabulary gunners to hold the fort. They were to be well supplied with ammunition and provisioned for fifty-four days ; but this only left half rations for one day for the remainder of the troops, who could not therefore spend more than one day in Kumasi. Much had to be done, however, before they left : the road must be cleared, and the surroundings of the fort were indescribable. On the 16th, therefore, a force of 400 men under Colonel Burroughs went down the road and destroyed the stockades and war camps that had been carried the day before. The Ashantis, always slow to rally after a defeat, made no attempt to oppose them, but had removed all their dead during the night, only one forearm having been overlooked. The camp behind the main stockade was found to contain over a thousand huts regularly laid out and fitted with raised beds of bamboo, and there were even small gardens with bamboo seats in them, while empty gin bottles lay around in hundreds. Meanwhile, 600 more men and 1,000 carriers worked throughout the day to clear the precincts of the fort. Tall elephant grass had grown up almost to its walls, and as this was cleared away, skeletons, and corpses in every stage of decomposition were found everywhere ; some even under the walls of the fort itself. Most of them were headless, but had died of starvation. Numbers were found lying among the rose bushes in the garden, and eight more were discovered in one hut alone within eighty yards of the fort walls. Many, again, lay close to the water supply, and over a hundred more in a single hollow near the gaol. There was no time to bury them all, and they were there-fore collected into heaps and burnt with the materials of the huts that still stood in the refugees' camp, poisoning the air with an acrid smoke far into the night.

At daybreak on the 17th the column left by the Peki road.   There were now plenty of unladen carriers available for the hammocks and stretchers, in which nearly every one of the old garrison had to be carried.   Only a very few of them could limp along slowly, and the column dragged out to four miles in length, but fortunately not a shot was fired at it.   Encumbered with its sick and wounded and the women and children from the refugees' camp, the pace was slower than ever, and halts also had to be made for the destruction of the villages on the road and as many of the farms as could be found in the time.   Peki, however, was reached on the second day, and Colonel Willcocks then pushed through to Bekwai with a flying column, leaving Colonel Burroughs to make two marches with the others.

Lieutenant-Colonel Morland, King's Royal Rifle Corps, 1st Battalion West African Frontier Force, and some Special Service Officers came into Bekwai with a large convoy of provisions and clothing on the day of Colonel Willcocks' return ; but the troops were suffering from the effects of the exposure and hard work of the last few days and the foul air of Kumasi, and it was necessary to give them a few days' rest and await the arrival of reinforcements before commencing the second portion of the campaign—the punishment of the Ashantis and pacification of the country.

It has been said that Colonel Willcocks might have relieved Kumasi very much sooner than he did ; that because he moved up rapidly during the last few days there was no reason why he should not have overcome the difficulties that confronted him very much earlier, and that he purposely left the relief until the very last possible day.   He has, in fact, been most unjustly accused of deliberately striving after dramatic effect at the cost of needlessly prolonging the sufferings and anxieties of those in the fort.   Such allegations, however, can only be the outcome of ignorance, either of the actual facts or of the local conditions, or of both combined.   They are absolutely without foundation, and, when all the circumstances are fairly considered, it will be seen that, so far from Colonel Willcocks having been guilty of any wanton or needless delay, his success was in reality a brilliant achievement, which he was only able to accomplish on the 15th of July by taking risks which it is unlikely that he would have thought justifiable, had it not been that he was driven on by dire necessity by knowing that it was the last day on which the garrison could be saved.

In the whole history of the country there is no parallel instance with which this campaign can be compared. The nearest is Sir Garnet Wolseley's march to Kumasi in 1874. He, however, landed on the 2nd of October 1873, and was in the country exactly three months before he reached the Pra and more than four before he entered Kumasi; whereas Colonel Willcocks relieved Kumasi seven weeks and one day after landing at Cape Coast. Both officers had to await the arrival of their troops; but still there was a vast difference. Wolseley arrived with thirty-six Special Service Officers and had Royal Engineers to prepare the road and build rest camps for him, and plenty of time for this and the collection and transport of supplies, which, even then, he found difficult enough. Willcocks, however, landed at Cape Coast with no Staff, found nothing ready for him, and had no time to improve the road and little enough for the collection of stores. When he landed, the garrison of the fort was numerically stronger than the whole force he had under him, and if they could not get out, it would have been palpably absurd for him to try to get in. The rising of the Adansis, who had been loyal in 1874, had also greatly increased the length of hostile country through which he must pass, while the necessity for affording protection to the white men at Obuasi created another fresh difficulty. Willcocks actually relieved Kumasi with less than half the number of troops that Wolseley employed, and, while his were all African mercenaries with no traditions of past glories won, and mostly young soldiers at that, Wolseley had the services of three picked British battalions and a Naval Brigade. It is true that he found the enemy in occupation of the country south of the Pra;

but they were already preparing to retire, and though, when he entered Ashanti territory he was opposed by an army that fought desperately in defence of its capital, yet it was an army that had suffered repeated defeats at Elmina, Esaman, Abakrampa and elsewhere, and whose subsequent retreat had been turned into a panic-stricken rout; while he was using troops whose march was an unbroken series of successes. Willcocks, on the other hand, had to rely on troops who had already met with disaster and failure, and whose first great success was not scored until they were outside Kumasi; while he was opposed to an Ashanti army already flushed with repeated victories Willcocks, too, was further handicapped by Colonel Carter's retreat and Colonel Burroughs' disastrous attack on Kokofu, both of which, though these officers thought the course they took was the best in the circumstances, were really undertaken contrary to his orders. But by far the greatest contrast lay in the fact that, while the expedition of 1873–4 was carried out during the dry season, the relief of Kumasi had to be accomplished at the unhealthiest time of year, when the rains were at their height. The tremendous difference that this one fact makes in the difficulties of campaigning or travelling of any kind can only be appreciated by those who have experienced them

When Colonel Willcocks landed at Cape Coast, besides having no Staff, he found that the few troops that had yet arrived had gone up country in small detachments with no settled plan, and were isolated and practically helpless in different posts on the line of communications, seventy miles of which was in the hands of the enemy. The available maps, too, though fairly accurate so far as the main road was concerned, were useless for anything else, and even such news as had come through from Kumasi was very misleading. It was useless to attempt to push through to Kumasi until not only sufficient troops, but also an adequate supply of food and ammunition could be taken there and this could not be attempted until the carriers arrived Even then small-pox broke out amongst them, and there were at one time as many as 500 cases. On the long marches over roads that were little better than swamps, with everyone obliged to walk and wet to the skin, the work was terribly hard and caused much sickness ; while the delays caused by specially bad stretches of road, swollen rivers and streams, and other obstructions were endless. Night after night it was dark when the column got in, and the rear-guard was, of course, later still ; while nights spent in drenching rain with little or no shelter deprived everyone of sorely needed rest.

It was only by a change of tactics and by taking considerable risks that Colonel Willcocks succeeded in reaching Kumasi by the 15th at all. After the first reverses, orders were issued that any column when attacked should only return the enemy's fire long enough to allow the troops to extend their front, and should then charge with the bayonet, thus saving the transport of an immense amount of ammunition and at the same time giving the men confidence in their ability to rout the Ashantis. More than once convoys had to be sent up with very insufficient escorts, trusting to chance that they would not be attacked, while the final advance and provisioning the new garrison were only made possible by practically abandoning the lines of communication, restricting officers to two loads each, commandeering all private stores, cutting everyone down to half rations, and allowing for a halt of only one day in Kumasi. It is evident, therefore, that so far from any needless delay having occurred, the relief of Kumasi was a remarkably fine piece of work, carried out in the face of almost insuperable difficulties.

CHAPTER XXVI

THE PUNISHMENT OF THE ASHANTIS

1900

COLONEL WILLCOCKS' plan for the second portion of the campaign was to keep the Ashantis in their camps around Kumasi, by making them believe that it was still impossible for him to occupy the place in force, while he cleared the flank of the line of communications by destroying Kokofu and defeating the main Adansi army. So soon as the whole of the southern district had been cleared of the enemy and the main road opened, the stockades around Kumasi were to be destroyed, after which a general advance would be made on Kumasi by several columns and that place used as the base of operations in driving the enemy north and trying to make them unite their forces, so that they might then be defeated in one final and decisive action.

A detachment of Sikhs and half a battalion of the Central African Regiment landed at Cape Coast two days after the return of the column to Bekwai, while 1,500 more carriers were on their way from East Africa, and the 2nd Battalion of the Central African Regiment and several thousand more carriers followed soon afterwards. Meanwhile, Captain Benson of the Shropshire Light Infantry, with whom was Captain Wilcox of the Gold Coast Constabulary, was in charge of the Eastern Akim Levies with orders to approach Kumasi gradually from the east, as Glover had done in 1874. Between this and the main column, the Western Akims from Insuaim, under Major Cramer, 3rd Battalion Highland Light Infantry, were to advance through Eastern Adansi as the country was cleared, while a force of several thousand Denkeras that had been raised by Captain Hall of the Gold Coast Police was to advance on the western flank of the main road under Captain Wright of the Manchester Regiment.

The attack on Kokofu was made on Sunday the 22nd of July. Colonel Morland was in command, and left Bekwai at daybreak with six companies, three 75-millimetre guns, two 7-pounders and four ·303 maxims. The strength of the column was increased to 800 men by drawing on the Esumeja garrison, and only the smallest possible number of carriers accompanied it. The small village that had been burnt by Captain Hall was soon reached and a short council held there. A little distance beyond this was the main stockade, built on a slope leading down to a swamp and small stream, on the far side of which was the Kokofu war camp and then the town itself. A proposal to cut a fresh path, so as to avoid the stockade altogether, was negatived on account of the density of the bush, and Major Melliss was therefore ordered to advance with one company, and, directly he came within sight of the stockade, to rush it at once without waiting to fire, and then extend his men along the near bank of the stream and hold it until the guns could be brought up. The men moved stealthily out of the village, and presently, round a bend in the path, sighted the stockade only thirty yards ahead. The whispered order to charge was passed down the line, the bugles rang out, and with a hoarse shout the men dashed headlong against the stockade and swarmed over it ; but only to find it empty. The enemy had once more been taken completely by surprise, and had been so confident that there was no force near them, that even the guard usually left in the stockade and the sentries themselves had gone back to the camp to join the others in their morning meal. Now, however, they came running back in hundreds. To halt would mean disaster ; so the Hausas, disregarding the hurried fire that was poured into them from the front and flanks, charged on with the bayonet, and the Kokofus in front, after a moment's hesitation, broke and fled in the wildest disorder. On rushed the men without a check, through the stream and war camp up the slope beyond, and into the town itself. Numbers of naked Ashantis were still pouring out of the houses and flying for their lives down the road beyond, and some thirty others lay dead in the street ; but the company was now far ahead of the column, and to have followed the enemy blindly into the forest beyond would have entailed a serious risk of being cut off. Half the company, therefore, was halted in the town, while the remainder continued the pursuit ; but the rout of the enemy was complete, and the whole road was found strewn with Chiefs' chairs, cloths, guns and other property that they had abandoned in their flight. By the time this half company returned, the rest of the force had come in without a single casualty, two companies thrown out on either side had finally silenced the snipers, and the men were busy eating the food that the Ashantis had been cooking for themselves. The town was then razed to the ground, a number of guns were collected and burnt, the powder exploded, the war camp and stockade destroyed, and the column returned to Bekwai. It arrived there just as it was getting dark, to be congratulated by Colonel Willcocks, who turned out with his whole Staff and paraded his body-guard to do it honour Kokofu was no more, and for the first time during the campaign a decisive victory had been gained without a single casualty.

The destruction of Kokofu was followed by the re-occupation of Kwisa on the 26th by a company of the West African Regiment under Captains Stallard and Tighe, thus opening the main road for convoys.

On the 26th a telegram was received direct from the Queen congratulating the Commandant and troops on their relief of Kumasi, with another from Lord Wolseley and one from Mr. Chamberlain informing Colonel Willcocks that Her Majesty had been pleased to promote him K.C.M.G.

The Adansi army now had to be defeated and dispersed It was known to consist of about 6,000 men and to be

encamped somewhere to the east of Dompoasi, and Major
Beddoes left Bekwai on the 26th with 400 men of the
Northern Nigerian Battalion of the West African Frontier
Force, one 75-millimetre gun and a 7-pounder to find it.
For this small column to enter the absolutely unknown
country beyond Dompoasi and seek out an immensely
superior force of the enemy, with no clue to its exact
whereabouts and while its own communications were
entirely cut off, was a sufficiently hazardous experiment,
even though it was known that Major Cramer and his Akim
Levies were moving up towards the same point from the
south-east ; but it would have proved far more difficult
had not Major Beddoes had the good fortune to capture a
prisoner near Kwisa on the 27th, who, on condition that
his life should be spared, undertook to act as guide. He
led the column rapidly through the forest in a north-easterly
direction towards Yankoma, on the Kokofu-Insuaim road,
and on the 29th a large deserted village was reached.
Traces of the enemy were visible everywhere, and when
the column moved out in the morning it was almost
immediately attacked in front and flank. Throughout
the day the enemy disputed every yard of the advance,
and were driven from position after position in the undergrowth by the fire of the maxims and extended companies.
More than once they made determined rushes to within a
few yards of the troops before they were repulsed by the
guns. Major Beddoes was severely wounded in the thigh
early in the morning, and had to hand over the command
to Captain Greer of the Royal Warwickshire Regiment ;
Lieutenant Phillips, Royal Artillery, and Lieutenant
Swabey, West India Regiment attached to the Northern
Nigerian West African Frontier Force, were also severely
wounded, and two more Europeans and twenty-five of the
rank and file were hit. Once, the enemy got to within a
few yards of a 7-pounder gun, which must have been lost
but for the steady volley firing of its crew. The column,
however, fought its way slowly on, in the hope of reaching
some village before nightfall, and a turning movement by
Captain Neal, 3rd Battalion Scottish Rifles attached to

the Lagos Constabulary, again drove the enemy back. But at about four o'clock they made another stand and fought really desperately. Not only did they hold the Hausas at bay, but made several most determined charges that were only repulsed with difficulty. Once, in trying to capture a temporarily disabled 7-pounder, they almost succeeded in breaking through the line ; but were driven back at the last moment by a countercharge by Captain Monck Mason of the Royal Munster Fusiliers at the head of a company. This was followed by a general charge, which finally routed the Adansis and carried the troops right through into their war camp.

The great number of dead that lay on the line of the advance and in the camp itself, where as many as ten lay in a single heap, was sufficient proof of the desperate nature of the fighting and the determined way in which the Adansis had defended their position. They had their great fetish Bondo with them, and all their women and children had been collected in this camp, which they had felt sure the white man would never be able to find. Throughout the day they had been fighting a splendid rearguard action to cover the retreat of these women, but could not stand against the hail of lead from the maxims, and their last stand had been made in the hope of defeating the column before they met the Akim Levies under Major Cramer, who, they well knew, were advancing towards them from the south. They failed, however, and then, fearing to be caught between two fires, fled northwards. Five white men had been wounded, three of them so seriously that they had to be invalided home, and thirty-five rank and file were killed or wounded. This precluded any possibility of pursuit, even had it been necessary, and the column set out next morning on its return march to Bekwai, where it arrived on the 1st of August.

On the 2nd, the Sikhs marched in from Cape Coast, and on the 5th, the Denkera Levies arrived at Esumeja, and Captain Wright reported that their King, Inkwantabissa, a man with many good points but much addicted to drink, had treated him with contempt and refused to allow the

men to obey his orders. Sir James Willcocks, therefore,
sent for the King, and, when he refused to come, threatened
to have him brought in by an armed party. He then
came to Bekwai in great state and evidently disposed
to stand on his dignity ; but some plain speaking by
the Commandant gave him a more accurate idea of his
own importance, and he afterwards gave no further
trouble, but did some really useful work with his
people.

When Sir James Willcocks left Kumasi, he had arranged
with Captain Eden to fire star shells every Sunday evening
to show that all was well with the garrison ; but, owing
to thick weather, it had been impossible to see these signals
on the last two Sundays, and it was rumoured that the
Ashantis had again attacked the fort. Moreover, a runner
had come in late on the 31st of July with news that the
enemy were preparing to attack Peki in revenge for the
help its people had given to the troops, and Sir James
therefore decided to send up a column at once to put this
place in a state of defence and then go on to Kumasi,
destroy the remaining stockades around the town, and
increase the garrison of the fort to ten Europeans and 300
soldiers. This was made all the easier by the opportune
arrival of further reinforcements and the occurrence of a
temporary break in the rains.

Major Melliss left on the 1st of August with one company of Hausas and two guns to strengthen Peki, but no
attack was made. On the 3rd, while a party of men were
out cutting materials for a palisade that was being built
round the village, they came upon a starving and wounded
soldier and brought him in. This was one of the Lagos
Constabulary who had been wounded on the day the
Governor broke out of the fort and been obliged to fall out.
From the 23rd of June till the 3rd of August he had been
hiding in the forest, often surrounded by numbers of the
enemy, keeping himself alive on such roots as he could find
by night, and crawling slowly and painfully towards
friendly country as his strength permitted ; but the
terribly slow progress that he had been able to make in

his weak condition was evident from the fact that he was still within eleven miles of Kumasi.

On the 4th, Colonel Burroughs marched in with the newly arrived half battalion of the Central African Regiment and Sikhs under Lieutenant (local Major) A. S. Cobbe, Indian Staff Corps, two more 75-millimetre guns and two 7-pounders. This brought the strength of the column up to 750 men, and on the 5th it advanced to Kumasi. No organized opposition was met with, but a party of the enemy hovered on the flanks for a time, killing one carrier and wounding four others before they were finally driven off. Kumasi was reached at six o'clock that evening, when the reports of an attack on the fort proved unfounded.

Next morning, the 6th, arrangements were made for the destruction of the remaining stockades. It was not known for certain whether they were still occupied by the enemy, but no one supposed that they would be held in force, and the intention was for two columns of 300 men each, under Majors Melliss and Cobbe, to destroy the stockades beyond Bantama and near the Wesleyan Mission during the morning, and those on the Ejisu and Accra roads in the afternoon. The capture of these positions, however, proved a far more difficult undertaking than had been anticipated.

Major Melliss' column, consisting of three companies of the West African Frontier Force and a millimetre gun, moved off towards Bantama at ten o'clock, followed by a number of unladen carriers to demolish the stockades. The enemy were seen running out of Bantama, and the column followed them down the Intimide road, where the stockade was presently discovered at about eighty-yards range. This stockade was loop-holed, and before the maxim could be got into position a terrific fusillade was opened on the leading company. The gun, however, was mounted, but its fire and the volleys of the men made no impression on the enemy. The bush, moreover, was so thick, and the fire from the flanks so heavy, that it was impossible to cut a way round, so the millimetre was

brought up and Sergeant Desborough, Royal Artillery,
fired six rounds of double-common shell. He failed to give
the gun sufficient elevation, however, and each shell
ricochetted over the stockade. He then changed to
shrapnel and fired four rounds ; but it soon became evident
that even this was making little or no impression on the
enemy's fire, which was becoming worse instead of better.
Several sharp-shooters, too, armed with rifles, were firing
steadily from a high tree on the right, but were cleared out
by the maxim.

Every white man and many of the rank and file of the
leading company had now been hit, and a heap of wounded
lay around each gun. After a quarter of an hour of rapid
but ineffective firing therefore, Major Melliss ordered a
charge, and, as the bugles rang out, the men sprang forward
down the slope with him at their head. This charge was
made in the face of a galling fire, for the Ashantis stood
firm ; but within a few moments officers and men were
dropping over the stockade into their midst and a fierce
hand-to-hand fight ensued. Still the Ashantis grimly
defended their position, and it was not until they found
themselves getting every moment more outnumbered,
and many of them had been laid low by sword or bayonet,
that at last they turned and fled, hotly pursued by the excited troops. When the enormous war camp was reached,
the last of its garrison were disappearing into the bush, and
the troops were halted while Captain Eden's company
went to destroy Intimide. The camp was then burnt,
the stockade demolished, and Bantama itself razed to the
ground on the return march.

This stockade was a very solid structure six feet high,
300 yards long, and crescent-shaped, so as to give a cross
fire. Major Melliss, Captain Biss, Colour-Sergeant Foster
and eight others had been wounded, several of them
severely, and the Ashantis' loss was very heavy. A bugler
boy named Moma was wounded in the head just before the
final advance, but stood quietly awaiting the order, and
then sounded the " charge " with the blood streaming
down his face and dashed at and over the stockade with

the rest. He was awarded the Medal for Distinguished Conduct in the Field.

Meanwhile, Major Cobbe's force of two companies of the 1st Central African Regiment, the Sikhs, one company of the West African Regiment and a millimetre gun, which had left the fort an hour later, could be heard heavily engaged on the Kintampo road. They had a very hard fight, and, as at Intimide, it was found impossible to drive the enemy out by rifle and gun fire. Major Cobbe, therefore, left the company of West Africans to continue the attack on the front of the stockade while be began to cut his way through the bush to the right with the Central Africans and Sikhs, so as to attack the enemy's left flank. The tall grass and undergrowth, however, made his progress so slow that the troops lost heavily, and the Sikhs, when at last they reached the stockade, found themselves still in front of it and had to fall back and move off to the right again. This stockade was also about 300 yards in length, but had been built in horseshoe form, so that the men were practically surrounded by it. At last, however, Major Cobbe succeeded in working his party behind it, and a simultaneous charge from front and flank then routed the Ashantis with heavy loss. The camp and stockade were destroyed, and the column reached the fort just before dark with a long string of wounded in hammocks, on stretchers, and in improvised litters made by slinging blankets from rough poles. Major Cobbe had been severely wounded in the thigh, and Sergeant-Major Rose was slightly wounded, while of the detachment of fifty Sikhs, one had been killed and one dangerously, seven severely, and ten more slightly wounded. The Central African Regiment had one man mortally, nine severely, and seven slightly wounded, and the West Africans one severely and two slightly wounded. Two carriers had been mortally wounded, two severely, and one slightly. Major Cobbe was afterwards decorated with the Distinguished Service Order.

The unexpected amount of resistance that had been met with in these two actions, the heavy casualties that had been sustained, and the quantity of ammunition that had been expended out of the 300 rounds per man that had been brought from Bekwai, precluded any possibility of making similar attacks on the other stockades before marching down the main road, where considerable resistance was expected and other stockades were known to exist. At the same time, the orders given to Colonel Burroughs had been most emphatic, and he had to be back in Bekwai by the 12th. He therefore decided to attempt the capture of another stockade by a night attack, trusting to the change of tactics so to disconcert the enemy that they would voluntarily abandon their other positions. The morning was spent in burying the dead from the previous day's fighting—the Sikhs, of course, burning theirs—and at midday Captain Loch went out with a party of West Africans to reconnoitre the stockade on the Accra road, which was the one chosen for attack. The men holding it had been strongly reinforced since the previous day's fighting, for the Ashantis themselves expected the next move would be made against it; but its capture would remove a danger from the flank of the column as it left by the Cape Coast road, and would also isolate the Ejisu road defences. While Captain Loch made a careful detailed sketch of the road, his men crept through the grass and succeeded in locating the stockade before they were discovered by the enemy's sentries, when they at once retired, leaving the Ashantis to believe that they had been preparing to attack them, but had thought better of it.

The attack was to be made by 500 men under Colonel Burroughs in person, and was to be carried out solely with the bayonet. At eight o'clock the men fell in, and, led by Captain Loch's company, stole quietly down the road. It had been arranged that when the stockade was reached the two leading companies, under Major Melliss and Captain Loch, should quietly extend on as broad a front as possible along the stockade, and then swarm over and dash into the enemy with a yell of triumph, while the companies in rear were to turn outwards, so as to guard the flanks from attack from the war camp and cover the retreat of the advanced party in case of mishap. This movement was being carried out as silently as possible, and the men were within ten or fifteen yards of the stockade, when Lieutenant Greer of the West India Regiment, who was with Captain Loch's men on the right, stumbled over a stone in the path and alarmed the enemy's sentries. They fired two signal guns, which were almost immediately followed by a volley from the stockade, which mortally wounded Lieutenant Greer. Further concealment was out of the question, so the order to charge was given at once, and the men, fresh from the sight of their fallen officer, sprang forward with a yell of rage, and, with their bayonets gleaming in the moonlight, poured over the stockade to avenge him. The Ashantis, already startled by the suddenness of the attack, could not stem this tide of infuriated men and fled in every direction with the troops in hot pursuit. " There, through the war camp's centre, ran a road, inundated with terror-stricken demons, as they fled in panic from their huts, struggling to force a passage down that living lane. Swords and bayonets could not be pulled out quick enough to be plunged afresh into another body. . . . The air was rent with shouts and groans ; the earth was strewn with corpses and reeking with blood. The headlong race continued to right and left, and down the road." [1] One camp after another was entered and passed in this fierce pursuit, but when the fourth was reached, the men had to stop from sheer exhaustion. A cordon of sentries was then thrown out while the camps and stockade were destroyed, and the column returned to the fort just before eleven o'clock. It afterwards became known that the panic had spread to the Ashantis on the Ejisu road also, who, thinking that they, too, were about to be attacked at dead of night, abandoned their stockade and never returned.

On the 8th, after having reinforced the garrison as arranged and left the wounded in the fort, the column returned to Bekwai, which, although heavy fighting had been expected, was reached without anything having been

[1] Biss, p. 258.

seen of the enemy : their stockades and camps had been
found deserted, and were of course destroyed. This was
partly because Ya Ashantiwa, the Queen-Mother of Ejisu,
had summoned all the Chiefs to a meeting to discuss what
had best be done now that the siege had been raised,
and what the white man was likely to do next after his
extraordinary and unexpected conduct the night before.

The scattered remnants of the Kokofu and Adansi
armies were believed to have retired to the fertile district
around Lake Busumtwi, and Sir James Willcocks therefore
sent two columns under Lieutenant-Colonels Henstock [1]
and Wilkinson to clear the country before the Levies
spread over it to loot the farms, and to make sure that
the Ashantis were not collecting on the flank before the
Headquarters were removed to Kumasi. Colonel Henstock
left Bekwai on the 14th to pass through Dompoasi and
Dadiasi and advance on the lake from the south, while
Colonel Wilkinson left a day later to follow the road
through Kokofu and approach it from the north. The
former, however, had to retrace his steps after reaching
Dadiasi for lack of roads, and because of the incompetence
of his guides, and, travelling by nearly the same route as
Colonel Wilkinson, overtook him at the lake. With the
exception of a few Ashantis in the villages round the lake
itself, who at once retired, nothing was seen of the enemy,
and, after reconnoitring the district for two days, the
columns set out together for Bekwai. Meanwhile, the
last reinforcements had arrived—namely, another weak
half battalion of the West African Regiment under Captain
Leveson, and ten officers and 481 men of the Central
African Regiment, and a few Sikh non-commissioned
officers under Captain (local Lieutenant-Colonel) Brake,
D.S.O., Royal Artillery. The latter met the returning
columns at Kokofu, having been sent out to warn them of
a rumoured reconcentration of the enemy at Ajimamu, a
little to the north of Esumeja. They therefore turned off
to Ajimamu, but found its rumoured occupation a myth,
and returned to Bekwai on the 24th and 25th, after a wet

[1] West India Regiment, Chief Staff Officer.

and tiring journey. Colonel Brake, in the meantime, had gone towards Jachi on the road to Ejisu, and succeeded in surprising and routing a body of the enemy, who were pursued into the village. A great deal of property, including a number of flags, Chiefs' chairs and umbrellas was captured, together with about 140 guns, several maxim belts, a quantity of ·303 ammunition, and about two hundred pounds' worth of gold ornaments and specie. Chief Opoku, who had commanded the Adansis in all their earlier actions, was among the killed.

The country to the south of Kumasi had now been cleared of the enemy, and Major Cramer's Levies were ordered up to the lake district to eat up the country, which was really one vast farm, while one company of the Central African Regiment was sent to support them and frustrate any attempt on the part of the enemy to return there. Colonel Wilkinson and Captain Haslewood were then ordered down to Accra to recruit and organize the Gold Coast Constabulary preparatory to their taking over the military control of the country at the conclusion of operations. The post at Bekwai, where small-pox was very bad and the deaths from this disease now amounted to twelve a day, was abandoned ; and the transport arrangements were re-organized so that carriers were posted to and worked between fixed depots, changing loads half-way between them. Detachments were left at Esumeja and Kwisa, while Fumsu and Prasu were held by men of the old Kumasi garrison who had now recovered sufficiently to be able to return to duty. Then, the line of communications having been secured, the Headquarters Staff and advanced base were removed to Kumasi, preparatory to following the Ashantis into the heart of their country and finally defeating them.

On the 28th of August, Colonel Burroughs left with 750 men and 3,000 carriers for Peki, the latter returning next day to bring up the remainder of the stores with the Commandant. He left Bekwai on the 30th with an even stronger column, and, joining Colonel Burroughs that night, the combined force reached Kumasi the next evening. So

bad was the road at this time that the column took twelve
hours to cover the eleven miles from Peki.

Meanwhile, Colonel Brake had marched out on the 29th
with 350 men of the 2nd Battalion of the Central African
Regiment, 350 of the 2nd Battalion West African Frontier
Force, 100 West Africans, 40 Sierra Leone Frontier Police,
2 millimetre guns, a 7-pounder, and the smallest possible
number of carriers to advance through Kokofu and attack
Ejisu before joining the others in Kumasi. Ejisu, which
was the headquarters of Ya Ashantiwa and her army, had
practically been made the capital since the relief of Kumasi,
and heavy fighting was expected there. It was even
hoped that the capture of this place might bring the
campaign to an end ; for it was well known that the rank
and file of the Ashanti army were tired of fighting and
camping out in such bad weather and with so little
success, and that the Kokofus had already sent to ask
the King of Akim to intercede for peace. A messenger
bearing a flag of truce had also come in from Jachi, but
was told that the Chiefs must come in person before any
negotiations could be opened.

This force arrived before a stockade outside Ejisu
shortly before ten o'clock on the morning of the 31st of
August. The leading company of the Central African
Regiment, under Captain Johnstone-Stewart, extended
across the front, while another company, under Captain
Gordon, began to work its way through the bush on the
left, and two companies of the West African Frontier
Force, under Captain Greer, moved off to the right. Owing
to the density of the bush and the number of rifle pits,
entanglements, and felled trees in their path, however,
their progress was very slow, and it took them two hours
to reach the enemy's flanks. Meanwhile, the millimetre
guns had been hurling double-common shell against the
stockade, and, for the first time during the campaign,
succeeded in breaching it. Shell after shell burst among
the timbers, tearing off huge splinters and hurling them
in all directions. At last Captain Johnstone-Stewart
reached a small clearing on the enemy's flank, and his

company dashed into the Ashantis with the bayonet, followed by Captain Greer's men and the reserve company of the West African Frontier Force, who made a frontal charge through the breach in the stockade. This ended the fight, the enemy flying northwards to Ofinsu. " The Ashantis showed a really brave front, and proved what excellent material for soldiers exists in their country. For two hours they stood up against a well-directed rifle fire, supplemented by quick-firing field-guns, which, as was seen after the fight, were killing and maiming large numbers of them ; yet only when both their flanks were turned and the bayonet called into play did they retire." [1]   The whole scene of the fight was strewn with their dead, and the bodies of as many as nine men who had been killed by a millimetre shell lay in a cluster. The British casualties were also heavy : Lieutenant Burton, Munster Fusiliers, was killed whilst leading his half company, and Colonel Brake and Sergeant-Major Slattery were slightly wounded, while the losses of the rank and file amounted to one killed, three dangerously, seventeen severely, and nine slightly wounded. Sergeant-Major Slattery, Scottish Rifles, and Sergeant Adada, Central African Regiment, both received the Distinguished Conduct Medal for this action.

During the search of Ejisu before it was destroyed, some papers and property belonging to Captain Benson had been found, and were brought in to Kumasi with the column on the 1st of September. This was the first intimation that disaster had befallen him ; but it was soon afterwards confirmed by a letter from a native clerk who had been with him, and a report from Captain Wilcox, his second in command. By the middle of August Captain Benson had succeeded in collecting a disorderly and undisciplined crowd of between 3,000 and 3,500 Akim and a few Kwahu Levies under their Chiefs at Abogu, to the north-east of Lake Busumtwi. He then moved to Odumasi on the Kibbi road and about twenty-five miles from Kumasi, where he was joined on the 22nd of August by Captain Wilcox. These Akims were as arrant cowards

[1] Willcocks, p. 377.

now as they had been when serving under Captain Butler in 1874, and Captain Benson had the greatest difficulty in getting them to obey his orders or advance in the direction of the enemy : indeed, so serious a quarrel took place between different factions that he was compelled to disarm and dismiss some of them on the 24th. It had never been intended that these men should do more than follow and lay waste the country to the east of Kumasi after the troops had defeated the enemy ; but Captain Benson seems to have become so run down by long-continued illness, and so worried by the delays caused by his timorous followers, as to fear that he might be blamed for their slowness. He therefore determined to push on towards Ejisu at all costs, and although Sir James Will-cocks, so soon as he heard of his intention, wrote telling him not to advance unassisted, the letter reached him too late. On the 27th of August the Levies advanced to within an hour's march of Boankra on the road to Ejisu ; but early the next morning, when Captain Benson moved out with his body-guard, he was attacked about a mile from the camp, and lost three men killed and two wounded. He therefore fell back on his main body, under Captain Wilcox, while the Ashantis, knowing that they only had Akims to reckon with, despatched 300 picked men to oppose them.

The enemy kept up a desultory fire for two hours ; but directly they began to press their attack home, the cowardly Akims fled one after another. Their King Amoaku Atta, and his Chief War Captain were among the first to go, and their men followed, while the carriers threw down their loads and joined them. The Akims deserted by scores and hundreds ; but others, too terrified apparently even to turn, fell on their knees before the Ashantis and begged for mercy. By two o'clock there was no one left but the Chiefs of Wanki, Asiatu and Bompata and a few of their men, whom they had been industriously flogging forward with cow-hide whips when they tried to bolt, with two native Government clerks, Messrs. Hammond and Hutchinson, and some non-commissioned officers of the Gold Coast Volunteers. These still stood by their officers in a hurriedly entrenched position and fought on until late in the afternoon ; but so much ammunition had been lost when the carriers bolted, that it soon ran short, and a retreat was ordered to Odumasi, which was reached at midnight. Captain Benson then sent Captain Wilcox to Abetifi to fetch stores and medicines, and, worn out by illness, worry and disappointment, shot himself.

Within a few hours of the receipt of the true story of this disaster, Captain (local Major) Reeve of the Leinster Regiment left Kumasi with 360 men and a millimetre gun to patrol the district and punish the villages that had taken part in the attack. He was away ten days and recovered much Government property, but could not come up with Captain Wilcox, who had already retired fifty miles farther east. The great number of headless bodies, with quantities of ammunition boxes, guns and baggage that lay strewn about the scene of the fight bore eloquent testimony to the utter demoralization of the Akims and the chaos that must have reigned when they fled. Major Reeve passed through Boankra, Bompata, and Abetifi to Odumasi, and returned through Jabin and Agogo, re-entering Kumasi on the 16th of September by the Mampon road, without having seen anything of the enemy.

Meanwhile, the outskirts of Kumasi had been systematically explored and all the remaining stockades destroyed. They proved to be far more numerous than had ever been suspected, forming a continuous cordon round the town just beyond the clearing, and must have involved an immense amount of labour in their construction. The sanitary condition of the town, too, was improved, and a market was established, to which the people were required to bring supplies, which were sold at prices fixed by the Provost-Marshal. Frequent reconnaissances were made along the roads leading out of the town, and a Military Commission sat to try such prisoners as were taken from time to time. This Commission had been appointed before the Headquarters left Bekwai, and several Ashantis had been sentenced to death and hanged there. Others

were tied to trees and shot in Kumasi until a proper
gallows was erected ; but a little later it was decided by the
Law Officers of the Crown that the disloyal Ashantis were
not technically rebels, and only those who were found
guilty of actual murder were afterwards sentenced to
death.   Flags of truce were constantly arriving, and many
Chiefs surrendered.   They all told the same tale ; that
they had tried to regain their independence, but had been
fairly beaten, and that their people were now tired of
fighting, but that some of the leaders would never surrender
so long as they could keep four or five thousand men in the
field.   But though this at first gave rise to hopes that the
campaign was over, it soon became evident that some
further fighting would have to take place.   Ya Ashantiwa
herself had sent in tendering her submission, which she
said was forced upon her by want of food and dissensions
amongst her followers.   She was given four days in which
to surrender, but, just before the time expired, sent another
defiant message, saying that she would fight to the end.
Kwaku Inkansa, Nantwi, Kofi Kofia, Kwesi Bedu, Kobina
Cherri and others were still in the field and must be secured
before the troops withdrew.

On the 16th of September Sir James Willcocks held a
review of the 1,750 troops and nine guns then in Kumasi,
at which the Ashanti prisoners and loyal Chiefs were
present.   They were much impressed by this display of
force, especially by the demolition of a stockade that had
been built to demonstrate the power of the millimetre guns.
In fact, the news quickly reached the Ashantis still in the
field, and they never again used stockades, but returned to
their old tactics.

On the 20th Captain Donald Stewart arrived and took
over the duties of Political Officer, and a strong column left
the same day for Kintampo to re-open the road and keep
the enemy on the move.   It was commanded by Captain
(local Major) Holford of the 7th Hussars, and consisted of
500 men and a millimetre gun.   With the exception of a
few scattered shots from the bush, no opposition was met
with, and on the third day Kwaku Inkansa of Adansi,

his son, his Chief War Captain, and eleven other Chiefs surrendered unconditionally and were sent back to Kumasi under escort. Kintampo was reached on the 1st of October. The garrison was well; but badly in want of news, having only heard of the relief of Kumasi a few days before Major Holford arrived. A company of the 2nd Central African Regiment, under Captain Brock, was left to reinforce the post, and the column returned to Kumasi, where, on its arrival on the 13th of October, its bedraggled appearance and the number of hammocks in its train plainly showed what a trying time it had had on this march of 200 miles in the worst possible weather. In addition to securing the surrendered Chiefs, it had captured a large number of guns and completed the destruction of Sekredumasi and the other disloyal villages on the road.

Meanwhile, a second column had left Kumasi on the 21st of September for Ofinsu. This was much stronger than Major Holford's, because it was known that a large force under Chief Kofi Kofia had been collected in the district through which it had to pass and would almost certainly give it battle. It consisted of 950 men with two millimetre guns, under Major (local Lieutenant-Colonel) Montanaro, and sufficient carriers for supplies for twenty-eight days. Major Cramer followed with 800 Levies. A village about ten miles from Kumasi was found occupied, but Major Melliss advanced with two companies of the Central African Regiment, under Captains Margesson and Luard, and the enemy at once fell back. The column halted in this village for the night; but though a few sniping shots were fired from the bush, killing one of the Levies, no real attack was made. Next morning the Ashantis were found in force near Dinasi, where they occupied a strong position on the top of a hill surrounded by dense bush; but the scouts of the Sierra Leone Frontier Police had advanced so quietly that they were taken by surprise, and the guns were got into position and opened fire on them with case-shot and shrapnel before they realized that the column was so close. They then poured in a tremendous fire from the front and flanks, parties advancing in turn and pouring in a volley at close range and retiring. A Northern Nigerian company of the West African Frontier Force, under Captain Grahame, and Captain Johnstone-Stewart's company of the Central African Regiment then entered the bush to the right, while Major Cobbe led the Sikhs and two more companies of the West African Frontier Force to the left, and, driving the Ashantis from the flanks of the column, forced them to re-enter the path. The " charge " was then sounded, and a fight at close quarters with the bayonet ensued before the enemy finally broke and fled in confusion through the village and into the forest beyond. Captain Stevenson of the Manchester Regiment fell dead, shot through the chest as he was leading his company in the charge, and one Hausa was also killed. The other casualties were three men of the West African Frontier Force and one Sierra Leone Frontier Policeman severely, and Major Melliss and two more men slightly wounded. The enemy left thirty-four of their dead on the path ; but their casualties must have been very much heavier, though, as usual, they succeeded in carrying off their wounded and probably many of the dead. Captain Stevenson's body was cremated to prevent any possibility of its being exhumed and decapitated. Ofinsu was entered next morning, and five Chiefs and a number of men surrendered, but Kofi Kofia and most of his army had retired to Fufu and were determined to make another stand. A two days' halt was then made, during which 341 guns were secured and Ofinsu and the surrounding villages and their fetish groves razed to the ground before the column returned to Kumasi, which was reached on the 28th.

On the return of this force, arrangements were at once made for another strong column to visit Berikum, to reinforce the detachment there, re-open the trade route, punish the disloyal villages on the road, and, if possible, capture Kobina Cherri. These preparations were almost complete, when news was brought in late on the 27th that Kofi Kofia, with an army of 5,000 men principally composed of the hitherto unbeaten Achimas, was waiting on the

Berikum road about twelve miles out from Kumasi to attack any force that was sent. He declared his belief that the British troops would not dare to face the fighting Achimas; but that if they did he should use no stockades, but fight in the open. The original orders were therefore countermanded and fresh ones issued for an advance at dawn on the 29th.

Sir James Willcocks himself took command, and the column consisted of 1,200 infantry, with three 75-millimetre guns and two 7-pounders. Captain Donald Stewart accompanied the Commandant as Political Officer. Bad as the weather had been before, it was, if anything, even worse when this column set out. From a steady drizzle as it left Kumasi, it rapidly developed into a deluge, and the rain fell in torrents throughout the whole day. The muddy road was as slippery as glass, while a constant succession of streams and swamps had to be crossed, which so delayed the column that the advance-guard had only reached Adada, a village about seven miles out of Kumasi, by sundown. Here a halt was ordered for the night; but the place had been burnt, and the troops had to bivouac in the rain and mud, officers and men alike seeking what protection they could beneath hastily constructed shelters of banana leaves. Even these were nearly all blown away by a tornado, and the men spent a thoroughly wretched night.

Next morning, the 30th of September, brought no improvement in the weather, as officers and men, stiff with wet and cold, threw off their dripping blankets and fell into their places. Fifty Dengiasi Levies were sent on ahead to scout, with orders to fall back immediately if they were attacked, and the column moved off at half-past six. Just before eight o'clock, as the head of the column was nearing Aboasa, the rain almost ceased. Suddenly shots rang out ahead, and the scouts fell back a few minutes later. The enemy occupied a long crescent-shaped rise in a low-lying patch of ground, fronting the road and overlapping both flanks. Their front covered about half a mile, and they opened a tremendous fire along

the whole length of the line. A company of the Central
African Regiment, under Captain Charrier, was ordered to
extend from the road into the bush on the right and work
round the enemy's flank, and Captain Eden's Yorubas
were sent to execute a similar movement on the left.
Captain St. Hill's company of the West African Regiment
then moved off to extend the line still farther to the right,
and a maxim was mounted on the path, as the millimetre
guns had not yet arrived, owing to the impassable state of
the road. The ground was fairly open, and the extended
line of troops crept slowly forward, keeping up a steady
fire. The enemy fell back a little on the left, but otherwise
held their ground, while the fact that they were shooting
up-hill to a great extent counteracted their usual tendency
to fire high. After about twenty minutes' steady firing,
Major Montanaro, who was in command of the advance-
guard, ordered the buglers to sound the " Cease fire "
and " Charge." The whole line rose as one man and
sprang forward ; but the Ashantis never wavered. Holding their fire as the troops rose to charge, they poured in
a quick succession of tremendous volleys, and for the first
time since bayonet tactics had been adopted, the men
failed to drive their charge home. In the face of this
terrific fire they were forced to lie down again before they
had gone more than ten or fifteen yards. Orders were
therefore given them to recommence firing, while word
was sent back to Major Melliss, who came up at the double
with Captain Luard's company of Central Africans, and
moved off to extend the line still farther to the left. The
casualties were now mounting up, and Major Melliss soon
came back to report that the men were losing touch with
each other in the bush, and that it would be dangerous for
Captain Luard's company to fire. Another charge was
therefore ordered, but with no more success than the first ;
for the Ashantis held their ground in the most determined
manner, and only fell back a little farther on the left.
Lieutenant-Colonel Henstock, the Chief Staff Officer, now
arrived on the scene, and at once went back to report to the
Commandant that further reinforcements were necessary.

Sir James Willcocks then came up with Captain Godfrey and the Sikhs, whom he ordered to charge straight down the road against the enemy's centre and try to break through. As they did so, Major Melliss dashed forward with them at the head of such men as he had been able to collect while they were forming up, and nearly all the Staff and Departmental officers joined in. Then, from either side, the long line of troops sprang up and swept forward against the enemy's position. Yet even before this determined rush the Ashantis would not give way, but stubbornly contested every inch of ground, and many a fierce hand-to-hand encounter took place. One Sikh, who already wore the Order of Merit, lay dead beside an Ashanti, and Major Melliss ran another through with his sword; but the man seized the blade and grappled with him, both falling and rolling down a bank together. Captain Godfrey ended the struggle by blowing the Ashanti's brains out with his revolver, but Major Melliss was almost immediately afterwards severely wounded in the foot and had to be carried in. Many others fell; but the Ashantis were now beginning to give way, and retreated slowly up the hill towards Aboasa until the companies closing in on the right threatened to cut off their retreat, when at last they broke and fled. Turning half left to avoid these troops, they ran into the advancing Yorubas: panic then seized them, and they dashed off through the forest in the wildest disorder, followed by shell after shell from the millimetres, which had now arrived and been got into position.

A large piece of ground had been cleared between their original position and the village, but whether this had been done preparatory to building a war camp or for some strategic reason is not clear. They left 150 dead on the field, some of whom lay in heaps of as many as seventeen, and had about 400 wounded. The British casualties were six officers wounded and three rank and file killed and twenty-eight wounded. Major Melliss' wound was severe, and when he was carried in the Commandant publicly told him that he would recommend him for the Victoria Cross

It was afterwards awarded him, and was well deserved; for he had been conspicuous for his gallantry in action, and, though he had been wounded four times, seemed to bear a charmed life. Several of the rank and file were also promoted for gallantry in the field directly Aboasa was entered.

The Ashantis, though finally defeated and now in full flight, had no cause to feel ashamed of themselves. They had fought splendidly. Major Montanaro wrote that "their pluck during the fight was the admiration of our officers, and, though they must have known that they were fighting in a losing cause, they stood their ground bravely for more than an hour." [1] Colonel Sir James Willcocks, too, joined Wolseley and others who had met them in the past in extolling their fighting qualities. In his despatch to the Secretary of State he wrote: "Who can but admire such splendid courage as these brave though cruel people displayed throughout the campaign? . . . The Ashanti does not like the combined sound of bugles and drums sounding the charge, but the brave fellows faced it this day right well, and as the Sikhs, with their warlike Khalsa cry, dashed into them, led by Captain Godfrey, they stood their ground and fired, killing some and wounding several severely." [2] In his book, again, he writes of the "superiority of the Kumassis and their immediate neighbours as fighting men over the other natives of the Gold Coast and its Hinterlands; for whereas over and over again did these gallant Ashantis face us in the field and fight like good men and true, yet in nearly every case except that of some of the Bekwais and Dengiasis, who, however, were themselves Ashantis, did the Levies who came to our assistance take to their heels the moment that danger threatened. It would, indeed, be good policy to treat the Ashantis so as to gain their loyalty, and having done that, to enlist them if possible in our forces, when I do not believe they would be surpassed as soldiers by any West African natives. They are not a

[1] Armitage and Montanaro, p. 193.
[2] Parliamentary Paper, *Ashanti War*, 1900, p. 105.

prepossessing-looking race, but I believe they are made of the right stuff for soldiers. At any rate, they are well worth a trial ; and a regiment of these people, well commanded and ruled by the laws of common sense as distinct from red-book discipline alone, which is not suited to them, might one day prove of even greater value in other parts of West Africa than did the corps which crossed the waters to crush the rebellion." [1]

The rain had now cleared off altogether, and after a short halt in Aboasa to take a hurried meal and partially dry their soaking clothes, the troops went on to Insansu, whither the Ashantis had fled after the battle. But they had already left, and traces of their hurried flight lay around on every side. Their Chiefs had called a hurried roll here, and their heavy losses had so alarmed them that they had pushed on at once and crossed the Ofin River. Only one old woman remained in the village, who sat wailing and crying " Run, run, the white men are coming, the white men are coming ! " A small column was sent out to clear the surrounding villages, but only came across one Ashanti picket, which at once retired, and then returned to Insansu, which was fortunately large enough to afford shelter for everyone for the night.

Next morning Major Cobbe was sent out with 800 men and two millimetre guns to follow the enemy. Guns and baggage of all kinds strewed the path, with here and there a wounded man who had been abandoned in the flight, and on reaching the Ofin River a starving Ashanti child was found lying on the near bank. The river was in flood, forty yards wide and with a strong stream running. A covering party of the Sierra Leone Frontier Police was sent across, however, and two rough bridges of trees were made, by which the whole column had crossed by five o'clock that evening. Another old woman was met, and reported that the Ashantis, who she said were carrying hundreds of wounded with them, had hurried on to Inkwanta, a village several marches up the Berikum road, only stopping to gasp out the warning to those they met that the white

[1] Willcocks, *Kabul to Kumasi*, p. 383.

man was coming. Major Cobbe, therefore, pushed on to Fufu, which was reached at ten o'clock that night after one of the worst marches of the whole campaign. Stumbling along over the rough road in the dark, the carriers were continually falling, and more than one officer left the soles of his boots in a swamp and had to complete the march in his socks. Fufu was found deserted, and the column re-entered Insansu late the next evening after another trying march of twelve hours.

The whole force re-entered Kumasi on the 3rd of October, and their recent decisive victory made it possible to give the troops a prolonged rest. It was sorely needed. Many of them had been on active service in their own country before coming to the Gold Coast, and they were now thoroughly worn out by their many hardships in the field during the rainy season, the ravages of small-pox, and the impossibility even now of always providing them with a full ration. As they always march bare-footed, too, their feet were now in a dreadful state, and they could not have continued working at such high pressure for much longer. The rainy season, moreover, was nearly over, and it was hoped that this delay would enable the final duties of the campaign to be undertaken in better weather.

During this period of inaction, the loyal Kings and Chiefs were received at official palavers, special honour being shown to the King of Bekwai out of gratitude for his many kindnesses to the sick and wounded. Osai Kanyasi was also sent to tell the Ashantis still in the field that the Queen had consented to regard them as belligerents instead of rebels, and that no more trials for high treason would therefore take place. Once they understood that their lives would be spared, unless they were proved guilty of actual murder, many of the enemy surrendered, though the most important leaders still failed to come in. Small flying columns, too, were sent out from time to time to destroy those villages near Kumasi that had been notoriously disloyal or were known to have sheltered the murderers of Mr. Branscombe and others, and 300 men and a 7-pounder gun were sent to the Northern Territories to replace those that Major Morris had brought down. Some trouble was caused at this time by the selfishness of mining prospectors and others, who took advantage of the cessation of hostilities to push stores and machinery up from Cape Coast, and, by paying exorbitant rates, attracted so many carriers to their service that the greatest difficulty was experienced in getting the necessary supplies for the troops to Prasu. This was soon put a stop to, however, by the issue of an order that no European should be allowed to cross the Pra without a written permit, which the Base Commandant was not to give without reference to Kumasi. The miners then found that if they went up country, they must either return to the coast or be content to halt for an indefinite period at Prasu, where they could not renew their supplies and their machinery rapidly deteriorated in the open. Their enthusiasm for visiting the interior then quickly cooled.

The fugitive Chiefs had sought refuge in the north-western district of Ashanti, which alone had not yet been visited by troops. On the 1st and 2nd of November, there-fore, two columns were sent out to march to Berikum, attempt the capture of these Chiefs, and inflict punishment on the disaffected towns and villages in that part of the country. The first consisted of 700 men with five maxims and a millimetre gun under Major Montanaro, and the second of 500 men with three maxims and a 7-pounder under Major Browne (Leinster Regiment), the recently arrived second in command of the West African Regiment. They were accompanied by 2,500 carriers with supplies for twenty-eight days. Although the real rains had now ceased, the roads were still in a terrible state, and heavy tornados constantly swept over the country. This march, therefore, proved quite as trying as those that had preceded it, and small-pox once more broke out amongst the soldiers and carriers. It was reported that Ya Ashantiwa had appointed Kobina Cherri her Chief War Captain, in place of Kofi Kofia, and, as it was believed that he might oppose the advance at Bechim, the two columns united at Insuta on the fourth day out from Kumasi. Messengers had

already been sent on to the Chiefs at Bechim, calling upon
them to surrender at Insuta, but they had asked for time
for consideration, which had of course been refused. On
the 6th, however, while the force was halted at Insuta,
an insolent message was brought in from Kobina Cherri,
saying that he would fight.

That same afternoon a most unfortunate accident happened. Two carriers, who had gone out in search of food,
reported that they had seen a number of armed Ashantis
in the bush building an enclosure for sheep and cattle, and
a company was sent out to surprise them and capture the
live-stock. These Ashantis, however, were the 150 Jabin
Levies who had accompanied the column to act as scouts
and messengers between it and Kumasi. They were
making their camp some distance away, when the company,
led by the carriers, came upon them and fired a volley ;
for although the Levies had all been given a blue and
white sash as a distinguishing badge, these were now so
dirty that it was difficult to distinguish them at a range of
fifty or sixty yards on a dull afternoon in the forest. The
Jabins, thinking they were being attacked by the enemy,
fell back and returned the fire, and it was not until three
or four more volleys had been poured in and the company
charged with the bayonet that the mistake was discovered
and the " Cease fire " sounded. The relatives of six of the
Jabins who had been killed were compensated with grants
of money, but some of the others fled to Kumasi, and it
was some time before any Jabins would take the field
again. Fortunately their return fire had done no harm.

On the 7th, the column moved to Bechim, where its
Chief and those of Inkwanta and Tekiman surrendered.
Kobina Cherri had been unable to get together a following
after the disastrous fight at Aboasa, and had therefore
retired. Foraging parties were sent out and Jemu was
destroyed. The Chief of Bechim had fought at Aboasa,
and, finding his retreat cut off, had escaped by lying down
and feigning death ; several soldiers had actually passed
over him, but directly they had gone he hurried off
through the forest. He complained that the Ashantis

thought the white man was taking an unfair advantage in using knives—meaning swords and bayonets—while they only had their guns.

There were now more than fifty cases of small-pox, and a portion of the town was railed off as an isolation hospital, and the remainder used as an advanced depot for the reserve ammunition and stores, with a garrison of 350 men under Major Gordon.   On the 9th, the remaining 850 men, with 1,200 carriers, moved to Inkwanta, raiding and destroying several villages, and on the 10th to Tanosu, where several more Chiefs surrendered. Odumasi was reached on the 11th, and a garrison of 300 men left there under Major Browne, while the rest of the force moved on through Suatru to Berikum, which was entered on the 13th. The loyal King gave the troops a great welcome, and was publicly thanked for his services. There was a small detachment of Gold Coast Constabulary here under Lieutenant St. John, and Captains McCorquodale and Hobart marched in with fifty more from Pamu during the afternoon. They reported that the whole of the western tribes were loyal, and permission was given to Pong Yow the King of Wam to send 1,000 of his men against the Ashanti fugitives in the Ahafu forest.

The return march was begun on the 14th, and just before the column reached Odumasi news was received of the capture of Kobina Cherri. Major Browne had heard from a daughter of one of the men he had murdered that he was hiding in Suinjam, a village about two hours' march from Odumasi, and sent four sections of the West African Frontier Force, under Lieutenants Kingston and de Putron, to surround it. When they entered the village, the people hurried out of their houses in great alarm, but found their escape cut off by the cordon of troops, and Native Officer Daniells, who understood Ashanti, heard them calling to one man in particular to run and hide himself. Feeling sure that he must be someone of importance, Mr. Daniells gave chase and seized him, when his identity was soon discovered. When brought before Major Montanaro, he was openly defiant, and called on the Berikum Levies to rescue him. The column marched into Kumasi on the 23rd with thirty-one captured Kings and Chiefs, 900 guns, 5,000 pounds of rubber, and a small amount in specie, having destroyed every village on or near the road. The burning of Odumasi on the 17th had nearly ended in disaster, for, owing to some mismanagement, the place was prematurely set on fire, and the sick were only got out with the greatest difficulty, while the officers and men of the rear-guard had to run for their lives through the flames.

Kobina Cherri was tried by a Military Commission, found guilty of murder, and sentenced to death. He maintained his defiant attitude throughout the trial, but afterwards sent for Sir James Willcocks and offered to buy his life by revealing the whereabouts of the Golden Stool and much buried treasure and denouncing other murderers. Whether or not he would really have divulged the secret of the stool, even assuming that he knew it,[1] is very doubtful ; but his offer was refused, and he was hanged in the market-place of Kumasi on the morning of the 25th in the presence of the whole garrison and population. Once he found his life was really forfeit, his courage never failed him : he walked firmly to the gallows, with head erect and his eyes glaring defiance at his enemies. As he passed some Krepis who had tremblingly given evidence against him, he spat contemptuously on the ground, and after he had climbed the scaffold, stood on the drop as erect as a soldier on parade. There was not a man present who was not impressed by his bearing, and an involuntary murmur of admiration arose.

The war was now over, and Sir James Willcocks left Kumasi on the 3rd of December, and was accorded an enthusiastic reception on his arrival in Cape Coast.

The Ahafu forest had been surrounded by a cordon of loyal natives, which was gradually drawn closer and closer until the fugitive Ashantis hiding there were located by hunters and secured. Kofi Kofia and Kujo Krum of Bantama were taken prisoners a few days after Sir James Willcocks left Kumasi, and Ya Ashantiwa was secured a

---

[1] It is known to very few indeed even of the principal men in Ashanti.

little later. All the principal leaders were now accounted for, and though some others still remained at large, they were captured or surrendered soon afterwards.

The casualties during a campaign carried out under such difficulties during the unhealthiest season of the year were naturally very heavy. They constitute a record that it is to be hoped will never be equalled ; but what they would have been had it been necessary to employ white troops instead of natives can only be imagined. The average strength of the Europeans was 152 ; and of these 9 (all officers) were killed in action, 7 died of disease, 52 were wounded, 54 were invalided, and there were 360 admissions to hospital. One officer, Lieutenant Payne, contracted fever almost as soon as he landed, and died within three days of reaching Bekwai ; but the largest proportion of deaths from disease was amongst the Medical Officers. Even the admissions to hospital given here afford no true indication of the amount of sickness ; for when there was work to be done officers frequently struggled on when they were really far too ill to be about. The average strength of the native force was 2,804, of which 113 (including one Native Officer) were killed in action, 102 died from disease, 680 (including three Native Officers) were wounded, 41 were missing, and 4,963 were admitted to hospital. The average strength of the carriers was 15,000, one of whom was killed in action, while 400 died of disease and another 5,000 were admitted to hospital. These figures, however, do not include the losses during the siege and the Governor's march to the coast, for the numbers were never known. Fifty Native Levies were also killed in action at Boankra.

CHAPTER XXVII

CONDITION OF THE COUNTRY AT THE BEGINNING OF
THE TWENTIETH CENTURY

AFTER the war, most of the troops that had been engaged
were withdrawn, leaving a strong garrison of 1,225 of the
Central African and West African Regiments, under Colonel
Burroughs and Major Gordon, to occupy Kumasi until
other arrangements could be made ; for the local force
was being re-organized. From the 1st of January 1901 the
Gold Coast Constabulary was amalgamated with the other
Colonial troops on the West Coast of Africa and became the
Gold Coast Regiment of the West African Frontier Force.
It consisted of two battalions of infantry, with artillery.
The 1st Battalion was stationed in Ashanti, with one company in the Colony, and the 2nd Battalion in the Northern
Territories. This corps, however, had suffered so severely
in the war, losing five officers out of an average strength of
eight, and eighty men, with nearly fifty per cent of wounded,
that it had to be extensively recruited before it could
again take over the military care of the country.

The responsibilities of the Resident, Captain Donald
Stewart, at this time were very great. Numbers of Kings
and Chiefs were prisoners of war, and many sub-Chiefs would
yet have to be deprived of their stools for the part they
had taken in the rising : the whole country had been
devastated, towns and villages burnt and farms destroyed,
and the people, deprived of their natural rulers, hardly
knew where to turn or how to begin to restore order.
Captain Stewart, therefore, released many of the sub-Chiefs
on parole, so that he might have some men in authority
to assist him in looking after returning fugitives, rebuilding

villages, making farms, clearing the roads and supplying carriers. By these means the country soon quieted down, and many prisoners who had been captured by the Native Levies and taken by them to their own towns were returned. The cantonments, prison, and other buildings that had been destroyed by the enemy were rebuilt by them without cost to the Government.

In March 1901 Major M. Nathan, C.M.G., R.E., who had succeeded Sir Frederic Hodgson as Governor, visited Kumasi. The imprisoned Chiefs were then classified according to the parts they had severally taken in the rising and sentenced. Sixteen of the leaders and originators were deported to the Seychelles, and thirty-one others, who had taken a prominent part, but been more or less forced to obey the orders of the leaders, were removed to Elmina as political prisoners. These sentences were read out at a meeting on the 14th of March, at which the Governor also announced the punishment to be inflicted on the disloyal tribes. None but a few licensed hunters were to be allowed to carry guns, and the people would be required to provide free labour for the erection of such military posts as were deemed necessary in their districts and for the repair of all damage done by them to Government buildings during the war ; while two Adansi villages, Kinabosu and Odumasi, were handed over to Bekwai. The Chiefs were then told that, though nothing would be added on account of the cost of this war, the tribute originally imposed would have to be paid. The Kings and Chiefs elected to the vacant stools were afterwards announced, and a list of those who had remained loyal and aided the Government, and to whom presents were to be given, was read out. The next day, the King of Mampon, speaking on behalf of the whole of the Ashantis, told the Governor that they were ready to abide by the decision he had given and pay the tribute.[1]

---

[1] Some of the Kings and Chiefs soon afterwards asked that this tax might be remitted in consideration of their loyalty during the rising. It was collected that year ; but, partly for this reason, partly because of the difficulty of collecting it, and mainly because the in-

On the 8th of June an amnesty proclamation was issued CHAP.
assuring pardon for all offences connected with the rising, XXVII
whether committed in Ashanti or the Colony, and only
excepting six named persons charged with murder, whose
arrest had not yet been effected.

Immediately after the Governor left Kumasi, towards
the end of March, the West African Regiment, which
formed part of the garrison, mutinied. When these men
were ordered to the Gold Coast from Sierra Leone, they
had been told that they would only be required to serve
during actual hostilities and would then be allowed to
return. Though only required to do garrison duty temporarily, they appear to have thought that this would be
permanent and that their officers had broken faith with
them : there also seems to have been some mismanagement
by which their pay had been allowed to fall into arrears.
Placing themselves under command of their sergeant-
major [1] and taking their arms and ammunition, they
marched in perfect order to Cape Coast, where they encamped on the parade ground and mounted a guard over
the Bank of British West Africa, where they thought their
money was. The Governor was then in the Castle, and a
few days afterwards the men paraded outside at his
request, when Assistant-Inspector Watson, a big, powerful
ex-Life Guardsman, on a pretence of dressing the ranks
before the Governor came out, suddenly seized the ring-
leader and pushed him inside the gate before his men had
time to realize what was happening and interfere. He
was afterwards brought out and shot against the tree
outside the Castle gate, and the men then started to march
along the beach to Sierra Leone. After an ineffectual
attempt to turn them back, they were fired on by a gunboat near Axim and lost several killed. The others then
divested themselves of their uniforms and, leaving these
and their arms and everything belonging to the Govern-

creased use of imported goods by the Ashantis enabled indirect taxa-
tion to be substituted for it, it was remitted in part the next year and
wholly a year later.

[1] Mandingo.

ment on the beach, escaped into the bush. These men honestly thought that the Government was treating them very badly. Apart from the fact that they had mutinied, they really behaved very well and observed perfect discipline during their march to Cape Coast and while they were in the town. Had they got out of hand, the situation would have been serious in the extreme, for the Government at the time had no means of opposing them.

Rumours of impending further trouble in Ashanti now became rife. It was said that the Kings of Mampon and Jabin had secretly " drunk fetish " together, that those of Insuta and Kumawu were preparing to do the same, and that this had caused much uneasiness among the other tribes. These rumours, however, really seem to have owed their foundation in part to official nervousness lest the conduct of the West African Regiment should have the effect of encouraging the Ashantis to disloyalty by leading them to believe that the Government's troops were not to be depended upon, and partly to false reports spread by the Kumasis against the King of Mampon in the hope of frightening him into running away or committing some other act that would discredit him in the eyes of the Government, and thus secure them some measure of revenge for his failure to join them in the rising.

In August, therefore, Captain Stewart left Kumasi with a column of 400 men and passed through Jabin, Kumawu, Insuta and Mampon, but found no sign of discontent at any of these places. The Kumasis had sent messengers to Mampon saying that the Resident was coming to arrest the King, and this had caused some alarm in the town and nearly induced him to run away. Fortunately, however, he did not do so; for this was exactly what the Kumasis wanted, and would have placed him in a false position at once.

On the 1st of January 1902, three Orders in Council were published relating to the Colony, Ashanti and the Northern Territories respectively. They defined the boundaries of these several divisions, and, in the case of the

Colony, amalgamated the former Protectorate with it by CHAP.
providing that all such territories within the boundaries XXVII
defined as had " not heretofore been included in His
Majesty's dominions shall be, and the same are hereby
annexed to His Majesty's dominions, and the whole of the
said territories are declared to be part and parcel of His
Majesty's Gold Coast Colony in like manner, and to all
intents and purposes as if all such territories had formed
part of the said Colony, at the date of the said Letters
Patent of 13th January 1886." Ashanti was formally
annexed, and it and the Northern Territories were each
placed under a Chief Commissioner, and the laws of the
Colony applied to them with certain modifications. Effect
was given to these orders by the Ashanti and Northern
Territories Administration Ordinances, which preserved
the judicial rights of the Chiefs in minor matters and
provided for appeal to the British Courts.

On the 12th of December 1904 Geraldo de Lema, who
had been the cause of so much trouble in the eastern
districts, died at Kitta. He had been released some years
earlier and was now an old man, and, being nearly blind,
tripped over a child playing on the steps of his house, and,
falling over the balusters, broke several ribs and died of
his injuries.

The last century had witnessed greater changes on the
Gold Coast than any other. The rise of British influence
and the advance of civilization had changed nearly everything, but only the principal differences can be mentioned.
The departure of the Danes and Dutch had left the English
in sole occupation, and their power and influence in the
country had steadily grown. At the commencement of
the century their authority was of little account, and
they were still merely the tenants of the Chiefs ; but partly
by the extension and improvement as opportunity arose
of the wise system originated by Maclean, partly by
gradual encroachment and the seizure of every opening
offered by " custom, usage and tacit assent," and partly
by their military successes, their power had increased until
their authority and jurisdiction were now universally

recognized, while the lands on which their forts stood had
become their own property. The abolition of the slave
trade, too, had entirely altered the system of trade and the
social condition of the people, though its effects were
to a great extent overshadowed by those of Maclean's
administration.

Ashanti, from its position as a great and growing independent empire, had now fallen to that of a conquered
and subject state, whose King was a prisoner in exile, and
whose territory had but recently been overrun and laid
waste by a victorious army. In considering the position
of affairs in Ashanti, however, it must not be forgotten
that the chief predisposing causes of the last rising still
remain to give rise to an undercurrent of dissatisfaction
and unrest which might once more be brought to the
surface by another ill-advised act of the Administration.
Moreover, although several important Chiefs remained loyal
in 1900, and might very possibly do so again should the
occasion arise, it must be remembered that in some cases
at least they were largely the victims of circumstance. On
the other hand, the fact that the Ashantis have now made
a gallant, if unsuccessful attempt to force the Government
to restore them their King has satisfied their national
honour and removed one powerful cause of the rebellion.

The acquisition of the Northern Territories has secured
to the Gold Coast Government an extensive, if not very
valuable hinterland, assured the safety of important trade
routes to the north, and provided a recruiting ground for
its troops.

The condition of the country a few years after the war
of 1900, indeed, bears little resemblance to that of a
hundred years before. Apart from the great facts of the
growth of British influence and the abolition of slavery,
the whole country, though still backward, has become
comparatively civilized. Commissioners' stations with
Courts have been established all over the country, roads
have been improved and others made, while a road, originally intended for motor traffic from railhead at Kumasi
to Tamali, the administrative headquarters of the Northern

Territories, has been made as far as Ejera. The completion of the line of railway from Sekondi to Kumasi in 1903 has been followed by the construction of another line from Accra to the cocoa-bearing districts behind it, and these two lines have enormously facilitated trade; while the former, which passes through the principal mining districts, has done much to aid that industry by providing a means of bringing up heavy machinery, and been responsible for the establishment of numerous European trading firms in Kumasi, which has become a great trading centre of exchange. Harbour works are being constructed at Accra, which have made landing in surf-boats much safer than before, though, unfortunately, owing to an unforeseen effect of the currents and tides in silting up the sand, little else has as yet been attained beyond the reclamation of a hundred yards or more of sandy foreshore at the landing-place. Other harbour works have been commenced at Sekondi and water works at Accra. The abolition of the slave trade and the demonetization of gold-dust, combined with the acquisition of most of the gold-bearing lands in the Colony by European concessionnaires, has done much to turn the attention of the people to timber, rubber collecting, and agriculture generally, which the Government has encouraged by holding agricultural shows and providing travelling instructors to assist cocoa farmers and others with expert advice. Trade, with its attendant revenue to the Government, has increased enormously, and the nature of the goods dealt in is greatly changed. A submarine cable to England was landed in July 1886, and telegraphic communication between different parts of the country has been extended even to the northern districts of the hinterland. Though cowries are still used in the markets of some of the outlying districts of Ashanti and in the Northern Territories, and gold-dust is still occasionally used, British silver coin is current everywhere in steadily increasing quantities, while the Bank of British West Africa, which was first established at Accra in January 1897, has branches in all the more important towns of the Colony and Ashanti.

After the war of 1900 there was a great boom in the gold-mining industry, and concessions were taken up in the most reckless way. Provided the samples produced showed a colour when crushed and panned, a speculator could generally be found to take up the concession without ever inspecting the land or having any guarantee that the samples even came from it. In some cases the experts sent out are alleged to have prepared their maps, plans and reports and returned to England with them without ever having left Cape Coast. The natural result was that many people lost heavily, and Gold Coast mines fell into disrepute ; but many valuable properties were acquired, which have since been worked with success, and since the railway provided means of transport for the necessary heavy machinery much progress has been made.

When the Gold Coast Constabulary was converted into the Gold Coast Regiment, it consisted of Artillery and two Battalions of Infantry, one of which had its headquarters in Kumasi and the other at Gambaga in the Northern Territories ; but early in 1907 the 2nd Battalion was disbanded, and most of the men re-enlisted in the newly formed Northern Territories Constabulary, which replaced it. The regiment, therefore, now consists of the old 1st Battalion and a Battery, many of the men in which have already proved their value as soldiers in the suppression of the Ashanti rebellion. This force, again, presents a striking contrast to the undisciplined and disorderly rabble of Fantis on which the Government had to rely in case of trouble a hundred years earlier.

Medical officers, provided with small hospitals and dispensaries, have been stationed in every district throughout the Colony, Ashanti and the Northern Territories, and a great deal has been done to improve the sanitary condition of the towns ; but although these improvements are very noticeable, the Gold Coast still retains, and fully deserves its reputation for having one of the most deadly climates in the world. The ever-present malaria, blackwater fever, and dysentery account for much sickness and many deaths, while epidemics of other diseases are by

no means infrequent.   There have been several outbreaks
of yellow fever, notably in Sekondi in 1910, when a number
of Europeans died ; and in January 1908 plague—a disease
hitherto unknown on the Gold Coast—broke out in Accra
and resulted in a total of 352 cases with 258 deaths before
the town was declared free from infection in May.   For
several years, too, epidemics of cerebro-spinal meningitis
occurred in the Lobi country in the north-western province
of the Northern Territories, and caused the deaths of
enormous numbers of people, decimating the population
over and over again, until the disease died out in 1908.

APPENDIX A

BIBLIOGRAPHY

THE following is a list of the principal published books and papers dealing with the Gold Coast and Ashanti, to which reference has been made. There are, however, a number of others which contain isolated pieces of information about the history of the country. Some of the later ones contain numerous inaccuracies, which can only be detected by reference to the earlier works.

ARMITAGE and MONTANARO: The Ashanti Campaign of 1900.[1] 1901.

ASTLEY: A New General Collection of Voyages and Travels.[1] 1745-1747.

BARBOT: Description of the Coasts of North and South Guinea.[1] 1732. (This is the fifth volume of Churchill's Collection.)

BEECHAM: Ashantee and the Gold Coast. 1841.

BENEZET: Historical Account of Guinea and the Slave Trade. Second edition, 1772.

BISS: The Relief of Kumasi.[1] 1901.

BOSMAN: New and Accurate Description of the Coast of Guinea.[1] First edition, 1705; second edition, 1721.

BOWDICH: Mission from Cape Coast Castle to Ashantee.[1] 1819. Second edition, without plates and appendices, 1873.

BOYLE: Through Fanteeland to Coomassie. 1874.

BRACKENBURY: The Ashanti War.[1] 1874.

BRACKENBURY and HUYSHE: Fanti and Ashanti. 1873.

BURLEIGH: Two Campaigns, Madagascar and Ashantee. 1896.

BURTON: Wanderings in West Africa. 1863.

BUTLER: Akim-foo. 1875.

CLARKE: Progress of Maritime Discovery. 1803.

CRUIKSHANK: Eighteen Years on the Gold Coast of Africa.[1] 1853.

DAPPER: Description de l'Afrique.[1] 1686.

[1] The more important books are marked thus.

Dupuis: Journal of a Residence in Ashantee.[1] 1824.

Dyer: The West Coast of Africa . . . from a Man-of-war. 1876.

Ellis: West African Stories. 1890.

—— West African Sketches. 1881.

—— The Land of Fetish.[1] 1883.

—— The Tshi-speaking Peoples of the Gold Coast. 1887.

—— History of the Gold Coast of West Africa.[1] 1893.

Fox: History of the Wesleyan Missions on the Western Coast of Africa. 1851.

Freeman, R. A.: Travels and Life in Ashanti and Jaman. 1898.

—— T. B.: Journal of Two Visits to the Kingdom of Ashantee. 1843.

Fremantle: The Navy as I have known it. 1904.

Gordon: Life on the Gold Coast. 1874.

Hakluyt: Principal Navigations, Voyages, etc.[1] (Reprint.) 1903-1905.

Henty: The March to Coomassie. 1874.

Hippisley: Populousness of Africa, Trade, etc. 1764.

Hodgson: The Siege of Kumasi.[1] 1901.

Horton: Letters on the Political Condition of the Gold Coast.[1] 1870.

Hutchinson: Impressions of Western Africa. 1858.

—— Ten Years' Wanderings among the Ethiopians. 1861.

Hutton: A Voyage to Africa.[1] 1821.

Kingsley: West African Studies. 1899. Second edition, 1901.

Lucas: Historical Geography of the British Colonies, vol. iii, West Africa.[1] 1900.

Major: Discoveries of Prince Henry the Navigator.[1] 1877.

Martin: British Colonies, Africa. 1852.

Meredith: Account of the Gold Coast of Africa.[1] 1812.

Mockler-Ferryman: Imperial Africa, vol. i, British West Africa. 1898.

Morel: Affairs of West Africa. 1902.

Musgrave: To Kumassi with Scott.[1] 1896.

Powell (Baden-): The Downfall of Prempeh.[1] 1896.

Ramseyer: Dark and Stormy Days in Kumasi. 1901.

Ramseyer and Kühne: Four Years in Ashantee.[1] 1875.

Reade: The African Sketch Book. 1873.

—— The Ashantee Campaign.[1] 1874.

[1] The more important books are marked thus.

REINDORF : History of the Gold Coast and Asante. 1895.

RICKETTS : Narrative of the Ashantee War.[1] 1833.

SARBAH : Fanti Customary Laws. Second edition, 1904.

—— Fanti National Constitution.[1] 1906.

SMITH : A New Voyage to Guinea. 1745.

—— Thirty Different Drafts of Guinea.[1] 1728.

SNELGRAVE : A New Account of some Parts of Guinea and the Slave Trade. First edition, 1734 ; second edition, 1754.

STANLEY : Coomassie and Magdala. 1874.

THOMAS : Adventures and Observations on the West Coast of Africa. 1864.

WILLCOCKS : From Kabul to Kumasi.[1] 1904.

WILSON : Western Africa. 1856.

WOLSELEY : Story of a Soldier's Life.[1] 1903.

PARLIAMENTARY PAPERS

Report from the Select Committee on papers relating to the African Forts ; 26 June 1816.[1]

Report from the Committee on African Forts ; 25 June 1817.[1]

Report from the Select Committee on the West Coast of Africa, together with the minutes of evidence, etc. ; 1842.[1]

Papers respecting the cession to the British Crown of the Danish Possessions on the Coast of Africa ; March 1850, July 1850, 1851.[1]

Copies of despatches relating to the warfare between the Fantees and Ashantees ; 1 July 1853.[1]

Further papers relating to the Gold Coast ; 4 August 1855.[1]

Despatches explaining the cause of the war with the King of Ashantee ; 14 June 1864.[1]

Further papers relating to the military operations on the Gold Coast ; June 1864.[1]

Plan to accompany further papers, etc. ; June 1864.

Correspondence from or to the War Department . . . troops for the Gold Coast in 1863 and 1864 ; 22 February 1865.

Report of Colonel Ord ; 29 March 1865.

Report from the Select Committee on Africa (Western Coast), together with the proceedings of the Committee, minutes of evidence, etc. ; 26 June 1865.[1]

[1] The more important books are marked thus.

Correspondence relative to the arrest and detention of King Aggery 5 April 1867.[1]

Correspondence relative to the cession by the Netherlands Government to the British Government of the Dutch Settlement on the West Coast of Africa; February 1872.[1]

Correspondence relative to the Fanti Confederation; 28 April 1873.[1]

Despatches respecting the transfer of the Dutch Possessions. . . Negotiations for the release of German missionaries . . . and the Ashantee invasion; 1873.

Despatch from Governor J. Pope Hennessy, C.M.G., and reply July 1873.

Despatches on the Ashantee invasion and attack on Elmina July 1873.[1]

Further correspondence respecting the Ashantee invasion; July 1873.[1]

Further papers relating to the Ashantee invasion; March 1874 1 June 1874, 23 June 1874.[1]

Return of the total strength of the force . . . in Ashantee; 10 July 1874.

Correspondence on the Queen's Jurisdiction and abolition of slavery; 1874–1878.

Affairs of the Gold Coast and threatened Ashanti invasion; 1881

Further correspondence on the affairs of the Gold Coast; 1882 1888.[1]

Correspondence respecting the West African Conference at Berlin 1885.

Further correspondence on Gold Coast affairs; 1888.[1]

Correspondence on the administration of the laws against slavery 1891.

Arrangements between Great Britain and France; 1892.

Correspondence relating to affairs on the West Coast; 1893.[1]

Memorial from merchants and traders and reply of the Secretary of State; 1893.

Further Correspondence on affairs in Ashanti; 1896.[1]

Correspondence relating to the Ashanti War, 1900; 1901.[1]

Correspondence relating to Ashanti, 1901; 1902.[1]

[1] The more important papers are marked thus.

APPENDIX B

LIST OF GOVERNMENTS

Nation.	From.	To.	Duration in Years.
French	1383	1413	30
Portuguese . . .	19 January 1482	9 January 1642	160
Dutch	1598	6 April 1872	274
English	1631	Present time	282 [1]
Danes	*Circa* 1642	6 March 1850	208
Swedes	*Circa* 1640	1657	17
Brandenburgers . .	May 1682	1708	26

[1] To 1913.

APPENDIX C

GOVERNORS OF THE EUROPEAN SETTLEMENTS ON THE GOLD COAST

ENGLISH

A. GOVERNORS UNDER THE EARLY COMPANIES

Very few of these are known. The only names of which trace has been found are as follows :

Sir William St. John	*Circa* 1621–1623
Greenhill	1660
Captain Henry Nurse	*Circa* 1685
Baggs	Died in 1701
Sir Thomas Dalby	1701 to 1708

John Bloome, mentioned in 1691, was probably Governor

B. GOVERNORS UNDER THE ROYAL AFRICAN COMPANY

Name.	Date of Appointment.	Remarks.
Thomas Melvil	23 June 1751	Died
William Tymewell	23 January 1756	Died
Charles Bell	17 February 1756	Acting
Nassau Senior	15 October 1757	Acting
Charles Bell	10 May 1761	
William Mutter	15 August 1763	
John Hippisley	1 March 1766	Died
Gilbert Petrie	11 August 1766	
John Grossle	21 April 1769	
David Mill	11 August 1770	Resigned
Richard Miles	20 January 1777	
John Roberts	25 March 1780	Died
John Bernard Weuves	20 May 1781	Acting
Richard Miles	29 April 1782	
James Mourgan	29 January 1784	
Thomas Price	24 January 1787	Died
Thomas Norris	27 April 1787	
William Fielde	20 June 1789	
John Gordon	15 November 1791	
Archibald Dalzel	31 March 1792	
Jacob Mould	16 December 1798	
John Gordon	4 January 1799	
Archibald Dalzel	28 April 1800	
Jacob Mould	30 September 1802	
Colonel George Torrane	8 February 1805	Died
Edward William White	4 December 1807	
Joseph Dawson	21 April 1816	
John Hope Smith	19 January 1817	

C. Governors during the First Crown Period

Name.	Date Appointed.	Remarks.
Brig.-Gen. Sir Charles Macarthy .	27 March 1822	
Major Chisholm	May 1822	
Brig.-Gen. Sir Charles Macarthy .	December 1822	Killed in action
Major Chisholm	21 January 1824	Died
Major Purdon	17 October 1824	
Maj.-Gen. Charles Turner .	22 March 1825	Died in March 1826 at Sierra Leone
Maj.-Gen. Sir Neil Campbell. .	18 May 1826	Died at Sierra Leone August 1827
Captain H. J. Ricketts . .	15 November 1826	
Lieut.-Colonel Lumley . .	11 October 1827	Died at Sierra Leone August 1828
Captain Hingston . . .	10 March 1828	
Major H. J. Ricketts . . .	5 June 1828	

D. Governors under the Committee of Merchants

Name.	Date Appointed.	Remarks.
John Jackson	25 June 1828	Acting
Captain George Maclean . .	19 February 1830	
William Topp	26 June 1836	Acting
Captain George Maclean . .	15 August 1838	Died at Cape Coast 13 December 1847

E. Governors during the Second Crown Period

Name.	Date Appointed.	Remarks.
Commander H. Worsley Hill, R.N.	1843	
Doctor James Lilley . . .	8 March 1845	Acting
Commander W. Winniett, R.N. .	15 April 1846	
James Coleman Fitzpatrick .	31 January 1849	Acting
Commander Sir W. Winniett, R.N.	19 February 1850	Died
James Bannerman . . .	4 December 1850	Acting

F. Governors during the Period of Independence of Sierra Leone

Name.	Date Appointed.	Remarks.
Major Stephen John Hill . .	14 October 1851	
James Coleman Fitzpatrick . .	June 1853	Acting
Brodie C. Cruikshank . . .	August 1853	Acting. Died in Lisbon on his way home
Major Stephen John Hill . .	February 1854	
Henry Connor	December 1854	Acting
Sir Benjamin Chilly Campbell Pine	March 1857	
Major Henry Bird . . .	14 April 1858	Acting
Edward Bullock Andrews . .	20 April 1860	
William A. Ross	14 April 1862	Acting
Richard Pine	20 September 1862	
William Hackett . . .	1864	Lieut.-Governor
Richard Pine	1864	
Brevet-Major Rokeby S. W. Jones	1865	Acting, died
W. E. Mockler	1865	Acting
Colonel Edward Conran . .	1865	Lieut.-Governor

G. Administrators under Governor-in-Chief at Sierra Leone

Name.	Date Appointed.	Remarks.
Herbert Taylor Ussher . .	February 1867	
W. H. Simpson	August 1868	Acting
Herbert Taylor Ussher . .	November 1869	
Charles Spencer Salmon . .	July 1871	Acting
Herbert Taylor Ussher . .	1872	
John Pope Hennessy . . .	April 1872	Governor-in-Chief
Charles Spencer Salmon . .	1872	Acting
Colonel R. W. Harley, C.B. . .	November 1872	
Robert W. Keate . . .	7 March 1873	Governor-in-Chief, died
Colonel R. W. Harley, C.B. . .	17 March 1873	Governor-in-Chief
Maj.-Gen. Sir Garnet Wolseley, K.C.M.G., C.B. . . .	2 October 1873	
Lieutenant-Colonel Maxwell . .	4 March 1874	Acting, died on voyage home
Colonel William W. W. Johnston .	30 March 1874	Acting
Captain George C. Strahan, R.A. .	June 1874	

H. Governors during the Period of Union with Lagos

Name.	Date Appointed.	Remarks.
Captain George C. Strahan, R.A. .	25 July 1874	
Charles Cameron Lees, C.M.G. .	7 April 1876	Lieut.-Governor
Sanford Freeling, C.M.G. . .	December 1876	Lieut.-Governor, Governor 5 June 1877
Charles Cameron Lees, C.M.G. .	13 May 1878	Lieut.-Governor
Herbert Taylor Ussher, C.M.G. .	June 1879	Died [1]
William Brandford Griffith, C.M.G.	1 December 1880	Lieut.-Governor
Sir Samuel Rowe, K.C.M.G. . .	4 March 1881	
C. A. Moloney	13 May 1882	Acting
William Brandford Griffith, C.M.G.	4 October 1882	Lieut.-Governor
Sir Samuel Rowe, K.C.M.G.	24 December 1882	
W. A. G. Young, C.M.G. . .	29 April 1884	Died [2]
William Brandford Griffith, C.M.G.	24 April 1885	Lieut.-Governor

I. Governors after the Separation from Lagos

Name.	Date Appointed.	Remarks.
William Brandford Griffith, C.M.G.	14 January 1886	
Colonel F. B. P. White . .	11 April 1887	Acting
Sir W. Brandford Griffith, K.C.M.G.	26 November 1887	
Frederic Mitchell Hodgson . .	30 June 1889	Acting
Sir W. Brandford Griffith, K.C.M.G.	18 February 1890	
Frederic Mitchell Hodgson, C.M.G.	12 June 1891	Acting
Sir W. Brandford Griffith, K.C.M.G.	24 November 1891	
Frederic Mitchell Hodgson, C.M.G.	12 August 1893	Acting
Sir W. Brandford Griffith, K.C.M.G.	7 March 1894	
William Edward Maxwell, C.M.G..	7 April 1895	K.C.M.G. 11 April 1896
Frederic Mitchell Hodgson, C.M.G.	19 April 1896	Acting
Sir William E. Maxwell, K.C.M.G.	23 October 1896	Died at sea
Frederic Mitchell Hodgson, C.M.G.	6 December 1897	Acting, appointed Governor 29 May 1898
William Low	27 December 1898	Acting
Sir Frederic M. Hodgson, K.C.M.G.	13 July 1899	
William Low	28 June 1900	Acting
Sir Frederic M. Hodgson, K.C.M.G.	11 July 1900	
William Low	29 August 1900	Acting

[1] Buried in the London Market Cemetery, James Town, Accra.

[2] Buried next to Mr. Ussher in the Cemetery at London Market, James Town, Accra.

J. Governors after the Separation from Lagos—*Contd.*

Name.	Date Appointed.	Remarks.
Major Matthew Nathan, C.M.G., R.E.	17 December 1900	
Captain L. R. S. Arthur, C.M.G. .	30 July 1902	Acting
Major Sir Matthew Nathan, K.C.M.G., R.E. . . .	20 December 1902	
Major Herbert Bryan . . .	9 February 1904	Acting
Sir John Pickersgill Rodger, K.C.M.G.	3 March 1904	
Major Herbert Bryan . . .	10 May 1905	Acting
Sir John Rodger, K.C.M.G. . .	12 November 1905	
Major Herbert Bryan, C.M.G.	2 April 1906	Acting
Sir John Rodger, K.C.M.G. .	2 September 1906	
Major Herbert Bryan, C.M.G. .	9 October 1907	Acting
Sir John Rodger, K.C.M.G. . .	28 March 1908	
Major Herbert Bryan, C.M.G.	30 March 1909	Acting
Sir John Rodger, K.C.M.G. . .	29 August 1909	Died on arrival in England
Major Herbert Bryan, C.M.G. .	1 September 1910	Acting
James Jamison Thorburn, C.M.G..	21 November 1910	
Major H. Bryan, C.M.G. . .	5 February 1911	
J. J. Thorburn, C.M.G. . .	16 June 1911	
Major H. Bryan, C.M.G. . .	29 June 1912	Acting
Sir Hugh Clifford, K.C.M.G. . .	26 December 1912	
W. C. F. Robertson . . .	1 May 1914	Acting
Sir Hugh Clifford, K.C.M.G. . .	27 August 1914	
A. R. Slater	5 May 1915	Acting

DANISH

Name.	Date Appointed.	Remarks.
Erik Tyllemann	*Circa* 169–	Died
Erik Oehlsen	*Circa* 1698	Died
Johan Trawne	*Circa* 1698	Died
Hartvig Meyer	31 August 1703	Died
Peter Sverdrup	23 April 1704	Died
Peter Petersen	6 June 1705	Died
Erik Lygaard	6 May 1706	Died
Frantz Roye	17 August 1711	Died
Knud Röst	26 November 1717	Died
Peter Ostrup	30 August 1720	Died
David Hernn	24 January 1722	Died
Niels F. Ostrup	22 January 1723	Died
Christian Syndermann . .	30 October 1723	Died
Hendrik von Suhm . . .	30 April 1724	
Fred Pahl	1 March 1727	Died
Andreas Willennsen . .	18 September 1727	Died
Andreas Waeroe	24 December 1728	
Severin Schilderup . . .	12 August 1735	Died

DANISH—*Contd.*

Name.	Date Appointed.	Remarks.
Enewold Borris	14 June 1736	Died
Peter Forgensen	20 June 1740	Died
Christian Dorph	26 May 1743	Died
Jörgen Bilsen	3 February 1744	Died
Thomas Brock	13 March 1745	Died
F. Wilder	23 March 1745	Died
A. F. Hackenborg . . .	23 April 1745	
Foost Platfusz . . .	21 June 1746	
Magnus Litzow	21 February 1751	Died
Magnus Hacksen . . .	8 March 1751	Died
Carl Engmann	21 July 1752	
Christian Fessen . . .	10 March 1757	
Carl Resch	14 February 1762	
Christian Tychsen . . .	20 October 1766	Died
Frantz Kyhberg . . .	11 January 1768	
Gerhardt F. Wrisberg . . .	2 July 1769	
Joachim Otto . . .	1 June 1770	Died
Johan D. Fröhlich . . .	13 June 1770	Died
Niels A. Aarestrup . . .	15 June 1772	
Conrad Hemsen	24 June 1777	Died
Jens Kioge	2 December 1780	
Johan Lipnasse	31 March 1788	
Andreas Biörn	23 October 1789	
Andreas Hammer . . .	25 January 1793	
Bendt Olrich	30 June 1793	Died
Baron Frantz Christian von Hagen	3 August 1793	Died
Johan P. D. Wrisberg . . .	17 August 1795	
Johan D. Anholm . . .	31 December 1799	
Johan P. D. Wrisberg . . .	1 October 1802	
Christian Schionning . . .	15 April 1807	Died
Johan E. Richter . . .	1 March 1817	Died
J. Reiersen	5 October 1817	Died
Christian Stanekjaer . . .	15 May 1819	Superseded
Peter S. Stiffens . . .	1 January 1821	Died
Mathias Thonning . . .	10 September 1821	
Johan Christian von Richelieu	23 December 1823	
Niels Bröch	16 March 1825	
Jens P. Findt	30 September 1827	
Henrich G. Lind . . .	1 August 1828	
Ludvig Vincent von Hein .	20 January 1831	Died [1]
Helmuth von Ahrenstorff .	21 October 1831	Died
Niels Bröch	4 December 1831	
Henrich G. Lind . . .	1 March 1833	Died
Niels Bröch	21 July 1833	Superseded
Frederick S. Mörck . . .	2 December 1834	Died
Hans Angel Giede . . .	18 March 1839	Died
Lucas Dall	18 August 1839	
Bernhardt I. C. Wilkens .	24 May 1842	Died [1]
R. E. Schmidt	26 August 1842	
E. J. A. Carstensen . .	April 1850	

[1] The graves of these officers are in the old cemetery at Christiansborg.

DUTCH

Name.	Date Appointed.	Remarks.
Adrian Jacobs	1624	At Mori
Nicholas Van Ypren . . .	1637	At Elmina
A. J. Montfort . . .	1638	
R. Ruyghaver . . .	1640	
J. Van der Well . . .	1644	
H. Doedens . . .	1649	
A. Cocq . . .	1649	
J. Ruyghaver . . .	1650	
Jean Valkenburg . . .	1655	
Jasper Van Houssen . . .	1658	
D. Wilré	1661	
Jean Valkenburg. . . .	1662	
H. Van Ongerdonk . . .	1666	
D. Wilré	1667	
J. Root	1674	
A. Meermans . . .	1675	
D. Verhoutert . . .	1679	
T. Ernsthuis . . .	1682	
N. Sweerts	1684	
Joel Smits	1689	
J. Staphorst . . .	1694	
John Van Sevenhuysen . .	1696	
William de la Palma . . .	1702	
P. Nuyts	1705	
H. Van Weesel . . .	1708	
A. Schoonheidt . . .	1709	
H. Haring	1711	
A. E. Robberts . . .	1716	
W. Bullier (or Butler) . .	1718	
A. Houtman . . .	1722	
M. de Kraane . . .	1723	
P. Valkenier . . .	1723	
R. Norri	1727	
Jan Pranger . . .	1730	
Ant. Van Overbeck . . .	1734	Died
M. Francis des Bordes . .	1736	Died
Francis Barbrins . . .	1740	Died
J. Baron de Petersen . .	1741	
Jan Van Voorst . . .	1747	
N. M. V. Nood-de-Gieterre .	1754	Died
Roelof Ulsen . . .	1755	Died
L. J. Van Tets . . .	1758	Died
J. P. T. Huydecooper . .	1759	
David Peter Erasmi . . .	1760	Died
Hendrik Walmbeck . . .	1763	Died
J. P. T. Huydecooper . .	1764	Died
Pieter Woortman . . .	1767	Died
Jacobus Van der Puye . .	1780	Died
Pieter Volkmar . . .	1780	Died
G. Servis Gallé . . .	1784	
Adolph Thierens . . .	1785	Died
G Servis Gallé . . .	1786	

DUTCH—*Contd.*

Name.	Date Appointed.	Remarks.
L. Van Bergen Van der Gryp .	1787	
Jacobus de Veer	1790	
L. Van Bergen Van der Gryp .	1794	Died
Otto Arnoldus Duim . . .	1795	Died
G. H. Van Hamel . . .	1796	Died
Cornelius L. Bartels . . .	1798	Died
J. de Roever	1804	
Pieter Linthorst	1805	Died
J. P. Hogenboom	1807	Murdered by the Elminas [1]
J. F. Koning	1808	
A. de Veer	1810	
H. W. Daendels . . .	1816	
F. Ch. E. Oldenburg . . .	1818	
J. Costhout	1820	
F. F. L. U. Last . . .	1821	Acting
L. J. Timmink . . .	1822	Acting
Lieut.-Colonel W. Poolman .	1823	
J. H. A. Mourve . . .	1824	Acting
J. D. C. Pagenstecher . .	1824	Acting 8 days
F. F. L. U. Last . . .	1824	Acting
J. C. Van der Breggen Paauw	1826	Acting
Lieut.-Colonel F. F. L. U. Last .	1828	
J. T. J. Cremer . . .	1833	Acting 1 month
E. D. L. Van Ingen . . .	1833	Acting
M. Swarte	1834	Acting 1½ months
Lieut.-Colonel C. E. Lans .	1834	
H. J. Tonneboeyer . . .	1837	Acting. Murdered by the Ahantas
A. Van der Eb	1837	Acting
Lieut.-Colonel H. Bosch .	1838	
Lieut.-Colonel A. Van der Eb	1840	Still in office in 1863
—— Derx	*Circa* 185–	Died at sea 1855
Colonel Elias	*Circa* 186–	In office in 1863
Colonel Boers . . .	*Circa* 186–	Superseded
Colonel C. T. M. Nagtglas .	1869	
Yan Helmes Fergusson .	1871	Acting

[1] The " Marble Stone " at Elmina marks his tomb.

Nothing is known of the PORTUGUESE GOVERNORS after Diego d'Azambuja, nor of the officers in charge of the FRENCH and SWEDISH Settlements. After Philip Peter Bloncq in May 1682, there is no record of the BRANDENBURG GOVERNORS except that quoted elsewhere from Bosman, about 168– to 1700 or 1703.

APPENDIX D

GENEALOGICAL TABLE OF THE KINGS OF ASHANTI

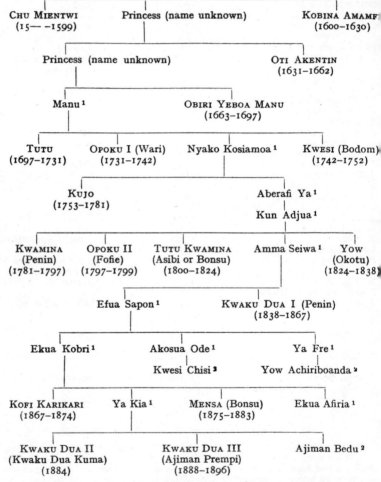

In the above table, the secondary names in brackets are the alternative titles or " strong names " of the Kings by which they are often referred to. Some of these are more commonly used than the actual names.

¹ Princesses. ² Princes.

APPENDIX E

LIST OF WARS, ETC., BETWEEN THE ENGLISH AND THE ASHANTIS

FIRST WAR, 1806

" Buinka," 1806.
Arbra, May 1806.
Anamabo, 15 and 16 June 1806.

Emperu, May 1806.
Egya, 14 June 1806.

SECOND WAR, 1811

Akim district, February 1811.
Pillage of Adda, March 1811.
Apam, 1 March 1811.

Volta River district, June 1811.
Krobo Mountain, August 1811.

THIRD WAR, 1814–1815

Egwa-arru, 1814.

Ajumaco, 1815.

FOURTH WAR, 1823–1826

Tuanko, 21 February 1823.
Essikuma, 13 August 1823.
Essikuma, 20 August 1823.
Essikuma, 21 August 1823.
Insamankow, 21 January 1824.

Dompim, 25 April 1824.
Efutu, 21 May 1824.
Cape Coast burnt, 22 June 1824.
Cape Coast, 11 July 1824.
Dodowa, 7 August 1824.

THE INVASION OF 1853

FIFTH WAR, 1863

Essikuma, April 1863.

Bobikuma, 12 May 1863.

Sixth War, 1873-1874

Yankumasi Assin, 9 February 1873.
Yankumasi Fanti, 10 March 1873.
Dunkwa, 8 April 1873.
Tetsi, 14 April 1873.
Jukwa, 5 June 1873.
Elmina, 13 June 1873.
Shama, 14 August 1873.
Esaman, 14 October 1873.
Iscabio, 27 October 1873.
Dunkwa, 3 November 1873.

Abakrampa, 5 and 6 November 1873.
Ainsa, 8 November 1873.
Fesu, 27 November 1873.
Atobiasi, 26 January 1874.
Boborasi, 29 January 1874.
Amoafu, 31 January 1874.
Kwaman, 31 January 1874.
Bekwai, 1 February 1874.
Fomana, 2 February 1874.
Odasu, 4 February 1874.
Kumasi burnt, 6 February 1874

The Alarm of 1881

The Expedition of 1896

Kumasi entered, 17 January.

Prempi arrested, 20 January.

Seventh War, 1900

Bali Road, 2 and 3 April.
Fomosua, 23 April.
Bantama Road, 25 April.
Bantama Road, 29 April.
Siege of Kumasi begun, 25 April.
Esiagu, 28 April.
Cape Coast Road, 29 April.
Kintampo Road Stockade, 2 May
Sekredumasi, 11 May.
Near Chichiweri, 14 May.
Buaman, 15 May.
Mampon Stockade, 20 May.
Dedisuaba Stockade, 20 May.
Intimide Stockade, 25 May.
Intimide Stockade, 29 May.
Patasi Stockade and Road, 23 June.
Near Kokofu, 23 May.
Dompoasi, 24 May.

Sheramasi, 2 June.
Dompoasi, 6 June.
Dompoasi, 16 June.
Dompoasi, 30 June.
Kokofu, 3 July.
Treda, 14 July.
Peki Road Stockades, 15 July.
Relief of Kumasi, 15 July.
Kokofu, 22 July.
Near Yankoma, 30 July.
Intimide Stockade, 6 August.
Kintampo Road Stockade, 6 August.
Accra Road Stockade, 7 August.
Jachi, 22 August.
Boankra, 28 August.
Ejisu, 31 August.
Dinasi, 22 September.
Aboasa, 30 September.

APPENDIX F

TABULATED HISTORIES OF THE FORTS

ACCRA

Circa 1565, the Portuguese built a fort.

1578, their fort was destroyed by the Accras.

1580, the French built a factory.

1583, the French were driven out by the Portuguese.

1642, the Danes built a lodge.

Ussher Fort

1642, the Dutch built a lodge.

1652, the lodge enlarged and fortified and named FORT CREVE CŒUR.

1782, the fort captured by the English under Captain Shirley.

1785, restored to the Dutch.

Circa 1816, abandoned.

Circa 1830, re-occupied.

10 July 1862, shattered by earthquake.

1868, transferred to the English and renamed USSHER FORT.

James Fort

1673, built by the English and named JAMES FORT.

10 July 1862, shattered by earthquake.

ADDA

1784, fort built by the Danes and named KONIGSTEIN.

15 March 1850, transferred to the English by purchase.

AKWIDA

1683, lodge built by the Brandenburgers.

1690, captured by the Dutch, enlarged by them, and named FORT DOROTHEA.

1698, restored to the Brandenburgers.
1708, abandoned, but re-occupied prior to 1816 and again abandoned later.

ANAMABO

Circa 1640, the Dutch built a lodge.
Circa 165–, captured by the Swedes.
1657, captured by the Danes under Sir Henry Carlof.
Circa 1660, recaptured by the Dutch.
1664, taken by the English under Holmes.
8 February 1665, capitulated to the Dutch under De Ruyter.
1673–1674, the present ANAMABO FORT built by the English.
4 September 1701, attacked by the Anamabos.
4 December 1794, bombarded by a French fleet.
15 June 1806, attacked by the Ashantis and capitulated to them the next day.

ANASHAN

1663, lodge built by the English.
1665, captured by the Dutch under De Ruyter.
1666, restored to the English.
Circa 166–, abandoned.
1679, turf redoubt built by the Portuguese.
Circa 168–, abandoned.

APAM

1697, fort begun by the Dutch.
1700, completed and named FORT LEYDSAAMHEID.
1782, captured by the English under Captain Shirley.
1785, restored to the Dutch and abandoned later.

AXIM

Circa 1502, Portuguese built a fort.
Circa 1514, their fort destroyed by the townspeople.
1515, the present fort built by the Portuguese and named FORT SAN ANTONIO.
9 January 1642, captured by the Dutch.
1664, captured by the English under Holmes (?).
1665, recaptured by the Dutch under De Ruyter (?).

April 1872, ceded to the English by purchase.

Circa 1650–1670, the Dutch had another small fort, FORT ELISE CARTHAGO, at the mouth of the River Ankobra.

BERAKU

Circa 1667–1704, fort built by the Dutch.

782, captured by the English under Captain Shirley.

785, restored to the Dutch.

Circa 1816, abandoned.

BEYIN

Circa 1750, fort built by the English and named APOLLONIA FORT.

833, abandoned.

835, ruins temporarily re-occupied by Governor Maclean's expeditionary force.

868, transferred to the Dutch and partly rebuilt ; but abandoned soon afterwards and pillaged by Afu.

April 1872, purchased by the English with the other Dutch Possessions ; flag hoisted on 11 August.

BUTRI

Circa 1598, lodge built by the Dutch.

644, the lodge fortified and named FORT BATENSTEIN.

816, abandoned.

Circa 1830–1840, re-occupied and again abandoned, but occupied intermittently until 1860.

April 1872, purchased by the English with the other Dutch Possessions ; flag hoisted in August.

CAPE COAST

Circa 15—, lodge built by Portuguese and afterwards abandoned (?).

630, lodge built by Dutch and afterwards abandoned (?) this lodge then occupied by the Swedes (?).

657, taken by the Danes under Sir Henry Carlof and afterwards abandoned by them also (?).

Castle

Circa 1662, built (? rebuilt and enlarged) by the English.

une 1663, surprised and captured by the Dutch.

7 May 1664, recaptured by the English under Holmes.
1673, improved and enlarged.
1681, attacked by the townspeople.
1703, bombarded by a French fleet.
1757, bombarded by a French fleet.
1803, bombarded the town.

Fort Victoria

1721, built by the English Governor Phipps and known as PHIPPS
    TOWER ; renamed FORT VICTORIA very much later.[1]

Fort William

April 1820, built by the English Governor Hope Smith and known
    as SMITH'S TOWER.[1]
Prior to 1838, converted into a lighthouse and renamed FORT
    WILLIAM.

Fort M'Carthy

1822, redoubt hurriedly built and named FORT M'CARTHY, but
    allowed to fall into ruins soon afterwards.

Queen Anne's Point

Prior to 1682, the Dutch built a lodge and had already abandoned it
Circa 1720, the English built a small fort and subsequently aban
    doned it.

Amanfu

1658, the Dutch built a fort and named it FORT FREDERICKSBURG
1685, purchased by the English and renamed FORT ROYAL.
1699, rebuilt by the English ; subsequently abandoned.

Connor's Hill

1863, a redoubt was built here by the Naval Brigade that was
    landed for the protection of the town : it was called FORT
    FREDERICK, but was not maintained.

    [1] Both these forts were hurriedly built of " swish " and strengthened
with masonry afterwards.

CHRISTIANSBORG

16—, lodge built by the Portuguese and named URSU [1] LODGE.

1645, captured by the Swedes.

1657, captured by the Danes under Sir Henry Carlof.

1659, enlarged by the Danes and renamed CHRISTIANSBORG.

1679, the Danish Governor murdered and the fortress sold to the Portuguese by a Greek employé and renamed SAN FRANCIS XAVIER.

1682, the Portuguese garrison mutined and imprisoned the Governor.

1682–1683, the Danes redeem the fort.

1693, captured by the Akwamus under Asameni and occupied by him.

May 1694, again redeemed by the Danes.

6 March 1850, purchased by the English.

13 September 1854, bombarded the town.

10 July 1862, shattered by earthquake.

The fort, thenceforth known as CHRISTIANSBORG CASTLE, was afterwards repaired, and, some years later, modernised by building a bungalow on the top of the main building, which is now used as Government House. Prior to this it was used for a time as a lunatic asylum.

DIXCOVE

1683–1690, the right to the ground was continually in dispute between the English and Brandenburgers.

1691, the English commenced building the fort.

1697, the fort finished and named FORT METAL CROSS.

1697, besieged by the Ahantas.

1868, transferred to the Dutch by exchange.

14 June 1869, bombarded the town.

6 April 1872, purchased by the English with the other Dutch Possessions. The flag was hoisted on the 9th.

EGWIRA

1623, the Portuguese built a fort up the Ankobra River and named it FORT DUMA.

1636, shattered by earthquake.

1694, rebuilt by the Dutch, and a second fort also built and named FORT RUYGHAVER.

[1] Ursu, or Osu, is the native name for Christiansborg village.

Circa 169–, one of these, probably fort Ruyghaver, was captured
by the Awoins and blown up during the negotiations for its
surrender to the Dutch. Both were soon afterwards abandoned altogether.

EGYA

1663, English built a lodge (it is doubtful whether the Danes
also had a lodge here at about this time).
June 1663, the English lodge captured by the Dutch.
1664, recaptured by the English under Holmes.
7 February 1665, blown up by the English to prevent its capture
by the Dutch and in an attempt to destroy the latter.

ELMINA
Castle

1383, fort built by the French and known as the BASTION DE
FRANCE.
1413, abandoned.
1482, fort built by the Portuguese and named SAN JORGE D'ELMINA.
29 August 1637, captured by the Dutch. Subsequently greatly
enlarged and improved by them and the Bastion de France
incorporated with it.
1680–1681, besieged for ten months and twice assaulted by the
Elminas.
1781, bombarded by the English from H.M.S. *Leander*.
6 April 1872, purchased by the English.
13 June 1873, bombarded the " King's town."

Fort Conraadsburg [1]

Circa 1556, the Portuguese built a redoubt on St. Jago's Hill.
August 1637, captured by the Dutch.
1638, fort built by the Dutch and named FORT CONRAADSBURG.
1680–1681, besieged for ten months by the Elminas.
1781, attacked by the English under Captain McKenzie.
6 April 1872, purchased with the other Dutch Possessions by the
English.

[1] This is generally known as Fort St. Jago at the present time ; but
St. Jago is really the name of the hill, derived from the fact that the
Portuguese built a small chapel on it and dedicated it to the Saint.

Other Forts

1810 or 1811, fort built on shore to the west of the Castle (by the Dutch) and named FORT DE VEER.

1810–1811 and 1828, other forts were built to protect the town during the Fanti-Elmina wars. One near the Cape Coast road was afterwards known as FORT NAGTGLAS, one on Java Hill as FORT JAVA, and others at the back of the town as FORT SCOMARUS and FORT BATENSTEIN.

KITTA

1784, fort built by the Danes and named PRINZENSTEIN.

Circa 1840, bombarded the town.

12 March 1850, purchased by the English.

1856, abandoned.

KOMENDA

British

1663, lodge built by the English.

1665, captured by the Dutch under De Ruyter.

1667, restored to the English by the Treaty of Breda.

1673–1674, KOMENDA FORT built by the English.

168–, abandoned.

1694, re-occupied.

1 January 1868, transferred to the Dutch by exchange.

31 January 1868, bombarded by the Dutch warship *Metalen Kruis*.

6 April 1872, purchased by the English with the other Dutch Possessions.

Dutch

1688–1689, fort built by the Dutch and named FORT VREDENBURG.

1695, attacked by the Komendas.

1782, captured by the English under Governor Mills and much damaged.

1785, the ruins restored to the Dutch.

1809, occupied by a force of Wassaws who completed its ruin.

6 April 1872, included in the Dutch Possessions purchased by the English.

French

Circa 1400, the French are said to have had a post here.
1688, the French established a factory.
1688–1689, the Dutch pillaged and destroyed it.

KORMANTIN

Circa 1698, the Dutch built a lodge, but soon abandoned it.
1631, the English built the fort.
Circa 1640, the Dutch rebuilt their lodge, but again abandoned it.
8 February 1665, the Dutch, under De Ruyter, captured the English
    fort and named it FORT AMSTERDAM.
1681–1682, the Dutch enlarged and greatly improved the fort.
1782, captured by the English under Captain Shirley.
1785, restored to the Dutch.
1806, surrendered to and occupied by the Ashantis.
1806, abandoned by them and re-occupied by the Dutch.
Circa 1816, abandoned.

KUMASI

1897, built (by the English).
25 April 1900, besieged by the Ashantis.
15 July 1900, relieved by force under Col. James Willcocks.

PRINCES

May 1682, some temporary defences raised by the Brandenburgers.
1683, the fort built by them and named GROOT FREDERICKSBURG.
1708, abandoned by them and either left in the care of Chief John
    Conny, or taken possession of by him.
1720, unsuccessfully attacked by the Dutch.
1725, besieged and captured by the Dutch, who renamed it HOL-
    LANDIA, but abandoned it soon after.

MORI

1598, fort built by the Dutch.
1624, rebuilt and named FORT NASSAU.
1664, captured by the English under Holmes.
1665, recaptured by the Dutch under De Ruyter.
1782, captured by the English under Captain Shirley.
1785, restored to the Dutch.
Circa 1816, abandoned.

NINGO

1734, fort built by the Danes and named FRIEDENSBORG.
? abandoned at an unknown date.
8 March 1850, the ruins handed over to the English with the other
  Danish Possessions purchased by them.

PRAMPRAM

Circa 1780, fort built by the English and named FORT VERNON.
? fell into ruins or was destroyed by the Danes.
1806, partly rebuilt by the English.
Circa 1816, abandoned.

SEKONDI

Dutch

Circa 1640, the Dutch built FORT ORANGE.
September 1694, the fort plundered by the Ahantas.
1840, abandoned, but re-occupied later.
6 April 1872, purchased by England with the other Dutch Possessions ; the flag hoisted on the 10th.

English

Circa 1645, the English built a fort.
1 June 1698, the fort plundered and burnt by the Ahantas.
Prior to 1726, the fort had been rebuilt.
1782, captured and destroyed by the Dutch.
1875, restored to the English, but not rebuilt.
1820, abandoned.

SHAMA

Circa 15—, lodge built by the Portuguese and named SAN SEBAS-
  TIAN.
Circa 1600, abandoned by the Portuguese and occupied by the
  Dutch.
1640, enlarged and improved (or entirely rebuilt).
1664, attacked and ruined by the English under Holmes.
1664, re-occupied and temporarily fortified by the Dutch.
1666, rebuilt by the Dutch, but abandoned before 1870.
6 April 1872, included with the other Dutch Possessions purchased
  by the English.

TAKORADI

1390, factory built by the French.[1]
? Lodge built by the Swedes (?).
1657, captured by the Danes under Sir Henry Carlof (?).
Circa 1660, the Dutch built a fort, FORT WITSEN.
9 April 1664, captured by the English under Holmes.
25 December 1664, recaptured by the Dutch under De Ruyter and blown up as useless.
1685, the Brandenburgers built a lodge.
1708, abandoned.
1708, it is doubtful whether the Dutch built another small fort which they quickly abandoned.

TAKRAMA

1684, a small fort built by the Brandenburgers.
1708, abandoned.

TANTUMKWERI

Prior to 1726, fort built by the English.
31 January 1820, abandoned.

TESHI

1787, the Danes built a fort and named it AUGUSTABORG.
7 March 1850, included in the transfer of the Danish Possessions by purchase, but not occupied by the English.

WINNEBA

1662–1663, the English built a factory.
28 May 1863, the factory plundered by the Agunas, but re-established a little later.
1665, captured by the Dutch under De Ruyter.
1667, restored to the English by the Treaty of Breda.
1679, plundered by the Agunas.
1694, WINNEBA FORT built by the English.
July 1812, the fort blown up and the town destroyed by Commodore Irby to avenge the murder of the Commandant, Mr. Henry Meredith, by the townspeople.
Circa 1816, the fort rebuilt and again abandoned some time later.
1844, re-occupied, but for how long is uncertain.

[1] There is little doubt about this : the natives still point out a hill on which they say the French fort stood at some distance from that on which they can still show the foundations of Fort Witsen.

INDEX

Ababio, Chief of Adukrum, his revolt, II, 300–302 ; deposed, 302
Abadama, rapids at, I, 130
Abakrampa, II, 26 ; attacks on, 61, 69–71 ; reinforcement of the garrison, 62, 70
Abankoro, I, 583
Abe-Teki, Chief of Komenda, I, 148 ; dispute with his brother, 148 ; murdered, 153
Abeille, the, I, 458
Abekum, burned, II, 457
Aberidwesi, his execution, I, 423
Abetifi, I, 583 ; II, 368
Abi, redoubt at, II, 42
Abiasi, camp at, II, 364
Abiasis, the, defeated, II, 363
Abina, attack on, I, 569
Abmussa River, I, 460
Aboadi, bombardment, II, 80
Aboasa, battle of, II, 556–558 ; casualties, 558
Aboasi, gold-mine, I, 88 ; falls in, 90
Abodum, burned, II, 511
Abodum, King of, signs a treaty, II, 408
Abodums, the, alliance with the Kumasis, II, 433
Abogu, II, 148 ; attack on, 116
Abomi, I, 456
Aborigines' Rights Protection Society, II, 432
Abosso, Gold Mining Company, II, 246
Abra, I, 240 ; battle at, 241 ; Fanti camp at, 258
Abramboe, I, 137
Abrobi, gold mine at, I, 43 ; falls in, 86 ; abandoned, 87 ; attempt of the Dutch to re-open, 146
Abrodi, II, 263
Aburi, II, 321 ; botanical garden at, 352
Accra, I, 56, 145, 155, 171, 263 ; II, 251, 345, 502, 548 ; French Settlement at, I, 49 ; Portuguese Settlement at, 55 ; fort, 59 ; II, 593 ;

outrages at, I, 267 ; slave trading, 317 ; British warships, 318 ; riot, 456 ; refusal to pay the toll tax, 499 ; earthquake, 501 ; ceded to the English, 560 ; Native Confederation, formed, 616 ; meeting at, II, 84 ; Harbour works, 573 ; outbreak of plague, 575
Accra, S.S., II, 396
Accras, the, I, 7 ; war with the Akwamus, 118, 121 ; attack on Ashantis, 341 ; war with the Awunas, 549 ; attack on Duffo Island, 607
Achiriboanda, his claim to the throne of Ashanti, II, 296 ; unpopularity, 297 ; supporters, 304 ; intrigues with women, 310
Achowa, attack on, II, 41
Acra, I, 17
Adada, II, 556
Adada, Sergeant, at the attack on Ejisu, II, 550 ; receives the Distinguished Service Medal, 550
Adafia, eastern frontier at, II, 164, 203 ; smugglers captured at, 205
Adams, Commander James, I, 497.
Adansi, I, 5, 192 ; independence of, II, 200, 201 ; intrigues of Ashantis, 213 ; destruction, 294
Adansi, King of, acts as intermediary in the overtures for peace, I, 395–397
Adansis, the, defeat at Boborasi, II, 114 ; secession, 155, 163 ; outrages, 284, 286 ; hostilities against the Bekwais, 285, 298 ; supposed claim to the protection of the Government, 286 ; victory at Akrokeri, 289 ; removal to Insaba, 305 ; treaty with, 398 ; attacks at Dompoasi, 511, 512, 515, 518 ; expedition against, 538–541 ; defeated, 541
Adasmadi, camp at, II, 70, 72
Adda, fort at, I, 221, 476 ; II, 593 ; taken by the Ashantis, I, 264